THE MEANING OF MARXISM

THE MEANING OF MARXISM

by

G. D. H. COLE

Ann Arbor Paperbacks
for the Study of Communism and Marxism
THE UNIVERSITY OF MICHIGAN PRESS

CONTENTS

PREFACE

This book is largely based on *What Marx Really Meant*, which I published in 1934. That work contained a good deal that was topical, especially in relation to the then recent conquest of power in Germany by the Nazis. So much has occurred since that, instead of merely revising the original text, I have thought better to use it as the basis for what is largely a new book. I have also altered the title, not only in order to mark this change, but also because what was said by reviewers and others at the time of the original publication convinced me that my title was liable to be misunderstood. What I was attempting then—and am attempting now—was not a summary of Marx's doctrines or merely an essay in interpretation of Marx's thought, but rather a revaluation of Marx's essential ideas and methods in relation to contemporary social structures and developments. Especially I was trying to consider the bearing of Marx's theories on the structure of social classes, which have altered greatly since he formulated his account of them. I think the new title better expresses what I had, and have, in mind.

I should like to thank Dr. D. B. Halpern for a very useful discussion of Marx's ideas, but I have of course no wish to saddle him with any of my conclusions.

G. D. H. C.

Oxford.
May, 1948.

ANALYTICAL TABLE OF CONTENTS

CHAPTER I

THE FOUNDATIONS OF MARXISM

This book of mine requires at the outset a few words of explanation; for otherwise there is a danger that some readers may search in it for what they will certainly fail to find. It is not meant primarily, or to any considerable extent, either as an exposition or as a criticism of Marx's doctrines, here paraphrasing, condensing and expounding the words of the master, or there seeking to set him right where I believe him to have been wrong. There exist plenty of expositions and abridgments of Marx by followers of his doctrine; and criticisms and refutations of him are as the sands of the sea-shore. There are even competent judicious essays upon his work, with which I have no desire to set up this book in rivalry.

My object is something different. It is to disentangle in his teaching, from what is dead or no longer appropriate, what remains alive and capable of that process of growth and adaptation which is the prerogative of living things. I am conscious that my own thought has been deeply influenced by Marx—the more so perhaps because I came to him after I had first received, and then repelled, the influence of the Hegelian doctrine. I am no Marxist, if to be one involves, as many of his followers seem to suppose, unquestioning acceptance of his opinions, or any sort of belief in the literal inspiration of the Marxian scriptures. Indeed, in a good many respects my mind recoils from Marxism, as a system, both because I have a deeply-rooted mistrust of systems, one and all, and especially of systems which attribute everything of importance to a single cause, and also because Marx's system appears to me to rest, as so many systems do, on a failure to analyse with sufficient clarity the master-cause on which everything is thereafter made to depend. Over and above this, Marx's system hits right up against my conviction that it is a profound error to attribute to "classes," of things or of men, any reality distinct from that of the individuals which compose them, or to regard the classes, as distinct from the individuals, as active forces shaping the course of history. In saying this, I do not of course mean to deny the possibility of statistical generalisations about the probable behaviour of the majority of individuals who belong to a particular class or group, in face of situations which broadly affect them in the same ways. I do, however, deny that such generalisations can establish more than probabilities, or that, in most cases, the classes or groups about which they can be made can be more than approximately delimited or defined. However deeply individuals may be influenced by their social environment, they remain individuals; and it remains true that all action, as well as all consciousness, is an attribute of the individual. Group or class action is the action of a number of individuals doing the same or interrelated acts: it is never the action of the group as such, even if the acts of the individuals are deeply influenced by their relation to the group, or are taken as representative acts on behalf of the group—as when an official acts on behalf of the members of a society or association. Marx, as against this, often wrote as if classes could act, and were even in some sense more real as active agents than the individuals composing them. In this important respect he never shook himself free of the Hegelianism in which he was brought up. In "turning it upside down," as he said he had done, he did not get rid of the metaphysical element: he only substituted a new form of metaphysics, masquerading as science. This had the disastrous result of making him think of individuals—of capitalists and workers alike—as abstractions, and of the capitalist class and the proletariat as realities. The individual worker came to be regarded as merely a "detail-labourer," an atom forming an element in the mass of social labour, and significant only in the mass; and, hardly less, the individual capitalist was thought of as no more than an element in the total force of Capitalism, which appropriated "surplus value" by exploiting the proletariat and then shared out this "surplus value," as rent, interest and profit, among the detail-capitalists. Here again, I do not of course deny that capitalists, through joint stock concerns and monopolies, and workers, through Trade Unions and Co-operative Societies, do act as impersonal forces, or that it is legitimate to speak of the actions of these collective entities, provided that care is taken not to forget that they can act only through the actions of individual men and women. What I do deny is that the "actions" of groups or classes can be *determined* apart from the actions of the individuals who make them up.

Nevertheless, despite this sharp dissent from certain of Marx's fundamental notions, I remain "Marx-influenced" to a high degree, because I have found in certain of his doctrines, and above all in certain of his methods of social analysis, clearer

12

light than anywhere else by which to seek an understanding both of certain key factors in the development of human societies and of fundamental economic and political problems of to-day.

In this sense alone, I claim, has anyone a sound intellectual title to call himself Marxist in 1948. For it is the rankest injustice to Marx to suppose that he would have written exactly as he wrote in 1848, or in 1859, or in 1867, or even in 1883, if he had been alive and writing to-day. No sense was stronger in Marx than the sense of change; and how much has changed almost out of recognition since Marx died two-thirds of a century ago! Only fanatics learn *The Communist Manifesto* and the key passages of *Das Kapital* by heart, and conceive themselves thereby to have unlocked the secrets of the capitalist world as it now exists. Only disciples who utterly misunderstood both the meaning and the method of their master can think that an analysis of the economic development of the first half of the nineteenth century, primarily in a single country, will serve in lieu of fresh thinking about the world-bestriding capitalism of a century later. No thinker thinks beyond his time, in the sense that his thought can be adequate for any generation later than his own. He may lay lasting foundations, good for later generations to build upon; but woe betide those who seek to save themselves the pain of mental building by inhabiting dead men's minds.

If Marx is to be of any service to us, we must neither parrot his phrases nor repeat his doctrines by rote, nor on the other hand denounce him for his failure to provide valid answers to questions which neither were being asked nor could have been asked in his day, but must let him help us to do afresh for our generation what he sought to do for his own. For this task we are likely, I believe, to find his methods more directly helpful than his doctrines. For if we begin with Marx's doctrines, and set out to discover where and how far they are still applicable to the world of to-day, we shall be in danger of producing either an apologia or a criticism, without throwing any real light upon our own problems. We shall run the risk of assuming that precisely the questions Marx asked are the questions that need asking now, and that the answers will be merely modifications, or perhaps negations, of the answers which he found. But in fact the questions that it is important for us to ask may be different questions, and the answers may have to be stated in radically different terms.

Yet, of course, the world we have to study has grown directly out of the world Marx studied. Our world, greatly though it has changed and much more closely interrelated though its elements have become, is continuous with his; and to some extent he was able to foresee aright how the one would develop out of the other. We shall doubtless find after all that many of his questions are our questions too, and derive from them answers of the same order as his own. But we must not, at our peril, assume in advance that this is so of any particular question. We must look closely at our own world, not only for the answers to our questions, but equally for the questions themselves.

That is why, if Marx helps us at all, his method is likely to help us more than his conclusions. For a method of study and analysis is likely to remain valid for longer than any set of conclusions arrived at by its use. This is not to say that method can remain static in a changing world; but it is reasonable to suppose that the general forms of thought will change more slowly than their particular content.

Of course, it is possible that Marx's method will not help us. There are, I know, some Marxists who hold his method to have been an unfortunate philosophical aberration, in despite of which he hit on a number of important truths. But these are either the parrots of Marxism, who learn diligently without reflection, or its mere hangers-on, in search of comfortable crumbs of congenial doctrine. Marx's method is integral, not only to his conclusions, but to the entire basis of historical study on which his conclusions rest. His method will fail to help us only if his whole analysis was from beginning to end upon the wrong lines. It may have been so; and those who hold *a priori* that it was so will be indisposed to attempt its use for an analysis of the world to-day. I have not found it unhelpful, when I have tried to use it; and all I ask of the readers of this book is that they should follow me in the experiment of seeking to discover how far Marx's method can be applied with success to a reading of the signs of our times.

The Dialectical Method

Having said this, I feel I shall be expected to proceed at once to explain what this wonderful Marxian method is, in order that my readers may be in a position to follow the analysis of the world of to-day with full knowledge of the method by which it is being made. This, however, is not what I propose to do; for the Marxian method is best understood not by reading a theoretical exposition of it, but in the first instance by seeing it at work. Later in this book, I shall attempt to state what I believe its essential qualities to be; but at this stage I shall say but a few words about it.

14

In the first place, all living things are subject to constant change, which arises partly from their environment and partly from within themselves. This is true of societies no less than of individuals; for societies are constantly changing collections of individual men and women. In order to understand any human society, we must study it not as something static, but as a continually changing thing, subject to an unceasing process of development, growth and decay. It is intelligible only in relation to its entire past history, as well as to its present condition, which is indeed only a cross-section of its history. Even if our aim is to understand the present, we have to think of the present as a constantly moving point; for even while we are making our analysis to-morrow is becoming to-day.

It follows that, even if our aim were only to understand, and not also to use our understanding as a basis for action, the method of static analysis could not, in the field of the social studies, yield us satisfactory results. For if a thing is in fact in constant motion, it is fatally misleading to analyse it on the assumption that it is standing still. And human society does not merely move: in our day it moves fast—faster than ever before. It has change—rapid change—as an essential part of its nature. A thing which has change as the very essence of its nature will not stand still for the student's convenience: it can be grasped only in and through its changes, and by an understanding of its processes of change. To ignore this fact has been, right up to our own day, the fundamental mistake of orthodox economics, which has set out first to analyse capitalist society on the assumption that it can be treated as standing still, and has then tried to introduce the dynamic factors at a later stage, as modifications of this static analysis. Such a method is radically wrong; for if the vital factor of change is left out of the original analysis, it cannot be successfully reintroduced. Man cannot breathe the breath of life into a dead body, or achieve concreteness by starting out from what is admittedly an abstraction.

The falsification inherent in static analysis of living and changing things becomes still more evident as soon as we ask ourselves what the purpose of the analysis is. For in our study of social affairs we are assuredly seeking not only to understand, but also to make our understanding a basis for action. Being men and members of a society of men, we cannot escape the necessity of acting, or dissociate our desire to understand society from our desire to act aright as members of it. We can, of course, seek to make our analysis as objective as possible, in order to avoid falsifying facts to suit our personal wishes and ideals;

and it is of vital importance that we should do this to the fullest extent of which we are capable. But, however objective we try to be, we cannot possibly even wish to stop our understanding from influencing our action, or exclude considerations of practice from our attempts to understand. All social studies, however objective they may need to be, have a practical aspect; and, if it is disastrous to allow our wishes to distort our observation of the facts, it is no less so to forget, or deny, that understanding of the facts is bound to influence action, and thereby to modify the facts themselves. For actions are facts, and men's understanding is a fact, which becomes a social fact as soon as it is diffused by speech or writing, or even as soon as it affects the actions of him who understands.

A sound method of social analysis must therefore be dynamic, in the sense that it must set out from things as they are, in continual change and growth, and not from dead abstractions from which the quality of change and the power to change have been carefully removed. It is above all at this point that Marx's method diverges at the very outset from that of the "orthodox" economists. For they, from the time of Ricardo[1] up to the present, have one and all, with varying degrees of consciousness, begun by constructing an abstract and static economic world as a field for their analysis, and have allowed change to intrude into this world of theirs only when they have completed its equipment with a full set of static institutions, and studied down to the last detail the hypothetical "behaviour" of these institutions in the absence of all changes which could operate as disturbing factors. This is the celebrated "equilibrium analysis," carried to its barren perfection above all by Pareto and by the economists of the Austrian school and their imitators, but used less consciously as a method by all their predecessors of the classical schools after Adam Smith.

For example, in this abstract world of the economists, there is no room for the influence of technical changes which affect the productivity of industry, the balance of machine and human power, the structure of the productive system, the character of the labour process, the supply of and demand for the various kinds of commodities—in fact, every aspect and element of economic life. Not, of course, that the economists are unmindful of these changes. They are not; but they treat them as disturbing factors which cause conditions in the real world to diverge from the pattern of the abstract world which they have devised. They fall in love with this creature of their minds, until they

[1] Not from that of Adam Smith, who had a strong historical sense.

come readily to believe that man's chief task in society should be to make conditions in the real world resemble as closely as possible this abstract world, in which things always work themselves out with the precision of mathematical equations, and nothing unexpected can ever happen. But, for this to be achieved, all possibility of progress would have to be emptied out of the world; for progress is essentially and inevitably a disturbing force, upsetting current adjustments and existing relationships, and changing the very nature of things as well as their relative positions.

Our first precept, then, is to begin with the real concrete world of things as they are, and not with a simplified abstract world of our imagination. But we must think of things as they are, not as standing still, so as to be reproducible by timeless portraiture, but as changing and growing while we regard them, and as carrying about in all their ceaseless movements and interactions the whole living history of their growth. It is often said that the origin of a thing can never explain it; and that is true enough. Its origin is but one fragment of its history, even as its present activity is another fragment. To study things historically is to set out to interpret them, not by their origins, but by the whole active force of which their entire history is the expression.

But that is not all. If we are setting out to understand a thing, we must look directly at the thing itself, and not primarily at men's ideas about it. This is not because ideas are unimportant, or uninfluential in shaping the world's history, as some Marxists seem to suppose, but because in the last resort ideas are about things, and not things about ideas. The thing is prior to the ideas men form of it, though the ideas, once formed, can exert a profound influence in changing the shape of things, and in bringing new combinations of things into existence. Throughout human history, things and ideas ceaselessly interact, but never so as to upset the primacy of things. For, in order to become a force in history, the idea, which is derived from things, must be made flesh, and become a thing.

The Conception of History

This, and neither more nor less than this, is the basis of the "Materialist Conception of History"—a name so misunderstood and so overlaid with wrong associations as to make clear explanation of it a terribly difficult task, not only because the conception itself is unclear at certain vital points, but also because the name is apt to conjure up a wrong picture which

17

it is a labour of Sisyphus to remove. For most people think instinctively of 'materialism' as asserting the supremacy of matter over mind, or even as denying the existence of mind save as a derivative quality of matter, whereas no such doctrine is involved in, or even reconciliable with, the "Materialist Conception of History."[1] What this conception does assert is that mind, as a formative force in history, works by embodying itself in things, changing their shape and potency, and combining them into relations and systems whose changing phases are the basis of the history of mankind.

Marx is never weary of asserting the primacy of things over ideas about them, or of denying the Hegelian-Platonic notion of the primacy of 'ideas'; but he is no less emphatic in denouncing the "crude materialism" which dismisses mind out of the universe. Marx's 'materialism' is to be contrasted not with philosophies which affirm the reality of mind, but with the kinds of Idealism that deny the reality of matter. In the sense in which most people to-day use the word, Marx was not a 'materialist' at all. He was a *realist* opponent of Idealism.

What are the "material" things that Marx conceived to be the active determinants of social change? Marx calls them the 'powers of production' and rests his entire account of historical development upon their influence. These 'powers of production' are not, though they include, mere natural objects, offered to man for his use apart from any activity of his own. They also include, more and more as civilisation advances, things which men have made by changing the form of natural objects, directing the labour of their hands with the informing power of the human mind. Moreover, even natural objects make their contribution to human history largely, though not exclusively, through men's knowledge of their use. The sea is barrier, and not highway, till men learn to make vessels that will carry them upon it. Coal becomes a productive power only when men have discovered that it will burn, and have learnt the art of mining. Storms and earthquakes may destroy, and climate may cause vegetation to grow or perish, or may influence men's bodies and minds without positive collaboration of men's minds with nature. But the advance of civilisation consists above all else of the growth of men's knowledge of the ways to make natural

---

[1] "The materialist doctrine that men are products of circumstances and upbringing and that, therefore, changed men are products of other circumstances and of changed upbringing forgets that circumstances are in fact changed by men and that the educator himself has to be educated." Marx, *Theses on Feuerbach*, III.

objects serve their ends, and to fashion out of them things that exist and work not by nature, but by art bending nature to man's will.

The external things, then, that Marx calls "material" and regards as the agents of social evolution come as man's knowledge increases to be more and more products of the human mind using and transforming what is given by nature. The 'gifts of nature' become products of human intelligence, as when barren wastes are converted by irrigation into fertile land. Not nature, as in Buckle's conception, but *man's power over nature* lies at the root of history. Indeed, for Marx, man himself, mind and all, is a "thing" and, in his economic capacity, one of the 'powers of production,' and the most important of them all. Why call such a conception "materialist," when it in fact embodies the fullest recognition of the conscious determining power of mind?

It is, I think, impossible to acquit Marx of having opened the door to serious misunderstanding by failing to make clear this dual character of the 'powers of production.' It is, indeed, implied throughout in the account Marx gives of them, as well as in his repeated insistence that "men make their own history"; but it is nowhere clearly stated; and the labelling of the powers of production as 'materialistic' is calculated, as we have seen, to foster misunderstanding of their real character. Indeed, Marx was probably unconscious, when he formulated his doctrine, that the distinction between the mental and environmental elements in the powers of production was of key importance. These elements were so intermingled in both land and capital goods—which in their historical forms are alike products of mind acting upon the gifts of external nature—that it may have seemed to him that to distinguish them would involve needless abstraction. It would, moreover, have blurred the contrast between his version of the dialectical process and Hegel's, which he wished to make as sharp as he could. The consequence, however, was that he appeared to many of his readers to be building his theory of history on a monistic foundation of determination by man's physical environment, whereas he was in fact building it on a dualistic foundation of the interaction between the mind of man and the physical world upon which man's mind has to work. Engels tended to worsen the confusion by insisting that the mind of man is part of the physical world, because it can operate on things only through the body. This method of statement does indeed save consistency, by explicitly including mind itself within the range of 'material' things; but it does so only at the cost of concealing the essential dualism of man's relation to things and, if pressed to an extreme, of annihilating mind and returning to the crude materialism which Marx so strongly denounced.

Idealism and "Materialism"

Marx called his conception of history "materialist," because he was determined to mark it off sharply from the metaphysical Idealism of Hegel and his followers. Where he wrote "materialist," it would be more natural in our day to write "realist"; for it is Realism, and not Materialism, that we are accustomed to contrast with Idealism as a philosophical point of view. In this book, I shall write "realist" in place of "materialist," wherever "realist" will convey better to the modern reader the meaning of Marx's doctrine. For I can see no point at all in that form of servility which clings obstinately to a name, even when it has been proved again and again to be a source of needless confusion and misunderstanding. This irreverence will doubtless annoy the theological parrots who screech about the Marxian temples. Let them squawk. Our business is neither to vilify nor to adulate, but to understand.

According to the Idealists, ideas and not things are the ultimate substance of being. The world we seem to know, the world of fact and event, is but a shadowing of a more real world of pure idea. The thing is nothing, save as a pale and unsubstantial reflection of the idea. Mind not merely shapes matter to its will, but makes it out of nothing save itself. Real things, or rather the appearances that masquerade as real things, owe such half-reality as is conceded to them solely to being emanations of mind or spirit. Consciousness, which is the attribute of mind, is therefore regarded as prior to existence in space and time, which is the attribute of things. There are no things: there are only thoughts thinking them.

But now even these thoughts begin to dissolve. For how shall thought subsist without a thinker? How shall many thoughts exist save in the substance of a unifying mind? But the minds of mere men will not serve; for they dwell in bodies which, being things, are but the unsubstantial wrack of thought. The Idealist proceeds at last to the One Universal Mind, wherein all thought has its source and ultimate substance, so that no thought is finally real, except it exist in the Universal Mind. Thus Idealism, which begins by upholding the claims of mind against matter, ends by annihilating minds equally with material things, leaving in substantial existence only the Universal One who bears the same suspiciously close resemblance to the

Absolute Nothing as a perfectly empty circle bears to the figure o.

Absolute Idealism is conceived most naturally in static terms; for how can the Absolute, which includes all, change? Change must be out of one form into another; but can the Absolute ever discard, or add to itself, even a single characteristic? It was left for Hegel to re-think Idealism in dynamic terms, so as to make of the Absolute, not a One existing from all time, but an immanent reality gradually achieving actual existence by the evolutionary process of its own thought, discarding ceaselessly the dross of partially conceived and incomplete truths, so as to draw nearer in actual as well as in immanent reality to the ultimate Oneness of the completely coherent and rational self-realisation of the Idea. If, at this point, the reader exclaims, "What a sentence!" I must answer that I can find no words less nonsensically grandiloquent wherewith to express without mis-representing Hegel's curious conception of the dialectical March of Mind. This process of developing actuality was expressed in the Hegelian dialectic, on which Marx built a "materialist"— say rather a "realist"—dialectic of his own.

For Hegel, human history was merely a phase in the dialectical self-realisation of the "Idea." Things were not, save in and for the developing Idea. Minds were not, save as stuff to be burned up to nothing more than the infinitesimal speck of reality distilled out of them in the fierce heat of the crucible of universal history.

In that fierce heat only the rational could live; and therefore only the rational was deemed to possess reality. But as everything of which we have direct experience falls short of rationality, all our experience had to be deemed an experience of unreality. All Idealism before Hegel resolved itself into this flat denial of the reality of things experienced. It was Hegel's achievement, by invoking the conception of degrees of reality, and by re-stating Idealism in evolutionary terms, to attempt, on Idealistic assumptions, to put back a shadowy element of reality into our every-day experience. But, in the Hegelian universe of becoming, the stigma upon common experience remained; for things possessed such imperfect reality as they had only as partial embodiments of the developing Idea.

To this Idealist conception Marx opposed an uncompromising Realism. Seizing upon Hegel's evolutionary conception of being, he applied it, under Feuerbach's influence, directly to the substance of the world of actual experience. The things we see and feel and experience directly with our minds and senses are real, but they are not static. They are constantly changing, becoming, waxing and waning, passing into something other than themselves, even as Hegel said; but their mutations are their own, and not reflections of anything external to themselves. According to Marx, the Hegelian dialectic is the right method of apprehending reality; but, as Feuerbach had already shown, it needs to be applied directly to the world of things, and used directly as a clue to the interpretation of ordinary human experience.

In Hegel's universe, the evolution of the Idea is accomplished dialectically by a ceaseless succession of ideological conflicts. Every idea that embodies a partial truth meets in the world its opposite and "contradiction,"[1] which is also the embodiment of a partial truth. Between the two there follows a conflict, out of which at length a new and higher idea, embodying new but still partial truth, emerges—to generate in its turn a new opposite and a new conflict. This struggle of ideas is fought out again and again in the dialectical form of thesis, antithesis, and synthesis; and each synthesis becomes, in the moment of its victory, a thesis in terms of which a fresh struggle is to be fought. This process must go on until finally the goal is reached in that complete and insuperable synthesis which embodies in itself the whole truth and nothing but the truth.

In Hegel's philosophy, these battling ideas can hardly be said to be in men's minds: rather are men's minds conceived of as being in the ideas, and as partaking of reality only by virtue of being so. The individual mind has, for Hegel, only the most shadowy reality, as a speck of 'mind-stuff' on its way towards absorption in the Universal Mind or Idea.

Marx took over, and applied directly to the world of human affairs, all the Hegelian paraphernalia of conflict—of theses, antitheses and syntheses succeeding one another in a ceaseless ascent of mankind towards more developed forms of social and economic organisation. But what he saw evolving in this way was not the Idea, but life itself—the multifarious social life men embody in the patterns of the successive epochs of human civilisation. There was no need to go outside the world of men and things for the clue to the evolutionary process. For men and things are themselves the subject-matter of evolution.

The life, however, which Marx saw as developing in this dialectical fashion is *social* life. It is the life, not of individuals, but of societies. For Marx, as for Hegel, the individual is not the "real thing," but an abstraction. He says in the sixth of his

[1] For the Hegelian meaning of "contradiction" see page 288.

Theses on Feuerbach that "the human essence is no abstraction inherent in each single individual: in its reality it is the *ensemble* of the social relations." He speaks of Feuerbach as compelled, by his failure to understand this, "to presuppose an abstract, *isolated*, human individual"; and he goes on to say that the older materialism was unable, from the same cause, to advance beyond "the outlook of single individuals in civil society"— meaning, by "civil society," what Hegel meant by it when he contrasted it, as the realm of individual relations, with the State as the concrete human reality. If Marx had intended by this no more than that the individual is subject to social influences and that the very notion of an isolated individual apart from such influences is an abstraction, he would have been correct. But he meant a great deal more: for him the class, and the State as a representative of class power, were endowed with the same sort of higher reality as Hegel attributed to his metaphysically conceived State, and the individual, social influences and all, was regarded as less real, and more abstract, than the class to which he belonged.

Mind, Matter, and Statistical Probability

In the conflict between Marx and Hegel, the issue is not whether the dominant power is mind or matter; for the Hegelian conception subordinates both alike to the supposed Idea, and makes men into abstractions in order the more to exalt the Absolute. Marx's so-called Materialism, which was in fact Realism, upheld actual mind, in its form as "social mind," equally with actual matter against the Absolute which was greedy to engulf them both. Marx did not pose the question of mind *versus* matter at all, because he conceived it to be wholly without meaning for the world of men. He was deeply influenced by the fact that, in the world of men and external things, mind and matter are so inter-penetrated and at one that he held it to be futile to ask which counts for more. Mind cannot exist save in the material substance of the brain, or receive impressions save through the material avenues of the sense-organs; and the material objects external to man amid which he lives and works, from the soil itself to the steam-engine and the electrical generator, owe their form and nature and productive power so largely to man's activity as to be essentially products of mind, constantly evolving and changing under the influence of man's inventive power.

It might have been supposed that this assertion of the essential unity of mind and matter would have led Marx to insist on the final reality of the individual; for it is only in individuals that mind and matter are conjoined. Neither State nor group nor class has a body, any more than it has a mind. The collectivity, to use Herbert Spencer's phrase, "has no common *sensorium*." But Marx did not draw this seemingly obvious conclusion, to which he was blinded by his sense of the overwhelming importance of social factors in the making of human character. Because the *isolated* individual is an abstraction, Marx rushed to the conclusion that Hegel was right in regarding the individual himself as an abstraction, and in attributing concrete reality to the whole to which he was attached. He attributed reality and potency in shaping the world not to individuals, but to classes. He did not realise that in taking up this attitude he was departing from his affirmation that bodies and minds could exist only in union, and that mind apart from body could have no real existence. He made the class an active reality, though it had no body wherewith to act, except the discrete bodies of its individual constituents.

In what sense, if any, can it be legitimate to speak of 'classes' as real things, despite their want of bodies or minds distinct from those of their members? Any statistician will be able to answer this question, after a fashion. If enough members of a class tend to act uniformly in any given situation to render unimportant, because uninfluential, the actions of the exceptional individuals, it is legitimate to speak loosely of the class as "acting" in such and such a way. If we find how, in this sense, classes have in fact repeatedly responded, we may be able to predict, with some degree of probability, how they will respond in similar situations in the future. Such predictions are, however, only statements of statistical probability, and they tell us nothing about the probable behaviour of any particular member of the class. Marx assumes that classes, in this statistical sense, act in accordance with their conceptions of class-interest (and also, I think, that their conceptions of class-interest tend to coincide with real class-interests). Thus, his theory of class-action says nothing about the motives that move any particular individual to act: it is a complete misunderstanding to represent Marx as saying that everyone always acts either in the interest of his class, or in his own private interest. What he does hold is that, on any occasion when great numbers are involved, most of the individuals will act in accordance with class-interests as far as such interests arise; so that there exists a statistical probability that the power of a class will be thrown predominantly on the side of its interest. Marx, of course, did not state his position in

24

this way. He did not distinguish between statistical probability and certainty: he regarded the correlation between class-action and class-interest as certain for practical purposes of historical interpretation and prediction. But what he regarded as certain was not how the individual, but how the class, would act.

Does the fact that it is possible to make highly probable statistical predictions about how a class will act justify treating the class as a "real thing"? That is mainly a question of terminology: if for "real thing" is substituted "real force," there cannot be much doubt about the answer. What is not justifiable is to conclude that any "reality" attributed to the class derogates in any respect from the "reality" of the individuals included in the class. Hegel did take this view; and Marx was enough under Hegel's influence at least to come near to taking it, and often to use language which appeared to imply it. How far he did consciously take it I am not sure. What is certain is that his belief that class-action was predictable in terms of interest, combined with his belief that class-action was the moving force in history, led him to relegate the individual to a quite subordinate rôle. This is the foundation of much of the ruthlessness and lack of humanism that has characterised the application of the Marxian doctrine. Marx and Engels would probably have said that it was essential to the "scientific" spirit, and would have rested their claim to be "scientific Socialists" at least partly on this ground. But is the best scientist he who ignores "variations"; and, if there is an analogy between Biology and Social Science, is it found in a practice of ignoring variations and relying exclusively on a study of statistical probabilities? The statistical method has been very fruitful in many fields of science, including Social Science; but, however fruitful it can be in studying and in predicting class-behaviour, does it cover the whole field? Does it, for example, even begin to explain that "variation" in the 'powers of production' which, on Marx's own showing, sets the whole process of social evolution to work, and creates the classes whose behaviour is regarded as the means of bringing human institutions into a right relation with the developing 'powers of production'? The human mind does not act *only* as an ingredient in the "class-mind," or in class-behaviour. It acts in many other ways as well, including the fundamentally important way of acquiring new knowledge.

True though the assertion of the essential unity of mind and body may be, it does not make the distinction between mind and external nature unimportant. When Marx first formulated his theory, the most pressing need may have been to confute the Hegelians; but the attribution of concrete reality to classes was illogical, and the consequence of setting up "Materialism" against "Idealism" was to let loose endless misunderstandings upon an age less ridden by Hegelian Idealism than that of Marx's youth.

The Powers of Production

When we speak, in Marxian terms, of the 'powers of production' as the fundamental forces responsible for social evolution, the phrase has no meaning unless it applies not only to the natural forces which are at men's disposal, but also to the artificial forces which men have made by their use, and not only to all these forces, natural and artificial, taken together, but also to men's knowledge of how to apply them—that is, to the human mind.

Suppose a horde of savages left, by the flight or massacre of every civilised inhabitant, in undisputed possession of all the resources of an advanced country, but with no knowledgeable human being at hand to teach them the use of their new possessions. What would be the 'powers of production' in such a case? The great engines and power-stations, the complicated machines in the factories, the equipment of transport and communication—all these would cease to be 'powers of production' determining the course of social development and would become mere "matter," useless except where the savage mind could devise, within its range of comprehension, some use for them—probably, in our eyes, mostly some peculiar or even ludicrous use. I remember reading somewhere of a motor car, captured by tribesmen who were ignorant of its use, and converted into a man-drawn ceremonial car for the chief. A thing becomes a 'power of production' only by virtue of a special relation to the mind of man; and this relation is not something given, but something achieved in the development of human knowledge. The Marxian Conception of History, in any interpretation of it that makes sense, is so far from representing men as merely the sport of things that it stresses more than any other theory the creative function of men in making the world after the pattern of their own knowledge. The outcome of the so-called 'Materialist Conception' is not to dethrone the mind of man, but on the contrary to assert that men make their own history against those who hold that God or the Absolute makes it for them, or that the whole course of human events is no more than a stream of undirected chance.

Men make their own history; but according to Marx they make it primarily in the economic sphere. The great history-makers are those human societies which, by invention or experiment, or by enlarging the boundaries of human knowledge, alter the character of the powers of production, and therewith the ways in which men get their living and organise themselves for economic ends, or those which, by destroying civilisations and sweeping away the works and knowledge accumulated by generations of toil and experiment, drive men back to painful new beginnings of economic and cultural activity. This is not to say that in Marx's view the dominant rôle in history belongs to great scientists and inventors on the one hand, and to great captains of destruction upon the other; for in his view the great advances in the arts of production are social products and often the great invention arises as the cumulative result of the work of many innovators—and the most destructive warfare in history has often arisen not from one man's ambition or military genius, but from the migrations of entire peoples, or the clash of rival groups within a common civilisation. Emphatically, the "great man" theory of history is not what Marx believed in; but to deny its validity is not to deny that great men do count, for both good and ill. There is no warrant for the view that the Russian Revolution would have followed the same course without Lenin, or the French Revolution without Napoleon, or that Europe would have been just the same to-day if Hitler had never existed, or that someone else would have been bound to hit on just the same inventions as Watt and Siemens and Marconi at just the same time even if these particular individuals had never been born.

It is fully consistent with Marxism to hold that great men do count; but the Marxist asserts that they count because their greatness fits in with the opportunities of their time. Nor will any Marxist agree that they count exclusively; for no Marxist will accept it as in the least true that in their absence the world would stand still, or that they are the only, or the principal, formative force in world history. According to Marx, what forms world history above all else is the continual interaction between what is given to men as their social inheritance, natural or acquired, and the minds of men in each generation.

Indeed, Marxists, though they do not rule out the influence of 'great men,' tend to regard such men as more the products than the creators of their age. Superior products, no doubt—or at all events products more influential than others for good or

27

ill—but essentially products, in the sense that their 'greatness' lies in giving exceptionally powerful expression to forces which would be operative even in their absence, because they arise out of the developing relations between man and his economic environment. Marx in his account of historical evolution makes little of 'great men' and much of the developing 'powers of production'; but the fact that inventions and discoveries are largely social products does not get away from the fact that one element in the growth of these powers is the contribution of the 'great men' who either devise new forms of mastery over external nature or obstruct their development by annihilating knowledge or imposing fetters upon its expansion and diffusion in and between human societies.

In considering how men's social heritage acts upon them, and how men act upon it, in any particular epoch, it is irrelevant how much of this heritage is natural and how much the product of the activity of earlier generations of men. For our own generation, the steam-engine and the electrical generator—and also, alas, the atomic bomb—are just as much parts of the objective situation which confronts mankind as the climate, or the minerals that are found near the earth's surface. It is, of course, true that there will soon be no steam-engines unless men go on making new ones, whereas there will be a climate (but not necessarily quite the same climate) even if men suspend all activity in relation to it. But that is not the point, which is rather that, within any given civilisation, each generation finds itself presented with a certain objective situation, including both natural and man-made elements, and that it is upon this situation that each generation of men has to build, within the limits imposed by it, and with the materials which it affords.

This view of history does not, as many people appear to suppose, imply any sort of fatalism. It does not involve saying that, given a certain objective situation *irrespective of the behaviour of the human beings who have to handle it*, there is only one possible outcome, so that the next phase of human history is utterly predestined however human beings may behave. It does involve insisting that, as history is a chain of connected development, the next phase of any civilisation must be of such a nature that it can be developed out of its predecessor, and that men's power of influencing the course of history is limited to a choice between alternatives which are practicable in face of the objective situation. It follows that, when the historian looks back on past phases of development within any given civilisation, he will be likely to find in the objective situations of the past sufficient reasons for history having followed the course which it has actually followed, rather than any other. But this will be because his view of the objective situations of the past will include the actions in them of the human beings who shaped their growth. This is only the familiar dilemma of free will and determinism in one of its sociological aspects. Every event that has happened must have had sufficient cause and must therefore have been determined; but it does not follow that events which have not yet happened are pre-determined apart from the influence of those who have still to act in relation to them. For the causes are not complete until the human beings whose action makes history have done their part. The free wills of men form part of the chain of causality; and those wills are limited only by the limitations of their own knowledge and capacity and by the conditions within which they have to act.

Is History a Straight-line Process?

The foregoing paragraph has repeatedly been qualified by saying "within a given civilisation." When the field of study is extended to cover all human history, including the impact of one civilisation upon another, much more complex issues have to be faced. The attempt, made in *The Communist Manifesto*, to explain *all* history as a single, continuous chain of economic development involves gross over-simplification, if not falsification, of the facts. To what extent Marx really believed in this simplified version of his theory we shall have to consider later on. Meanwhile, let us bear in mind that the *Manifesto* was a propagandist pamphlet, and not a theoretical treatise, and that we cannot necessarily take its sweeping generalisations quite *au pied de la lettre*. Engels, in editing it, had to except 'Primitive Communism' in a footnote; and its practical morals would be unaffected even if its account of the march of history were to be regarded as applicable, in the form given to it in the *Manifesto*, only, say, to the Western World, seen as in broadly continuous development from the dawn of civilisation in the Near and Middle East up to its present phase.

Marxism is determinist, in the sense of rejecting the causeless as a formative force in history; but it is not fatalist. No one who reads Marx's political writings, or his elaborate plannings of Socialist strategy, can reasonably suppose that he considered the victory of Socialism to be predestined as to both time and place, and the behaviour of men in the objective situations which faced them to be limited to an inevitable reaction to economic circumstances. He clearly held that it made a quite vitally significant difference to the prospects of Socialism how Socialists behaved, and that their behaviour was capable of being influenced by instruction and exhortation and example.

The Coming of Socialism

It is, however, sometimes suggested, with more plausibility, that Marx did believe the coming of Socialism to be inevitable, and held that men could, by their conduct, only advance or delay its coming, or cause it to come in a more or less satisfactory form. It is quite possible that Marx did hold this view; but, whether or no, it does not follow as an inexorable deduction from his conception of history. If he held it, his case presumably would be that the objective conditions facing the modern world were of such a nature as to make some form of Socialism the only possible next main stage in the development of Western civilisation. On this view, nothing except Socialism would be compatible with the limiting conditions of objective possibility, and men's power of influencing history would be restricted to making Socialism well or ill, and in this or that of its variant possible forms. Such a judgment, whether correct or not, does not form a necessary part of the Marxian Theory of History, in the sense that anyone who holds the Marxian theory is bound to assent to it. It is a deduction from that theory when it has been brought into contact with the available facts of a particular historical situation, and its validity depends not on the soundness of the theory alone, but also on the observer's skill in selecting from and interpreting this particular set of facts. If something other than Socialism should succeed to Capitalism as the next historical form of social organisation, that would not at all prove the Marxian Conception of History to be wrong. It would at most only show that Marx had made a mistake in interpreting a particular set of facts in the light of his theory.

It is no doubt possible to hold, as an integral element in a theory of history, that historical epochs do succeed one another in a predestined order, so that there *can* never be more than one possible successor to any given system. But what conceivably valid ground can there be for such a view? If it is held at all, it must be held simply *a priori*; for it is by its nature incapable of verification or even of plausible demonstration in the light of the facts. It is, in effect, a piece of mysticism, wholly out of keeping with the realistic temper of the theory we have been discussing. Hegel could plausibly have held such a view, because

30

for him all history was the logical unfolding of the Idea, and freedom consisted solely in furthering this cosmic process. But nothing can square it with a realistic approach to the facts; for to the realist there can be no logical reason why a given objective situation, considered apart from those who are to handle it, should not have more than one possible outcome.

It is of course fully possible for a realist to consider that Socialism is both by far the best and by far the *most probable* successor to Capitalism as a form of social organisation, or even to reach, on the basis of his study of the facts, the conclusion that there is no *positive* alternative. But by this he can mean only that he can see or imagine no positive alternative, and that in his judgment there is none. He cannot rationally mean that in the very nature of things there *can be* no alternative, or even that there can be none of a positive kind. It follows that, in judging that there is no positive alternative, he *may* be mistaken.

Moreover, even if his judgment is objectively right, the possibility of a *negative* alternative remains. It may be a case of Socialism or—chaos. The only alternative to the building up of some sort of Socialist system may be the sheer dissolution of the civilisation that has reached this critical stage. And, in such a situation, the behaviour of men in facing it may make just the vital difference between the collapse of a civilisation and its advance to a new phase of development. Men's choice is confined to the objectively practicable; but how vital that choice may be when the alternatives are delicately poised!

Beyond doubt, Marx took it as "scientifically" certain that Socialism would be the next phase in the history of Western civilisation. Always he wrote as if he regarded the coming of Socialism as inevitable, and only the time and manner of its coming as open to doubt. But this judgment of his rested on two assumptions which are fundamentally quite distinct from his assertion of the primacy of economic forces—of the 'powers of production'—in shaping the course of history. The first of these assumptions was that all human history is to be regarded as a continuous process of development from lower to higher forms, analogous to that which biologists were discovering in his day in the field of organic nature. Engels later declared that Marx had done for the study of social evolution what Darwin had done for Biology, and had thus provided a foundation for "Scientific" Socialism, which rendered the earlier, 'Utopian' forms of Socialism obsolete. The analogy was, however, false. Darwin by no means divided the course of biological evolution into a series of great epochs, each marked by the emergence of a new and higher single dominant species. It was Herbert Spencer, rather than Darwin, who attempted to present biological development as a teleological process of unified advance from lower to higher forms—from the simpler to the more differentiated types of organic life. There was in Darwin's theory nothing at all corresponding to Marx's (or to Comte's) epochs—much less to Marx's conception of social evolution as the instrument of change from one epoch to another.

The Belief in Progress

The plain truth is that Marx worked out his conception of historical development under the spell not of Darwin but of Hegel, who in turn had worked under the spell of earlier theorists inspired by the notions of human perfectibility and continuous underlying progress of the human spirit. Marx, in discarding the Idealistic philosophy of these thinkers, did not discard the framework of their thought, which was a belief in the inevitable "march of man." For his predecessors this belief had been founded on the idea of divine government of the universe and of human affairs, and God's benevolence towards man was the ultimate guarantee of progress.[1] Marx of course rejected this notion of divine governance; but he somehow, like many other nineteenth century atheists, kept the belief in progress which had rested on it. He continued to think that history must work out well even though there was admittedly no *deus ex machina* to ensure this result.

Marx was able to hold to this position, because he substituted for divine providence a conception of the inevitable march of nature, as expressed in the development of the "material" powers of production. This, however, even if it could be held to guarantee development, could by no means logically be treated as guaranteeing that the development would make for men's happiness or well-being. The force of nature had to be regarded as wholly neutral in relation to men's ends and desires save to the extent to which men were themselves operating as a part of nature. To the extent to which they were, nature could be said not to be neutral in relation to their desires; but there could be no assurance that this unneutral element in nature would always be strong enough to prevail against the neutral elements, so as to ensure continuous human progress from epoch to epoch. Marx, however, always assumed that this human element in

[1] This was the basis, for example, of Kant's Philosophy of History.

nature would be able to co-operate with the rest of nature in such a way as to shape nature as a whole to its developing ends.

Social Conflicts

Marx's second assumption, derived directly from Hegel, was that the method of historical development was essentially 'dialectical,' in Hegel's sense of the word. That is to say, it was by way of conflict. In Marx's inverted Hegelianism, this conflict could not be between ideas: it had to be between 'real' forces. These forces Marx saw in economic classes, each historical epoch embodying the supremacy of a particular class. Granted this, he felt he could point to the proletariat as the only class capable of succeeding the *bourgeoisie* in power; and, regarding the proletariat as essentially a single, indivisible class, in process of being more and more completely unified by subjection to a common exploitation, he felt he could regard the victory of the proletariat as leading directly to Socialism, because its emancipation would leave no subject class to be exploited. These are issues to which I shall return later; for the present we need only observe that Marx's rightness or wrongness on this point does not in any way affect the validity of his fundamental theory about the preponderant influence of the powers of production.

Marx, then, regarded Socialism as the inevitable next stage in social evolution, because he regarded each stage as involving the supremacy of a particular class, up to the stage at which the very notion of class would be done away with by the institution of a 'classless society.' Under Capitalism there remained, he insisted, only one exploited class capable of taking upon itself the historical function of organising the fuller use of the developing powers of production. The victory of this class over Capitalism would therefore clear the way directly for the institution of a classless economic order, of which Socialism would be the institutional expression.

This view rests upon at least three distinct foundations: first, that the proletariat is the only class capable of taking over from the capitalist class the ruling power in society; secondly, that society is destined to pass through successive phases of class-domination into classlessness, and cannot simply break down and revert to a more primitive phase; and thirdly, that Socialism is the only form which can be taken by the institutions of a proletarian revolution. These views may all be correct; but they are not self-evident, and they cannot be deduced directly from the primary affirmation of Marxism that what determines the course of human history is the development of the powers of

33

production. They are derived rather from the secondary doctrine of Marxism, that the way in which human institutions are adjusted to fit the requirements of the developing powers of production is the way of class-struggles. It would be quite possible to agree with Marx's primary affirmation, but not with this secondary affirmation about the mechanics of social evolution. It would also be possible to hold that the proletariat is not in fact so completely unitary a class as to exclude the possibility of continued class-exploitation even after a section of it had won political and economic power; and finally it could be held that some economic system other than Socialism might prove to be consistent with the further development of the powers of production.

Of course, any Marxist will deny that these are real possibilities. This denial, however, rests on an unproven assumption that the technical evolution of the powers of production is necessarily such as to require for their effective use the increasing 'socialisation' of control by placing authority in the hands of wider and wider classes, and finally of the whole society. But is there any finally valid reason why the powers of production should not develop in such a way as to call for their control by a narrower, and not by a wider, ruling class? If Marx thought there was, may not the reason have been, not anything 'scientific' in the basis of his thought, but rather an acceptance of the widespread contemporary belief in the inevitability of human progress? We are more disposed than were his generation to ask ourselves whether this belief has any scientific basis, and also whether, in its absence, there would be any reason for taking the inevitability of Socialism for granted.

I am not attempting to answer any of these questions at this point. I am only raising them in order to affirm that there can be ample scope within a "Realist" Conception of History for the constructive influence of the minds of men. Indeed, the practical value of such a conception as a guide to method lies largely in the warning which it gives men against banging their heads uselessly against brick walls. It directs men's minds away from the Utopian, the unrealisable save in fancy, towards the real possibilities of the objective situations in which they are placed, and teaches them, by thinking and acting realistically, to control the course of history far more than they could if they were content with Utopias of the mind. For it is no less indispensable for the social than for the mechanical engineer to accept the qualities and limitations of the forces and materials with which he has to work.

34

The Class-struggle

The Marxian theory of the method of social evolution, however, involves, as we have seen, not only the primary assertion of the overriding influence of the powers of production, but also the secondary assertion that social evolution works itself out by means of the struggle of classes. In the Hegelian dialectic, development takes place always and essentially by means of conflict. In the realm of ideas, antithesis joins battle with thesis, till out of their conflict a new synthesis is born; and this struggle is mirrored in the phenomenal history of men and things. Marx, in turning the Hegelian conception upside down, took over from it the central importance assigned in it to the notion of conflict, and equally with Hegel made conflict the necessary dynamic of social change. But of what nature was the inverted conflict to be? It is easy to master the notion of a conflict of ideas leading to the discovery of a new idea based on both the contestants and incorporating the valid elements in each of them; but in Marx's inverted Hegelian world, what are the contestants? If Marxism were truly "materialism," as most people understand that term, they could be only material things apart from the minds of men. Social evolution would have to take the form of the non-human powers of production fighting one another—a process which it would be exceedingly difficult to express plausibly or lucidly in dialectical form—or indeed in any form at all. But in Marx's view the combatants in social conflict are not mere things but men, or rather groups of men ordered in economic classes in accordance with their differing relations to the non-human powers of production and one to another.

This is the theory of the class-struggle, as repeated in changing forms through human history till its end is reached with the final abolition of classes and the institution of a classless Society. There will be much to say about this theory in later chapters, when we come to discuss the class structures and loyalties of the world of to-day. Here we are concerned with the theory only as an element in the Marxian method.

In reading Marx's writings, above all *Das Kapital*, one is continually reminded of his tendency to regard the class as somehow more deeply 'real' than the individuals who make it up—certainly as a more important influence on historical evolution. Despite his insistence on the priority of things over ideas, he gives the class priority over the individuals who make it up, and treats the class as a thing, and not as an idea. Especially does he tend to speak in this way of the modern world;

for he conceives that, under the capitalist system of large-scale machine production, the individual workman has lost the status and character of an individual producer, and has become merely a "detail-labourer" whose work has meaning only in relation to the work of numerous other labourers working at the same or at related processes within a complex productive unit of which they are part. Even the individual capitalist has largely lost his independence, and has become a contributor to a chain of related processes linking one commodity to another from the first raw material to the final output of consumers' or of capital goods. This rapidly developing interrelation of the entire economic system is called by Marx the process of economic "socialisation," to which Socialism is the appropriate institutional counterpart. Capital is becoming "socialised," and is above all "socialising" the workers who are employed in conjunction with it as elements in a growingly social productive process; and this indispensable "socialisation" of the productive powers of society is laying the necessary foundations for the socialisation of the ownership of the means of production, of the control of the political machine, and of the economic classes which it will merge into the social solidarity of the coming classless society.

It is of vital importance to state this conception of the 'reality' of classes aright. Marx sometimes seems to be playing dangerously—all the more so because but half-consciously—with the Hegelian conception of degrees of reality, as if the reality and historical influence of classes somehow condemned their individual members to a subordinate order of real existence.[1] But it is quite unnecessary for the validity of Marx's primary assertion of the predominant influence of the powers of production to entertain any such metaphysical view. Groups can be real forces, and can exert a real influence on their members, without derogating at all from the reality of the individuals of whom they are made up; and a man may be a "detail-labourer" in a factory, with no isolable individual product of his own, without losing his individuality as a person, however much he may act and think as a member of a group.

Social Action

At this point we are confronted once more with the same question as we met with in the discussion of men's freedom to

[1] Marx himself says that in the first volume of *Capital*, in treating of the theory of value, he "here and there coquetted" with the modes of expression peculiar to Hegel, and that he "avowed himself the pupil of that mighty thinker." In fact, Hegel's influence on Marx's mode of thought remained strong to the end.

make their own history within a system of economic necessity. For here again the status and implications of membership of a group or class set limits within which the individual is compelled to work in order to get what he wants. All action is in the last resort action by individuals, but the individual who occupies a defined place within an established social system can act effectively either to uphold or to change it only if he acts appropriately in relation to the objective conditions. This means, in social matters, acting in association with others who are similarly placed, or whose circumstances, even if they differ, are so related to his own as to afford a basis for co-operative action. It is of course always possible for an individual to dissociate himself from those who are similarly placed with himself, and to act in opposition to his own group or class. But, even in this case, he will be able to act effectively *in social matters*[1] only if he transfers his allegiance to some other group or class, within which he can find like-minded collaborators. In any society of men, collaboration is the prerequisite of effective social activity. There has never been a human society in which each individual acted by himself, without group loyalty or collaboration. Such a society can be imagined by mad philosophers or by *laissez-faire* economists; but it is quite out of the question that any real society of men should ever bear a significant resemblance to it.

This collaboration among men is by no means based exclusively either on a rational calculation of self-interest, or on a merely passive acceptance of the implications of a common status. It is neither Benthamite nor sheerly determined apart from men's wills and desires. Based largely on community of needs, experiences and purposes, it is informed by a spirit of loyalty and fellowship. It affects men in their altruistic as well as their egoistic impulses; and the strength with which it is felt differs greatly from man to man, quite apart from differences in their economic and social experience. For this reason a class cannot be defined, when it is regarded as an active agent of social change, simply in terms of its common economic experience. It becomes fully a class, in this positive sense, only to the extent to which it is permeated by a spirit of loyalty.

[1] I.e. on the plane of those activities which, according to Marx, form the "superstructure" reared on the foundations supplied by the "powers of production." It may be quite possible for an individual to act on his own in devising some new invention or discovery that may have prodigious social effects.

Class and Class-consciousness

It is sometimes suggested that a class becomes a class, in this positive sense, only to the extent to which its members become "class-conscious." But this is not wholly so, if class-consciousness is held to imply a clear formulation of the notion of class-solidarity in the members' minds. Class loyalty can be very strong, at any rate in its negative reactions, without the notion of class-solidarity being clearly present in the minds of most of the members. But class-consciousness, through which loyalty becomes a reasoned conception of solidarity without losing its emotional content, is a powerful agent in strengthening the ties of the class-group. The sense of loyalty becomes the stronger for being made the basis of a rational idea; and classes become powerful instruments of social change when the instinctive class-loyalty of the majority passes under the leadership of a rationally class-conscious minority. Marxian Socialism, which could have no wide appeal if there were no foundation of class-loyalty for it to build upon, has been a means of equipping large sections of the working classes in the industrial countries with this reasoning class-conscious leadership. For, if Marxism is essentially rationalistic in its methods and doctrines, it has its roots deep down in the simple sense of a common fellowship among the oppressed.

That class-loyalty need not imply class-consciousness in the individual is seen far more clearly among the upper than in the lower strata of human societies. Those whom the existing social and economic arrangements suit best are often least conscious of acting together on a basis of class. They feel themselves to be acting in defence, not of a single class, but of the whole society, as it is actually constituted; and they repudiate angrily, and often quite sincerely, the suggestion that their attitude is influenced by considerations of class. Yet such people have usually a very high degree of class-loyalty and of solidarity one with another, as we can see by their eagerness to sustain common and exclusive cultural and social standards of their own, by their intermarriages one with another, and by their care in preserving from invasion their own educational institutions and their monopoly of certain professions and callings, as well as, in "open" societies, by their skill in assimilating such outsiders as do penetrate from above or from below inside the circle of their class. To classes in this position, class-consciousness of a reasoned and explicit kind is unnecessary; indeed, it is a positive danger. They are the stronger if they, and even their leaders, can believe that they are acting, not in any narrow spirit of class-egoism, but as the

38

protagonists of the community as a whole. The British upper class in the eighteenth century, and the British middle class in the generation following the Reform Act of 1832, alike possessed this spirit almost to perfection; and despite the confidence-disturbing experiences of the 1930's, which a great many of them are doing their level best to forget, the main body of the American middle classes has it to-day.

On the other hand, for a class which has still to win power, in order to become a controlling agent of social change, a considerable degree of positive class-consciousness is indispensable. For a far higher degree of deliberately organised co-operation is needed for changing the form of society than for preserving the *status quo* under conditions which make for its continuance. A governing class comes to need class-consciousness only when the onslaught upon it is already being pressed hard, and when it has been forced into a posture of defence. In such circumstances the most hopeful line of defence is prompt and vigorous counter-attack; and class-loyalty without class-consciousness is incapable of taking the offensive.

Class-consciousness, however, is essentially a matter of degree. Any class contains some members who possess it in a high degree, some who possess it not at all, and some who are at every intermediate stage between the extremes. The objective conditions are the most important determinants of the strength and diffusion of class-consciousness. But they are not the only determinants; for the turning of class-loyalty into class-consciousness is largely a matter of propaganda and organisation. Trade Unions spring up everywhere as capitalist production develops; but both the numbers of their adherents and the degree to which they are animated by a class-conscious attitude depend greatly on the character of their leadership. It takes a highly organised class-conscious minority to imbue the collective organisations based on common interests and loyalties with any high degree of class-consciousness.

Class and Group

We begin to see now what is meant by Marx's insistence on the "reality" and efficacy of economic classes. They are 'real' in and through their capacity for organised collective action. The creation of Trade Unions, of Co-operative Societies, of rudimentary political organisations formed largely on a class basis, is the first step towards the collective self-expression of the working class. But it is only the first step; for such bodies are formed first sporadically, among groups here and there, under the impulsion of immediate needs and experiences. They are not class-organisations, but group-organisations formed on such a basis as to have the potentiality of cohering at a second stage into larger units and associations, under the influence partly of developments in the objective situation—the growth of larger-scale Capitalism, for example—and partly of constructive leadership using the opportunities which the developing situation presents. But, though they have this potentiality, there is no certainty of it being realised; for the objective situation by itself will not suffice to create a consciously organised class. That is the work of men—of leaders; and, though the developing situation is a powerful agency in calling latent leadership into active life, the successful conscious organisation of a class is no more inevitable than the advent of a Lenin or a Napoleon or a Hitler.

Indeed, even when class-organisation has been brought to a high pitch of mechanical efficiency, under the inspiration of leaders possessing a reasoned class-conscious point of view, success is not assured. For, if the leadership subsequently fails, the imposing mass-organisation may rot away inwardly, preserving only the semblance of the class-solidarity and the class-consciousness which gave it its original driving-force. Nothing in human history is ever inevitable until it has happened, not because things happen without a cause, but because no chain of causation is ever complete until it has actually produced its effect.

Leadership, then, is essential to make a class an effective agent of social development. But if classes need constructive leadership, leaders are nothing unless they are able to place themselves at the head of forces upon which the objective situation confers the opportunity of real power. Marx's point is not merely that effective action in the sphere of world history is always collective action, involving the collaboration of a group, but also that these groups must be of a particular kind. A man may collect a group of followers round him on the basis of an idea, or groups may arise on a foundation of neighbourhood, race, nationality, or religion; but in Marx's view no group plays a dominant rôle in world history unless it appears as the representative of a class. This does not mean that Marx regards the part played by other groups as unimportant or ineffective, but only that he deems it secondary, and holds that no group that is not also a class is ever the main agent of transition from one stage of social evolution to another. A group which is not also the embodiment of a class may be able to make history within

40

the framework of a given social system, and to exert a powerful secondary influence on the character of the change from one system to another; but in Marx's view no such group can itself effect a major change of system.

Why does Marx hold this? Because each social system—that is, each stage in social development—corresponds in his view to a particular arrangement of the powers of production, and therefore involves a particular set of class-relationships. There is, in his view, a particular relation between the powers of production and the class-system. He holds that a group which is not the embodiment of a class does not stand for any particular way of arranging the powers of production. It does not stand for a particular social system based on a particular stage in the development of man's power over nature, and expressing itself in a set of economic class-relationships calculated to secure the most effective use of this power. It cannot therefore stand as the representative of an existing social system, or as the protagonist in the struggle to replace it by a new one. For as soon as it came to be either of these things, it would have become the representative of a particular economic class.

Be it clearly understood that Marx does not suggest that the groups which stand as the representatives of classes must always be consciously aiming chiefly at economic ends, or must express their aspirations always in economic terms. On the contrary, he affirms that class-struggles are often fought out in terms which have apparently little or nothing to do with economic questions or with class-relationships. A group may become the representative of a class even if it begins and develops without any conscious reference to class issues. Men, Marx says, have often fought out essentially economic struggles in religious or ideological terms, making the will of God or the dictates of universal justice in the image of their own class-needs, or taking over and turning to a class-purpose an institution or a doctrine which had no class-implications in the minds of its original makers. Everyone is familiar in these days with Max Weber's view that there has been an intimate connection between the growth of Protestantism and Puritanism and the rise of the capitalist system, not because Protestants and Puritans were conscious hypocrites, eager to throw a veil of religion over their economic rapacity, but because "the Protestant ethic" provided a basis for "free" and "rational" business activity. Others have reversed this judgment, and have argued that the developing class of traders and industrial *entrepreneurs* seized avidly on an ethic which fitted in admirably with the economic practices appropriate to the objective

41

situation with which they had to deal. Similarly, in eighteenth-century England, Wesleyanism exactly suited the needs of the new class of abstinent capitalists because it not merely strengthened them for money-making by encouraging their abstinence, but also gave them the satisfying sense that they could make money to the glory of God. This glorification of money-making, on the ground that money made and saved is the outward and visible sign that a man has wrought hard in this world of tribulation, runs as a strange thread of self-deception through one early Wesleyan apologia after another.

Groups and associations are not classes, but they can and do become in varying degrees the representatives of class aspirations and points of view. To this power, Marx argues, they owe their ultimate efficacy as agents of social transformation. But this is not to say that any group can become an agent of social transformation by coming to represent a class. For not all classes at all times are either the protagonists in the defence of an existing social order, or the leaders of a crusade against it. There are classes to which, at least at a particular stage of social evolution, a rôle of dominance is necessarily denied—for example, the class of landlords in a situation already dominated by large-scale industrial Capitalism. A class, in Marx's system, plays the leading rôle in defence or attack only if its class point of view coincides with the requirements of the existing arrangement of the conditions of production or with those of an alternative arrangement calculated to advance the development of production to a higher stage. The class thus occupies an intermediate position between the active groups which lead and represent it and the economic foundations on which it rests.

How Classes Arise

How, then, does a class come into existence? Marx holds that it arises out of the requirements of the objective situation of the powers of production. At any stage, men possess certain natural and acquired resources of things and of knowledge of the use of things, and these together form their equipment for carrying on the work of production. But this work can be carried on only if there arises in fact, or by conscious adoption, a social arrangement for its conduct. There must be laws or conventions or customs regulating the right of use, or ownership, of the instruments of production; and there must be operative relationships between men as producers, whether these relationships arise out of force or by consent. Someone must dig, fetch and carry, organise and give orders; there must be some way of dividing the products of associative labour; and finally there must be some way of enforcing conformity with the rules and conventions of the established system, whatever it may be, and some way of assigning to each man his place and function. In other words, every arrangement of the powers of production necessarily implies a social system—an ordering of the relationships between men and things and between men and men, on a basis consistent with the development of the available productive resources. But this in its turn has involved, at every stage of human history up to the present, a set of class-relationships; for the arrangement of men into groups with different economic functions and claims has been at every stage[1] an arrangement of them into economic classes.

Observe that I say "has been," and not "must be"; for it is not suggested that the division of society into economic classes is inevitable for all time. What is suggested is that the class-systems of the past and present, however much evil they may seem to embody when they are judged by ideal standards, have been, at the time of their origin, instruments for organising the advance of men's power over nature, and the enlargement of the opportunities for welfare. They have not been necessarily the best instruments possible at the time of their advent to power—to believe that would be to relapse into fatalism—but they have been the means of improving, economically, on what went before.

Or rather, they have been so, subject to one qualification of outstanding importance, the omission of which has vitiated much Marxist thinking. This qualification is that the entire process with which we have been dealing seems to be envisaged as relating to the internal development of a given civilisation, and not to the impact of one civilisation upon another. For it must surely be admitted that, where a whole civilisation is overthrown, as happened at the decline and fall of the Roman Empire as a world system, the course of development follows the lines made possible by the economic power and knowledge and assimilative capacity of the conquerors, and not of the defeated civilisation—so that in such a case a higher stage of economic evolution and knowledge may be displaced by a lower. No doubt, where this happens, some part at least of the civilisation of the conquered will usually be assimilated in time

[1] Except perhaps at the most primitive; for Engels at any rate believed in a "Primitive Communism" as the classless starting point of human history, and therefore, in a footnote to *The Communist Manifesto*, exempted this first stage from the operation of the general formula.

by the conquerors, and so preserved and caught up into a fresh advance. Moreover, what is from one point of view a regression may be from another the basis for an advance. The fall of the Western Roman Empire opened the "Dark Ages"; but it also got rid of slavery as the basis of the productive system, and replaced it by serfdom, which is undoubtedly a higher economic form. Nevertheless, as soon as we begin to think in terms, not of a "straight line" evolution of mankind as a whole, but of the impact of one civilisation upon another, a good many complications arise to make questionable the adequacy, and even the correctness, of the Marxian formula.

The Historical Process

This question of the impact of one civilisation on another presents for the pedantic adherents of the "Materialist Conception of History," in precisely the form in which it was originally enunciated by "the master," the most difficult and perplexing problem. *The Communist Manifesto*, in which the doctrine was first plainly set out for popular consumption in an essentially propagandist form, appears to treat all human history from beginning to end, and with no limitations of either space or time, as a continuous process of world development from one all-embracing primitive Communism through a series of world class systems to a world system of advanced Communism, or Socialism. But is there really any warrant for such a view? Is not Marx in reality starting out from an analysis of the social development of Western Europe and of the countries brought from time to time within its orbit from the Dark Ages to the growth of an advanced system of Capitalism, and then attempting to extend the results arrived at by this analysis to cover human history as a whole? May not the first of these steps be largely valid, and the second invalid, in the popular form in which it is made in *The Communist Manifesto*?

I hold this to be so. I believe that the Realist Conception of History—by which I mean the interpretation of the course of social development primarily in terms of the changing powers of production—embodies a large element of truth, but that it is wrong and absurd to attempt to interpret all history by it as the growth of a single civilisation. The civilisation in which we are living to-day has no doubt been immensely influenced by the civilisation which culminated and fell in the extension and disruption of the Roman Empire; but it is in no sense continuous with that civilisation, or merely developed out of it in accordance with any internal rhythm of social evolution within a single

44

system. The roots of our civilisation are to be sought not only in Imperial Rome, but also in the tribal institutions of the barbarians whom Tacitus described, and of all those mingled racial and cultural elements which swept down upon the Western Empire and destroyed it. What we owe to Rome is to be explained in terms not only of the internal rhythm of the economic development of a continuous civilisation, but also of the impact of one civilisation upon another.

To envisage the matter in this way is to remove the greatest obstacle to the acceptance of the large element of validity in the primary Marxian analysis. For the puzzle for those who have regarded all human history as a continuous process has always been to explain why, in order to advance from a slave-economy to a serf-economy—an admitted economic advance—mankind had, in so many respects, to fall back so far. Were the Dark Ages really an advance on the *Pax Romana* of the Roman Empire? Civilisation for civilisation, can anyone possibly believe that they were? But, if they were not, what becomes of the notion of mankind's continuous advance to higher stages of social development?

This difficulty disappears if it is accepted, on the one hand, that all human history is not the history of a single civilisation, and on the other that human progress is not inevitable, but has to be struggled for by men at every stage of development. Why, historians have often asked, did not the Roman Empire emancipate itself from slavery, and advance to a higher stage of economic organisation, without the need for men to undergo the searing experience of the Dark Ages? I should answer that this did not happen because the Roman Empire decayed internally through failure to use its opportunities. It could have survived and continued to advance, if the progressive social forces contained in it had been able to find leadership and organisation strong and intelligent enough at once to readjust its conditions of economic life from within and to resist the disintegrating forces pressing upon it from outside. In default of this, its culture fed upon its body till, like the ill-fated heroines of Victorian romances, it fell into a decline and died. Its fall may look inevitable, in retrospect; for, looking back, we can see all the factors which brought it about. But this does not mean that it *was* inevitable, until all these forces had actually come into play. It is mere mysticism to suggest that, because a man can live only for a limited time, the same must be true of a civilisation. A man has a body, which cannot be renewed when it wears out: a civilisation has not such a body, and *can*

45

be renewed indefinitely if its members act in the appropriate ways to ensure its survival.

It has often been said that this fate overtook the Roman Empire because the plenty and cheapness of inefficient slave labour deprived it of all incentive to improve its productive power. The slaves themselves were too weak, too scattered and too disorganised to achieve more than a few sporadic revolts; and on a basis of slave labour there could arise no active class of industrial *entrepreneurs* powerful enough to make a bid for the control of the political machine. But the attempt to re-write Roman history in terms of class-struggles expressed in slave revolts has always seemed to me a most unsatisfactory—and indeed absurd—proceeding. Slave labour was no doubt antithetical to the growth of machine-production because in general the mass of slaves could not have been trusted to operate the machines. What calls for explanation is not that the slaves failed to make a successful proletarian revolution, but that the capitalists of the Roman Empire failed to establish a successful and progressive capitalist system. Reliance on slave-labour may have been in part the explanation of the ancient world's failure to apply to economic uses the inventions of Alexandria, or to make, except in the unique field of civil engineering, any significant advance in the arts of large-scale production. But what ancient civilisations **did** achieve in the erection of buildings and aqueducts shows that they could develop in the economic field when they gave their minds to it; and this familiar explanation of their failure seems to be inadequate. It would be more plausible if they had tried to apply machinery and had failed; but in fact they did not try. It is a far more probable view that undue extension and parasitical reliance on tribute, rather than slavery, killed Imperial Rome. For the Empire was too large to be held together under centralised control except by vast military and administrative expenditure; and it may be argued that the magnitude of the tribute levied on the provinces for these and for other purposes and the centralisation of the entire system prevented the capitalists of the Roman Empire from accumulating the resources needed as the basis for economic advance.

My point here, however, is not that the Western Roman Empire fell from this or that cause, but that its fall was the end of a civilisation in Western Europe, so that the social development of Western Europe since then is to be regarded as belonging to the history of a distinct, though of course a related, civilisation. To recognise this is to escape the fantastic misrepresentations involved in trying to squeeze all classical history within the confines of a shape made to explain the development of modern Europe, instead of working out a distinct pattern, on the basis of the same Realist Conception, for the interpretation of the Ancient World in terms of its own problems and productive powers. No one who looks at the matter in this light will be tempted to equate the slaves of the Roman Empire with the modern proletariat, or to ransack ancient history for isolated events in which he can trace a fanciful resemblance to the class-struggles of to-day.

The Interaction of Civilisations

World history has to be written in terms not only of the internal evolution of a number of distinct civilisations, but also of their impact one on another. The conception of class may suffice to explain the essential phases of the internal development of a single civilisation from stage to stage, or at any rate those of the particular civilisation with which we are practically concerned in the world of to-day; but I am convinced that it does not suffice to explain the action of one civilisation upon another.

It does not follow that for the explanation of other civilisations, or of the impact of one civilisation upon another, we have to go outside the powers of production. A distinction needs to be drawn between the theory that economic forces are the final determinants of social change, and the secondary theory that these economic forces are in all cases necessarily personified by economic classes. Mass migrations of hungry peoples in search of the means of living are assuredly due to economic causes; but they are not class-movements. Yet they are capable of determining the fate of an entire civilisation, of checking or turning aside its internal course of development, or of bringing its growth abruptly to an end. War and conquest have played in human history a part which can by no means be explained as a mere by-product of class-struggles, even where they admit of explanation in economic terms. Similarly, the explanation of the internal history of some civilisations—China and India, for example—may be largely economic, and yet be quite incapable of being brought within a formula of class-struggle designed primarily to explain the history of Western Europe since the fall of Rome.

It is a sound principle of theoretical method never unnecessarily to extend a generalisation. There is always a temptation for anyone who hits on a limited truth to see in it the philosopher's stone that turns the whole universe into a blaze of light. But the light of reasoning is apt to become feebler as it proceeds from its centre to the circumference; and what may be a convincing explanation of the facts which originally suggested a theory may fail to be even plausible when it is stretched to cover a wider ground. Or, at best—even when the central truth is all pervasive —it may need to be quite differently stated in applying it to different groups of facts. A Realist Conception of History, closely akin to Marx's, may be universally valid without Marx's statement of it in terms of class-struggles possessing the same universality. There are other possible dialectical forms besides the class-struggle.

More Marxist than Marx

But if, at one extreme, it is dangerous to claim too much extension for the application of Marx's theory in the form in which he set it out, at the other extreme it is at least as dangerous to apply it too intensively even nearer home. There are some Marxists who cannot see a flapper use her lipstick without producing pat an explanation of her conduct in terms of the powers of production and the class-struggle. It is, of course, undeniable that the prevalence of lipstick at a price within the normal flapper's purse is a by-product of capitalist mass-production, and has therefore an economic cause; but in relation to world history it is a phenomenon completely without significance, and also quite irrelevant to the class-struggle, as Marx would have been the first to agree. Nor is there any sound reason for attempting to trace all important and historically influential events to economic causes—much less for regarding all such events as manifestations of the class-struggle, whatever outward forms they may assume. No one in his senses really doubts that men are constantly acting on grounds that are non-economic, or that non-economic actions and organisations can and do influence history. All that the most rigid Marxist needs to claim is that the influences which are not manifestations of underlying economic forces are of a secondary order, and exert their effects, however important they may be, within limiting conditions set up by the evolution of the powers of production.

Thus, to take a few modern examples, if two countries go to war, it is not necessary for Marxists to prove that their conflict is the outcome of a rivalry inherent in the development of modern Capitalism. It may be so; but the war may also be due to some quite different cause. If a particular people, or section of a

48

people, manifests a spirit of violent nationalism, it is not necessary to prove that this nationalism is really but a perverted form of class-feeling, or that it depends finally on economic grounds. Possibly it is, and does: possibly not. Or again, if a particular body of men is strongly Catholic or Protestant, it does not follow that their creed is merely a cloak for the pursuit of their economic ends. Perhaps it may be so, or half so, in certain cases. But assuredly war and nationalism and religion, greatly as their manifestations have been affected by economic forces, are not to be explained away as purely economic things.

There are many causes at work in history, even if it be true that one set of causes has dominated the rest and shaped the general course of social development within a particular civilisation. Moreover, as Marx and Engels again and again insisted, what is originally derivative has the power of becoming an independent cause. Thus Marx held, as we saw, that the need of mankind to organise social structures for the use of the developing powers of production gives rise to legal and political systems for the enforcement of the class and property relationships required at any given stage of economic development. These legal and political powers are thus, according to Marx, in the first instance derivatives of the powers of production at the stage which had been reached when they were set up; but, once established, they become independent factors with a power of their own to influence history and to react upon the course of economic development. Even if the feudal State be regarded as the political expression of a particular set of economic relations based on a particular stage in the development of the powers of production, it can hardly be questioned that some forms of feudal State were much more able than others to hold back for a time the growing forces of Capitalism; nor can it be denied that some forms of the capitalist State are more effective than others in resisting the advance of Socialism. Any institution, whether it be economic or non-economic in its origin, and whether or not it is or has become an embodiment of the standpoint of a class, can act upon men's minds, and upon other institutions, and can therefore influence the course of history. The only question that is at issue between Marxists and non-Marxists is whether class-institutions, based on the changing powers and conditions of production, play the dominant part in social evolution, and set limits within which the other forces have to act. The independent and important influence of these other forces is not in dispute.

The worst enemies of Marxism are those who harden it into a

universal dogma, and thus conceal its value as a flexible method of social analysis. For the Realist Conception of History is a clue to the understanding of social realities, and not a complete explanation of them. Nor was it meant primarily as a theory; for Marx's object in formulating it was not simply to understand, but by understanding to gain the power to control. He sought a theory, not for a theory's sake, but because he wanted to find a guide to action, and did not believe that men could hope to act aright unless they could gain a correct working appreciation of the objective facts with which they had to deal.[1] But a theory which is to serve as a guide to action can afford least of all to decline into a dogma, or to be formulated rigidly on mechanistic lines. The first essential of successful action is flexibility in the application of principles—a quality often confused with opportunism, but in truth its very opposite. The opportunist does not apply principles: he flouts them; whereas the successful man of action holds fast to his principles, but at the same time understands the need to restate them constantly in relation to changes in the objective situation. In this opening chapter, I have tried to set out the fundamental ideas of Marxism not as dogmas, but primarily as a way of approach, embodying in its method principles which, rightly understood, are too realistic to harden into dogmas, and too closely related to the objective situation for it to be legitimate to state them to-day in the same terms as Marx used in formulating them a hundred years ago. Some Marxists will say that what I have been stating is not Marxism at all, but a radically different doctrine. Even if that were so, it would not matter, provided that my interpretation were the more valid basis for the formulation of a doctrine for to-day. But I think what I have written rests in essence on Marxism, in that sense in which Marxism is to-day a living force, and not the opium of a Socialist orthodoxy which is determined to bid thought stand still in a world in which everything else is subject to rapid and violent change. In asserting this, I am expressing at this stage neither agreement nor disagreement. I am not saying that Marxism, as I have here interpreted it, is true or untrue. I am only trying to clear the ground for an examination of this issue by eliminating from my restatement of Marxism what simply cannot be true, before proceeding to enquire how much of what *can be* true is in fact true and relevant to-day.

[1] "Social life is essentially practical. All mysteries which mislead theory to mysticism find their rational solution in human practice and in the understanding of this practice. . . . The philosophers have only *interpreted* the world in various ways: the point however is to *change* it." Marx, *Theses on Feuerbach*, VIII and XI.

CHAPTER II

THE MATERIALIST CONCEPTION OF HISTORY

IT SEEMS BEST TO begin this chapter with three quotations, which give the most direct summary of the Marxian Theory of History. The first of these is taken from Friedrich Engels's Introduction to the authorised English translation of *The Communist Manifesto*, published in 1888. It runs as follows:

"The *Manifesto* being our joint production, I consider myself bound to state that the fundamental proposition which forms its nucleus belongs to Marx. That proposition is:

"that in every historical epoch the prevailing mode of economic production and exchange, and the social organisation necessarily following from it, form the basis upon which is built up, and from which alone can be explained, the political and intellectual history of that epoch;

"that consequently the whole history of mankind (since the dissolution of primitive tribal society, holding land in common ownership) has been a history of class-struggles, contests between exploiting and exploited, ruling and oppressed classes;

"that the history of these class-struggles forms a series of evolution in which, nowadays, a stage has been reached where the exploited and oppressed class—the proletariat—cannot attain its emancipation from the sway of the exploiting and ruling class—the *bourgeoisie*—without, at the same time and once and for all, emancipating society at large from all exploitation, oppression, class-distinctions, and class-struggles.

"This proposition, which, in my opinion, is destined to do for history what Darwin's theory has done for biology, we, both of us, had been gradually approaching for some years before 1845."

The second, still more famous, passage comes from Marx's own Preface to *The Critique of Political Economy*, an advance sketch of the theory which he later formulated more fully in *Das Kapital*. The *Critique* was published in 1859; and Marx prefaced it with an account of his mental development up to the point when he arrived at his fundamental sociological doctrine. The relevant passage, which is very condensed, runs as follows:

"The first task I undertook for the solution of the problem that was troubling me was a critical revision of Hegel's *Philosophy of Law*;[1] and the introductory part of this appeared in the *German-French Year-books*, published in Paris in 1844. My investigations led me to the conclusion that relations of Law,[1] like forms of State, can be understood neither by themselves nor in the light of the so-called general development of the human spirit, but that, on the contrary, they have their roots in the natural conditions of living, which Hegel, after the fashion of eighteenth-century English and French thought, summed up under the name 'civil society,' and further that the anatomy of civil society is to be found in Political Economy. My research into this subject, begun in Paris, was continued in Brussels, whither I betook myself in consequence of an order of expulsion issued by M. Guizot. The general conclusion which I reached and thereafter continued to be guided by as the leading thread in my studies can be briefly summarised as follows:

"In the social production of the means of life men enter into circumstances which are determined, necessary, and independent of their wills—circumstances of production which correspond to a definite stage in the development of the material powers of production. The sum-total of these circumstances of production constitutes the economic structure of society, the real basis on which a juridical and political superstructure is reared, and to which correspond determined forms of social consciousness. The mode of production of the material means of life conditions in general the social, political and spiritual process of living. It is not men's consciousness that determines their existence, but on the contrary their social existence that determines their consciousness.

"The material powers of production, at a certain point in their development, come into contradiction with the existing circumstances of production, or—what is simply an expression of them in Law—with the circumstances of property-holding within which they had hitherto operated. From forms for the development of the powers of production these circumstances are transformed into fetters upon them. Then comes an epoch of social revolution. With the variation of the economic foundations the entire immense superstructure turns itself slowly or rapidly about.

[1] = *Recht*.

52

"In considering such revolutions a distinction should always be drawn between the material revolution in the economic conditions of production, which can be determined with scientific accuracy, and the legal, political, religious, artistic or philosophical—in a word, the ideological forms under which men become conscious of the conflict and fight it out. Just as our judgment upon an individual is not based on what he thinks of himself, in the same way a revolutionary epoch cannot be judged by its own consciousness: on the contrary, its consciousness has to be explained in terms of the contradictions of material life, that is, of the actual conflict between the social powers of production and the relations of production.

"No social system ever perishes until all the powers of production which can find scope in it have been developed; and new, higher relations of production never manifest themselves until the material conditions of their existence have been hatched within the womb of the old society itself. Accordingly, mankind always sets itself only such problems as it can solve; for, when we take a closer view, we shall always find that the very problem arises only when the material conditions of its solution already exist, or are at least in process of coming into existence.

"In broad outline, we can point to the Asiatic, the ancient, the feudal, and the modern *bourgeois* modes of production as successive epochs in the progress of the economic structure of society. The *bourgeois* relations of production are the final antagonistic form of the social process of production—antagonistic in the sense, not of individual antagonism, but of an antagonism arising out of the conditions of the social life of individuals; at the same time, the powers of production as they develop within the womb of *bourgeois* society create the material conditions for the resolution of this antagonism. With this social form, therefore, the pre-history of human society comes to an end."

The third quotation comes from *The Communist Manifesto* itself:

"The history of all hitherto existing society is the history of class struggles. Freeman and slave, patrician and plebeian, lord and serf, guild-master and journeyman, in a word, oppressor and oppressed, stood in constant opposition to one another, carried on an uninterrupted, now hidden, now open fight, a fight that each time ended, either in a revolutionary reconstitution of society at large, or in the common ruin of

53

the contending classes. In the earlier epochs of history, we find almost everywhere a complicated arrangement of society into various orders, or manifold gradation of social rank. In ancient Rome we have patricians, knights, plebeians, slaves; in the middle ages, feudal lords, vassals, guild-masters, journeymen, apprentices, serfs; in almost all of these classes, again, subordinate gradations. The modern *bourgeois* society that has sprouted from the ruins of feudal society has not done away with class antagonisms. It has but established new classes, new conditions of oppression, new forms of struggle in place of the old ones. Our epoch, the epoch of the *bourgeoisie*, possesses, however, this distinctive feature; it has simplified the class antagonisms. Society as a whole is more and more splitting up into two great hostile camps, into two great classes directly facing each other: *Bourgeoisie* and Proletariat."

In the light shed by these three quotations, we can now proceed to a more careful study of what its authors elected to call the "Materialist Conception of History."

Men and Things and Men and Men

All economic systems are ways of applying the power of human labour, by hand and brain, to the available instruments and materials of production. These instruments and materials—the means of production apart from human labour—consist for any society of the resources afforded by nature in the condition to which they have been brought by the labour of past generations. They include, that is to say, in the first place, only such gifts of nature as men have found ways and means of using for human ends; and secondly, in addition to these sheer gifts of nature, all usable instruments of production accumulated in the past, and all stores of usable things that are available as a result of past labour. The power of human labour, which is to be applied to these means of production, includes all forms of active work, by hand or brain, that are capable of being expended in the making of useful things or in the rendering of useful services; and in this labour are embodied the acquired knowledge and skill which are the legacy of the labours of previous generations of men. The economic problem for any society is that of establishing the "right"[1] relations between men and the things

---

[1] "Right" is, of course, here a relative term: it means right in relation to the ends that dominate a particular society at a particular stage. It means right from the standpoint of the controlling influences in a society, not right from the standpoint of promoting maximum welfare in any absolute sense.

upon which they are to labour, so as to make the most advantageous use of the available resources of production, including both men and things.

Any relationship between men and things involves also a relationship between men and men. For men, in arranging for the social exploitation of the means of production by their own labour, must of necessity establish certain corresponding relations among themselves. There must be some form, rudimentary or advanced, of the division of labour between man and man; and there must be some defined relationship between men and things to regulate the rights of men to the use of the available means of production. Marx held that these relations between men and men, involving the definition of rights of property and of personal freedom and obligation, have in the past been embodied in successive class systems, so that each class system has corresponded to a particular stage in the development of the social use of the powers of production, including both things and men.

The question, "What is the right relationship between men and things, and between men and men, for the exploitation of the resources of production?" can therefore be answered, if Marx is right, only in relation to a particular stage of economic development, and not absolutely. For the answer must depend on the character of the available powers of production, including the stage reached by men's knowledge of their use. There can therefore be no absolutely best economic system, desirable for all times and places; for different economic systems best fit the circumstances of mankind at different stages of historic development.

The Economic Foundations

Marx assumes that the system which is economically "right" for any particular civilisation at any particular period is that which is best adapted to improve the use of the available powers of production, both by advancing the efficiency of production itself and by affording an outlet for the distribution of the largest possible amount of real wealth, or material welfare. This, he assumes, holds good for any stage of social development in which the scarcity of real wealth is the dominant economic consideration, in the sense that there is not enough produced to ensure to everyone a standard of life which is regarded as adequate by the consciousness of society. It holds good, not because men, at any hitherto existing stage of development, have set before themselves the object of promoting the largest practicable

55

welfare for all, but because improved methods of production and economic organisation tend to drive out worse methods by the force of competition. At each stage, in Marx's view, the ruling class seeks to develop the powers of production, for its own advantage, and not for that of the entire society, and distributes productive resources with a view to its own requirements. It is, however, compelled to apply superior methods of production, as they are discovered, because otherwise it will not be able to stand up to the competition of those who do apply them. Moreover, any capitalist who applies them before others stands to appropriate a surplus resulting from the higher efficiency of his methods. That is why, in Marx's phrase, Capitalism continually "revolutionises the methods of production," even at the point where their further development is threatening to exceed the limits of capitalistic consuming power.

Thus, the continual development of the powers of production presents itself as a *sine qua non* for capitalist society right to the end. A similar need, however, would not drive forward a classless society in which the problem of producing and distributing enough real wealth for everybody had already been solved.

No system of organising the powers of production can hold good for all time. For, as these powers are continually being altered by changes in men's skill and knowledge of the use of natural forces, the appropriate forms of economic organisation must need to be continually changing as well. Economic systems therefore have to be reconstructed from time to time if they are not to get calamitously out of adjustment with the developing powers of production. The study of social evolution, from the economic point of view, is the study of the changing phases of the powers of production and of the adjustment to them of the economic and social systems which men construct for their use.

The "Superstructure"

Any economic system, involving as it does a particular set of relations between men and things and between men and men, requires the support of a corresponding system of political and social relations. It cannot function successfully unless the individuals and classes who are its active agents are protected in, or compelled to, the rights and duties assigned to them under it. In other words, any economic system connotes a legal, political and social system of which the concepts and precepts have to correspond to the needs of the underlying economic situation. The economic purpose of the legal and political system is to secure the appropriate conditions for the effective use of the powers of production, and to repress any claims or activities that are calculated to interfere with these conditions. No economic system can develop its full potentialities except with the aid of a legal, political and social system in harmony with its needs.[1] This is why economic revolutions always carry with them the necessity for corresponding political, legal and social revolutions.

The form and content of public and private law, and the political structure of the society which upholds it, are intimately connected with the underlying requirements of the economic system. A society of hunters or fishers is bound to organise itself in a number of respects, politically as well as socially, after a different fashion from a society of men who live by agriculture or by industrial production, or depend on international commerce for the means of life. It is easy to trace broad correspondences between the underlying economic structures of different types of society and their political organisations and social systems, and to see how, in the past, political and social structures have been adapted to changes in the fundamental economic conditions. It is, however, dangerous to press this too far. It is by no means the case that societies which are at the same level of productive technique have necessarily the same economic institutions—much less the same social patterns of family and group relations, of political and religious organisation, or of ideas of value and morality. Anthropological investigations have shown widely divergent culture patterns which can by no means be explained in purely economic terms. Such correspondences as are found to exist bear out, at the most, only the contention that social institutions are *influenced* by economic conditions—not that they are exclusively determined by them. The economic foundation of society is only one factor, even if it be the most important, in settling the general pattern of culture. It cannot, however, be denied that it is a factor of primary importance. This can be seen most plainly of all in the different forms which the institution of property assumes in different civilisations, or phases in the growth of civilisations, and in the changing status of the human beings who perform the ordinary labour required. Marx, in a sweeping generalisation, laid down that slavery corresponds to one phase, serfdom to another, and "free" wage-labour to a third; and of course slavery, serfdom and wage-labour are all legal, political and social as well as economic concepts, expressed

[1] Or, in the more primitive forms of society, of a customary social system which covers the ground occupied by legal and political systems in more advanced societies.

57

in different systems of law, in different political institutions, and in different social relations between man and man.

In the Marxian view, political, legal and social systems, and the theories which men frame in explanation and justification of them, are derived from the necessities of the economic order. They embody in laws, political institutions, theories of juris- prudence and politics, and in social conventions, the precepts required to uphold particular economic systems which arise out of the development of the powers, or resources, of production; and they are subject to change, in face of whatever resistances, in response to changes in the underlying economic conditions of society. Economic changes, by forcing upon men new methods of exploiting the available powers of production, compel them to modify the relations of men to things and of men to men, and accordingly to readjust the political and social systems which uphold such relations. It is inconceivable that a modern society, employing the resources of large-scale machine production, should continue for long to be organised politically after the fashion of a feudal monarchy, or that the localism of the medieval system of city government should survive the impact of the world market. At every stage of civilisation, there must be a sufficient degree of correspondence between the conditions of production and the political and social system embodied in law and custom; for otherwise there will develop a conflict between the developing economic forces and the established political system, and the latter, so far from upholding the conditions required for further economic advance, will be found to stand in the way of the effective use of the available productive resources and to give rise to social conflicts which can be resolved only by fundamental changes in the legal and political structure.

Economics and Politics

According to Marxism, economic forces play throughout history the creative and dynamic part. The powers of production are in continual evolution as men's knowledge and command over nature increase, and consequently there is a continual need for changes in the political structure of society. But political systems do not change continually and gradually in step with the development of the powers of production. According to the Marxian view, any system of government, once established, embodies the authority of a particular class; and this class, having seated itself in political power, is by no means willing to yield up its privileges without a struggle merely because the

58

economic conditions have so changed as to make its supersession desirable. Its authority is the guardian of countless vested interests and claims, for the defence of which it exists. The entire system of law which has grown up within it is the expression of these claims in the form of rights and prohibitions; and the government itself is the political representative of the dominant class. Accordingly, though political systems do change in response to changing economic needs, they change tardily and against the will of those who control them; and their adaptation usually both lags behind the changes which occur in the economic sphere, and is limited to what can be done without departing from their essential class character, or admitting claims inconsistent with the vested rights of the dominant class.

This resistance to necessary changes, Marx contended, causes major change, when it does come, to take a revolutionary form. The need for changes accumulates, in face of increasing resistances, as the proposed modifications threaten more deeply the essential institutions of the dominant order, until at length the forces making for a change of system grow too powerful to be resisted, and the old political system is broken by revolution and superseded by a new system embodying a different set of class claims and ideas. The class struggle, which has been in progress within the dying system, enters on a revolutionary phase; and a new class, previously held in subjection, assumes in its turn the powers and responsibilities of making a new State.

We shall have to examine this Marxian concept of revolution more fully later on. Here the point to notice is that the political institutions of society are regarded as a *superstructure* raised upon economic foundations, and embodying the rule of the class which is predominant in the economic field.

This, however, does not mean that Marx held all political developments to be capable of explanation in purely economic terms. Even if the roots of political systems are in the economic order, any set of institutions which men create is bound to acquire a life and a potency of its own. A system of government, when once it has been established, has therefore a secondary power of influencing the movement of history, and of reacting on the course of economic development. Human history does not proceed solely under the impulsion of the underlying economic forces, but is also affected by the forms which the social and political life of society assumes. What is itself at bottom the outcome of economic forces is capable, Marx agrees, of becoming an independent, though still a secondary, cause of historical events.

59

Social Values

What is true of political institutions Marx holds to be no less true of other forms of social organisation. Any underlying economic condition of society, embodied in a particular system of organising production, involves a corresponding set of values, not only in an economic but also in an ethical sense. Things and forms of conduct are regarded as good or bad at different stages of civilisation according as they further or hamper the carrying on of production in accordance with the requirements of the predominant economic system. This is held to involve, in ethics as well as in law, a system of values which reflects the ideas and interests of the controlling economic class, that is, of the class upon which devolves the responsibility for the successful organisation of production.

Marx further asserts that these ethical ideas, appropriate to a particular phase of social evolution, acquire, like the political institutions of society, a sanctity of their own, and become highly resistant to change. Equally with the law, they help to uphold and to sanction conduct in harmony with the needs of the established economic order; and, equally with law, they become, when once established in men's minds, independent causes, capable of influencing the further development of historical events. For men think within a social framework, and the shape of the prevalent thought on political and economic matters is derived from, and corresponds to, the shape of the society within which the thinking is done. The forces which arise within a given social system, as a challenge to its economic and political institutions, have perforce to challenge also those elements in the established morality which reflect the needs and notions of the system that is to be attacked. But it is often harder to get the attacking forces to attack ideas than institutions; for every dominant class teaches the absoluteness of moral precepts which fit in with its interests with even more fervour and assurance than the finality of the established type of State and of the existing class-relationships. Besides, morals are entangled with religion, and for this reason men are less accessible to rationalistic argument about morality than about political or economic matters which are not tied up with their religious beliefs.

It is nevertheless clear, and it is indeed affirmed by all sociologists, that moral ideas about social relationships are not absolute, but are deeply affected by the needs and conditions of different types of society. Even if there is an absolute moral law, it can have, in such matters, no absolute and timeless content.

There is no positive individual human action that will be pronounced *a priori* to be absolutely right or wrong by the prevalent opinion or sentiment of all types of society, wholly without regard to the circumstances in which it is performed. When once this is recognised, it is easy to accept the view that the positive precepts of social morality must change with changes in the economic and political conditions of society, and that current codes of conduct are profoundly influenced by the character of the contemporary economic and political system.

Nor does this apply only within the field of moral ideas and precepts. Men's entire way of thinking is obviously conditioned, even if it is not fully determined, by the nature of the society in which they live. This is not so much because contemporary social conditions affect the answers men make to the questions which they ask themselves—though of course this is the case— as because these conditions affect the framing of the questions. Each society has its own problems, dictated to it by the conditions in which it lives, and imperatively demanding solution: and the philosophies and sciences of every age, though they are built upon the legacies of the past, are essentially attempts to find answers to contemporary problems.

Of course, this does not mean that every individual is limited to thinking only in terms of the problems of his own age. No one, indeed, can help being influenced by his age, however much he may try to escape from it; but, subject to this, individual thought is free, and can range at will over all questions that individual men are in a position to frame. A man can live in a past age, and think in terms of its problems; or he can construct a dream-world of his own, and do his thinking in terms of the imaginary concepts appropriate to his dream. He can think about something which exists in his age, but is largely ignored by his contemporaries because it does not appear to raise any problem imperatively demanding solution. A scientific inquirer can pursue his researches, without caring a whit about their practical results, in a spirit of disinterested curiosity. But even so he will not be able to escape the influence of his age and environment, however strongly he may seek to be 'objective,' or set himself in revolt against his age. Nor will he be able even to ask questions which are not suggested to him by the materials presented to him by the knowledge of his day, or to advance beyond guesswork where the materials for an assured answer do not yet exist. Men think, not *in vacuo*, but with the aid of the ingredients for thought which their situation supplies. Within this limiting condition, however, individual thought is free.

But, out of all the welter of contemporary thought, the age will select. More thinkers and inquirers will be attracted to those problems which peculiarly vex the age than to others; and thinkers, no matter how subtle or profound, who have no message for their age, will be passed over—to be rediscovered, perhaps, centuries later, when their thought has become appropriate to the problems of a different stage of social development. The Marxian contention is not that men can think only in terms dictated by current economic conditions, but that out of men's thoughts only those which are relevant to contemporary problems will influence the course of social evolution.

Clearly, then, human thought is not a mere mechanical product of the economic conditions of society. It is an independent force, itself powerful in the shaping of the economic conditions. But it is a force which builds upon what it finds in being, and takes its form and direction, as far as it is influential in the contemporary world, from the problems which the objective situation presents. Marx's point is not that thought is impotent in the shaping of man's destiny, but that it is neither arbitrary nor capricious in its influence, but is, in its social aspect, fundamentally a seeking of answers to questions set by the conditions of contemporary society, which is itself a product of men's past thought as applied to similar objective conditions.

We have seen that there is in this view of thought, as in the entire Realist Conception of History, nothing derogatory to the powers of the human mind. What is emphasised is that the thought which makes history is not "pure" thought, or a pure emanation of the 'human spirit,' divorced from the material and substantial things of the workaday world, but thought which can be directly applied to these things, thought which is largely stimulated by them, thought which acts upon them so as to elicit their latent powers of social development. Marx, true to his principle that being is logically prior to thought, exalts thought by enlisting it in the service of being. Not the thought of men, but Hegel's disembodied thought, is the object of his attack. But his conception of thought is essentially practical: thought, for Marx, is essentially a means to action.

Nevertheless, the Marxian view shocks many people because it exalts the thinker who keeps his nose to the grindstone of fact above the pure contemplator beloved of the Idealist philosophers. If that is shocking, then Marxism is shocking; for Marx's view emphatically is that in any age the thought which counts is thought which bears a close relation to the practical problems of mankind in that age and civilisation.

But what, it will be asked, of mankind's theoretical problems, which have nothing to do with current political or economic affairs, but arise out of a disinterested desire to understand, or out of a wish to solve the purely personal problem of a man's own place in the universe? Marx says nothing to deny or to affirm the value of disinterested curiosity, or its power to discover vitally important truth, and to react upon social development; but he is impatient of that type of thinking which seeks, apart from society, a purely personal interpretation of man's place in the world of being.[1] He is profoundly convinced that social ideas are social products, and lose their meaning when they are cut away from a social context. The problem of man's place in the universe is for him a social problem, involving questions to be asked and answered afresh by each generation in social terms, and in close relation to the objective conditions of contemporary society. He does not deny that men can think in abstraction from their social environment; but he appears to hold that such purely individualistic thinking will be abstract, and therefore barren of social results. Real and creative thought must be about real things; and abstractions are never real. Thought divorced from being is an abstraction: thought divorced from social being is no less an abstraction. It ends in a futile solipsism, or in a no less futile denial of all reality save the Universal that annihilates the universe.

What shocks people most in Marx, however, is not his aversion from this type of thinking, but his insistence that, when men think they are thinking of one thing, they are in fact often really thinking of something else. It is, above all, his contention that the great struggles of history have all been at bottom economic, even when men have fought them out consciously in religious or ethico-political terms. It infuriates a religious man to be told that the form and substance of his religion are really at bottom expressions of his economic interests and desires, or a philosopher to be told that his philosophy is really a thought-projection of the conditions appropriate to a particular class-structure of society. No wonder it infuriates him; for he may be sincerely conscious of having thought out his position in religious or philosophical terms, without having been deflected from the

[1] "The question whether objective truth can be attributed to human thinking is not a question of theory but a practical question. In practice man must prove the truth. . . . The dispute about the reality or non-reality of thinking which is isolated from practice is a purely scholastic question." Marx, *Theses on Feuerbach*, II.

process of thought by any consideration of class or personal economic interest.

It is important, if we are to regard Marxism objectively, to get as clear a view as possible of Marx's meaning at this point. He is not accusing the religious or philosophical thinker of hypocrisy or of deliberate mystification, though of course both these things do often occur—as when infidel prelates in the eighteenth century defended their position by urging that religion was good for the poor, or when a religious person makes his observances a cloak for living an immoral life. These abuses, however, are accidental, and beside the present point. What Marx says is that men who hold certain religious or philosophic beliefs in full honesty may in fact be fighting under their banner in a struggle which has at bottom an essentially economic content.

Religion and History

In advancing this doctrine, Marx had doubtless most of all in mind the circumstances of the Reformation. Since his time, numerous writers have attempted to show the intimate connection between the spirit of Protestantism and the needs of the commercial classes which were beginning in the sixteenth century to claim emancipation from the restrictions imposed on capitalist enterprise by the ethical code of the Catholic Church. It is significant that Protestant societies openly broke away from the medieval tradition concerning usury by authorising the receipt of interest, while Catholic societies were still trying to square commercial practice with a nominal adherence to the older doctrine, and that the Protestant communities were everywhere those which broke most easily with the old codes of business ethics. But the argument goes much deeper than this. It is, fundamentally, that the new Capitalism was in its essence individualistic, and therefore found itself in strong hostility to the social doctrines and atmosphere of medieval Christendom. The rising merchants and manufacturers wanted to go their own ways, untrammelled by codes of conduct which had been framed to suit the localised and regulated economy of the Middle Ages. They were emancipating themselves from the control of the gilds and corporations and manorial institutions which had dominated medieval economic life, and from the conception of status and limited gild or other localised fellowship which went with them. They were getting away from the notion of a "just price," based on the conditions of production, to the rival idea that the right price for a thing, or for a worker, was what it, or he, would fetch in the competitive market—neither more nor less. Ethics and economics were being torn apart by the rapid changes in the conditions of manufacture and exchange; and the Catholic Church, conservative in social doctrine, stood in the way of the fuller development of the new powers of production.

Accordingly, when Protestantism, in some one of its many forms, presented itself to a community of traders or manufacturers, it came reinforced not so much by conscious considerations of economic interest as by an appeal which fitted in admirably with the new conditions of economic life. The trader became a Protestant, not because he put it to himself that Protestantism squared better than Catholicism with his business interests, but because he was already thinking individualistically in connection with the everyday problems of life, and a religion which emphasised his individual relation and responsibility to his Maker gave him the kind of spiritual attitude that he wanted. It was not in the least that his religion was insincere: he was but following the example of men in all ages by re-making his religion after the model of his desires and values.

Only in this sense can the religious struggles of the sixteenth and seventeenth centuries be held to have had an economic basis. The underlying forces which broke up the Catholic Church and set in its place a number of Churches were by no means all economic; but the new Churches which based themselves on Protestantism did to a great extent develop a doctrine and an outlook well adapted to the needs of the rising capitalist system, and the forms which the various Protestant Churches assumed were profoundly influenced by the economic conditions of the countries in which they grew up.

Capitalism and Nationalism

The break-up of Catholicism was, however, obviously connected with the rise, not only of the capitalist system, but also of the new national States. It was fully as much a "nationalisation" of religion as a change in doctrine. It cannot therefore be explained satisfactorily in economic terms unless the rise of the Nation-State admits of a similar explanation.

This undoubtedly raises a very difficult question. It is of course beyond doubt that the movement towards political nationalism found stout supporters in the majority of the commercial classes, and that kings owed much, in their struggles both with feudal barons and with the claims of the Universal Church, to the support of burghers and craftsmen. For the

65

traders and master-producers wanted above all things order, and saw the chief hope of this in strengthening the hands of the King's Government against both feudal potentates and the overriding authority of Pope and Holy Roman Emperor alike. They were opposed too to Church exactions destined to go to the support of a central Church organisation at Rome; and this led them to support monarchs who were prepared to set up a National Church as the auxiliary of the National State.

Almost everywhere, the main body of the commercial classes was on the side of the new Nationalism. But it does not, of course, follow from this that the rise of the Nation-State can be explained wholly, or even mainly, in economic terms. Certainly there were other forces, as no one who has read Machiavelli can doubt, besides those of economic change that made in the direction of a strengthening of national consciousness and national control. What above all, marks off Machiavelli from earlier political thinkers is the completely secular character of his conception of politics and of the State. Order is his political objective, as it was that of the traders; but he brings home the truth that order could be ardently desired for other than economic ends. The Nation-State, based on secular principles, triumphed because, amid the collapse of the medieval system, it provided, not for the traders alone, but for everyone who was frightened or beggared by the confusions of the times, the best available guarantee of order and of personal security. This is of course the argument which Hobbes put forward in an extreme form when he advocated absolute government as the only way of estab-lishing order and security for the individual.

To admit the claim of the Nation-State, however, is only to push the question a stage further back. For the root cause of the rise of political Nationalism must be sought in the forces which led to the dissolution of the medieval system. These forces were undoubtedly in the main economic. Medievalism broke up in face of the alterations in the economic condition of Europe which followed the taking of Constantinople by the Turks and the discovery of the New World. Shut off from traditional contacts with the East, and offered instead the vast opportunities of the New World in the West, European civilisation rapidly ceased to base itself upon the Mediterranean. The countries whose seaboards lay along the Atlantic Ocean ceased to be at the world's circumference, and found themselves at its centre. Spain, France, Great Britain and the Low Countries became the strategic points for the next advances of European civilisation; and the rivalries between their adventurers and monarchs for

66

a share in the new opportunities for wealth provided the most powerful incentive to strengthen the national State, and to cast off the outworn allegiance to a civilisation based upon the Mediterranean Sea. Only strong national States could hope to claim a part in the riches of the great new world that was being opened up; and among national States that which was least powerfully organised for backing up its claims was certain to lose the prize.

The rise of political Nationalism does in this way go back to economic causes. But it cannot be regarded as the creature of a coherent economic class. For, though the commercial classes gave it their support, and were powerful allies of the monarchs in their struggle against the medieval system, these classes were not nearly strong enough to carry the day by themselves; and most of their power came after the battle for the Nation-State had been decisively won. Kings needed burgher help; but the new national States were real monarchies and not disguised commercial oligarchies such as many of them became later on. In this first struggle associated with the rise of Capitalism, the growing capitalist class won, not power over the State, but only the conditions necessary for its subsequent rise to dominance. The capitalist class did not overthrow the feudal State and set up at once a new State made in its own image: it gave its support to a kind of State which it did not control, but within which it found greater opportunity to pursue its own purposes. Social evolution need not proceed by the simple and immediate substitution of one form of class-power for another. There are hybrid forms and transitions which may take centuries to work themselves out before a new class-system is thoroughly and completely established.

Moreover, the rise of strong, centralised Nation-States was largely the consequence of the growing need for the enforcement of law and order over a wider area. With the extension of the market and the breakdown of local isolation, there came a more pressing demand for a strong hand wielding a wider justice, both to keep turbulent local barons and freebooters in order, and to supplement and co-ordinate the local jurisdictions of city and manorial courts. The traders, as the chief journeyers from place to place, compelled by the nature of their calling to carry about with them large values in merchandise or money, were especially urgent for protection that would enable them to go their ways in peace and security over the widest possible area. They also wanted a system of uniform law and administration that would reduce their trading risks and would enable them to increase the scale of their ventures with more assurance. The growth of agricultural production for the market and of settled systems of manufacture created a lively demand for the suppression of internal disorder and destructive civil warfare, including the abolition of private armies of retainers living on the neighbourhood. Strong States, with fairly extensive territories and high centralisation of armed force, alone could meet these claims; and consequently the weight of the developing economic forces was usually thrown on the side of the Crown against the barons, as the readiest way of creating the conditions required.

This brief discussion of one particular critical phase in social development has been designed to clarify the meaning of the Marxian contention that political and ideological struggles which appear to exert a dominant influence in shaping the general course of history are in the last resort the outcome of changing economic forces and conditions. Given the economic situation of Europe at the close of the fifteenth century, it was necessary, Marx argued, that the loose unity of medieval Christendom should be broken up, that the claims of the Universal Church should be repudiated, that strong Nation-States should be brought into existence, and that the capitalist *entrepreneur* should escape from the restrictions imposed on him by gild and manor and Church, and should take to himself an ethic and a religious outlook in harmony with his changed economic opportunities. The alternative to such developments would have been, not the continuance of the medieval system, but its sheer dissolution with nothing to take its place—the death of a civilisation instead of its rebirth into a new phase. These things may not have been inevitable, any more than the coming of Socialism is inevitable to-day—for nothing is built unless men build it—but in retrospect they do look very much as if they were the only alternative to a chaos which would have ushered in a new Dark Age.

How Men make Their History

The point is this: men make their own history; but they can make it, in any constructive sense, only by accepting the limitations and opportunities of the age in which they live. This implies, not only that they must act in ways appropriate to their age, but equally that they must think and feel in terms appropriate to it. For men's thoughts and feelings, as well as their habits and conventions, are the foundations of their actions; and it is only by thinking and feeling appropriately to the needs and

68

opportunities of their time that men can become the constructive agents of social development.

It is to this extent only that men's social ideas, as well as their political and social institutions, rest upon an economic basis. Thoughts and feelings are man's weapons in his struggle to make the best of things. Their biological purpose is practical—to make man more at home in his environment, and to help him in adapting his environment to his needs. He has, of course, a private as well as a social environment; and the use which he makes of his mind has reference to this private environment as well as to its wider social context. But when we speak of the thought or mind or spirit of an age we are referring, not indeed to any mystical 'spirit' existing apart from the minds of individual men, but to those ideas and feelings which are characteristic of the age and enter, as the product of many individual minds, into its collective consciousness. These are the social ideas and feelings which, arising out of the common factors in the objective situation, find lodgment in the minds of many different individuals, become incorporated in the working rules and practices of many social institutions, and form the substance of current intellectual and social intercourse. It is to these alone that the Marxian doctrine refers, when it asserts that social ideas and attitudes are ultimately traceable to economic causes.

However, even if the major movements of history are unintelligible except in relation to the development of the powers of production, it is foolish to ignore the fact that any institution, or any form of thought, when it has once come into being, is capable of exerting an independent influence of its own. Even if the fundamental forces behind the broad sweep of historical development are to be regarded as economic, the actual course of events is being continually affected by forces of any kind and every kind—by political, ideological and religious as well as by economic factors. Any institution, or any idea or notion present in the minds of men, is part of the objective situation, whatever its origin and whatever the forces that have shaped its development. Thus, the State, as it is shaped at any particular stage in the history of a society, may be in a broad sense the outcome of a special phase in the evolution of the powers of production. But it is also, since it exists, a force not without influence on the course of economic development. It reacts on the very conditions which brought it into being; and, still more, it can delay and obstruct readjustments of social relationships that are required to make them correspond to a new phase in the development of the productive powers. Similarly, if an idea once finds lodgment in the minds of men, the fact that its acceptance may have been largely due to its original harmony with the economic needs of the time will not prevent it from persisting after this harmony has disappeared, or from reacting upon the ways in which men reorganise their social relationships in face of economic change.

No one who appreciates this vital point will make the absurd mistake of trying to interpret all history in exclusively economic terms. To do this is to empty out the human content of historical development, and to represent men as mere automata responding blindly to stimuli from the world of economic experience. No such denial of personality is implied in, or consistent with, a Realist Conception of History. For according to that conception men act in the light of the entire objective situation; and this situation includes not only the economic factors in the environment, but all the factors. It is ridiculous to argue that in every case the economic factors are bound to prevail over the rest; for how is it possible to say that men's minds will always act in one particular way in evaluating the relative importance of the factors concerned? It is the judgment of men that co-ordinates the several factors, so as to arrive at a basis for purposive activity; and in making such judgments men are free to make their own estimates of value. Only the crudest pseudo-Benthamite psychology can support the conclusion that always and in all circumstances they will be swayed by the economic factors in preference to the others.

Determinism and Freedom

It is, no doubt, possible to argue that, even though each individual may be free to think and act as he chooses, there is nevertheless a statistical predictability about the actions of men in the mass, or of classes of men, in the sense that, whenever the objective results of their individual and group actions come to be added up, it will be found that these results coincide with the interests of the groups concerned, to such an extent that deviations by some of the individuals do not significantly affect the general outcome. It may be impossible to predict how each individual will act, and yet remain possible to predict the behaviour of a majority—even of a majority large enough to sweep aside the dissentients.[1] Thus, in a British General Election, we can say confidently of a number of mining constituencies that they will not return Conservatives, or of the City of London that it will not elect a Socialist. Obviously groups of men who

[1] On this point see also p. 24.

have a strong common interest do tend to act in accordance with that interest, even if minorities dissent. It is, on this basis, quite legitimate to conclude that, where such an interest preponderates over all others among the members of a group, the action of the group can be predicted with a high degree of probability in terms of that interest. Marx treats class as the type of group to which this condition pre-eminently attaches. He asserts that classes always act predominantly in their own class-interests, as far as they understand them; but this does not involve any assertion about the action of any particular individual belonging to the class.

It can also be argued that, however men may attempt to act, either individually or in the mass, the economic forces will in the long run make their action ineffective unless it is in sufficient harmony with the requirements of the economic situation. On this showing economic conditions circumscribe, but by no means abrogate, human freedom; for, in a given situation, there may be many alternative courses open, none of which is impracticable on economic grounds. Within this range of choices, even on the assumptions of the economic interpretation of history the non-economic, as well as the economic, forces are free to operate, inducing men to do one thing in preference to another on whatever grounds may appeal to them, and thus vitally influencing the movement of historical events. Only when men try to pass beyond the limits set by the absolute practicabilities of the economic situation are they sharply pulled back by the confusions which ensue into a path consistent with the requirements of economic development.

It can, however, be argued that, although non-economic forces can be of great importance in the shaping of historical events, their influence is in fact either secondary or mainly negative. It can be contended that such forces, where they are old, are powerful to the extent to which they have already become embodied in strongly entrenched social institutions, or in ideas widely received as axiomatic. But nothing becomes embodied in an institution, or a received idea, or dogma, until it is already old; for it takes time for ideas and institutions alike to grow and to acquire the sanctity of being past question. The established ideas and institutions of an age, unless it be an age that has accomplished a successful revolution, are the legacy of the age that preceded it. They are not creative, but conservative of established values. They are, to be sure, challenged and contradicted by rival ideas and institutions; but these rivals are powerless against them unless they can embody themselves in movements powerful enough to challenge the authority of the established order. In other words, the ideas and institutions which appear to play a creative rôle in history are those which are identified with living and growing social forces. New ideas which lack this foundation can exert only a secondary influence on the course of historical events. They may inspire a faction, or a coterie. They cannot, it is argued, give form to a new historical epoch.

Marx held that social forces which are the exponents and embodiments of new ideas arise primarily in the economic field. To them, he argued, are attached the ideas, selected out of the welter of contemporary thought, which meet the needs of groups and classes created or enlarged by the development of the economic forces. Thus ideas, in Marx's theory, are powerful in history in two ways. They can add strength and resisting power to groups and classes which are threatened by the development of the powers of production. That is their negative and obstructive rôle, in which they serve as the allies of the established order, whatever it may be. But they can also lend consciousness and attacking power to the rival groups and classes which the development of the powers of production has called into being; and this second is their constructive rôle in history, whereby they become the slogans and premonitions of the future. In both these ways they exert a vital influence on human affairs. For no established order can effectively resist change unless it believes in itself and possesses a code of ideas justifying its own authority; and equally no movement challenging the established order can succeed unless it is able to equip itself with a philosophy corresponding to its own needs and aspirations.

The rôle of ideas in history, as seen by Marx, is thus vitally important, but at the same time secondary. For ideas have their influence, not as disembodied notions, but as the creeds of bodies of men whom they inspire to action. The idea is nothing without a thinker: the social idea is nothing unless it is embodied in a social movement. Even as there can be no mind without a body, there can be no socially influential conception without a social movement to make it real.

Class-struggles in History

The social movements which "make history" are in Marx's opinion essentially *class* movements. He interprets the entire course of history in terms of class-conflict, in the sense that he regards every major historical epoch as embodying a particular form of class-domination and as yielding place to another

72

epoch in consequence of the emergence and victory of a rival and hitherto exploited class. Obviously, this view is closely connected with a general evolutionary standpoint which looks on history as a continuous process of development and seeks to define this process in very broad terms, so as to break the entire movement up into a small number of stages, or epochs, each with an underlying common character of its own, and each arising out of its predecessor by a logical succession. Such a view of history both necessarily throws into relief the most persistent factors—those which are least amenable to the influence of the wills of men—and also draws attention away from any factors, however influential, that cannot be represented as following a logical order of succession throughout history. Because it is a fundamental need of men to find the means of subsistence, the economic factor is always operative at the very root of all societies; but it does not follow from this that all human history is a continuous process of evolution from lower to higher economic forms. Still less does it follow that such advances, even where they can be traced, are adequate measures of historical achievement. Serfdom may have been an economic advance on slavery; but it does not follow that the civilisation of the age in which serfdom became the prevalent system represented an advance on the civilisation of Greece and Rome. The conception of a continuous evolution from lower to higher forms may or may not be valid for biology: even if it is valid in the realm of biological development it does not follow that it is equally valid for the history of mankind.

In effect, Marx makes it appear so by taking for granted what he is setting out to prove. Just as, in his economics, he sets out from the assertion that the only common element in all commodities is that they are products of labour and concludes from this that labour must be the sole source of their value, so, in his conception of history, he begins by looking for something which is a common underlying characteristic of all human societies—the pursuit of a living—and concludes that all human history must be interpreted in the light of this persistent factor. He never disproves either the contention that it is illegitimate to regard all history as a record of continuous progress from lower to higher forms, or the view that, even if the economic factor is the most persistent, other factors can at any point exert, in conjunction with it, an independent influence of their own, which cannot be resolved into economic terms. Having established the perfectly sound point that economic need is primary and universal, and that the foundations of economic life (the 'powers of production') are subject to change, he goes on to treat all other factors as derivative from the economic.

The Social Outlook of Primitiv Peoples

When, however, we study the history of primitive societies—a study which, as Engels said, had been but little developed when Marx formulated his conception of history—we cannot but be struck by the fact that the need of primitive man to accommodate himself to his environment and his environment to himself has to do fully as much with his fears as with his physical needs. He seeks to propitiate, as much as to produce. His religion, which consists mainly of observances, is as necessary to him as his food, and requires as much an organisation in terms of social structure and convention. In our eyes, primitive religion rests largely on sheer ignorance, or misunderstanding, of the operation of natural forces; but this does not alter the fact that religion, equally with economic organisation, changes its forms with advancing knowledge, and is equally a developing response to human need. Comte, in his *Positive Philosophy*, which Marx condemned, constructed an evolutionary theory of religion, relating fetishism, polytheism and monotheism to successive stages of human development, corresponding to an increasing awareness of causation and natural laws. Marx swept all this aside with the broom of his Economic Sociology; but he was able to do this only by asserting that men's religious ideas were a part of an ideological superstructure built on economic foundations. What Marx never did explain was how men came to adopt this curiously mystifying habit of fighting out their essentially economic conflicts in theological terms. Could they have done so, had there not been some independent basis for their having any theological ideas at all?

Economics and Theology

If it is answered—as I myself should answer—that theological ideas are men's reactions to the unexplained factors in their environment, and that these factors present themselves as things, or even as persons, it is none the less true that the range of things to which men respond by constructing ideas about them is by no means limited to things of economic importance, and that there is accordingly no valid basis for resolving all men's ideas into derivatives of *economic* environment. Once this is admitted, the explanation of human history in economic terms ceases to be a full explanation, and room is made for the independent activity of non-economic forces.

74

Marx does not admit this independence. Having asserted the sole dominance of the economic factor in settling the succession of historical epochs, he goes on to explain its working in terms of economic classes and of class-conflicts. For Marx, class is essentially an economic conception: he does not admit that there can be significant class distinctions that do not rest primarily on the relations of classes to the exploitation of the powers of production. This, as we shall see, raises difficulties over the position of warrior-classes; for, even if one function of such classes is the seizure of the possessions of other tribes or peoples, this seizure is achieved, in the more primitive societies, by means of military and not of economic power. It does not rest on a particular class-relation to the powers of production. It can be used to achieve command over these powers; but such use of it demonstrates the independent validity, under certain conditions, of what is basically a non-economic force.

Class as an Economic Category

To this point it will be necessary to come back: for the moment let us set it aside, and agree to regard 'class' as a phenomenon of economic origin and significance. We can then treat class as an economic category; but even so the conception of class is a social and not solely an economic idea. There can be in fact a working class, or a capitalist class, without the persons who compose it being conscious of themselves as a class. But only as they become conscious of themselves as a class, at least to the extent of accepting a leadership which possesses this consciousness, or acts in pursuance of policies which are adapted to the furtherance of class-interests, do they become capable of acting effectively as a class. The fact of class comes first, and the consciousness of class is secondary to it; for always and everywhere a thing must exist before men can become conscious of it. But among conscious beings the existence of a thing provides the essential condition for the growth of consciousness about it. Given the existence of a class, some degree of class-consciousness is likely to follow. How much is another matter.

No particular degree of class-consciousness arises by any logical necessity. An idea, vaguely present in men's minds, can remain indefinitely inchoate and unclearly formulated, as a feeling undeveloped into a positive conception. The creative function of thought is to give clarity and distinctness to vague feelings presented to men by the crude experience of events.

Without this added clarity, the members of a class may act, under stimulus, as a class—as has happened again and again in history, whenever men have shown an instinctive solidarity unexpressed in any common creative purpose. The rising capitalist class fought its early battles in this way, holding together by instinct even before there had been any clear formulation of capitalist objectives or philosophy. Strikes among the workers have repeatedly revealed the same instinctive solidarity, among men who could certainly not have formulated with any clarity the foundations of their loyalty. The General Strike of 1926 in Great Britain evoked a response far transcending the class-consciousness of the British working class. But a class that fights by instinct alone fights with feeble weapons; for instinct may help it to resist, but not to construct. As long as its action remains on the plane of instinct or feeling, and does not rise to the height of a conscious idea, at any rate among its leaders, it cannot win more than sectional and occasional victories; for it cannot formulate a plan of campaign, or define the objectives of its action. Thus, Marx holds that a class must rise to the stage of class-consciousness, at least to the extent of accepting a class-conscious leadership, before it can be fit for the exercise of authority, or hope to remake society after the image of its own desires.

Ideas and Social Evolution

Thus, on the basis of the Realist Conception, ideas, though they are secondary to economic forces, are nevertheless the direct agents of historical evolution. Where there is no idea, no consciousness expressing itself in a positive policy, there can be no effective historical movement. That there can be no such idea without a movement in which it can be embodied goes without saying: the complementary, and no less important, truth is that there can be no creative movement without an idea.

But, whereas the economic forces, however much they are themselves the result of human activity, are necessarily always present—for men must always set out to get their livings in particular ways, and thus create an objective economic situation—there is no corresponding necessity in the development of ideas. Ideas arise out of situations: there is no other way in which they can arise. But they do not arise of necessity, or of necessity attain in men's minds the strength of social convictions. To express in clear-cut ideas the needs and desires appropriate to the objective situation is the task of great thinkers: to impose

76

these ideas upon the minds of those whose needs and desires they are fitted to express is the function of education and propaganda. But neither thinkers nor propagandists of the required calibre are produced automatically by the objective situation alone. The situation acts as a stimulus; for it suggests the problems, and arouses the sense of need. But a stimulus does not necessitate a response. The universe is full of abortive stimuli.

The social thinker and the social propagandist arise in response to the objective situation; but they arise not of necessity, but of their own motion—of course, under the influence of this situation. The needs of a situation may fail to be met because no one thinks and articulates the thoughts required to give coherence and direction to an instinctive social movement, or because the propagandists and educators fail to use the thoughts that the thinkers and planners have placed at their disposal. There is no inevitability in history, because there is no inevitability in men's response to a given objective situation. They cannot act outside the possibilities which it presents; but they can, and often do, fail to take full advantage of these possibilities. That is what is meant by saying that mankind makes its own history; but let us add that mankind can fail to make it sensibly.

Is the Economic Factor Determinant?

So far, in discussing Marx's conception of history, I have adopted Marx's own standpoint without question, and have assumed that it is methodologically legitimate to begin by postulating the economic factor as an "independent variable" and to proceed to explain the course of social development as a derivative of this single factor. Is this a valid method? Obviously, if the economic factor is important, it will be possible plausibly to explain a great deal in terms of its influence. If, however, some other factor were to be taken, hypothetically, as an independent variable, might it not be possible to explain a great deal in terms of this other factor, so as to make the influence of economic forces appear secondary, just as, given Marx's approach, the non-economic factors appear to be reduced to a secondary rôle? This, as we have seen, was precisely what Max Weber did, when he started by taking men's religious conceptions as an independent variable and proceeded to derive the practices and institutions of modern capitalism from the "Protestant ethic." Marx, his critics have suggested, did not *prove* that the economic factor is primary, and everything else secondary to it. He simply asserted that this was so, and backed up his assertion by a series of illustrations which went to show that the economic factor was highly important, but in no way proved its exclusive determining power.

This criticism of Marxism can by no means be summarily dismissed. A great many sociological writers have offered rival explanations of the general course of human development by taking each a different factor in social evolution and treating this factor as an independent variable from which they have then attempted to derive the other elements as functions. Thus Buckle, following a number of earlier theorists, treated climate as the determining factor and collected a large mass of material to illustrate the influence of climatic conditions on the characteristics of different peoples. The main difficulty inherent in this explanation was that climate, though it could be plausibly represented as a cause of many differences between peoples, could be of little service as an explanation of historical development. The same difficulty applies to other theories which put exclusive stress on factors in the geographical environment. Obviously, no one will deny that such factors exert an important influence on social differentiation; but theories based exclusively or mainly upon them do not go far towards any comprehensive conception of the rationale of social development.

Another group of theorists has set out from the concept of biological evolution, and sought to explain social development by transferring to human societies the notion of the "struggle for existence." This type of explanation, which came into wide favour in the second half of the nineteenth century, after the publication of Darwin's *Origin of Species*, suffers from the defect, among others, of ignoring the complementary influence of "mutual aid," to which Kropotkin has drawn special attention. It rests, moreover, on a crude transference of biological conceptions to the social sphere. Again, no one is likely to deny that a sort of struggle for existence, in the two forms of a struggle to master natural forces and of a struggle of man against man and society against society, has played a part in human development; but to stretch this factor to cover the whole of man's historical evolution is plainly absurd.

Yet other theories, also biological in their line of approach, place exclusive emphasis on the factor of heredity. To this group belong the numerous theories which stress, in various ways, the preponderance of racial factors, and also those which put the main weight on eugenic and dysgenic influences or on other demographic factors. Other sociologists set out to interpret human history in terms of the concepts of individual psychology, whereas yet others regard the individual mind as essentially a social product and frame theories in terms of a social-psychological approach which sometimes involves an assertion of the real existence of a "group mind." Max Weber, as we have seen, attempted, though in a less dogmatic spirit, to compose a sociological theory on the basis of treating the development of religious ideas as an independent variable and deriving such other social phenomena as the development of capitalism from this source. Gumplowicz and others have offered explanations mainly in terms of man's warlike instincts: Pareto, in terms of non-logical "residues" which underlie man's ideological beliefs.

In effect, there is no end to the rival sociological theories which put the main, or even an exclusive, emphasis on some one particular factor in man, in society, or in the natural or social environment, and attempt to explain everything, or at any rate everything of primary importance in the history and structure of human societies, in terms of the chosen variable. The question that confronts us here is whether Marx's theory is simply one of these rival universal explanations, with no claim to be regarded as scientifically more valid, or intellectually more convincing, than a number of others.

On the face of the matter, it seems improbable that human history, or even the great turning points in it and the main phases through which it has passed, can be satisfactorily explained in terms of the operation of a single cause. Where there have been admittedly at all stages many different forces simultaneously at work, it seems unlikely that any one among them has consistently exercised a proponderant influence. The tendency of the speculative mind to seek this type of explanation is of course undeniable—witness the many rival one-factor theories that have been advanced. This, however, is no good reason for accepting any such theory as valid. It seems much more likely that human history has been the product of a number of interacting and mutually determining forces than that any one has been at all stages so powerful as to overshadow all the rest.

Marx's theory, however, turns out an analysis to differ from most of the others in not being really monistic. The economic factor which Marxism treats as primary is, as we have seen, essentially complex. It is not an environmental theory, which attributes everything to "nature" as against man; nor is it environmental in the other sense of putting all the stress on the social, as distinct from the natural, environment. The 'powers of production,' which Marx makes his independent variable, are in fact a highly complex set of phenomena, arising out of the interaction between the natural and social environment and the contemporary activity of the human mind in devising new ways of exploiting it. Such a theory leaves a great many questions open. Marx has nothing to say about the factors in men which make them better or worse at increasing their mastery over environmental conditions. He does not discuss whether one race is better than another at doing this, or whether inventive capacity belongs to many men or to few, or whether some groups of men receive new inventions and discoveries more readily than others (or, if so, why?). He hardly concerns himself at all with the different histories of the various peoples, because he is attempting to formulate a general law of development applicable in its broad sweep to the history of mankind as a whole.

It is, of course, perfectly true that one thing common to all human societies is that they must find the means of living. This necessity is enough to make the economic factor always and everywhere a primary factor; and this is the point on which Marx fastens in formulating his general law. But it does not follow, because the economic factors are always present, that they are always predominant as influences making for change. It is possible for a civilisation—witness that of China—having solved its primary economic problem after a fashion, to stagnate economically for an indefinite period. Marx might have answered that, where this happened, the economically stagnant civilisation would cease to play a significant part in the course of human evolution, and would in due course become the victim of economically more progressive branches of the human race. Humanity has, on this view, but a single history, and the leadership in social evolution rests in every age with those peoples which show the greatest power of adapting their environment to suit their wealth-creating purposes. Such a formulation may fit the fate of China under the impact of modern Economic Imperialism; but it is not easy to see how it can be applied to the barbarian conquest of the Roman Empire— for even if Imperial Rome was economically stagnant, it can hardly be maintained that the barbarians were ahead of it in the development of the powers of production, or stood for a higher stage of social evolution. The notion of a simple, unified history of all mankind, proceeding in accordance with some inner necessity from lower to higher forms, is really a metaphysical assumption, for which there is no warrant in the known facts.

It is, however, possible to eliminate this metaphysical element without abandoning the theory that all major developments in human history have been due primarily to economic forces. Is this amended version of the Marxian theory worthy of acceptance? It rests on the assumption that, in all types of society, the economic factors can be isolated from other factors, so that their influence can be separately studied. But is this true? It is to a large extent true in those modern societies which have, over several centuries, been making rapid strides in the natural sciences and in the arts of production. It was also to a large extent true of those earlier societies which revolutionised their ways of life by making great innovations in the domestication of animals and in the development of improved agricultural techniques. But it was not true to anything like the same extent of the history of the European peoples in the Middle Ages: nor was it true for the great periods of classical history when the civilisations of Ancient Greece and of Rome were making their most rapid advances. Take but one case, that of Rome. The growth of Roman civilisation and empire was not based primarily on the development of the powers of production. Its basis was military, much more than economic; and it was not the case, in classical times, that military power could be based only on a highly developed economic technique. Rome's technical prominence (save in civil engineering) was military rather than economic: it was not marked by any outstanding development of the powers of production. No doubt, it developed the institution of slavery, and the use of slave-labour; but it did not devise this institution, and the use made of it came rather as a by-product of military activity than as an independent economic advance.

Thus, although every society must find the means of living, it does not follow that the achievement of every society can be measured in terms of its mastery of the powers of production. This is the case to-day, more than at any earlier epoch, because of the intense economic requirements of modern war. But the growing together of military and economic power is a modern development; and all human history can by no means be interpreted by taking it for granted.

This reinforces the point that Marx's theory of history was evidently formulated—as he himself declared—primarily as a guide to action and with a view to explaining the forces at work in contemporary Western society. If it was cast into a universal form, so as to appear to cover in its broad sweep the whole of human history, this was rather because universal explanations were in Marx's day the fashion, and because of the deep influence which Hegel's universalist theory of history exercised on Marx's mind, than because Marx had really considered the relevance of his theory to human societies in all places and at all times. Obsessed by the notion of the history of mankind as a straight-line progress from its beginnings to a final classless perfection in which social solidarity would be fully realised over all the world, Marx and Engels felt that a single comprehensive explanation of this single world process must be discoverable: rejecting Hegel's Idealist formula, they sought for a parallel to it in the realm of actual being. An inverted Hegelianism seemed exactly to fit the case, with the underlying dualism of man and man's physical environment made one in the conception of the 'powers of production.' Had they not begun by assuming that all history made up a continuous story of straight-line progress—a matter which they never argued, but simply took for granted—they would hardly have been looking for a single all-embracing explanation. They could have rested content with a formulation of the law of development limited to the particular civilisation which they were attempting to influence. Whether, formulated in this narrower way, their theory would have exercised as powerful a spell as it has in fact exercised may be doubted; for its universalism was undoubtedly not the least of its attractions and played a large part in converting it from a rationalistic doctrine into a belief which could be held with the intensity of a religion. Perhaps its authors would have regarded this, had they been capable of looking at it coolly, as a sufficient justification for putting it as they did; for was not their purpose that of inducing men to act, and not merely to accept? They could have argued, pragmatically, that their theory was "true" because it worked, and would have been less "true" if it had been less effective in inspiring enthusiastic belief. Being no pragmatist, I cannot study it in this spirit. I find myself compelled to ask whether the theory really fits *all* the facts, and not only those which are relevant to contemporary social action. My answer has to be that it does not, but that, as an interpretation of the social trends of modern times, it comes in its general outline much nearer to adequacy than any alternative formulation of which I am aware.

CHAPTER III

THE GROWTH AND DECLINE OF CAPITALISM

A GREAT DEAL OF unprofitable discussion has taken place about the date at which the capitalist system came into being. Some writers refuse to speak of Capitalism as existing before the machine age which began, broadly, towards the end of the eighteenth century, and thus regard Capitalism as the child of the "Industrial Revolution." Others, tracing back its development from the nineteenth century, find it already in existence in a rudimentary form at the latter end of the Middle Ages, gradually superseding and pushing out of existence the localised economy of the medieval city and the manorial system. Yet others, connecting it with the wars of religion, credit it with a birthday somewhere in the sixteenth century; and another school of thought, working back from the great age of mechanical inventions and discovering that the "Industrial Revolution" did not, after all, begin in 1760, lands up somewhere in the seventeenth century—perhaps about the date of the foundation of the Bank of England.

These discussions are of little real value. Obviously Capitalism was not born, as a child is born, at any precise moment of time. It did not come into existence at any definite period. It grew gradually, out of capitalistic elements which had existed in previous stages of economic development. There were plenty of capitalistic features in the economic life of the Middle Ages in their prime, and not merely at their latter end—to say nothing of the Ancient World. What happened was that these elements developed, ousting stage by stage and bit by bit the other characteristics of the medieval system. The so-called "domestic system," widespread but never anything like universal in the seventeenth and eighteenth centuries, was a development of these earlier capitalistic qualities, based especially on the growth of the capitalist merchant. The advent of power-driven machinery on a large scale enabled Capitalism to spread directly from the sphere of commerce to that of industrial production over a growing number of its branches. It is a matter of definition, and not of knowledge, to say when the Age of Capitalism began. What can be said with assurance is that Merchant Capitalism rose to a position of economic predominance in the seventeenth and eighteenth centuries, and Industrial Capitalism in the nineteenth. Some would proclaim a new age of "Finance Capitalism" in the twentieth century; but that is a point which we can for the moment leave aside.

Some of the most forcible chapters of Marx's *Capital* are devoted to an account of the development of the capitalist system. For by "Capital" Marx meant not merely the existence of an accumulation of resources or instruments of production, but a particular form of social organisation in which the ownership of these resources, at a certain stage of their development, assumed a particular character and involved a particular set of relationships between men and men. The essence of "Capital," as Marx saw it, lies in the ownership of the resources of production by a class of persons distinct from those who perform the bulk of the productive labour of society, in such a way that the personally "free" possessors of labour-power and the "free" possessors of accumulated productive resources confront each other as two distinct and opposite economic classes, one of which must employ the other before production can take place. "Capital," in this sense, comes into being as a corollary to the divorce of the main body of producers from the instruments of production; and the value of capital to its owners depends on the existence of a supply of labourers available for employment at a wage. In other words, "Capital" is monopolistic ownership of the resources of production other than labour-power; and the value of capital is simply the power of exploiting labour which this monopoly confers.

Capitalism and the Workers

This thesis is often stated as if it involved the view that the coming of Capitalism carried with it the degradation of labour, and a fall in the workers' standards of life. So it did, for particular groups of skilled artisans whom it deprived of their craft independence, and for particular bodies of peasants whom it displaced from their holdings in the interests of capitalist farming. At every stage, the advance of Capitalism has involved, as it still involves to-day, the displacement and degradation of particular bodies of persons whose traditional methods of living it supersedes. But this does not at all imply that its historical effect has been to lower the standard of living for the poorer classes as a whole. Any such view would be quite unrealistic, and indeed plainly nonsensical. For obviously the advance of capitalist methods of production took place precisely because they were much more efficient in the creation of wealth than the methods they superseded. By whatever injustices and oppressions the rise of Capitalism was accompanied, it did undoubtedly lead not only to a large positive increase in total wealth, but also to a wider diffusion of consuming power. It would be sheer nonsense to contend that the poor became in the mass poorer under Capitalism than they were under the systems which it displaced. This was not even true of the period which was chiefly in Marx's mind as he wrote; for it is scarcely possible to argue that even in the earlier decades of the nineteenth century, when the abuses of the Industrial Revolution were at their worst, there was more material poverty in England than there had been in the eighteenth century, or, to go back further, when the medieval economic system was in its most flourishing phase.

It is indeed quite misleading to compare the lot of the general body of workmen under Capitalism, at any stage of its development, with that of, say, the very limited groups of skilled craftsmen in the medieval towns, or the small minority of peasants who possessed adequate holdings of their own, without taking into account the mass of sheer poverty which existed in the medieval villages as well. Nor can such instances of the tragedy of a craft as the decline of the handloom weavers in the course of the Industrial Revolution, or such special cases as the wrongs wrought under the Enclosure Acts during the same period, be taken as representative of the effects of advancing Capitalism upon the living standards of the poorer classes as a whole. It is practically certain that at any time after the first few decades of the Industrial Revolution the average real income of the poorer classes was higher than it had ever been before; and it is utterly beyond question that the further development of Capitalism in the nineteenth century was accompanied in every capitalist country by a real and rapid advance in working-class standards of life.

Moreover, the rise of Capitalism, apart from the improvement in the standards of living for the wage-earners which has marked its successive phases, has also at every stage increased the relative as well as the absolute numbers of the middle classes, and of all those who are better off than the manual workers. It created, in its earlier phases, a large new middle class of self-made men who rose from relative poverty to affluence or comfort by the exploitation of the new powers of production. At every stage, it has swollen the numbers of the professional classes; and in its later phases it has created a new class of well-paid salary-earners—technicians, managers and administrators—who enjoy a high economic standard as the servants of joint stock enterprise. The creation of this great middle class is the characteristic social achievement of Capitalism; but it cannot possibly be argued that this achievement was purchased by a positive lowering of the standards of life of the poor below what they had been under earlier systems.

Nor did Marx ever attempt to argue in this way. His contention was that Capitalism routed the earlier systems precisely because it was a superior way of exploiting the developing resources of production. It destroyed in its coming many vested interests among the privileged bodies of workers as well as among the higher privileged classes of landlords and ecclesiastics. It did lower the standard of life for groups of small masters who found themselves degraded into the wage-earning class, or for peasant farmers whom it deprived of their land, as well as for some skilled workers whose craftsmanship was superseded by new methods of production. But it also brought with it higher standards, not only for the new industrial employers and the rising professional groups, but also for large bodies of workers who exchanged the status of serfs, or virtual serfs, or of very poor peasants and cottagers in the rural areas, for that of wage-workers able to sell their labour to the highest bidder, and to move far more freely from place to place in search of employment. It is safe to say dogmatically that Capitalism, wherever it cáme (except perhaps in some colonial areas), raised the material standards of living for a good many more persons than it drove downwards in the scale of material comfort. The age of the Industrial Revolution was insanitary and unhealthy enough, in all conscience, as Marx and Engels, drawing on the reports prepared by Edwin Chadwick and his fellow-reformers, were able to show with a wealth of graphic example. But was it, taken as a whole, as insanitary or as unhealthy as the centuries before? Save in exceptional areas, where new factory towns were run up at top speed so as to dwarf the feeble efforts of the sanitary reformers, there is no sufficient evidence that it was.

Of course, it is open to argue that the workers under Capitalism, though they had on the average larger real incomes than the generations before them, suffered spiritual degradation and unhappiness in the loss of craftsmanship and independence. But this view also is suspect; for does it not rest on comparing the spiritual condition of a privileged minority of craftsmen and substantial peasants with that of the worst-placed bodies

86

of workers under the new system? How much spiritual independence or pride of craft had the typical peasant of the Middle Ages, or the typical English villager of the eighteenth century under the rule of the squires, or again the typical worker under the domestic system? The view that Capitalism degraded the general condition of the poor in the advancing industrial countries is based on sentimentalism, and not on an objective study of the facts.

This attitude is in no wise inconsistent with the doctrine that Capitalism is founded upon the exploitation of labour. For so were the systems which preceded it, in an even greater degree. The exploitation of the wage-workers is not disproved by arguing that serfs, or slaves, were exploited even worse. The conception of exploitation is relative, not to the absolute standard of living, but to the discrepancy between the standard actually achieved and the standard attainable at any particular stage in the development of the powers of production. The labourer under Capitalism may live absolutely much better than the medieval serf—as he obviously does—and may yet be exploited if the full use of the available resources of production and a more even distribution of the product would enable him to live much better still. His exploitation is to be measured, not by what he receives, but rather by what he fails to receive.

In a later chapter, this question of the exploitation of labour will have to be argued out in its theoretical aspect, as it arises in connection with the Marxian theory of value. Here the purpose of mentioning it is only to make clear that Marx's theory of exploitation does not involve, but explicitly contradicts, the view that the advent of Capitalism made the lot of the labouring class as a whole absolutely worse. The manual workers' share in the total product of the economic system may possibly have fallen under Capitalism—it is difficult to say—but their absolute standard of living has assuredly risen.

It would indeed be most surprising if this had not occurred, as a concomitant of the great increase in productivity which resulted from the rapid advance in the techniques of both agricultural and industrial activities and from the opening up of virgin territories in the New World. Whatever the degree of labour exploitation accompanying these developments, it would have been impossible that the vast additional supplies of goods thus made available should not to some extent have found their way into popular consumption. No small wealthy class could possibly have consumed the bulk of these products, nor could the enlarged production have been profitable without a great widening of the consumers' market. Marx never denied that this widening had occurred: what he asserted was that Capitalism, like preceding economic systems, would in due course exhaust its expansive capacity and, from acting as a stimulus to more intensive development of the 'powers of production,' would turn into a fetter upon them. This would happen when it could no longer find fresh external markets to open up and accordingly resorted to increasingly competitive exploitation of such markets as were open to it, coupled with restrictive measures of each national capitalist group designed to limit supplies and competition in its own home market. Marx held that Capitalism, in this phase of arrested expansion, would reveal its 'contradictions' by turning more and more to the elimination of the small masters and to wage-cutting at the expense of the workers, though in so doing it would be limiting the market for its products. It was at this stage that Marx expected 'increasing misery' to set in, and more and more of the middle groups to be flung down into the proletariat to the accompaniment of a falling rate of profit and a worsening of working-class standards of life. To those issues I shall return later; for the present I wish to follow the argument in a different way.

The Exploitation of Labour

The sense of riches or poverty is essentially relative. Men feel rich or poor, not absolutely, but in relation one to another and to the available supply of wealth. Consequently, a rise in the absolute standard of living in a society does not carry with it a corresponding increase in the sense of material well-being unless it comes about in such a way as to reduce economic disparities between class and class and, where such disparities exist, to give men the sense that their wealth has risen in relation to the total available supply. Increases in the absolute standard of life which do not satisfy these conditions are speedily absorbed into the current conception of the minimum required to support a reasonably tolerable way of living. This is what both Marx and Ricardo had in mind when they estimated "real" incomes in terms, not of the goods they would buy, but of the amounts of effort the production of these goods had cost—or, in other words, as shares in the social income. Wages, says Ricardo, have fallen, even if they will buy more goods, when they absorb a smaller proportion than before of the total value of production. Exploitation, says Marx, has increased, even if the standard of living has risen, when the labourer's proportionate share in the total product is less than before, or, as he preferred to phrase it, when the proportion of 'surplus' to 'necessary' labour-time is increased.

Marx envisaged the process of capitalist production as involving a continual struggle between capitalists and labourers over the sharing-out of the product of industry. On the one hand, the labourers are pressing constantly for improved conditions, in the form both of higher wages and of shorter hours and better working environment, and, through their Trade Unions as well as through their power to change their jobs, are becoming more alert to take advantage of favourable conditions in the labour market. And on the other hand the capitalists are constantly revolutionising the methods of production, and trying to make labour more intensive within the hours of work, so as to secure a larger return upon their capital, and to have more left for themselves after meeting such claims from the workers as they are compelled to concede.

Marx argued that the competitive character of capitalist industry, even apart from the pressure of the workers for improved conditions, forces upon the capitalist *entrepreneurs* the necessity continually to revolutionise the processes of production, so as to keep down costs and make industry more productive. This competitive pressure ought to make possible a steadily rising standard of life; for it involves a continual advance in the productivity of the economic system as a whole. But the increased productivity of each hour of direct labour applied to industry is secured only with the aid of an enlarged mass of capital, which is required not only for the provision of more expensive machines, but also by the growing roundaboutness and complexity of the business of production and marketing. In order to keep up the rate of profit on this increasing mass of capital, the *entrepreneur* has to decrease the share of labour in the final product of industry; and Marx represents him as constantly fighting against a tendency for the rate of profit on capital to fall, as the mass of capital grows larger in proportion to the total costs of production. The capitalist, Marx points out, is aided in this struggle by the fact that the progressive substitution of machinery for labour diminishes the pressure of demand on the labour market, and thus makes it harder for the Trade Unions to insist on better terms of employment. Nevertheless Marx held, in common with the classical economists, that the rate of profit on capital would tend to fall, even while the total amount of profit was rapidly increasing; for the increased profit would have to be spread over a still more rapidly growing mass

89

of invested capital. This tendency would strengthen the capitalist resistance to working-class claims; for any attempt to press these claims to a point at which they would seriously lower the rate of profit would lead to a fall in the volume of capital investment, and this would react in turn on the demand for labour and so bring about a situation favourable to wage-reductions, or to the more intensive exploitation of labour.

Even so, the rapidly growing productivity of industry ought to lead to a rising standard of life, on account of the greater volume of goods available. Indeed, Capitalism has a strong incentive to aim at a rising standard, because of the tendency of most machine industries to obey a law of increasing return, or decreasing cost, as the amount produced increases. Capitalism, as it is under the necessity of continually raising productivity, requires a continually expanding market for its wares; and where is it to find such a market save in the growing demand of the general body of consumers? For the commodities which most obey the law of increasing return are chiefly those which cater for mass-demand.

Capitalist Competition

Capitalism, however, because of its competitive character, cannot set out to increase the incomes of the general body of consumers up to the limits of productive capacity. For all the incomes paid as wages and salaries, and also incidentally those paid as rent and interest, appear to it in the guise of costs of production, which each *entrepreneur* must keep down if his margin of profit is not to disappear. In the early stages of capitalist development, this pressure arises out of the competition of individual capitalists, or businesses, within the same economic area. But even when, at a later stage, combination has largely replaced competition in each leading industry within each advanced country, the necessity to keep costs down remains, both because the integrated capitalist groups continue to a great extent to compete internationally, and because each trade group is in rivalry with every other in trying to persuade the consumers to spend on its products as large a fraction as possible of their total incomes. It is possible, in theory, to imagine a completely combined capitalist world, from which both these remaining forms of competition would have been eliminated; but, despite the growth of international cartels and combines in certain trades, there is no sign of this happening in practice. In fact, international competition, and in some fields also the

90

competition between trade and trade for a share in the consumers' total incomes, come to be much more intense in the later phases of capitalist development.

Marx explains this tendency by reference both to the increasing advantages of expanding the scale of output under the conditions of modern machine-production, and to the growing pressure upon the world market as the number of highly industrialised countries becomes greater. When only one or two countries are industrialised, it is relatively easy for them to find foreign markets for a large part of their expanding output, by displacing in the less advanced countries the more expensively produced commodities of craft and peasant industry, and, at a slightly later stage, by setting out to equip those countries with machinery and modern transport services with the aid of the export of capital. This export of capital is indispensable; for the less developed countries cannot afford to pay at once for the expensive equipment which the advanced countries are eager to sell. The conditions required for the export of capital are, however, in being; for the large mass of profit made in the advanced countries is seeking outlets for profitable investment. It is clogging the home market for new capital, and is threatening to force the rate of profit down. But the less developed countries offer a field in which invested capital is likely to find even more profitable, though perhaps more hazardous, outlets than at home; for with great untapped natural resources, or an abundance of cheap labour, or in some cases both, to draw upon it should be possible to produce many types of goods at lower cost in the more backward than in the more advanced countries.

Consequently, capital emigrates in search of higher profits; and its emigration, by creating a demand for goods which the advanced countries are well equipped to produce, keeps up the rate of profit in these countries. But this process involves a patent contradiction. For, broadly, the capital invested abroad will be profitable to its owners only in proportion as the goods made with its help enter subsequently into competition with the goods produced in the more advanced countries, where their competition will have the effect of keeping down wages and thus restricting home demand.

As long as the number of countries carrying on advanced industrial production remains small, and the number of new countries to which the expansive process of foreign investment and supersession of native industries can be applied remains relatively large, the effect of this contradiction is not seriously felt. It was not seriously felt in Marx's own day; but he predicted that it was bound to become serious in the next phase of capitalistic growth. For he foresaw that the application in a number of countries of an advanced technique of capitalist production was bound to lead to a rapidly increasing rivalry between these countries for the right to exploit and develop the less advanced areas, with a view both to securing markets for their products and to assuring themselves of adequate supplies of such foodstuffs, raw materials, and tropical products as the conditions of their own territories compelled them to import. Marx foresaw the advent of the age of Economic Imperialism, dominated by the rivalries of the advanced countries over markets, spheres of influence, territorial expansion, and the building up of alliances and groupings designed to foster their several economic interests. He foresaw—and his successors, above all Lenin, elaborated the theme in the light of later events—that these rivalries would inevitably lead to wars of colonial conquest, and finally to wars between the great Imperialist Powers, and that these wars, and the huge economic losses and piling up of debts which they would involve, would endanger the stability of the capitalist order, and would afford an opportunity for the forces of social revolution. In these internecine wars between capitalist countries Marx held that the capitalist system was destined to perish.

The Contradictions of Capitalism

But in Marx's view imperialist wars would be, not the ultimate cause of the fall of Capitalism, but themselves the consequence of the inherent contradictions of the system. For the wars would arise out of the sheer necessity for each national capitalist State to develop markets and spheres of influence outside its own frontiers, owing to its inability, under the exigencies of the profit-making system, to find at home an outlet for its expanding productivity. Marx undoubtedly held that a time would come when, by reason of its internal contradictions, Capitalism would no longer be able to meet the expanding claims of the working class for an improved standard of life. It could meet them, as long as it was able to press on with the development of the resources of production and to find an outlet in the world market for the growing product of industry. But there would come a time when this resource would fail it, and thereupon the increasing pressure of international capitalist competition in the limited world market would force the capitalists in each country into an attack on wages. Each national group of capitalists would be set on reducing its costs of production in order to secure a larger share in the limited market; and any group which failed to do this would find itself left behind in the race. The result of being left behind would be both a fall in profits and a rise in unemployment, which would be no less effective than a fall in wages in reducing consumers' demand, and would, moreover, soon bring about a fall in wages by diminishing the power of the Trade Unions to resist.

This process of reducing costs in face of international competition is, however, fatally self-contradictory. For reduction of costs, at the expense of wages, leads also to a restriction in the volume of demand. Capitalism, therefore, when it once embarks upon this process, condemns itself to an inability to make use of the advancing powers of production; for it can no longer find a market for the increased supply of goods which it is in a position to produce. At this point, according to the Marxian theory, Capitalism becomes ripe for supersession by an alternative system.

In Marxian language, whereas the capitalist method of production has been hitherto a means of promoting the development of the productive powers of society, it turns at this stage of its history, and by an inherent tendency which it cannot escape, into a fetter upon the effective use of the available resources. At this stage, but not until this stage has been reached, Marx holds that the capitalist system involves, by virtue of its essential character, a fall in the working-class standard of life.

The contradiction which thus becomes manifest in the capitalist order is simply the consequence of the commodity status of labour. A system under which labour-power is bought by private *entrepreneurs* at a price, just like the materials and implements of production, and therefore ranks as a cost of production, is inevitably committed to regarding the incomes distributed in wages as a necessary evil, to be kept down to the lowest possible point. Even when individual capitalists preach the doctrine of high wages, they cannot escape the net of this contradiction. For, save to the extent to which they are able, by securing more efficient production than their competitors, to reconcile high wages with low wage-costs per unit of output—and to this there must be quite narrow limits—they cannot afford to pay higher wages than their competitors at home and abroad. As we have seen, a perfectly combined World Capitalism might in theory be able to transcend these limits; but no such system is within the bounds of practical possibility. Capitalism remains essentially competitive, despite the growth of combinations

93

within it; and if it became completely combined it would cease to be Capitalism at all. Such complete combination would imply the unified control of all the powers of production by a single world authority; but who can suppose that Capitalism is consistent with the creation of such an authority, or could survive its establishment?

As long as Capitalism retains its competitive character—that is to say, as long as it continues to exist—there are narrow limits to the application within it of the policy of high wages. Although an individual *entrepreneur* who is far-sighted enough to pay higher wages than his rivals, and clever enough to make good use of the high-quality labour which his offer of higher wages will secure, may find that high wages pay, the "economy" of these high wages depends mainly, not on their absolute level, but on their superiority to the wages offered by other employers. As soon as they become general, they lose most of their effect, because they can no longer be effective in attracting the best workers or in securing a more-than-average response. They retain, of course, their effect in expanding home demand; but unless a country is in a position—as very few are—to isolate itself from international competition under a régime of Economic Nationalism this advantage will be speedily offset by the pressure of foreign competitors. The lower costs of foreign producers who pay lower wages will enable them to capture the external markets of the high-wage country, and, unless it adopts a high protective system, to invade its home market as well.

Economic Nationalism

It may be answered that Capitalism in a particular country can escape this dilemma by resort to Economic Nationalism. But only under very rare conditions can Economic Nationalism be a way of escape. For it involves a deliberate refusal to take advantage of the economies of international specialisation, and the production at home of goods which could be produced with less expenditure of effort elsewhere. It therefore tends to lower to a serious extent the productive capacity of the country which adopts it; for it means that productive resources must be diverted from more to less efficient uses. A country which has so wide a diversity of natural resources and so large a population that it can produce, without serious economic sacrifice, nearly everything it needs for an advancing standard of life is in a position, by adopting Economic Nationalism, to escape the fatal barrier to a high-wage policy which international competition sets up.

But in all the world to-day there are at most only two countries which can possibly be regarded as even coming near to satisfying these conditions—the United States and the Soviet Union. One of these countries has already thrown Capitalism over. The other presents a particularly interesting problem. Having developed through all the earlier phases of Capitalism in a peculiar way, which arose out of scarcity of labour in relation to abundant land and other natural resources, the United States was acclaimed as an example of a Capitalism which could offer high wages without adverse reactions on profits, and could therefore escape the class-conflicts characteristic of capitalist development under less happy conditions. Then came, in the 1930's, a slump of unprecedented intensity, which appeared to give this optimism the lie; and under the influence of this slump the United States was impelled to embark upon a 'New Deal' which was an experiment in controlled Capitalism largely on a basis of Economic Nationalism. As part of this experiment, a deliberate attempt was made to apply a policy of high wages for limited working hours as a means to the absorption of the goods which were not being produced, or were even being deliberately destroyed, for want of purchasers.

No sooner, however, did the conditions which had led to this experiment cease to exist, as a consequence of the outbreak of world war, which created a market for all that could be produced, than the Americans started roundly denouncing President Roosevelt's 'New Deal'; and no sooner was the war over than they set to work to make a holocaust of their 'controls' and showed every intention of reverting as fast as they could to the 'free,' unplanned Capitalism that had failed them so signally in the pre-war decade. This, for the time being, they were in a position to do without internal disaster because the sheer needs of the war-devastated countries provided an outlet for everything they could produce beyond their own require-ments, which were in addition swollen by arrears of demand unsatisfied during the war, as well as by war gratuities and by the high earnings established during the war in every important productive occupation. But, as the needy countries could not afford to pay for what they received from America, production in the United States could be kept going only by what amounted to giving the goods away, first under the Loan made to Great Britain, virtually as a continuation of Lend-Lease, in 1946, and thereafter, on a still larger scale, under the Marshall Plan of 1948—the outcome of which is still hanging in the balance as I write these words.

High-wage Policy and Its Limits

The degree of central control which is indispensable for the consistent carrying-through of a high-wage policy except under conditions of labour scarcity is exceedingly great. In the first place, the natural tendency of each *entrepreneur* to desire to keep his wage-costs, like his other costs, down to the lowest possible point must be successfully overcome by a control which will give him the assurance that all his competitors in the same trade will raise wages at least as much as he is compelled to raise them. This, however, is not enough. If costs rise more in one trade than in others, the higher-cost trade will be at a disadvantage in selling its products. Demand for its products will fall off, and consumers will transfer their purchases to other goods. There must therefore be, in the second place, a sufficient assurance that the rise in wages-costs will be spread, with approximate evenness, over all industries that are competitive in this wider sense.

Even this, however, is not all. The policy of high money wages in all trades will, if manufacturers are left to their own devices, be likely to be speedily counteracted by the raising of prices in response to the expansion of demand, until the higher wages will purchase little if any more than the wages previously paid. Indeed, they may purchase less, if the initial expansion of demand is seized on as an opportunity for speculative activity, and gives rise to an uncontrolled inflationary movement of bank credit. In order, therefore, to give the policy of high wages a chance of success, and at the same time to avoid a cumulative inflation, the controlling authority of the experiment must take effective steps to regulate prices of commodities, and also to control the expansion of bank credit.

Capitalism and Political Democracy

In effect, then, sustained maintenance of a policy of high wages, designed to enable Capitalism to escape from its inherent tendency to a failure to employ the resources of production to the full, involves, even in a single country, however well placed for its adoption, a highly co-ordinated control over all the vital factors in the economic system. It means the abdication of the private capitalists as the controlling agents, and their supersession by a unifying authority which, even if they begin by dominating it, is bound to have a political rather than an economic character. It is, however, impossible, when once this authority does assume a political character, to prevent it from responding to the will, not of the capitalists alone, but of all politically influential forces in the society. In any country which works under a system of responsible parliamentary government, resting on a wide franchise, the policy of the groups which in fact exercise the ruling economic and political authority will have in the long run to be made consistent with the desires of the preponderant elements in the entire electorate. In face of any serious breakdown or recession, the electorate will insist at the least on a 'New Deal' of the Roosevelt type, and, if this is refused them or fails to achieve recovery, will transfer its support to those who are seeking to convert the system from State-controlled Capitalism into some form of Socialism. Therefore, in the long run, in the absence of exceptionally favourable factors, the maintenance of controlled Capitalism of the sort under discussion will depend on the destruction of the democratic-parliamentary form of government, and on its supersession by some form of unconcealed political autocracy under capitalist control. Some form of either Fascism or Socialism is the logical outcome of the attempt to establish a planned and unified capitalist régime.

If the outcome be naked capitalist autocracy rather than Socialism, what will happen next? Will the capitalist autocrats be able so to overcome their instinctive opposition to working-class claims as, even after they have destroyed for their own security the independent organisations of the working class, to persist in handing over to the defeated workers the higher and higher incomes required to afford an adequate outlet for the expanding product of industry? If they do not, subject to one condition, the old capitalist contradiction will recur, with a renewal of unemployment and business losses and stagnation, and a consequent re-emergence of the forces of discontent, to threaten and in the end to cast down their autocracy. The one condition which allows a way of escape is the diversion into preparation for war of so large a proportion of the productive resources as to maintain the level of employment despite the consumers' lack of purchasing power. This, of course—guns instead of butter—is what happened in Nazi Germany after 1933. If, on the other hand, we can imagine the autocrats using their power to put more goods and services at the disposal of the people, the rising standards of the workers will strengthen their feeling of power, and will make them less ready to submit to the continuance of the autocratic régime. For why, they will ask, should not they control the system on democratic lines? That way, too, the autocracy will break in the end, and give place to some kind of Socialism. But it is more likely to break in the other way; for it is most improbable that a capitalist autocracy could deliberately set out to raise the working-class standard of life.

All this relates only to a policy of high wages and Economic Nationalism pursued by a country well situated for its adoption. It cannot apply fully to any capitalist country in Europe, because no such country could embark on a thorough-going policy of Economic Nationalism without such economic loss as to lower, and not raise, the standard of life. In Western Europe at any rate, Economic Nationalism is irreconcilable with high wages; and there is not even a temporary way of escape by this method from the contradictions of the capitalist economy. West European Capitalism is irrevocably dependent on the world market, and therefore cannot evade the limitations imposed upon it by international competition. Capitalist autocracy in Germany, working on lines of Economic Nationalism, was never in a position to choose between high and low wages. Low wages were forced upon it, whatever expedients it might adopt, unless it could build up an overwhelming military power and thereafter use this power to levy tribute on an enslaved Europe.

Recent History of Capitalism

It is undeniable that, in this matter of the inherent contradictions of capitalist economy, the recent history of Capitalism fully bears out all the essentials of the Marxian analysis. A generation ago, it was common to laugh Marx's predictions to scorn, and to point, in refutation of them, to the advancing standards of life which Capitalism had been able to offer to the workers in all the advanced countries. To-day no one can dismiss Marx's contentions in this facile fashion. World Capitalism in the period between the two World Wars stood convicted of a lamentable failure to make use of the rapidly increasing productivity which the progress of knowledge and invention had put within men's power; and world unemployment and the cry about "over-production" were sufficient witnesses to its failure. World Capitalism in the 1930's appeared to have reached a point at which, so far from being able to promise confidently a progressive advance in the standard of life, it was busy cutting wages on the plea of international competition, and endeavouring to retrench upon the social services on the ground that high taxation was strangling business enterprise. Finally, instead of relying confidently on a popular electorate to keep it in power because it did at any rate "deliver the goods," it was turning in

98

one country after another to the forcible suppression of its critics, and to the establishment in one form or another of Fascist or semi-Fascist political system as a means of preserving its economic authority.

The Decline of Capitalism

The Marxist contention is that this situation arose because the capitalist system had already lost its appropriateness as a method of developing the resources of production. As the scale of production expands and machine-technique improves, the economies arising out of the large-scale organisation of the productive processes continually increase, both in the sphere of actual manufacture and in those of marketing and the purchase of raw materials. Consequently, in the more developed industries, each enterprise has a powerful incentive to expand output, in order to lower costs. But the expansion of output is limited by the extent of the available market; and this factor makes strongly against any system of Economic Nationalism save in vast countries. It leads rather to Economic Imperialism; for in each great country the larger producers are eager not only to absorb their smaller rivals, but also to secure the largest possible markets outside their own territory. They are, however, save to the extent to which they can make themselves positively more efficient than their competitors, or can subject their neighbours to some form of imperialist power, unable to expand their foreign markets without unfavourable reactions on the home market. For, except where they can build up closed markets for their products by the method of Imperialist expansion, their share of the world market depends on the prices at which they are prepared to sell, and therefore largely, though not of course exclusively, upon the wages they are compelled to pay. In face of the increasing number of highly industrialised countries, the possibilities of an expanding world market for any one of them may dwindle; and the contraction of the home market—or at least the failure to expand it in proportion to the advance in productive power—causes a disuse or underuse of available productive resources, manifested in a growth of unemployment, which is further swelled by the efforts of the producers to reduce their costs by still more mechanisation of industry.

In this dilemma, the capitalist world has been turning more and more to the use of combination as a means, not of promoting efficiency, but of holding up prices by the systematic restriction of output. Factories have been bought up in order that they may be put out of action, so as to ease the pressure on the remaining firms; and differential prices have been introduced, according to what the markets will bear. This has usually meant the charging of higher prices to home than to foreign buyers, in an intensive effort to sell abroad by methods of "export dumping." It has reacted further on the home market, by reducing the purchasing power of the wages and other incomes distributed to the producers. Such practices can benefit one group of *entrepreneurs* as against another or as against their employees; but they are bound to react disastrously on the total volume of wealth produced. They amount to a positive confession of the failure of Capitalism to fulfil any longer its function of developing the powers of production.

Clearly this situation did not arise out of any real satiation of human needs or desires. Not only have vast communities, including the majority of the human race, been left still in a condition of primary poverty which contrasts tragically with mankind's expanded productive power: there have remained also, even within the most advanced economic societies, both a mass of destitution and a standard of living, even for the main body of the wage-earners, far below what is necessary to satisfy those current aspirations which are embodied in the contemporary conceptions of a minimum of security and comfort. There is no lack of wants, but only of what economists call "effective demand"—that is, of wants which capitalist producers can see their way to supplying at a profit.

Now, clearly, the satisfaction of human wants ought not to stop short of the point at which all the available resources of production are fully employed in meeting them, up to the limit at which the cry for more leisure becomes more insistent than the cry for more goods. It was the indictment of Capitalism in its inter-war phase that it found itself impotent to apply this elementary rule of common sense to the working of the economic system. It failed, as we have seen, because instead of setting out to produce as much as possible, subject to the demand for reasonable leisure, and to distribute incomes sufficient to ensure a market for all it could produce, it was based on treating only one particular form of income—profit—as the end to be aimed at in production, and all others—above all, wages—as evils, or costs, to be kept down to the lowest possible point.

The Socialist Remedy

As soon as this contradiction became manifest in the actual working of the capitalist system, the general character of the requisite remedy irresistibly suggested itself. It could be nothing else than the institution of a system which would aim at the distribution of the largest total income consistent with the available resources of production, in such a way as to create a demand corresponding to the magnitude and the nature of these resources. But this can be brought about only if a single authority is responsible both for the planning of the social production as a whole and for the distribution of the incomes which will be used in buying it. In other words, the remedy is some sort of Socialism—involving the socialisation of the essential means of production, distribution and exchange.

The tendencies which exist in growing strength within the capitalist system point the way towards this solution. For, whereas Capitalism in its early stages was a system of unrestricted individual competition between rival *entrepreneurs*, it has been compelled in its later stages more and more to deny its own premises, and to resort to combination as a way out of the difficulties which the competitive system involves. Trusts and combines, and more recently what is called "rationalisation," embody this denial of the validity of the competitive principles, and point the way towards the positive socialisation of forms of enterprise which have already taken on a social, or collective, as opposed to an individualistic, character. Moreover, the growth of the joint stock system, with its increasing divorce between the ownership of industrial shares and any constructive contribution to, or responsibility for, the conduct of industry, has made sheer nonsense of the old view that business can be successfully carried on only by enterprising capitalists who stake their personal fortunes upon a concern that is their private property. The capitalists as a class have long ceased personally to conduct business enterprise in its more highly developed forms; for the most part they only see to it that such business shall be conducted in their interest. There are, of course, still capitalists who personally run businesses which are largely their own; but they are less and less typical of Capitalism as a controlling power. The typical *entrepreneur* of to-day is far less a capitalist than a salaried nominee of the capitalist interest.

The Conditions for Socialisation

Under these conditions industry becomes ripe for socialisation. For the capitalists as a class become functionless; and there is no valid economic reason why the salaried conductors of business should continue to be appointed at their bidding, as the servants of their interests. The right way of appointing those who are to be responsible for the policy and conduct of business operations is the way that will ensure that industry shall be so carried on as to use all the available productive resources for the balanced satisfaction of human needs. This implies a control constituted in the interests, not of a limited class of owners, but of the entire body of consumers whose needs are to be met. It implies not merely the socialisation of each essential industry or the co-ordination of all industries in accordance with a socially devised and controlled economic plan, but also Socialism as a political system, organising the national economy in accordance with a democratic conception of welfare; for no conception of welfare which stops short of seeking the means of good living for all the members of society can any longer be made consistent with the full use of the available resources of production. Industrialism has become too productive to be consistent with oligarchy: Socialism is the indispensable system for an age of technically practicable, if not of actual, sufficiency for all.

For a working model of the new socialised system of production and distribution of incomes it is natural to turn to Russia. In doing this, we have, as theorists, the inestimable advantage over Marx that we can watch the system which resolves capitalist contradictions in actual process of growth. The Russian system, of course, still falls far short of being Socialism, in any completed sense. It is transitional; and even the essential institutions have by no means yet taken on a final form. But it is already evident that, under the system which has been built up in the Soviet Union, it is impossible for the characteristic dilemma of Capitalism ever to arise. There can be no question at all, however much Russian production may increase, of any inability of the Soviet system to ensure a market for as much as can possibly be produced. The Russians, to whatever criticisms their economic arrangements may be open in other respects, do at any rate begin by discovering how much their resources will enable them to produce, decide how much of the available productive capacity to devote to the needs of war preparation, how much to the accumulation of means of production for the future, and how much to the provision of free collective services, and then distribute to the consumers enough income to buy the entire remaining product. A system organised on these lines can never suffer from the disease of being unable to use its productive resources for lack of demand.

Of course, this does not mean that the Russian system is proof against errors of judgment. No system is. It is possible for the controllers to make mistakes about the proportions of their incomes people will want to spend on different things, so as to produce relatively too much of one thing and too little of another; and it is possible for them to anticipate wrongly the future course of demand, so as to accumulate new means of production in the wrong proportions. It is possible for them to spend too much, or too little, on armaments. It is also quite possible both for the controllers and for the workers to be inefficient in actually carrying out the plan, as undoubtedly is the case over a large part of Russian industry to-day. I am not contending that the Russian system ensures the Russian people a high standard of life—obviously it has been up to the present very far from doing this—but only that it does ensure that as much as they can contrive to produce will readily find a market, so that over-production and under-consumption, and also unemployment, save as a temporary consequence of friction in the process of industrial change, simply do not arise.

In effect, the Russians, despite their present inefficiency as producers and their low standard of life, have solved the dilemma which Capitalism has found insoluble, and have ensured that, within the limits set by expenditure on armaments, every advance in technical efficiency shall be passed on to the consumers in the form of a rising standard of life. If other countries, far ahead of Russia in their mastery of productive technique, were to apply the same method of planned socialisation, they would be able promptly to secure results which can come in Russia only at the end of a long and painful process of learning the new techniques.

The Accumulation of Capital

For Socialism does appear to be the only appropriate economic system for an age of potential plenty. While scarcity continued to be the law dictated to men by the condition of the powers of production, the development of these powers to a higher point could most easily be secured under a system based upon the exploitation of the majority and on the private accumulation of wealth. In order to ensure an advance in productivity, it was necessary to provide for the withholding of a large part of the scanty productive resources of society from use in supplying current needs, and for their application to the building up of additional productive resources for the future. Capitalism provided the readiest way of achieving this accumulation at a time when there were no means to hand of securing it by collective action, as there are to-day in Russia. The private capitalist, spurred on by the incentive of the profit or interest to be earned on his accumulated capital, was prepared to abstain from reckless consumption in order to increase his future wealth and his power. He was prepared to keep down the standard of life of his employees in order to swell his profits, and thus to get more capital for accumulation. In doing this, he caused much misery; but he did also add to the productive power of society, and make possible improved standards of living for the future.

This system, despite all the miseries and injustices which it involved, and despite its effect on the minds of the accumulators, was defensible as long as the primary need of society was to ensure a sufficient accumulation of capital, and as long as no better means of accomplishing this end could be found. But it was defensible only on condition that it did put all the available productive resources to the fullest possible use in supplying either consumers' goods or instruments of production for the future. As soon as it began to leave productive resources unused in order to maintain its profits, its claim to be an efficient system for the accumulation of capital was fatally undermined. The accumulation of capital is not an end in itself, but only a means to increased consumption in the future. It is of no conceivable advantage to expand the instruments of production, except as a means to an increased provision of consumers' goods. The entire process of capital accumulation has meaning and justification only if it does actually issue in a higher standard of living: if it does not, the accumulation is sheer waste.

When, therefore, Capitalism reaches a point at which it can no longer guarantee a rising standard of life as a result of increasing productivity, that means either that it has ceased to make adequate provision for the accumulation of wealth, or that it is allowing its accumulations to run to waste by failing to put them to proper use. It is then ripe for supersession by a different system. In fact, the recent troubles of Capitalism have been due not to the failure of the individual capitalists to save enough, but to its inability to find outlets for the savings which under it individuals and companies have been attempting to make. The root problem for society in the 1930's was no longer that of ensuring adequate accumulation, but that of providing a sufficient outlet for what it was technically practicable to produce.

Capitalist and Socialist Accumulation

This does not mean, of course, that accumulation is no longer necessary. It is; but in the advanced countries it presents no

104

serious difficulty, except when an economy has been subjected to drastic disinvestment as a consequence of war. It used to be argued, against any form of Socialism or economic democracy, that if the poor controlled the economic system they would always prefer immediate to future satisfactions, and would therefore never consent to a sufficient accumulation of wealth. It is a significant comment upon this view that the one Socialist economy which has existed long enough for judgment to be passed on its economic effects is that in which by far the largest proportion of the productive resources has been applied to the increase of future rather than present wealth, despite the extreme poverty of the country. Accumulation on the scale on which it has been practised in the Soviet Union would be utterly self-destructive for any capitalist country. It is not so for the Soviet Union, because under a Socialist system there is no obstacle to the increased productive capacity issuing in a higher standard of living. But a more advanced industrial country, even if it became Socialist and thus removed the limits of useful accumulation, would not need to save on anything like the Russian scale. It would set out with an established industrial equipment, whereas the Russians have had to build up their economic system from the very foundations. Even if an advanced country had undergone quite extensive destruction of capital as a result of war, the re-building of its capital resources would be a task much less onerous than the general industrialisation undertaken by the Soviet Union.

In the next stage of economic development the accumulation of capital, like the conduct of industry—of which indeed it forms a part—is due to become a social function under collective control. Fundamentally, capital accumulation consists not in saving money, but in directing a certain part of the available resources of production to the making of capital goods rather than of goods for direct consumption. Money, except in the form of hard cash, cannot be really saved or accumulated: it can only be used to promote accumulation by being spent on capital goods. Money that is saved, and not spent, is wasted: it has no real existence. For money is only a token of spending power, and realises itself only in being spent. Accordingly, the real accumulation is done, not when money is saved, but when productive resources are directed to the making of capital goods. This direction of productive resources is clearly a function of the control of industry, which will fall to any authority which undertakes the planning of production. A Socialist economy connotes the socialisation of the process of accumulation: it is wholly inconsistent with the maintenance of the practice of relying on individual saving to provide the capital needed for economic development.

This does not mean that individuals must cease to save, but only that the amounts of current productive power devoted to the making of investment goods will cease to be in any way affected by their greater or less willingness to save out of their private incomes. If individuals continue to save, it will remain open to the State to borrow their savings, and to reduce proportionately what it deducts from the total social product before allocating the residue to be distributed as spendable private incomes.

If the private capitalist is no longer necessary in order to ensure the adequate accumulation of capital, the last economic defence of Capitalism goes by the board. For, as we have seen, the capitalist has already ceased to be necessary as an active agent in the conduct of large-scale industry. He has become, *qua* owner of capital, a passive recipient of a share in the proceeds, who contributes nothing to the efficiency of the productive process.

The Drive towards Socialism

The overwhelming strength of the economic case for Socialism is, however, obviously in itself no guarantee of its coming; for systems are created not by logical arguments but by men. The logic of the case may help the coming of Socialism, but only to the extent to which it works on men's minds so as to strengthen the movement of those who are seeking to institute a Socialist system. But the strength of a movement depends not only, or even mainly, on the cogency of its arguments, but also on the forces behind it. Marx believed that Socialism would supersede Capitalism not only because it was the system best fitted further to develop the use of the powers of production, but also because it was the creed of a growing movement, based on the working class, which would in due course become powerful enough to overthrow the capitalist autocracy. He believed that this would come about because he held that Capitalism, by the very necessities of its own development, was bound to lead to a polarisation of economic classes and to the creation of a more and more powerful and class-conscious movement among the exploited. Large-scale production, he insisted, requires the aggregation of the workers into large masses subject to common conditions and to a common discipline, and thereby makes easier the task of organising them in Trade Unions; and the growing interrelation of capitalist industries and the growing pressure of international competition drive home the lessons of class-solidarity on both a national and an international scale. This is an aspect of the Marxian doctrine, vital to Marx's attempt at scientific demonstration of the certainty of the coming triumph of Socialism, that we have so far left unexamined. We must proceed now to ask how far he was right about this increasing polarisation of classes, or about the consequent growth of national and international working-class solidarity. In fact, we must consider Marx's doctrine of the class-struggle, in the light of the actual development of class-relationships in advanced economic societies during the most recent period of capitalist evolution.

CHAPTER IV

ECONOMIC CLASSES

MARX'S THEORY OF THE class-struggle was first explicitly formulated in *The Communist Manifesto* of 1848. Marx never restated it in a similar full and explicit form, though of course it underlay the whole of his thought. Actually, the unfinished final chapter of the third volume of *Capital*, edited from Marx's papers by Engels after his death, is the beginning of what promises to be a thorough discussion of the nature of economic classes and of their relationships. But this chapter remains the merest fragment, broken off before the exposition has fairly begun, and highly provocative in the wonder which it arouses. Would Marx, if he had expounded the nature of classes towards the close of his life, have written of them in the same terms as he had used more than thirty years before? Or would he have recognised that there had been, in the interval, vitally important changes in the class-structure of advanced industrial societies, and that these changes were, to some extent, different from the anticipations which he had entertained? The question is probably unanswerable; but let us at any rate remember that the familiar Marxian account of the class-struggle was written near the beginning of Marx's public life, and reflects the capitalist conditions of the first half of the nineteenth century, and not of Marx's later years.

This is of great importance; for *The Communist Manifesto* was written before joint stock enterprise had become the accepted form of developed capitalist production over the greater part of industry, and before the middle classes had assumed the new character given to them by the increased wealth of modern industrial societies, and by the greater complexity of modern technical and financial processes. The middle classes, that is, the classes between the governing groups of the capitalists and the wage-earners, have increased markedly as a percentage of the entire population with the more recent developments of capitalist enterprise, and have assumed, under the joint stock system, new relations to the processes of production. Any modern theory of classes must take full account of these changes: it is merely beside the point to repeat without modification a statement of the basis of class-divisions conceived in terms of the very different economic conditions of a century ago.

The Theory of Class-struggle

Let us begin by outlining the theory, in the form in which it is stated in *The Communist Manifesto*. We are there presented with a theory of world-history as a succession of class-struggles for economic and political power. We are concerned in this chapter only with Marx's picture of the most recent of these struggles—the conflict between the exploiting capitalists and the exploited proletariat, which is conceived to be the dominant theme of contemporary Western society. These two classes are represented as so dominating the society of to-day that the admitted existence of other classes, or of groups which cannot be adequately classified as either capitalist or proletarian, is regarded as, not indeed unimportant from the standpoint of the day-to-day political struggle, but irrelevant to a consideration of the general historical movement. It is admitted that these other groups may exert here and there, or now and then, a temporarily decisive influence on a particular phase of the struggle; but it is inconceivable, in Marx's view, that they should finally determine the issue, or play a truly creative part. For they have in them, he believes, no power to create an alternative social pattern of their own; and accordingly they can act only so as to obstruct or fog the issue, or as secondary allies of one or the other of the major classes.

Moreover, Marx undoubtedly wrote as if these secondary class-groups were already in process of disappearance, or destined to disappear with the further advance of Capitalism. He thought of the two great classes of capitalists and proletarians as destined, for all practical purposes, to become in the final phase of the struggle between them co-extensive with the whole of society, or at least so nearly co-extensive as to reduce any remaining groups outside them to the rôle of impotent spectators or obviously subordinate assistants. From the standpoint of the broad process of social evolution, only the proletariat and the capitalists were held to count.

We must ask, then, first of all in what terms Marx sought to define these outstanding classes. He admitted that their precise limits were unclear, and that there were, in capitalist society, many border-line cases. But he held that both proletariat and capitalists could be sufficiently defined by the places which they occupy in the capitalist system. The proletariat he defined as that class which consists of persons who depend for their living on the sale of their labour-power, and are unable to secure an income except by resigning all claim to the product of their labour. The proletariat is made up of workers who are shut off from direct access to the means of production, and live by the alienation of the only commodity they possess—their power to produce wealth by labouring upon machines and materials which they do not own. The distinctive characteristic of this class is not so much that its labour is paid for by a wage—though it is—as that its product belongs, not to its members, but to the purchasers of their labour-power.

The proletariat thus defined must, of course, be held to include not only those who in this way alienate their labour-power but also their dependants, who, equally with them, live out of the proceeds of the sale of labour-power as a commodity. It includes, obviously, the employed wage-workers in agriculture as well as in industry and commerce; but it does not, by the terms of the definition, include anyone who is not either an employed worker or the dependant of an employed worker. How far it can be held to include employed workers who receive not a wage but what is called a salary we had best leave over for consideration at a later stage. Whatever limits may be assigned to the proletariat as a class, obviously its central mass consists of the general body of manual wage-earners, and it is thought of as predominantly a manual-working and wage-earning group.

Marx, however, warned his readers against attempting to define economic classes by the forms in which they receive their incomes. There are, he held, many more distinct forms of income than there are separate economic classes. The distinctive characteristic of the proletariat is not the receipt of a wage, however important that aspect of the status of the majority of its actively working members may be, but the alienation of its labour-power,

109

based on its divorce from ownership of, and direct access to, the means of production on which it is required to work.

The Bourgeoisie

This warning becomes far more important when we turn to consider the character of the capitalist class, called by Marx the *bourgeoisie*. For the class which Marx calls *bourgeois* receives its income not in a single form, but in many different forms. It is the class which predominantly lives by the receipt of profit, interest and rent—all three of these, and not any one or two of them. Marx states this by saying that the *bourgeoisie* lives by the receipt of "surplus value," which he conceives of as a fund, arising out of the exploitation of labour, out of which rent, interest and profits are all paid. The *bourgeoisie* lives out of surplus value to much the same extent as the proletariat lives out of the proceeds of the sale of labour-power. But the *bourgeoisie* as a class must be defined strictly, not as the recipients of surplus value, but as the owners of those resources of production upon which the proletariat is employed to work. The *bourgeoisie*, even though it derives a part of its income from the remuneration of its own labour of superintendence and of its performance of the *entrepreneur* function of co-ordinating the factors of production in risk-bearing ventures carried on under its control, is essentially a class of owners of the means of production; the proletariat is essentially a class of employed persons who do not own the means of production, apart from their own labour-power.

The power to labour is merely useless and abstract without access to the means of production; and accordingly the proletariat as a class has, under Capitalism, no power to produce wealth unless the capitalists are prepared to employ it. But the means of production are also useless and unproductive unless labour is applied to them. The labourer has to find an employer, in order to get the means of life. But it is also true that the employer, or capitalist, has to find labourers whom he can employ if his capital is to possess any value. Marx again and again stressed this point, insisting that Capitalism is fundamentally a relationship among men, and that its essence consists not of the accumulation of a stock of goods or instruments of production, but of the availability of a proletariat from which surplus value can be extracted. This is the point of the argument of the closing sections of the first volume of *Capital*, in which the rise of the capitalist system is discussed and traced to the emergence of a propertyless class of free labourers compelled to live by the sale of their labour-power.

The Petite Bourgeoisie

This, however, takes us beyond *The Communist Manifesto* to a subsequent formulation of Marx's doctrine. In the *Manifesto*, there is only a brief historical section of which the sole purpose is to bring into relief the dominant importance of the class-struggle and of the two great classes between which it is carried on. There is much said of the rôle of a group to which Marx gives the name of *petite bourgeoisie*, as well as of the two outstanding classes, but always on the assumption that the *petite bourgeoisie* is a dying or decaying class, because its very existence is bound up with the survival of the small-scale forms of production which are being remorselessly crushed out by the advance of capitalist industry. The *petite bourgeoisie*, as it appears in *The Communist Manifesto*, consists chiefly of small master craftsmen and independent artisans, small traders, and small farmers, who are being driven from one position after another by the development of large-scale methods of production. This section of society is thus, in Marx's view, essentially a threatened and obsolescent class, attempting to retain for itself a status and an economic position which the advancing powers of production are rapidly making untenable.

This decaying class is represented as placed, in the contemporary phase of the class-struggle, between the protagonists, hovering doubtfully in its allegiance, but unable to stand by itself or to formulate a policy of its own. Marx characterises it as hating and fearing the advance of large-scale Capitalism, which threatens it with submergence, and as animated by democratic sentiments on account of its hostility to the greater *bourgeoisie*, and of its desire for equality with the class above it and for a share in the formulation of policy. But he describes it as even more fearful of the class below it, towards which some of its members stand in the relation of employers and others in a relation of petty profit-seekers through the sale of the products of small-scale agriculture and workshop industry, or as retailers of goods produced under large-scale capitalist auspices; and he represents it as desiring not social and economic quality, but the maintenance of its own position of petty economic privilege. Consequently, while it is willing to accept the support of the workers for an attack on the greater *bourgeoisie*, it will do this only on condition that the attack is directed to the realisation of its own limited objectives, and not to the overthrow of capitalist society as a whole. It wants to clip the wings of large-scale Capitalism; but even more it wants to preserve the decaying system of small-scale Capitalism. Its attitude therefore, even when it appears to be radical and democratic, is in Marx's view always really reactionary; for its supreme desire is to preserve conditions which are inconsistent with economic progress. In a serious crisis, though it may begin by siding with the proletariat against the *bourgeoisie*, it will always, he argues, change sides as soon as the *anti-bourgeois* movement threatens to develop into a fundamental attack upon the capitalist system. For, in the last resort, it will always prefer gradual erosion by the further development of large-scale industrialism to complete supersession as the consequence of a proletarian victory.

This analysis of the attitude of the *petite bourgeoisie*, set out in general terms in *The Communist Manifesto*, was applied with much more detail by Marx and Engels in their occasional writings commenting upon current affairs, especially in their studies of the actual events of 1848 and the following years. *Revolution and Counter-Revolution in Germany, Class Struggles in France*, and other writings of this sort amplify and illustrate with a wealth of examples the teaching of *The Communist Manifesto* concerning the historic rôle of the *petite bourgeoisie*. Nor is there any doubt that Marx and Engels were essentially right in their diagnosis both of the economic position of the *petite bourgeoisie* of 1848, and of its political attitude. It was, in the economic sense, at this stage mainly a decaying and reactionary class; and politically it did seek to use the proletariat to help it to increase its own power in relation to the greater *bourgeoisie*, but did at once rally to the side of the *bourgeoisie* when there was any risk of the proletariat getting out of hand, and attempting to fight its own battles, or to deliver a frontal attack upon the capitalist system.

The essential struggle, as Marx conceived it, could be obfuscated or temporarily sidetracked by the attitude of the *petite bourgeoisie*, but could not be prevented from dominating the situation in the long run, precisely because the preservation of small-scale industry and trade as a significant form of economic organisation had ceased to be a possible policy in face of the advance in the powers of production. The *petit bourgeois* might be a long time dying; but Marx regarded his doom as certain, and his power even to cloud the fundamental issues as destined to become inevitably less and less.

The Proletariat

What then of the proletariat, of which Marx thought as essentially the rising class destined to accomplish the overthrow and supersession of the capitalist system? The position of this class was contrasted by Marx and Engels with that of previous subject classes which had accomplished their emancipation and had risen to a position of economic and social dominance. For, whereas the embryonic capitalists had managed, under feudalism, to prosper and to develop into full-blown *bourgeois* on their road to power, Marx believed the modern labourer was faced with the prospect of an increasing exploitation which, as Capitalism developed further, would cause him to sink deeper and deeper into misery and distress. The capitalists had conquered political and economic power by becoming prosperous enough to assert their claims with success; but, paradoxically, the modern proletariat was to force its way to power along the road of "increasing misery."

The Theory of Increasing Misery

That this is the doctrine of the *Manifesto*, and that it remained Marx's doctrine in his later writings, there is simply no doubt at all. But Marx nowhere explained why, if the capitalist class managed to rise to power, in most countries, not by catastrophic revolution overthrowing the previous ruling class, but rather by a gradual process of encroachment and adaptation of the established social structure, increasing misery should be the means to the conquest of power by the proletariat, whereas increasing prosperity had been the weapon of the *bourgeoisie*. Yet the view is plainly paradoxical; for, on the face of the matter, the increase of misery would be much more likely to weaken and dispirit a class than to aid it in the prosecution of the class-struggle. There are in fact, at this point, two unresolved and imperfectly co-ordinated elements in the Marxian doctrine. On the one hand Marx argued that the capitalist system would in its development reach at a certain point, because of its inherent contradictions, a position in which it would be unable to carry further the evolution of the powers of production, or even to carry on at all, and would be plunged into a series of economic crises of growing amplitude and severity which would in the end involve its destruction. On the other hand he argued that this destruction would come upon it at the hands of a proletariat forced into misery by the growing difficulties of the capitalist system, and powerful enough, in its misery, to set manfully about the construction of an alternative system.

If, however, the further development of Capitalism seemed to promise both a laying bare of the inherent contradictions of capitalist production and the increasing misery of the working classes, what was the outcome likely to be? The first of these developments would threaten Capitalism with destruction; but the second would make less likely its supersession at the hands of the proletariat. In effect, if Marx had been right, the probable outcome would have been the collapse of Capitalism under conditions in which the proletariat would have been too weakened by its misery successfully to establish an alternative system. In these circumstances, if there had been no other aspirant to the succession, a collapsing Capitalism would have been likeliest to be succeeded, not by Socialism, but by sheer chaos, and by the dissolution of the entire civilisation of which Capitalism had been a phase.

It can be objected to this view that the proletariat might get both more miserable and stronger, because its misery would make it more revolutionary. But surely the essence of the Marxian conception is that revolutions are made by economically advancing, and not by decaying, economic classes?

One answer is that domination comes, in the evolution of the historical process, to that class which is best adapted to further the development of the powers of production, and that this law designates the proletariat as the successor of the capitalist class. But does it? Or rather, would it, if Marx were correct in holding that the proletariat would, before the final crisis of Capitalism, have been reduced to an undifferentiated mass of 'detail-labourers'—surely a class highly unsuited to take over the task of controlling and of carrying to a more advanced stage of development the exceedingly complex processes of modern production and exchange? The theory of 'increasing misery,' plausible as it must have appeared to anyone surveying the phase of developing machine-production in Europe in the first half of the nineteenth century, simply does not square with the view that victory in the struggle of classes goes to the class that is best qualified to advance the use of the powers of production to a higher stage. Marx's general economic analysis, which is on this point essentially sound, leads rather to the conclusion that the further development of the powers of production will be best advanced by the institution of a classless society, which will make the satisfaction of the individual and collective needs of all its members the guiding principle of its economic organisation. The solution of the contradictions of capitalist society is to be sought, on this showing, not in the domination of a new ruling class, but in the abolition of classes and the complete socialisation of the economic system to serve the needs of a classless society. The dictatorship of the proletariat is indeed advocated by Marx only as a necessary means of bringing about the transition to the classless society. The "proletarian State" stands not for a new epoch in social evolution, but only as an instrument for effecting the change from Capitalism to Socialism. But, if the proletariat were really destined to be ground down by "increasing misery," what chance would there be of the "proletarian State" ever coming into existence?

The Rôle of the Proletariat

There are in this part of Marx's doctrine two distinct elements —the assertion that the contradictions of Capitalism can be resolved only by the institution of a classless society, and the assertion that a temporary dictatorship of the proletarian class is necessary in order to bring such a society into being. These two assertions are quite independent, and acceptance of the one need not carry with it acceptance of the other. It may be true that the proletariat is the only agency through which Socialism can be brought into being; but this conclusion neither squares with the doctrine of 'increasing misery' nor follows immediately from the demonstration that Socialism is the appropriate method of resolving the contradictions of Capitalism.

Marxists, however, hold that the instrument of the transformation of society cannot be anything other than a class, and that, in the present phase of history, the proletariat is the only class that can possibly fulfil this revolutionary function. To Marx, surveying the actual conditions of 1848, this conclusion seemed obvious, because there was no other serious claimant to the rôle of revolutionary leadership. The *petite bourgeoisie*, as he saw it, was ruled out of court because it was a decaying class, whose powers and conceptions were bound up with a declining and obsolescent method of small-scale production. The proletariat, on the other hand, seemed clearly designated for the rôle of revolutionary saviour; for it was in fact a rising class, developing with the advance of Capitalism, and growingly disposed to advance claims inconsistent with the maintenance of the capitalist system. It was not in fact being converted into an undifferentiated mass of detail-labourers, without pride of craft or capacity for control. On the contrary, whatever the sufferings of the main body of less skilled operatives in mine or factory, the skilled workmen, even in the first half of the nineteenth century, were improving their economic and social position; and new kinds of skill, based on new machine techniques, were creating new bodies of skilled workmen to take the lead in building the modern Trade Union movement. It has, however, to be considered whether these conditions hold good nearly a century later, in face of large changes both in the class-structure of advanced industrial societies and in the workings of Capitalism. Moreover, even if Marx's thesis concerning the dominant rôle of the proletariat is reaffirmed, it has to be considered how far Marx envisaged correctly the actual method of the rise of the proletariat to power.

What is "Increasing Misery"?

This last point is partly bound up with the question whether Marx was right in holding that, with the advance of Capitalism, the proletariat was destined to fall into a period of increasing misery. The doctrine of "increasing misery" seems to have been interpreted by Marxists in a number of different ways. One interpretation is that the proletariat is destined to become more miserable only in a relative sense, in that, although the working-class standard of living may rise in terms of the goods that wages will buy, the degree of exploitation is destined to increase and the capitalist to pocket a growing *proportion* of the total product of industry. This interpretation is, however, plainly inconsistent with Marx's own words. He did quite explicitly prophesy for the poor a fall in the standard of living, and not merely a failure to improve it in proportion to the increase in capitalist wealth. The second interpretation, which seems the most natural for some of the passages, especially for *The Communist Manifesto*, is that Marx regarded the tendency of Capitalism to force down working-class standards as already in action, and expected it to become more marked with every stage in the further development of capitalist production. This view, though it is consistent with what Marx wrote, is plainly wrong in relation to the facts. For undoubtedly for half a century after *The Communist Manifesto* was written, working-class standards of life were rising, and rising most of all in the most rapidly developing capitalist countries.

Accordingly, resort was had to a third interpretation. Working-class standards could continue to rise as long as Capitalism continued to be a developing system, consistent with the further advancement of the powers of production. On this showing, the tendency to increasing misery would come into force only as this condition ceased to be satisfied, and as Capitalism turned into a fetter on the further development of these powers. Only as the inherent contradictions of Capitalism were brought into actual operation by the later manifestations of the system would the pressure of capitalist competition begin actually to force down the working-class standard of life.

This interpretation hardly accords with what Marx said; but it alone can be made to look consistent with the subsequent evolution of Capitalism. On this view, the first foreshadowings of increasing misery appeared in the first decade of the twentieth century, when, at any rate in Great Britain, the most advanced industrial country, the increase of international competition began seriously to check the rise of wages, and even to cause some actual fall in the purchasing power of money wages in face of a rising cost of living. The first World War, by creating a scarcity of labour and inducing an increased pressure for the provision of social services, for a time reversed this tendency; and the strength of the adverse forces was not again manifested until well after the war, when it appeared to come back first in the slump and in the working-class setbacks of 1921 and the following years, and then, far more devastatingly, in the world depression which set in after 1929. Even then, however, the tendency to depression of working-class standards manifested itself very unequally as between trade and trade, hitting hardest the workers engaged in the industries most subject to international competition, including that of the developing capitalist economies of the Far East.

The result of this pressure was, not an even fall in working-class standards, but a pressing down of certain sections of the working class, whereas other sections were relatively well able to maintain their position—the more so because the world depression brought with it a sharp fall in the prices of foodstuffs, which benefited the workers in the industrial countries at the expense of primary producers. There were also large national differences: the German workers suffered more than the British, and the Americans, relatively, most of all. Among industrial workers coal-miners and textile workers suffered much more than workers engaged in the services or in production for a less competitive market. Pockets of working-class misery were the consequence, rather than a general depression of standards for the working class as a whole. This caused cleavages in the working-class ranks, because it made the hardest-hit sections far more amenable than the rest to extreme types of propagandist appeal. There was moreover in a good many countries a continuing growth of the social services, which took the edge off the sufferings of the unemployed and of others near the bottom of the social ladder; and, as these improvements were maintained when the slump grew less severe, it can hardly be maintained that the working classes as a whole were worse off in 1939 than at any earlier stage of Capitalism.

117

The interruption of capitalist development and the growing difficulties of the capitalist system did, however, react for the time not only so as to depress working-class standards in many trades, but also so as to decrease the organised power of the workers. Unemployment lessened, or even undermined, the authority of Trade Unionism in the industries in which the pressure was most intense; and these were precisely the industries in which capitalist expansion had been greatest, and working-class organisation strongest and most effective. Moreover, the new phase of Capitalism carried with it the adoption of a new technique of rapidly growing mechanisation and standardisation of industrial processes, and a new complexity of organisation. These developments diminished the proportion of workers engaged in productive industry—the stronghold of Trade Unionism—and increased the proportion in the less easily organised and less class-conscious service occupations, such as distribution and clerical work. They also diminished, in productive industry, the proportion of skilled to less skilled workers; and this too tended to weaken the organised Labour Movement, which had rested largely upon the strength of organisation among the more highly skilled groups.

Thus, as the contradictions of Capitalism grew more obvious and menacing between the wars, the *industrial* strength of the working-class movement, instead of increasing, tended to decline; and the class-conscious section of the "proletariat," composed mainly of wage-workers, came to form a smaller proportion of the total population in the most advanced industrial countries. This decline in industrial power, it may be argued, was more than offset by a spread of class-consciousness to other groups and by an advance in *political* strength. Trade Unionism might grow weaker in consequence of unemployment and technical change; but the general pressing-down of the working-class standard of life which seemed to be threatened by the growing difficulties of Capitalism would create in its place a class-conscious and militant Socialist Movement.

Capitalist Crises

Marx's theory of "increasing misery," we have seen already, was closely bound up with his view that the growth of "monopoly Capitalism" and of imperialist rivalries between the great capitalist countries would lead to economic crises of increasing severity. It was in the throes of such a crisis, he thought, that Capitalism would finally be brought down by proletarian revolt. We can follow him, in his correspondence with Engels, speculating whether the next crisis—and then the next after that—would prove to be the final crisis of Capitalism, bringing the dialectical process of contradiction to a head and leading to social revolution. Marx in effect wrote as if the growth of capitalist crises and the increasing misery of the proletariat were simply two aspects of one and the same thing. Actually, this has not so far been the case. Even if large sections of the working class have been flung into misery by crisis, this has not meant that their misery has been lasting, or has involved a permanent fall in their standards of life. Neither in the United States nor in Great Britain was the average standard of living of the workers worse in 1939 than it had been ten years earlier, before the greatest crisis in the history of Capitalism began.

There was in truth no necessary connection between the theory of the developing contradictions of Capitalism (as leading to more and more severe economic crises) and the theory that the misery of the proletariat was bound to increase. A crisis such as overtook the capitalist world in the 1930's was more and not less calculated to stir up working-class revolt if it came as a sharp reversal of an upward trend in standards of living. A continuously declining standard is the worst of preparations for revolt, because it steadily saps working-class power and undermines the spirit of the sufferers. A sharp and sudden reversal of fortunes is likely to create conditions which fit in very much better with Marx's affirmation of the approach of the proletarian revolution.

It may be objected that the devastating crisis of the American economy in the 1930's did not in fact lead to revolution. Of course it did not; for the conditions were not ripe. No system, Marx tells us, ever gives way until it has exhausted all its power of developing the powers of production; and this point American Capitalism, as its subsequent history shows, had by no means reached in 1931. Nor was there in 1931 any American Labour movement capable of constructing, or even of wishing to construct, a Socialist system. What the crisis did achieve was a 'New Deal' which, in rescuing Capitalism from its difficulties, also gave opportunity for an immense growth of Trade Unionism and class-consciousness among the American workers in the mass-production industries.

In Germany, on the other hand, the crisis of the 1930's did lead to revolution, but not to revolution of the type Marx had counted upon. There, however, the working class had not been suddenly flung down from a condition of advancing prosperity, but gradually beaten down as a consequence of the economic repercussions of defeat in war. What happened in Germany plainly illustrated the truth that "increasing misery," far from helping on the proletarian revolution, is much more likely to ensure working-class defeat. No doubt, conditions in post-first-war Germany did lead *some* workers to draw revolutionary conclusions; but they also disastrously split the working class, leading others to Fascism and yet others to apathy or hopelessness of achieving anything. "Increasing misery," at any rate in Germany, helped Fascism a great deal more than it helped Socialism. Instead of uniting the workers, it divided them: instead of strengthening them, it made them easy victims of the capitalist-Fascist alliance.

It is therefore by no means reasonable to conclude that, under all conditions, the developing contradictions of Capitalism will drive the proletariat solidly to Socialism. They may, under some conditions, have a very different effect; and they pretty certainly would have, if the proletariat were really in process of being steadily ground down into an undifferentiated mass of unskilled wage-slaves living at sheer subsistence level. The task of building Socialism calls for a high degree of skill and directive capacity in many fields: a strong and differentiated working class stands a much better chance of success in building it than a pack of dispirited starvelings, the victims of that "increasing misery" which Marx foretold.

The Russian Revolution

And yet . . . a kind of Socialism came in the Soviet Union as a sequel to the first World War, whereas no proletarian revolution was forthcoming in the more developed capitalist countries. True; but that in no way invalidates my contention. The Russian Revolution assuredly did not occur because in Russia Capitalism had passed its zenith, or because the contradictions of Capitalism manifested themselves there more than elsewhere. Nor was it the outcome of a protracted period of *increasing* misery. The Revolution of 1917 took place because the Czarist system, which was in the main pre-capitalist, broke down utterly under the strain of modern war, and because the resulting economic and political chaos gave a small but solid proletariat, under strong and self-confident leadership, the opportunity to overthrow a decadent feudal monarchy which could find neither prop nor alternative in an inchoate and undeveloped *bourgeois* class. The task of building Socialism would have been not harder but immensely easier if the leaders of the revolution had been able to call upon a stronger and more highly developed working

120

class, without having to encounter a no less strengthened Capitalism.

But, of course, this could not have happened. The strength of the working class and that of the capitalist class normally grow together. In the making of revolutions the strength that counts is not absolute, but relative. A revolutionary situation may arise where the proletariat is weak absolutely, as well as where it is strong. It will not, however, arise, as a situation favourable to *proletarian* revolution, where the proletariat is getting steadily weaker in relation to the forces ranged on the other side.

In order to see how and how far Marx's theories of class-war can be adapted to fit the conditions of the modern world, it is obviously necessary to make a careful study of the actual class-structure of the capitalist societies of to-day. We cannot assume that this structure is the same as that which Marx studied in 1848: indeed we know that it is not. We must try to look at it objectively, as Marx tried to study objectively the conditions of his own day. What, then, are the salient classes, and class-divisions, in the highly developed industrial countries of to-day?

The Capitalist Class

First, what of the capitalist class? Evidently there has been, during the past century, a profound change in its character and economic position. Marx began writing at a time when, above all in England, the new type of industrial capitalist created by the development of power-driven machinery and the factory system was rapidly supplanting the older type of merchant capitalist who made his money by trade rather than by the direct exploitation of the productive process. The great capitalists of the seventeenth and eighteenth centuries had been pre-dominantly merchants rather than industrial employers, though even under the domestic system of manufacture the rich merchant was tending to become virtually a large-scale employer as well. This tendency foreshadowed the coming of the phase of Capitalism which Marx saw developing fast in his own day. With the advent of power-driven machinery, capital had to be aggregated into large masses for the actual carrying on of production; and the factory-owner began to displace the merchant as the typical representative of the capitalist system. This rise of a new and numerous section of industrial capitalists who could not be readily assimilated to the old order was accompanied by the struggle for reform of parliamentary institutions, and by the creation of a political system based on a suffrage wide enough to admit the middle classes to an increasingly effective share in political power. It led to the evolution of the nineteenth-century capitalist State, within which the older groups of landowners and merchants were more and more assimilated to the new industrialists, so that land came to be a form of capital not differing greatly from other forms, and merchant capital was more and more fused with industrial capital under the dominance of the new industrialists.

Marx foresaw the further evolution of this process, based essentially on the further development of machine technique. He saw that the scale of production was bound to grow larger and larger, and to call for the aggregation of capital into larger and larger masses in the industrial field. He foresaw that this growth in the scale of production would lead to an increasing restriction of competition within each developing national economy, both because small businesses would tend to be crushed out, and because large businesses would grow more and more aware of the advantages of combination. Accordingly, he envisaged, on the national scale, an increasing concentration of control in the hands of the great capitalists, accompanied by the beating down towards the proletarian class of such of the *petite bourgeoisie* as could not become fully fledged *bourgeois*.

Imperialism

But Marx also looked, in two important respects, beyond the tendency towards capitalist concentration of control, within any national system of Capitalism, in the hands of the great industrialists. He did not believe that this concentration would or could assume in general a cosmopolitan form. He held rather that in the more advanced countries each national group of capitalists, having acquired control of its national State, would use its power to institute an intensified and State-supported international competition with similar capitalist concentrations in other countries. He prophesied that each national capitalist group, unable to find within its own borders markets for its constantly expanding output, would be driven outwards in the search for foreign markets, as well as for the raw materials needed to keep its growing factories at work, and for concessions and openings for foreign investment that would afford profitable outlets for its mounting accumulation of capital. Thus the industrialist phase of Capitalism would pass into Imperialism, which would express itself in fierce international competition between huge capitalist groups, and would lead, by way of economic rivalries, to destructive Imperialist wars.

This development of Capitalism into Imperialism could not, however, occur without bringing with it far-reaching changes in the internal characteristics of Capitalism as well. The phase of Capitalism which Marx was observing in 1848 was that in which the capitalist merchants were being superseded by the industrialists as the dominant group; but he foresaw that with the further evolution of the system the industrialist was destined either to be superseded by, or to develop into, the financier. The Imperialist phase of Capitalism would be also the phase of the domination of Finance Capital, as distinct from either Merchant Capital or Industrial Capital.

Financial Capitalism and the Shareholders

In this phase, the predominance would belong, no longer to the industrial employers as such, but to the owners and manipulators of huge blocks of accumulated money capital. These might be either bankers, in effective control of a mass of deposits far exceeding their own capital, and able by this means to set in motion a still vaster mass of credit created by themselves; or the heads of finance houses and investment agencies, powerful enough to swing great blocks made up of the savings of a host of investors in any direction they chose, and influential especially as the ministers of Imperialism in the financing of undeveloped areas; or the controllers of great industrial combines who, still remaining in form large employers of labour, would become in effect far more the manipulators of mass production for purely financial ends, and would owe their power and influence over the State rather to their financial than to their industrial pre-eminence. The dominance of Economic Imperialism and of Finance Capital would be the significant characteristics of this phase of Capitalism, and would clearly differentiate it from the preceding phases of Merchant and Industrial Capitalism.

In these two foreshadowings of the future of Capitalism Marx was indisputably correct, and showed an astonishing prescience. In these fundamental respects he prophesied with absolute correctness the subsequent course of capitalist development. But it does not follow that he was equally correct in everything else. It has often been pointed out that, whereas Marx often wrote as if the advance of Capitalism would be bound to involve a growing concentration of the *ownership* of capital in the hands of the great capitalists, actually throughout the remainder of the nineteenth century there went on a rapid increase in both the absolute and the relative numbers of those who had a share in the ownership of capitalist industry, and drew "surplus value" from it in the form of rent or interest or profit. Marxists have sometimes contended that this fact is of no importance, because the diffusion of the ownership of capitalist industry over a larger section of the population has been accompanied by a steadily increasing concentration of control. The number of small owners, it is said, is irrelevant, because the small shareholder or *rentier* has in effect no control over the uses to which his capital is put, and is thus wholly in the hands and under the domination of the great capitalists.

That the smaller shareholders and *rentier* have, economically, no real control is, of course, perfectly true. The simultaneous development of diffused ownership and of concentrated control has been made possible by the evolution of joint stock enterprise, of which the chief advance came after Marx had formulated his doctrines, and largely after his death. The joint stock system did solve some of the most difficult problems of nineteenth-century Capitalism. It made possible a more effective mobilisation of the money resources of all those who had any capital to invest, including the main body of the middle classes as well as the owners of larger masses of capital, for the development of industry; and at the same time, by giving the entire middle class, and also the old landowning class, which came to invest largely in commerce and industry, a direct stake in the capitalist system, it greatly broadened the political basis of Capitalism, and made the dominance of large-scale industrialism compatible with a far more extended franchise than could otherwise have been co-existent with it. It reconciled the need for concentration in the control of capital with diffused ownership, by putting the great capitalists in a position to manipulate far larger masses of capital than they could possibly have owned without provoking an overwhelming hostility from every other section of society.

The Divorce between Ownership and Control.

As the joint stock system developed, it took on more and more this characteristic of divorcing ownership from economic control. Small investors, unable to take large risks, and eager to insure against them, found the great capitalists always ready to oblige. The preference share, commonly carrying with it either no voting right, or at most a restricted voting right, in the enterprise, gave the small investor greater security in return for the abnegation of even nominal control. But, even in the case of ordinary shares, the control exerted by the small investors was usually quite unreal. They were many and scattered, and could have no real knowledge of the working of the enterprises to which

124

they entrusted their money; and under the system of "one share, one vote,"[1] they could almost always be swamped by the few big holders of shares. Moreover, in pursuit of security, the small and middle investors usually "spread" their risks, entrusting their money in small doses to a number of different concerns, either directly or through Investment Trusts, and so reducing their potential influence on any one of them to nothing. The growth of Stock Exchanges, which spread the excitement of gambling in stock values, meant that large numbers of shares were continually changing hands, and caused their momentary owners to have no sustained interest at all in the businesses in which their money was placed, but to regard their shares merely as potential sources of money-income and of capital appreciation, so that it was a matter of no concern to them to know whether the companies in question made rifles, or church furniture, or whisky, or cotton goods, but only what dividends they were likely to pay and whether the money prices of the shares were likely to go up or down. The consummation of this divorce of the investor from control over, or interest in, the use of his money was reached with the growth of Insurance Companies and Investment Trusts. For in both these cases the investment of the small investor's resources in actual productive enterprise was removed right out of his hands, and was taken over directly by large capitalist concerns which were able to operate with greater skill and knowledge.

Thus, under modern conditions, the small investors and even the middle-sized investors in large-scale enterprise have hardly any control at all over the economic working of Capitalism. When once they have invested their money, control of it passes right out of their hands; and even the control they can exercise over its direction to this or that form of enterprise has been increasingly surrendered by the growth of indirect investment through Insurance Companies, Investment Trusts, and other agencies of large-scale Capitalism. The ordinary investor does not control; and, what is more, he does not want to control, and cannot possibly know how to control.

The Small Masters

The small-scale capitalist whose capital is invested in his own small business stands on a different footing; for he is usually the manager of his enterprise, alone or in partnership with others, and does take the risks of organising production for the market.

[1] To be contrasted with the democratic principle of "one member, one vote," which is the basis of Co-operative enterprise.

This is the type of enterprise which Marx expected to be ground out of existence by the development of large-scale production and of centralised financial control; and it has in fact been subject to continual erosion ever since the Industrial Revolution. Nevertheless, even in the most advanced countries, there has been no tendency for small-scale business to disappear. It is still in most countries the commonest type, not only in agriculture but also in distribution and in a large number of trades in which there are no great economic advantages in mass-production and no great attractions in large-scale financial control. Moreover, many types of big business tend to create around them swarms of little firms, which act either as sub-contractors making special components or undertaking auxiliary tasks, or as agents and distributors for the products of the great concerns. Brass-foundries are an example of the first type: motor garages, small tobacconists, newsagents, and confectioners illustrate the second. These small firms are in a sense independent; but they are as a rule dominated by the great firms on which they depend for orders or for supplies. The sub-contractor is in the hands of those who place orders with him: the small dealer is strictly regulated in most cases in respect of prices and conditions of sale, and may be absolutely dependent on the trade credit allowed him by the large-scale producer or wholesale merchant.

The continuing existence, under developed Capitalism, of this large body of small *entrepreneurs* is nevertheless a highly significant fact, of which, as we shall see, full account must be taken in assessing the class-structure of modern capitalist societies. But the survival of this type of enterprise does not invalidate the generalisation that the characteristic feature of modern Capitalism is the dominance of large-scale businesses in which control is highly concentrated, even though ownership may be widely scattered.

The Growth of the Middle Classes

Marx, then, was absolutely right in holding that Capitalism tends to a growing concentration of the control of capital; and the fact that the ownership of shares in large-scale capitalist enterprise has tended to become more diffused does not in the least affect this part of his argument. But the diffusion of the ownership of large-scale business enterprise over the whole of the classes above the wage-earning level—and even to a small extent over a section of the wage-earners, especially in the United States—is nevertheless also a highly significant and important social phenomenon.

For this broadening of the basis of Capitalism acts with the persistence of small-scale enterprise to prevent effectively the complete polarisation of classes which would result from a concentration of ownership as well as of control in the hands of a shrinking class of great capitalist magnates. By diffusing the ownership of property, not over the whole of society, but over a fraction fully large enough to offset the effects of concentration, it protects Capitalism against the massing in hostility to it of all the remaining elements in society, and provides it with a body-guard of retainers who feel their economic prospects and social status to be bound up with the continuance and prosperity of the capitalist system. Every shareholder or *rentier* who draws an appreciable part of his income from capitalist enterprise has a stake in its success, and feels himself menaced by any attack upon it. This sentiment even extends, by way of insurances, savings deposits, and the collective investments of Friendly Societies and Trade Unions, well beyond the boundaries of the investing groups and classes, and affects the attitude of leaders of working-class opinion. Meanwhile, the Co-operative Movement, imitating in part the joint stock structure, albeit in a more democratic form—"one member, one vote" instead of "one share, one vote"—and compelled to work within an environment of capitalist industry, necessarily reproduces in some degree the same social attitude. Thus Capitalism, by creating a large body of dependent capitalists, as well as by using small-scale enterprise as its agent over a wide field, averts the menace of a complete proletarianisation of all who are not able to amass enough wealth to gain an effective place in the control of the expanding process of mass-production.

Nor is this all. The typical capitalist of 1848 was still his own manager, despite the existence here and there of large *entrepreneurs* controlling a number of separate producing plants. But with the further growth in the scale of enterprise, there was a great differentiation of functions. The large capitalist, becoming more and more a financier, resigned the actual management of productive business increasingly to salaried officers; and round these new managers there grew up an increasing host of departmental managers, buyers, and agents, technicians and professional consultants, superior clerical workers and cashiers, all in receipt of incomes intermediate between those of the large capitalists and those of the general mass of clerical and manual employees. These rising grades in large-scale industry coincided in income and social status with the grades of professional men outside industry—lawyers, doctors, the better-off teachers and a host more—whose numbers grew with the increase in total national wealth and in the size of the intermediate class as a whole. They came, indeed, to be themselves small investors out of their savings; and some of them were remunerated in part by commissions or shares in the profits of business. They thus acquired a double attachment to Capitalism, as the source both of their salaries or fees, and of the return upon their investments.

Thus, whereas the diagnosis of *The Communist Manifesto* appeared to foreshadow a narrowing of the basis on which Capitalism rested proportionate to the advance of capitalist concentration, and the flinging down of the intermediate groups, including the small capitalists, into the ranks of the proletariat, actually the basis of Capitalism grew broader with concentration, and the absolute and relative numbers of the intermediate groups increased. There was no polarisation of classes, but rather a growing difficulty in marking off one class clearly from another—a blurring of the lines of division, even if the essential characteristics of the outstanding classes remained plain and distinct. That this did not happen in Russia, where a small sector of large-scale capitalist enterprise came into being in a country otherwise primitive, and remained a sector apart, largely under foreign influence, was one great reason why the Marxist analysis appeared to apply much more completely to the Russia of 1917 than to the more advanced capitalist countries. Czarist industrial development neither created a large class of inactive shareholders belonging to the middle groups nor became linked to a host of small-scale enterprises which acted as its sub-contractors, agents and distributors. Czarist Capitalism was *narrowly* based, and confronted the proletariat much more nakedly as an exploiter than the Capitalism of Great Britain or of the United States.

I do not mean to suggest that the tendency to blurring of class-divisions went unnoticed by Marx. There are references in *Das Kapital* and in his writings and correspondence to show that it did not. But even in his later writings Marx continued to regard this blurring as a matter of secondary importance, influential in shaping the course of particular phases and incidents of the fundamental class-struggle, but incapable of altering its essential character or its ultimate outcome. He regarded the middle groups in society as incapable by their very nature of pursuing a coherent and constructive policy of their own, and as able only to get in the way of the principal combatants. Moreover, he continued to hold, even in his later writings, that in the long run the forces making for polarisation were bound to come into play more and more as the difficulties of Capitalism increased: so that the decisive class-struggle between capitalists and proletarians could be delayed, but by no means averted or changed in its essential character by the emergence of any new class.

Were Marx's Prophecies Correct?

It is clearly of the greatest importance, for any critique or re-statement of Marxism in twentieth-century terms, to determine whether this view is correct. Marx was right, we have seen, in predicting the growing concentration of the control of capital. Was he also right in predicting, as the inevitable outcome of Capitalism, the growing polarisation of economic classes?

Before we attempt to answer this question, we must pursue further our description of economic classes as they exist to-day. The great capitalists, as Marx foresaw, form a small group in effective control of huge concentrated masses of capital—great bankers and financiers, the heads of great trusts, combines and concerns engaged in production or distribution, great newspaper proprietors, and a few more. These men have little to do directly with the day-to-day work of industrial or commercial management. They are great financial manipulators, conducting to a money tune a vast orchestra of subordinate business execut- ants, and controlling masses of capital vastly larger than they personally own. By themselves, they clearly do not form a class: they are the leaders of a class extending far beyond their own ranks.

Of whom, then, does the rest of this class consist? In the first place, of business *entrepreneurs* of the second rank, who are in command of large-scale businesses, but have not risen to the heights of that financial control which transcends industrial boundaries, and lays its commands so heavily upon the capitalist States. Secondly, of the leading officials of the great business enterprises under the joint stock system, including both those which are controlled directly by the great financiers and those which have become, as the railways had become prior to nationalisation, mere impersonal concentrations of capital belonging to many scattered owners. Thirdly, the men at the top of the leading non-industrial services, from Cabinet Ministers and other major politicians of the capitalist parties to the heads of great Public Corporations and similar enterprises and to the most successful lawyers, doctors, accountants, applied scientists, and even teachers who have ceased to teach and have become administrators of great educational concerns.

CHAPTER V

THE NEW MIDDLE CLASSES
AND THE RISE OF FASCISM

IT IS, OF COURSE, impossible to say where the capitalist class ends and the class below it—the *petite bourgeoisie*—begins. There are infinite gradations of wealth and social status at every point of the scale, from the greatest capitalists to the lowest-paid labourers and the chronically unemployed. But undoubtedly there is a real division, as real and important as the distinction which Marx drew in *The Communist Manifesto* between the *grande* and the *petite bourgeoisie*, but of a radically different nature.

For Marx's division between these two was based on their essentially different relations to the powers of production. The *grande bourgeoisie* was for him the class which was waxing in authority and economic strength with the development of the new powers of machine-production upon which it was based; whereas the *petite bourgeoisie* he regarded as a declining class, certain to decrease in authority and strength, because its very existence depended on the survival of methods of production and trade which were already becoming obsolete. The *petite bourgeoisie* of 1848 consisted mainly of small-scale producers and traders whose position was bound up with workshop production or with retail shopkeeping on an undeveloped capitalist basis and of a comparatively small group of professional men. Within it, or very closely allied to it, was the main body of farmers above the peasant level. But for the moment let us leave this agricultural section aside, as its position calls for special discussion.

The Old Middle Classes and the New

To a great extent, Marx was right in predicting that the influence of the *petite bourgeoisie*, in this sense, was bound to wane. There has, indeed, been no such complete submergence of the small-scale producer—much less of the small-scale trader—as he seemed sometimes to expect. The small shopkeeper still holds on, despite the growth of the Co-operative Societies and multiple stores, and, driven from one part of the field, he continually finds new openings elsewhere, especially in new forms of supply—wireless shops, garages, and so on. But the small shopkeepers are tied more and more by the need for credit to the large-scale producers and suppliers, as well as to the banks; and this dependence subordinates them increasingly, in the economic sphere, to the large-scale control of financial capital. The small-scale industrial producer, though he survives to a considerable extent, has been driven more and more back to the fringes of industry. He carries on, especially in new trades not yet ready for large-scale organisation, in luxury branches of production where the market is necessarily small and diversified, and in supplying secondary needs of the large-scale producers, often as a sub-contractor to the great firms. But he too has largely lost his independence; and though the type strongly persists, the survival of the individuals of whom it is made up is apt to be precarious, since they are liable at any time to be evicted by a fresh development of the economy of large-scale production.

As far as these groups are concerned, and can be isolated, Marx was certainly right in his prophecy that their economic importance and strength would dwindle. But can they be isolated, as a factor in the class-struggle? To a considerable extent, they belong to the same family groups as the new *petite bourgeoisie* of small investors, senior officials, administrators and technicians employed in large-scale businesses, and minor professional men—that is, to the same social group as sections of the population whose numerical and economic importance, so far from dwindling, has been increasing fast with the advance of capitalist industrialism. How are we to classify a family in which the father is a local grocer, the mother the daughter of a works manager in a big factory, one of the sons a garage proprietor, another a municipal official, and a third a technician in large-scale business, while one daughter has married a school-master, one a small-scale employer with a tiny workshop of his own, and another a Trade Union official? There is nothing out of the ordinary in such a case, which represents well the inter-mingling of the old *petite bourgeoisie* based on small-scale methods of production and the new *petite bourgeoisie*, which owes its rise to the development of large-scale capitalist enterprise.

Faster than the old *petite bourgeoisie* has gone out, the new *petite bourgeoisie* has come in. Of course, the new group does not stand for the same ideas and policies as the old, any more than land-owners and capitalists, at the time when they were contending with each other for mastery, stood for the same ideas and policies, though they are now, in the most advanced societies, practically fused into a single class. To some extent, the ideas and policies of the old and the new *petite bourgeoisie* are antagonistic; and this antagonism is capable of becoming a factor of great political importance. For, whereas the newer group on the whole thrives on the further development of Capitalism, and has therefore hitherto been favourable to it, the older *petite bourgeoisie* has cause to fear a further decline in its power and position as capitalist organisation becomes increasingly rationalised, and as more and more trades are brought within the range of mass-production and mass-distribution.

This antagonism, however, has not hitherto developed far. To a much greater extent both groups, having intimate family connections and a similar social status, have been disposed to unite whenever they have felt their positions of petty class-privilege and economic superiority to be threatened by the advance of Socialism. For one thing they have had in common, and have in general united to protect, is that they have both felt themselves as standing above the proletariat, and as depending for their incomes and status on the maintenance of economic inequality as the basis of the social system.

The Salariat

There has, however, been of late years a quite noticeable change in both the composition and the attitude of the section of the salary-earners attached to large-scale industry. Many more of them have been prepared to entertain the notion of Socialism, if not positively to throw in their lot with the Socialist movement. There has been a substantial growth of Trade Unionism among technical and supervisory workers, in new Unions such as the Association of Scientific Workers, the Association of Supervisory Staffs, Executives and Technicians, and other more specialised societies; and these bodies, unlike the older professional associations, have joined the Trades Union Congress and have thus recognised their membership of the working-class movement. This change has been partly due to a change in the scientific outlook, which is much less dominated than it used to be by biological individualism of the type popularised by Herbert Spencer and has come to be more influenced by ideas of the social functions of science. It is also partly due to a dawning realisation among both supervisory and technical workers that they are likely to find wider opportunities for the successful exercise of their capacities under a public, planned economic system than under a declining

132

Capitalism at perpetual loggerheads with the workers and less and less able to make use of advanced technical knowledge in expanding the application of the powers of production.

These newer attitudes are naturally found mainly among the younger technicians and administrators and have not spread far among the largely non-technical managements of the less up-to-date business concerns. Their emergence is, however, significant, among groups which occupy a key position in industry and, unable to play by themselves a controlling part, can nevertheless powerfully reinforce the main body of the working class in its efforts to democratise industrial relations and to gain for itself a measure of control both over economic policy at the national level and over the day-to-day processes of workshop organisation and discipline.

These developments, though they have not yet advanced very far, are auguries of hope that the new middle class of salaried technicians, administrators, and professional workers may not be so socially recalcitrant a group as the older *petite bourgeoisie* based on small-scale industry and commerce. There is at least, given a soundly conceived Socialist policy, the possibility of an alliance, here and now, between the proletariat and a substantial section of the salaried intermediate class against the large capitalists and the more reactionary *petit bourgeois* groups. An alliance of this sort offers the only possible prospect of achieving Socialism by peaceful and constitutional means, and probably the only way of averting a dangerous recurrence of Fascist tendencies. The proletariat by itself is not strong enough or technically well enough equipped in any country either to win and hold a parliamentary majority, or to carry through the construction of a new industrial system by constitutional means. If it has to fight alone, it can win only by revolution, accompanied by a forcible destruction of all the opposing forces. Such a victory can be achieved only by the accident of a highly favourable conjuncture, or by help from outside; and the winning of it will leave the constructive task of building Socialism far harder than it need be, because of the immense destruction that will have taken place, and because of the proletariat's inevitable lack of adequate resources of trained knowledge and administrative experience. It may be possible to build Socialism successfully in face of these handicaps; but the building of it, under such conditions, would be bound to involve a tremendous amount of suffering and, in all probability, a serious temporary fall in the standard of life.

On the other hand, if the proletariat could be reinforced by the adhesion of even a minority of the technicians, administrators, and professional men and women who form the active section of the new *petite bourgeoisie*, it could be strong enough both to resist Fascism and to build Socialism against the united hostility of the great capitalists and the more reactionary *petit bourgeois* groups, and even, with good fortune, to do these things by peaceful and constitutional means. That this should come about is by far the best hope for Western civilisation in its present plight.

Socialism and the Middle Classes

But will it come about? There has been no indication at present in most capitalist countries that a sufficient section among the new middle class to make it possible is prepared to rally to the Socialist side. Moreover, the condition of its coming about is not only that a sufficient section of this class should be won over, but also and above all that this should be done without any dilution of the Socialist policy. For if the proletarian Socialists, in their efforts to win middle-class support, water down their policy to one of mere social reform, and abandon their frontal attack upon the capitalist system, they will merely fall headlong into the contradictions from which Socialism provides the way of escape. In trying to find money for social reforms without destroying the capitalist control of industry, they will dislocate the capitalist machine without replacing it, and will both fail to find means of satisfying their own followers and create the conditions most favourable to the growth of Fascist reaction. The proletariat needs support from the technically and administratively competent section of the middle classes in order to win Socialism; but that support would be worse than useless unless it were secured upon decisively Socialist terms.

The Farmers

In a society as highly industrialised as Great Britain, the farmers, albeit still a large economic group, and to-day one of increasing importance, can only hope to play a secondary part. In face of a world shortage of food and of difficulties over the balance of payments which compel the urban population to rely more on home-grown foodstuffs, the farming interests are well placed for striking a favourable bargain for themselves; but, even so, they are neither numerous enough, nor politically competent enough, to take an independent leading part in public affairs. In countries where, despite industrialisation, agriculture is still the occupation of a large part of the people—

as it is in France, in Germany, and even in the United States—
the farmers, or upper peasants, form a much more important
group. There is, even to-day, no sign of an extensive introduction
of large-scale capitalist farming in the industrially advanced
capitalist countries, and in many of the less developed countries
the tendency has been strongly towards the breaking-up of
great estates and the multiplication of small and middle-sized
peasant holdings. Farmers and peasants are indeed, even to-day,
notable in most countries for their incapacity for effective
political organisation or for the formulation of constructive
policies—Denmark, as well as some of the countries of the
New World, being, of course, notable exceptions. But the farmer
and peasant groups in the older countries are capable of bringing
a most powerful reinforcement to the other groups and classes
hostile to Socialism, and of either being used as instruments of
large-scale Capitalism in its struggle against Socialism, or
reinforcing the middle groups in their attempts to preserve their
privileged positions. The question is whether Socialism can
come to terms with the farming interests by offering them fair
prices and secure markets for their produce, while encouraging
better farming through Co-operative organisation and improved
distribution through Co-operative or State-controlled agencies.
The farmers, under the conditions of to-day, are a doubtful
political factor, most influential where the major forces in a
society are fairly evenly poised.

Middle-class Power, Economic and Political

As we have seen, the new *petite bourgeoisie*, despite its great
and growing importance in the conduct of modern industries
and services, has hitherto had very little influence over economic
policy. Although it is the chief repository of technical and
administrative competence and of inventive power, and thus
plays the leading part in shaping the evolution of the forces of
production, it has been able to act hitherto only under the orders
of its great capitalist masters, who have been interested in its
achievements only as means to the extraction of profit, rent and
interest. Large-scale Capitalism has paid the piper, even if it
has got the money largely from small investors; and large-scale
Capitalism has accordingly called the tune. In capitalist societies
the power over economic policy of the rising salaried groups of
technicians and administrators has therefore been hitherto very
limited indeed—despite all that has been written about Technocracy and the so-called "Managerial Revolution." But can the
same be said of its political power?

I am aware that it is often argued that "economic power precedes and dominates political power," which is only a reflection of it, and that accordingly the new industrial middle class cannot call in its political influence to redress its economic subservience. At this point, however, we must beware of an ambiguity in the use of phrases. The "economic power" which this class lacks is the power to control economic policy. But it possesses potential economic power in a more vital and fundamental sense. It has the capacity to organise and carry on industry under its own control, without the aid of the great capitalists, if it can ensure either the co-operation or the subservience of the proletariat. It and the proletariat, and not the great capitalists, are the classes which to-day perform the functions indispensable for the carrying on of industry and the further development of production, to which indeed the authority exercised by the hierarchs of banking, investing and financial manipulation constitutes a serious obstacle. There is, accordingly, no barrier in the way of the creation of a successful political movement by the technicians and administrators on account of any lack in their understanding and mastery of the technical requirements of economic progress; and there is a positive foundation for such a movement in the form of economic power which is already theirs.

The unity and strength of the middle classes of the twentieth century are certain, if they are manifested at all, to take shape primarily in a political movement. Economically, they cannot act together as a class, but only in sections, often with conflicting aims and policies, because they lack a common relation to industry such as binds the wage-earners together, and are too much mixed up with ownership, both by direct shareholding and by participation in profits, as well as by family connections, to be able to take a clear line. Politically, on the other hand, they can act together, and have often done so with considerable effect, for the protection of the rights and privileged inequalities of the recipients of unearned incomes. They have done this sometimes against the rich, but more often against the enactment of expensive social legislation or the improvement of municipal services. They have been found banded together against high taxation on middle incomes, against high local rates, and against Trade Unions which threaten the maintenance of essential services, as in the British General Strike of 1926.

These forms of combination are, however, merely negative and unconstructive; and they are, in any advanced industrial society in which the peasants and farmers do not form a group powerful enough to determine the issue, unlikely to be effective in the long run. They have succeeded hitherto in France and in a number of countries, though not on the whole in Great Britain, in checking the growth of social services and in offering a resistance to the proletariat and at the same time restraining the political influence of large-scale Capitalism; for in such countries as France, Holland and Switzerland, peasants and urban *petite bourgeoisie* are still, despite the high finance of Paris and other great centres and the growth of the proletariat, economically powerful groups. Not even in these countries, however, is a purely negative policy likely to suffice for long to hold a balance between the main contending forces in society: nor is there any certainty that it can suffice much longer even in the United States. In highly industrialised societies, among which France still barely counts, in the long run the pressure of the proletariat for improved conditions is bound to overbear a purely negative policy of resistance, if the affairs of State continue to be conducted upon a basis of universal suffrage with reasonable freedom of elections and of political organisation.

Middle-class Policies

Accordingly, the middle classes, if they desire to preserve their cherished inequality, are in the long run compelled either to look for a constructive policy of their own or to acquiesce, on such terms as they can secure, in the policies of the capitalist class. Hitherto, they have for the most part preferred the latter of these alternatives, and have acted politically as well as economically as the faithful servants of large-scale Capitalism, getting in return an increasing supply of crumbs from the rich man's table. Acting in this way, they have often been strong enough to help the capitalist interest to prevail in elections, even under adult suffrage; but this electoral success, at any rate in the more highly industrialised countries, has been bought only at the price of concessions to the proletariat, which have of late increased in scale and cost, and have been paid for to a growing extent by heavier taxation of the middle classes. The difficulties of Capitalism between the wars at the same time increased the need for these services, by swelling the numbers of the unemployed, and added to the awkwardness of paying for them. The proletariat, in face of these difficulties, became more clamant for some form of Socialism, which threatened the privileges of the middle classes as well as of the class above them. The middle classes responded, to a small extent, by blaming the financiers and the financial machine for their troubles, but to a much greater extent by banding themselves together to resist the proletariat, of which they stood in more fundamental fear. For most sections of the middle classes still regarded it as preferable to remain in subordination to the capitalist system rather than run the risk of forfeiting their unequal privileges under Socialism. This was the ultimate rationale of the inter-war growth of Fascism, which naturally developed first and furthest in those countries in which Capitalism was most in difficulties, and the demand for Socialism had accordingly become most insistent. Middle-class fears of Socialism were no doubt often exaggerated, and they were of course deliberately worked upon by the use of modern propagandist techniques. There was, however, substance behind them, wherever the capitalist system did appear to be in imminent danger of sheer collapse.

The Rise of Fascism

Where the middle classes set out to aid the capitalists to defeat the proletariat, they need some stronger weapon than their mere voting strength. In the advanced industrial countries which have been pressed hardest by the growing difficulties of Capitalism, this weapon has already proved its inadequacy as a means of resisting the gradual encroachment of democratic social reform. In these circumstances a large section of the middle classes may go Fascist, under whatever name, with the aid of parallel elements in the country districts. It may repudiate Parliamentarism, and clamour for authoritative government. But this cry for a form of dictatorship to keep the proletariat in its place cannot be effective if it is put forward as an open defence of the vested interests in present-day society; for the proletariat is too strong, and has too many allies scattered among the other classes, and among a considerable part of the middle classes prejudice in favour of Parliamentarism is too strong, for a naked appeal to violence on a basis of privileged self-interest to be successful in overbearing them. Fascism has, therefore, needed to assume the outward form of an alternative ideal to that of Socialism, appealing to sentiments as deeply rooted as those of democracy, and capable of attracting not only a considerable part of the middle classes, but also a substantial section of the proletariat itself.

This appeal was found in aggressive Nationalism, reinforced according to local conditions by any form of anti-foreigner complex likely to arouse a widespread response in the country concerned. All right-minded citizens were called upon, in the name of national honour and manhood, to take arms against

138

the insidious propaganda of pacifism, against Jewish penetration, and against the open cosmopolitanism of the Socialist ideal. The sentiment of the class struggle was countered by an appeal to the sentiment of national solidarity against the rest of the world; and a specious ideal of national service and self-sacrifice was held up against the allegedly materialist objectives of Socialism. These ideologies, which would have been powerless by themselves, proved able to become great powers when they were made the allies of class-interest; and a section of the worst-off part of the proletariat, the "submerged tenth," reinforced by many of the long-term unemployed, who had been ground down to despair by the attrition of economic distress and saw little prospect of early relief in face of the deadlock reached between the capitalist and Socialist forces, was won over by large, vague hopes and promises of the rewards certain to accrue from a Fascist victory, not unaccompanied by advance bribes, to go over to the Fascist side.

Where this happened, and the working-class forces were divided, the path was made easy towards a Fascist victory. For the power of the proletariat depends essentially upon substantial unity among its leading elements. But, in the circumstances here described, disunity was pretty certain to arise. In face of the growing difficulties of Capitalism there were some who urged an immediate advance towards Socialism, by revolutionary methods if no other way were immediately open; whereas others held that it was necessary to wait until a majority had been won over to Socialism by constitutional methods of propaganda and electioneering. In most countries such a majority was by no means easy to secure, in face of the combined voting strength and the propagandist resources of the upper and middle classes reinforced by the agricultural interests; and, condemned to prolonged inaction under stress of serious economic adversity, enough of the proletariat became disillusioned at the slow progress of Socialism, especially where the Socialist cause was poorly led, to result in a disastrous division in the proletarian ranks. This provided the Fascists with their opportunity to jettison the substance of Parliamentarism, though they usually preferred to keep its shadow, and enabled them to institute some form of dictatorship in the name of the "national spirit."

Working-class Disunity

Division in the ranks of the working class would have developed in any case; but it was both facilitated and deeply aggravated by ideological conflict. After 1917 the Soviet Union, as the one country in which the proletarian Revolution had been successfully made, exercised a powerful spell upon the minds of the workers—especially the younger workers—in every country. The Bolsheviks had carried through their Revolution in strict accordance with their interpretation of Marxism and, attributing the failure of parallel revolutions to occur in Western Europe largely to lack of correct Marxist leadership of the working-class movements of the West, were continually calling upon the workers of other countries to throw over their "reactionary" leaders and to rally behind the Communist Parties created in imitation of the Communist Party of the Soviet Union. The long ostracism of the Soviet Union by the capitalist countries and the news of the tremendous efforts in economic construction that were being put into the successive Five Year Plans made the Soviet Union appear as the key position in the world struggle for Socialism, and lent immense authority to whatever advice its leaders chose to tender to the working classes of the capitalist countries. At the same time the sharp contrast between the strict authoritarianism of the Soviet régime, based partly on the continuing conditions of 'cold war' and partly on the heritage of Czarist autocracy and centralisation in a vast, mainly pleasant country, and the relatively liberal and unbureaucratic traditions of the West rendered the Communist approach quite unacceptable to more than a small minority in Great Britain or in the 'smaller democracies' of the West, and resulted in disastrous divisions among the workers of Germany and of France. In Germany, which had long been a battleground between liberal and autocratic conceptions, and in France, where centralisation had been the historic weapon of the opponents of privilege ever since 1789, the working-class forces were split through and through. In the one case, these divisions prepared the way for Nazism: in the other, though no such extreme result has so far followed, the action both of the Trade Unions and of the whole Republic was paralysed, and there developed that fatal mood of disillusion and disorientation which led up to the collapse of 1940 and is still following its unhappy course in the frustrations and tumults of the period since the liberation. If France is now facing de Gaulle, with an unpleasing likeness to the mood in which Germany once faced Hitler, the principal cause is to be found in the disunity of the French working-class movement; and the principal cause of this disunity is to be found in the ideological conflict between Soviet-based Marxism and the traditional Socialism of the West.

The consummation that was reached in 1933 in Germany

and the consummation that appeared to be threatening France in 1948 were alike the outcome of extreme economic difficulty and dislocation; for nothing short of this would have served either to bring about the necessary division in the proletariat or sufficiently to unite the middle classes under the nationalist banner. Where economic difficulties are less pressing, parliamentary forms and methods are likely to be preserved, and, in countries where there is a strong parliamentary tradition, nothing worse is likely to happen than a setback to social reform, and perhaps a period of national "economy" and reaction under the ægis of a "national" Government that will not do more than nibble at the existing provision for the poorer classes. In such countries severe strain on the economic system is needed to bring Fascism or any variant of it to boiling point, and to secure the necessary support for a forcible overthrow of the parliamentary system in the interests of the propertied classes. British people, however, are apt to exaggerate the strength of parliamentary institutions in other countries, judging of them by their own, and to mistake what is only a façade of parliamentary government for a deeply-rooted social habit; whereas those whose experience of parliamentary institutions has been entirely of the sham varieties are apt to fall into the opposite mistake of regarding all parliamentary government as essentially a sham, a cloak for the operations of a hypocritical ruling class. These misunderstandings lead British people to pay an exaggerated respect to the profession of parliamentarist principles even where they have no real roots, and they similarly lead Soviet propagandists and their fellow-travellers to dismiss with contempt the adherance of Socialists anywhere to the methods of parliamentary government. Each side interprets everything in the light of its own experience; and a disastrous game of cross-purposes and mutual recriminations is the result.

The Real Nature of Fascism

For British Socialists it is important never to forget that the strains of the inter-war years and of the war period were very much more severe in many other countries than they ever became in Great Britain, and that in most parts of Europe there was no deeply-rooted parliamentary tradition at all corresponding to the British tradition. It is not at all surprising that many Socialists outside Great Britain saw the crisis of Capitalism as a thorough fulfilment of Marx's prophecies, and were consequently attracted to Communism as preached from the Soviet Union. It is not even surprising, though it is lamentable, that some of them were induced by their belief in the inevitably impending doom of Capitalism to underrate the importance of Fascism, or even to suppose that a Fascist victory would help to prepare the way for Socialism by sweeping obsolete pseudo-democratic parliamentary institutions aside. This attitude, as we shall see, rested on a fundamental misunderstanding of the nature of Fascism, which was regarded as merely the final stage of Capitalism in decline. This complacent attitude towards the Fascist menace created a situation in which the working class, instead of uniting to destroy it, divided itself into warring factions, of which one set itself to defend the existing parliamentary system against Fascist attack, while the other stood aloof, hoping either to profit immediately by the conflict or, at any rate, to inherit the control of society when "Fascist Capitalism" speedily broke down through its failure to solve the inherent contradictions of capitalist production.

The truth, however, was that Fascism, far from being merely the final stage of Capitalism in decline, was a new social phenomenon of the greatest independent significance. Although it owed its rise mainly to economic distress, it was not in itself or in its driving force mainly an economic movement. It rested rather, like the mass-movements of earlier ages, on the will to domination and conquest, on the hope to escape from the oppression of circumstances by forceful aggression, and on the exaltation of the "national spirit" as a liberation from the restraints and inhibitions of a customary morality made irksome by adversity. It was no accident that Fascism's gods were tribal gods or that it revived, in modernised form, the ancient myth of the "god-warrior-king." These things were not merely trappings, put on for propagandist purposes: they were of Fascism's very essence. If there is in history an analogy to Fascism, it is to be looked for, not in the record of class-conflicts, but in the great migrations of warrior peoples which have again and again set the world in turmoil. Nowadays, whole peoples cannot migrate: the foundations of their living are too deeply rooted in the places they inhabit, and if they were to move *en masse* they could only starve. It was not, however, impossible for a modern people to seek *Lebensraum* without mass-migration—by conquering and subjecting, by levying tribute on the conquered, and even by bringing their enslaved victims to labour for them in the fields and factories of the Fascist homeland.

All this, it may be said, is an interpetation of Fascism in essentially economic terms. It is, and yet it is not. I agree that the roots of Fascism were in economic distress, and that economic

142

purposes ranked high among its objectives. But I deny, not only that the appeal which gave it strength was mainly economic, but also—what is really the critical point—that it can be correctly interpreted *as a class-movement*, or simply as the last manœuvre of Capitalism to avert the proletarian revolution.

Fascism and Capitalism

No doubt Fascism, where it has triumphed, has climbed to power only with the help of a powerful section of the capitalist class. Neither in Italy nor in Germany could the forces which destroyed the parliamentary State have been brought to the required strength without the financial backing of a sufficient number of great capitalists. The creation of a revolutionary force based mainly on the declassed middle classes, the soldiers of fortune out of a job, and the most helpless sections of the proletariat required a large amount of money, which could in practice be supplied only from the resources of large-scale Capitalism. The great capitalists would, of course, not have financed such a movement unless they had considered that it was calculated to serve their ends. The leaders of Fascism had, therefore, to give to the great capitalists pledges of intentions which these paymasters would regard as good, and had to promise to turn their weapons upon the proletariat and not upon "Big Business." In the earlier stages of Fascist development the armies of counter-revolution fought the proletariat as the allies and upholders of Capitalism, which was represented under the guise of social solidarity as an integral element in the greatness of the National State.

Petit Bourgeois Attitudes

This alliance with large-scale Capitalism was by no means welcome to all the members of the *petite bourgeoisie* whom the Fascists were attempting to attract into their ranks. The small-scale producers and traders in this group had a fear of high finance and of rationalised enterprise which was second only to their dread of a proletarian victory. Farmers and peasants shared this attitude and wanted to fight for their own interests and not for large-scale Capitalism. Fascist programmes, therefore, usually contained many projects designed to appeal to *petit bourgeois* sentiment, and had often an anti-capitalist seasoning, even where Capitalism was in fact giving them its support. The support was given none the less, because many capitalists believed that, if once the proletariat could be thoroughly defeated, there would be no real difficulty in keeping in proper

143

subjection the forces which had been used to compass its defeat.

There have been, indeed, at periods of less intense social conflict, middle-class groups which, unwilling to become the instruments of large-scale Capitalism in the fight against Socialism, have attempted to devise constructive programmes of their own. Such groups were to be found in Great Britain at the time of the Industrial Revolution; and J. C. L. de Sismondi's "New Economics" of 1819 were an attempt to give their aspirations a theoretical basis in opposition to the classical Political Economy. From the days when Marx, at the outset of his career, arraigned Sismondi and Proudhon as *petit bourgeois* reformers— indeed, from even earlier—this has always meant largely the formulation of projects of monetary reform. These projects have to some extent changed their nature with the changes that have occurred in the composition of the middle classes. In the time of Proudhon they were predominantly schemes for securing to the small-scale producers and traders a sufficient supply of credit to enable them to stand up to the competition of large-scale business and to the vicissitudes of the trade cycle. They retain this character to a great extent even to-day in the agricultural areas of Canada and the United States; but among industrial communities the emphasis has shifted in modern times from the small-scale producer to the consumer, and recent projects have been designed to bring about low prices for consumers' goods, or issues of free credit to consumers to enable them to buy the greatly enlarged product of which modern industry is technically capable, but of which it has appeared disastrously unable to dispose. Currency and credit cranks are to-day, as they were a century ago, foremost among those *petit bourgeois* reformers who want their class to put forward a programme of its own, in order to fight Socialism in its own interest and not for the benefit of the great capitalists.

Technocracy

Nowadays, side by side with the monetary reformers go the technocrats, who emphasise the creative rôle of scientist, inventor and technician in the advance of material wealth, and urge the claims of the new *petite bourgeoisie* of experts to reform and govern society by virtue of their technical and administrative competence. Both the monetary reformers and the technocrats often have the merit of generous sympathies, and of a desire to raise the general standard of life by setting free the vast forces of productivity which have been chained up by the capitalist system. They mostly aim, however, at reconciling the advent

144

of the new age of plenty with the maintenance of privileges and economic and social superiority for the technical and administrative groups in society over the manual workers, whom they dismiss as too ignorant to rule, and they usually repudiate the conception of the class-struggle because it appears to threaten their superiority of income and status.

This attitude condemns these "radical" movements among the middle-class technicians and experts to sterility, for they cannot possibly make themselves strong enough to stand alone, or expect to rally the main body of the middle classes behind them. A large section of the middle classes, including the small-scale producers, the small traders, and the farmers, acutely dislikes technocracy, which it rightly regards as standing on the whole for mass-production and for the elimination of the independent "small man." The great capitalist financiers naturally repudiate the claims of their hired servants to call the tune; and the workers are naturally not at all attracted by the offer of a new set of masters to order them about. Intellectually, technocratic theories have little appeal to the proletariat, unless they can be combined with an appeal to sentiment; but such an appeal is inconsistent with the desire of the technocrats to hold on to their superior status. Accordingly, though in a number of countries technocrats and monetary reformers have temporarily commanded considerable followings, there has never been any real chance of their rallying behind them, at any rate in any developed industrial country, a sufficient following to enable them to put their notions to the test of practice. The monetary reformers have had their best chance in predominantly agricultural countries, such as Canada, especially in the prairie provinces where the farmers' movement is in a position, if it can become united, to dominate the political situation. But even where monetary reformers have won elections they have been able to achieve little; and in industrial countries such creeds as technocracy and credit reform can but create diversions: they cannot win power

Fascism and the Middle Classes

In such countries the middle classes, when they are driven into political activity as a reaction to economic crisis, are apt to become the allies of large-scale Capitalism in the fight against Socialism. They see no hope of preserving their petty privileges without the support of the great capitalists. But, when these classes unite in the struggle against Socialism, it remains to be seen which of them will carry off the victory in the contest

145

between them which is certain to follow if they achieve the rout of the Socialist forces. Large-scale Capitalism starts with the great advantage of being in possession of the field, and of being able to claim that any attempt to disturb its vested interest will result in economic dislocation and will menace both the consolidation of the victory over Socialism and the attainment of the Fascist objective of national strength as a means to national aggrandisement and predatory aggression. But the leadership of the Fascist forces, and the power of Fascism to spell-bind the people, is bound to rest not with the capitalists but with a motley group of perverted idealists, thugs, swashbuckling adventurers, careerists, thwarted aristocrats, and assertive militarists, whose chief bond of union is a hatred of democracy, and by no means a love for Capitalism; and the main body of their followers will necessarily consist of the middle-class elements and of those sections of the peasants and of the working class which have rallied to the Fascist appeal. These groups will claim the fulfilment of the promises made to them in the course of the struggle, while the section of the aristocracy which has thrown in its lot with Fascism will also clamour for the reward of its collaboration. In face of the difficulties of the economic situation, these conflicting claims will not be easy to satisfy; and the centralised, authoritarian State set up for the purpose of destroying Socialism will be an instrument which can readily be applied to the issuing of positive orders, in the name of the awakened Nation, to the capitalists themselves as well as to the defeated workers and to the middle classes. In these circumstances, a drastic régime of State control over industry will have to be instituted, so that the State, even if it seeks to respect the interests of the big capitalists as a class, will not scruple to lay rough hands on the individual capitalist who refuses to work in with its National Plan of economic reform. There will arise a State-controlled Capitalism which will no doubt serve to protect the interests of property-owners, both large and small, against the proletariat, but will afford this protection only to the extent to which the rights of property can be turned into instruments of national consolidation and reconciled with the discipline of the civil population. Consequently, within the Fascist ranks, there will be a struggle for the control of the new State which is to exert this authority over all the people.

Fascism is not a Class Movement

In this ensuing struggle, the victory goes neither to the great capitalists nor to the small. It does not go to any *class*; for

146

Fascism, though it wages war upon the working class and uses other classes as its instruments, is not fundamentally a class-movement. Its claim to transcend classes is in a sense quite genuine; for it reaches back, behind the class-divisions of modern society, towards primitive conditions of tribal solidarity. It is not a *class* but a *horde*-movement, profoundly antagonistic to every rational form of social structure and therefore to the rational utilitarianism which lies at the root of capitalist enterprise as much as of every form of 'liberal' philosophy. It may no doubt be able to reconcile the great capitalists to accepting its domination; for it can offer them the retention of their wealth and the re-establishment of their direct authority over the workers in return for their acceptance of its ends. Far, however, from controlling Fascism, the great capitalists come to be controlled by it, and are compelled to subordinate their money-making impulses to the requirements of the Fascist State as an organiser of national aggression. As for the small property owners, they soon discover that their property rights and social privileges are left to them only to the extent to which they can be fitted in with the requirements of centrally organised national power, and that no pledges given to them in the course of the counter-revolution are of any validity when they come into conflict with the power plans of the totalitarian State. The technicians and administrators fare better, on the whole, than the rest of the middle classes; for Fascism has need of them for the detailed execution of its national projects, and they can most readily square their ambitions and interests with its ideology and thus act without sense of frustration as members of the Fascist hierarchy. Fascism and technocracy make good bed-fellows; for the *"Fuehrer* principle" in practice involves the placing of immense delegated authority in the hands of an official class made up largely of expert administrators and technicians. Under Fascism, however, the technician is compelled to subject his technical mastery to the requirements of the totalitarian State. He changes masters, and works no longer mainly to pile up profits for the capitalist, but to make the State strong for aggressive war. With the change he acquires the possibility of a higher status, through promotion, under the *Fuehrer*, into the ranks of the dominant *élite*.

The victory of Fascism in a single country thus sets up a new set of internal power-relations. It vests power, not in an economic class, but in a "god-warrior-king" who gathers round him a military, administrative and technical bureaucracy devoted under his inspiration to the service of national aggrandisement; and it subordinates all classes to this horde concept of national solidarity. It tramples most heavily upon the working classes, both because they are the principal rival of whom it is afraid, and because their desire for better living and greater security conflicts with its creed of national glory. It seeks guns before butter, whereas the working-class movements everywhere put butter before guns. Fascism, however, tramples also—albeit much less heavily—on the classes which have been its allies in its capture of power. It erodes the class of small capitalists to whom it has promised succour; and it subordinates even large-scale Capitalism to its quest for national aggrandisement. If the situation which ensues upon its victory could last, it might be able to reduce the elements thus subjected to it to a condition of equilibrium, such as the Italian Fascists romanticised in their static phantasy of the Corporative State. But Fascism is in fact essentially unstable because it looks outward upon other nations and can realise its nationalist aspirations only by subjecting them to its rule. Fascism, as long as it is contained within one country, involves unremitting preparation for wars of conquest, leading to actual war; and when war comes as a natural consequence of its aggression it must either win outright, and make other nations its helots, or go down to a defeat in which its power is utterly broken. Its ambitions being irrational and unlimited, it cannot come to terms with any other power: it cannot be appeased or contained. It must win or lose everything.

The Effects of Fascism

If it loses, there is left behind a most intractable legacy of spiritual and economic disaster. The beating of its swords into ploughshares would be a hard enough task even if it had not done its utmost to uproot from the midst of the nation all the elements to which such a task would appeal, and to destroy national faith in all decencies of behaviour and aspiration. As things are, it has scorched the soil of humanity, leaving only bitterness and frustration behind, save among the few who have been strong enough to resist the brutal reinforcements of the mass-appeal—nor are even those few unscathed. Economically, its legacy is mass-privation and that very ruin of the middle classes which it claimed to prevent. The re-building of either the economic or the political and social foundations of a defeated Fascist nation presents a terrible problem because the very conditions which it leaves behind can serve as a breeding-ground for new forms of Fascism much more easily than for any demo-cratic or Socialist system.

On the other hand, if Fascism were to win, what would the outcome be? It is still worth while to consider the answer to this question, though for the time German, Italian and Japanese Fascism have gone down together in defeat. For the world may not have done yet with the Fascist danger, even if a recurrence of it is likely to take somewhat different forms. Victorious Fascism, in its Nazi form, would have meant a Europe of helot peoples condemned to labour for the *Herrenvolk*, or in its Japanese form a "Co-prosperity Sphere" of Asiatic helots. But that could not have been the end. Even if the Soviet Union had been overwhelmed and divided up, these two could neither have lived in the world side by side with an unsubdued American continent nor have kept the peace with each other. War upon war would have laid the whole world waste, each waged with more frightfulness than the one before; and all the time the processes of Fascist indoctrination would have been intensified and decent sentiment and morality more and more savagely rooted out from the minds of the young in every country.

But, up to the final disaster, would the *Herrenvolk*—German, Japanese, and probably American—have been living well or ill? From any standpoint that takes account of decent human values, obviously very ill indeed; but how, in a sheerly material sense? With the tribute of a prostrate world to draw upon, it would seem that the conquerors should have been able to wax fat, even if they spent much of their substance on policing their victims and on arming against each other. Nor could there be any inherent reason why a Nazi State, ruling over subject peoples, should suffer from unemployment on account of any inability to distribute the products of the labour either of its own people or of its foreign slaves. In full control of the use of its resources and of the distribution of incomes, it would be in a position to raise the standard of life of its people to any extent consistent with the proportion of its man-power devoted to war services, including the garrisoning of subject territories and preparation for actual war against its remaining rivals, as long as any were left.

Could Fascism Succeed?

It was, I am sure, a fatal error to suppose that Nazism, even if it triumphed in arms, would be bound speedily to break down because of its continued liability to the contradictions of Capitalism. The view that this would necessarily happen was based on the erroneous belief that Fascism was simply a form of

149

Capitalism, and therefore could not escape from its contradictions. If, as I have tried to show, Fascism was not a form of Capitalism, but an essentially different system, using certain capitalist institutions for its own aggressive nationalist ends, there was no presumption that it would break down *from this cause*.

The real reason why Fascism would in all probability have been unable to endure was its inherent insatiability. In attempting to conquer the whole world, it could hardly have avoided tearing both the world and itself to pieces, and collapsing under the immense strain which its effort would have placed upon its own nation as well as upon every other.

This view is of course highly unacceptable to rigid Marxists because it involves recognising that non-economic factors can play a primary part in determining the course of history. I have suggested earlier that Marx's theory of history was thought out as a theory of the continuous development of civilisation regarded as a unified whole, and took no adequate account of the impact of external forces on the internal process of development. Indeed, if all the world were one civilisation, developing in a straight line from lower to higher forms, there would be no question of an external impact deflecting the course of its evolution. In fact, however, the world never has been covered by a single civilisation; and the course of development has again and again been diverted by the impact of one civilisation upon another, in the form of mass migrations and wars of conquest. What I am suggesting is that the Fascist aggressive totalitarian State is the modern equivalent of the great conquering migrations of earlier history, and though, like them, greatly affected by economic forces, can no more than they be explained in terms of classes or class-struggles. To say this is not at all to deny that class-struggle played an important part in the development of Fascism. But I am contending that this part was secondary, and that the mainspring of Fascism has to be sought elsewhere. The factor of class-conflict played in the rise of Fascism a part analogous to that secondary influence which Marx recognised as affecting the course of history within the general movement determined by economic forces. His mistake lay in concluding that, because all civilisations rest fundamentally on the use made of the powers of production, and change as these powers develop, therefore the mode of change must be always and universally the same. In other words, it lay in not merely treating class-struggles as the sole mode by which the development of the powers of production could be translated

150

into terms of social structure, but also asserting that the evolution of the powers of production could not be either interrupted or deflected by any human agency.

This error arose directly out of the confusion which I have already noted in Marx's thought about the powers of production themselves. In failing to stress their dual character, as consisting not only of things usable by men but also of men's knowledge of their use, he obscured the important fact that the powers of production are fundamentally altered if the same *things* fall into the hands of *men* better or worse equipped with knowledge of their use, or with an essentially different attitude towards them. This is precisely what has happened in the past as the result of great migrations and wars of conquest; and that is why such movements form the great element of discontinuity in human history.

It may be answered that, even if this be true, it has no bearing on the question of the fundamental character of Fascism, because Fascism was an outgrowth of Capitalism, and the Fascists were equipped with the same knowledge of the use of things as their victims. Agreed. That is a valid reason for holding that the victory of Fascism would not have involved a break in the continuity of development of the powers of production. But I have not argued that it would have had this effect. What I am arguing is that the powers of production, though *a* fundamental factor in social development at all stages, are not always the sole major factor, and that there are other forces in men's natures that can operate as major causes in history. Fascism, even if it had triumphed, would not have involved a break in the development of man's technical mastery over nature (though it might have deflected it in a number of ways): what it would have involved would have been the advent as successor to Capitalism of a system other than Socialism, which Marx regarded as the only possible claimant. Fascist victory would have continued the development of the powers of production, but, instead of transferring power from the capitalists to the proletariat, would have handed it over to an exploiting national group, and replaced the subjection of the working class in each country by the subjection of whole peoples to the victor nation. This is where the situation would have been analogous to past conquests based on mass-migration of peoples. There would no doubt have been an element of class-conflict in it; but to attempt to explain it exclusively in terms of class-conflict involves travestying the facts.

151

CHAPTER VI

THE PROLETARIAT

IN THIS ANALYSIS OF economic classes in the twentieth century, the proletariat has been left until last; for, though the winning of Socialism may be held to require the collaboration of other elements, it is evidently upon the proletariat that the main burden of the struggle is bound to fall. What, then, is the proletariat in the advanced societies of modern Capitalism, and of what groups and sections is it made up? How far can it be clearly marked off from other classes, and how far has it a distinct interest and point of view which hold it together as a coherent class? The attempt to answer these questions demands a chapter to itself.

The proletariat, or working class, is essentially that class in society which gets its living by the sale of its labour-power, and, even though some of its members may possess some income from property, does not possess resources which enable it to command the means of living except by this sale. It consists primarily of those wage-earners who, having sold their labour to an employer for a contractual payment, work under the employer's orders, and take part in creating a product which becomes the property of the purchaser of their labour-power. This characteristic of employability at a wage is the distinguishing feature of the proletariat, just as the act of employing labour, directly or indirectly, is the distinguishing mark of the capitalist class.

Obviously, it is not possible, in terms of this definition, to say precisely who is a member of the proletariat, and who is not. For, in the first place, there is clearly no essential economic difference between a wage and a salary. They are both incomes obtained under contract by the sale of labour-power. It would be absurd to exclude all salary-earners from the ranks of the proletariat, especially as both wage-earners and salary-earners may be employed by the same employer, with no fundamental difference of income or status. But it would be equally absurd to include in the proletariat all salary-earners, up to the most highly-placed Civil Servants or the managing directors of great capitalist concerns; for the richer salary-earners clearly belong to a quite different economic class from the main body of wage-earners. No sharp line can be drawn between those who do belong to the proletariat and those who do not. In this case, as in those discussed in the last chapter, class-divisions become blurred at the margin, and the doubtful group at the margin is here very large.

This difficulty of exact denotation does not in the least invalidate the conception of a proletarian class. For, if the outer limits of this class are vague, its central nucleus is evident enough. It may be disputable how large a proportion of the salariat are to be regarded as proletarians, or how far down the scale of physical or mental deficiency the margin of employability is reached; but there is no doubt that the central mass of the proletariat consists of the manual-working wage-earners in industry, and especially of that section which has become organised in the Trade Union movement. Larger or smaller elements of the salariat, or of the submerged groups below the regular working class, may gather round the central mass, and think and feel themselves part of the proletariat. The central mass itself is the essential proletariat: the outlying groups belong to it only to the extent to which they attach themselves to it, and identify its interests and attitudes with their own.

To a certain extent, then, proletarian is as proletarian feels. But, in general, this applies only to the outlying groups whose classification is doubtful. These have to "contract in" to the proletariat, by associating themselves with it; whereas the members of the central mass belong to the proletariat unless they definitely "contract out," and abjure allegiance to the class that is theirs by economic status. The proletariat as a whole is thus $x+y$; x being a nearly fixed, and y a highly variable magnitude.

The proletariat is often spoken of as if it were integral to the very idea that its members should possess no property of their own, but should subsist solely upon their wages, except where these are supplemented by some form of public relief. But this is not really essential. What is essential is that the proletarian should be a person who gets his chief means of living from the sale of his labour-power. Such a man or woman does not lose the proletarian status by virtue of possessing some small amount of property, but only if the property is considerable enough to constitute an important element in total income, outweighing the wage or salary. The proletarian can be, and in advanced societies often is, at the same time an owner of some small capital resources, which eke out but do not replace the larger income derived from the sale of labour-power.

It is, of course, true that any ownership of capital, in the sense of individual property yielding an income, tends to some degree to give the possessor the attitude of a property owner, and thus to align him with the class of property owners. But a man's class must be interpreted normally in relation to his major interest; for this will be likely to be decisive in the majority of instances in determining class allegiance in economic matters when a conflict of allegiances arises. It is by no means irrelevant to a study of the modern proletariat to observe that, in the more advanced countries, it includes a large number of members who also own some property, from money in the Savings Bank or shares in a Co-operative Society to the ownership of a house or even of a few industrial shares or some Government Stock. In Great Britain, for example, as a result of National Savings Movements and post-war credits, the holding of small amounts of government paper has become very widely diffused. Nor is it irrelevant that working-class bodies, from Friendly and Co-operative Societies to Trade Unions, are considerable collective holders of property. These facts do affect the economic attitude both of individual workers and of working-class organisations. But that conflicts of interest and loyalty may spring from this source is no reason for denying to the individual or collective holders of such property the status of proletarians, if they continue to depend primarily on their labour-power for the means of life.

A further difficulty which is sometimes raised is that a section of the class which lives by selling its labour-power is definitely parasitic, in the sense that the type of employment which it follows depends essentially on the existence of a rich class. To this group belong certain types of domestic servants and workers in luxury trades providing exclusively for a wealthy clientèle. It is sometimes suggested that all such workers ought to be excluded from the idea of the proletariat as a class. This, however, is quite irrational. These workers, provided they comply with the definition already given, must be regarded as proletarians, even if many of them are likely, when a conflict arises, to fight against the rest of the proletariat rather than on its side. For it is no less possible for a proletarian than for a capitalist to take sides against his class. The proletariat is a class, and not an army: it is not necessarily all-obedient to a common discipline of its own.

The proletariat, then, consists principally of what ordinary people ordinarily mean when they speak of the working class. Its boundaries are ill-defined, but its central mass is always easily recognisable. A class cannot be defined in terms of its marginal members, but only of its central mass. But this definition is fully adequate for purposes of both practice and theory.

Differentiation within the Proletariat

The proletariat, as a class, emerges gradually with the rise of Capitalism. There were, of course, wage-workers, and a rudimentary proletariat, before Capitalism became the dominant system, just as there were capitalists, and a rudimentary capitalist class. But both proletariat and capitalist class reach full stature only under a developed form of capitalist system, in which contractual wage-employment by a capitalist, or a group of capitalists, becomes the prevailing mode of organising production.

At all stages, there are marked differentiations within the proletariat. In the earlier phases of Capitalism, when the great capitalist is still predominantly a merchant and only secondarily an employer, the number of small master-craftsmen is still relatively very great, and there is no sharp line of social or economic division between these small masters and the upper strata of skilled artisans working for a wage, from whose ranks they are largely recruited, and to whose ranks they may easily return. The gulf is often wider between the skilled artisan and the unskilled labourer than between the artisan and his master; and it is hard to distinguish between the independent small master and the piece-working sub-contractor who is virtually a wage-earner. At this stage the proletarian class is not yet fully differentiated or developed, any more than the capitalist class is. But the further advance of Capitalism alters this situation, though many relics of it remain in the industries of to-day, wherever small-scale production persists. The rise of larger-scale production both drives out many of the small masters and greatly alters the relation between the artisan and his employer, impelling the skilled artisan towards a closer unity with the less skilled workers below him. The technical development of machine-industry also blurs the old distinctions between craftsmen and labourers, undermining the institution of apprenticeship, which kept them apart, and creating numerous gradations of semi-skilled labour intermediate between the two extremes. These two factors work together to solidify the wage-earners as a class; and the growth of compulsory State education, required by the demands of the industrial system as well as in the name of democracy, narrows the cultural gap. The working class becomes far more recognisably one, and recognises itself much more as one, than under the earlier conditions. Moreover, as the capitalists come to have large resources locked up directly in the instruments of production, that is, as Merchant Capitalism gives place to Industrial Capitalism, the class employed upon these instruments of production comes to be more clearly marked off in terms of economic status from the employing class.

But this does not mean that differentiation disappears, or is even diminished. It reappears within the now solidified class, but in different forms. There is at this stage not a sharp contrast between skilled and unskilled workers, but a much greater diversity of skill and status in which one grade merges into another to an increasing extent, but new grades are also constantly appearing as the techniques of industry change. To some extent the workers in the more skilled occupations, who have built up Trade Union monopolies of labour, struggle against technical changes, and still more against the attempts of employers to invade their monopolies by the use of less skilled types of labour; and antagonisms exist on this score between skilled and less skilled workers. But as mechanisation grows, and as the scale of production becomes larger, in spite of these antagonisms the skilled and the less skilled are increasingly driven to recognise their common interests and to join forces in collective bargaining. Technical changes weaken the old craft monopolies; and new ones equally strong seldom arrive in their place. Diversity increases; but it comes to be of a sort more easily compatible with united class-action among the manual workers.

The "Black-coated Proletariat"

There is, however, another process of differentiation at work. As mechanisation advances, a smaller proportion of the entire labour force is employed upon directly productive operations or in transport, and a larger proportion in clerical, technical, administrative and supervisory work, and in the distribution of goods and the rendering of personal services. This process, as we have seen, is an important factor in creating a new *petite bourgeoisie* in place of the small masters supplanted by the growth of large-scale Capitalism. But it also creates, corresponding in some degree to the upper strata of craftsmen under the old system, an upper proletariat of "black-coats," closely akin in income and way of living to the lower strata of the middle classes as well as to the upper strata of the manual workers. We have seen that, among this group, it is impossible to say where the proletariat ends and the middle classes begin; for at the doubtful margin the question is largely one of feeling rather

156

than of economic condition. In any event, this upper proletariat, fading into the *petite bourgeoisie*, is of much more doubtful allegiance to the central mass of the proletariat, which forms the class-nucleus, than any important section of the manual workers.

Marx sometimes argued as if the subjection of this group to the same experience as the manual workers, in the cutting down of salaries, the increased speeding up of work, and the danger of unemployment, would in due course drive it helter-skelter into conscious allegiance to the proletarian cause. As long as this group can improve its economic position within an advancing capitalist system, it is more likely to look away from the proletariat, out of which it is striving to emerge, than to act solidly with the rest of the proletarian class, though even at this stage some sections of it will organise Trade Unions and associations for the furtherance of their group interests, and some, but by no means all, of these bodies will ally themselves with the Trade Unions of the manual workers. But it is argued that when the process of advance slows down and turns to adversity as Capitalism begins to decay the "black-coated proletariat" will be speedily converted to a clear recognition of its proletarian status, and to an alliance with the manual workers in an attempt to change it. This view, however, needs large qualifications. In the first place, the ability of the "black-coats" to form Trade Unions is greatest in economic prosperity and falls off when Capitalism gets into difficulties; for the great mass of "black-coat" labour is easily transferable from job to job, and in face of widespread popular education the "black-coats," save in a few instances, are in the worst position for building up sectional monopolies of labour. Moreover, their desire to hold their status of social superiority to the manual workers is strongest when that superiority is most threatened. The desire to rise individually out of the proletariat weakens their power of collective action, and tends to make each individual play for his own hand by courting the employer's favour. "Black-coat" Trade Unions, except in occupations in which there is a high security of life-long employment,[1] are apt to be mushroom growths, and to die out in bad times as rapidly as they arise under conditions of favourable trade. Even where they persist, as in the public services, they have in most cases nothing like the cohesion or loyalty which exists among the Unions of the manual workers. They are apt to think of strikes as beneath their dignity; and employers do everything they can to foster this feeling of superiority as a means of keeping manual and non-manual

[1] E.g. Civil Service, Post Office, Railways, Banks and Insurance.

157

workers apart. The non-manual worker who ventures to become an active leader runs as a rule a far greater risk than the manual worker, both because he has often more to lose, and because his fellows are far less likely to protect him successfully against victimisation.

Secondly, if the "black-coats" feel their position to be seriously threatened, and are stirred to defensive action, it is not certain what side they will take. Too weak and with too little coherence to act alone or to lead, they have the choice of joining forces with the manual workers or of taking sides against them under whatever leadership offers to preserve their social superiority. To join with the manual workers means, in the end, sacrificing social superiority in the interests of economic defence; whereas the leaders who seek to mobilise them against the workers offer to defend both their economic interests and their superior status, by re-establishing a Capitalism that is henceforth to be controlled in the interests of the middle classes and made prosperous again by the defeat of the manual workers. Offered this choice, the "black-coats" are likely to divide, in different proportions according to the particular situation, but with a strong disposition, except in a few well-organised groups, to rally chiefly to that side which seems to have the better prospect of victory.

It is, of course, to some extent misleading to speak of the "black-coats" as a single group. The section among them that is nearest to the proletariat consists of shop assistants and other distributive workers—a numerous group, but difficult to organise except in large establishments or in Co-operative service. Next nearest are the general run of clerks and typists, among whom organisation is strong in a few groups, such as the lower ranks of the Civil and Local Government Services, the railways, the Post Office, and the banks, but usually very weak elsewhere, where the clerks form only small groups in industries employing chiefly manual workers. The expression "clerk" covers a wide range of differences of social status, from mere routine workers to persons of high skill and responsibility. In some cases, where the occupation is highly stratified—e.g. in the Civil Service—there is a fairly clear line between the elements which are near-proletarian and those which belong more with the professional classes. In other cases, e.g. railways, the line is less clear, and higher and lower clerical workers tend to be organised together, even when their class status differs. Side by side with the clerks, and with similar internal differences, are the draughtsmen, industrial chemists, and other routine technical workers in

158

industries and services, with their higher elements merging into the professional classes. Teachers and health workers, other than qualified doctors and dentists, form another group of which the lower levels are fairly near to the proletariat, but the higher much nearer to the professional middle class. These groups tend to hold themselves aloof from organised alliance with the manual workers, though a good many of them are individually Socialists or near-Socialists.

In general, there are three impulses which may drive sections of the "black-coats" into alliance with the proletariat proper. One is the trade union impulse, based on a common interest in maintaining the conditions needed for effective collective bargaining: the second is an impulse towards Socialism as a technically superior way of organising the industries and services in which they are employed; and the third is a common interest with the manual workers in the development of public social security services. This last has been the most powerful factor in those States which have gone furthest in creating, under popular pressure, welfare agencies involving an element of redistributive taxation in the interests of the poorer strata of the people.

The Change in Manual Labour

But the "black-coats," though they can be distinguished as a large and rapidly growing group lapping over from the proletariat into the middle class, are not separated from the manual workers by any clear line of division. Indeed, in the more advanced industrial countries, a growing section among the manual workers becomes "black-coated" both in its dress and habits of living and in its mental attitude. The more recent developments of industry not only cause a transference from manual to non-manual occupations, but also, by greater mechanisation, make many types of productive labour lighter and less rough, so that, even when the pace of work is speeded up, the exhaustion to which it leads is nervous rather than muscular, and many manual jobs no longer make those who labour at them dirty or uncouth in manner or appearance. This change in the quality of labour combines with the spread of popular education to make the manner and appearance, and also the minds, of a growing proportion of the manual workers more like those of the non-manual workers, who have been hitherto regarded (albeit often falsely) as their superiors in culture and education. Despite the persistence of slums and over-crowding in the towns of to-day, the conditions of housing in the new estates and suburbs assist in this process of making

159

a large part of the better-off members of the manual-working section of the proletariat more *bourgeois* in their habits and ways of living. The manual and non-manual workers often cannot be told apart nowadays, when they are off duty. They dress alike, talk alike, live alike, think alike, to an ever-increasing extent. Of course, this change affects some sections of manual labour much less than others. Until very recently it has touched the miners least of all, both because of the nature of their work, and because they live largely isolated in mining villages apart from other sections of the population. But among them too a change, social as well as technological, is rapidly coming about; and cheap motor transport, bringing the towns within their reach, helps towards their assimilation to the new type, as it does in the case of the agricultural labourers.

This change in the manual-working class cuts both ways. On the one hand, the assimilation between manual and non-manual workers makes co-operation between them easier within a common movement, as appears plainly in the Labour Party and in other political organisations. But, on the other hand, fighting spirit tends to be weakened, and the sense of solidarity is often less strong in the newer industries than in the old. The worker who has come to live more like a *bourgeois*, at any rate in externals, has more consciousness of what he has to lose by kicking against the pricks, and is inclined to be more cautious in action. Mechanisation, in making labour more readily transferable, diminishes craft-consciousness and solidarity; and in many cases there is really nothing more "manual" in operating an automatic machine than a typewriter or a calculating instrument in an up-to-date office. The decrease in the dirtiness of industrial occupations makes heavy, distinctive clothing less necessary than it was; and this too diminishes the sense of belonging to a separate social class.

The Proletariat in a Declining Capitalism

In these circumstances, it becomes easier to organise the proletariat politically, but harder to maintain the strength and vigour of its industrial organisation. Up to a point, this may aid the growth of class-consciousness; but beyond this point it makes class-consciousness less militant and less intense. It leads most easily to the growth of a vague, half-Socialist sentiment, which finds expression in a mild desire for reforms rather than in a determination to change the basis of society. Class-consciousness becomes more prevalent, but also more diluted and less determined in action.

These, however, are to a great extent the effects upon the proletariat of a Capitalism advancing in wealth and prosperity, and therefore able without endangering its solvency to grant progressive improvements in the standard of life. If, as seems to be the case over a large part of Western Europe, Capitalism is already passing out of this phase into one of declension and increasing embarrassment, is this situation likely to continue? Will the conversion of proletarians into marginal members of the new *petite bourgeoisie* still go on; or will the tendency of the past generation be sharply reversed?

It is a familiar theory among certain Marxists that it will be reversed, as Capitalism in its decline sets about cutting down wages and flinging the "black-coats" down into the growing mass of the impoverished. But is this theory correct? However Capitalism as a system may decline, the process of transferring workers from heavy to lighter mechanical operations and from direct productive jobs to distributive and clerical occupations seems certain to continue. Moreover, on the evidence of the inter-war years capitalist depressions impinge very unevenly upon the standard of living. They are more apt to create "pockets" of misery and destitution in declining industries, and to widen the gulf between the employed and the chronically unemployed, than to oppress the entire working class with a common oppression. When they do act in this way, they make some members of the proletariat more, and others less, amenable to forthright Socialist propaganda, or to any alternative form of "extremism" that promises redress. They tend to make Communists at the one extreme, and Fascists—under whatever names they may pass—at the other, out of those upon whom the conditions press hardest; but they also hinder the acceptance of either extreme by those sections of the workers upon whom the scourge of unemployment and depression does not seriously fall. Extremism of both types makes headway among those who suffer extreme experiences; but even in times of severe depression there are many who, relatively undisturbed in their own lives, remain sceptical of extreme courses.

Of course, where the disintegration of capitalist society goes beyond recurrent crises into absolute decay, this ceases to be true. Economic adversity, if it becomes deep and persistent enough, is bound to spread throughout the entire working class, in such a way as to drive all sections into resistance to a common misery. The whole proletariat, including the "black-coated" section, may have its standard of living so beaten down as to drive most of it into revolt. But, even where this happens, it does not follow that all sections will revolt in the same way. To assume this is to assume that Capitalism, threatened with utter destruction, will passively await its doom, and will allow the entire proletariat to concentrate for the attack upon it without resorting to any fresh expedients of defence. It is to assume, further, that the onset of "increasing misery," accompanied by more and more insistent claims from the proletariat for relief as well as for a change of system, will cause the middle groups to join the proletariat in its demands rather than to rally to the capitalists in an attempt to break its power, and thus rebuild the system of class-exploitation on a new basis. If the proletariat could be thoroughly crushed, might not the middle groups, as well as the capitalists, who cannot hold power without their aid, continue to live well enough even under an economic system that would be unable to carry further the development of the powers of production, or even to make full use of the powers already at men's disposal? Moreover, in such a situation, might not the capitalists and the middle groups be able to suborn a section even of the undoubted proletariat, by offering it a share in the spoils of victory?

Both the course of events in Germany after 1918 and the development of affairs in Europe since 1945 give support to a positive answer. The German capitalists did not wait for the decay of German Capitalism to unite all the other elements in society against them: they supported and subsidised Fascism, as a means of detaching a section of the malcontents from the working-class movement and of using these apostates as auxiliaries in the struggle against Socialism. The course of events in Western Europe since the liberation has not been quite the same; but it illustrates the same point in a different way. The peoples of the liberated countries, as they emerged from Nazi occupation, showed at first a pronounced tendency to "go left," on the basis of an alliance between all the groups, or nearly all, that had been active in the *résistance*. But, as the depth of Europe's economic disaster came to be more generally apprehended, this mood passed, and there was a swing from "left" to "centre," above all among the black-coats and other marginal groups that had ranged themselves temporarily with the Left. There was, at this second stage, not much thought of a Fascist policy of violent attack upon the Left: what was looked for was some middle way that would save the middle classes from being crushed between the proletariat and the reaction. In France, however, there had appeared by 1947 clear signs of a third phase, in the emergence of General de Gaulle's *Rassemblement du Peuple Français*, with its demand for an authoritarian State and for an outright war against Communism—which meant, for many of his supporters, nothing less than war upon the main body of the working class. Even if a large share in the responsibility for this must be assigned to the French Communists, or rather to the line which they followed in obedience to Moscow's wishes, the fact remains that in France adversity, so far from uniting the proletariat and driving the declassed black-coats and *petit bourgeois* groups to collaborate with it, appeared in 1947-8 to be producing an alignment of social forces closely analogous to that of Germany shortly before Hitler's conquest of power—with the difference that Communism and Social Democracy had changed places in the leadership of the main body of the working class.

It can by no means be taken for granted that, the more Capitalism decays, the more solidly united the proletariat will be, and the more recruits it will gain from the marginal groups of salary-earners and independent workers. Even in Great Britain, where the Labour electoral victory of 1945 was won as the outcome of such a rally, increasing realisation of the seriousness of the economic situation has done something—no one can yet tell how much—to drive the marginal supporters of Labour over to the other side. The Labour Government has, indeed, been able to carry out a policy which has greatly increased social security for the middle groups as well as for the manual workers, and has protected the basic standards of living of all sections of the relatively poor. But it remains to be seen whether this will suffice to earn the Labour Party the continued support of the large marginal fraction of the electorate under the conditions of an unavoidable "austerity" which each income group will instinctively wish to pass on to those above or below it. Perhaps in Great Britain the "left front" will hold. If it does, that will be mainly because solid unity does exist among the central part of the proletariat, or in other words because there is no serious division into Communist and Socialist factions. Even, however, if there are hopes of the alliance of forces holding in Great Britain, it has to be admitted that there are few other parts of Western Europe about which the same hope can be easily entertained.

The Prospects of Revolution

War, no doubt, is the proletariat's opportunity; for war is usually followed by a period of dislocation and unrest that

163

opens the door wide to revolution, at any rate in the defeated countries. In war, both sides cannot win. The struggle must either be indecisive or end in someone's defeat. But an indecisive struggle discredits the ruling class that wages it, and stirs up discontent; and defeat strains the political as well as the economic system of the defeated country, often to breaking point. Therefore, some Socialists after 1918 saw the chief, if not the only, prospect of Socialist victory in another war. War begat the Russian Revolution of 1917: what fresh revolutions would not the next war bring?

To those who envisaged the future in this way, the prospect of Socialist electoral victories made little appeal. They were much less concerned with winning for some form of Socialism a wide basis of support than with the creation of a proletarian movement which, even if it were small, would have the fighting quality and the determined temper that would ensure full advantage being taken of a revolutionary opportunity when it came. Some of them were not even much disturbed when the fear of Socialism led to a successful Fascist revolution, which celebrated its victory by breaking up the entire mass-organisation of the working class, and succeeded in sweeping a substantial section of the proletariat behind it into a mood of hysterical Nationalism. For, they said, their time would come. The Nationalists would lead the deluded multitude into war: war would beget unrest and disillusion; and then the mass would be ready to follow, in a hardly less irrational fashion if to a better end, the lead of a determined Communist minority.

It happened so in Russia, where the repressions of the years following the unsuccessful Revolution of 1905 broke up the mass organisations and drove the working-class movement underground, and where imperialist war and collapse made the way plain for the proletarian Revolution of 1917. It happened so in Russia; and therefore, some people imagined, it was bound to happen so everywhere else. But was it? In Germany, perhaps, or even in Italy, things might wear that look; for when a Fascist Revolution had once occurred, and the mass organisation of the workers had been successfully broken, it seemed as if there might be no alternative method left for the winning of Socialism. But was it supposed to follow that Fascist Revolution was inevitable in every country, or that everywhere the existing mass organisation of the workers was destined to be broken up, in order to be re-created in the fiery furnace of war? Some Socialists acted almost as if they thought so; but the basis for such a conclusion is not self-evident.

164

Parliamentarism and Revolution

It has to be borne in mind that neither Russia nor Germany ever became parliamentary democracies in any real sense. In Russia the attempt to establish parliamentary democracy in 1917 was made in the face of complete economic and political collapse of the old autocracy, and never stood any real chance of success. In Germany the ill-fated Weimar Republic was similarly founded on the ruins of a defeated autocracy—for pre-war Germany was never really a parliamentary State—and the Socialists could have pushed it over quite easily at the outset if they had wished. That they did not wish is true and important in its place; but it is not my present point, which is that German parliamentarism, born out of defeat and presented with the impossible task of governing Germany as a subject-Power at the orders of the victors, never had even half a chance. Even in Italy, which was rather more a parliamentary country before the war, the roots of parliamentary government were always weak and the system had little hold on the mind of the population; and though Italy emerged from the first war nominally a victor, the disappointment of her imperialist aspirations and the pressure of economic difficulties, with which her weak Governments were quite unable to cope, smoothed the way for the victory of Fascism over the divided Socialist and Syndicalist forces.

On the other hand in Great Britain, Holland, Belgium and Scandinavia, the parliamentary system is strongly entrenched, and has behind it a long record of economic success. In these countries autocracy was superseded long ago, while Capitalism was still a progressive system with most of its victories still to come, by the rule of the *bourgeoisie* exercised through parliamentary institutions. The suffrage was extended, working-class organisations were allowed freedom to grow, economic pressure from below was met by concessions as well as by repressions, and the State became a machine for the dispensing of social services as well as for the maintenance of law and order and of the rights of property. Parliamentarism got the credit of these achievements, as well as of the rising standards of life characteristic of an advancing capitalist system. And, though there was even in these countries some sign of a growing reaction against Parliament as the difficulties of Capitalism increased, Parliamentarism remained strongly entrenched in the minds of all classes, including the workers.

In France the situation is somewhat different. For a variety of reasons the French State lagged a long way behind the other

165

advanced countries of Western Europe in the development of welfare services. French Socialism, denied the backing of the Trade Unions, which followed an anti-political Syndicalist policy, was unable to exert anything like the same pressures upon government as the Socialist and Labour Parties of other advanced Western countries. French parliamentarism remained unstable; and the French working class never identified itself with the parliamentary system or with the Socialist Party in the same way as the British, Belgian or Scandinavian working classes. In certain notable respects, Syndicalism and Marxism were poles apart; for the Syndicalists were deeply hostile to all forms of centralisation and mass-discipline. They relied instead on spontaneity and guerrilla struggle, and dismissed legislation as a mere ratification of victories won in the economic field. As against this, however, the Syndicalists fully agreed with the left-wing Marxists in regarding the existing State as essentially an instrument of class-power, as well as in emphasising the doctrine of class-struggle in an extreme form. These character-istics of Syndicalist propaganda prepared the way for a conversion of the main body of French Trade Unionists, at any rate in the manual occupations, much more readily to Communism than to Social Democracy: so that when the workers were forced into politics by the pressure of world events, the Communist rather than the Socialist Party fell heir to the Syndicalist traditions of revolutionary struggle. Something of the same sort occurred in Italy, which had also been a Syndicalist stronghold; but there the course of events was somewhat different because of the intervening period of Fascist rule, which uprooted the old parliamentary institutions. Of course, the influence of Syndical-ism in France and Italy (and also in Spain) was not causeless. It was partly due to the relative prevalence of small-scale business enterprise under localised control. In comparison with Great Britain or Germany, neither France nor Italy was a country of highly advanced capitalist structure; and neither had acquired the range of State services which elsewhere in Europe has accompanied the development of democratic electorates largely concentrated round factories and mines in teeming industrial areas.

In France, then, and also in Italy, there was a basis for the mass-influence of Communism on the organised working class. But, the more Communistic the workers became, the less chance had they of securing any substantial support from the middle groups in society. The middle classes, in these countries, con-tained much larger elements of the old *petite bourgeoisie* of small employers, small traders, small farmers, and small *rentiers,* and much smaller elements of the new *petite bourgeoisie* based on large-scale business and administration, than was the case in economically more developed societies. There was accordingly no basis in either France or Italy for any stable electoral victory of the "left"; and when victory was secured at the polls, as in the short-lived triumph of the *Front Populaire* in 1936, the result was only to show up the deep divergence of policies within the victorious coalition of forces.

In such a situation, with the proletariat divided unevenly between Communism and Social Democracy, and with revolution and counter-revolution threatened from the two extremes, the Social Democratic section of the proletariat finds itself driven, as the German Socialists were driven under the Weimar Republic, into an alliance with the middle parties to sustain parliamentary government. Such an alliance is paralysing; for it prevents any constructive policy from being put into effect. It can endure only as long as the extreme forces on both sides cancel each other out because neither dares to risk revolutionary action. Even so, the central parties tend to lose support to both the extremes, because they have, in practice, only negations to offer. It is, however, by no means the case that, in such a situation, the proletarian extremists are likely to gain more recruits outside the manual working class than their counter-revolutionary opponents. The probability is very much the other way. The chance of proletarian revolution succeeding depends not on numbers but on cohesion and skill in organisation and on the failure of the counter-revolutionary elements to display these qualities in equal measure. It depends also on the skill shown by the middle groups in playing off the extremists against each other, and in holding the social and economic structure precariously together—a task which is likely to be a good deal easier for the capitalistic middle groups than for the Social Democrats, who cannot apply their own remedies and have to support measures acceptable to their capitalist allies. Thus Social Democracy is further eroded, as it was in Weimar Germany, and as it has been in France since the liberation.

If a country has to work out its problems mainly in isolation, as Germany did in the struggle which culminated in the Nazi victory, the outcome is a matter of the relative strength of the internal forces and of the skill shown in leading them. Where, however, the forces are delicately poised, external influences may make all the difference. Thus, in France in 1948, the prospect of avoiding a revolutionary trial of strength evidently

167

depended very much on two external factors—Marshall Aid, and the amount of reinforcement the Russians were able to bring to the French Communists. The first of these external factors could have operated either to induce a sufficient economic recovery to enable the middle groups to regain support at the expense of both extremes, or in default of this to reinforce the right-wing extremists for a *coup d'état* against the Left. The second factor, largely dependent on Communist success in either Italy or Western Germany, so as to give the Russians direct access to their French supporters, could have made only in favour of a revolution of the Left.

In effect, the Communist strategy of propaganda designed to prepare the way for social revolution stands little chance of success in countries with a strong parliamentary tradition unless they have been reduced to serious economic straits, and even so involves at least an equal danger of counter-revolution, unless the Communist elements in the country concerned can get real help from outside. If the balance of forces remains such that neither extreme section ventures to precipitate a revolution, the effect is likely to be—again in the absence of external help— a creeping paralysis of the entire social system. On the other hand, when the forces are thus balanced, external help in economic recovery may serve to reinvigorate the middle groups, and may even pass the initiative over to the Social Democrats and rally not only the main body of the proletariat proper, but also a large section of the "black-coated" proletariat, to its side. In the absence of economic prostration, which is always a force driving men to extremes, the predominant struggle in such countries will continue to be between parties still employing parliamentary methods, and endeavouring to gain their ends by lawful means. The principal immediate effect of Communist policy under such conditions can be only to weaken the chances of a constitutional Socialist victory, just as Fascism can only lessen those of the successful constitutional defence of Capitalism. Hence the established parties will excommunicate the rival extremists and do all they can to prevent the spread of their doctrines. Messrs. Baldwin and MacDonald did not love Sir Oswald Mosley any better than the present leaders of the Labour Party love Mr. Harry Pollitt.

To this ostracism the extremists on both sides will reply that they are being excommunicated because the older parties are selling the pass. The capitalist parties will be told that their weakness is leaving the door wide open for the Socialists to come in; and the Socialist parties will be accused of being traitors to the proletarian cause. But in fact on both sides the leadership will be expressing with fair accuracy the minds of most of those to whom it is seeking to appeal. For, in countries with a strong parliamentary tradition, most men do not want to fight until they have lost hope of gaining their point by peaceful means.

To this both groups of extremists will answer that, even if most people do still hold these views, they are demonstrably mistaken. The capitalist extremists will point to the gradual increase of Socialist legislation, and will explain that Socialism is the inevitable outcome of parliamentary "democracy"; while the Communists will demonstrate that Capitalism in its decline must increasingly grind down the proletariat, and will certainly resort to force on the model of Italy and Germany, as soon as the proletariat refuses to be ground down. Up to a point, both these views are correct. Socialism is the natural long-run outcome of a democratic franchise in an advanced industrial country; and Capitalism, if it relies on parliamentary methods, is bound most of the time to be fighting a rearguard action, because it must find means of keeping a majority of the electors on its side. And, on the other hand, a declining Capitalism must oppose the claims of the proletariat with increasing vigour if it is to survive at all.

Nevertheless, the conclusions drawn by the extremists do not follow; for a premature attempt at Fascism may be the surest means of bringing about a Socialist victory, and the growth of Communism may be the means of preventing the Socialists from placing themselves constitutionally in a position to render impossible a successful capitalist appeal to force. For even if the making of Socialism involves much more than the winning of a parliamentary majority, possession of the machinery of State is a most powerful instrument for the suppression of counter-revolutionary activities.

The case against the Communist policy in those parts of Western Europe in which parliamentarism remains strong is not that it misinterprets the attitude of the proletariat, but that it is likely, in the existing circumstances, to divide the forces of the proletariat at a crucial juncture, and so to make more difficult a parliamentary Socialist victory and perhaps, in the measure of its own success in attracting adherents, open the door to a real growth of Fascism. This does not deter the Communists, because they have no belief in the value of a parliamentary victory, and are intent only on building up a revolutionary movement capable of assuming the leadership when its opportunity arises. But how is this opportunity to arise?

It could come, first, as a result of the progressive decline of Capitalism even in the absence of war. But this is to contemplate either an indefinite postponement of victory or the outbreak of a third World War; for there is no evidence that, save as an outcome of war, Capitalism in Great Britain or the Dominions, or in Scandinavia or Belgium or Switzerland or Holland, is likely to break up finally for a long time to come. The history of the inter-war years has very plainly illustrated the toughness and resisting power of Capitalism in these countries even in face of prolonged world depression; and who is bold enough to say that the present difficulties of West European Capitalism, serious as they undoubtedly are, will not be overcome, and may not be succeeded by a phase of capitalist revival aided by the great power of Capitalism in the United States? Capitalism may be doomed to be pulled down by its own inherent "contradictions"; but, unless war intervenes to hasten the process, it may well take a considerable time for this destruction to be completed, save as the result of a victory of Socialism won by parliamentary methods.

It may be argued that the Communists' chance will come only after parliamentary Socialism has been tried, and has failed. But, if that is so, should not the Communists help the Socialists to power, rather than do their best to destroy their chances? Moreover, is the failure of parliamentary methods really so unavoidable as the Communists would have us believe?

In France, however, and in Italy the situation is by no means the same; for in both these countries the major part of the organised working class is at present aligned with Communism rather than with parliamentary Socialism. This, unless the Communists and their allies are powerful enough to carry through a social revolution, or unless they are defeated by counter-revolution, involves a stalemate which is disastrous in its immediate economic effects. Such a situation is inconsistent alike with the application of Socialist remedies and with the re-building of Capitalism on any efficient footing. It can hardly last for long, even if the reconstruction of capitalist industry is aided from outside, as it is presumably meant to be under the Marshall Plan. It is bound to be ended, either by revolution or counter-revolution or, conceivably, by a change in social attitudes among sufficient sections of the people to restore the possibilities of effective parliamentary government. Of this third alternative there is, however, at present little sign.

The main discussion of these issues must be reserved for a later chapter, in which we shall be dealing with the Marxist attitude to the State and to parliamentary action. For we must first complete our picture of the modern proletariat, upon which the victory of Socialism by *any* method must be mainly based, whatever other forces may come to the aid of the victors in the course of the struggle. What the proletariat is, and what it can become, are the vital questions which must be answered before any attempt can be made to work out a sound and practical Socialist strategy.

The Mind of the Proletariat

What the modern proletariat is, in the advanced countries of Western Europe, we have seen in outline already. It consists of a central mass of manual workers and their families, shading off at one end into the unemployables and at the other into the "black-coats" of the middle class. It is greatly differentiated within itself, into many grades of labour and levels of incomes and education, without anywhere a sharp break between one grade or section and another. A large number of its members, while depending on wages or salaries for the means of life, are small owners of property, and its collective organisations are holders of property to a considerable extent. Its better-off groups, which have a standard of life permitting of some modest comfort, certainly do not echo the sentiment that they have nothing to lose but their chains. They are very conscious of having also their jobs, their houses and gardens, their small savings, and their share in social services provided by the State, Local Authorities, Trade Unions, Friendly Societies, and numerous other bodies. They value these things, and are prepared to defend them if they are attacked; and they want more of them, with an appetite that grows with experience. They are therefore mostly "progressives" in their political attitude, and ready to support parties which promise to defend what they have gained and to improve upon it by further reforms. Many of them, but not perhaps most, are Socialists of a sort; but Socialism means to them mainly the cause that stands for giving them more of what they want, and does not mean any clear idea of an alternative kind of society—much less a kind to be won by violent revolution.

These people are, for the most part, capable of becoming Socialists in a more positive sense only if and when they realise that continued progress along the familiar lines is impossible within the capitalist system, and that they can secure a further rise in their standards of living, or indeed protect the standards which they have already, only by changing the basis of economic

171

organisation. Even so, they need to be convinced that the Socialists, in calling upon them to deliver a frontal attack on Capitalism, do mean and also know how to create a Socialist system that will give them what they want. The Socialism to which they will listen must be a "bread and butter" Socialism, offering tangible benefits and appearing competent to make its promises good. If Socialists can appeal to them on these lines, many of them will be disposed to follow; but they will insist that the change be brought about with the minimum of dislocation and violence, and that the attempt be made on constitutional lines if the road remains open for attempting it in that way. This applies to a great majority of the better-off wage-earners and of their allies among the "black-coats" and in other social groups.

There is, indeed, a substantial section of the proletariat to which this diagnosis does not apply. This section consists primarily of those who have suffered prolonged unemployment and had their accustomed standards of living badly beaten down, as well as of a minority of the people who grew to manhood during the years of depression between the wars. These elements have dwindled, because the renewal of war brought with it full employment, and there has been no serious recurrence of unemployment since 1945. If, however, the old conditions were allowed to return, even for a few years, the old attitudes would come back with them. There would be again, among a substantial section of the proletariat, a greater readiness to listen to extreme policies—to become Communists, and perhaps thereafter in not a few cases to turn Fascist if and when they lost faith in a Communist victory. From having fewer roots in the present order, they would again be much more unstable in their allegiance. They would be good revolutionary material; but they would also be a favourable source of recruits, as they were in Germany, for the counter-revolution.

This section of the proletariat has been, under any conditions that have so far existed in Great Britain, quite incapable either of making a Socialist revolution, or of gaining the leadership of the general body of the working class. It has never been more than a small fraction of the whole proletariat: even in Germany, where it came to be a very large fraction, those who became its leaders never succeeded in winning over the majority of the workers to their point of view. A movement based upon this section alone cannot be a class-movement, but only a fractional movement within a class. It can destroy the solidarity of a class, but it is impotent to build up any new solidarity in its stead.

172

Only national defeat in war, or the utter decay of Capitalism, plunging the majority of the workers down to its economic level, can avail to make such a movement the representative of a united working class.

In the parliamentary "democracies" of Western Europe, unless and until this stage is reached, any advance towards Socialism has to be made by means of a strategy that will unite rather than divide the proletariat. This means not only the use of parliamentary methods of agitation and an attempt to capture the machinery of State, as long as these methods remain open, but also building upon the existing mass-organisations which the proletariat has created for itself. It means using the Trade Unions and the Co-operative Societies, as well as the Labour Party, as instruments both of working-class defence and of the furtherance of Socialist policy. It means preserving the unity of these movements, and preventing them if possible from being torn asunder, as Trade Unionism has been again and again in France and Spain, by doctrinal differences. For, in the industrial field, disunity is even more fatal than in political action. Rival Trade Unions, fighting one another and pursuing opposite policies, are plainly impotent to protect the workers' standards of life—much more to further the coming of Socialism. If there is a conflict of industrial policies, as there will be, it has to be pursued within a united organisation, unless the workers are to court disaster.

The Prospects of Trade Unionism

This is the more important to-day because the forces of the time are in many respects inimical to Trade Unionism. At times of crisis in the national economy the Trade Unions are inevitably put on the defensive, and are compelled to hold fast to existing positions rather than to seek new fields to conquer. They have even to restrain their members from making full use of their bargaining strength for fear of upsetting the export trades, or of putting an uncontrollable inflationary process in motion. Such tactics require unity even more imperatively than attack does; for they are harder, and call for much greater patience and persistence as well as for greater loyalty. It is, however, when Trade Unionism is forced to assume a measure of responsibility for the maintenance of production and for the stabilisation of costs that unity is most difficult to maintain. There can be no easy and spectacular victories to attract members and to inspire ready confidence in the value of the Unions; for it looks much more successful to secure a rise in wages than to prevent an inflation from leading to a fall in the standard of living, though the latter may be by far the greater accomplishment. Moreover, leaders who have always to be preaching caution cannot easily sound inspiring, and may easily have their own spirit worn away; and members, finding their Unions dull, may discover more exciting things to do than to maintain the steady round of necessary work for keeping the machine efficiently in order. Trade Unionism, far more than political Labour, has to trim its sails according to the winds of economic opportunity. As long as Capitalism is there, it has to live on terms with Capitalism; and in difficult times it dare not insist on terms that, in adding to the difficulties of Capitalism, will also react on the entire national standard of life.

It is, however, when Trade Unionism looks least inspiring that it is most important to keep it alive, both for the immediate protection of working-class standards and because it can be relied on to come alive again when the conditions require greater activity, and is at all times indispensable as a means of organising working-class solidarity in a primary way. Where there are no Trade Unions, the working class is reduced to a merely atomistic mass, incapable of concerted action in politics as well as in industry, or of being rallied effectively behind a Socialist policy. Trade Unionism may be incapable of supplying the positive driving-force towards Socialism; but without it there could be no working-class army to be led. No delusion is more foolish than the delusion that Socialists could do without Trade Unions, or afford to advance without their support.

It is, however, true that there have been at work other forces besides inter-war depression and post-war national economic dislocation that have tended to lessen the power of Trade Unionism. For this power has in the past been concentrated in a high degree in a few great industries and among certain special groups of workers possessing a valuable monopoly of technical skill. The more recent developments of industry have tended to decrease the numbers of workers employed in these older industries, and to increase employment in industries less dependent on highly skilled manual labour, in transport and distribution, and in the public utility and other services; and they have also, by the greater use made of automatic and semi-automatic machinery, broken down in part the established monopolies of the skilled crafts and made much harder the creation of solid blackleg-proof organisations on sectional lines.

It would have been much easier for the Trade Unions to adapt themselves to these changes in industrial technique and in the employment of labour if their advent between the wars had not coincided in time with serious depression of trade, so that technological and cyclical unemployment increased side by side. But even if there had been only the technological problem to face the Trade Unions would have needed to revise their methods of organisation and bargaining to a considerable extent. For the new industrial conditions demand both a wider solidarity embracing all sections of workers and a greater concentration of bargaining in each separate establishment as well as on the general adjustment of wage-rates and hours of labour over a wider area. It was, however, exceptionally difficult to establish machinery for workshop bargaining under conditions which involved the existence of a surplus of labour; for such Trade Union agents as shop stewards could be readily singled out for victimisation and dismissal, and the Unions, when trade was bad and unemployment prevalent, might not be strong enough to protect their active members against such treatment. Consequently, there went on between the wars, side by side with the introduction of new technical methods of production, a progressive undermining of established Trade Union customs and a worsening of conditions quite apart from the actual reduction of wage-rates; and only the most fortunately placed Trade Unions were able to stand out against these innovations with success. There was much speeding up, both by stricter factory supervision and by the introduction of new methods of wage-payment such as the unpopular "Bedaux" system; much use of less skilled or juvenile labour at lower rates on jobs previously reserved for skilled men; much nibbling at the privileges which the Trade Unions had managed to build up by long years of effort. All these causes naturally produced a large amount of irritation in the factories; but this irritation was held in check by the fear of dismissal which was bound to be always present in the workers' minds at times of super-abundant labour supply.

Trade Unionism and Politics

For these difficulties of the Trade Union movement between the wars no remedy could be found in terms of industrial action alone. The Trade Unions were driven irresistibly towards political action as a means of reinforcing their economic power. They wanted a satisfactory system of maintenance for the unemployed in order to reduce the pressure to accept jobs on any conditions which the employers chose to offer. They wanted, in industries where wages were being seriously pressed down by

175

adverse trade conditions, a legal minimum wage. They wanted shorter hours of labour as a means of sharing out the available work. And, especially in the depressed industries, such as coal and cotton, these claims impelled them towards a stronger demand for complete socialisation, or at least for the reorganisation of these industries under State control. Trade Unions thus turned to political action as a means of securing their industrial demands; and the Labour Party became more important in their eyes as an indispensable agent of economic policy.

This pressure of the Trade Unions upon the Labour Party was capable of taking, upon the surface, opposite and inconsistent forms. Sometimes, it seemed to be pressing the Party to promise a further squeezing of the capitalist orange, without any frontal attack upon Capitalism itself; for the Unions, with the immediate needs of their members most in mind, were apt to press for pledges that the Labour Party, when it came back to office, would concentrate on questions of "bread and butter," to the exclusion of more ambitious objectives. At other times, the Trade Unions—especially the miners—seemed to be intent on pushing the more timid political leaders further towards Socialism than, in their fear of offending other sections of the electorate, they were disposed to go. In Great Britain Trade Union votes, fully as much as the votes of constituency Labour Parties, were responsible for the marked stiffening up of the Labour programme at inter-war Labour Party Conferences, often despite the reluctance of the Party Executive. The truth is that the Trade Unions, when they were acting as industrial bodies, had to be moderate because they were conscious of their weakness; but this very consciousness tended to make them favour an advanced political programme because that alone offered the prospect of strengthening their hands in the industrial sphere.

Nevertheless, when the Trade Unions were presented with such an issue as that of constitutionalism *versus* revolution, their answer was always unhesitatingly in favour of constitutional action. In this the leadership rightly interpreted the feeling of the great majority of the members, who, not being Socialists in any considered theoretical sense, thought in terms of possible remedies for particular grievances rather than of a complete change in the basis of society. The Trade Unions, in a sense, were all the time gradually becoming more Socialist; but they were becoming so only as it was gradually forced upon them, in relation to one practical issue after another, that Capitalism was unable, as well as unwilling, to grant their demands.

To what extent, if at all, have the years since 1939 altered

176

this situation? In one respect—the diminution of unemployment—they have obviously altered it very much indeed. Trade Unions in recent years have been under no necessity of holding back from demanding improved wages or conditions because of the existence of a reserve of unemployed labour. On the contrary, they have been in a very strong bargaining position *vis-à-vis* the employers in almost every industry. That they have still felt the need to hold back has been due to essentially different causes—above all to the changed position of Great Britain (and indeed of many other European countries) in world economy, and to the consciousness that pressure for higher wages or for shorter hours would be to a large extent necessarily self-defeating. In face of shortage of goods, the higher wages would inevitably be cancelled by higher prices; and the shorter hours would only render the scarcity of goods yet greater, and prejudice the export trades in their endeavour to earn the means of paying for indispensable imports. Under these conditions, not even socialisation could offer much prospect of real improvement in standards of living, except in the long run. The first national interest was to develop national productivity to make up for the severe losses incurred in the war. Socialisation, over a wide field, was doubtless all the more desirable as a long-run means of promoting efficiency; but it had to be recognised that there was, for the time being, little more to be squeezed out by re-distribution of the national income, either through taxation, or by insistence on higher wages. In these circumstances, the Trade Unions had to accept a measure of responsibility for the effective conduct of industry; and they could do this much least against the grain in partnership with a non-revolutionary Socialist Government that would at the same time seek to control and to work in with the capitalist directors of industry outside the field to which socialisation could be immediately applied.

In other respects, the second World War has not greatly altered the position of the Trade Unions, except in affording them an opportunity to re-build the machinery of workshop bargaining and consultation, which had been largely destroyed during the years of depression. To a limited extent, this has been done; but there has been as yet no thoroughgoing re-organisation of Trade Unionism to fit it for taking its place as an effective factor in the control of industry within a system of public planning and state ownership or regulation. The Trade Union movement has still not overcome the factors making for less intense interest in Trade Union affairs as the scale of bargaining grows larger, and the process therefore removed further from the individual member and the local group. There has been no adequate realisation of the character of the new tasks that must fall on the Trade Unions as the capitalist incentives to production lose their force. Yet the rising of Trade Unionism to the task of helping positively in the construction of the new economic order is absolutely necessary, if the political attempt to build Socialism on a libertarian basis is not to fail.

The Trade Unions are indispensable to the Socialists; but in these days Socialism cannot be founded on a Trade Union basis only. It has to get behind it a body of support wide enough to include, not only the Trade Unions, but the great mass of people outside the Unions who are of the proletariat or are capable of acting as its allies. The Trade Union is still predominantly a male institution; but the enfranchisement of women makes indispensable an organisation wide enough to include housewives as well as employed women in its scope, and to give them an increasing share in its conduct. This need the Labour and Socialist Parties, with their strongly organised Women's Sections, are now beginning satisfactorily to supply. The Party also affords room for the unorganised "black-coats" and "independent" workers, and for all the miscellaneous converts from other groups and classes whom conviction and sympathy induce to rally to the Socialist cause. The problem of uniting all these elements in one mass organisation, so as both to preserve the allegiance of the Trade Unions and to give the other sections a real share in the framing of policy in face of the Trade Union "block vote," is not easy to solve. But in Great Britain it is on the whole being solved with fair satisfaction in the gradual evolution of the Labour Party machine.

For the Trade Unionists are aware that, if they stood alone, on the basis of a predominantly Trade Union party, they would have little chance of conquering a majority in Parliament, or of using political action as an effective reinforcement to their industrial power. If the proletariat were merely the manual-working group, it would be, not only a minority, but also a minority incapable of leading the majority, or of acting unitedly with itself. For, as we have seen, while the main body of manual workers forms the central core of the proletariat, the manual workers are not to-day marked off sharply as a single group from the non-manual workers, but shade off into the other sections of the proletariat, with which they have increasingly a common standard of culture, income, and way of life. Political action—even if the Trade Unions continue to play a vitally important part in its organisation, as they do and must—has

178

to be developed on a basis wide enough to include the whole proletariat, in a very broad sense, and all the elements sympathetic to its aims, and not its Trade Union elements alone.

The Co-operative Movement

This brings us to a consideration of the place of the Co-operative Movement. The Co-operative Movement has travelled far since the days of Robert Owen; and its great success as a trading institution has caused it in the main to stand aside from the industrial and political phases of the working-class struggle for power. Becoming a great employer in competition with capitalist industry, it has been compelled to adopt towards its employees an attitude not differing greatly from that of capitalists, save that it has usually afforded securer employment and quite often better working conditions than the general run of private firms. Seeking a wider membership, it has been disposed until lately to eschew political discussion and activity; and it would hardly have been drawn much into politics even now but for the ill-advised attacks launched on its privileges at the instigation of private traders jealous of its commercial success. It tends, by the very nature of its activities, to throw up to the top men marked out by business qualities rather than by propagandist zeal; and as long as it has been able to live and grow within a capitalist setting it has been inclined to forswear attacks on Capitalism that might bring its own rights into jeopardy. The Co-operative Movement is never likely to place itself in the vanguard of the working-class's political advance. It is far more likely to come lumbering along behind, like the commissariat in the wake of an advancing army. But it is of high importance to the success of Socialism that it should not lag too far behind; and those who seek to frame working-class policy would be well advised to pay more attention to assuring Co-operators of a satisfying place in the coming reorganisation of society, and to securing that Trade Unionists and Socialists who are also Co-operators shall more actively carry their Trade Union and Socialist principles into the Co-operative Store.

The preceding paragraph refers to the movement of Consumers' Co-operation: not to the great Agricultural Co-operative Movements which have their main strength in the peasant countries. These movements have tended inevitably to come under the influence mainly of the better-off peasants, who have been most active in taking advantage of them and best at organising them. Consequently, they have been in many cases a force making for social peace, and have not uncommonly received encouragement even from very reactionary Governments. Under Fascism they were left intact, provided that they accepted a leadership that was prepared to fall in with Fascist agricultural policies. Politically, they were usually the allies of, and often a powerful force in, the peasant parties of Eastern and Central Europe; and they were consequently potential focusing points for opposition to Socialism and Communism. Communist policy, in the countries falling within the Soviet sphere of influence, has been to impose new leadership upon them much as the Fascists did, and to refrain so far from any frontal attack on peasant ownership. In Western Countries, such as Denmark and Sweden, where the Agricultural Co-operatives are also a powerful influence, they have for the most part kept out of organised political action and have certainly never thrown their weight on the side of Socialism. Agricultural Co-operation, even if it is a form of economic organisation compatible with industrial Socialism, is necessarily in the main a movement based on the collective self-interest of agricultural producers who cultivate the land for profit. It can become the ally of the Socialists when it needs their help in order to stabilise agricultural prices and secure capital for land development; but it is usually altogether indisposed to take a revolutionary line except in rare cases under the impulsion of nationalist rather than of economic motives. This, of course, does not apply—or at any rate applies much less—to the special form of Agricultural Co-operation that has been developed in the Soviet Union—the *kolkhoz*, or collective farm—for the *kolkhoz* is in effect the whole village organised as a co-operative community, and not an association of independent cultivators each farming for profit. Even, however, in the Soviet Union, the agricultural part of the population has followed, rather than led. The *kolkhoz* is a creation, not of the peasants, but of the Communist Party.

Communism and Socialism in Advanced Countries

The proletariat, in the advanced countries which have a strong tradition of parliamentary democracy, is then a widely differentiated class, with many and increasing claims, but by no means of revolutionary temper as long as it is left room to organise freely and sees a chance of realising its claims within the existing framework of society. Compared with the proletariat of Marx's day, it is not more, but very much less, "miserable," though it came between the wars to include a substantial depressed section upon which fell the main brunt of the difficulties of Capitalism. In Great Britain this depressed section almost

180

disappeared under war conditions, and has not since reappeared in view of the continuing shortage of man-power. In countries where the capitalist game is being played out to the end, and constitutional Socialism has failed to supplant it in time, the dislocation of industry has exerted its depressing effect on the whole working class, which has thus been rendered much more responsive to Communist appeals for a revolutionary Socialist policy. There is, however, no sign as yet of the emergence of similar tendencies either in Great Britain or in such other countries of Western Europe as have a strong parliamentary tradition and have been able to maintain tolerable living standards by means of effective systems of rationing, price-control, and progressive taxation of the larger incomes. In these circumstances, it appears that Socialist policy in these countries should, in order to maintain working-class unity, be based on the proletariat as it actually is, and not as it may come some day to be if a number of not certainly foreseeable contingencies occur. But this point—what the appropriate Socialist strategy should be—we can discuss best when we have considered the Marxian attitude to the State in the light of States as they actually are in the world of to-day.

CHAPTER VII

MARXISM AND THE STATE

ONE OF MARX'S MOST FAMOUS phrases is his character-isation of the modern State. "The executive of the modern State," he and Engels wrote in *The Communist Manifesto*, "is but a committee for managing the common affairs of the *bourgeoisie* as a whole." In these words Marx characterised the modern State as essentially an organ of class-dictatorship.

Later on in *The Communist Manifesto*, Marx and Engels set out to define the policy of the proletariat towards the *bourgeois* State. "The first step in the working-class revolution," they wrote, "is to raise the proletariat to the position of ruling class, to win the battle of democracy." They added that "the proletariat will use its political supremacy to wrest, by degrees, all capital from the *bourgeoisie*, and to centralise all instruments of produc-tion in the hands of the State, *i.e.* of the proletariat organised as the ruling class."

Much later, in 1875, Marx wrote in his criticism of the Gotha

Programme of the German Socialists a passage which further clarifies his meaning. "Between capitalist and communist society lies a period of revolutionary transformation from the one to the other. To this also corresponds a political period of transition during which the State can be nothing else than the revolutionary dictatorship of the proletariat."

There are two important points to notice in these passages. First, in the contrast which they draw between the two types of State, *bourgeois* and proletarian, each is regarded as embodying the rule, or dictatorship, of a particular class which is the holder of political power. There is not, in Marx's idea, any such thing as a classless State, or any State which is not the embodiment of the ruling authority of a particular class. This is made abundantly plain in Marx's criticism of the Gotha Programme, and also in his manifesto, drafted for the First International, on the Paris Commune, and published under the name of *The Civil War in France*. The State, according to Marx, is simply the police power of an organised ruling class.

Secondly, Marx clearly envisages a period of transition from Capitalism to Socialism or Communism, during which there will exist a new form of State, based on the authority of the proletariat. This State will be, not the *bourgeois* State simply "captured" by the proletariat and applied to the ends of the proletarian Revolution, but an essentially new State made by the proletariat to serve its own revolutionary purpose. But the proletarian State will not be lasting; for the object of the proletarian revolution is to abolish classes and to institute a classless society. When this has been done there can be no room for any State at all, in the sense in which Marx uses the word. The State, which is by Marx's definition an organ of class-domination, obviously cannot remain in being in a society wherein all class-distinctions have ceased to exist. In such a society there will be no need or room for a State, in the Marxian sense. No organ will be needed to keep one class in subjection to another. Government will endure no longer: there will be left only the problem of administration. In a familiar phrase, "the government of men will give place to the administration of things."

It is, of course, above all on this part of Marxist doctrine that the political theory of modern Communism has been built up. Lenin's *The State and Revolution* is in essence a simple amplification of this view. At this point the divergence between the Social Democratic and Communist interpretations of Marxism is widest; and round it centred the bitter controversy between

Lenin and Kautsky as the outstanding theorists of the rival schools. In this controversy, there can be not the smallest doubt which side can rightly claim to be "orthodox," in the sense of basing itself firmly upon the writings of the master. Marx's conception of the State and of the transition was utterly plain and unequivocal. There is not the smallest question about the view he took. Lenin, and not Kautsky, said what Marx said. Kautsky was only continuing to say what the German Social Democrats so angered Marx by saying in the Gotha Programme of 1875. For Kautsky, and the Social Democrats as a party, had come to think in terms of the capture and democratisation of the existing State, and not, like Marx, in terms of its overthrow and replacement by a State of a quite different sort.

This, of course, does not settle the question whether Marx was right or wrong; for we are not accepting the view that anything Marx said or held must of necessity be either. But it is well to be clear before we approach the discussion of the merits of the case that, despite all the casuistry that has been used in trying to represent Marx as holding a different view, there is no uncertainty at all about his own words, either in 1848 or, much later, in 1875. On this issue, Marx was unquestionably a Communist, and not a Social Democrat.

What Marx's View of the State Involves

With this in mind, we can go on to examine rather more closely the implications of Marx's view. Whereas other schools of social theorists have usually defined the State in terms of political right, or obligation, and on the assumption of a common relation existing among all the citizens, or subjects, Marx defined it in terms of force. The State is, in his view, the political embodiment of a certain form of class-domination, corresponding to a certain set of economic relationships, which in turn arise out of a certain stage in the development of the powers of production. Accordingly, the State is, in Marx's theory, neither an association of citizens bound together in pursuance of a common purpose, nor a body of subjects owing allegiance to a common sovereign, but essentially a coercive instrument, standing for the power of the ruling class to punish all offences which threaten the established system of class-relations. Any State has, of course, other functions besides these; but the other functions are, in Marx's view, secondary. The fundamental purpose of the State, in terms of which alone it can be correctly defined, is class-coercion.

It follows from this that the forms of State organisation upon which Marxists chiefly concentrate their attention are those which most clearly embody this coercive character. Whereas other modern thinkers dwell mainly upon the existence of representative institutions, the extent of the franchise, the growth of the modern State as an instrument for the provision of common welfare services and for the protection of the weak against the aggressions of the lawless and the unduly powerful, the Marxists think of it chiefly as a set of institutions for the maintenance of the capitalist system of property-holding, for the punishment of subverters of the established order, and for the coercion of the proletariat to labour in the service of the capitalist class. The law courts suppressing "sedition," the police bludgeoning demonstrators or haling "dangerous agitators" to prison, and the armed forces standing ready to put down rebellion at home, as well as to fight in international wars, loom much larger than the legislative body in this conception of the State; and the legislative body itself—King, Lords and Commons, or whatever it may be—is thought of less as an authority for the passing of fresh legislation than as the authority under whose auspices the existing body of legislation has been enacted, to serve as the instrument of the existing dominant class. Emphasis is therefore laid rather on those features of the legislative machine which check or prevent radical innovation— the powers of the Second Chamber, and the Royal Prerogative— than on those which make possible the introduction of changes into the existing system of law.

This does not mean that Marx and his followers deny the possibility of securing progressive legislation from the capitalist State. On the contrary, Marx was well aware of the growth of such legislation; and all the programmes of the bodies which he led or inspired were full of demands for more. He believed it to be entirely possible to bring pressure to bear upon the capitalist State, and to secure social legislation by this method, at any rate at the stage of a Capitalism still advancing in wealth and prosperity. He believed, further, that the struggle for such measures of social amelioration formed, at that stage, a vital part of the training of the proletariat in solidarity and class-consciousness. But he did not believe that the cumulative effect of measures of this sort could be a change of system, or that such methods could be employed for the attainment of Socialism, or to any extent inconsistent with the maintenance of Capitalism as a working system. For such ends as the establishment of a new social order he believed an utterly different instrument to be required.

It is obvious that Marx's conception of the State was greatly influenced by the States of which he had, in his formative years, direct experience—especially by the Prussian State and by the French State under Louis Philippe and Napoleon III. He was for most of his life one of a band of exiles who could not live in their native countries because the "police State" was pursuing them; and the kind of State that he denounced as an organ of class-domination existed in his day over most of Europe. The States with which he was most familiar were not based, even nominally, on representative democracy and engaged in practically no welfare activities. Even in Great Britain, the franchise remained very narrow in the towns up to 1867 and in the country areas up to 1884, and there was hardly any social legislation except the highly offensive Poor Laws and a few Factory Acts applying only to women and children. The idea of the State as primarily a welfare agency had arisen in the minds of some social reformers; but no actual State of this sort existed or seemed likely to exist at the time when Marx formulated his theory. The States which he surveyed in the 1840's *were* instruments of class-domination, and little besides. They were at various stages of conversion from instruments of autocratic or aristocratic to capitalist domination; and the British State, despite the Ten Hours Act of 1847, was still mainly an agent of the alliance between aristocrats and capitalists which had been the outcome of the Reform Act of 1832. The Chartists were beating their heads vainly against the solid wall of opposition which it presented to all major working-class claims. There was, then, nothing surprising in the fact that Marx, in 1848, regarded the State as incapable of being used as the instrument of a voteless proletariat, and set out to devise a method of compassing its destruction rather than its reform.

Proletarian Dictatorship

This method was revolution, involving the complete destruction of the capitalist State, and the substitution for it of a quite different type of State made by the workers in the image of their own needs, as the instrument of a proletarian dictatorship. The establishment of this new State would involve not only the setting up of a totally new legislative authority, resting directly on the organised economic power of the working class, but also the establishment of a new proletarian judiciary and code of law, a new proletarian police and military force, a new proletarian Civil Service, both national and local—all under

185

the authority of a proletarian party organised as the representative agent of the new governing class. It was equally inconceivable to Marx that the Socialists should attempt to govern, after their victory, through a Parliament of the *bourgeois* type, and that they should leave the old civil service and judiciary in possession, or the armed forces and the police under their old leaders. He envisaged, at the very outset of the Revolution, the complete smashing and putting out of action of all the coercive machinery of the capitalist State, and the setting up in its place of a wholly new organisation, conceived throughout in accordance with the needs and interests of the proletariat organised as a ruling class.

The Civil War in France, in which Marx passed in review the successive phases of the Paris Commune of 1871, clearly brings out this point of view. When Marx praises the Commune, it is for destroying the institutions of the *bourgeois* State and establishing instead new institutions of its own on a definitely proletarian basis. When he blames, it is for not going far enough or ruthlessly enough towards the immediate goal of proletarian dictatorship.

Obviously, this view runs directly counter to the policy actually followed by the modern Social Democratic Parties of Western Europe. These parties, in the more advanced countries, set themselves not only to work for meliorative legislation, as Marx himself desired, but also to use the existing State as an instrument for the gradual establishment of Socialism by evolutionary means. They set out to capture the existing State with a view, not to destroying it as a whole, but to transforming it into a democratic State, by lopping off the incurably undemocratic parts of it, and by amending the rest under the influence of responsible government based on a fully representative Parliament elected by the entire people. That this was to be the method of Social Democracy was already plain enough in the Gotha Programme endorsed by both sections of German Socialists—the Marxists and the followers of Lassalle—in 1875; and that it was so was the gravamen of Marx's sweeping condemnation of the programme on which these two parties agreed to unite. For to his mind to think of the existing State as a potentially democratic body and a possible instrument of Socialist construction was in itself a complete betrayal of the Socialist cause.

The Social Democrats, for their part, were looking at the State in quite a different way. They thought they saw it in process of being transformed gradually from an engine of class-coercion into an institution for social service—a grand Co-operative Society of all its citizens. They thought of the widening of the franchise, up to the final establishment of universal suffrage, as making the State an essentially democratic body, within which it would become possible, by steady pressure and electoral success, to create the requisite system of responsible executive government. They believed that the anti-democratic powers of Crown and Second Chamber would not be able to stand out long against the popular will, and that law courts, police, and armed forces would become, by a process of evolution towards fully responsible government, the loyal servants of a triumphant democracy. The first step was to get the whole people the vote; the second was to educate the people to use the vote aright; the third was to institute Socialism by a series of evolutionary changes under the sanction of the popular will.

Marx utterly rejected this conception. To his mind, there was, and could be under Capitalism, no such thing as "the people," which he regarded as a mere figment of the *petit bourgeois* imagination. There were classes, contending for power, exploiting and exploited; but there could be no "people," because social solidarity could not exist within the framework of a capitalist society. If Socialists came to believe in the figment of "the people," and to base their electoral policy on an appeal to "the people," that, he held, would be the end of their chance of getting Socialism; for it would cause them to dilute their programme in order to win this mythical "people" to their side, instead of coming out plainly in support of a revolutionary attempt to substitute working-class for capitalist dictatorship. It would cause them to attempt to use the capitalist State as an instrument of Socialist construction, instead of setting out to smash it and build on its ruins a new proletarian State of their own.

The "people," Marx held, can come into being only within the framework of a classless society; for in his view, as long as States exist, classes exist, and social solidarity does not. The entire conception of evolutionary Socialism, as something that can be achieved by progressive modification of institutions under the auspices of a democratised parliamentary State, is therefore thoroughly un-Marxian, in the sense that it is in sharp opposition to what Marx said and thought. Socialism, Marx thought, would indeed come gradually; but Socialism, as distinct from mere social reform, could not begin to come until after the proletarian Revolution had been successful in establishing the proletarian State. The Marxian conception of "gradualism" was that of a gradual development of Socialist institutions and ideologies under the authority of a proletarian dictatorship.

187

There have been many followers of Marx who, admitting that this was Marx's opinion, have argued that he would not have held to it if he had lived on into the age of Social Democracy's parliamentary advance. The master, they have said, formulated his essential doctrines before the modern democratic State had come into being, or even into view, before the great growth of social legislation and redistribution of wealth through taxation, and before, save here and there, the advent of manhood or universal suffrage and popular education had created the possibility of a truly democratic electorate. They contend that, if he had lived on, he would have changed his views, and would have realised that the State was merely a piece of machinery capable of being used for the most diverse purposes, according to the ideas and class-affiliations of the persons placed in command of it by a more or a less democratic constitution. Surely, they say, it is undeniably possible to convert a majority of the electorate to support the Socialist Party, and for a Government thus returned to power to make what use it pleases of the machinery of State, so as to effect the Socialist Revolution by strictly constitutional means, and avoid all the dislocations and dangers which are involved in revolution and in the smashing of the existing State. What waste, to smash a perfectly good instrument, which has gone wrong only because it has been hitherto controlled by the wrong people!

This is, of course, the Fabian conception of the transition to Socialism, which profoundly influenced not only the German "Revisionists" at the opening of the twentieth century, but also their opponents who professed to remain true to the orthodox Marxian doctrines. It rests on a denial, not necessarily of the class-struggle—though it often comes to that—but of the idea that the State is to be regarded as essentially a class-institution, adapted to a particular sort of class-domination, and not adaptable for use in the interests of a different class or of a classless society.

As we have seen, this evolutionary conception is always defended by stressing the parliamentary nature of the State as a representative institution capable of becoming completely democratised. It is assumed that, in the existing State, the representative and democratic elements are in process of triumphing over the other elements, and will be strong enough, with the popular will behind them, to complete the extermination or subjection of these other elements—to destroy or democratise the Crown, the Second Chamber, and the judiciary and

188

magistracy, and to exact in the name of democracy loyal obedience from the armed forces and the police. This, however, is precisely what Marx believed to be out of the question. He held that these other institutions of the capitalist State would be strong enough to resist the process of democratisation, and at need to destroy the democratic elements, as they had done in the course of the counter-revolutions which followed the "Year of Revolutions," 1848.

Moreover, Marx held that, if the Socialists attempted to conduct their political action on the basis of an appeal to the "people," rather than to the working class, and of an evolutionary instead of a revolutionary programme, they would inevitably fail to create among the proletariat the will and driving force requisite for the winning of Socialism. For Marx, though he has often been wrongly accused of preaching a fatalist doctrine, in fact laid overwhelming stress on the need for creating among the workers a vigorous revolutionary consciousness, and believed profoundly in the educative influence of the day-to-day class-struggle in bringing this consciousness to maturity. A policy of social peace seemed to him to stand in open contradiction to the revolutionary aim of Socialism, and to be therefore inadmissible as a Socialist technique. It might be necessary at times to step back, and it might be exceedingly foolish to promote a revolutionary outbreak that could, in the circumstances, be nothing more than an abortive *émeute*, because it lacked the support of the working class as a whole; but Marx held as firmly as he held any of his doctrines that the basic policy of Socialists must be to develop the class-consciousness of the workers into a revolutionary opposition to the capitalist State, and to make no compromise with the forces of Capitalism or with the *petite bourgeoisie*, or with any other force that might stand in the way of this consciousness.

In effect, Marx held that the capitalist State, though it might make compromises with the claims of the workers and admit real social reforms as long as it continued to rest upon an advancing and prosperous capitalist system in the economic field, would be bound in the end to turn upon the workers, and to attempt to intensify exploitation, as Capitalism passed into a phase of decline and was no longer able to reconcile the encroaching demands of the workers with its own need for an expanding volume of rent, interest and profits. He did not believe that Capitalism would be successfully superseded until it had arrived at this impasse, which he thought to be much nearer at hand than it turned out to be. He held that it was the task of the Socialists to prepare the working class for the advent of this final phase of Capitalism, and in the meantime to keep clear of all forms of entanglement with the responsibility for the successful working of Capitalism. For he insisted that if, at the final hour of Capitalism, the workers should find themselves lacking the requisite revolutionary Socialist leadership, the means for achieving the transition to a Socialist economy would be fatally wanting.

The Social Democratic Parties, on the other hand, came more and more to assume that their sole tasks were to take advantage of the opportunities for the promotion of democratic reforms presented by the parliamentary system, while preaching Socialism itself as a more distant goal, and that the governing class would permit itself to be constitutionally superseded by the political party representing the workers, without either making any attempt to invoke against the advance of Socialism the non-democratic elements in the capitalist State, or resorting to any new methods of action designed to seduce a sufficient part of the popular electorate to render a Socialist majority unobtainable. They ignored the fact that the capitalist State possesses large authoritarian elements, and that these can be so used as to divide as well as forcibly to resist the proletarian forces. They tended to leave too much out of account the need of their working-class followers for immediate material victories as an earnest of the coming change of system, and to rely far too exclusively on an appeal to common humanity and reason rather than to an organised following consisting primarily of proletarians. Moreover, in pursuit of this policy of social reform leading gradually towards Socialism, they tended inevitably to find themselves committed by implication to keeping Capitalism as prosperous as possible pending their readiness to advance towards a Socialist system. This desire to keep capitalist industry successful was, however, in sharp conflict with the task of building up a revolutionary consciousness among the workers; for it involved damping down industrial unrest, and abetting resistance to working-class demands whenever they were liable to interfere with the successful operation of the capitalist system. A Socialist movement of this type found itself reluctant to attempt any rapid advance towards Socialism, or to encourage working-class unrest, because of the dislocation of capitalist enterprise which continuous frontal attacks upon it were bound to involve.

Thus, in face of Marx's clear-cut revolutionary doctrine, the orthodox Social Democrats were apt to find themselves engaged, not in attacking Capitalism, but in deliberately bolstering it up until they felt strong enough to make a real advance in the direction of Socialism. Nor was this policy, either as an electoral method or as a means of securing social reforms, without its advantages; for, on the whole, strange as it may at first thought appear, a larger fraction of the electorate was likely under ordinary conditions to vote Socialist at periods of prosperity than in adverse times, and it is certainly easier for a Socialist Party to press successfully for social legislation when trade is good. Under the conditions of adversity, the majority of the *organised* workers might be as ready as ever to support the Socialist cause through thick and thin. But such support was likely to be weakened in times of bad trade by defections from the Trade Union ranks; and Trade Unionism itself inevitably tended to be less aggressive, and more disposed to social peace, in times of adversity than when trade was good and employment plentiful and relatively secure. Moreover, bad times are apt to arouse cries for "national economy," of which the social services are usually the first victims. It was natural for the Trade Unions to long in bad times for the return of capitalist prosperity, which would enable them again to secure concessions and to increase their following by the winning of economic advances; and it was natural for a party dominated by Trade Union influence to be more concerned over restoring the conditions necessary for effective Trade Union bargaining and the improvement of social services than over building up proletarian consciousness even at the cost of aggravating the difficulties of Capitalism, and therewith multiplying Trade Union and political difficulties as well.

When, however, a Socialist party definitely devotes itself to an attempt to make Capitalism prosperous, in order to increase the bargaining strength and improve the immediate conditions of its own supporters, it is hard for it to avoid placing itself in the power of Capitalism. The conditions requisite for the restoration of capitalist prosperity may easily be irreconcilable with the simultaneous pursuit of a constructive Socialist policy. This contradiction arises partly because capitalist prosperity is largely a matter of capitalist "confidence"—confidence, that is, in the prospect of sustained profit-making, but even more because a further instalment of Socialism may easily undermine capitalist incentives without putting anything effective in their place.

A Socialist Government, if it pursues a Socialist policy, is committed to destroying as fast as it can replace them the very foundations on which the opportunities for capitalist profit-making rest. It can therefore hope to secure capitalist confidence only to the extent to which it is prepared to forswear Socialism, and can press on with Socialist measures only to the extent to which it is prepared to forswear capitalist confidence.

In this dilemma a Socialist party which is trying to rest on a wide basis of "popular" support rather than on a determined working-class following can all too easily be driven to preferring the confidence of the capitalists to an attempt to advance towards Socialism in the teeth of their opposition, especially if it finds itself faced by economic difficulties which may lead into a deep depression as a result of their want of confidence in its measures. It may hope by its moderation not only to reassure the more timid of its supporters among the middle classes, but also to command the assent of the Trade Union leaders by improving the conditions under which collective bargaining has to be carried on.

Where circumstances are favourable to capitalist prosperity, there is no reason why a professedly Socialist Government which follows a non-Socialist policy limited to moderate measures of social reform should not govern a capitalist country quite as successfully from the standpoint of immediate economic prosperity as a capitalist Government could, or why it should not at the same time secure some real improvements in popular welfare; for the inferior degree of confidence it is likely to inspire among the general run of capitalists will be offset by its greater success in maintaining full employment and industrial tranquillity. When, however, conditions are not favourable to capitalist prosperity, a Government of this sort is bound to find itself in a very difficult position. It cannot create capitalist confidence in the absence of favourable objective conditions: it dare not attempt Socialist measures for fear of provoking a crisis and estranging its own more timid followers: it cannot create favourable conditions for Trade Union bargaining, and so expiate its failure to make a constructive advance towards Socialism. It can, in effect, only dither, as the German Social Democrats dithered after the first World War, and as the second British Labour Government dithered from 1929 to 1931.

A Government so placed is lucky if it does nothing worse than dither. For, if the economic circumstances are sufficiently adverse, it is likely to be faced by a revolt among its own working-class followers, and to be compelled to choose, in the last resort, between acting as the policeman of Capitalism against its own adherents, and convicting itself of sheer failure to govern— unless, indeed, it is able and willing to revise its entire strategy and to come out boldly with a constructive Socialist programme. Even in that event its lot is not likely to be easy. It will be compelled to enforce many measures which, however necessary, will be unpopular with làrge sections of the people, including many of its own supporters; and it will be pretty certain to forfeit a proportion of the "popular" support with the aid of which it rose to power. Nor will it have prepared the workers for backing it up in an attempt to maintain its authority on a definitely Socialist basis. The sort of Government I have been describing is, in fact, unlikely to make the attempt: it is much more likely to break up in the course of an internal quarrel about the right course to pursue, as happened to the British Labour Government in 1931, and to be compelled ignominiously to resign and to hand over the task of bolstering up Capitalism to more appropriate defenders of the capitalist régime.

The Essentials of Socialist Policy

If this diagnosis were both correct and complete, it would follow that Marx was right, at any rate in one part of his contention—that is, in holding that no Socialist party can make a firm advance towards Socialism unless it bases its authority, not on the "people," but on a class-conscious and politically educated working class. It would also follow that a Socialist Government which sought to govern by gaining the confidence of the capitalists would be doomed to the complete stultification of its efforts. How can the capitalists be expected to feel confidence either in a Government of which the avowed and explicit intention is to supersede and dispossess them as rapidly as it can organise production upon an alternative basis, or in one which, in abandoning this objective, has in effect left itself without any constructive policy at all? Surely a Socialist Government in possession of the confidence of the capitalists is nothing less than a monstrosity. Either it does not really possess that confidence, or it is not really a Socialist Government.

This, however, is by no means the whole story; for we have still to consider the case of a Socialist Government which does from the outset make a real attempt to follow a constructive policy leading towards Socialism, and does not allow itself to be deflected from its purpose by the fear of a 'crisis of confidence' even in face of serious economic difficulties. Marx would have argued that such a Government, equally with the type just

193

considered, would be bound to fail, because a policy really leading towards Socialism could not in any event be carried through save on the basis of a revolution in the character of the entire State. He would have held that the Government's efforts would inevitably be sabotaged, not only by the capitalists in the economic field, but also by the civil service, the law courts, and all the undemocratic elements in the existing political and social structure.

No doubt, this is precisely what would happen if the State were, through and through, in all its elements except the one element represented by a Socialist Government resting on a Socialist parliamentary majority, as capitalistic as Marx assumed all existing States to be. If all the other parts of the State did without limit all they could to thwart and destroy the Socialist Government, the next step could be only either the fall of the Government without more than a show of resistance, or civil war. But can we say that all existing States that are not definitely Socialist would necessarily react in this way, or even that the capitalists would so react in all circumstances? I feel sure that, in the world of to-day, we cannot make such a generalisation. In Great Britain, for example, though it is true enough that up to a point the judges, the higher civil servants, the main bodies of employers, and the financial agencies will try to put spanners in the works of a Socialist Government, they will be restrained in doing this to the extent to which they believe that the Socialist policy has real popular support; and they will also be held back by fears that what they do will react upon themselves, either by weakening their support among the people or by ruining the industries on which their incomes depend. They will be held back especially if the country is in real external difficulties; for by prejudicing its position in the world they would be endangering their own, perhaps even more than they would feel it to be endangered by the Socialist Government's actual measures. Above all, if the Socialist Government were in office under a parliamentary system which involved before long a fresh appeal to the electors, and if there seemed to be a fair chance of turning it out, the capitalists and their allies would think twice before staking everything on an attempt to destroy by sabotage a Government which they could hope quite soon—and before it had done too much to overturn Capitalism—to evict in a strictly constitutional way.

Of course, I am not suggesting that the capitalists and their allies in the State machine will always be ready to behave in this accommodating way. They would be unlikely to do so, if they felt that accommodation would make their doom inevitable, whereas out-and-out resistance and sabotage offered them a fair chance of success. The sort of policy Marx advocated—involving the immediate destruction of capitalist State and power—would obviously provoke out-and-out resistance wherever resistance offered any hope, and even in some cases where it did not. We are, however, now discussing, not that policy, but the quite different one of attempting to construct Socialism by stages, using rather than destroying the existing State machine, wherever it can be adapted to the new purposes, and accordingly proceeding on the basis of an electoral and party system that leaves the way still open for the overthrow of the Socialist Government should a majority of the electors turn against it. I am not denying that such a policy *might* be resisted by violence and sabotage: I am denying the validity of any assertion that it always and necessarily would be.

The British Labour Government of 1945

In fact, it has not been,[1] in the case of the Labour Government which took office in Great Britain in 1945. Some sabotage there has been, especially in relation to foreign affairs. But most civil servants have carried out the spirit as well as the letter of their orders; most employers in trades not subject to early socialisation have worked in without resistance with the various Controls; the House of Lords has contented itself with pinpricks; and the defiance of reactionaries of most kinds has been confined to words. Yet this Labour Government did undoubtedly, during its first two years of office, carry through quite a number of real advances towards Socialism and a number of measures highly distasteful to the more reactionary part of British society.

I am not arguing now whether the British Labour Government of 1945 was too socialistic, or not socialistic enough, but only that it was socialistic in the sense that it did make a real start on the task of constructing a Socialist system. Those who accept the Marxian view of the State will no doubt retort by stating *a priori* that this cannot be so, because the existing State cannot be used for Socialist construction, which cannot be started until there has been a proletarian revolution. The plain answer to this is in the facts. The instalment of Socialism so far achieved[1] is admittedly small; but it exists; and the State machine itself has not been unaffected by it.

Of course this kind of gradualist Socialism requires that a Socialist Government shall keep capitalist institutions at work

[1] Up to 1948.

in every sphere which it is not prepared at once to take under its own operational control. Manifestly, it must do this; for the collapse of capitalist industries and services before the Socialists were ready to take them over would result in a dislocation of economic life that might easily leave the people to starve. This, however, does not mean that the Government is compelled to keep capitalist industry running by winning the confidence of the capitalists. Industry has somehow to be kept running without that confidence—that is to say, by making the conditions more unfavourable for the capitalist who closes his business down, or contracts its operations owing to his loss of confidence, than to the capitalist who does his best to maintain employment and output despite his dislike and distrust of the Socialist Government. This involves control, and, in the background, a knowledge that the Government is prepared to take over and operate any useful businesses which their owners may elect to close or to contract; and it involves further a well-considered economic plan for achieving the right distribution of materials, man-power, licences for necessary work, and so on, and for the maintenance of adequate inducements to capitalist firms to fall in with these conditions, rather incur the penalties of non-co-operation.

Must Revolution come First?

The pursuit of such a policy implies strong and authoritative Government, more amenable to pressure from a working class demanding higher wages and better conditions of employment than to clamour from other classes for less 'austerity' or more profits, but at the same time courageous and candid enough to tell its own followers what it is practicable to concede to them, and what not. It involves that the Government shall so act as to feel secure of solid backing for its policy from the greater part of the working class; and this in turn involves that the working class shall have been educated in advance to expect a Government of this forthright type, and shall have consciously helped to place such a Government in power. For the Government will be impotent to govern on these terms unless the greater part of the working class is prepared to see it through.

I am, then, questioning whether Marx was right in holding that any real Socialist Government would have to begin by revolutionary measures designed to smash entirely the *bourgeois* State, and at once to build up a new proletarian State of its own, before it could make a start upon a constructive Socialist policy. Marx's contention rests on denying that the conditions for such a policy as I have been outlining can exist. First, is it

196

possible to win a parliamentary majority, and so to capture control over the existing State machine, on the basis of a policy appealing directly to the proletariat rather than to the "people" as a whole? And secondly, even if this is possible, can a Government elected on such a programme successfully carry on its task without being compelled first to attack and overthrow those elements of the *bourgeois* State which are not directly amenable to conquest by means of a majority vote for the election of Members of Parliament?

Both these questions raise highly interesting and important points. On the first, it is clearly out of the question for the Socialists to secure a working majority in the "popular" Chamber by the votes of the manual workers alone. Even in highly industrialised countries they must, if they are to climb to office by constitutional means, with a clear majority behind them, attract a substantial number of voters from the black-coated proletariat and from various sections of the middle classes, including if possible the farmers. This, however, cannot be done if their appeal is limited to the Trade Unions, or even to the manual workers as a whole. They must find issues wide enough to enlist the support of other elements as well, and must do this without abandoning or diluting their essential working-class appeal.

This is by no means impossible, if the problem is tackled in the right way. For the appeal of a constructive Socialist policy does extend far beyond the manual workers, especially among technical, administrative and professional workers who can be made to see in Socialism expanding opportunities for the carrying on of their own types of service. It can appeal to the technician to see a chance of getting his industry rationalised, not for the purpose of contracting its output, but in order to enable it to pour out needed commodities in greater abundance. It can appeal to a good many administrators to see a prospect of straightening out the confusions and anomalies of the system within which Capitalism compels them to work. And it can appeal to a good many doctors to offer them the hope of a great crusade for the improvement of the health and living conditions of the entire population. Nor are the members of any of these callings necessarily deaf to the appeal of economic equality and of a classless society, though this appeal has to wage war in their minds with the more familiar counter-appeals of snobbery and of the desire to retain a superior economic status. Finally, it can appeal to farmers to be offered a secure market at a satisfactory price, on conditions which will leave them in

197

possession of their farms as long as they agree to follow the inducements offered them to produce what the Government regards as necessary in the public interest.

In these circumstances, everything depends on how the case is put. But it is a great mistake to suppose that the more moderately Socialists state their case the more convincing they are. For the evolutionary, or "gradualist," Socialist case can all too easily be presented so as to look like an advance confession of defeat, and to promise not Socialism, but only semi-socialistic interferences which are calculated to hamper Capitalism without setting anything else in its place. The more clearly constructive the Socialist programme is, and the further it promises to go with rapidity towards the positive construction of a Socialist system that will work, the more likely is it to appeal to those non-proletarian elements of the population which are most capable of acting as the efficient allies of the manual workers in putting Socialism into practice.

Capturing the State Machine

There is, at any rate in advanced industrial countries which have a strong tradition of political compromise, a real possibility of capturing the State machine, as far as it can be captured as the result of a parliamentary election, on the basis of a policy that is not merely social reform, but constructive Socialism. But what is the prospect that the capture of a part of the legislative and executive machine in this way will suffice to equip the Socialists with an adequate instrument for carrying their policy into effect? Clearly, the House of Commons, or "popular" Chamber, is not the whole State; and there are narrow limits, even in the most democratic parliamentary system, to the power of the "popular" House to govern in opposition to the remaining elements in the State.

In this matter, conditions differ widely from country to country. In the United States, where both Senate and House of Representatives, as well as the Presidency, would have to be captured in order to give the policy a start, the next obstacle to be encountered would probably be the Supreme Court interpreting a written Constitution which was drawn up on the assumptions appropriate to a pre-capitalist society of independent farmers and small-scale producers and contemplated a government authorised to act only within a very narrow field. In Great Britain, on the other hand, a Socialist majority in the House of Commons would have no written Constitution to deal with, but would come immediately up against the powers of the

198

House of Lords and the still extensive prerogatives of the Crown—to say nothing of the massive conservatism of a large part of the social structure. Everywhere the path of Socialism to political power involves much more than the simple conquest of a majority in the "popular" Chamber. It is bound to mean serious clashes with the elements in the State which are less susceptible to conquest by constitutional means.

A great deal, of course, would depend on the strength of sentiment and opinion at the back of an incoming Socialist Government. Were this to be evidently strong enough to threaten serious trouble if the Government were obstructed in the use of its constitutional powers, the hostile elements in the State would doubtless be disposed to hold their hands, and to await a convenient opportunity before taking action. But if they were left in possession of their authority such an opportunity would be certain to come; for, as omelettes cannot be made without breaking eggs, Socialism certainly cannot be introduced, either as a whole or by stages, without large dislocations of the social mechanism or without serious mistakes being made by the Socialists themselves. These dislocations and mistakes are bound to afford the hostile elements in the State their chances; and unless the Socialists are prompt to meet their challenge, or even to anticipate it by taking the offensive against them, there are likely to be large masses of disgruntlement and discontent on which the forces inimical to Socialism will be able to call.

That this is so is the substance of the Marxian case. The Marxists hold, in effect, that a Socialist Party, on assuming power,[1] ought to proceed at once to the complete disarmament of all State forces likely to be able to offer effective opposition to its policy, from Crown and Second Chamber to judiciary and police and the armed forces. This does not necessarily imply any complete change of personnel in these branches of the State; but it does involve the drastic purging of their leadership, and the positive elimination of any elements which cannot be successfully purged by less drastic methods. The German Republic, though it did something to alter the leadership and personnel of the Prussian police, paid dearly for its mistake in leaving the judiciary and most of the public services in reactionary hands, and for allowing the *Reichswehr* to be officered for the most part by extreme reactionaries, and developed in the heart

[1] Communists recognise, however, that in certain circumstances there may have to be a preparatory period of coalition government, which they will use in order to occupy as many as possible of the key points of authority, such as control of the police, and to do all they can to "purge" and disorganise the parties which are nominally their allies.

of the Republic as a potentially counter-revolutionary force, on which no Government of the Left could ever depend. On the other hand, both the Bolsheviks in Russia and the Nazis in Germany at once followed up their accession to power by a drastic purging and reorganisation of all the elements in the State that were suspect of hostility to their point of view. This process of *Gleichschaltung*, as it was called by the Nazis, was pushed to the extreme limit in every branch of the public services, and was also extended by them into industry, the professions, the Churches, and every form of private association which seemed to them important for the secure establishment of their political and economic power. More slowly, and by less sensational methods, the Fascists carried through in Italy a similar process of political purgation.

Socialism and the Parliamentary Tradition

In its more extreme forms, this method is certainly possible only under revolutionary conditions, and not for a Government endeavouring to govern on democratic lines. In most parliamentary countries, there is a powerful tradition hostile to what is known as the "spoils system," or at any rate definite limits are set by tradition and public sentiment to its use. As the name "spoils system" implies, this tradition is designed primarily to prevent corruption and jobbery within an established parliamentary régime in which rival parties govern alternately. It has relevance to a situation in which the change of Government involves a change of system that is meant to be permanent only on the assumption that the public officials, or most of them, will in fact be capable of adapting their conduct to a set of principles radically different from those on which they have acted previously, so as to serve as the executants of policies of which they cannot possibly approve unless they had been acting quite against their convictions before. So remarkable a feat of adaptability is possible in general only for subordinates, who have been accustomed to executing policies rather than to forming them. It is too much to expect of the leading civil servants, who have been used to wielding great powers of policy-making under a succession of Ministers shifting from post to post and in and out of office too fast to get any real mastery of departmental practices, and for the most part quite content to be run by their civil service advisers on all matters not under immediate parliamentary consideration. The tradition, however, of civil service 'impartiality' puts serious obstacles in the way of a Socialist Government making more than a limited number of changes in the personnel of its salaried advisers—the more so because it is of the very essence of the parliamentary system to leave open the return to office of the opposing party, and accordingly to assume that the rival parties are not divided by any fundamental difference of opinion about the proper constitution of the State. As long as this assumption can rightly be made, the "spoils system" is evidently an abuse; for it means the displacing of one group of persons by another on grounds not mainly of divergent policy but rather of sheer job-finding. When, however, the contending parties are fundamentally divided about the entire basis of government, it becomes impossible for either side to act on the assumption that the opposite party may soon return to office, and that nothing must be done to depart from a tradition which rests on an understanding that no Government will do anything that its successor will feel strongly impelled to undo. A Government which is really seeking to change not merely this or that special feature of social arrangements but the social system as a whole cannot possibly carry through its policy with the same instruments as its opponents would be content to use. Under these circumstances, some changes in the controlling personnel of the vital State services become indispensable to the carrying out of the Government's policy, and something which the opponents of the Government will be certain to denounce as a revival of the "spoils system" becomes unavoidable.

It does not of course follow that this process of displacement has to be extended over a wide field. For example, it may be true that the British Civil Service has developed in general so high a tradition of impartiality in carrying out the policies laid down for it by Ministers as to be capable of serving adequately a Socialist Government, subject only to a few changes in the occupancy of the leading positions in the key departments. This is, however, a wholly exceptional situation; and it is more than doubtful if the same can be said either of the judiciary and the local magistracy or of the leading persons in the armed forces or in the police. A Socialist Government, if it intended to carry through a really extensive Socialist policy, would have to find for the key positions executants who believed in such a policy, and would have to safeguard itself against the risks of sabotage in high places and of possible counter-revolutionary action. But it would not find the taking of these steps at all easy, in face of the powerful parliamentary tradition and the widely diffused public opinion against them; and in practice the attempt to establish Socialism by constitutional methods, before it had advanced very far, would almost certainly involve a great deal of compromise upon these vital points.

The whole question goes, indeed, much deeper than appears at first sight. As we have seen, the assumption underlying the parliamentary system is that there exists always an "Opposition," which is capable of supplying an alternative Government should the Government get into serious difficulties, or lose public support, and that this "Opposition" has enough in common with the views of the Government to make the party game of the "ins" and the "outs" a workable affair. This is, however, obviously an impracticable assumption when the rival policies differ in fundamentals. Under such circumstances, the aim of each side is bound to be the permanent exclusion from power of its opponents—and this, in relation to the parliamentary system, is an essentially revolutionary aim, which involves using power, however secured, to bring about such changes as will render the restoration of the displaced policy as difficult as possible, if not wholly out of the question. The existence of this dilemma of parliamentary Socialism may remain concealed during the earlier stages of the attempt to build up a Socialist system by evolutionary methods; for as long as the elements of Socialism introduced into the social structure are limited, it may be possible for a non-Socialist Government to take them over and operate them while pursuing a mainly capitalist policy. But the larger the element of Socialism becomes, the more difficult it is bound to be to alternate between Socialist and capitalist Governments; and beyond a certain point this alternation is surely bound to become quite unworkable. The point of impossibility is reached when the alternating Governments can no longer accept each other's doings as accomplished facts, but feel compelled to spend their main energies on undoing each other's work; for the consequence of such a situation is bound to be sheer paralysis of the social system, with neither the socialistic nor the capitalistic elements able to work efficiently, and with the whole population suffering a sharp upset in its living conditions. Peasants may be able to carry on under such circumstances: town-dwellers cannot. Urbanised civilisation requires strong and efficient government, and falls to pieces at once when such government fails.

I think those Marxists right who contend that, for the reasons just given, it is not possible to construct a Socialist system by means of an alternating series of Socialist and non-Socialist Governments, depending on a fluctuating majority dominated by a 'floating vote.' It is partly on the ground of this impossibility that Marxists rest their theory of the State, and their rejection of ordinary parliamentary action as the means of effecting the transition from Capitalism to Socialism. Such a change, they contend, is so far-reaching in its effects that, however it began, it is bound to develop into a revolution if it continues at all.

The Question of Revolution

The question, then, is whether the attempt to establish Socialism must in all circumstances begin as a revolution, or can begin as a constitutional assumption of political power, and then take on a revolutionary character in the actual process of carrying it into effect. The Communist view is that it must begin, as well as develop, as a revolutionary movement, and that it is, in nearly all countries, if not in quite all, bound to be accompanied by violence because of the violent opposition which the present governing classes are certain to offer to its advance. The opposing "left-wing" Socialist view is that, in countries equipped with powerful parliamentary institutions, the transition can and should begin as a constitutional movement, and thereafter develop into a social revolution under the ægis of the constitutional authority under which it has been begun. It is noteworthy that even Mussolini and Hitler made large use of constitutional forms in carrying through their several revolutions. Mussolini, indeed, began with the revolutionary action of the "March on Rome"; but thereafter he was careful to execute his policy as far as possible in formal consistency with the law of the Italian Constitution. Hitler actually came to power in the guise of a constitutional Prime Minister, at the head of a Coalition Government. Both used the Constitution, wherever it was usable, to give formal sanction to what were in essence clearly revolutionary acts and policies.

Hitler and Mussolini, equally with Lenin, were prompt, having assumed power, both to purge the State machine of all actually or potentially hostile elements, and, by their methods of government, to render as nearly impossible as they could the subsequent return of their opponents to power. Lenin, indeed, simply destroyed the old State and built up, in accordance with Marx's precept, a totally new proletarian State in its place; whereas both Mussolini and Hitler, aiming at less fundamental economic changes, and having the support of a large part of the upper and middle classes because they appeared as the destroyers of the working-class movement, preserved much more of the structure of the old State, and sought rather to make themselves completely its masters than to tear it up by the

203

roots. But even in Germany and Italy the changes in State structure went very far, and before long the Fascists replaced a large part of the old official hierarchies by instruments of their own, who could be relied upon to act in the spirit of the new totalitarian State. The Fascists, even where they preserved a shadow of parliamentary institutions, based their new systems on a decisive repudiation of representative democracy. The Russians, on the other hand, claimed to be making democracy real and effective for the first time, by giving it an economic basis. The claim of the Fascists and Nazis was that representative parliamentary institutions were not of the State's essence, but were a mere excrescence upon it. They sought to recall the State from its declension into parliamentary democracy to its historic character as an instrument of authority wielded from above; and they were able to build upon their existing States more largely than Lenin could precisely because this coercive and authoritarian character did exist in the States which they took over, even where it had been to some extent overlaid by the growth of parliamentarism.

We must conclude, then, that the extent to which a revolution needs to detroy the State, or can build upon it by a process of transformation rather than of destruction, depends on the relation of the aims of the revolution to the essential character of the State in which it conquers power. Lenin could not use the Czarist State, because its essential character was that of a military and aristocratic autocracy with aims utterly inconsistent with his own. Hitler could use the German State, though not without large changes, including the sweeping away of some of the elements of federal autocracy which it embodied, because there was much in it, inherited from the pre-war *Reich*, that could be adapted to serve his needs.

Can West European Socialists hope to use the States which now exist in their countries as instruments for the attainment of Socialism? The question is not easy to answer. Clearly the German Social Democrats failed to use the German State for this purpose, and were continually checkmated in such attempts as they did make to advance towards Socialism by the resistances generated within the State structure. Still more clearly, they cannot use the ruins of the Nazi State for this purpose, even if many of the controls which it established over private groups and corporations were fully capable of being turned to Socialist ends. For the Nazi State was essentially an aggressive nationalist State, which needed to be broken irretrievably, and was entirely unadaptable to pacific ends. German Communism, if it should ever come to

204

power, might make a new State resembling the Nazi State in many vital respects. But it would have to be a new State.

The case is different in the parliamentary countries—as long as they remain parliamentary. For these States, while they retain their essentially *bourgeois* character, do embody in varying degrees considerable elements of democratic service as well as elements of coercive capitalist authority, and have been "liberalised" to such an extent as to afford means of carrying their adaptation further by constitutional methods. If they can be seized and controlled, there are forces in operation within them that are consistent with the purposes which Socialists have in view, as well as forces making in the opposite direction. As long as these States continue to offer to the workers both certain positive services and a freedom of constitutional agitation, it is most unlikely that any frontal attack upon them will command general working-class support. Only where the constitutional States, torn asunder by internal dissensions and unable, because of these divisions, to cope with their pressing economic difficulties, seek to withdraw these real benefits and meet the protests against their withdrawal by curtailing the freedom of agitation, is the main body of the workers likely to join in a frontal attack upon them and to demand their supersession. Unless this impasse is reached, enough of their citizens are likely to rally round the parties which present themselves in constitutional guise, rather than behind any party which preaches the necessity for a thorough destruction of the existing State as the prerequisite of all Socialist (or Fascist) construction. For enough people are likely to hope for a continuity that will preserve without interruption those elements in the society as it is which they have learnt to value, while making away with those which are inconsistent with the changes which they desire.

Parliamentary Systems

There is, however, an important condition. Under the British parliamentary system the scales are weighted in favour of large parties, and there is a reasonable chance for a single party standing for Socialism to win a clear majority. As against this, a good many other electoral systems, especially those which are based on Proportional Representation, favour a multiplication of parties, and tend to involve government by coalition, on a basis of inter-party compromise. These systems are defended by some doctrinaire democrats on the ground that they result in Parliaments which accurately mirror public feeling; but they are also upheld by a great many people who see in a multiplicity of parties a powerful bulwark against major changes in social structure. It has always puzzled me that any Socialist in a capitalist country can advocate Proportional Representation: so plain is it that the struggle for Socialism requires a succession of strong Governments, with unified policies and with clear majorities behind them. Moreover, weak Governments, though there may be much to be said in their favour in tranquil conditions and when no major changes are deemed to be needed, are disastrous in difficult times, when great problems have to be faced. Nothing has contributed more to the political plight of France than the tradition of weak government, based on fluctuating party groups. The existence of a political system which encourages this tendency may make it impossible for Socialism to make any real progress by constitutional means, and may thus drive the main body of the working class over to a belief in the necessity of revolutionary action.

A new British Revolution at any rate can most naturally begin (as indeed it has already begun) in a strictly constitutional way, with an endeavour to amend, rather than end, the existing State, and to use it meanwhile as an instrument in the positive work of Socialist construction. But this way of proceeding might at any time be made impossible if the anti-Socialist forces, fearing the advent of Socialism by constitutional means, set themselves so to alter the structure of the State as to strengthen its authoritarian and anti-democratic elements, and thereby to make it less usable as an instrument of Socialist policy. In Great Britain, for example, if the anti-Socialists were to come back to power in a militant mood, a Conservative reform of the House of Lords might render quite impossible the execution of a Socialist policy within the limits of the Constitution; and in France, where the working of the parliamentary system is already most seriously threatened, the strengthening of the powers of the President demanded by General de Gaulle might have a similar effect.

Where the structure of the State is, or becomes, such as to exclude an advance towards Socialism by constitutional means, there remains for the Socialists no recourse save a resort to unconstitutional action. For this reason, many opponents of Socialism have been unwilling to support their more intransigeant colleagues' desire to put further constitutional barriers in the way of Socialist advance. They have entertained hopes of side-tracking a purely constitutional Socialist Government, and they have feared that the taking away from the Socialists of the chance of constitutional action for the establishment of a

Socialist system might lead to the development of a much more militant and dangerous Socialist agitation. But how long such moderate counsels will be listened to if the threat of Socialism is felt to be imminent, who can say? In both Italy and Germany Fascism provided the answer to constitutional Socialism by taking full power into its own hands, and by using this power both to render the State proof against democratic tendencies and to crush out remorselessly any form of organised opposition. Where this has been done, Marx's analysis comes into its own, as it does wherever any State is of such a sort as to be beyond the reach of lawful working-class or democratic pressure. For there is under these conditions no alternative to a revolutionary method as well as a revolutionary objective, and no means of carrying out a Socialist policy without first destroying the old State, and setting up a new State in its stead.

Where Constitutional Gradualism is Impracticable

I have been speaking so far mainly of States which possess, in a significant degree, the tradition of parliamentary government and of elections in which the spokesmen of rival parties are free to put their several cases, and the electors can go to the ballot without direct intimidation and with an assurance that their votes will be fairly added up. Where, as over most of Eastern Europe and in a good many other countries, none of these traditions exist, the situation is necessarily a good deal different. States whose Governments rig the elections to suit their convenience; where opposition leaders can speak out only under continual threat of arrest and liquidation; where all the main instruments of propaganda and intimidation are monopolised by the party in power; and where differences are tolerated at all only as long as they are regarded as harmless, evidently cannot be captured by the constitutional exercise of popular voting power. The only chance for an opposition in such States comes when the ruling groups fall out among themselves; and even then the result is more likely to be a *coup d'état* than a free, democratic election. Socialist parties under such conditions are bound to be either ineffective groups allowed to function because they offer no real challenge, or revolutionary bodies, employing underground methods as well as such open forms of propaganda and organisation as are permitted to them by the ruling powers. Social Democratic Parties, where they exist at all in such countries, are usually no more than middle-class reformist groups with some following among the skilled artisans and black-coated workers. The main body of the working class either remains unorganised, with occasional outbreaks of chaotic revolt against oppression, or comes under revolutionary leadership. That is why Communist Parties have been so easily able, with Russian backing, to liquidate or subordinate the other "left" parties in such countries as Roumania and Hungary, which have behind them no tradition of parliamentary give-and-take or of success in using the legislative machine as an agency for the furtherance of popular welfare. It was doubtless necessary in most of these States for the national Communists to have Russian help in order to establish their supremacy; but it is an entire mistake to suppose that, had this help been lacking, the countries in question could have settled down quietly to order their affairs in a parliamentary way. Parliamentary institutions, in any form in which they can be expected to work, cannot be simply planted upon a country which has no tradition adapted to them. They are a matter, not simply of paper constitutions, but of a way of life. They imply, for their successful working, both a habit of give-and-take among the legislators and parties and an administrative machine with some tradition of impartial execution of the orders of the Government in office, even against the private opinions of the administrative officials. Such traditions cannot be developed in a day or a year: they have to grow gradually. In the parliamentary countries, they have grown up under conditions of alternating party Governments divided only on a limited number of secondary issues, but united in their will to uphold the general structure of society without fundamental change. They have broadened down, in most cases, from aristocratic beginnings to responsiveness to successive accretions of electors and representatives drawn from wider social and economic groups; and they have become adaptable to changes which can be fitted in to the existing structure piecemeal, even if the cumulative effect over a period may be to alter substantially the ethos of the society. How far even these traditions of parliamentary government and adminis-tration are capable of standing the strain of any comprehensive attempt to change the economic foundations of society is a moot point. At all events, where in the absence of such a "liberal" tradition the mere forms of parliamentarism are introduced into a country accustomed to quite different political behaviour it is utopian in the extreme to expect that they can work as they have done, say, in Great Britain or in Switzerland.

Accordingly, whatever may be the position in countries which do possess "liberal" traditions, in countries which do not the Marxian conception of the State fits the facts very much better than the Fabian, or Social Democratic, conception; and it is futile to ask the Socialist Parties of such countries to behave as if it did not. There is in such cases no possible foundation for Socialist construction except social revolution; and the institutions set up on the morrow of the revolution will inevitably be ineffective unless they embody a large element of dictatorship. Socialist construction in Russia would have been quite impracticable except under the auspices of the Communist Party, or of some other party prepared to adopt no less authoritative methods. The same was true in 1945 over most of Eastern Europe; and anyone who denies this is merely kicking against the pricks of social necessity.

Marx, however, and Lenin alike advocated the dictatorship of the proletariat only as a temporary instrument, to be used for the purpose of consolidating the gains of the revolution and of laying firmly the foundations of the new "classless society" in which the State—that is, the proletarian class State—was to "wither away" as fast as it could accomplish its socialising mission. Neither Marx nor Lenin contemplated dictatorship, or any kind of authoritarian State machine or class-party, as permanent, or even, I think, as destined to endure for long. The present rulers of Russia still hold in theory by this doctrine, and look forward to the time when "the government of men" will give place to "the administration of things." It can, however, hardly be denied that the vision of the free, classless society has receded a long way, or that the dictatorship of the dominant party looks like being very difficult to do away with. For the present, of course, the leaders of the Soviet Union argue that it cannot be done away with, or even relaxed, because the countries in which the social revolution has occurred, however successful they may be in liquidating the counter-revolutionary classes and in "socialising" the minds of the peoples, are still confronted with the immense danger of counter-revolutionary war from the countries still under capitalist control, led and provisioned by the still massively capitalist United States. This danger is held to necessitate the maintenance of a dictatorial régime; and it may reasonably be doubted whether anything short of world-wide Communist victory would be regarded as removing it. For, as we have seen, Marx's theory of history and class rests on the idea of the entire human race following a single evolutionary course, and as destined to undergo a common social revolution extending over the whole earth. On the basis of this theory, dictatorship must continue at any rate until the social revolution is victorious everywhere, and thereafter until it has been everywhere consolidated by the socialisation of men's minds and attitudes, as well as of their economic and political institutions.

It is accordingly out of the question, as long as this theory is believed in by the rulers of any great country, to arrive at anything more than a temporary and provisional accommodation between those countries which are dominated by it and those in which it is rejected in favour of either Capitalism or Social Democracy. Truce there can be; for Communists, sure that the future is on their side, feel they can afford to wait when waiting is expedient. But the Marxian theory of the State and the revolution, echoed by Lenin and now erected into a universal dogma over a large part of Europe, utterly excludes any final compromise or sharing of spheres of influence. Such compromise can come, on any enduring basis, only if the dogma itself comes to be modified in face of a plain demonstration that world-wide conquest involves too great a task even for the self-confident representatives of the Marxian revolutionary tradition.

CHAPTER VIII

THE THEORY OF VALUE

Every theory of value I have ever heard of, with the single exception of the Marxian theory, has for its object the explanation of prices. But Marx's theory of value is so little a theory of prices that it is hard in the end to say whether it has any point of contact at all with prices. For it explains, or tries to explain, neither why prices are what they are, nor why they fluctuate; and such elucidation of these questions as Marx does attempt comes in quite a different part of his book from his account of value and has little relation to it. In face of this fundamental difference of object, it is not surprising that economists who persist in criticising the Marxian theory of value on the assumption that it is a theory of prices succeed in demonstrating, to their own complete satisfaction, that as a theory of prices it makes nonsense.

If the Marxian theory of values is not a theory of prices, what is it? If it does not seek to explain prices, what does it seek to explain? The answer is easy. It is an attempt to explain how labour is exploited under the capitalist system. It is a theory, not of prices, but of capitalist exploitation.

It follows that the Marxian theory of value is applicable only to capitalist societies, and does not apply, save in its one broad assertion that value is created by labour and by nothing else, to the process of value-creation under Socialism. Indeed, Marx holds, as we have seen earlier, that all social and economic theories are valid only in relation to the actual objective conditions which they are called into being to explain, and need re-making if they are to be invoked for the explanation of different social systems. Not only does the Marxian theory of value not explain prices at all: it seeks to explain value itself only within a certain limiting set of conditions.

Price and Value

But what is value, apart from prices? Up to a point, all economists recognise a distinction. But again the Marxian distinction differs from all the rest. To most modern economists value and price differ only in that price is value expressed in the dimensions of a particular currency—value in money form—whereas value is the quantitative exchange relationship between commodities as distinct from its monetary expression: 'x tons of coal $= y$ pounds of rubber $= z$ ounces of gold' expresses the values of certain commodities in equivalent form, whereas 'x tons of coal $= £z$' expresses the value of one of these commodities in the form of a price.

Many of the earlier economists saw a good deal more than this in the distinction between value and price. For they thought of the prices of commodities as moving continually up and down in the market under the fluctuating influence of supply and demand, and yet as having a constant tendency to return to a particular price which was regarded as more "natural" or "normal" than any other, and as being the price that would exist if the forces of supply and demand were in perfect balance. To this "natural price," or rather to the exchange relationship underlying it, many of the earlier economists gave the name of "value," or "exchange value," denying the name to the constantly fluctuating exchange relationships expressed in actual market prices. Of course, "values," in this more restricted sense, were not fixed, and were subject at any time to change as the conditions of production changed; but they were thought of as changing far less often than ordinary market prices, and for quite different reasons—though changes in them would affect market prices by their influence on the balance of supply and demand.

Economists who defined value in this way all held that the "values," and the normal prices, of commodities, as distinct from the day-to-day market prices, were determined by the conditions of supply. They gave, from Adam Smith to John Stuart Mill, many varying explanations of the manner of this determination—from the simple view which represented values, and normal prices, as depending exclusively on the "amount of labour" expended in the production of a commodity to J. S. Mill's more complex "price of production" theory. With the soundness, or unsoundness, of these various views we are not at present concerned: all that concerns us now is that they were one and all advanced primarily with the object of explaining prices.

Value, then, in non-Marxian economic writings, means either market price stripped of its specific monetary expression, or normal price, similarly stripped, and regarded as depending on the conditions of supply. Since all non-Marxian economists have in modern times dropped the conception of a normal price so determined—though vestiges of the ancient doctrine are often to be found in their writings—we can say that in modern non-Marxian economics value = the exchange relationship expressed in market prices.

Marx, however, began writing at a time when the earlier conception of the nature of value was still dominant among orthodox economists, and was indeed practically unchallenged. In 1867, when the first volume of *Das Kapital* was published, with its formal exposition of Marx's own theory of value, the position in this respect was not vitally changed. If Ricardo no longer dominated economic thinking, John Stuart Mill did; and Mill's theory of value was fundamentally only a modification of Ricardo's. Jevons and Menger had yet to propound their radically different theories: it was still generally assumed that values had to be equated to "normal" and not to "market" prices, and that normal prices were somehow determined by the conditions of supply, whereas market prices depended on the interaction of supply and demand.

Marx built his theory of value upon a critique of the orthodox theory of his own day. But, when he came to discuss prices, so far from seeking to show that there was any tendency for market prices to return to the level of natural or normal prices determined by the conditions of supply, he set out to demonstrate exactly the opposite—a point which his critics have almost unanimously ignored, and often bluntly denied in the face of Marx's explicit statements. Yet Marx's view of the forces determining prices is, in its essentials, nearer to the view held by modern economists than to that of the classical school. He held that prices are determined by the interaction of supply and demand, and that there is and can be under Capitalism no tendency for commodities to return to a level of prices corresponding to their "values" in the classical sense.

The Labour Theory of Value

This, however, has nothing directly to do with Marx's theory of value. For prices, in the Marxian system, are merely the means of realising value by the sale of commodities in a market, and value is regarded as coming into existence quite apart from prices as a consequence of the labour process. The orthodox economists of the Ricardian school had contended that the values, by which they meant the normal prices, of commodities were determined by the amounts of labour incorporated in them. Ricardo did not hold this doctrine in an unqualified form—for he modified it in order to find room for interest on capital—but he did make it the basis of his general theory of value. Marx took the doctrine over from the Ricardians, as he took the dialectic over from Hegel, in order to apply it to a quite different purpose and endow it with an utterly different meaning. For in Marx's writings "value" came to mean what commodities were really worth in consequence of the amounts of labour directly or indirectly incorporated in them, as something quite distinct from the prices which they actually fetched, or tended to fetch, in the market.

The Marxian theory of value begins in fact with a dogma— that, whatever may be the measure of prices, one thing alone— human labour—is capable of creating value. The productive powers of society consist of two elements only—men, and the things which are at men's disposal. These things consist in part of natural objects, existing independently of men's minds and wills, and in part of things which men have created by changing the form of natural objects. No productive power exists at all without being embodied either in a man or in a thing which men can use. But the things men use, as far as they are not mere natural objects, are products of men's activity in the past. They are products of men's labour, acting upon natural objects. Capital, then, except to the extent to which it consists of natural objects, is a product of human labour, is simply human labour in a stored or accumulated form. It is past human labour, stored up in things. But natural objects, merely as natural

213

objects, have no value. They acquire value only by being mingled with men's labour. Ricardo had, indeed, admitted that certain natural objects might possess a value, by which he meant a price, by virtue of their natural scarcity. But Marx, who does not mean "price" when he says "value," is under no necessity to admit this exception. Value consists, in his definition, of that which men add by their efforts to what is conferred upon them by nature. Defined in this way, value is clearly neither more nor less than a product of human labour; for no commodity can be more than a mingling of human activity with natural objects.

Of course, "labour" in this connection must be understood as including every sort of human activity in the field of production. It includes the labour of the brain-worker and the organiser as well as that of the manual worker who engages in the physical task of transforming matter from one shape to another or of moving it from place to place. No distinction is drawn at this stage between the different types of labourers, and no claim is made that the manual worker is more productive than the others. The claim is simply that nothing except human labour in some form can add value to the resources which are at man's disposal by the sheer gift of nature.

Stated in this way, and released from its entanglements with the question of prices, the proposition is one that cannot be denied. But there lurks in it an ambiguity, which Marx must be held responsible for failing to remove, though it was none of his creating. The ambiguity lies in the use of the term "value." Following the tradition set by Adam Smith and observed by the whole classical school of economists prior to Jevons and the Austrians, Marx distinguished sharply between "use-value" and "exchange-value." "Use-value," or "value in use," is simply the qualitative usefulness of a commodity considered as an object of human need or desire; whereas "exchange-value" is the measurement of its quantitative relationship to other commodities. In non-Marxian economics of the classical school, "exchange-value" corresponds to normal price, whereas "use-value" bears no relation to price. In modern economics, of the schools which regard prices as depending upon utility, the distinction between "use-value" and "exchange-value" disappears, and the qualitative difference between commodities is regarded as being transformed into a quantitative difference directly by means of prices. But, for the classical economists, this direct transformation does not take place. Nothing can be a commodity, or have an exchange-value or a price, unless it possesses use-value to make it an object of human desire. But this use-value is never regarded in a quantitative aspect: it is something which a thing either possesses or does not possess, and the amount or degree of it which a thing has is regarded as irrelevant to the determination of exchange-value or normal price, since these are thought of as determined by the conditions of supply and not by those of demand, which is treated as affecting only day-to-day market prices as distinct from values.

Now, when it is said that value can be added to natural objects only by human labour, is the reference to use-value or to exchange-value? In the sense in which the term "exchange-value" is used by Ricardo and the other members of the classical school, the statement is not true of "exchange-value"; for other things besides human labour can add to the price at which a commodity tends to sell—that is, to its value in the Ricardian sense. Monopoly, for example, can do this, whether it takes the form of cornering the supply of a particular commodity or means or production, or of a scarcity in the supply of the means of expanding productive activity. That is to say, under a system of private ownership of the means of production and private appropriation of the product of industry, the cost of capital as well as the cost of labour affects exchange-value, in the sense of normal price.

Ricardo saw this, and attempted to modify his labour theory of value in order to meet the point. According to him, the exchange-value of commodities depends primarily on the amounts of labour incorporated in them, including of course the labour indirectly incorporated *via* the materials of which they were made and the wear and tear of the machinery employed in making them. But allowance has to be made for the requisite inducement to the capitalist to apply his resources to production instead of consuming them, or in other words for interest on the capital used in industry at a sufficient rate to induce and maintain an adequate supply.

In arguing in this way, Ricardo was guilty, on the face of the matter, of a childish illogicality; for he was attempting to measure the values of commodities by the impossible feat of adding together the *amounts* of labour directly or indirectly incorporated in them and the *cost*, in terms of interest, of the capital employed in their production. But clearly an amount of labour and a money cost are incapable of being added together. This did not seem to Ricardo to matter, because what he was mainly thinking of under the heading of interest was the time over which certain quantities of stored labour (= capital) were being locked up in the process of production, and it seemed to him no less natural for this stored labour than for current labour to receive a daily or weekly reward. Moreover, Ricardo thought of the relative amounts of labour as in fact sufficiently measured by the wages paid to the different bodies of labourers, so that in effect the cost of capital was being added to the cost of labour in order to arrive at the value. John Stuart Mill made this explicit, by expressing the entire theory in terms of costs, or prices, in his "price of production" theory of value.

If, however, things other than labour enter into the determination of "value," in the sense of normal price, what becomes of the Marxian theory? It remains totally unaffected, because "value" in the Marxian sense is not equated to normal price. Thus the decline and fall of the classical theory of value, which has often been regarded as dragging down with it the Marxian system, does not in fact affect the validity of Marxism either the one way or the other. It is, however, most unlikely that Marx would ever have formulated his own theory of value in the way he did had he not been casting it into the shape of a "critique" of the classical Political Economy.

The ambiguity, however, remains. For the "value" which human labour adds to natural objects is surely, in its fundamental aspect, "use-value" rather than "exchange-value," and modern economists are surely right in contending that "use-value" as well as "exchange-value" has a quantitative aspect. However hard it may be to measure the utility of one thing against that of another, we are in fact constantly performing this miracle, not only in the demand-prices we assign to different commodities, but whenever we choose between things that are offered to us as alternatives, whether any question of a price arises or not. It may be objected that such valuations are purely subjective, unless and until they receive objectivity in the form of market prices. But the so-called "objectivity" of market valuations can be nothing more than the resultant of a number of private estimates, and cannot therefore be different in character from them. On the other hand, a valuation is not made any the less quantitative by being subjective.

Objective Value

Marx and the classical economists shared the desire to objectify value, so as to find in it some valid principles underlying the subjective valuations of the market. The classical economists sought to achieve this result by objectifying prices, as "natural" or "normal" prices underlying the actual day-to-day prices

216

arising in market transactions. Marx, on the other hand, sought to objectify not prices but in effect use-values, by transforming them into expressions of the quantities of human labour incorporated in various commodities. Thus, whereas for Ricardo "exchange-value" = objective price, for Marx "exchange-value" = objectified use-value. And again, for an orthodox economist of the dominant modern school, exchange-value = objectified use-value = price. But for Marx there is no equation involving prices in any form.

It may be objected to this view that there is no reason for supposing that the amounts of labour applied to the production of different commodities correspond in any way to the amounts of use-value which they possess. But there is. The rational object of all production is to produce use-values. If a certain amount of labour can be used in different ways so as to produce either a larger or a smaller amount of use-value, obviously the preferable use is that which will lead to the former result. Unless, then, the system of production is at this point wholly irrational, there will be a tendency to prefer the creation of a larger to that of a smaller amount of use-value, and therefore to distribute productive resources in such a way as to achieve this result. The classical economists obscured this truth by treating normal prices as depending exclusively on conditions of supply; for the influence of demand is in fact the means whereby the tendency to prefer the creation of a greater amount of use-value is made effective. But this criticism of the classical school applies much less to Marx, whose notion of "socially necessary labour" includes an explicit reference to the importance of the demand-factor in achieving this result. For, in the Marxian theory, not *all* labour, but only "socially necessary" labour, creates value. The "socially necessary" labour is that amount of labour which is needed to create a thing for which there is a demand. Labour which exceeds the necessary amount, either because the labourer is exceptionally slow or clumsy or because he wastes his time in making unwanted products, does not, according to Marx, create any value.

Marx's "value," or "exchange-value," is, then, neither the "exchange-value" of the classical economists nor that of their modern successors, but purely and simply objectified use-value. It is the real amount of objective utility which a commodity possesses as a result of the labour directly or indirectly bestowed upon it under a system which tends to distribute the available resources of production so as to maximise the amount of use-value.

Again it may be objected that, whereas this might be the tendency of a socialised system of production, it is emphatically not the tendency inherent in the capitalist order. But this too is a misapprehension; for Capitalism, as far as it functions successfully as Capitalism, does tend to maximise the creation of use-values. The misapprehension arises from thinking of objective use-values in an absolute, or ideal, instead of a relative and concrete sense. Objective use-values are relative to the objective situation in which they are being created, that is, to the valuations of the social system in which they exist. If the capitalist system appears, from an absolute or ideal point of view, to fall far short, even when it is functioning most successfully, of creating the maximum amount of use-values for the satisfaction of human needs, that is because the object of Capitalism is not the satisfaction of all human needs in proportion to their urgency from an ideal standpoint, but the satisfaction of some needs—of the needs of those persons who are in possession of purchasing power, in proportion to their possession of such power—in preference to others. Capitalism, in other words, has its own scheme and calculus of "use-values"; and its success in maximising "use-values" must be judged in relation to this calculus, and not to any ideal standard.

It is, of course, true that in practice Capitalism often falls far short of success in living up to its own standards. It is compelled, as a condition of survival, to make concessions to standards which it does not accept—witness the growth of the social services and of industrial legislation and Trade Union bargaining. And it has its breakdowns, when it not only throws millions of workers out of work and wages, but also makes the capitalists themselves go short of their anticipated returns. But that is only to say that Capitalism does not work wholly according to capitalist desires, or as a perfect Capitalism would work. Assuredly it has, through all its ups and downs, a tendency so to distribute productive resources as to maximise the creation of the objective use-values appropriate to the desires and needs of a capitalist society.

We can, then, regard Capitalism as tending to maximise objective use-values in a capitalist sense: and we can equate this objectified use-value with "exchange-value" in the Marxian sense. But why does Marx choose to call it "exchange-value," at the cost of getting it confused with the quite different "exchange-value" of the classical economists?

In one sense he does not call it "exchange-value," but rather simply "value," which is manifested only in the exchange relationship. His point here seems to be that things of different sorts assume a quantitative and comparable character only in their exchangeability, apart from which each use-value remains a thing apart, quite without ascertainable relation to any other. This view is based on the sharp distinction drawn between use-values and exchange-values by all the classical economists from the time of Adam Smith, and discarded only by the economists of the late nineteenth century. If Marx had been able to advance beyond his time and to think of use-values as quantitative, some of the most confusing parts of the opening chapters of *Das Kapital* need never have been written.

The Source of Value

The truth is that Marx's "value" is not really exchange-value, but something radically different, drawn directly from a realistic analysis of the conditions of production. There is at any time at men's disposal a limited supply of energy for working upon the available non-human resources of production. The using up of any part of this energy in the making of particular goods or the rendering of particular services leaves so much the less available for all other uses. It involves a transformation into particular use-values of a part of the available supply of use-value-producing energy. This energy is the source of the use-values generated by its consumption: it alone has the power to create value. But clearly it can be so used as to create either a greater or a less amount of use-value; and the object must be, within the limitations stressed earlier in this chapter, to employ it to create as much as possible. Capitalist society uses the price-system as the means of bringing about this optimum distribution of productive resources, which in a monetary economy presents itself in the guise of the distribution that will create the greatest sum of money-values. This optimum is however only relative: it is the optimum for a society which accepts money-value as its standard. Marx seeks to look behind the money form to the real value-creating resources of which it is necessary to arrange the distribution; and he finds these resources to be neither more nor less than the available supply of human labour. Accordingly, he proclaims that human labour is the sole source of the power to create value.

But, it may be objected, the value which is created is the result of using up, not only part of the limited supply of human labour, but also part of the no less limited supplies of available materials and instruments of production. In what sense can it be maintained that the labour which is used up creates value, whereas the materials and instruments of production do not?

It is, of course, true that animals and plants, as living beings, have the power to create. A sheep creates wool, and a tree leaves. Even the earth itself creates one thing out of another, when it gradually converts other substances to coal, or, with the aid of rainfall and sun, causes crops to appear. But these acts of creation belong to nature, and are not of man's making. They are the forces which are available for man's use; for animals and plants, as well as lesser forms of organic matter, are by mankind relegated to the world of "nature," and are set in contraposition to man as a creative agent. Men work upon animals and plants, as well as upon the earth itself, to make values. The values, when they are made, belong to men. The sheep creates wool, and the tree fruit; but men, in appropriating these gifts of nature to their own use, give them value.

Marx's answer, therefore, is obvious. Materials and instruments of production and even animals and plants are, from the economic standpoint, passive things, which can create no values. They can doubtless embody, and transfer to the commodities which they are used to make, such values as they possess for men; but they are clearly incapable of being themselves the creative agents of additional values. Mere things can never create values: that is the prerogative of human beings.

If, then, the materials and instruments of production cannot create, but can only embody or transfer, values, it is left to inquire whence they have got the values which they are able to embody or to transfer. They get their values, Marx answers, from being themselves products of previous labour, each embodying the result of a past using up some of the limited supply of this sole source of value. It is true that in each case we come ultimately to some element which is not a product of labour, but a part of the natural resources available for men's use. But in developed societies it is usually impossible to disentangle even in the rawest materials that which is the gift of nature from that which is the product of man's past labour upon natural objects. Marx does not deny that natural objects, even if no human labour has been spent upon them, can, where their supply is limited, have a price—an exchange-value in the classical sense. He does deny that they can possess value in his sense; for value in his sense *is* simply the character of being a product of labour.

But, non-Marxists object, the using up of a scarce[1] natural

[1] "Scarce," in this context, of course, means simply limited in supply.

object or of a scarce product of past labour is just as much a subtraction from what is left for all other uses as the using-up of a part of the available supply of labour. Surely then the owners of materials and instruments of production contribute by allowing them to be used in production just as much to the creation of value as the owners of labour-power; and if value means exchange-value, in the sense of normal price under capitalist conditions of exchange, of course they do. For it is the entire principle of Capitalism to distribute the product of industry on precisely this assumption. But it is a very different thing to say that materials and instruments of production create value, and to say that *the owners* of these things create value. The first statement is open to dispute because it attributes a creative property to mere things; the second is wrong because it assumes that the fact of ownership can be in itself a source of value. Ownership is not a creative act, but a claim to share in the results of the creative acts of others. It is easy enough for a social system to exist in which the ownership of things is regarded as conferring a title to share in the product of industry, or even one—slavery—in which the ownership of men confers a similar title. But no social system can make either things or the fact of ownership into positive agents of creation. The fact that ownership confers a recognised claim to appropriate things of value does not constitute the owner a creator of value, though of course he may be such a creator if he works as well as owns.

There is, then, no inconsistency between the recognition that all the costs of production enter into prices, whether they arise out of the payment for labour or the claims of ownership, and the contention that human labour alone can be creative of value, because it alone is the using up of a scarce *active* agent of production. On the basis of Marx's theory, the amount of potential value in any society is simply the amount of labour, including the surviving products of past labour, which is at that society's disposal: the amount of actual value is that which is created by the actual expenditure of this labour. The Marxian theory of value is a theory, not of prices, but of the social distribution of the resources of production.

The Amount of Labour

At this point, objection is taken to Marx's theory on the ground that there is in practice no way of measuring the amount of labour. Labour is of many different sorts and qualities. An hour's labour of one man is not so good as an hour's labour of another, even within a single trade; and there is the greater difficulty of comparing labour of very different kinds. If we had to deal only with one kind of labour, we could doubtless express quantitatively the difference between the productivity of a good and bad plumber, or cotton weaver, or electrician, or perhaps even bank manager or writer of books on economics—though the two last would present a problem. But how are we to compare quantitatively the labour of the plumber with that of the weaver or the bank manager? The differences are here surely qualitative, and not quantitative; and no process of reasoning can reduce them to quantitative terms.

To the orthodox economist, this problem presents no difficulties; for he solves it in exactly the same way as he has already solved the problem of quantitative comparison between different commodities. He compares the labour of the plumber and the bank-manager by comparing their remuneration, which he assumes to coincide with their productivity of value. But this method is not open to the Marxist, who is setting out to measure the productivity of labour in terms not of exchange-values in the classical sense, or of prices, but of value in the Marxian sense—that is to say, directly in terms of quantities of labour. Marx attempts to meet the difficulty by invoking his own form of the subsistence theory of wages, or rather a conception closely akin to it. The respective values of different kinds of labour coincide with the values which it is necessary to use up in order to produce a sufficient supply of each kind. If more values must be used up in order to produce a bank-manager, or rather a unit in a sufficient supply of bank-managers, than to produce a unit in a sufficient supply of cotton-weavers, the difference in the real unit costs of production is the measure of the difference in value.

I find this explanation unconvincing—as a complete explanation of the problem. It would be valid only if all kinds of human skill and productivity were producible at will, just as most commodities are producible, by an appropriate real expenditure of materials and means of production. It is valid, to the considerable extent to which this is true of the various kinds of technical competence—for skilled manual labour of many sorts as against unskilled labour, for example. But it ceases to be valid for any sort of skill or competence that men owe to their original endowment of mind or body, or to influences that cannot be brought within the field of commodity production, or multiplied at will. This is of course precisely the same problem as presents itself in the case of naturally scarce materials or sources of energy which cannot be reproduced at will. Probably Marx would have been prepared to accept this limitation, and to answer that he was speaking of labour-power only in its ordinary forms, as reproducible at will by the appropriate outlays.

Within this limit, Marx's explanation is clearly valid. To the extent to which all labour-power is the product of an appropriate real expenditure of the means of life—as to some extent all labour-power is bound to be—the using up of any part of it is in effect the using up of the commodities required for its production and maintenance. Thus, a decision to erect a power-station that calls for the labour of a thousand skilled mechanics for a year is, quite apart from the question of the materials and plant required, a decision to use up more productive power than a decision to build a road with the aid of a thousand less skilled workers for the same period. The Russians, faced with an acute shortage of skilled labour, are to-day very conscious of this difference in making their successive Five Year Plans; and both Great Britain and other belligerent countries became acutely conscious of it under the impact of war. We remain conscious of it to-day: it is indeed felt in capitalist fully as much as in Socialist countries whenever there is a shortage either of labour in general or of a particular kind of skilled labour. It arises, however, equally for the time being whether the form of labour of which there is a shortage is or is not capable of being reproduced by additional expenditure on training and education. For these things take time, even if there are workers available to be trained. It is not, however, possible to contend that the "value" of all labour-power depends on the amount of the products of labour required for its production and maintenance; for clearly labour-power, when it has once been produced, has a productive quality which exists irrespective of the nature of the forces which produced it.

Value and Expenditure

It would have been better, I think, if Marx had defined value not as the quality of being a product of labour, but rather as that which arises out of the expenditure of any scarce agent or instrument of production. This would not have upset his vital contention that value can be *created* only by positive human agency, and that things have the power only of transferring, and not of creating, value. But it would have enabled him to recognise that scarce natural objects can possess value apart from any contribution added to them by human labour, simply because they are scarce, and that forms of human labour-power which

223

are not reproducible at will have a value which cannot be measured in the same terms as the value of ordinary acquired technical skill. Such a recognition would in no way have weakened Marx's argument, or have diminished the force of his contention that all values, however embodied, are ultimately social, in that they depend on the objective social situation in which they exist.

We can now come back to our question about the possibility of measuring the amount of available labour-power. The analogy of "horse-power" has often been invoked in this connection—by Robert Owen, for example, in his *Report to the County of Lanark*. We measure the power of machines in terms of this abstract unit of mechanised energy: why not employ a similar unit for measuring the power of human labour? The analogy does not hold; for the thing that horse-power is most obviously unable to measure is the power of actual horses.

If we could assume, with the classical economists, that things tend to sell at their values and that labour-power, which is bought and sold as a commodity, tends to sell at its value, so that the wages actually paid to different workers can be taken as tending to measure their varying productivities, we should have in wages a common standard for measuring the amount of labour. But Marx, as we have seen, explicitly denies that commodities do tend to sell at their "values" in his sense of the term, that is, at prices corresponding to the amounts of labour incorporated in them. Are we, then, to conclude that wages are of no help in measuring one kind of labour against another, or that labour-power differs from all other commodities in that it alone does tend to sell at its "value" in the Marxian sense?

Marx, I believe, did hold that labour-power possesses this exceptional characteristic. In order to understand why, we have to inquire why he held that other commodities do not tend to sell at prices corresponding to the amounts of labour incorporated in them. The answer is that this lack of correspondence is due to what Marx called the different "organic composition of capitals" in different branches of production. If all commodities were produced under identical conditions, with a precisely equal mingling of labour-power, materials and instruments of production, they would all tend to sell at their values in terms of the amounts of labour incorporated in them. But in fact the conditions of production differ widely from one branch of industry to another. One industry is highly mechanised, and uses up a great quantity of machinery in proportion to the amount of labour which it employs; while another industry

224

relies far more largely on manual labour, and requires comparatively little fixed capital. Moreover, even when two industries mingle labour-power and machinery in equal proportions, one may involve a far greater lock-up of capital than another, because it uses more, or more costly, raw materials, or involves a longer period of turnover before the outlay can be recovered. If the prices of commodities normally coincided with the amounts of labour incorporated in them, it seems at first sight as if, on Marx's theory, it would always pay better to employ much labour and little machinery, because a machine can only transfer to the product a value which it already possesses, whereas labour alone has the power to create an additional value. In that case, technical progress would never arise under Capitalism, because it would always be against the interest of the capitalist to displace labour by machinery. Which is absurd; for notoriously Capitalism has thriven upon technical progress, and has been an active agent in forwarding the mechanisation of industry.

Surplus Value

Yet it does seem at first sight as if the truth of the Marxian theory of value carried with it the implication that it should pay better to spend money on that which possesses the power to create value than on what does not. According to Marx, the entire source of capitalist profit, and also of rent and interest under Capitalism, is to be found in the exploitation of labour. Profit, rent and interest together, with certain other elements which need not concern us now, Marx calls by the collective name of "surplus value," or rather he regards "surplus value" as forming the fund from which profit, rent and interest are entirely drawn. This "surplus value" consists wholly of the difference between the value which labour has the power of creating and the value, called by Marx the "value of labour-power," which the capitalist has to pay away to the labourer in return for his service. Why this difference exists we shall have to inquire later; at present we are concerned only with the point that, if surplus value does arise entirely from labour, and if the object of capitalists is to appropriate as much surplus value as possible, it appears as if they ought greatly to prefer employing the labour which possesses this magical property to laying out their money on machines which can only transfer to the product the value which they already possess as the outcome of earlier labour processes.

The Distribution of Surplus Value

Marx's answer is that surplus value constitutes a fund, divisible among all capitalists, but not accruing directly to the particular capitalist in whose service it is brought to birth. All capitalists are in competition one with another to secure as much of the total amount of surplus-value as they can; and the system of prices is the means whereby the available amount of surplus-value is shared out among them. The share which each gets, *qua* owner of capital, tends to correspond to the total amount of capital which he embarks in production, irrespective of the ways in which the capital is expended as between the purchase of labour-power and of other requisites of production. For, if this were not so, capital would obviously flow in undue measure, in relation to demand, towards those branches of industry which offered the opportunity of appropriating the largest profits. The effect of this would be to depress, through relative over-production, the prices of the goods produced in these branches of industry, and so to reduce the profits on the capital embarked in them. Thus, the ebb and flow of capital from industry to industry in search of surplus-value tends to bring about an equalisation of the expectation of profit in all branches of production. But this process is wholly inconsistent with any tendency for commodities, except those which happen to be produced with precisely the average organic composition of capital and at precisely the average rate of turnover, to sell at their values in terms of the amounts of labour which they embody.

Commodities would tend to sell at their values if they were all produced under precisely the same conditions by capitals of the same organic composition. But they are not. On the other hand the commodity, labour-power, does tend to be produced under conditions in which differences in the organic composition of capital do not affect its production to any significant extent. Accordingly, Marx can say that labour-power does tend to be sold at its value, though other commodities do not, and that differences in the wages paid to different kinds of workers do tend to reflect real differences in the values of different kinds of labour.

This seems to be the view underlying Marx's argument. Appreciation of this point helps incidentally to clear up a problem in Marx's presentation of his case that has puzzled many Marxian students. Why does Marx, in the first volume of *Das Kapital*, so often speak as if commodities did tend to sell at their values, whereas such a view is plainly inconsistent with his case, and he makes it abundantly clear later on in his book that no such tendency can in fact exist? The answer is that, in Volume I,

Marx is concerned chiefly with the conditions governing the sale of labour-power, which he does hold to take place normally at its value, and he does not want to complicate his argument at that stage by introducing considerations more appropriately to be treated when he is dealing with questions of profits and prices. He does not assert that commodities do tend to sell at their values: he only implies the existence of such a tendency when differences in the organic composition of capital are left aside.

To the extent to which labour-power tends to be bought and sold at its value, in the Marxian sense, apart from day-to-day fluctuations in its price, the wage-system, as a particular manifestation of the pricing process, does serve as a valid measure of the amount of labour, and does establish a quantitative measure for labour of qualitatively different types. Wages thus appear to be unlike all other prices under the capitalist system, in that they tend to be a valid phenomenal expression of real values.

The Source of Profit

If, however, "labour" does tend to be sold at its value, whence can capitalist profit arise? Marx is at pains to show, in opposition to certain earlier anti-capitalist writers, that profit cannot arise out of any general tendency for capitalists to sell commodities for more than they are worth. Every bargain has two sides: it involves a buyer as well as a seller. If, then, things tended to be sold for more than their values, it would follow that they tended to be bought for more than their values as well. Conceivably the producers might in this way cheat the consumers; but this would involve the capitalists tending constantly to cheat themselves. For they spend in one way or another what they get; and presumably they would tend to lose as buyers whatever they stood to gain as sellers.

Marx concludes from this that, on the average, things must tend to sell at their values—a statement which has often been misinterpreted as implying a tendency for each class of goods to sell at its value. In fact, this is not implied at all, but only that on the average of all commodities values and prices must balance. As the sum of values must be equal to the sum of goods and services available for purchase, and the sum of prices must be the aggregate price of the entire supply, it is clearly out of the question for the two to be different magnitudes. In the aggregate, things must sell at a total price expressing their total value; for, whatever the total of prices is, it can express nothing except this total value. It is, and must be, the money-name of the total value that is bought and sold.

Capitalist profit cannot, then, be the result of over-charging; for, if it were, the total of profit would be nil, as each gain would be balanced by an equivalent loss. It may be objected that the capitalists might still make a net profit at the expense of the wage-earners, by selling them things at too high a price. But Marx would reply that any attempt to do this would be bound to lead to a rise in money-wages, which are finally no more than the money-expression of the real values of the various forms of labour-power. The labourer's real wage is the quantity of goods and services which represents the value of his labour-power; and the capitalist has to pay him, apart from market fluctuation, enough money to buy this quantity of things, whatever they may cost. If, then, the capitalists tried to cheat the labourers by overcharging them, the effect in the end would be to raise money-wages so as to counteract the capitalists' gain.

We come back, then, to the original difficulty. If (*a*) the sum of commodities cannot be sold for more than its value, (*b*) labour-power tends to be sold at its value, (*c*) labour is the sole source of value, whence can capitalist profit arise? The Marxian theory of surplus value is an attempt to explain this paradox. In order to master Marx's explanation, it is necessary to understand the distinction which he draws between "labour" and "labour-power." The thing which the labourer has to sell, and is compelled to sell in order to supply himself with the means of living, is his "labour-power"—his power, by working upon things, to create value. This labour-power—and not, as under slave-systems, the labourer himself—is a commodity; and its "value" is determined in the same way as the "value" of other commodities, by the amount of "value" that is used up in its production. But "labour" itself, when it is actually being expended in the creation of value, is not a commodity; and the value of the product of labour is by no means the same thing as the value of the labour-power which is expended in making the product. The difference between these two values is what Marx calls "surplus value."

In plainer terms, the capitalist has to pay the labourer as wages whatever is requisite in order to produce and maintain an adequate supply of the type of labour-power that is in question. But the labourer sells, in return for his wage, his entire power to create value, subject only to such limitations as are involved in the terms of sale. Normally this means that the labourer produces more than is needed for his maintenance, in other words, that the value of his product exceeds the value expressed in his wage. The capitalists, Marx says, get their

228

profits, and the landlords and money-lenders their rent and interest, out of this difference between the value of labour-power and the value of the product of labour. This, as we have seen, is "surplus value," and the pricing process is the means by which it is distributed among the various capitalist claimants to profit, interest and rent.

This allegation that the entire capitalist system rests upon the exploitation of labour is the focal point of Marx's economic doctrine; and it therefore deserves the closest scrutiny. It appears, in the first place, to involve a strict adherence to a form of the Subsistence Theory of Wages; for, if workers can receive wages in excess of what is needed for their maintenance, what certainty is there that Capitalism will be able to exploit them at all? May they not, by improving their bargaining strength, so raise their wages as to absorb the entire surplus value into their own remuneration?

The Subsistence Theory of Wages

Let us be clear, first of all, what the Subsistence Theory of Wages is. In the form in which it appears in Malthus, it is bound up closely with the question of population. Wages tend to a physical subsistence level because as soon as they rise at all above this level more children are born, or survive, and the supply of labourers is before long so increased that their competition for work forces wages down again to subsistence level. On the other hand, wages cannot fall for long below this level because, if they do fall below it, population is before long so reduced, by fewer births or by more deaths, as to bring them up again because of the shortage of labour. In Ricardo, the substance of this doctrine remains; but its severity is modified so as to allow more room for the recognition of conventional standards of living. Population is still regarded as the chief factor in keeping wages at or about subsistence level; but it is recognised that this level itself can change if, in an advancing society, the growing demand for labour keeps wages above the old subsistence level long enough for the labourers to incorporate into their established expectations a higher standard of living, which will thus become the new minimum needed to induce them to breed a sufficient supply of workers possessing the requisite qualities of strength and skill. Of course, in a declining society these factors would work the other way round, so as to reduce subsistence levels when the supply of labour fell off less rapidly than the demand for it.

In Marx's version of the Subsistence Theory of Wages,

insistence on the conventional element in the subsistence standard becomes much stronger. The attempt to base the theory on the Malthusian dogma about population is abandoned; and so is the tendency of wages to subsistence level, in any purely physical sense. All subsistence levels are treated as relative to a particular time and place, that is to say, to a conventional standard of living. The point to which wages tend is, then, not that which will just suffice to keep the labourer in health and physical energy, but that which, given the labourer's own state of mind and expectation of living conditions, will in fact induce him to give labour, and to reproduce supplies of labour of different kinds, in the requisite quantities and qualities to meet the capitalists' demands. If the established wage-standards are too low to induce the labourers to do this, wages will have to rise, and the higher wages will then be incorporated in a higher subsistence standard.

Of course, it must be understood that, in Marx's sense, the wages which tend to subsistence level are not merely those of the least skilled and worst-paid labourers, but equally those of the better-paid workers. For the subsistence wage is the wage needed to secure an adequate supply of any given class of labour, and the higher equally with the lower wage-rates fall within this definition. A subsistence wage, in the Marxian sense, is in fact little different from the wage fixed by the forces of long-period supply and demand for the commodity, labour-power, in any of its specialised forms. As we have seen, Marx holds that, as labour-power tends to sell at its value, the differences between the wages of the various kinds of workers tend in fact to coincide with the differences in the real costs of producing them in the necessary quantities. But the "real cost" of production of the labourer includes a psychological element; for it depends in part on the labourers' own estimates of what they are worth.

In these circumstances, does not any wage that is paid under Capitalism, unless it is due to quite exceptional and transient circumstances, become a "subsistence wage," in Marx's sense of the term? The answer must be that it does. The only wages that are not, for Marx, subsistence wages are those which are due to a temporary market shortage, or redundancy, of labour. But, if this is so, why should not the workers, by raising their psychological standards and refusing to supply labour-power save at a higher price, absorb the surplus value which the capitalists now appropriate?

Marx's answer was twofold. It was, first, that a rise in the

230

demand-price of labour tends to cause less of it to be bought, unless it can be made by some other adjustment of conditions to ÿield as much surplus value as before. But if less is bought, this will mean unemployment, which will reduce the workers' bargaining power, and compel them to readjust their psychological valuations of the commodity which they have to sell. For the bargaining power of the workers under Capitalism depends on the state of the labour market; and the workers can effectively raise their psychological valuations of their own labour-power only in conditions which make it worth the capitalists' while to pay more for it. In other words, only an advancing Capitalism can concede rising wage-standards. The capitalist system depends for its working on the profit-incentive offered to the capitalist, and therefore on the continued manufacture of surplus value on a sufficient scale.

In the second place, Marx pointed out that the capitalist and the labourer are not on equal bargaining terms. Economic progress under Capitalism consists of an advancing "socialisation" of the processes of production based on the fact that the combined labour of a number of men in a complex industrial unit can be made more productive than the isolated labours of the same number of separate individuals. This progressive "socialisation" of the labour process is one aspect of the growth of Capitalism. But this same development, seen from another angle, consists of the progressive expropriation of the individual and small-scale producers from the ownership and control of the instruments of production. Beaten in one industry after another by the superior efficiency of combined production, these smaller producers go to the wall, and are compelled to surrender their independent power to produce value.[1] They become wage-workers within the capitalist system—"detail-labourers" who have no individual product of their own, but are contributors only to an essentially social process of production. As this happens, whoever controls the new and more efficient instruments of production is in a position to hire labour at a wage-standard set by the lower productive capacities which are being superseded, and to appropriate for himself the increased productivity which arises out of the growingly social character of the productive process—that is, in the language of Marshallian economics, to secure a "producer's surplus." Under Capitalism, Marx argues, the main benefits of the growth of productive "co-operation" accrue, not to the workers, but to the capitalist owners of the means of production. No amount of collective

[1] For qualifications to this generalisation, see pages 126 and 130.

bargaining through Trade Unions can counteract the influence of the capitalist monopoly of the means of production, so as to enable the labourers to bargain with the capitalists on equal terms.

This being so, the power of the labourers to raise the subsistence level of wages is limited by the pace of capitalist development. Wages can advance, as long as Capitalism can advance from economic triumph to triumph; but the power of the workers is only that of taking full advantage of such opportunities for raising the wage-level as the advance of Capitalism affords. They may take or miss such chances; but they cannot by mere will-power create chances which do not independently exist.

Under Capitalism, labour-power must have this property of creating values beyond the value which it possesses as a commodity; for otherwise there would be no inducement at all to employ it. But labour conditions under Capitalism can improve; and Marx fully recognised that at the time when he was writing improvements were actually coming about. These improvements had always a tendency to diminish the ease with which it was possible for the capitalists to appropriate surplus value; but there were also means at hand whereby the capitalists were able to counteract this tendency. Marx concentrated his study of the rival forces tending to the improvement of labour conditions on the one hand and the maintenance of surplus value on the other mainly round the question of the length of the working day; for it was above all upon this issue that the industrial struggles of the early nineteenth century had turned. This accounts for the form in which Marx presented his doctrine of surplus value, though the doctrine itself is independent of the particular form in which he set it out.

According to Marx's presentation, the labourer, in selling his labour-power to the capitalist, contracts to work in his service for the normal working day of so many hours. After working a certain number of hours, he has created enough value to meet the real cost of his own subsistence, and thus to cover the wages which he receives. But his obligation does not end there; for he has still to work for the capitalist the remaining hours of the normal working day. In this form the doctrine presents the worker as working so many hours for his own subsistence—"necessary labour time," in Marx's phrase—and so many hours at the creation of surplus value—"surplus labour time." It is of course only a way of presentation thus to split the working day into "necessary" and "surplus" hours: the point is that in the course of his employment the worker produces more value than he receives.

But now the workers, aided to some extent by other elements in society, begin to struggle for a shorter working day, and succeed in getting the hours of labour reduced by legislation, or by collective bargaining, or by both means. They could not do this at all unless Capitalism could afford the limitation; but even so the effect of the shorter working day must be, if other things remain equal, to reduce the surplus value accruing to the capitalist. What, then, can the capitalist do? There are two resources open to him. In the first place, he can seek to increase the productivity of labour by supplying it with more efficient machinery and in other ways improving the technique of production. To the extent to which this happens, the labourer will be able to reproduce his means of subsistence in a smaller number of working hours, and thus, if this reduction in the "necessary labour time" is equal to the reduction in the working day, to work as much "surplus labour time" as before. In that case, he will continue to produce for the capitalist as much surplus value as before; and this surplus value will be embodied in a greater quantity of goods. For a given amount of "value" is not a given quantity of goods, but the product of a given amount of labour-time, and the "values" of commodities will accordingly fall as the productivity of labour increases. The labourer, on the other hand, will receive as many goods as before for his subsistence; but he will receive less "value." Actually, of course, as productivity rises and as the length of the working day is reduced, the conflicting forces may not balance. Either side may make a net gain or loss in the amount of "value" appropriated, within limits set on the one hand by the difficulty of combating the workers' resistance to a fall in their subsistence standard or their insistence on a higher standard and on the other by the necessity of continuing to afford the capitalists a sufficient incentive to maintain the employment of labour.

The Productivity of Labour

It is essential at this point to observe the difference between the amount of "value" and the amount of commodities obtained by capitalists and labourers. An increase in productivity increases the volume of commodities available for distribution; but it does not increase the amount of "value" in the Marxian, or in the Ricardian, sense—for the change in productivity does not affect the amount of labour expended, on which the "value" depends. Accordingly, as productivity increases, it is perfectly possible for the real wages of the workers to increase in terms

233

of the goods they can buy even while the "value" of labour-power is falling. The "value" of labour-power rises only if wages are advancing faster than productivity. Similarly, the capitalist may appropriate more commodities, but less "value," as a result of a fall in the working day. In face of rising productivity, it is unlikely that either real wages or the amount of commodities appropriated by the capitalists will fall; but it is quite possible that the "value" of labour-power may fall. On the other hand, a reduction in the working day, accompanying a rise in productivity, may reduce the amount of surplus value without reducing the real profits of the capitalists below their previous level.

But an advance in productivity is not the only means of counteracting the influence of a shorter working day. Faced with a contraction in the total length of the working day, the capitalist will also seek to keep up the surplus value by causing workers to labour more intensively than before. Marx distinguishes sharply between an increase in output which is due to technical advances in the processes of production—greater "productivity" of labour—and an increase which is due to harder work—greater "intensity" of labour. The former adds to the supply of commodities, but not to the amount of value, whereas the latter increases both. For more intense labour is a greater amount of labour, and is therefore productive of a greater value. In Marx's view, the worker who works for hour harder than the pre-existing standard caused him to work works in effect for more than an hour, and therefore produces more than an hour's "value."

Accordingly, when the intensity of labour is increased, normally wages will tend to rise in compensation for the additional labour-power supplied. The previous proportions between necessary labour time and surplus labour time will tend to remain undisturbed, and the value of labour-power and the surplus value will tend to retain the same proportions as before. But the amount of commodities appropriated by the capitalist, and also the amount of value, will be greater, unless the working day is reduced. Here then is another means open to the capitalist of counteracting any tendency for surplus value to fall off as the length of the working day is restricted.

These means may avail to keep up both the rate and the amount of surplus value. But they will not normally suffice to maintain the rate of profit. For normally any steps taken to increase productivity (and some steps designed to increase intensity as well) will involve changes in the organic composition of capital. The capitalist will get as much surplus value as before, or most likely more, out of each unit of labour that he employs; but in order to get it he will have to employ a larger mass of capital, over the whole of which this surplus value will have to be spread. For the owners of all the capital will demand their profit or interest, whether the new capital is used to employ labour directly or to purchase machinery and other means of production upon which the labourers are to work. Accordingly, the rate of profit on the total capital will tend to fall unless the rate of surplus value on each unit of labour employed can be made to rise so fast as to offset the change in the organic composition of capital. Marx, in common with other economists of his time, believed firmly in the existence of a tendency towards a falling rate of profit on capital; but the explanation which he offered differed from other economists' in linking the fall directly to the continual change in the organic composition of capital.

Constant and Variable Capital

Before we discuss this question further, it will be well to restate in Marx's own phraseology the gist of the foregoing argument, using as far as possible his own technical terms. According to him, the capital used in industry can be regarded as consisting of two elements—Constant Capital and Variable Capital. Variable Capital is that which is spent in employing value-creating labour—that is, on wages and salaries paid as a return for production. Constant Capital is that which is spent on machinery, buildings, other instruments of production, materials, fuel—in fact, on anything and everything except the employment of productive labour. The two names, taken together, express Marx's view of the character of the value-creating process. Constant Capital is so called because it is spent on things which cannot create, but can only transfer, value. Its value therefore remains constant throughout the productive process in which it is expended. On the other hand, Variable Capital is so called because it is spent on something—labour-power—which creates more value than it costs to buy. Accordingly the value of this kind of capital varies: it emerges from the productive process more valuable than it went in.

Surplus Value and Profit

The capitalist, as we have seen, reckons his profit on the total capital he expends, irrespective of the method of expending it, and profits tend to be equalised, through the pricing process, over the total capital employed. But surplus value, which is the

235

source of profit, arises, according to Marx's contention, only out of the use of capital in its "variable" form—that is, only out of the exploitation of productive labour, or, in other words, out of the difference between the value of the product of labour and that of labour-power. Marx, then, draws a sharp distinction between the rate of profit, which he defines just as his predecessors defined it, as a rate per cent on the total capital invested, and the rate of surplus value, which he calculates as a percentage on the variable capital alone. If one employer locks up £100 in his business, and has £5 gain at the end of a year, we say his profit is at the rate of £5 per cent per annum. But suppose he spent £80 out of the £100 on raw materials and wear and tear of machinery and only £20 on wages, Marx would say that the rate of surplus value was not 5, but 25 per cent; for he would reckon it on the £20 alone.

Suppose the degree of mechanisation increases, so that wages account for only £10 out of every £100 invested, and other expenses account for £90, then each labourer who previously produced a value 25 per cent in excess of his wage will have to produce a value 50 per cent in excess, if the profit on the total capital is not to fall. Marx believed this to explain why Capitalism, in its attempt to counteract the tendency to a falling rate of profit, is always trying to increase the productivity of labour, and so to decrease the "necessary labour time" in which the worker reproduces the value of his subsistence, and leave more time available for the production of "*relative* surplus value," whereas "*absolute* surplus value" proceeds from the prolongation of the total working day or from an increase in the intensity of work. In Marx's terminology, increased intensity of labour thus adds to absolute surplus value, while increased productivity adds to relative surplus value.

But the increase in productivity is accomplished only by altering still further the organic composition of capital in such a way as to increase the proportion of Constant to Variable Capital. It therefore continually recreates the problem of the falling rate of profit, by calling for a larger and larger total capital in order to set any given amount of labour in motion.

The Falling Rate of Profit

In considering the validity of this doctrine, it is necessary to ask first of all whether there is in reality any tendency for the rate of profit to fall. The classical economists all thought there was, as an observed fact which needed to be explained; but their data related chiefly to the rates of interest at which money could be borrowed at different periods rather than to profits in a strict sense. The fall in interest rates was, however, largely due to two factors—the increased plentifulness of capital as societies became more wealthy, and the reduced risks of lending as the capitalist system became more settled. The reduction of risk would tend to reduce interest rates; but it would not tend to reduce profits, but rather to increase them, if it stood alone. But the greater plentifulness of capital would tend to reduce the rate of profit, by driving capital into less productive uses than would be worth while if it were scarcer. Thus the increase in the wealth of capitalist societies, especially if the accumulation passes mainly into the hands of the rich, does tend, by making capital more abundant, to lower the rate of profit. But on the other hand this abundant supply of capital also tends, by making labour more productive, to reduce necessary labour time, and thus to increase the production of surplus value, and to expand the opportunities for the profitable employment of capital. There seems so far to be no necessary reason why the one tendency should outweigh the other.

There is, indeed, no reason to suppose that, throughout the period since the Industrial Revolution, the rate of profit has continued to fall, though it has tended to be higher in less than in more developed societies because of the greater scarcity of capital. It is, however, undeniable that the principal factor in preventing a fall in profits has been the expansive power of Capitalism, which has enabled it to find markets for its rapidly growing output in the less developed countries, both by the investment of capital abroad and by successful competition with native industries in their home markets. Without this power to expand, Capitalism must soon have encountered the difficulty that its ambition to maintain profits and opportunities for the accumulation of capital was bound to conflict with its desire to find a market for a rapidly increasing output of goods and services. In the last resort, the size of the market for ultimate products is bound to determine that of the market for capital investment; for capital is needed in the last resort only for the production of ultimate products. To a great extent, however, the capitalists have wanted not to spend their money on such products, but to accumulate it by investing it in additional instruments of production. Their desire to get profits by keeping down wages has, therefore, been in constant conflict with their desire to sell the growing product of industry—or rather would have been so if new external markets had not continually been found. Marx saw in this most fundamental of the inherent

237

contradictions of capitalist production the root cause of the impending breakdown of the system, when once its power to overcome the recurring difficulty by finding fresh markets and spheres of investment abroad began to give way.

This part of the Marxian doctrine, however, belongs rather to the theory of capitalist crises than to the theory of the normal working of the system. Normally, in Marx's view, the development of capitalist enterprise sets up a tendency for the rate of profit to fall, because, as mechanisation increases, larger and larger amounts of capital are used in setting a given amount of labour in motion, so that the surplus value derived from the exploitation of labour has to be spread thinner over these growing accumulations of capital. This does not mean that the total amount of profit tends to fall: on the contrary, it grows steadily whether it is measured as a quantity of commodities or as an amount of "value." Increasing population has provided a growing supply of labour-power, and has thus swelled the sum-total of "value." Growing intensity of labour has had the same effect, even where the working population has been stationary. Increasing productivity has reduced the necessary labour time, and has thus added to the amount and proportion of surplus value; and all these factors together have increased the total real wealth of commodities and services. Against these forces have been arrayed the demand for a shorter working day and the movements for legislative restriction of the right to exploit labour. These have tended to decrease the sum-total of "value," save to the extent to which they have been counteracted by an increase in the working population or by a greater intensity of labour. There has also been arrayed against the forces making for exploitation the pressure of the labourers for a higher level of subsistence, which has the effect of increasing the necessary labour time and of decreasing the surplus labour time available for the extraction of surplus value.

Marx thought that the normal resultant of these forces would be a falling rate of profit, but a rising rate of surplus value. In other words, he thought that the effects of a shorter working day in reducing the rate of surplus value would normally be outweighed by the reduction in necessary labour time due to increasing productivity, and that the labourers would not normally be able so to raise their subsistence level as to redress the balance. But he also held that the increase in the rate of surplus value would not normally be enough to prevent a fall in the rate of profit as the total mass of capital increased and as a far larger amount was used in proportion to the amount of labour. Both these judgments are evidently not logical necessities, applying to Capitalism at every phase of its development, but empirical conclusions based on an attempt to measure the relative strength of conflicting forces. It is quite possible to reach a different judgment on either point in relation to a particular phase of capitalist growth, without questioning any fundamental doctrine of Marxism. In fact, either or both may be true of Capitalism at one phase of development, such as the phase of British Capitalism in the early nineteenth century, which Marx was chiefly observing, and may not be true of it at another phase, owing to a change in the balance of the opposing forces.

It may, however, be contended that Marx's two conclusions are valid, not for Capitalism at every phase, but as statements of what is bound to happen to it in the long run. For, in the first place, the bargaining strength of the labourers clearly depends on the demand for labour in relation to the supply, and the growth of mechanisation is continually reducing the quantity of labour needed for the production of a given quantity of goods. If the demand for goods expands fast enough to offset this influence, there need be no decrease in the labourers' bargaining strength. But this condition requires a very rapid expansion; and whence is this expansion to come? It cannot come from the capitalists' personal spending; for the limits to their consumption of mass-produced goods are soon reached, and their desire is to find means for the creation of further surplus values through investment rather than to consume more. It can come from the workers only if wages rise so far as not merely to represent as much "value" as before, despite the fall in the "value" required for keeping up the established level of subsistence, but also to encroach on the surplus value previously appropriated by the capitalists. But is this possible? The general run of individual capitalists cannot pay higher wages, except for more intense labour, without suffering defeat at the hands of their competitors at home or abroad, and in the same or in different industries; for producers of different types of goods are always to some extent in competition one with another to attract the consumers' purchasing power, by offering more "utility" in return for money. Accordingly capitalists, unless they are in a strong position of monopoly, always tend to keep wages as low as they can, even where the need exists to raise them over industry as a whole in order to expand consumption. As soon as Capitalism develops on an international scale, this condition applies through international competition to the capitalists of each country regarded as a combined group; for no national group of capitalists in internationally competitive industries can afford to pay wages higher than those which exist in other countries save to the extent to which the national productivity is greater. But the demand for commodities cannot expand on a sufficient scale until wages have risen, and the labourers cannot be strong enough to enforce a sufficient rise in wages until the demand for commodities has expanded. Accordingly, the argument runs, in the long run Capitalism is bound to get caught in a vicious circle of low wages and inadequate demand. Marx insisted that the final cause of all capitalist crises is to be found in the limited consuming power of the mass of the people.

Capitalist Contradictions

This inherent contradiction of Capitalism need, however, manifest itself only "in the long run." It will indeed, Marx holds, tend to appear speedily in the working of any capitalist system which is confined to a single country, and depends exclusively on the home market. But, for a capitalist system which has scope for foreign trade and investment, the nemesis may be long postponed. For the capitalists in such a country may create a demand for their goods abroad by successfully destroying the less developed industries of pre-capitalist or semi-capitalist countries, and by the investment of surplus resources in the development of such countries. This was on the whole the position of Great Britain in the latter half of the nineteenth century, as it is of the United States to-day; and Marx has much to say about it in the third volume of *Das Kapital*.

Any such situation, however, Marx argued, is inherently unstable. For the more other countries develop economically, the more widely the same conditions are reproduced. Other countries come in their turn to depend for the maintenance of their Capitalisms on finding markets and spheres of investment abroad; and competition to exploit and develop the still undeveloped areas becomes more intense. This competition, as we saw, reacts on the home market; for it leads to competitive pressure to keep down the wage-level, and thus limits the growth of domestic demand. But at the same time it intensifies the efforts to make industry more productive, and thus increases the quantity of goods that can be produced. Greater productivity, however, in face of limited demand means decreased employment; and this further limits demand, and causes wages to be actually reduced by the competition of the labourers for jobs.

Critics of Marx have sometimes written as if he supposed that this state of affairs, plainly manifesting the inherent contradiction of Capitalism—its tendency at once to increase productivity and to restrict demand—would arise only when the whole world had become industrialised, so that there were no longer any backward areas to develop and exploit. But this was not Marx's view. The difficulty begins as soon as the competition among capitalists to secure a share of the market becomes severe; and it becomes critical as soon as the extent of economic development in the advanced countries makes it impossible to press forward the exploitation of the less advanced countries fast enough to meet all their needs. At this point, Marx held, the conflict between rival Capitalisms was bound to become intense; and the Economic Imperialisms which would have already grown up through the inner need of each developed country to expand would come into serious conflict one with another, and would lead on to wars which would become world struggles endangering the very foundations of the capitalist system.

This question, in its relation to the historical tendency of Capitalism as a whole, is discussed in another chapter of this book. It has been introduced here only to the extent to which some mention of it arises necessarily out of the consideration of Marx's theory of value. That theory could not be adequately discussed without raising this question, because Marx's view of the inherent contradictions of capitalist production is bound up with his theory of profit, which in turn has to be understood in relation to his theory of surplus value. The reader is referred back to earlier chapters both for a fuller treatment of this problem of capitalist contradictions and for the consideration of the closely connected doctrines of the "concentration of capital" and the "increasing misery" of the working class.

The object of the present chapter has been only to get at what Marx really meant by his theory of value, and to reveal its intimate connection with the previous economic theories as a criticism of which he built it up. This has involved some passing of judgments upon the soundness of the theory at certain particular points; but the main object of this chapter has been expository rather than critical or constructive. In general, however, the conclusion is that the Marxian theory of value remains untouched by the criticisms which have been levelled against its fundamental consistency, though there is much in its expression and in its secondary doctrines that is either invalid or of no relevance to-day, partly because Marx never escaped from invalid assumptions which he took over from his predecessors, partly because circumstances have so changed that provisionally valid criticisms of an earlier phase of Capitalism have lost their meaning now, and also partly because Marx never completely straightened out his own thinking, or escaped from ambiguities and uncertainties in his own mind.

We cannot, however, be content to leave matters there; for if the Marxian theory of value has a living virtue in relation to our own time, we must attempt to restate in terms appropriate to our own problems whatever of it appears to be still valid and important, with such modifications and additions as are called for both by changes in the objective situation and by the further development of economic thought. That this is difficult, and that the attempt will fall short of complete success, goes without saying. Nevertheless, the attempt needs to be made.

CHAPTER IX

THE THEORY OF VALUE (*continued*)

Value, in the fundamental economic sense of the term, depends on scarcity. Valuable things are things which are scarce in relation to the quantities of them men would use if they could be had without effort. Anything that is capable of being scarce in this sense is capable of having a value. It follows that nothing has a value in itself, without reference to men's need or desire for it. All values are social; and no such thing as the "intrinsic value" of any commodity exists.

If no one needs or wants a thing, even though it can be had for nothing, that thing has no value, however much effort its production may have required. If humanity finally gave up war, the instruments of war could have no value, unless they were capable of being applied to other uses. Thus the mere fact that a thing is a product of human labour does not suffice to give it value.[1]

But clearly no one in his senses will intentionally expend labour in making things that nobody wants, unless he does it either as part of a technical process of training, or because he takes pleasure in the activity itself, apart from its product. Bad water-colour paintings that nobody wants have no value, but the painting of them may give the artist pleasure. An

[1] Marx recognises this when he says that only "socially necessary" labour is productive of value. See p. 217.

uneatable pudding has no value, but its making may be part of the necessary expense of producing a cook. Apart from these special cases, the aim of all human labour is to produce things that are wanted, and that cannot be had without effort. In other words, the general object of human labour is to produce values.

Human labour, in the wide sense in which it includes all human labour directed to the production of values, is scarce. There is not enough of it to produce all the things men would use if no effort were involved in their production. Accordingly, the production of any particular thing always involves the non-production of something else that could have been produced instead. The cost of producing a thing can therefore be reckoned in two ways—either as the actual expenditure of effort which its production involves, or as the forgoing of the alternative things that might have been produced with the same expenditure of effort. This latter is the "Austrian" School's way of looking at value.

Things of which the production involves the same expenditure of effort have accordingly, subject to the reservation stated below, the same real cost; for their real cost is measured by the amount of effort, or productive power, that they use up. This is the truth underlying the contention that labour is the measure of value.

We cannot, however, conclude that things of which the production has involved the same expenditure of effort have the same value. For, in the first place, some men may take longer than others in making a thing, or may make a better thing in the same time. Secondly, the effort may have been well or ill applied to meeting the needs or desires of mankind; and thirdly men's needs or desires may change between the time when the production of the thing is undertaken and the time when it passes into use. In any of these cases, the value of the thing made depends on men's need or desire for it; and not on the actual cost of producing it.

Effective Demand

All production is based on an estimate of future needs, nearer or more remote according to the nature of the economic system and of the commodity produced. The purpose of the economic system is always to select for production those things which are needed more, in the sense that there is a greater demand for them, in preference to those which are needed less. But the conception of "need" is not absolute or ideal. It is always

243

relative to the valuations and to the social structure of the particular economic system in which the production is being undertaken. Under the capitalist system, need is equated to "effective demand," by which is meant the willingness and ability of some possessor of purchasing power to expend money on the acquisition of a commodity. Capitalism thus recognises the possession of more money as carrying with it the existence of greater need. Capitalism takes no account of "needs" which cannot somehow find expression as "effective demands."

Capitalist economics is therefore based on the conception that effective demand is the sole measure of value. It equates value with market price, as determined by effective demand. Modern capitalist economists sometimes go so far as to insist that the expenditure of effort involved in producing a commodity is wholly irrelevant to its value, which is derived exclusively from the effective demand for it. The nature of the effective demand, they say, will determine the amount of effort that will be put into making each commodity, and will thus decide the amount of it that will be produced. The cost of producing a thing, they argue, will never determine how much people will be prepared to give for it; for that must depend on the intensity of their desire for it as against other things.

This was not the view of the earlier capitalist economists, who held that the value of things—meaning the exchange relationship with other things expressed in their "natural" or "normal" prices—depended on the conditions of their production. This view, however, was incapable of explaining why one thing was produced in preference to another; for, if value depended on the conditions of production and not on demand, the same value would be created by the same expenditure of effort, no matter what might be produced. This is of course nonsensical. If all human effort were directed to producing fire-grates, and none to producing fuel to burn in them, the same value would not be created as if fire-grates and fuel were produced in balanced quantities. The term value has no meaning except in relation to some sort of need or desire.

But capitalist economics picks out one sort of need or desire—effective demand[1]—and makes this alone the arbiter of value. Other economic systems, corresponding to other forms of economic society, could select other criteria instead, and thus give the term "value" a radically different meaning. Thus a purely communistic society might make its criterion its collective

[1] Including, of course, the effective demands of public and other collective bodies as well as those of individuals.

view of what was really most useful to men, and not what they were willing and able to pay for, or individually wanted.

The criterion of effective demand has the obvious attraction that it enables every commodity to be measured against every other in terms of its price. The money offers which the possessors of money are willing to make for goods become the determinants of their relative values. In capitalist societies, goods always sell at their values, because their values are simply the prices at which they sell stripped of their expression in a particular monetary unit. This way of measuring values is valid for capitalist societies; for it measures them appropriately according to the capitalist standard.

The basis of this method of measuring values is the taking for granted of the money-incomes available for the buying of commodities. These incomes are assumed for the purpose of making the valuation as existing absolutely; for apart from them there could be no effective demand, and no values could come into existence. This is a legitimate assumption for capitalist economics; for capitalist economics is based on assuming the existence of the capitalist system as a going concern, and within that system money-incomes do actually exist.

Nevertheless, this assumption involves a circular argument; for actually these incomes come into existence only as a result of the productive processes which they are invoked to explain. Incomes are prices, are values in the capitalist sense: they are the prices set upon the factors of capitalist production. Or, where they are not this directly, they are derived from incomes which possess this character. No incomes can exist apart from products to which they are claims.

Capitalist economists recognise this fact at a second stage, when they go on to explain incomes—as the prices of the factors of production—in the same terms as they have already employed in explaining prices in general. Wages, salaries, rent, interest and profits are all explained as prices *derived from* the prices which the possessors of effective demand are prepared to pay for goods and services. Thus incomes are derived from incomes, at the end of a fallaciously circular process of reasoning. In the end the incomes which have been taken for granted at first are explained; but the explanation is that they are derived from themselves.

This vicious circle of capitalist economics does not destroy its validity as an analysis of capitalist production. But it does reveal that the economics of Capitalism are valid only for Capitalism and upon capitalist assumptions. Capitalist economics constitute a theoretical system built up within the assumptions of an existing capitalist world.

The Critique of Capitalist Economics

In order to make a critique of Capitalism, or of capitalist economic theories, it is necessary to go outside the assumptions of Capitalism. This involves going outside the assumption that effective demand, as it arises out of the actual distribution of incomes under Capitalism, can be regarded as a satisfactory measure of value. But if we reject this standard, what alternative standard can we adopt?

The quest for an absolute standard is vain; for any standard of economic value must be relative to a particular economic system. We can criticise capitalist standards only by some other standard which is no less relative in its nature. For there can be no absolute standard of the right criteria for meeting human needs or desires. Conceptions of what men need arise out of the social conditions in which they live; and what men actually desire is also relative to their social environment.

On this basis, certain alternative standards suggest themselves as relevant to the conditions of the modern world. With alternatives that are not relevant we need not concern ourselves here; for any useful critique of Capitalism must be in terms of real and practicable alternatives to it.

The first alternative is one that discards effective demand altogether as the measure of values, and accepts instead as its basis a collective estimate of human needs. Such a standard could be appropriate only to a society in which the entire mechanism of production and distribution was under collective control, so that the society itself decided collectively what to produce and how to distribute the product in accordance with its collective view of men's needs. Such a society might institute unlimited free supply of certain kinds of goods; but for all other goods it would have to work by means of some sort of rationing or "points" rationing system—unless indeed it had reached a situation in which there was as much available of *everything* as anybody wanted. Its economic arrangements would express the principle "To each according to the collective estimate of his needs."

The second alternative is one that continues to accept effective demand as the means of distributing goods and services, but discards it as an independent and self-sufficient measure of values, and undertakes to control effective demand itself by collective regulation of the distribution of incomes. This is of course done to a certain extent in many modern societies; but such a standard would be appropriate in a complete form only to a society in which the collective control of the incomes of the members was undertaken in accordance with a collective estimation of their needs. The society itself would determine the distribution of incomes, leaving the business of deciding what to produce—whether actual production were collectively undertaken or not—to depend upon the preferences of the possessors of incomes, as is done under Capitalism. Such a society would dictate the general character of effective demand by regulating incomes, but it would leave demand for particular commodities free to fluctuate within the general conditions so dictated. Its arrangements would not involve either free distribution of some commodities, or rationing of others; and they would involve the continuance of a monetary economy.

Both these alternative standards differ essentially from the capitalist standard in refusing to take the distribution of incomes in accordance with the capitalistic principle of competitive bidding for the use of the factors of production as a basis for the determination of values, and in setting up instead a standard based ultimately on collective control and estimation of needs, or of the needs and desires to be given priority. They both discard the underlying assumptions of *laissez-faire*—the assumption of a fundamental economic harmony which exists in the absence of collective regulation. They both appeal from men as self-interested individuals to man as a social being. In this sense, they are both socialistic.

The difference between them is indeed at bottom a difference of mechanism, and not of principle. This can be seen from the obvious fact that a society might exist embodying both of them in part, without any friction or contradiction arising from their coexistence within a single system. There would be no inconsistency in a society deciding collectively to distribute certain goods freely without limit, and to ration others, while leaving yet others to be bought at a price within a system of incomes collectively settled and distributed. Indeed, it is plausible to suggest that any actual Socialist system is likely to rest on a combination of these two alternative standards.

But both these alternative standards are in sharp opposition to the standard of capitalist society, because they rest alike on a collectively determined conception of human needs. Now, it is formally possible that men might collectively decide that Capitalism is the best of all possible systems and the distribution of incomes under Capitalism the best possible distribution. In that case, the substitution of the Socialist for the capitalist standard would make no practical difference. Socialism and Capitalism, as opposites, would meet at the extreme. But this is possible only in a purely formal sense. Practically, it is quite out of the question.

For, if once the appeal is made to a collective standard of valuation based on needs, or away from the standard which actually exists to any other, the existing distribution of incomes at once becomes irrelevant, except as a starting point from which to work towards a different distribution. It is no longer merely a question of taking an existing set of facts as a basis for economic analysis, but of deciding, within the practical opportunities which the situation presents, what alternative set of facts to substitute for them. Economics, which can never establish universal truths beyond the merest truisms, inevitably becomes normative, and ceases to be primarily descriptive or analytical, as soon as it begins to question the standards accepted in the existing economic system. It comes to concern itself with preferring one standard to another, on grounds which are never purely economic, even though its preferences have to conform to the economic requirements of the time. Accordingly, the critique of the capitalist economics and of capitalist standards must rest on a belief in the practical desirability of an alternative economic system. For the alternative standard on which the critique is based can have no real content unless it is capable of being embodied in an alternative system.

Systems, however, come into being not of themselves, but as the result of active forces operating upon the objective situation. To any alternative standard of valuation that is to be historically valid there must therefore correspond a set of forces capable of bringing it to realisation. Any valid critique of capitalist economics must base itself not only upon an alternative theoretical doctrine, but also, and more fundamentally, upon a movement powerful enough to act as the agent in replacing Capitalism. But, in the economic situation of to-day, the only self-consistent alternative to Capitalism is some sort of Socialism—the substitution of some form of social for individual and private control over the powers of production and distribution.[1] The main force corresponding to this alternative system, and capable of

[1] Fascism is here ruled out as a "self-consistent alternative" on the ground that it is not fundamentally an economic system, and does not provide any basis for an economic distribution different from those of Capitalism and Socialism. For the general discussion of the nature of Fascism, see pages 138 ff. and 280 ff.

bringing it into being, is the working-class movement. The workers may indeed find allies in the struggle; but the working-class movement is the only possible point of focus for the forces capable of becoming the active agents in the supersession of the capitalist system. Any valid critique of capitalist economics must therefore be in terms appropriate to the aspirations of the working-class movement. In other words, it must logically be in essence a Socialist criticism. The standard by which it criticises capitalist economics must be that which Socialists are seeking to establish in place of the capitalist standard.

Now, the aspiration of the working class is to cease to be a working class. This does not mean that it wants to cease working, but that its aspiration is to lose the stigma of social and economic inferiority which at present attaches to it because of its work. The fundamental aim of all working-class movements,[1] whether it be explicit or not, is to abolish class-distinctions, and to reorganise society upon a classless foundation.

An Alternative Standard of Value

The valid standard whereby to criticise capitalist economics must therefore be a standard appropriate to a classless society. But a classless society means, in the modern world, a society in which the distribution of incomes is collectively controlled, as a political function of society itself. It means further that this controlled distribution of incomes must be made on such a basis as to allow no room for the growth of class-differences. This does not necessarily involve equality of incomes among all the members of society; for it allows scope for differences corresponding to recognised differences of service. But it does involve that these differences shall not be so great, or so permanent through inheritance, as to form a basis for the survival or reintroduction of a class system. To that extent at any rate, the appropriate system of distribution must aim at keeping economic inequalities within the narrowest limits that can be made compatible with the offering of necessary incentives to effort.

An equalitarian system of distribution, even in this limited sense, is clearly out of the question unless the processes of production are brought decisively under collective control. For either incomes will continue to be distributed, as they are in capitalist societies, mainly in connection with the productive

[1] That is to say, of all movements based on the working-class as a whole, not necessarily of all sectional movements—witness the American Federation of Labor.

249

processes, or they will not. If they do so continue, the control of incomes will involve the control of production. If they do not, production will have to be carried on collectively, because the entire basis for its conduct in any other way will have been destroyed. The controlled distribution of incomes therefore carries with it as a logical necessity of its working the socialised control of production.

If, however, production and distribution are to be controlled in accordance with the requirements of a classless society, the only possible primary standard of value for a society organised upon this basis will be one of the collective estimation of human needs. Value will belong to things because the society holds them to be valuable for meeting real needs and wants. Value will become completely a socialised conception.

Under these conditions, the social conception of value will be embodied directly in the collective decisions about what is to be produced, and indirectly in the collective decisions about the distribution of income. Many things will be produced directly for collective use, or for free distribution among the members of the community. Every decision to produce such things will be a decision that it is worth while to produce them, in a double sense. It will mean both that they are worth the effort which their production involves, and that they are better worth this effort than any other products which could be produced by the same expenditure of effort but are not in fact being produced. Society will have constantly to make such collective judgments of value, weighing the value of things against the claims of leisure and against the hypothetical value of other things which it decides not to order to be produced.

This is easily seen; but it is equally true that, where goods continue to be produced for sale at a price, so that consumers are left free to guide the course of future production by deciding what to buy and what to refrain from buying, and thus intimating their wishes to the social agencies responsible for planning production, collective judgments of value will be involved, again in a double sense. For, first, the distribution of incomes collectively established will of itself profoundly influence the character of demand, so as to make the relative demands for different products radically different from those which exist in capitalist societies; and, secondly, society, since it controls production, will also control prices, and will be in a position to influence the direction of demand to any extent it may think fit by its policy in fixing the relative prices of different goods. Thus, individual "effective demand," to the extent to which it survives, will be itself a result of the controlled social forces of the new collective system.

Under these conditions, on what will the collective estimates of value be based? Clearly not, in any primary sense, on the prices things will actually fetch in the market; for these will be largely the controlled results of social decisions previously made. Society will think of value as existing in commodities or products of any consumable sort only in a secondary sense, and purely by virtue of the scarce factors of production which have had to be used up in their manufacture. Value will be regarded as belonging primarily to the means of production rather than to the products, and above all as existing in human beings as sources of productive energy. The value which will be predominant in the new society will be the value of human labour. And human labour will have value, as it has now, because it is a scarce factor of production.

Ultimately, scarcity is of two kinds. Some things are scarce in the sense that the quantity of them that *can* be made available on any terms falls short of what men would demand if they could be had freely in unlimited supply. But the great majority of things are scarce only in the sense that their production involves an expenditure of human effort and materials and capital equipment, which are themselves scarce in the other sense. Thus the scarcity of things is in the great majority of cases only a manifestation of the scarcity of human labour. This, as we saw, is the fundamental truth behind the assertion that labour is the source and measure of value.

It is sometimes objected that the production of useful things involves an expenditure, not only of human effort, but also of raw materials and instruments of production, which must be equally a source of value. But these things are, as we saw, in the great majority of cases, themselves the results of a previous expenditure of human effort. The value which they represent is ultimately the value of the human effort which produced them, though the value of the things may no longer be equal to that of the effort which was applied in their production.

It is, however, true that in the last resort the processes of production go back to things provided by nature, which are not the products of human labour. Such natural goods can embody a value, if they are scarce in the first sense in relation to the quantities of them which men desire to use. Their value, being like all value social, in that it depends upon men's needs and desires, is created by society itself, and exists in natural objects only by virtue of the entire activity of the society in

251

which they exist. For they are scarce, not absolutely, but only in relation to social demand. Above all, their value cannot be due to their ownership by any particular person or class of persons, though under a particular social system it may be appropriated by such persons or classes, and their prices may be enhanced as a result of monopolistic ownership. But, by the standard of a socialised system, their value is simply the expression of their scarcity in relation to social need. Thus, if in a socialised system a choice has to be made between two possible acts of production, it will be a relevant consideration that one involves using up more of an absolutely scarce means of production than the other.

In any developed society, it is often difficult or impossible to distinguish the value which belongs to natural objects from that which is the product of past human effort. The Ricardian theory of rent slipped up on this difficulty. For land, as it exists in any developed country, has incorporated in it the results of the labour of past generations. There is no possible means of distinguishing its original properties from those given to it by the expenditure of human labour.

Fortunately, whatever Ricardo and his followers may have supposed, it is not of the smallest importance to achieve this feat. For, if a thing exists, it does not matter in the least how it came into existence, from the standpoint of determining its value. The conception of value is of importance only in relation to things that are to be made in the future, and not to things that have been made in the past, save to the extent to which things that have been made serve as the means of making other things. The conception of price may be of great importance in relation to consumable goods: that of value, as distinct from price, is of none at all, except within the assumptions of capitalist economics, in which value is equated to either normal or market price. Value, as distinct from price, is an important conception only in relation to the using up of scarce real factors of production.

A socialised economy is necessarily a planned economy. It involves collective decisions about what is to be produced. These collective decisions are in fact decisions about the use of the scarce real factors of production, including both the available man-power and raw materials, and the machines and other instruments of production already in being. Value, which is the power to create useful things, exists in all these factors of production. The magnitude of the value in any one thing depends on that of the utility which it can be used to create. But as the actual utility of a consumable thing can never be known until that thing actually reaches the point of being consumed, the actual utility that will result from the expenditure of a factor of production can never be accurately known. It can only be imputed, by anticipation, on the basis of a collective estimate of what society is going to need. The value of the factors of production is thus always the outcome of a process of imputing to factors of production the power to produce useful things.

In this process of imputation, the value of a factor of production must always be estimated on the basis of its use as a whole, to create the largest possible sum of utility—utility being measured, of course, by the collective standard of social need. Thus, for all practical purposes, the value of a factor of production corresponds not to the utility which it actually produces, but to that which the society deems it to be capable of producing. This explains the divergence between the values used up in producing a thing and the value of the thing when it has been produced.

We have, then, a conception of value as existing primarily in the scarce factors of production, and only secondarily, and in a practically unimportant sense, in consumable goods. We have, further, the conception of society as determining collectively the use of the productive values available to it, so as to produce the largest total of utilities in accordance with its collective estimation of human needs.[1] Values, in this sense, are the scarce things which are used up in producing utilities.

Socialism and the Price System

But, it will be objected, if we once depart from the use of prices as a standard for the measurement of values, shall we be left with any standard that we can practically apply? Under Capitalism, all capitalist values are commensurable by means of prices; and this commensurability is the very basis on which capitalist economics rests. If we take this away, what is left? For the capitalist price-system enables us to measure, not merely one kind of labour against another, and one kind of goods against another, but also labour against goods, and both goods and labour against capital itself. Is not this commensurability essential to any sound judgment in economic matters? And, if

[1] These "needs," of course, include not only basic needs of which society lays down that enough *ought* to be produced to allow everyone to get an adequate provision, but also supplementary needs, which are not for specific quantities of particular things, for everybody, but for whatever people happen to want, provided it is not socially too noxious to be allowed them.

so, is not this the final vindication of capitalist economics, and even of Capitalism itself?

It can be admitted at once that the capitalist system of prices, whereby all things are reduced to a money measure, possesses very great conveniences, and that it is so rooted in men's way of living in the modern world that in any change of system they are certain to retain much of its form, even if they alter its meaning. But though it may seem convenient to measure all things by a common standard, such measurement may be appropriate to one situation, but wholly inappropriate to another. Capitalism is able to measure men and things by the same standard, because it is based—though not in the same crude way as the slave system—on treating men as things. It can measure labour as a commodity, because it treats labour as a commodity. If, however, labour emancipates itself from this commodity status, it becomes by virtue of its emancipation incapable of being measured in commodity terms. A new standard of measurement comes to be needed for measuring something that has come to be regarded in an utterly different way from the commodities with which it has been hitherto confused.

In effect, under the changed conditions the value of labour-power ceases to be a money-cost of production. As a consumer, the labourer has now become a claimant to share, according to his need, as modified by the need of society to offer him adequate incentives to give of his best, in the social dividend which comes out of production. His claim as a consumer has been partly divorced from his contribution as a producer, to the extent that his remuneration is now determined socially, and not simply by the higgling of the labour market, or by the incentive element in it—which indeed it is the aim to keep as small as can be made compatible with the requirements of production, by substituting social motives for individual money incentives to the fullest practicable extent. The value of a man's labour cannot therefore be measured any longer by the income which he receives; for the two magnitudes are becoming increasingly independent of each other. How then is the value of his labour to be determined at all, in comparison with that of other labourers? Or again, how is the value of his labour to be made commensurable with that of the materials and instruments of production which he uses for the creation of utilities?

The Problem of Socialist Accountancy

This is the fundamental problem of the accountancy of a socialised system; and it is no more possible to solve it fully in advance than it was for pre-capitalist thinkers to anticipate how the money-system would develop under Capitalism. For theory follows facts, and cannot march ahead of facts into the future. Humanity solves its social problems only when they have been presented to it in a practical form. Consequently, all we can hope to do at present is to decipher such partial anticipations of the solution of this problem as are already being offered by actual experience of socialisation. Obviously Russian experience is likely to offer the most significant suggestions.

The Russian experience is of special value for this purpose because the Soviet leaders have been faced so dramatically with the problem of scarcity. This scarcity is indeed neither of sheer human labour-power nor of natural resources; for they have both of these in plenty. The Russian scarcity has been above all of skilled labour and technical competence, and of a sufficient inheritance of means of production in the form of capital goods derived from past labour. The problem of production has therefore presented itself to them very plainly. It has made them realise that crude labour-power, as well as crude productive resources still undeveloped, has no present value. It has been brought home to them that inherited means of production, as well as skilled labour, have a very great present value. This has caused them to visualise their problem as, above all, that of using the presently valuable resources at their command in such a way as to realise as rapidly and fully as possible the potential value which exists in at present valueless labour and natural productive resources.

In seeking this end, the Russians have necessarily been concerned above all else with making the best possible distribution and use of their limited supplies of skilled labour and of real capital in the form of productive resources. Their problem has been, in its fundamental character, inexpressible in money terms. Its valid units of accounting have been scarce workers and technicians and machines, and not the sums of money these factors of production are supposed to be worth or were worth in the old society which has been overthrown. But throughout, as the heirs of a capitalist economy used to thinking in money terms, and recognising the convenience of money as a unit of account, they have been anxious to re-express in monetary language as many as possible of the judgments they have made about the use and distribution of the real factors of production.

Russian accounting, however, differs, and is bound to differ, radically from the accounting of capitalist society. For the items of which it is made up are almost all controlled items, socially determined by one or another of the collective organs of the Soviet system. They are not prices arrived at by the higgling of a free market, but prices deliberately and to some extent arbitrarily imputed for the purpose of using them as units of account. Such prices are of vital importance in the system as "control prices," for the purpose of enabling the responsible authorities to discover how far the processes of production and distribution are actually going on in accordance with the collective plans. But they have no independent validity, and no commensurability save as the expression of collective judgments made by the planning authorities themselves. They are in that sense arbitrary, and the responsible authority can alter or adjust them at will. Perhaps this can be put most clearly by saying that the profits or losses made by Soviet enterprises are always "accounting" profits or losses, and bear no necessary relation to the real efficiency of the enterprise. They measure its success or failure in living up to the expectations of the planning authorities which set the prices, or in comparison with other enterprises producing under similar conditions—that, and nothing more.

In other words, the commensurability in *terms of money* which appears to exist to a great extent in the Soviet economy is really an illusion. Things are, and must be, constantly measured one against another, and men against men, and men against things. But these measurements are actually made in terms of scarce real factors of production and are turned into monetary expressions only for convenience in social accounting.

When capitalist economists discover this, they are apt to regard it as a sufficient reason for dismissing the entire Soviet experiment as economically unsound. But why? Individuals in their private lives are constantly making judgments about the use of their time which they cannot possibly translate into monetary terms. In pre-capitalist societies, similar judgments were constantly made by peasant households (as indeed they are to-day), by entire tribal communities, and by such institutions as the manor. Modern States and municipal bodies have to make the same sort of judgments whenever they are deciding what to undertake and what not to undertake in the sphere of commercially non-reproductive public works and services; for though such decisions involve the consideration of factors which can be expressed in terms of money they can never be based solely upon these considerations. Why cannot a whole economic system similarly rely in the last resort on judging between real things, instead of between monetary expressions which are supposed to stand in the place of real things?

Capitalist economy seeks inevitably to universalise the money-measure because it is based on private property and the individual appropriation of values under a system of exchange. Seeking to make all its means of production, as well as all its products, capable of exchange and of individual appropriation, it must try to make them all commensurable in money terms. But a socialised system, while it will doubtless retain the buying and selling of products in an amended form, will discard the buying and selling of the means of production in any save a book-keeping sense. Apart from human labour, these will be socially owned, and therefore incapable of being bought and sold; and there will be no need to place a money valuation upon them unless this continues to be done purely for purposes of book-keeping and social accounting. For money is essentially relative to exchange. Labour itself will not be socially owned, but will be collectively the social owner of things; so that it will no more be bought and sold (save in a purely transitional stage) than the material means of production. Labour will have an income, but not a price in the capitalist sense; for the wage-system will have disappeared. There will, then, be no need to measure either labour-power or any other factor of production against consumable goods in terms of a common money standard.

But there will be a need to measure in some way one kind of labour against another, and each kind of labour against the other factors of production. An example will make this plain. Without some standard by which this can be done, it would be impossible to decide when to introduce machinery in place of labour, or to prefer the use of one kind of labour to another, or how intensively to cultivate a particular piece of land. For this sort of measurement a socialised society will have to discover and establish a standard; but there is no reason why its standard should be the same as that of Capitalism. Indeed, there is every reason for using for such measurements a standard different from that which is employed for the pricing of exchangeable goods.

A Social Standard of Value

This standard can be nothing else than that of productive power, or value. Society itself will establish this standard, to meet the requirements of the new system of production; and society will sustain and work it by means of a continual process

257

of collective decisions. In correspondence with the requirements of an individualist economy, the price system under Capitalism undergoes constant adjustment under the influence of individuals exercising their power of effective demand or of business concerns exercising their monopolistic control over supply. But in the collective economy the standard of value will be set not by individuals or private combines, but by the "collective," which will assign its appropriate value to each scarce factor of production, and will constantly readjust its valuations in accordance with changes in the objective situation. Thus, if skilled engineers are scarce in relation to the collective need for them, a high valuation will be set upon their services in terms of the new collective standard; whereas if they become relatively abundant this valuation will be lowered by collective decision of the same authority as fixed it in the first place. Any enterprise which demands the services of highly valued workers or the use of highly valued implements or materials of production will be debited in the collective accounts with a proportionately high social cost, and will be expected to deliver a proportionately large sum-total of utilities. But the accounting charge on account of the scarce kinds of labour will bear no *necessary* relation to the incomes allowed by society to the workers in question: nor will the prices charged for the goods produced be *necessarily* proportionate to the accounting costs of production, which may indeed come to be expressed in terms of a totally different standard. Many of the products of industry may come to have no money prices, being produced either for collective use, or for free or rationed distribution, or for employment as means of production in further processes in relation to which there may be no need to attribute definite money costs.

I am, of course, aware that these adumbrations of a new collective standard bear some resemblance to certain proposals put forward by various schools of currency reformers for adoption under the capitalist system. There have been proposals for an alternative currency standard, to be called the "erg," or unit of work-energy, or by some similar name; and there have been plans for a double standard, based on separating "money of account" from the "current money" supplied for use in ordinary retail transactions. This resemblance is not merely accidental. These monetary reformers have been feeling, at one point, after a standard whereby to make a critique of existing economic conditions; and they have been feeling after a real thing. But they have made the mistake of supposing that their new standard can be grafted on to Capitalism, and used as a means of reforming

258

Capitalism; whereas its entire validity is relative to a quite different economic system, based on the recognition of collectively estimated need, instead of effective demand, as the rationale of production. The energy unit, or unit of productive value, is a conception highly appropriate to the accounting of a socialised economy; but it is entirely inapplicable to the practice or theory of the capitalist system.[1]

Further than this it is, I believe, impossible to push the analysis of the new standard at the present stage. Its exact form and substance can be determined only in practice, in the course of growth of an actual socialised economy. But it is surely clear that the working out of such a standard is fully practicable, and that it can meet the need of a socialised economy for a means of estimating the real economic costs of different projects far more valid, in relation to the needs of such an economy, than any standards based on the higgling of the market could possibly be. For always and everywhere the root problem for a socialised economy will be that of distributing its available productive resources so as to yield the best possible return in terms of its own collective conception of social needs. In establishing its calculus of needs by a series of acts of collective judgment, it will be also inferentially setting values on all the scarce factors of production with the aid of which these needs will have to be met. Its valuation of the factors of production will thus follow from its estimates of social needs. It will of course be fully possible for the "collective" to go astray in making its estimates, both by estimating wrongly what men need or desire, and by misjudging the productive quality of this or that factor of production. But the possibility of such errors is inherent in the entire business of production, however it is organised. They are constantly being made and painfully corrected under Capitalism in relation not to need, but to effective demand; and they will be constantly made and corrected, it is reasonable to hope less painfully, under a collective economy. The utility of things when made will inevitably diverge from the values used up in making them; but the entire collective system will be directed to making such errors as small as possible, and to eliminating them promptly when they are found to exist. A collective system, worked on a basis of collectively estimated needs, will clearly be in a far better position both to anticipate and to correct than a capitalist

[1] The reader who wishes to see the point of this and the foregoing paragraphs elaborated is referred to my treatment of the matter in *Money, Present and Future*, and especially to my booklet, *Fifty Propositions about Money and Production*, which is reprinted as an appendix to that work.

system, working to meet an uncertain flow of individual effective demands, can possibly be. Nor will anything make more surely for successful planning than the severance, within a system of collective production and distribution, of the structure of prices and incomes from the structure of real costs involved in the using up of scarce factors of production.

It should be observed at this point that there will be, under a collective system of planned production, abundant opportunity for retaining, and indeed for developing much further, the principle of "consumers' choice" which is often claimed as one of the chief advantages of a capitalist economy. The needs of the consumers, as we have seen, are made up of two elements, (a) certain basic needs, not uniform for all individuals, but broadly so for large groups, which are among the fundamental requirements for healthy and decent living, and (b) the need to enjoy, over and above the satisfaction of these basic requirements, the means of satisfying, in reasonable measure (which must vary with the wealth of each society) personal preferences for things which are not basically necessary. No sharp line can or need be drawn between (a) and (b); but it can be said broadly that a well-organised society must aim at ensuring that all its members get *the actual things*—goods and services—required for (a), whereas in relation to (b) it should aim at providing a wide diversity of supplementary goods and services for people to choose from according to their personal preferences. This involves that the social planners must aim at getting produced what the society regards as an adequate quantity of goods and services of the (a) type, whether individuals demand them or not. (Education is an obvious instance in which the demands of individuals might fall short of what would be deemed socially necessary, and water is another.) On the other hand, in the case of (b) goods, the task of the planners is to find out what people *want* individually, and to respond with the appropriate quantities of the various things they want, fixing prices which do not discriminate in favour of one class of goods as against another, except where there is a special social reason for discouraging (or perhaps for encouraging) a particular type of consumption, *e.g.* alcohol or pool-betting or some form of "going to the dogs" or to the opera.

There is no reason whatsoever why a Socialist society should not give the fullest freedom of choice in relation to goods and services of the (b) type. It would, indeed, in proportion as it led to closer approximation of incomes, spread "consumers' choice" much more widely, and thus maximise the utility afforded by it.

From this point we can come back to our more immediate critique of capitalist economics and of the capitalist system. The fundamental tenet of the capitalist economists is that every factor of production does tend to be paid for at its value, in accordance with its specific productivity; and that accordingly it is nonsense to speak of the exploitation of labour. In a limited sense, this statement is perfectly true. Under Capitalism, the factors of production are put into competition one with another, so that each is employed and paid for up to the point at which it pays the capitalist better either to call a halt to further production or to employ some other factor of production instead. The remuneration paid for the use of the various factors does tend to be determined by their competition at the margin, in such a way as to make their marginal productivities equal; for if they were not equal, it would pay better to alter the proportions in which the various factors were employed. Of course, marginal productivity in this sense must be understood as referring entirely to productivity of money values, and not to quantity of output. It is therefore productivity in a purely capitalist sense, in relation to the capitalist standard of effective demand.

With the fact that this tendency towards equality of productiveness at the margin works out very imperfectly in practice I am not for the moment concerned. It is sufficient that it does exist as a tendency, and that its existence is vital to the working of the capitalist price-system in relation to the pricing of the factors of production. In a capitalist sense, as Marx showed long ago, labour is not exploited; for the commodity, labour-power, is paid for at its capitalistic value. The exploitation of labour cannot be demonstrated within the circle of capitalist economic ideas, but only by going outside them and making a critique of capitalist economics and institutions in terms of an alternative standard.

This alternative standard we now possess, in a provisional form which suffices as the basis for a critique of Capitalism. For the capitalist valuation of labour-power now appears to us as valid only within the assumptions of the capitalist system. It measures the productivity of labour on certain assumptions—that this productivity is to be measured in terms of the money demand for its products and not of physical product, and that labour, as a factor of production, is to be equated to all other factors in terms of a common commodity standard based on the existing distribution of purchasing power.

As soon as we adopt the standpoint of a collective economy, these assumptions cease to be valid. For we are now considering the factors of production not as things privately owned and offered for sale, or used as the means of procuring private incomes, but as parts of a socially controlled supply of productive power, to be directed collectively in accordance with a collective estimate of social needs. All claims to productivity or value based upon private appropriation or on the capitalistic system of income distribution therefore disappear; and the production of value has to be considered from a social point of view—from the standpoint of a society collectively attempting to make the best use of its productive resources for the general welfare.

The Sources of Value

Value in this sense exists in all the scarce factors of production, and not in living labour alone. For the most part these factors of production, apart from living labour, are the products of past living labour working upon things which would have no value—because they would have no scarcity—apart from the labour expended upon them. They are thus also products of labour, which has been incorporated in them. But their present value cannot be equated in any way to the amount of labour incorporated in them in the past: it depends entirely, like the value of living labour, on their anticipated potency in the creation of future utilities.

There are, however, certain natural goods which are very limited in supply; and any natural good is capable of becoming scarce under certain objective conditions. Thus, unimproved land has no value in an undeveloped country, but it can acquire a value as it becomes scarce with the growth of population. All values belonging to natural objects by virtue of their scarcity are the creation of society itself; for scarcity is essentially a social conception.

When a factor of production is scarce, it is irrelevant to its value whether it is a product of labour or not, or to what extent it mingles labour with purely natural resources. Its value lies in its scarcity: its scarcity is its value. The question of its origin does not arise in this connection.

Labour therefore is not the sole source, and still less is it the sole measure, of value, though it is by far the most important source and measure of value. Labour, in the wide sense which I have throughout been assigning to the word, is, moreover, the source of value to which, in any normally working economic society, the power actively to create new values exclusively belongs. Existing things have a value; but living labour creates new values whenever it is productively applied. It is true that the value of existing things—natural goods or instruments of production—can rise if they become scarcer with the growth of population or with the development of the society in which they exist. But to the extent to which their value is raised by positive action in the society, it is due to the activity of living labour in creating new values. Similarly, the activity of living labour can lower or destroy the value of scarce natural objects, as when means are found of reproducing synthetically a scarce good previously available only in its natural state.

We can therefore legitimately speak of living labour—including of course all forms of human productive energy by hand or brain—as the sole *active* source of new values. It follows that labour is exploited, in the sense of receiving as the reward of its energy less value than it produces, unless the sum-total of the new values created in society accrues to it—or, in other words, whenever any unearned incomes exist as claims upon the product.[1] Capitalism, on the basis of its own standards, pays the labourer the full value of the productivity of the commodity, labour-power. But, on the basis of any collective or socialised standard of value, Capitalism definitely exploits the labourers by paying them collectively less than their collective product.

It may be answered that the labourers are constantly receiving a share, not only in the new values currently created, but also in the store of previously created values which is being used up, and that accordingly the existence of exploitation is not proved. But all previously created values, to the extent to which they are the products of past labour, were at some period new values created by labour, and labour has accordingly the same title to them as to the products of current labour. Moreover, such values as exist in natural goods by virtue of the social situation are, as we have seen, indirect products of the labour-process, and belong to labour by the same title as the rest. The exploitation of labour is therefore clear, in the light of the collective standard of value by which the capitalist standard has been replaced for the purpose of this critique.

[1] It may be retorted that on this showing labour would still be exploited even under Socialism, because the young, the aged, and the disabled would have to be supported out of its product. Anyone who feels like using this argument to convict me of illogicality may use it, and welcome. I am, of course, referring to unearned incomes accruing on the score, not of need, but of claims to ownership. See the next page.

We are now explicitly criticising capitalist economics and the capitalist system of distribution, by the criterion of a standard which belongs not to Capitalism, but to a socialised economy. In doing this, we are *not* laying down how value ought to be distributed in such an economy, or making any claim that the labourer should have, under Socialism, a right to his entire product.

For, in the first place, we are dealing with the general exploitation of the class of labourers as a whole, and not with the wrongs of any particular labourer or group of labourers; and it is clearly impossible, under modern conditions of production, to determine in any save the capitalist sense what the value of the product of any particular labourer or group of labourers is. Value has become even under Capitalism essentially a social product; and only the capitalist method of estimating it in terms of marginal productivity serves to conceal its social character, and to give a veneer of individualism to the social process of production.

Secondly, our socialised standard of value has nothing to do with the distribution of incomes. It is a standard for the right distribution of productive resources, and not for the repartition of the incomes arising out of production. Its standard of distribution and its criterion of the worth-whileness of production are based on collective estimates of need; and it is therefore irrelevant to its standard of distribution how much value this or that labourer is capable of producing, though it is relevant to consider what incentives are needed in order to secure good productive service. It would be wholly inconsistent with our collective standard to recognise any claim by the labourers to the whole produce of labour, save in the sense in which for a classless society the labourers and the community constitute an identical group. By our collective standard, all value, however created, accrues to the society as a whole, to be either consumed collectively or distributed in accordance with the collective estimate of social needs and the necessity of offering adequate incentives to good work.

The thesis that labour is exploited under Capitalism can thus be expressed in the following form. The capitalist pays the labourer the full capitalist value of his labour-power. But, as Marx insisted, the capitalist value of labour-power is an entirely different thing from the social value of labour. Capitalist exploitation consists in applying to the remuneration of labour a capitalist standard, by equating the labourer to a commodity. The labourers, as soon as they repudiate this commodity valuation, set up a claim to be judged by a different standard. Under Capitalism, this leads to a claim by the labourers to receive collectively the entire product of their labour. But such a claim arises only as an antithesis to the capitalist claim, within the class-struggles that develop in capitalist society. It has no relevance as a principle of distribution for a socialised economy, though the principle which serves the labourers under Capitalism as a fighting claim will find its true place in a socialised economy as a standard for the measurement of social value.

This I conceive to be correct development of the truth inherent in the Marxian theory of value. Expressed in this way, it appears stripped of the forms in which Marx set it out as a critique of the capitalist economics of the early nineteenth century, and is reshaped as a critique of the capitalist economics of the twentieth century. As Marx built upon Ricardo, this post-Marxian theory builds, by way of criticism, upon the 'utility' economics of the modern schools. It is twentieth-century Marxism—in any sense in which Marxism is not merely a meaningless repetition by rote of the phrases rather than of the essential meanings of its founder.

The Institutional Basis of Capitalism

This fact of capitalist exploitation can also be expressed in another way, not as critique of capitalist economics, but as an historical interpretation of Capitalism itself. Obviously, the antithesis between the capitalist standard and the collective standard of value, which have been analysed in this chapter, rests upon the antithetical institutional shapes of capitalist and socialised economic systems. A socialised economy is an economy that rests upon the principle of social ownership and control of all the factors of production; whereas a capitalist economy is one that rests upon the rival principle of private ownership and control. For the socialised economy, there is but a single owner and controller of all the resources of production—the classless community itself. Accordingly, there can be for this single owner only one final standard of value and principle of production, the key to which is to be found in the single conception of social need. Even to the extent to which such a society retains monetary incentives, it does so only as means to the better satisfaction of socially estimated needs. On the other hand, for the capitalist economy there is no such self-evident standard; for there are many owners and controllers, each exerting his private claim and pull upon the forces of production. Capitalism has therefore to use the money system as a means of reducing to commensurability all the discrepant claims that exist within it; and, as a result of this reduction, its standard becomes one of effective monetary demand. Human claims are reduced to money claims; and the creative power of human labour is reduced to the commodity claims of vendible labour-power possessing a certain amount of marginal productivity, not of goods, but of money.

Private ownership is thus the institutional basis of Capitalism, and is recognised under Capitalism as the only title to appropriate a share in the social product. The non-human means of production are privately owned and controlled; and the labourer has his claim only because he is regarded as the private owner of the commodity, labour-power.

Given this institutional basis of private ownership, in a society subject to economic change and advancing in productive power as man's command over the forces of nature grows greater with the improvement of knowledge, it is inevitable that a large part of the economic benefits of growing productivity should accrue to the capitalist owners of the means of production. This does not mean that the owners of labour-power alone will secure no share in these benefits. They can and will; for in an advancing society there will tend to be a growing demand for labour; and the labourers, especially those who possess skills for which there is an expanding demand, will be able to make some gains both by means of collective bargaining, when the barriers in the way of Trade Union organisation have been broken down, and, even in the absence of Trade Unions, by using their opportunities to shift from declining to expanding occupations, in which the brisk demand for workers will tend to make wages relatively high. In advancing capitalist countries, labour standards will improve; and some share in the growing wealth will pass to the exploited class. Indeed, in new countries, where labour is a scarce factor of production, and there is no large mass of impoverished peasants who can be drawn as required from the land into capitalist industry, labour may be able to appropriate a large share in the fruits of developing industrial productivity. This is the main explanation of the difference between the history of labour in the United States and in the older countries where Capitalism developed under conditions of abundant labour supply.

But the class of labourers is normally at a fatal disadvantage in relation to the capitalists in the struggle to appropriate a share in the benefits of advancing productivity. For the labourer

266

must work in order to live; and his power to withhold his labour, though it can be increased by effective combination, is always and inevitably more limited in the last resort than the capitalists' power to hold out against him. This does not prevent the labourers from gaining some victories; for on occasion the capitalists deem it more profitable and expedient to give way, if they are not pressed too far, or asked to sacrifice any vital part of their control. But it does mean that in the last resort the capitalists can defeat the labourers, as long as the struggle remains on the purely economic plane, and is carried on upon the assumption of the continuance of Capitalism.

Moreover, the capitalist can shut his factory, not only in consequence of a labour dispute, but whenever it suits him to do so. Whenever he does this, or curtails the number of his employees, he deprives some of the labourers of their incomes, by refusing to buy their labour-power. It follows that, if Capitalism is to afford the labourers their incomes, the capitalist must be offered a sufficient monetary incentive to keep the labourers employed. This necessity, except where labour is a highly scarce factor, constantly sets limits to the power of the Trade Unions to secure higher wages or improved conditions of labour, and thus to lessen the degree of exploitation; and the limits become narrower when Capitalism becomes strongly competitive internationally, on a scale transcending the power of labour to organise effectively for collective bargaining or political pressure. In addition, as Capitalism develops, more and more capitalist claims upon the product of industry are converted into fixed claims to receive rent or interest, so that they become debts which the active capitalist *entrepreneur* has to meet. It then becomes necessary, if factories are to be kept open and the labourers are to retain their incomes, to acquiesce in the active capitalist retaining a sufficient profit after meeting all the claims to rent and interest which fall directly upon industry, as well as his share in taxes levied on behalf of the creditors of the State.[1]

Thus, while Trade Unionism can be a considerable force for the raising of wages at those stages of capitalist development at which there is a considerable profit-margin over and above the incentives necessary to the system, its power becomes narrowly limited, or valuable only in defence, when international competition reduces profit-margins, or when for any other reason the prosperity of the active capitalist *entrepreneurs* tends to decline.

[1] Inflation, by reducing or even annihilating these *rentier* claims, can of course greatly alter the situation in this respect.

For even if the Trade Unions were in a position to enforce higher wages, they could then do so only at the cost of diminishing employment, and thus of undermining their own bargaining power as well as depriving a section of the labourers of their incomes.

This, it may be argued, will cease to apply if capitalist States really and truly come to apply the policy of maintaining full employment. I have, however, still to be convinced that any capitalist State will, or can, consistently do this without destroying its capitalist character. A Fascist State can; but it deals with the problem of Trade Union pressure by the simple method of suppressing Trade Unions.

Even when, under systems of universal suffrage, the labourers in capitalist societies invoke their political influence to aid their economic strength, the same limitations remain. If Capitalism is to go on providing them with incomes, they must consent to these incomes remaining low. Under Capitalism it is always impossible for the working class to get more than a pint out of a quart pot.

Accordingly, exploitation of labour is not merely an accidental accompaniment of a particular phase of capitalist development, but is always and everywhere inherent in the capitalist system, though its incidence can be greatly modified in new societies in which labour is scarce. As long as the means of production are privately owned, the claims arising out of private ownership are bound to involve the exploitation of labour. For the capitalist recognition of the labourer's ownership of his labour-power is also by implication a denial of his right to the ownership of the product of his labour.

Of course, it is perfectly possible under Capitalism for a capitalist to labour and for one who labours to own property as well. Capitalists and labourers, as individuals, do not fall into perfectly distinct and isolable groups. In all capitalist societies, many capitalists perform productive labour; and, in highly developed capitalist societies, a substantial number of labourers become small owners of property. In some capitalist societies, there is a good deal of individual interchange between the two classes. But, from the standpoint of an analysis of Capitalism, these points are irrelevant, though they are important, as we have seen, in relation to problems of political and economic strategy. Whatever minglings and blurrings there may be, in every capitalist society capitalists and labourers exist as well marked and clearly distinct social classes, having different and contrasting economic functions and a radically different status.

268

The labour class is none the less exploited as a class because some of its members, as small owners of capital, obtain some part in the fruits of the exploitation: nor is the capitalist class less an exploiting class because it includes active producers as well as passive *rentiers* and mere financial manipulators. Colours are none the less colours because they run into one another; good and bad are none the less opposites because they are often hard to disentangle. To deny the reality of economic classes under Capitalism is merely absurd; the analysis of their composition and changing detailed relationships belongs to the discussion not of the theory of value and exploitation, but of the strategy and tactics of social transformation.

CHAPTER X

THE DIALECTIC—CONCLUSION

Finally, we come back to the question of Marx's method—Dialectical Materialism, as it is commonly called. There is, among professing Marxists, an extraordinary divergence of opinion about the interpretation of this method, most regarding it as the corner-stone of the Marxian system, but with many differences of view about its range of application and even about its essential content; whereas a few dismiss it as a tiresome fad of the master, who could never escape from the trammels of the Hegelianism of his youth. We shall have to ask which of these extreme views is right, and to come down on the one side or the other—for in this matter there is no possibility of splitting the difference. The Dialectic is either Marx's strength, or his weakness: it cannot be a matter of no account whether it is right or wrong.

First, then, wherein does the Marxian Dialectic consist? Like Hegel's Dialectic, it rests on a denial of the *all-round* validity of the concepts of Formal Logic. The fundamental principle of Formal Logic is the exclusion of the contradictory. Within the categories of Formal Logic a thing cannot both be and not be, cannot be at once itself and that which it is not. Obviously, if reality is conceived as static, this standpoint of the logicians is correct. A thing incapable of change cannot both be and not be, and cannot be both itself and that which it is not. As long as we remain within the realm of the unchanging, Formal Logic holds the field.

But, as Marx and Hegel both insist, the realm of the static is not the world of reality. It is a world of abstractions, which can be static only because they are not real. The mind of man can make for itself static conceptions; but such conceptions can never adequately express real things. Every thing that is real is in constant process of change, is continually becoming something other than what it was before. Reality never stands still, nor can man call a halt to it: all he can do to make it stand still is to make abstractions from it in his own mind—abstractions which he is then prone to mistake for the reality itself, or at least for a true and sufficient representation of reality.

As soon as this is admitted, the inadequacy of the categories of Formal Logic for dealing with real things, as distinct from abstractions, must be admitted too. For, of things that are in process of change, the exclusion of contradiction postulated by the logicians no longer holds good. A thing can be in process of becoming that which it was not; for it can change into something else. Indeed, it must do so, since by the very law of its being it cannot remain the same. Reality is not static, but dynamic and evolutionary; and any Logic that sets out to explain the fundamental nature of things must partake of the same dynamic and evolutionary character. It cannot exclude contradiction: indeed, it must be based on admitting contradiction as a vital part of the law of development. Change *is* contradiction. This, of course, does not invalidate Formal Logic in the fields to which it applies. It means only that a different Logic is needed for the handling of dynamic problems.

This need the Hegelian Dialectic attempted to meet, on the plane of the Idea. Hegel saw the universe as the expression of a divine Logic working itself out by a process of perpetual contradiction and conflict. All human history—and with that alone we are here concerned—spread itself out before him as a long process of ideal conflict, leading irresistibly towards the final exclusion of contradiction in the perfect self-realisation of the Universal Idea. The evolution of societies upon the physical plane of existence was for him but the derivative expression of this ideal process. What was happening in human history was not what seemed to be happening, but the gradual and progressive actualisation of the reality immanent in the Absolute Idea. Everything was present in potentiality throughout the entire temporal process of development; but the potential could become actual only by means of the long struggle of the Idea towards self-realisation through the conflicts of imperfect ideas, as manifested in history.

Thus, the understanding of the universe required, according to Hegel, a Logic of a different order from Formal Logic, which could fulfil the needs only of the secondary world of abstractions. Formal Logic had its due place in this world; but infinitely superior to it was the Dialectical Method, which alone could give the clue to the understanding of developing reality. To this higher Logic the syllogisms of Formal Logic, with their premises and their conclusions based on the exclusion of contradiction, were bound to be utterly inadequate. Instead of the syllogism the higher Logic required an appropriate form of its own, expressive of a dynamic process of becoming, instead of a static condition of being. For major premise, minor premise, and conclusion Hegel accordingly substituted thesis, antithesis, and synthesis, as the expressions fittest to be used in explaining the true rhythm of developing reality.

This was the basis of the Hegelian Dialectic of becoming and of conflict. In terms of human history, every phase of civilisation is regarded as a thesis, the embodiment of an incomplete and imperfect version of the Idea. But the incomplete necessarily suggests some part at least of what is needed to complete it. It suggests a contradictory phase, embodying a different facet or aspect of the Idea. Thus, the posing of any proposition, or the establishment of any institution, at once involves the posing of a rival proposition, or the establishment of a rival institution, based on a different conception of truth and value. Between these opposites a struggle is bound to follow; for neither the human mind, nor human civilisation, can finally accept contradictions without an effort to resolve them. But out of this struggle of thesis and antithesis neither can emerge absolute victor. The contest between them will necessarily, as they are not static but changing things, set up within them, and within the universe in which they exist, forces which will alter their character and the conditions of their conflict. In this process, reality and the institutions which reflect the advance of the Idea will move on to a higher plane. Out of the struggle of thesis and antithesis will emerge a synthesis which is neither of the combatants, but embodies the valid elements in them both. This synthesis will thereupon become the thesis for a new conflict, evoking in turn its own antithesis, and so leading on to a new synthesis which embodies a yet higher validity. By these stages, repeated again and again, human history, reflecting the march of the Idea from potentiality to actuality, gradually approaches perfection. Such is the March of Mind upon earth.

Marx and Hegel

Marx, of course, did not accept the Hegelian Dialectic; but he did accept Hegel's notion of conflict as the essential form of progress, and on the basis of this notion he built his own very different Dialectic upon Hegel's method. In Marx's conception, as in Hegel's, thesis, antithesis and synthesis replace and transcend the categories of Formal Logic, and reality is conceived in dynamic instead of static terms. What is, is becoming: nothing ever stands still in the real world.

Marx's real world, however, is very different from Hegel's; for it is nothing other than the phenomenal world of everyday experience. The things we experience in ordinary life are not, Marx holds, abstractions or derivative and imperfect expressions of a superior reality existing outside space and time, but ultimates beyond which we cannot and need not go—for beyond them there is nothing. They *are* reality—the one and only reality on which all thought, all ideas, all purely mental or spiritual constructions are built. Men can seek to understand this reality, and, what is more, to make themselves increasingly masters of the laws which govern its development. But men cannot go outside or beyond it; for it and nothing else is the universe in which they are. Being precedes thought; for thought can be only thought of being, and about being. There can be no perception without something to perceive; no conception without a mind reflecting upon its experience of things. The external world is the external world, and is not either an idea in our minds or a reflection of some ideal substance outside and beyond our experience. The description "phenomenal" is thus, in Marx's use of it, applicable not to things but to ideas about things. Things are real, and are not mere appearances, but they often appear to men distorted by the notions men entertain about them. Reality and phenomenon, in Marx's usage as compared with Hegel's, change places.

But the real world of experience is not static. Nothing is static save the abstractions which men make in their own minds in their attempts to rationalise their experience. Everything changes: human history is the process of human change writ large in the common experience of mankind. In that Hegel was abundantly right; but Marx held that, as things are real and are not mere reflections of the Idea, the dynamic Logic which Hegel applied to the Idea must be applied directly to the things themselves, and used directly in explaining the course of historical movements. Things change. Things, in the ordinary temporal process of human development, are continually becoming that which they were not. But by what law do they change? Marx answered "By the dialectical law of human conflict." What, then, are the nature and the method of this historic law?

The Powers of Production

Since things, and not ideas, are the ultimate realities, things and not ideas must, it seems, be the ultimate motive forces of human history. But what things? Marx, as we have seen in earlier chapters, made answer that the underlying forces of history are the changing 'powers of production.' As these expand with the increase in men's knowledge and opportunities, human history passes through corresponding phases of development. To each broad phase of development of the powers of production corresponds a phase of human evolution.

Marx, then, regards the 'powers of production' as things, and not as ideas about things. The 'powers of production,' however, as we have seen in previous chapters, are not and cannot be merely material things as such, in the ordinary sense of the word "material." A machine is no doubt a "thing"; but it becomes a 'power of production' only in the hands of someone who knows how to make it work. It is, moreover, a thing in which is embodied someone's knowledge of the means of constructing it. These forms of knowledge—how to make instruments of production and how to work them—both became social forms of knowledge, as possessions of the society in which they exist and are handed on from man to man and from generation to generation. Most "inventions" are really improvements on what was previously known: most inventors use the work of many men's minds in devising their improvements: most skill is taught by men to men, even if there is in it a factor of natural aptitude. Thus, the powers of production embody in a social form not only the natural materials of which they are made but also immaterial factors of human mental achievement. Nor are all the powers of production embodied in material things: a chemical formula may be as much a 'power of production' as a machine. Of course, such a formula has to be in someone's mind, and that mind has to be in a body. But this can be said also of ideas of the most abstract sort. The 'powers of production,' then, though they include many material objects and cannot be exercised except in connection with material objects, cannot be defined exclusively in terms of "matter" in any sense in which "matter" excludes "mind." They exist in fact as the outcome of a relation between mind

273

and matter, and are made up of both material and mental elements.

We have, then, a picture of the 'powers of production' developing, as a result of the advance of men's practical knowledge, and of each major advance involving a change in men's social organisation, and also, therewith, in men's ideas and beliefs. But where, in this presentation, are we to find the Hegelian dialectical process at work? The powers of production advance as men's knowledge and command over the forces of nature increase; but in this advance there appears so far no necessary element of conflict, save the perpetual conflict of man with the niggardliness and reluctance of natural forces. Clearly this is not Marx's conception, any more than it is Hegel's. The conflict of which Marx is thinking is a conflict between men, and not between mankind and nature. Where, then, are we to seek for the thesis, antithesis and synthesis which the Dialectic postulates?

The Basis of the Marxian Dialectic

Each stage reached by the powers of production, Marx holds, gives rise among men to a set of economic relationships designed to further their use; and to these economic relationships correspond appropriate political and social relationships which arise out of, and react upon, the economic conditions. We have been over this ground in an earlier chapter, and there is no need to go over it again here. Marx's point, as we have seen, was that throughout human history these relationships have hitherto necessarily ranged men in economic classes, and that it is between these classes that the struggles which make human history have been waged. The theses and antitheses, according to Marx, are these classes; and the syntheses are the new classes which arise out of the struggle of class against class at each turning point of history, up to the conflict which succeeds at length in establishing a classless society, and therewith brings the dialectical process of class-conflict to an end.

We have seen already that this process, as Marx describes it, cannot truly be regarded as "materialist," in the most familiar sense of that term, because the forces upon which the entire movement rests—the 'powers of production'—are not forces of matter as opposed to mind, but embody the result of mind's action upon matter—man's command over nature, for short. For this reason Marx's Conception of History has often been called in this book "realist" rather than "materialist." Still more clearly, the struggle by which the process of historical evolution is carried on is not one of matter with matter, in any sense in which matter can be contrasted with mind, but of men with men. According to Marx, it is a class-struggle, or rather a series of class-struggles which continues to its end in the total obliteration of class-distinctions and in the establishment of a classless society.

What then becomes of the dialectical process? Clearly it cannot continue to obey the formula of class-struggle; for no classes remain in being. For the new phase of human history which then begins, and for the further phases that are to follow, a new formula is needed. "Pre-history ends," Marx writes, "and history begins." But what is to be the law of this new history of a classless world?

The Marxists' answer is that they do not know. For Marx held, as we have seen, that each age sets itself only the problems which it needs to solve, and is in a position to solve; and mankind is neither able nor in need to solve as yet the problems of the Socialist future. Clearly this need not mean that the Dialectic will no longer apply; for the law of the Dialectic admits of many different formulæ besides that of the class-struggle, and the formula may be changed without changing the dialectical character of the historical process. Struggle can proceed upon other planes than that of class, and in higher and less brutal forms. But what these forms will be the Marxist neither pretends nor even wishes to know in advance of the event. All he does pretend to know is that, whatever is to come after the winning of a classless society, it is not in the nature of reality ever to become static and unchanging. As long as mankind exists, mankind will have a history, and that history will proceed dialectically, in some form.

Such is the Marxian theory. What, now, of its validity and of its value? It has, in the first place, the merit, which is by no means always borne in mind by its professing adherents, that it excludes "once-and-for-all" dogmatism. For, as it regards social ideas as the expression of class-attitudes, and classes themselves as corresponding to the continually changing powers of production, it must regard social ideas as subject to change and development as changes in the powers of production alter the class-structure of society. If the structure of classes has changed since Marx's day, as I have tried to show that it has, the theory which Marx formulated as appropriate to the class-conditions of his day can no longer be adequate to meet the needs of the present time, at all events until it has been modified and adapted in conformity with these changes. Every Marxist

275

is logically compelled by his Marxism to be a "revisionist," though of course his revisionism need not agree with that of Bernstein, or with that of Sorel, or with that of Trotsky, or with that of Stalin, or with that of any of the other schools of thought which have set out to adapt Marxism to current needs and conditions. It is, no doubt, easy under cover of revising Marxism really to abandon it; and this tendency has given all attempts at revision a bad odour among Marxists, and has often driven them towards a defensively dogmatic interpretation of Marx's doctrines. But, in fact, no Marxist can escape revisionism without denying the dialectical principle. For to lay down hard and fast dogmas is to fall back from the evolutionary Dialectic into the static categories of Formal Logic.

Marxism and the Class-struggle

Marx's method is, indeed, fully as important as his doctrine. For it is fundamentally an injunction to look again and again at the changing facts of the social situation, to relate them to the changing character of the powers of production, and to draw freshly at each stage of development the practical conclusions which this process of observation suggests. Some Marxists will doubtless object to this interpretation on the ground that the vital factors of social development change in essence only over very long periods, corresponding to the entire span of the conflict between two rival classes, so that the essential character of the struggle between capitalists and proletariat can be expressed in a single comprehensive generalisation, which can become a dogmatic theory valid for the whole duration of the capitalist system, or at most needing only minor modifications in the province of Socialist tactics. Capitalists and proletariat, they will argue, are definite economic classes, the denotation of which may vary from moment to moment, but not so as to affect their general character or the nature of the opposition between them. Accordingly, it is argued, for the complete duration of the struggle between them the Marxian presentation holds good; and observation of changing facts can do nothing to modify any essential point, indispensable though it undoubtedly is as a guide to day-to-day strategy.

There is an element of truth in this view. The major antithetical relation of capitalists and proletariat does endure for the whole span of the capitalist system; and to this extent Marxism is and must be dogmatic. But for any correct development of Socialist strategy it is no less important to observe the variations within the general class-structure of capitalist society

276

than to grasp the fundamental antagonisms which it involves. In earlier chapters it has been argued that there have been in fact highly important variations in the arrangement of social classes, corresponding to the further evolution of the powers of production, since Marx formulated his doctrines; and it is a fatal error to ignore the significance of these variations, or to assume that they do not affect the correct formulation of the Marxian theory. For within the general antithetical relationship which exists in society over a major phase of development there are many lesser relationships which possess a similar antithetical character. Nor do these result, though Marx often wrote as if they did, merely from the survival within capitalist society of obsolescent elements left over from an earlier phase. If they did, they could be ignored, except as secondary factors complicating the day-to-day struggle between the major combatants. But, in fact, the most significant of them are, as we have seen, themselves products of an advancing technical mastery of men over natural forces—a mastery to which Capitalism has responded by changes in its own structure, not least in finding means of diffusing industrial ownership while continuing to concentrate the effective control of economic policy in fewer hands, and in creating a large and increasingly influential class of salaried and fee-taking professionals who form the nucleus of a new intermediate class very different in character from the old, and infinitely superior in initiative, driving-force, and powers of resisting the working class where it takes sides against them. To ignore or to minimise the importance of these changes in the class-system is to be guilty of wilful blindness; and to recite in face of them an unrevised Marxian creed is to prefer a dogma to a workable policy of Socialist advance.

It is evident that Marx was mistaken in supposing that the further development of Capitalism would result, in advance of the advent of the proletarian revolution, in driving the entire intermediate element in society down into the ranks of the proletariat. There have been, so far, no signs of this happening in any country, though in times of crisis there has appeared a large and dangerous threatened group of unemployed members of the non-proletarian classes. These, however, so far from joining the proletariat, have been its most vehement assailants, and have joined forces with its major enemies to overthrow it, even if they have not been powerful enough to make on their own behalf a bid for social and economic authority. They have been among the principal recruits to Fascism, and have in fact supplied a high proportion, if not of its leaders, at all events of its non-commissioned officers, and even of its leading executants. Marx appears—very naturally—to have foreseen neither the extent to which the further advance of capitalist prosperity would, with the aid of joint stock structure and technical invention, swell the ranks both of the functionless small capitalist shareholders and of the active and functioning professional and technical groups, nor the form which their reaction to the threat of the decline and suppression of Capitalism was likely to take. If there had not been the great increase in the absolute and relative numbers of these two closely connected and over-lapping groups, and the great advance in their incomes and status, which accompanied the expanding phase of Capitalism in the half century preceding the advent of Fascism, the develop-ment of capitalist concentration would doubtless have forced down more and more of the members of the old intermediate groups into the proletariat, and would have given them in due course the attitude of proletarians when they had lost hope of recovering their old position in society. But in fact the inter-mediate groups, having achieved a great advance and become more and more conscious of their economic importance, received the narrowing of their opportunities and incomes which the crises of Capitalism between the wars involved, not with acquiescence in proletarianisation, but in, a mood of angry revolt and determination to preserve or to retrieve their economic and social superiority against the threat of Socialism. They were antagonistic to the large capitalists, and especially to high finance, which they often blamed for their economic adversities; but they did not become antagonistic to Capitalism itself. Indeed, they became determined to defend their claims to privilege at all costs against the exponents of equalitarian creeds, by attempting to reconstruct society on a basis which they hoped would subordinate the conduct of large-scale industry and finance to their own claims within the framework of the Totalitarian State.

Intermediate Classes

Marxism, as Marx expounded it, assumed that there could exist between the capitalists and the proletariat no class capable either of winning power for itself, and of creating a new social system in the image of its own needs, or of serving as the auxili-aries of a force, not embodied in a class, which would revive, in a modernised form, the ancient behaviour of the conquering horde, and would seek to overcome the contradictions of

278

Capitalism by turning Capitalism itself into a subordinate agency of national military aggrandisement leading to the mass enslavement of conquered peoples. Marx further assumed, not only that the scale of capitalist industry was bound to increase, and to lead to a growing concentration of capitalist power—wherein he was quite right—but also that the capitalist era would end and give place to Socialism when the great capitalists were no longer able further to develop the use of the powers of production, or to resist the claims of the advancing proletariat, within the limits of Capitalism itself. This last view is, however, a far less obvious deduction to-day than it seemed in the light of the facts upon which Marx based his conclusions. For the rise of the new intermediate classes made it indispensable to consider the alternative that these groups, created and strengthened by the advance of Capitalism, might be powerful enough, in alliance with the other forces hostile to democracy, to defeat the proletariat and to put Fascism into power.

The orthodox Marxist answer to this argument is that the groups in question could hope to do this only if they were in a position either to reconstruct Capitalism, or to construct a new type of society, on a basis consistent with the further development of the powers of production. But it is illegitimate to exclude out of hand the possibility of this being done. It certainly could not have been done unless the new masters of society had been prepared to borrow, and to apply to their own ends, many of the techniques and instruments of control hitherto chiefly associated with the propaganda of Socialism. For assuredly the powers of production cannot be developed, or advantage taken of the modern possibilities for the expansion of the wealth-creating process, without a high degree of centralised control and operation of the productive and financial machine. The new economic system of the Fascist counter-revolution when it came did in fact turn out to be a form of State-controlled Capitalism—called "National Socialism"—under which industries and services were operated on the grand scale under State direction and protection, whether they were in form nationalised or left in private hands. Sorel, a courageous Marxian "revisionist," visualised this possibility in one of its forms, when he spoke, well before Lenin, of the possible alternative form of "State Capitalism." Sorel, indeed, envisaged this system as one in which the State would take over industry, and would run it, against the workers, in the interests of the bondholding, shareholding and salaried elements in society.

The Fascists and Nazis developed "State Capitalism" in a different form, in which industries were left mainly in private ownership, but were made subject in all essentials of national policy to the overriding authority of the Totalitarian State.

Marxism and Fascism

Orthodox Marxists were quite incapable of understanding what was happening in the rise of this new Fascist type of society. It was a part of their creed that the only social forces of which account needed to be taken in considering historical development were those which were embodied in economic classes; and, correctly holding that the new intermediate social groups were incapable, by themselves, of cohering into a class capable of seizing power and using it for the development of the powers of production, they mistakenly concluded that the rise of these groups could not significantly affect the course of social evolution. They might have taken warning from the fact that the capitalists, at the time when they appeared as a significant group exercising social influence, were at least as incapable as the new middle classes are to-day of taking over complete power and making a new State in the image of their own needs. The rising capitalist class did not revolt against the old ruling class, destroy the old feudal State, and make a new capitalist State of its own by a creative act of social revolution. Far from it. The capitalists took sides with whatever elements in the old ruling class they could get to help them in furthering their own ends. They did not destroy the old State: they entered into it, and set to work gradually to transform it from within—a thoroughly un-Marxian proceeding, but one in which they met with a very large measure of success. They did not replace the rule of the old governing classes by a new "dictatorship" of their own: on the contrary, they were content with a share of power—at the outset a quite small share—as the subordinate allies of the more progressive elements in the old aristocracy. They did not wait until they were strong enough to make their own revolution: instead, they took whatever concessions they could get, and therewith whatever responsibilities came their way as sharers in the administrative and legislative functions of a State which was not of their making. The rising capitalists in effect behaved after the manner of Fabians, and not at all in accordance with Marx's precepts. One can readily imagine a dogmatic "materialist" of those days explaining that the capitalist class could be neglected as a major factor in the class-struggle, because it was not powerful or coherent enough to do more than hover ineffectively between the landed aristo-cracy and the common people.

Of course, Marxists will reply that the capitalist class *was* the destined heir of feudalism, whereas the new middle class is not the destined heir of Capitalism. In the first of these statements they have the advantage of speaking with knowledge of what did actually occur, whereas the second is merely dogmatic. I am not suggesting, and I do not believe, that the second statement is wrong; for I am not at all disposed to take seriously such arguments as are put forward by Burnham in *The Managerial Revolution*. I am, however, suggesting that there is a clear similar-ity between the capitalist class, as it appeared in the earlier stages of its rise to power, and the technical and managerial groups of to-day. What they have in common is above all a mastery of the knowledge and skill needed for the effective exploitation of the 'powers of production.' This it is that marks off the new *petite bourgeoisie* from the old, and suffices to make it, if not a claimant for class power on its own account in any full sense, at all events a force which has to be reckoned with seriously in estimating the social outlook.

In effect, the mistake of many of the contemporary Marxists lies principally in ignoring the danger that groups not strong enough by themselves to control society may nevertheless become the instruments and auxiliaries of forces not primarily of a class-character and may be able to give to these forces the additional strength that will enable them to become the masters of society. Faulty psychology here co-operates with an over-simplified theory of history to lead to a wrong conclusion. Marx's psychology, being of his time, was unduly rationalistic, and made altogether too little allowance for the persistence in modern man of the primitive characteristics of the horde. Marx thought of man primarily as a subsistence-seeking social organiser, who made use of rational methods to improve his command over nature. He left out of account man's responsiveness to primitive appeals to the solidarity of the horde, and therewith neglected the possibility that economic forces could be diverted away from class channels into channels of nationalistic predatory self-assertion.

It is, of course, the case that Fascist economic policy involved at the very outset a practical contradiction. If the intermediate social groups were to be strong enough to aid the forces of militarist nationalism to seize power, the new middle class of *rentiers*, shareholders and salaried professionals had to succeed in carrying along with it the surviving elements of the old *petite bourgeoisie* of small-scale traders and producers, including the farmers and the peasant-owners engaged in small-scale agriculture. These latter groups, however, by no means wished for an advance of large-scale production and State control, but still hankered after the destruction of their large-scale competitors and exploiters. Accordingly, Fascist movements presented the paradox of appearing at once as the advocates of planned Capitalism, and as the enemies not only of Socialism and of the working-class movement, but also of trusts and combines, of centralised banking, and of large department and chain stores and large-scale merchanting. They had even at times to present themselves as the defenders of small-scale craft production against the encroachments of the machine. These reactionary elements in their programmes were indeed almost entirely window-dressing; and no serious attempt was ever made to carry them into effect when once they had served their purpose in attracting recruits to the Fascist movement while it was in the phase of opposition. There was, however, one important exception to this generalisation; for the Fascist Revolution, where it succeeded, did commit itself to upholding the position of the peasants, and therewith to maintaining the system of small-scale agriculture.

This one necessity would have been enough, even if there had been no others, to drive Fascism in power to adopt a policy of Economic Nationalism, even apart from the fact that it was based upon nationalist sentiment and on the use of this sentiment as a means of defeating the internationalist aspirations of Socialism. Some misguided Socialists, relying on the doctrines of orthodox Political Economy, believed that this necessity to pursue Economic Nationalism would inescapably condemn Fascism to failure, because it would make impossible the further development of the powers of production, which could not be fully utilised except on a basis of continually expanding international exchange. This view was, however, for large States, highly disputable; and it would not have applied to the Fascist States, if they had been able to win their projected wars of conquest. Undoubtedly, in order to secure the maximum production that is technically possible for the world as a whole, it is necessary to have a highly developed system of international exchange, based in the main on the valid principle of comparative real costs. But in relation to the gross under-production that was characteristic of capitalist society between the wars it was fully possible for a large country to add greatly to its output of goods and services by organising its economy to a substantial

282

extent on a basis of national self-sufficiency and production mainly for the domestic market. Economic Nationalism, although it was bound to be less productive from the standpoint of the world as a whole than a well organised economic internationalism could have been, could thus offer to particular countries the prospect of greater wealth and prosperity than was possible for them under an unregulated Capitalism more dependent on production for the world market; and this possibility sufficed to give such a system the chance of establishing itself, at least for a time, on foundations more compatible with the development of the powers of production in the prevailing circumstances of capitalist confusion than adherence to the principles of the international division of labour would have been.

The Fascists had, however, never the smallest intention of living for long on a basis of nationalist economic isolation. The organisation of their home economic resources was meant to serve them only as a basis for predatory war-making, leading to conquests which would enable them to lay hold on as much as they wanted of the products of other countries, either without paying for them at all, or at any rate without giving an equivalent return. Their real economic policy was not Economic Nationalism, but an Economic Imperialism that went far beyond anything that had hitherto been practised by capitalist States.

. It was ludicrously unrealistic in face of possibilities such as these—already to a great extent made actual in two great countries—merely to go on reciting the Marxian *credo* about economic classes, as if Capitalism were still identical in its class-structure with the half-grown Capitalism of 1848. For matters are not so simple as to remove the need for all further thought when the fundamental antagonism between the capitalists and the proletariat has once been grasped; nor does the Dialectic serve its purpose once and for all in revealing the existence of this antagonism and pointing the way towards its resolution by means of Socialism. The picture of the class-struggle thus presented needs to have its empty spaces filled in; and the candid user of the dialectical method will keep his eyes open for changes in the class-structure of society that may give him cause to modify his tactics and perhaps also his general diagnosis of the social situation.

The real question, of course, was whether the new force of Fascism that was interposing itself in the struggle between the capitalists and the proletariat was capable of reconstructing the economic system on a foundation strong enough to give it a

283

new lease of life without Socialism. We have seen reason to suppose that the spirit of Nationalism, by enlisting all the forces of reaction on its side and also by coming to terms with the new intermediate classes as well as with the older types of *petit bourgeois* and with the peasants, could for the time being do something to combat unemployment and to restore economic activity on a basis of Economic Nationalism. Such success, to be sure, could not have lasted for long on a foundation of economic isolation, or even on the wider basis given to it by Dr. Schacht's currency manipulation of economic relations with the countries which were marked out for inclusion, in due course, within the economico-political empire of the conquering German Reich. But it was never meant to last, as a self-contained national system: it was intended only as a temporary base for the system of domination which was involved in the realisation of the Fascist will to power over other peoples. Had this Fascist form of Economic Imperialism prevailed in war—and there was no necessary reason why it should not have prevailed—the road towards Socialism could have been blocked for much longer than Marx and his successors ever supposed; for to that extent there could have intervened between Capitalism, as we know it, and Socialism an entirely new phase of social development, resting on a system of State-controlled capitalist enterprise under the influence of a predatory nationalist Imperialism based on the exploitation less of class by class than of nation by nation.

For the time being, Fascism has been defeated in war, and the danger has receded, though it would be rash indeed to proclaim that we have heard the last of it. The defeat was at the hands of a singular alliance between the forces which Fascism menaced, including both the Capitalism of the countries which, immediately or remotely, felt themselves cast for the part of subject tribute-renderers to the Fascist power and the Socialism of the Soviet Union—which was cast even more obviously for the rôle of helot to the triumphant *Herrenvolk*. In addition, there was ranged against the Fascists every working-class movement in the world and, side by side with the proletarians, all the liberal-democratic elements which had escaped extinction. These ill-assorted allies could all unite to do battle with Fascism, which was their common enemy. But how much else had they in common; and, having defeated Fascism, with what hope of agreement could they set about the task of filling the void left by its overthrow? The history of the years since 1945 furnishes the beginning of the answer to this question—but only the beginning.

284

The Claimants to Power

Broadly, apart from Fascism, there were in the world after 1945 three major claimants, and one minor claimant, to the rôle of world-maker. There was, first, the still vital and developing Capitalism of the American Continent, which, after passing through a phase of serious internal contradictions in the 1930's, had been enabled, *by war*, to make a great further leap forward in the development of the powers of production. War, by providing an insatiable market, snatched American Capitalism out of its difficulties, and gave it, with a new lease of life, a new confidence in its superiority. This confidence was reflected in its ideological war-making on Communism and on Socialism— between which it did not pause to draw fine lines of distinction. Left by the war as the most powerful country in the world, because its vast resources were not devastated but developed by the conditions of the struggle, the United States emerged militantly capitalist—indeed, the more so because in the 1930's its capitalists had had so serious a fright.

Secondly, there was the newly emancipated Communism of the Soviet Union, seriously damaged by Nazi devastation and, even more, twisted ideologically by the terrible ordeal through which it had passed, but immensely resilient, with the sense of standing for a great new stage in social evolution, and at once confident and full of fears—confident that, could it but gain time to recover, it would emerge the strongest power in the world, immune from the contradictions of capitalist economics and able to develop the powers of production to a higher level than any other country, but at the same time fearful that American Capitalism might succeed in uniting all the rest of the world against it before it had regained its strength. Thus, the offensive-defensive of American Capitalism encountere ι the defensive-offensive of Soviet diplomacy on the 'cold' battle fields of Europe in the repeated deadlocks of the Security Council and the Council of Foreign Ministers; and Germany's was the body at which the contestants tugged hardest, because Germany, even in devastation and defeat, remained the key position in Europe.

Thirdly, as the minor claimant among the four, the old liberal Capitalism remained alive, but had undergone a strange metamorphosis; for who, even a little while ago, could have foreseen that Catholicism would become the principal standard-bearer of the European capitalist system? It has become so, because, in face of the decline of European Capitalism, Catholicism, covering itself with a veneer of social doctrine, alone has the toughness to resist the demands of economic progress, and can therefore serve as a rallying point for all the motley elements opposed both to Communism and to Socialism in its Western forms. This "third force," however, though it is powerful in obstruction, has so far shown itself altogether lacking in constructive quality and, to the extent to which it retains influence, has become unavoidably the pensioner and dependant of American Capitalism, which alone can lend it the power to keep the peoples it rules over from starvation leading to mass-revolt.

Fourthly, as the third major claimant, there is Western Socialism, variously called "liberal Socialism" or "Social Democracy." This force, over a large part of Europe, has been seriously weakened by the advance of Communism, which in France particularly has secured for the time being a preponderant position in the working-class movement. It retains, however, its hold on the working class in Great Britain, in Scandinavia, and in several other Western countries; and it is a force to be reckoned with in Germany. It may, moreover, regain much of its lost power in other Western countries if Western Communists are forced into fighting the battles of the Soviet Union to the detriment of their own peoples' standards of living.

The Outlook for Socialism

The fundamental creed of liberal Socialism is that, given the conditions provided by "liberal" Capitalism and a parliamentary system with real roots among the people, Socialist victory can be won without revolution or the use, save quite incidentally, of totalitarian weapons. Clearly, the chance of establishing Socialism by constitutional means in any country depends on the failure of all the other elements in the population to unite against the proletariat, and on the success of the proletariat both in maintaining its own unity and in attaching some elements drawn from other classes to its cause. There is the best prospect of this where the economic conditions are such that the question of Socialism comes to a head while both the middle groups and the proletariat—and, therefore, the capitalists also—are in general prosperous enough not to be driven by despair to extreme courses. In other words, Capitalism must be in difficulties, or the impetus towards a fundamental change of system will be wanting; but it must not be in sheer collapse, or the possibility of a smooth and peaceful transition will have disappeared, and revolutionary influences will have become powerful on both sides. Under such intermediate conditions,

286

most elements in the society will be inclined to give and take. The Socialists will be prepared to ease the transition in order to prevent undue dislocation and to weaken opposition; and considerable elements in the middle groups may be prepared to tolerate the advance towards Socialism, and even to help it on, provided that it comes without violence and without too much or too sudden upsetting of their accustomed ways of life and offers them the prospect of greater economic security than they can see ahead of them if capitalist forces are allowed to have their way uncontrolled. A considerable number of the technicians and minor administrators and professional men, who form the key elements in the middle group, may be ready to welcome and help Socialism if it can come in this form.

This possibility, as we have seen, makes it a vitally important matter for the Socialist appeal to be cast into such a shape as will attract these doubtful elements, provided only that the attempt to do this is not made by watering down the Socialist policy. Such watering down would defeat its own ends; for the Socialist policy can appeal only if it does offer a workmanlike solution consistent with the successful development of the powers of production; and this is impossible unless it is thorough-going in its methods and objectives. The Socialists can afford to do everything that is possible to minimise the hardships and dislocations of the transition; but they cannot on any account afford to demand less than plenitude of power over the entire economic system.

In Great Britain and in some other countries of Western Europe the chance of a constitutional transition to Socialism still exists. But its continued existence depends on the maintenance of conditions which do not drive the contending parties to the unrestrained extremisms of despair. If a large part of the British proletariat were to be converted to Communism, or a large part of the British middle classes to Fascism, then the possibility of such a policy as the British Labour Government of 1945 set out to follow in home affairs would promptly disappear; and the serious development of extremism on either side would inevitably lead to a parallel growth on the other. The reason why there has not been as yet in Great Britain a large-scale growth of either Communism or Fascism lies in the relative solidity of the British "liberal" tradition, which rests mainly on the foundations laid under Capitalism while it was still an expanding system, developing under British leadership. The loss of British revenue from overseas investment and the large setbacks encountered by British world trade have already knocked away the foundations on which this structure of liberalism has hitherto rested, so that it now hangs precariously in the air. It still remains, however, powerful as a psychological force; and it will retain its influence for some time yet if only Great Britain can find means of accommodating its way of life to its changed position in the world by readjusting both its commitments and its national economy to its lessened resources. The only practicable basis for such an accommodation is some form of Socialism; for it is abundantly clear that British Capitalism is unable to bring it about. The possibility of achieving it by way of constitutional Socialist advance depends, first, on the advance towards Socialism being speedy enough to forestall sheer economic disaster, and secondly on British Socialism finding enough like-minded collaborators in other countries to make possible the creation of a group of Socialistic countries able to stand out against engulfment by either American Capitalism or Soviet Communism, and so to preserve—by finding a new foundation for it—what is valuable in the "liberal" tradition.

Contraries and Contradictories

But where, it may be asked, in all this discussion of class-changes and national policies, does the Marxian Dialectic come in? It comes in all the time; for what I have been saying is in effect a criticism, not of the Dialectic itself, but of Marx's much over-simplified way of formulating it. It was, no doubt, highly convenient for purposes of simplified presentation, merely to replace the major and minor premises and the conclusion of the syllogism of Formal Logic by the thesis, antithesis and synthesis of the Hegelian dynamic "trinity." But the doing of this involved the unwarranted assumption that the conflicts which go to the making of history are all simple conflicts between two rival "statements," embodied in rival classes, and that any third "statement" that appears on the same stage of history must be of minor importance, and indeed without influence on the general outcome. This unwarranted assumption is the more easily made because the rival statements are misleadingly described as "contradictions"—which they are not, in any legitimate use of the word. To no "statement" can there correspond more than one contradictory statement (A is B: A is not B) but against any "statement" there can be brought up a number of different, or of *contrary*, "statements." A is B; A is C; A is D are not contradictions: they are *different* "statements," which may also be contrary, if there is any inconsistency in being at once B and C, or C and D.

288

Nor are social classes contradictories. Being a proletarian does not consist in not being a capitalist. It may involve that; but the status of a proletarian is a positive status, which cannot be defined simply by saying what it is not. There is no reason in the nature of things (at least, none can be given, except on purely metaphysical assumptions) why all major social conflicts should involve only two major combatants: nor does a realistic study of historical development bear out such a conclusion on an empirical test.[1] It is pure metaphysics, and not science, to assume that all class-struggles are simple combats between two embattled classes.

It is also very puzzling that, in Marx's version of the Dialectic, the exceedingly diverse and manifold changes that take place in the 'powers of production' always manage somehow to find representative embodiment in a single rising class. If we ask *why* this occurs, Marx provides no answer. He does not feel the need for an answer. Yet surely, even if he cannot say why, he should be able at any rate to back up his assertion with inductive evidence drawn from world history. He does not attempt to do this, unless the answer is to be taken as embodied in the very brief, and highly popularised version of ancient and medieval history that takes up a few paragraphs of *The Communist Manifesto*. In any case, these paragraphs are not an answer. The slaves of the Ancient World were clearly not the antithetical class to the ancient governing class. What classes did Marx suppose to have played the rôles of Thesis, Antithesis, and Synthesis in Ancient Greece or Rome? Goodness only knows.

The Thesis, Antithesis, Synthesis formula, in the simple form in which Marx applies it to the contemporary struggle between capitalists and proletariat, can by no means be made even plausibly applicable to human history as a whole. Nor, I feel sure, can it be made applicable even by presenting it in a more complicated form, with more than two contestants. Class-conflicts may have existed at all stages of historical development; but that is a very different thing from their having existed always in the form requisite for the Marxian analysis. The Marxian "class" that plays a rôle in history is not simply a class: it is a class which, at a particular stage, possesses the mastery needed for the further development of the 'powers of production.' Class-conflicts that do not conform to this pattern can have no relevance to the dialectical conception of history, in the shape in which Marx expounded it. A great deal of human history

[1] Nor did Marx think it had, in the past stages of history. See the quotation on page 54.

can, I agree, be elucidated by considering the influence of changes in the 'powers of production' on social and economic structure; but in a good number of the instances in which this part of Marx's theory is helpful no question of class-struggle appears to arise. The adoption of pastoral or of agricultural techniques greatly affected the social institutions of the peoples which resorted to them; but did it always create a corresponding class-struggle, and, if so, was there one sort of class-struggle among pastoralists, another among agriculturalists, and another among fishermen—and so on? If there was, what becomes of the unitary, straight-line, conception of human history as a whole?

Conclusion

It is, indeed, no more sensible to make the Dialectic, than any other part of the Marxian system, into a dogma. I find that it sometimes helps me to think in dialectical terms, rather than in the terms of Formal Logic, about the factors of social development. When I do this, however, I use the Dialectic merely as an aid to thinking, and use it only as much, and push it only as far, as I find helpful in any particular process of thought. I employ it, not as a dogma, but as a thought-shape, useful on condition that it remains a servant and is not allowed to become the master of thought. I feel that it ought to help others to use it in this way. But, if it does not help them, even after they have tried it, there is no more to be said; for no one can think outside his nature, and I know that the processes of thought go on very differently in different people's heads. A man can think realistically without the Dialectic, though I am sure he cannot think realistically about society if his thinking is shut up within the categories of Formal Logic. With this caution, let him think in the way that suits him best; but, if he wants to understand Marx, he will have, even though he reject the Dialectic, to make himself master enough of it to understand the form in which Marx actually thought. Failure to do this has been responsible, as we have seen throughout this book, for much supposed refutation of Marxism that is merely beside the point, as well as for a tendency, among Marxists, to make of Marxism a dead dogma instead of a living source of fresh observation and inference. Having said this, and presented in this book my conception of what Marxism really means, I can only ask the reader, if he is in any doubt, to go and study for himself what Marx wrote, and not merely what others have written about him.

A NOTE ON BOOKS

I DO NOT PROPOSE TO append to this book any large bibliography of Marxian writings, which are, except in Great Britain, almost co-extensive with the literature of modern Socialism. It is enough to give references to the most important of Marx's own works, and to those of his collaborator, Engels, with only a very few books expository or critical of his doctrines.

Among Marx's own writing, pride of place must be given to his *magnum opus*, *Capital*. This consists, apart from supplementary studies, of three volumes. The first of these, *Capitalist Production*, originally published in 1867, is now available, translated by Eden and Cedar Paul, in Everyman's Library (2 volumes), with an introduction by me. There are also a larger edition of the same translation, and an older translation, by S. Moore and E. Aveling, edited by Engels, and therefore regarded as sacred by some Marxists. This was the only volume of *Capital* published by Marx himself. The remaining volumes were edited by Engels after his death. Vol. II, *Capitalist Circulation*, is available in a translation by E. Untermann, originally issued in America. It is important for students of the details of Marx's economic theories, but far less important for most readers than Vol. III. Vol. II was left by Marx in a fairly finished state, whereas Vol. III, *Capitalist Production as a Whole*, was put together by Engels from many papers written at very different dates. It is less a book than a vitally important quarry for the Marxian student. Without it, Marx's theory of value cannot be fully understood—especially in relation to the connection between value and price; and it contains most of Marx's doctrines on such questions as the causes of capitalist crises and the changing class-divisions in capitalist society. It is available in E. Untermann's translation, published only in the United States.

There have been several attempts to summarise *Capital* in a single volume. By far the best of these is Julian Borchardt's *The People's Marx*, translated by S. Trask. Most of this is incorporated in a useful volume of selection from *Capital* and other writings, edited by Max Eastman, published in the United States in the *Modern Library*. Emile Burns's *Handbook of Marxism* contains, in addition to a selection from Marx, large extracts from the writings of Lenin and Stalin.

As a pendant to *Capital*, invaluable to students of Marx's economic theories, is his posthumous book, *Theorien über den Mehrwert*, also available in French as *Histoire des Doctrines Économiques*, but not in English. This contains Marx's detailed studies of the theories of the classical economists, especially Ricardo, and throws indispensable light on the formation of his own economic doctrines. Of Marx's other definitely economic writings the most important is his *Critique of Political Economy*, published in 1859, eight years before Vol I of *Capital*. This is available in an American translation by N. I. Stone. Apart from its importance in economic theory, it contains in the preface (and also in a draft introduction found among Marx's papers after his death, and published as an appendix in the American edition) the only direct exposition he ever made of the Materialist Conception of History and of his method of arriving at it. These few pages are quite indispensable for anyone who wants to grasp the essential foundations of Marxism. They should be read together with *The Communist Manifesto* of 1848, by Marx and Engels, the earliest clear formulation of Marxism as a system. The *Manifesto* is available in many editions. The fullest is that of D. Ryazonoff, which makes a stout volume of over 350 pages, with elaborate notes and comments.

Students of the Materialist Conception of History and of the philosophical basis of Marxism will also need to read *The Poverty of Philosophy*, Marx's answer to Proudhon, published in 1847 and available in an English translation by H. Quelch. They should also read Marx's *Theses on Feuerbach*, reprinted as an appendix to the English translation of Engels's *Ludwig Feuerbach* and, if they know German, the two volumes, *Aus dem literarischen Nachlass von Marx, Engels und Lassalle*, edited by F. Mehring, Marx's biographer. For English readers, some of Marx's early writings are available in *Selected Essays by Karl Marx*, translated by H. J. Stenning. *The German Ideology*, an early joint work of Marx and Engels, is also now available in English.

For Marx's views on the State and on Socialist policy, the best introduction is Marx's *Critique of the Gotha Programme*, written in 1875 as an attack on the policy of his German followers in connection with the fusion of the Marxian and Lassallian Socialist parties in Germany, and suppressed at the time by the German leaders. It is available in an English edition. With this should be read *The Civil War in France* (written in English), originally published as a manifesto of the First International on the occasion of the Paris Commune—a most important book for the understanding of Marx's political attitude. His views of

Socialist strategy, especially in relation to the position of the *petite bourgeoisie*, should also be studied in his earlier works, *The Class-Struggles in France* and *The Eighteenth Brumaire of Napoleon Bonaparte* (translated by E. and C. Paul) and also in *Germany: Revolution and Counter-Revolution*, which was written for Marx by Engels. These three books deal with the revolutionary and counter-revolutionary movements of 1848 and the following years.

Of Marx's other writings, two important pamphlets may be mentioned here. These are *Value, Price and Profit* (1865) and *Wage-Labour and Capital* (1849), both important for the development of his economic doctrines. For the student of Marxism there is an immense wealth of material in the volumes of his *Correspondence*, including the long series of letters which passed between him and Engels (available in German or French: in English there is only a selection, edited by Dona Torr), and his letters to Sorge and Kugelmann. Some of Marx's other writings (*Herr Vogt*, 3 vols., *Œuvres Philosophiques*, 3 vols., *Œuvres Politiques*, 8 vols.) are available in French as well as German. A complete French edition of the writings of Marx and Engels was in course of publication in the 1930's, but was interrupted by the outbreak of war.

Of the works of Engels, the most important are his *Condition of the Working Class in England in 1844* (translated by F. K. Wischnewetzky), his *Origin of the Family, Property and the State* (available in English), his *Peasant War in Germany* (translated by M. S. Olgin), his *Dialectics of Nature*, and his *Anti-Duehring*, now available in English. A part of *Anti-Duehring* is also available in an American translation, under the title *Landmarks of Scientific Socialism*, translated by A. Lewis, and in another partial version, *The Development of Socialism from Utopia to Science* (various pamphlet editions). See also another pamphlet *Historical Materialism*, and Engels's book on *Feuerbach*.

The standard life of Marx is by F. Mehring. A useful short book is Max Beer's *The Life and Teaching of Karl Marx*, and the next best life that of O. Ruhle, *Karl Marx* (translated by E. and C. Paul). See also D. Ryazonoff, *Karl Marx and Friedrich Engels*.

Of many books about Marx, I select a very few. First, small critical works include *Karl Marx*, by A. Loria (translated by E. and C. Paul), *Karl Marx's Capital*, by A. D. Lindsay, *Historical Materialism and the Economics of Karl Marx*, by Benedetto Croce (translated by C. M. Meredith) and *Karl Marx*, by I. Berlin. For Marxian philosophy, see G. Plekhanov, *Fundamental Principles of Marxism*, and S. Hook's two volumes *Towards the Understanding of Karl Marx*, and *From Hegel to Marx*. For a criticism from the standpoint of orthodox economics, see F. Böhm-Bawerk, *Karl Marx and the Close of his System*. For a "Trotskyite" interpretation, see various books by Max Eastman, especially *Marx, Lenin and the Science of Revolution*. Lenin's own writings, especially *The State and Revolution*, *The Proletarian Revolution*, and *Imperialism*, are all of primary importance. See also Lenin's *Materialism and Empirio-Criticism* for Marxist philosophy. Of works not in English, G. Sorel's *La Décomposition du Marxisme* is exceedingly interesting from a Syndicalist standpoint, and Arturo Labriola's *Karl Marx* (in Italian or French) is one of the best critical expositions.

INDEX

Accounting, Socialist, 254 ff., 258

Accumulation of Capital. *See* Capitalism *and* Investment.

Administration, 147, 182, 197. *See also* Civil Service.

Agriculture, Development of, 68, 86, 111, 126, 134 f., 144, 145, 290. *See also* Land.

Alexandria, 46

America. *See also* United States.
Agriculture in, 135
Discovery of, 66, 87
and Fascism, 149, 285

American Capitalism. *See under* Capitalism.
Labour Movement, 119, 249
Loans, 95

Anthropology, 57

Anti-foreigner Complex, 138

Anti-Semitism, 139

Armaments, Cost of, 103

Asiatic Mode of Production, 53

Atlantic Ocean, 66

Atomic Energy, 28

Austrian School of Economics, 214, 243

Baldwin, S., 168

Bank Clerks, 157, 158
of England, 83

Bankers, 123, 136, 137, 194

Bedaux System, 175

Belgium, 165, 166

Bentham, Jeremy, 37

Bernstein, E., 276

Biology, 25, 51, 69, 78, 132

Bourgeoisie, 33, 51, 53, 64 f., 67, 85 ff., 110 ff., 120 ff., 130, 165, 181, 205. *See also* Capitalism *and* Capitalist.
Petite. See Petite Bourgeoisie.

Buckle, H. T., 19, 78

Burnham, J., 281

Canada, 144, 145

Capital, Marx's, 13, 35, 36, 51, 84, 107, 110, 128, 212, 226 f., 240

Capital, Accumulation of, 237. *See also* Investment.
Concentration of, 122, 126, 241, 278, 279. *See also* Combination.
Constant and Variable, 235 ff.
Export of, 91. *See also* Investment.
as Factor of Production, 19, 251, 255
Organic Composition of, 224, 226
and Value, 215

Capitalism, American, 285 f., 288
Contradictions of, 88, 91, 92 ff., 98 ff., 113, 115, 116 ff., 120 ff. 149, 238, 240 ff., 278 f., 285
Development of, 13, 36, 40, 41 f., 44, 49, 54, 56, 67 f., 77, 83–107, 108, 113, 155 f., 239, 280
and Fascism, 97, 140 ff. *See also* Fascism.
Financial, 84, 123 f., 127, 129, 136
Industrial, 84, 121 ff., 156
Merchant, 83 ff., 121 ff., 155
National, 122, 146, 239 f.
Recent History of, 98 ff., 116 ff., 121 ff., 129, 137, 160 ff., 169, 170, 189, 277 ff., 285, 286 f.
State, 279, 280, 284
as a system, 31, 33, 36, 84, 101, 189 f., 240 ff., 246 ff., 265 ff.

Capitalists, 12, 36, 121 ff., 152

Catholicism, Roman, 49, 64, 65, 66, 68, 285 f.

Chadwick, E., 86

Change, Social, 13, 15, 16 ff., 21

Chartism, 185

China, 47, 80

Churches, National, 66, 200

Civil Engineering, 46, 81
Servants, 152, 157, 158, 194, 195, 200
Service under Socialism, 185, 200 f.
Society, in Hegel, 23, 52

295

Great Men, Historical Influence of, 27 f.
Greece, Ancient, 73, 81
Group Action, 12
'Mind', 79
Guilds. *See* Gilds.
Guizot, M., 52
Gumplowicz, 79

HANDLOOM WEAVERS, 85
Health Service Workers, 159
Hegel, G. W. F., 12, 18, 19, 20 ff., 24, 25, 26, 30, 32, 33, 35, 36, 52, 62, 82, 213, 269 ff., 288
Heredity, 78 f.
Herrenvolk, 149, 284
History, Theory of, as a Straight-line Process, 29 ff., 43 ff., 73, 80, 150, 209 f.
    Materialist Conception of, 17 ff., 27 ff., 34 ff., 44 ff., 50, 51–82, 150, 269 ff., 276 ff., 289 f.
Hitler, Adolf, 27, 40, 140, 163, 203, 204
Hobbes, Thomas, 66
Holland, 66, 137, 165, 170
Horde Movements, 147, 278, 281
Horse-power, 224
Hours of Labour, 176, 232 f., 236, 238
House of Lords, 187, 188, 195, 199, 206
House-Ownership, 15 f.
Humanism, 25
Hungary, 208

IDEALISM, 20 ff., 30, 32, 82, 270
Ideas and Things, 17, 18 ff., 35 f., 63, 272 ff.
Ideology as a Social Force, 41, 53, 68, 69, 72, 76 f., 139. *See also under* Thought.
Imperialism. *See* Economic Imperialism.
Imputation, 253
Incentives under Capitalism, 191
    under Socialism, 254
Incomes, Distribution of, 246 f., 249 ff., 254, 257, 262, 264 f. *See also* Labour, Exploitation of, Interest, Profits, Rent *and* Wages.
    Source of, 245
    Unearned, 263

298

Increasing Misery, Theory of, 88, 113 ff., 116 ff., 162
    Returns, 90
India, 47
Individual, Marx's View of, 22 ff., 35 f., 37, 38
Industrial Revolution, 83 ff., 126, 144, 237, 239
Inequality, 136, 249
Inflation, 173 f.
Insurance Companies, 125
    Workers, 157
Interest, 110, 124, 189, 215, 236 f., 245
International Working Men's Association, 182
Inventions, 27, 28, 273
Investment under Capitalism, 103, 122 ff., 128, 135, 136, 237, 238, 240
    under Socialism, 104 ff.
    Trusts, 125
Italy, 165, 166, 168, 169, 170, 203 f.

JAPAN, 149
Jevons, W. S., 212, 214
Joint Stock System. *See* Companies, Joint Stock.
Judiciary. *See* Law.
Just Price, 64
Justice, 41

KANT, IMMANUEL, 1, 32
Kapital, Das. See Capital.
Kautsky, Karl, 183
Knowledge, Growth of, 18 ff., 25, 273
Kropotkin, Peter, 78

LABOUR, CHANGING NATURE OF, 159 f.
    Differentiation of, 155 ff., 174
    Division of, 55
    Exploitation of, 84 ff., 87, 93, 210 ff., 225 ff., 238, 261 f., 263, 266 ff.
    Intensity of, 89, 234 f., 236, 238
    Marx's View of, 12, 54, 84, 109, 214. *See also* Labour-power.
    Measurement of, 221 ff.
    Parasitic, 154
    Productivity of, 89, 231
    Semi-skilled, 155 f.
    Socially Necessary, 217, 232

ANN ARBOR PAPERBACKS FOR THE STUDY OF COMMUNISM AND MARXISM

For a complete list of Ann Arbor Paperback titles write:
THE UNIVERSITY OF MICHIGAN PRESS / ANN ARBOR

THE AUTHOR

ETHEL WILSON was born in Port Elizabeth, South Africa, in 1888. She was taken to England at the age of two after her mother died. Seven years later her father died, and in 1898 she came to Vancouver to live with her maternal grandmother. She received her teacher's certificate from the Vancouver Normal School in 1907 and taught in many local elementary schools until her marriage in 1921.

In the 1930s Wilson published a few short stories and began a series of family reminiscences which were later transformed into *The Innocent Traveller*. Her first published novel, *Hetty Dorval*, appeared in 1947, and her fiction career ended fourteen years later with the publication of her story collection, *Mrs. Golightly and Other Stories*. Through her compassionate and often ironic narration, Wilson explores in her fiction the moral lives of her characters.

For her contribution to Canadian literature, Wilson was awarded the Canada Council Medal in 1961 and the Lorne Pierce Medal of the Royal Society of Canada in 1964. Her husband died in 1966, and she spent her later years in seclusion and ill-health.

Ethel Wilson died in Vancouver in 1980.

THE INNOCENT TRAVELLER

"And as if on a stream I fixe mine eye,
That drop, which I looked on, is presently
Pusht with more waters from my sight, and gone."

JOHN DONNE

ETHEL WILSON

AFTERWORD BY
P.K. PAGE

First New Canadian Library edition 1990.
This New Canadian Library edition 2008.

This book was first published in 1949 by The Macmillan Company of Canada
Limited. Reprinted 1990.

Library and Archives Canada Cataloguing in Publication

Wilson, Ethel, 1888-1980
The innocent traveller / Ethel Wilson ; with an afterword by P.K. Page.

(New Canadian library)
Originally published: Toronto : Macmillan, 1949.

ISBN 978-0-7710-8888-9

    I. Title. II. Series.
PS8545.I6215 2008   C813'.5   C2007-906236-9

We acknowledge the financial support of the Government of Canada through
the Book Publishing Industry Development Program and that of the
Government of Ontario through the Ontario Media Development Corporation's
Ontario Book Initiative. We further acknowledge the support of the Canada
Council for the Arts and the Ontario Arts Council for our publishing program.

Typeset in Garamond by M&S, Toronto
Printed and bound in the United States of America

McClelland & Stewart Ltd.
75 Sherbourne Street
Toronto, Ontario
M5A 2P9
www.mcclelland.com/NCL

2 3 4 5   12 11 10

To
Wallace
My Dear Husband

CONTENTS

AUTHOR'S NOTE

This is the story – part truth and part invention – of a lively woman who lived for a hundred years and died triumphant in Vancouver and is nearly forgotten after all her commotion of living.

The metaphors are not mixed. The drop of water, the bird, the water-glider, the dancer, the wind on the canal, and Topaz, are all different and all the same.

"I have a Father in the Promised Land" originally appeared in the *New Statesman and Nation,* and "The Innumerable Laughter" in *Orion IV.* I am indebted to the editors for their kind permission to republish them here.

E.W.

Vancouver
British Columbia
1947

DINNER AT NOON

Far away at the end of the table sat Father, the kind, handsome and provident man. At this end sat Mother, her crinoline spread abroad. On Mother's right was Mr. Matthew Arnold. On each side of the table the warned children ate their food gravely, all except Topaz on Mother's left. Topaz, who could not be squelched, was perched there on the top of two cushions, as innocent as a poached egg. Mother sat gracious, fatigued, heavy behind the majestic crinoline with the last and fatal child.

Said Mr. Matthew Arnold in large and musical tones, speaking across the children and three jellied fowls to Father who with divided attention carved, "It is now my hope to make a survey of the educational systems of France and Germany with a view to the establishment in this country of reasonable educational facilities for every child, rich or poor. You will agree with me, Mr. Edgeworth, that a modicum of education, given under healthy and happy conditions, is the right of every boy. This I would extend to girls also." Thus spoke Mr. Matthew Arnold.

Father, as he carved for ten people, made encouraging sounds, although he had not yet considered this novel idea.

He was, however, prepared to do so. He looked forward to a pleasant afternoon with this agreeable and enlightened person who was a coming Inspector of Schools, a present poet, and a son of Arnold of Rugby.

Mother's quiet sombre gaze swept round the table, dwelt for a moment thoughtfully on the poet, rested on Father busy with the jellied fowls, rested on the two young grown-up daughters, on the four sons, on the little Topaz at her side, and on the ministering Cook and Emma.

Topaz was anxious to be noticed. But nobody was noticed today except Mr. Matthew Arnold. Not Annie, Mary, Blakey, George, John, nor Joe. She determined to be noticed immediately, so she spoke across the table to the guest.

As she was so unimportant no one paid her any attention at first until she was heard to say, ". . . and it's got a lovely yellow glass handle and you pull it and it goes woosh! Woosh, woosh!" she trumpeted, and smiled happily at Mr. Matthew Arnold.

"What goes woosh, my child?" he asked.

"Our new —"

"TOPAZ!" thundered Father, and Mother put out a grieved and loving hand. The outraged brothers and sisters looked across and downwards. Only Mr. Matthew Arnold regarded Topaz without horror.

"Topaz, eat your bread and butter," commanded Mother. But Topaz had succeeded. She had been noticed, although she had failed to tell Mr. Matthew Arnold about their new plumbing. All ordinary friends and relatives had witnessed the behaviour of the Edgeworth's revolutionary plumbing, which was the first of its kind to be installed in the town of Ware in North Staffordshire. Its fame had spread, and even strangers accosted Father in the street and asked him if it really worked. It was the joy of Topaz and the pride of the

Edgeworths. It took the family a few moments to recover from the near-horror of the indelicate child.

The desire of Topaz to be noticed intoxicated her, and she went on. She looked only at the kind and unshocked face of Mr. Matthew Arnold, and she desired ardently to impress him now, at this very moment, while she still had the chance.

"Would you like me to say some poetry?" she asked.

"Topaz," said Mother half rising, "Emma shall take you upstairs to your room."

"Please, Mrs. Edgeworth," said Mr. Matthew Arnold, "let the child say her poetry, and I will then, if I may, expound a favourite theory of mine."

Topaz sparkled and began:

"Two are better far than one
For comfort or for fight.
How can one keep warm alone,
Or serve his God aright?"[1]

"And I'll say you another," she said quickly, "'How doth the little busy –'"

"TOPAZ – THAT – WILL – DO," said Father in a terrible tone. Topaz looked at Father. His eyes and his whiskers looked larger and darker than usual. She hung her head. Dear Father was angry. She slithered down from her cushions, down from her chair, and vanished under the table. The outraged brothers and sisters waited.

Mr. Matthew Arnold took things in hand and addressed both Father and Mother. "This is an interesting little child of

---

[1] From an old Methodist hymnal.

yours. Will you, as a favour to me, let her stay under the table? She has not really offended. She is young, and she wishes to entertain. Don't make her shy. Leave her to herself. She knows in her heart that she has been rather forward. Let her think about it. Now, on the subject of coercion, I feel strongly that . . ."

Father listened. The children watched the good guest and the good food. Mother rested her graceful head on her hand. She gazed attentively and sweetly on the expounding Mr. Matthew Arnold, and did not hear a word that he was saying. Upstairs with the nurse was Hannah, the youngest, labouring with croup. Within Mother the last and fatal babe moved and moved. "It will be tonight," thought Mother, "I feel it will be tonight, and Joseph will be greatly disturbed. Dear Father. But I . . ." She turned her troubled look on Father and on the food. Swish went the white cap-streamers as Emma set down the sweet. "Cream pudding," murmured Blakey, looking with greedy eyes across to George, unchecked. Mother looked upon George, upon all her brood. "Now, according to Rousseau . . ." said Mr. Matthew Arnold.

Underneath the heavy mahogany table sat Topaz in a world of shoes. She had recovered from fear and shame. Now she crawled from shoe to shoe. Each pair of shoes told Topaz a story. Mother had no shoes, no feet at all, just a beautiful rustling spread of purple silk. Topaz studied the silk without touching. Then she crawled to the large visiting boots of Mr. Matthew Arnold. Mr. Arnold wore elegant old-fashioned trousers which had straps under the feet. His feet were large, impeccable, neatly placed together. Topaz touched a leg with a friendly tickling finger. Above the table the great man checked his speech, smiled to himself, and continued. Topaz in the pleasing gloom of tablecloth, legs, and feet, crawled on.

Next to Mr. Arnold sat her nearest and favourite brother Joe. Joe's slippered feet curled round his chair legs. He listened, understanding a little, to the great man. Joe, gentle and frail, destined for early death, was never impatient with the chattering Topaz. Topaz dared to stroke Joe's ankle softly. Pussy pussy pussy. He gave no sign. She crawled on.

She put her head on one side and looked at Blakey's clodhoppers. What a smell! Blakey smelled of the stable and Father's horse. Topaz regarded Blakey and his boots coldly. He, the sharp-nosed boy, was already the farmer, the jockey. He was to sail cheerfully across an ocean and a half to Australia. Yes, Blakey said goodbye to the narrow streets of Ware and lived to be a happy horsey patriarch in a wide world of his own choosing. Happy Blakey. Topaz crawled on.

Here were the good shoes of Mary. Out she went to India, poor Mary, to marry a missionary. Glory surrounded the absent Mary who soon bore two little spinsters in the heat and died. Poor Mary, buried almost as her eyes closed, in that distant consuming heat. Topaz passed from Mary's shoes without interest and crawled on.

Here was Father. Two well-shod feet rested side by side on the thick carpet. Topaz looked at Father's boots with respect. Father never buttoned his own boots. Godlike he extended a foot, and his boot was put on and fastened by a reverent son, or daughter, or Emma, or Nurse, or Cook, or sometimes by Mother. Topaz dared not touch these hallowed and angry feet. She crawled on.

Oh, the beautiful slippers of Annie. Topaz made little passes with her hands over Annie's tiny feet. Annie was as pious as beautiful. She was eighteen and modestly in love. She was to marry James Hastings, Father's brilliant young man at the Works. She was to be the gentle and obeyed mother of nine. She was, in her charming matriarchal old age, to go far away across sea and land to join distant sons yet unborn. She was yet in mildness and in formidable and unquestioned piety to infuse the lives of her sons, of her daughters Laura and Rachel, of her orphaned granddaughter Rose, of a wicked Chinaman, of more, of more, unborn, unknown. She was to be the refuge and comfort of her bereft young sister Topaz. She was to die in Vancouver (yet undreamed of), tiny, ancient, beautiful, gently amused, pure in heart, greatly beloved. Here she sat, as yet the young and filial daughter, neat feet, tender eyes, unknown thoughts, and ringlets of brown. Topaz looked long at the slippers of Annie. She fingered Annie's grey silk dress with pleasure, and then she crawled on.

She did not stop at the plain and lumpish shoes of George. George was red of face, genial, soon to be ardent, to be much wived. George was kindly, lazy, earthy, petted, and at last to be tamed. Topaz was never to be tamed, never. She crawled on.

Here were the neat and respectable feet of John. John was pretty. When Topaz called John "pretty," Blakey and George were rude. But so he was. He grew more elegant and fastidious as years increased. It became inevitable that John should be called Giovanni, that he should marry an heiress, that he should mingle with lords, that he should move with conscious distinction through several decades of public service. These neat feet of John's globe-trotted. They carried him busily among the great and the near-great with correctness. These quiet feet will hasten to many a directors' meeting. ("Hear-hear. Hear-hear.") John, the correct one, who could make you feel sneaped.[2] John never felt sneaped. If you were

---

[2] Sneaped – a good Staffordshire word. Used by William Shakespeare too.

6

a dog, being sneaped would be the same as going off with your tail between your legs. If you were Topaz, people tried to sneap you, but you were hard to sneap. Even the proud gentle Annie, the eldest, could be sneaped by a look, but never John. Those who cause others to feel sneaped are vulnerable. Brother John, your day will come. Topaz pondered the neatness of John's feet and then curled up and fell asleep.

Above the table the future hung implicit, almost palpable, around the family. Above the table Mother sighed, caught the adult eyes, smiled her sad smile, and arose.

It was the next night that Mother died.

MOTHER, MOTHER!

The day of Mother's funeral was long remembered in Ware. It was so sad that people almost enjoyed it. The chapel was "Packed! Packed!" as Great-Aunt Topaz used to say enthusiastically nearly a century later with her special genius for repetition. She remembered this funeral, with Father leading her by the hand, the youngest walker of the family, down the aisle, and all the other boys and girls following after. This dark pageant and slow procession of the black-clothed and bereft father and children smote with pity and tears those who were gathered to do honour to Mrs. Edgeworth. A hushed warfare had raged amongst Aunts and other next-of-kin during the days intervening between Mother's death and burial. Should Hannah, still almost a babe in arms, go to the funeral? If so, the nurse must carry her. If so, Hannah should be dressed in black. "A baby in black! What a dreadful idea, Aunt! Better keep her at home!" whispered an innovator. "White at a funeral! Certainly not. If Hannah goes – and she *must* go – the nurse must carry her and she *must* wear black. It would be an insult to her Mother's memory to allow her to appear in white. A blot!" (of white!)

8

trumpeted Aunt Chalk lifting her high nose. "Merriman can run up a nice cap and cape of this good black very quickly, can't you, Merriman?" Such a snipping and cutting out and running up as there was now for this large family. Mother was badly needed to administer her own funeral. Decorum, decorum, sorrow and decorum. Hannah solved the whole question by having the sniffles before the cape was cut out.

"Aunt Chalk," said Mary, coming in timidly, "Nurse says that little Hannah's running at the nose again and should on no account go out." The disputants looked at each other across the cutting-out table and nodded. Heaven had decided, and Hannah stayed at home in white where only Heaven and Nurse could see her, neither of whose feelings would be hurt by this unsuitable child.

"See *me*, look at *me*, Mary!" said Topaz importantly, revolving in black on the cutting-out table where she stood because it was more convenient to fit one so doll-like there. "I'm all in black, you see! I'm all in black! I'm going to the funeral tomorrow!" as the dressmaker tried a nice bit of crape on the body of her dress ("the scraps will do for that, Merriman"). There was silence. Topaz hearing the silence, glanced from face to face, and saw the looks. Her features puckered, she opened her mouth wide and wept loudly. "Mother, Mother!" she cried out loud in face of these looks. But Mother was not there. Sister Annie's arms went round her.

Father had the kind of handsomeness of a happy dignified extrovert inspired by a strong and simple faith and the equanimity that shone from his fine eyes. If Father had ever faltered in his faith, how deep would have been the crack, the fissure, the ultimate chasm into which he would have fallen. You and I, who pick our way unsurely amongst the appalling wreckage of our time, patching the crack here, avoiding the split there, anticipating the unsure footing, rejoicing in a bit of solid ground and going ahead until we again trip and fall on our noses – we can take our troubles much more easily than Father could have done. But Father never tumbled down. Both he and his partner Mr. Cork walked along with a grave and simple integrity that was neither smug nor proud.

Father had a fine nose with generous nostrils, the kind of nose which, when surrounded by other suitable features, causes more trouble among females who are responsive to a bit of trouble than people suspect. He was tall, with good strongly-growing hair and whiskers. All these attributes, together with his deep sorrow and helplessness, touched the heart of every woman in the Chapel and of every man too. Each woman knew in her heart that Mr. Edgeworth, with all those children and bereft of his wife, was, for all his vigour, ability, and good looks, much more vulnerable than Mrs. Edgeworth would have been if her Joseph had been taken from her. Every wife and mother yearned over him, and so did others who were neither wife nor mother.

At home things were rudderless and difficult. There were times when the gentle Annie and the young Mary were taxed too much, and when the inroads of Aunt Chalk made for dispute and confusion. Each night Father knelt for guidance beside the silent bed that gaped for his Mary who had never failed him before, and when he got into the abominable bed where she was not, his spiritual loneliness exacerbated his physical loss. It was all bad and sad for the children – Father's heaviness of spirit and the vacancy where Mother had been. As for Father, he had done with Love.

It is all very well to say that Father had done with Love, but there remained the need for companionship and a sharing of the household's cares which were inescapable. Hannah's intermittent croup, the broken nose of Blakey caused in a fight whose fame and shame defaced the name of Edgeworth, the finickyness and indifferent progress at school of John, Annie's projected marriage, the flightiness of Topaz, the fragility of Joe – all these things, combined with new activity at the Works, an unexpected extension of the American china market, and a sudden large irrational order for earthenware poes (said Great-Aunt Topaz with authority, nearly one hundred years later) for an African tribe (these articles were prized as hats by the savages, it was said at the time, although this seemed unlikely) – all these things drove Father into a second marriage, whether he would or no. The foundations of this marriage were respect and integrity.

It seemed to Father (who within two years became Grandfather Edgeworth and within a twinkling of the century's eye became Great-Grandfather Edgeworth) that beyond his personal preference and delight was his need for a house partner who would maintain the standards by which he wished his children to grow up, and could run smoothly and easily his pleasant home and keep it happy. With all the propriety that was observed in such a home as this, we know that there was also fun of a fairly robust kind. There must have been fun. For from this sober home there bubbled up the sparkling volatile Topaz, the pleasant and tittering John, the guffawing George, and the crackling laughter of Blakey. You couldn't down these people. There was not much humour, but a good deal of fun.

Let us look at noses. Most people do not pay enough attention to noses. Noses are significant features and should be regarded more carefully by those about to marry and bequeath. Take Aunt Chalk, for example, Mother's eldest sister. She had a nose like the august beak of the great Duke of Wellington soon to be lamented by the nation ("Pull down the blinds, Topaz. The Great Duke has died.") and she walked in an unpleasant aura of command. When Aunt Chalk's nose was seen coming up the driveway, the young Annie and Mary gazed stricken at each other and felt guilty in advance, the poor little housekeepers. Mother's nose had been a pleasant enough nose to live with, neither here nor there. The nose of Jane, Mother's younger sister, was a perfect pug, like THIS – as Great-Aunt Topaz used to recall, suddenly flattening her own mobile and rather boneless feature up against her face, with her hand. But Father saw past the pug nose into the kind heart and sound judgment of his majestic spinster sister-in-law, and it was revealed to him that here, in his Deceased Wife's Sister, was the stepmother that his children needed. But the Law was not, up till then, on his side.

At this moment of Father's dilemma Fate took a timely hand and beat the Law, since a Peer of the Realm found himself in much the same boat as Father, and the Law was revoked for a while to oblige this exalted man. Democracy was then only in bud, and Justice and Privilege were still related, and although the unfairness of the whole thing was noticed by a good many Radicals who made it their business to notice everything, the Repeal of the Act was welcomed by many more in the same plight as Father. There was a temporary rush to the altar of Deceased Wives's Sisters. For some reason often explained by Great-Aunt Topaz to her Great-Niece Rose three or four generations later (but not understood), Father went to Switzerland to be married. He travelled alone to Switzerland, and after two weeks, which seemed to be a chaste and fairly safe interval, Jane followed him, pug nose and all, chaperoned by Aunt Chalk. After a suitable honeymoon among the surprising mountains, Mr. and Mrs. Joseph Edgeworth returned home.

—

"Did you know," said George, "that Father is going to Grin-del*wawld*?" The Edgeworth family took no notice of that silly foreign habit of pronouncing w like v.

"Where's Grindelwawld?" asked Topaz and no one paid any attention.

"On business?" asked Blakey.

"What's Grindelwawld?" asked Topaz.

"What for?" asked Joe.

"I don't know. I think there's Something Up," said George.

"What's Grindelwawld?" implored Topaz. "John, *what's* Grindelwawld, is it that sweety shop?"

"That's Grimble's, Topaz," said Mary.

"What . . . ?" began Topaz.

"Look at the map," said Blakey shortly.

"What's a map? Show me a map. *Show* me," said the aggravating Topaz.

"*Be* quiet!" said Blakey. "Little girls should be seen and not heard."

"Come, dear," said Annie, "we will look at the map. See, there is Switzerland, and look – that's Grindelwawld."

"Oh . . . well, what is it?" asked Topaz, who couldn't see anything that looked like anything. "Why is it pink? What is it? What do you do with it? Why is it pink?"

"It isn't pink."

"Well, it looks pink."

"Hold your peace," roared George.

"See, Hannah, look," said Topaz to her little playmate Hannah, and pointing at the globe, "Father's going to Grindelwawld and it's pink and if we're good he'll bring us a piece back."

Father did not bring back whatever it was that Topaz expected, but their stately Aunt Jane who was now their mother and their stepmother, and she began to live in Father's bedroom with Father. The household moved again into smooth accustomed gear.

The Stepmother's first achievement was the successful wedding party of Annie. Pretty Annie was now "our sister Mrs. Hastings," and after a year was out Annie's first baby, Laura, changed Father into Grandfather Edgeworth.

And while the years passed over Grandfather Edgeworth, Joe gently died; Blakey departed to Australia where he practised the two R's of Rearing a family and Racehorses; and Mary, poor child, went to her distant land.

George married the first of his three diverse wives, the daughter of Father's partner Mr. Cork, and from the earthy ground of George sprang three strange flowers of temperament. From the elegant and Italianate John, no children; but from the uninhibited George a poet, an artist, and a beauty of distinction. All these three had a splendour of du Maurier-esque beauty not again seen in the Edgeworth family.

All this time Topaz and little Hannah played together with a twin-like affection.

"BY OUR FIRST STRANGE AND
FATALL INTERVIEW"

Somehow the whole family was surprised when Edward Shaw wanted so much to marry their second sister Mary. If it had not been for young Edward Shaw's pertinacity in forcing a meeting with her when he did, Mary would have had a different life – and death – and would no doubt have followed what seemed to be her predestined uneventful course as her stepmother's helper. But Edward Shaw changed that in one single interview.

Across the Chapel Edward Shaw looked at Mary Edgeworth.

So strong was the woven fabric of their large domestic life that the Edgeworth family were first of all members one of another, and next, each became aware of his own individuality. They were sons, daughters, sisters, and brothers before they were people. They rapidly became cousins, nieces, and nephews. Also uncles and aunts. Quickly one child, slowly another, apprehended its own condition as a person. Only the small and irascible Topaz was an individual from the time she uttered her first sentence ("Oh, yes, I spoke clearly and fluently at the age of nine months; my Mother *was* surprised!"

"Now, Aunty . . . !") until that day nearly a century later when, still speaking clearly, she died. But even she was bound for a hundred years and beyond to this powerful family. For, speaking clearly, the words she said as she died were, "Me, the youngest!" and although the last of her generation had twenty years ago departed, her life was still tied to her powerful assembled family which had slipped one by one with acceptance or amazement through the strangely moving curtain of Time into another place. But the docile Mary, who preceded Topaz there by ninety years, had hardly discovered her own identity, apart from being a daughter and a sister, by the time that Edward Shaw looked at her and loved her.

Upon the plain and serious Mary the young man looked. He had made up his mind. During the service he regarded with apprehension the noble Mr. Edgeworth, as far removed from him as Jove. Mr. Edgeworth had often nodded kindly, as might Jove perhaps, at young Shaw. He had nodded kindly because he felt kindly disposed towards a young man who, having finished his term at the Theological College at Manchester, had come home for a furlough before sailing for the Mission Field in India. Horizons of yellow grain floated before the eyes of the young Edgeworths when they heard of the preparations of Edward Shaw – Edward, with his young and confidence-inspiring beard, waist deep in billowing grain, from which appeared here and there black and easily recognizable heathen. Edward was well thought of, and the Edgeworth family regarded him warmly. Even his newly developed beard was a suitable sign of responsibility and of inner grace. So when young Edward Shaw, his youth armoured by the deceiving beard, cleverly joined the spreading and multiple Edgeworths as they left the Chapel, nobody was surprised, except young Edward Shaw. He, breathing quickly, knew that not Chance but Edward Shaw was now taking a hand with Fate. Edward was nearly sick with excitement.

At the Wesleyan Chapel at Ware, greetings did not begin between Chapel-goers until they were free of the Chapel door. Only the faintest and most religious of smiles might be exchanged in the slow progress of the congregation towards the Chapel door. This was well done. How should one spring at once from the heights of spiritual contemplation down to the level of the five senses and their curiosities? This was well done, and a right recognition of things great and things small. Do not mix them, do not admit the mundane. But outside the Chapel door the House of God became the street of man. Edward, in the dark, beyond the chapel porch, successfully isolated the surprised Mary and walked home with her.

They walked slowly but without loitering along the narrow dark pavement where few lights shone. The large Edgeworth family walked ahead in twos and threes, their numbers augmented by friends and relatives. Edward had been adroit, for in the darkness of the ugly street, Who could see Who walked with Who, or that Edward Shaw walked alone with Mary Edgeworth.

As Edward walked with Mary on the narrow pavement, sleeve rubbed sleeve and arm touched arm. It was enough. For Edward it was almost too much.

"Miss Mary," said Edward in a low voice, grateful for the darkness which made him bold, "I am sailing for India in less than two weeks' time." (As Edward said these words he could hardly believe them. India. Staffordshire. India.) "I may not see you again. Do you mind if I walk home with you? I have longed to talk to you a little before I go. There is so little time left now and I must tell you Something. What you will say I don't know." The young man's voice shook and was husky.

This agitation was something special and Mary in the darkness caught his agitation. "What is this? What can Edward Shaw have to say to me? I know what Edward Shaw is going to say to me. What shall I say to him? What would Father say? Well, I'm a woman." She asserted herself. "I'm a woman. Annie got married. But Annie is different. Oh, Annie, are you happy? I think you are. What is Edward Shaw going to say? Keep still. This is your life. Wait."

In the family, Mary was not important. She was not even the eldest. Annie was the eldest and the beautiful one. Annie was a wife, already the admired head of her small household, soon again to be a mother. Mary was the rather unregarded helper of the kind and important Stepmother. ("Oh yes," said Great-Aunt Topaz ninety years later, "very strict and important was our Stepmother, but a good mother to us children, with a little pug nose – like this!") Mary had never yet been Mary, a person in her own right. And here she was, a person, with Edward Shaw walking beside her in the dark and speaking to her in urgent husky tones, and a future coming quickly towards her. She was inexperienced, but she knew.

"Oh, Mr. Shaw, Father told us that you are going into the Mission Field. We do hope that you will be happy, and we do hope that God will bless you in your work," she said simply. She endeavoured to still her little trembling. "Aren't you excited at the prospect of going so far away to such a strange country? Ware, I know, is very quiet and dull." Mary was astonished to hear herself say this in the darkness. The life of her family in Ware, the catastrophic death of Mother, Father's marriage, the boys growing, the comings and goings of Father, the life of school, of Chapel, of relatives, of the busy home – all these things had not seemed quiet and dull. Mary was hardly prepared to see the future leap out into the open and transform her past into something which was not enough. But this was now achieved by the young man in black walking by her side.

He seized her arm, not roughly. "Mary," he said, speaking rapidly, "no, don't stop me. I've watched you every time I've been at home, and I've dared to think about you, but I've never dared to come nearer you – your family" – (the Edgeworth family, strong barrier against the young and uninvited) – "I love you and I want to marry you, Mary, and now time's going so quickly, and if I go away without some hope from you, the future – well, I can't bear it, not even to do God's work." The young man spoke unhappily, and while he spoke he felt his case suddenly become desperate. His hopes that this young girl so near him in the darkness would leave her home of comfort to join him whom she knew so little, in a land yet unknown – these hopes seemed preposterous.

To Mary these hopes were not preposterous, but she did not at once enquire of her heart. She relaxed her arm in his and experienced an unfamiliar confidence. She honoured him; she trusted him; she, the big sister of once motherless young boys, pitied him in his need of her. His nearness was welcome. She did not shrink and she controlled her little trembling.

"Stop, Mr. Shaw," she said gently, "let me be. Just for a moment. Please. You've surprised me. I didn't think. This is such a big thing. No – don't talk to me for a minute." And they walked close and quietly, saying little until Edward again poured out his heart. ("And where can Mary be?" demanded the majestic Stepmother, far in front, of the dark.)

When Mary and Edward left the pavements and, walking slowly, reached the lane's end beside the gate of the house, Mary stood still. How displeased Father would be if his eyes could behold his daughter, Mary Edgeworth, standing in the shelter of the hedge in the arms of a young man in love, be he never so much a missionary! For that is where Mary was. "Edward, very well, dear Edward, I will, I will marry you if Father will let me, and if Mother can spare me. I will try to make you a good wife – no – not yet, not again. Let me go! I shall slip in at the side door. It's better that you should see Father alone."

As she left him Edward could have sung aloud. He was a King. He owned the world. A few minutes later he sat in Father's heavily curtained and lamplit study. He was no longer a King. He was a young and importunate theological student without proper means of support for a wife. Except for the importunity that shook him, he was nothing more than that.

One year later Mary sailed for India from Tilbury Dock, in the care of the Rev. Charles Pickering and Mrs. Pickering. All the family went to Tilbury with the travellers. "I'll tell you something," said Topaz to little Hannah in the corner of the railway carriage, "Mother said to Father, 'The girl's very innocent, Joseph. I do believe she's going to her first kiss.' What d'you think of that?" Hannah, aged five, did not know what she thought of that.

As the ship drew out they all waved. The departing Mary waved. "Can you see them now?" Topaz waved and waved. She jumped up and down flapping her white handkerchief. "Going to her first kiss," she chanted, "going to her first kiss." The family whirled round. "TOPAZ!"

But really, never since the time that young Edward Shaw and Mary Edgeworth had walked home from Chapel and stood clasped in the shelter of the hedge had they been alone together. The Stepmother had not thought it fitting. But "Dear Mary," "Dear Edward," they wrote. People had said, "Mary Edgeworth is going out to India to marry a missionary. She'll be such a good suitable wife for him. Not pretty like Annie, but a very nice girl." The whole family from Father to Topaz, and even little Hannah, were proud of Mary now because she was going to the Mission Field. Mary had begun to feel that she was nothing but Mr. Edgeworth's good girl who was going to marry a missionary, no longer Mary who was going to marry Edward. On the ship, in the constant company of the reserved Mrs. Pickering, Mary began to feel frightened and homesick. She longed to return to the safety of the large family, but the disregarding days brought her nearer and nearer to India and to Edward from whom she sometimes fled.

After Mr. and Mrs. Pickering had seen Mary safely married to Edward Shaw, they departed at once to their mission station. Mary, dressed in the grey of a dove, found herself arrived at the inevitable moment. She stood alone facing this man who was Edward, but who was nearly a stranger. She was more alone than she had ever been in her whole life. She was in India. She had reached the Mission Field. She looked steadily, almost fearfully, at Edward and tried to smile. This little lonely smile smote Edward. He looked at his Mary and saw the frightened courage in her face. He took only one step towards her. He overflowed with tenderness, compassion, and his desire. Mary broke into weeping which she could not restrain, sprang forward and cast herself, more in homesickness than in love, upon Edward's beard.

On the scorching day that followed the suffocating night when the babies were born and Mary died, Edward buried the young girl his wife with violent and shocking haste.

He sat at his desk with the notepaper lying in front of him. He sat there suffering and helpless and blinded by his loss. Was it for this that he had brought Mary to the land that had killed her? He gazed unseeing through his desk and at last summoned and steadied himself and wrote slowly, "Dear Mr. and Mrs. Edgeworth. It has pleased God in His Infinite Wisdom to take from us my beloved Mary." He read, and tore up the paper savagely.

He wrote, "Dear Mr. and Mrs. Edgeworth. It has pleased God to take from me –" He stopped, read, tore the paper across and flung it down.

He wrote, "Dear Mr. and Mrs. Edgeworth. I regret to tell you that Mary died last night. Our two infant daughters are well. Accept my deep sympathy. Yours faithfully, Edward Shaw." He folded and sealed the letter. He bowed his head upon his empty arms in his anguish, and wept.

"A very strange letter indeed for that young man to write!" said the majestic Stepmother, turning the pages this way and that, seeking lamentation and finding none.

MR. AND MRS. PORTER

It was not long before the six Edgeworth children who
remained at home became used to seeing the kind and
portly Stepmother, who was Mother's sister, who had
always been Aunt Jane, who was now "Mother," sitting in
Mother's place at the head of the table. In orderly families,
such as the Edgeworths', Father and Mother, flanked and separated down a fairly long table by a double row of children,
might consider themselves to be practically alone. At the
Edgeworth table no child, save one, raised his or her voice
unless addressed. All, save one, behaved with astonishing
decorum, while Father and Mother carried on their own
Olympian conversations. The six remaining sons and daughters were as nearly inaudible as six normal children could be
except for Topaz, who could not keep silent (how should she,
who talked persistently for over ninety-seven years?), and was
often admonished by both parents, and sometimes had to be
sent from the table because she was too bumptious; and Topaz
annoyed only in the same way that a fly annoys. Father and
Mother, being alone then, except for at least eight other people
in the room counting Emma and Cook or Betsy, spoke freely

to each other and settled much of their domestic business at the table.

As Father dealt with his letters, he retailed them to Mother.

"Dear, dear, dear!" said Father one morning.

"What, Joseph?" asked Mother.

"Mrs. Porter."

"What about Mrs. Porter, Joseph?"

"Mr. Porter has left Mrs. Porter," said Father, forgetting his children who should not be aware that husbands left wives.

Topaz always followed these conversations closely, turning her head and her intelligent grey-green eyes towards each speaking parent. Images evoked by these adult conversations sprang at once to Topaz's mind, but they were often incorrect images as they were limited by her own experience, which was slight. Topaz took part at once.

"Where did Mr. Porter leave Mrs. Porter?" she asked. Never having heard of a Mr. and Mrs. Porter before, she pictured Mr. Porter in a peaked cap taking Mrs. Porter for a railway journey (a novelty) and leaving her in a strange Ladies' Waiting Room all alone, as Mother had left her and the alarmed Hannah, only a week ago, with instructions not to budge.

Her parents took no notice.

"Oh, Joseph, *poor* Mrs. Porter! Whatever will she do?" exclaimed the Stepmother, deeply shocked.

"Was it in the Ladies' Waiting Room?" persisted Topaz.

"Was what in the Ladies' Waiting Room, Topaz? Speak clearly, if you speak at all," said Father sharply.

"Where Mr. Porter left Mrs. Porter."

George choked on his guffaw.

"Be quiet, Topaz. This does not concern you."

"I cannot believe it, Joseph!" said the Stepmother, incredulous.

"Was she in the Waiting Room all night?" asked Topaz, sympathetic to the fate of Mrs. Porter.

The Stepmother gave Topaz her attention. "What are you talking about, Topaz? Tell me and then keep quiet."

"She meant like you left me and Topath at the thtation the time I cried," explained little Hannah.

"Mr. Porter did *not* leave Mrs. Porter in the Ladies' Waiting Room. Now that will do, Topaz. You must learn to hold your peace." Then to Father, "But I thought Mr. Porter was such a *nice* man, Joseph!"

"Porter always seemed a nice enough fellow, but I have reason to think that he has been given to fast friends," said Father.

"Who gave him? Who gave him? Did Mrs. Porter give him? Why did she give him to fast friends?" demanded Topaz, horrified at the thought of this nice fellow being given by his wife, like a bundle, to these fast friends who had galloped off with him, probably on horseback.

"*Silence!*" said Father, turning wrathful eyes on her. "Mother, either Topaz may have her meals in the kitchen or she may behave at table. I do not propose to spend my meals in disturbance!"

"You hear what Father says, Topaz!" said the Stepmother in awful tones. Topaz's pink and white face flushed, and she made no sound but applied herself to her porridge.

"And," continued Father, still holding the letter in his hand, "Mrs. Porter writes to say that she has decided to open a school for girls at Brighton, and she is writing to all her father's old friends . . . she has little Fanny to support . . . she will take about twenty boarders. It will soon be time for Topaz and Hannah to go to boarding-school, and I cannot think of anyone I would rather send them to than Emily Porter. She is quite a Blue Stocking." ("A blue stocking?" puzzled Topaz.) "What do you think, Mother? Pass your Mother this letter," and he handed the letter to John.

"Oh . . . to America! . . . well, no wonder! . . . I see she hopes to have Mrs. Pocock's girl Lily to help her," said the Stepmother, perusing. ". . . I gather that she prefers to board all her pupils." (Topaz and Hannah looked at each other; would they be strapped to it, the board? How would they stay on?) ". . . Yes, but that entails a deal of work! Ah, yes, she will not take day girls. All the pupils will have to board. But I do wonder why ever Mr. Porter did such a dreadful thing!"

And this was why.

"THE DARK HOUSE AND THE
DETESTED WIFE"

The last term that Mary Davis (who became Mrs. Joseph Edgeworth) and Jane Davis (who also became Mrs. Joseph Edgeworth) were at school in York, there came a little beautiful motherless girl named Emily Fanshawe who was put, for a while, into Mary's charge. Shortly after Mary and Jane left school, the child returned home, and there she lived, cloistered in the country, with her father who was a Greek scholar. And so it was that the beautiful child, who was her father's most diligent student and devoted companion, became old for her years and a little too grave. About six years ago, so they had heard, Emily had made a journey with her father to Greece, and next they learned that Emily had married young Edmund Porter, whom Joseph Edgeworth knew, in Brighton. And then nothing more. And now "Mr. Porter has left Mrs. Porter." However could this be?

"The isles of Greece, the isles of Greece," murmured Emily, as the wind filled the sails and the small sailing ship beat slowly to the south of Cape Matapan. Many an evening she saw the Grecian islands melting away, mauve and pink and purple and a dying grey, into the darkening sea. "The winedark sea," thought Emily. What had she expected to see? Sea the colour of wine? No. At this moment the colours of the Mediterranean slid from steel-blue into sapphire into indigo into purple into bronze, and this, this was the sea which the Hellenes had smitten with their oars and which Odysseus had sailed for adventure and for home. Emily was romantic. The death of Lord Byron in Greece, not two decades before, had warmed the hard-headed and romantic and freedom-loving English people to the land where he had died. Yet it was not because Lord Byron had lived rashly, and had been a poet, and had died in Greece for Greece that Mr. Fanshawe and his daughter Emily had sailed on this pilgrimage down the Adriatic Sea, past the shores where Nausicaa played and the shipwrecked Odysseus slept, round the tip of the Peloponnese and north to the Piraeus, but because Mr. Fanshawe was fulfilling his life's dream of seeing, together with his daughter, before he died, the height of human truth and beauty, the small hill of the Acropolis, in Athens, and upon it the ruined Parthenon.

Emily wrote in her diary, "Papa and I today ascended the Acropolis. It was very strange and it pleased Papa very greatly that our guide is called Socrates. 'Are you indeed Socrates?' enquired Papa smilingly. 'No,' replied the old man gravely, 'I am not Socrates himself but I am his favourite nephew.'

"Up the stony steps we went and over the flintstrewn hill and upon our left was the small temple of the Erechtheum with the tall maidens, standing there these twenty-three hundred years, and still as noble as ever. Oh, unconquerably noble! The full sight of the pale honey-coloured pillars of the Parthenon sent us into a dream that went back to Pericles and the great days of Athens, and to Socrates and to Plato who must have walked on this very hill and up the wide steps which look so level and yet have a hidden architectural perfection of curve. It seemed to me as Papa and I stood with the old man Socrates that there was something timeless in the air. All truth, all beauty, has blown about this place that Papa and I have so long desired to see. We looked across at Hymettus which was growing violet in the darkening rays of the sun. Papa and I will go there again and again, but today we just stood and looked and felt the thousands of years go by. As the violet glow touched Hymettus, Socrates drank the hemlock, and tonight the violet touched Hymettus again and I could not contain myself, but wept as I looked."

It will be seen that Emily was a learned and romantic young girl with a large share of what was called "sensibility," and that Joseph Edgeworth was not wrong when he called her a Blue Stocking. It was on the way home from this studious journey which crowned Mr. Fanshawe's life, and perhaps was the crown and sorrow of Emily's life too, that the travellers met young Edmund Porter who was carried away by Emily's beauty, fell in love with her, followed her back to England, and married her.

It was unfortunate for Edmund Porter that the studious and poetic girl with whom he fell in love had the beauty and gentleness that promised him everything that he wanted, but promised him in vain. He was not long married (and still under the spell of his infatuation for the girl) before he knew that Emily's large dark-fringed eyes, her creamy skin, her soft grace, meant nothing for him, nothing. "My God," he thought in anger with her, "how cold she is." Never once did Emily's soft limbs melt willingly into his arms. When he approached her she became sealed away from him. He grew diffident and morose with her. Emily herself was uncertain and unhappy. She knew that she had failed. She did not want to fail, but her new life was repugnant to her; she was helpless and she was proud. When, before a year was out, their only child, a daughter, was born, Edmund saw with bitterness that the child aroused in his wife a passion of tenderness that he could never evoke. He detested seeing Emily bending over the baby and lifting it to her breast. He absented himself from home whenever he could. He was an easy, natural, sensual man, and she an academic beauty who had better have married one of her father's old friends, and spent her life puttering about a library with a lot of bloodless old scholars with their academic jokes, thought Edmund bitterly. He knew by this time that she had begun to bore him. All her high-falutin ideas bored him to fury. He no longer noticed that she was beautiful.

One day he came into his wife's room. She was sitting in front of her mirror, brushing her long hair with slow sweeping strokes. Edmund was impelled to go to her and place his hands upon her shoulders. Over her head he looked into the mirror and their eyes met there. His wife became motionless and in the mirror he saw the indifferent sweet expression of her face grow defensive and become almost the face of an enemy. He took his hands roughly from her shoulders and said angrily, still watching her immobile face in the mirror, "What made me fool enough to marry a woman like you! I'd as soon live with one of your damned Greek statues!"

Edmund took two steps to a bookshelf and lifted a small white sculptured goddess from the corner of the shelf. He dashed it to the ground where it broke into fragments. He looked at his wife and saw her involuntary gesture and her look of anger and distress. "That moves you, does it?" he said. Her face resumed its marble look. Edmund went out of the room. At the door he turned and said shortly, "I am going up to London," and he left her, hating her.

Emily was deeply humiliated, yet she was unable to do anything. She kept a silence which was both proud and stupid, because she did not know what to say, or what to do. When Edmund returned, as he did from time to time, a light in her room showed where Mrs. Porter was reading, and a light in Mr. Porter's study showed where he was. There were no bright lights or pleasant people in the young house when Edmund came home. Emily could not bear to show their estrangement to their acquaintance and he did not care. The house became dark and, except for the love of Emily for the child, sad and empty.

One day after a long interval, a man came to see Mrs. Porter. He was commissioned, he said, by Mr. Porter, to give some information to her. Edmund had left her, and he had left her destitute. She was now, in fact, a deserted wife.

When Mrs. Porter received the positive assurance that Mr. Porter had really left her and was on his way to America and would not come back, she walked to the fireplace and looked long into the fire, seeing not the fire but Edmund and his ways. "Please go and leave me alone," she said, without turning, to the quiet man standing behind her. The man standing behind her bowed gravely and went away.

Emily heard the door close behind her. She heard the house door close and knew that for a few minutes she would be alone. She was afraid. She was very much afraid of being afraid. "If I can prevent myself from being afraid," thought Emily, feeling very cold all of a sudden and shaking all over, "if I can stop myself from being afraid, I can manage, step by step. I think I will go out. I think perhaps if I walked . . ."

She went to the library door, opened it, and listened. There were only distant sounds from the kitchen. The child, Fanny, and her nurse had gone for their walk along the Front.

Mrs. Porter walked upstairs disdaining the banister. She held herself rigid so as to stop shaking and went towards the wardrobe. She took out her bonnet and mantle. She rummaged blindly on her neat shelves and found gloves and a heavy veil. "Do things," something at the back of her mind told her, "don't think, yet. Especially don't think about Edmund and the future." She stood in front of the glass and with cold hands tied her bonnet-strings and put on her veil. She did not see what face looked from the glass. She felt very cold. She threw back the veil from her bonnet and walked downstairs. She would not go out from the house as a woman humiliated and concealed. At the front door she looked to the right and to the left, turned to the left, walked quickly towards the Front and took the direction to Rottingdean. The wind blew in from the sea and the waves assailed the shore with rhythm. The rhythm. Roar, crash, withdraw. Slowly. Roar, crash, withdraw. She dropped the veil over her face, slackened her steps, and with assurance of solitude within and without, felt herself relax. Roar went the waves, crash, withdraw. She walked on slowly and at last descended towards the beach. She found a low rock on the shingle and sat down. Her large skirts spread around her on the shingle.

"What a shipwreck it's been!" she said. And that was all she dared to think about Edmund. Thinking of Edmund would come later. That was a luxury she could not afford now. She took off her bonnet and veil and the wind blew her brown hair. Solitude and the wind would free her thoughts. She must make a plan. What plan? She now forced herself painfully to think. What plan?

She sat, looking out to the grey sea, and sometimes looking down at the shingle, stooping and running the smooth pebbles slowly through her fingers. She found her thoughts straying and with great effort jerked them back. Her thoughts then went to Fanny and she became angry. "Don't waste your emotion. Don't let yourself suffer. Pull your thoughts back. What will you do? What can you do? What is there that you know how to do? What . . ."

A plan. What plan? Books. Her father's books. When Mrs. Porter had learned to read books with her father the whole world had opened before her. "A Blue Stocking," said Edmund's friends commiserating among themselves, "poor old Edmund!" "Let me see," thought Mrs. Porter astonished at her own boldness, "I can't teach them sums; I can't teach them to play the piano but I can teach them manners; I can teach them a little French and I can teach them to read and I can teach them the Classics. And I can get Lily Pocock to teach them sums and the piano and take them for walks. They shall read their History and Geography. They shall read quietly and they shall read out loud, and before they leave my school they shall be educated. And as for Edmund, he shall never come back and make me so unhappy. I must begin at once. I must waste no time. Here is my plan. I can do this. I shall be strong. I do not need Edmund. I don't want him. I can live without him very much better – if I can live."

At last she got up. She took a deep breath and smoothed back her blowing hair, pressing her hands firmly against her temples. She put on her bonnet and secured the fluttering veil. She walked slowly over the shingle and up the slope to the road leading to the promenade. "I am a strong woman," she told herself with satisfaction and surprise. "I can do this. I am not afraid. Fanny. Darling. You will have little girls to play with and learn with. We shall be more happy than we have been. I am not afraid any more. Yes – oh, I am afraid – no, no, I am not afraid . . ."

—

That was why in about 1853 Topaz and Hannah were sent to Mrs. Porter's School for Young Ladies at Brighton. And it explains why Topaz received there not a classical education but the English reflection of a classical education which tinctured her whole life, and particularly an unknown pagan part of her.

At Mrs. Porter's School Saturday night was homeletter night. All the pens were scratching. Topaz Edgeworth wrote:

My Dear Father and Mother

I hope you are very well. Thank you very much for the 2/6 for me and for Hannah. Hannah's cold is still bad so Mrs. Porter kept her in bed. I like it here. Every afternoon we have a walk. The waves are lovely. There are goat carriages drawn by goats and little Fanny Porter had a ride. She is an amewsing little child. It is sixpence and if I were not a great girl I should like to have a ride too. There is a place called the Pavilion that the Prince made for a friend of his. There is nothing like it in Ware. We do a deal of reading. Mrs. Porter made us copy out our timetable with black ink and red ink and we are to send a copy home. After Scripture we sing and Miss Pocock teaches us our sums. Miss Pocock is our pupil teacher I like her. Her mother brought her here. Her mother has big eyebrows. We think Miss Pocock is only 16. Her mother is a friend of Mrs. Porter and she is a friend of Miss Caroline Hershel the famous lady Astronomer and she is going to lecture to us next week about the Plannets. It is very nice to meet all these famous people. After dinner we read aloud a Leading Article from The Times and then we talk about it. Everything we read aloud we talk about after. Mrs. Porter reads about the Greeks and

Pan and Midas and the Golden Fleas. For our Geography we are reading the Journeys of Marco Polo with a great big globe and then we talk about it. We are reading a play of Shakespeare's King John and I am the bastard Faulconbridge. I wanted to be King John too where he says his soul will not out at windows or at doors. But I like the bastard. Eliza Pinder is King John although she reads indifferently. Mrs. Porter says that Eliza Pinder and I are bound to confess to our Parents that we did not behave like a lady. Mrs. Porter reads our letters. I am going to cross my letter now and I will do it very carefully so that you can read it. Eliza Pinder said that Topaz Edgeworth was very fond of the sound of her own voice and I said I was thankful indeed that I hadn't a Yorkshire accent to listen to and she said I was a rude cow with no manners from Staffordshire and I said no one should say such a thing to me unscathed and I slapped Eliza Pinder and Mrs. Porter came in. And Eliza and I had to apologize in public to each other after prayers for not being a lady. I make my Confession and hope my Parents will forgive me as Mrs. Porter has told me too. That is my Confession and I will now resume. For Ancient History we shall read aloud some parts of Gibbon's Decline and Fall that Mrs. Porter has chosen. For Modern History we shall first read Mr. Charles Dickens' Child's History. For serious reading we shall have Mr. Pope's translation of Homer's Iliad for Profane and Milton's Paradise Lost for Sacred. I like reading aloud and saying poetry. When somebody reads the others sew. I hope little Tilly and Sassy are all right. Now that Miss Lizzie Shaw is looking after them I suppose Edward Shaw will not send them to England although we are their auntys too. Hannah is afraid Tilly and Sassy may be a little black after living in India so long. Mrs. Porter wishes to know if you have any objection to Hannah and me joining in a card game. It is called Old Maid and is very amewsing. And she says will you please send the red flannel for Hannah. Miss Pocock is teaching us to sing songs and take part songs. I am beginning to sing seconds very nicely in hymns. We are learning a beautiful song called "Star of the Evening Beautiful Beautiful Star." I like this school better than Miss Astys. Mrs. Porter is very kind and so is Miss Pocock though she is not very old. Adieu my dear Parents j'espère que vous allez très bien. Pray give my love to Blakey and George and John and to Sister Annie. How are her babys. Pray accept my love my dear Parents. I beg to remain

Your respectful and affectionate daughter

Topaz Edgeworth

P.S. Miss Pocock is very jannock and she has cruley hair.

Topaz considered this for a moment. Then she stood up. "Please, Miss Pocock," she said, "do you spell curly with an 'e'?"

As the girls went upstairs to bed "Listen to the wind!" said Topaz, "And the sea how it's pounding tonight!" said Eliza Pinder.

"Yes, listen," said Mrs. Porter, "these are the Equinoctial Gales."

And the wind was blowing, too, among the great undiscovered pine trees in the yet unnamed place far away where some day Topaz Edgeworth would live and die. In this place Topaz would some day write and receive many letters, but no one could yet send letters there. This place was still silent and almost unknown.

IN ELDER HOUSE

Father and the ponderous Stepmother and Blakey and George and John and Joe and Topaz and little Hannah lived now in a large square house called Elder House. Elder House was set back by its own grounds which surrounded it from the Waterloo Road which, as the main thoroughfare from Bloxum to Ware, bore most of the traffic between the two manufacturing towns and their small grim satellites, and was, owing to its general undeniable drabness, a depressing street. Yet it was an exciting street, too. The Waterloo Road was exciting to Topaz and to Hannah because it carried the daily life of the towns, and because it was important, and because of its multiplicity of small brick shops which contained people, sporadic genteel rows of brick houses which contained people, incroppings of residential brick splendour which contained magnates, brick public-houses radiating their own peculiar stale allure, posters advertising shockingly the dramas at the Bloxum Blood Tub, here a brick Chapel and there a brick Chapel, and, walking up and down the rather narrow pavements in front of all these bricks, the people of the towns with their own private stories. These people of the towns were mostly working people, factory hands. Many were poor, and they all possessed for the two young girls a strong and secret fascination. The poverty of many of these people exalted them in the apprehensions of the two girls. Topaz, for all that she was the child of a strong up-springing persistent breed and fed upon comfort, took for granted the formidable quality of the poorest people who, unlike her, ate the cheapest of food, lived in the meanest of dwellings, were clothed in the sorriest of garments, and yet walked with a dare, and talked and gesticulated with an economy of violence. The Waterloo Road was not a Waterloo Road. Its "the" was its distinction and its crown. "They say they're going to have trams in *the* Waterloo Road." "There is a funeral going down *the* Waterloo Road." "Where does Dr. Russell live?" "In that there big 'ouse in *the* Waterloo Road."

In Elder House, which had a comfortable Victorian splendour, Father and the Stepmother continued their long uninterrupted life with an eternalness which seemed to make them immortal to their children, who now had begun to demonstrate vicissitude and change.

Joe died of phthisis in Elder House. Blakey went to Shropshire to farm, and then had his trunks packed at Elder House and left rejoicing for Australia. Hannah, after a short lifetime of croup and coughs, sickened, rallied, sickened again, and died of phthisis. Topaz, white of skin, pink of cheek, and voluble, had things called sniffly colds and was dosed with ale and stout in Elder House (and lived to be a hundred). The elegant bronchitic John was packed off to Italy for a year, and for some time after his return to Elder House had to be called Giovanni. George, strong and noisy, left the family and went into Father's partner's brother's bank in London. Four miles away from Elder House Annie, a devoted wife and already a pretty pocket matriarch, administered with gentle rectitude her growing family. Mary, who had never seen Elder House, had long vanished into an Indian grave. Father and the Step-mother and their biddable lively daughter Topaz now lived together with serenity and much quiet dignity, comfortably served and attended, removed by trees and garden from the busy thoroughfare, and by lack of imagination from the bitter realities of their world, to which, however, Mr. Charles Dickens and others had begun to call their attention.

It is hard to fathom how so lively a person as Topaz spent her allotment of twenty-four hours in the day, month by month and year by year. Time slides into time, and the extroverted Topaz did not consider that time, even one's own specific personal piece of Time, slides into eternity. After the death of Hannah, her dear companion, she turned to books, for which Mrs. Porter's School had well prepared her. She read every English and French book that was permitted her. She could write Greek, and wrote the enchanting characters with enthusiasm. She could not read much Greek and so she bought a Greek Testament of the parallel translation kind, and amidst fountains of ejaculations of surprise and pleasure ("Oh, what a pretty word, 'εἰρήνη,' I do declare!") Topaz read the Greek Testament. At Mrs. Porter's School she had been nourished on the pagan deities. Mrs. Porter, that strange and beautiful Blue Stocking, with a passion for the classics and a fair knowledge of Greek, had sent her pupils back to their homes in Bradford, Middlesbrough, Birmingham, and Ware, fairly convinced, in secret, of the existence of the Greek gods – as far as Greece was concerned at all events. Pan in Bloxum? . . . Well . . . Topaz did not consider the Greek gods in connection with the Waterloo Road, although it was true that her own private god lived there.

"Come, Topaz," the pug-nosed imperious Stepmother

would say as she sailed into the breakfast-room, her rotundity entering first, "put away your books now. I have ordered the brougham for eleven. We are going to Bloxum. We will see about your clothes for your London visit. And I hear that Huntbach's have some very handsome plush, old gold, the right shade, just what I need for draping the piano. And some Leek silks. I have an authentic Persian design on raw silk for the border, which I think you can embroider nicely." And Topaz, diverted and exclaiming, would hasten upstairs for her mantle, hat, and gloves.

"We are going to Bloxum, Cook!" she would exclaim on the stairs.

"We are going to Bloxum, Sarah!" she would announce to the parlourmaid on the landing.

"We are going to Bloxum, Austin!" she said delightedly to the housemaid upstairs.

And as she embroidered the elegant Persian design in the faded yet permanent exquisite silks from the neighbouring town of Leek, and related and re-related to the Stepmother, majestically inattentive, the account of her visit to Annie and the children the day before, the Stepmother would interrupt her, saying, "Topaz, is there fresh frilling in the neck of your grey?" and Topaz knew that the Stepmother's mind was on the Book-Meeting-Party to which they would go that evening.

And as Topaz drove home from the Book-Meeting-Party that evening, sitting facing her Father – who nodded – and her resplendent Stepmother, and talked eagerly of Eliza Pinder's rendering of Guinevere, and hummed her own cooing melodious part of "We fell out, my wife and I," her Stepmother said suddenly, "Topaz, you may help Austin wash the chandeliers in the drawing-room tomorrow, or it will take her all day." Topaz fell for a moment silent, wondering if, the last time that she helped Austin wash the two great cut-glass chandeliers which reflected themselves interminably in the large end-mirrors of the room, she had detached and attached two hundred and sixty, or two hundred and sixty-four pointed lustres. It was a good thing that Father and the Stepmother did not listen to Topaz overly much, or they might have stilled her incessant happy talking – and one must do something. Now that Hannah was gone, her pleasantest listeners were Cook and Austin and Sarah and her friend Tottie Hay in London and a few school friends who were within driving distance; so she enjoyed helping Austin, in an inept fashion. When she was with any of these listeners she was fed with applause and enjoyment, and often became very funny. But it was a fact that although Father had a sense of fun, he had no sense of humour, and the Stepmother had neither the one nor the other. But Topaz, uncritical, did not notice this. Rocking home in the brougham she put the thought of the chandeliers aside and continued to recapitulate the party to the indulgent elderly smiles and yawns of her parents.

And as she stood on the step-ladder the next morning and detached each lustre and, talking, handed it down to Austin who washed it carefully in light suds and rinsed it, and when she helped to dry each lustre in turn, and then mounted the ladder again and, receiving each gleaming pointed piece of glass from Austin's careful hand, attached it in its place, still merrily talking, she did not think that her life was uneventful. Her life was happy and eventful. She had found her god in the Waterloo Road. She had fallen deeply in love with William Sandbach who lived there.

I suppose that when Topaz Edgeworth realized that she had fallen in love with William, Mr. Sandbach must have been about thirty-five. He was easily the most distinguished person in the Waterloo Road, which runs straight or slightly curving for some miles. He was a widower, and, as mortality among wives was high, this seemed almost according to nature. He was a tragic widower who had lost both wife and child together under shocking circumstances when he was a very young man, and had borne his sorrow with a proud silence that distinguished him. He lived in a small and admirable Georgian house a little way down the Waterloo Road, which, with its well-tended and hedged garden, was hidden from the dingy thoroughfare. He was the only man in the two towns who gave dinner-parties. His voice was not the voice of the two towns, but had a quality of beauty that was almost suspect. His natural courtesy was a thing apart. He showed some friendship and hospitality to the Italianate young John Edgeworth. He had a handsome presence, kindly eyes, and an admired beard. He was Member of Parliament for the Borough. He had for the first time invited both John Edgeworth and his sister Topaz to a dinner-party the following week, and Topaz adored him. How should she not adore such a man? She had idolized him from afar ever since her school-days. And yesterday he had stopped her and her Stepmother in the Waterloo Road and, taking Topaz by the hand and looking kindly and directly into her eyes with the charm that had won him many an honest vote, had expressed his pleasure that she and her brother were able to dine with him, and to meet the Prince and Princess Colonna. And when this first time he took her by the hand and looked at her, Topaz ceased chattering, and her long adoration turned to the love which she now recognized. An extraordinary sensation flooded her. As she looked up, rapt, plain, and silent, at the grey eyes and light brown beard of Mr. William Sandbach she felt within her the ancient disquieting question arise, "Is this indeed love?" And it was. It was the very passion of love.

There was a distinction in dining with Prince and Princess Colonna who, owing to an interest in Italian and English china, had come to visit some of the factories in the two towns. Because they could not dash from factory to factory in a motor car, since there were no motor cars in which to dash, but drove from factory to factory in a barouche, the day being fine, and because the Princess, instead of climbing rapidly and unimpeded up and down stairs, moved with the slowness of gracefully manipulated skirts, swaying, bending gracefully to examine, to exclaim, to compare, the whole leisurely performance took a long time, and the Prince and Princess spent the night in the pretty Georgian house of Mr. Sandbach. Young Giovanni Edgeworth with his easy Italian and his pretty manners, his rather tittering wit and his kissing of hands when required, so satisfied William Sandbach's need of a good dinner guest, that whenever Mr. Sandbach again entertained distinguished visitors, and he often did, John and Topaz Edgeworth – that pleasant and presentable young brother and sister who could carry their weight in conversation in two or three languages – were always included in the Sandbach parties. They became almost indispensable. Topaz loved the sound of music, and, twittering, flew as a bird to where the other thrushes were. She was not aware of the deep knowledge, the frustration, and the exultation of the conductor as he moulded the plastic impassioned air into sound. "*What* a good concert! The Mozart, beautiful!" She did not assess the sustained cry of violin and flute, or the controlled fury of brass and drum, but when she met the conductor the next evening at dinner at William Sandbach's, she rejoiced to cry, "Ah, Herr Stein! Your Beethoven, magnificent!" She enjoyed music as she enjoyed food, with pleasure, but without passion, like a warbling unimportant bird; and perhaps she was as musical as any other bird. John and Topaz were full of amusing talk following each party, and people said what lucky young things they were to have all this experience, which was true. And after a time people said, too, "You'll see, Mr. Sandbach will marry Topaz Edgeworth one of these days. She's not pretty, and it's a pity she doesn't wear her clothes well, but she's entertaining, and, my word, she *can* talk! She'll be Mrs. William Sandbach, M.P., you mark my words, and she'll make a good wife for Holy Willie." People went on saying this for three or four years.

And the Stepmother said to Father, "Joseph, I hope William Sandbach intends to marry the girl. She's in love with him, I am convinced, and he is making her conspicuous. Couldn't you say something, Father?"

And William Sandbach said to himself, "Shall I marry again? . . . I wonder if Topaz Edgeworth . . . she's very good at a dinner-party . . . but I don't love her and I don't think I ever would love her, and I can*not* go through all that misery again. I'm free. And yet . . ."

And Austin said as she unhooked Miss Topaz's yellow moiré that was so good and so unflattering, "Cook said to me, Miss, only this very evening, 'Mr. Sandbach will pop the question any day now, see if he doesn't,' and Cook says that Mr. Sandbach's Mary said that the way Mr. Sandbach looked at Miss Topaz anyone could tell that there'll soon be a second Mrs. Sandbach. There then, you step out of it and I'll loosen the stays."

All these cruel things Austin said, and when Topaz was in bed, and the light was out, and the evening beat brightly about her brain, she said to herself, "Can it be possible that he could not love me when I love him so much? What do I do wrong that he does not love me? What will please him that I can do? I would lie down and let him tread upon me. When he is there, everyone else is just a shadow. Until he comes back into the room the room is empty. Just to touch his sleeve. Oh God, what shall I do? I cannot live like this."

And still Downs drove John and Topaz to Mr. Sandbach's evening parties and William Sandbach greeted them with the same urbane charm that he gave to each guest – or perhaps a little more. Topaz became rather more animated, a little more gay, but pale. Before she went into a room, now, she furtively pinched her cheeks that were so pale. ("Like this, you see? Like this . . ." she said fifty, sixty, and seventy years later, vigorously pinching her wrinkled but soft cheeks, "a great help to the complexion!")

Austin at last stopped her warm exciting welcome hints to Topaz as she undressed her after a party, although in the kitchen she (Austin) and Cook and the new Betsy talked commiseratingly.

"*I* could learn her how!" said young Betsy, boasting.

"You hold your tongue, miss," said Cook sharply, "our Miss Topaz needs no lessons from such as you!"

And upstairs Topaz wept alone. She really wept. Many a night she wept in the dark, and slept on a hateful moistened pillow.

And when three more years had passed, John made a runaway marriage, and this affected the happiness of Topaz a very great deal.

WHAT A DELIGHTFUL EVENING!

When, at Elder House, the letter arrived from John in London announcing his sudden marriage, Father faced Mother across the breakfast table, and Mother faced Father. They looked at each other and for some moments were unable to speak. It was nothing to them that in John's letter a general trembling could be discerned plainly. Let him tremble. So he should. But that John – the dilettante, the indolent, the elegant, the diner at good tables, the indifferent apprentice at Father's Works, without an income, with hardly a wage – should have slipped away to London and become a married man, and should have done it without their permission, shocked Father and Mother to their strong foundations. And that Mrs. Grimwade, the rich and miserly friend of their childhood, who each year entertained the young Topaz in a niggardly fashion, should, in her house in Lambeth, connive, and should abet this marriage, and should chaperon the bride, and should lend her an ancient silver bouquet-holder which appeared to be the only visible sign of celebration, was incomprehensible to them.

And Uncle Montague, at his breakfast table, glaring above his long beard – in which crumbs had lodged – at a letter from London, cursed so horribly that the parlourmaid went out to the kitchen door and beckoned Cook to listen. In Uncle Montague's letter, which was also tremulous in tone and matter, Anne Edgeworth informed her father, oh, so timidly, that she had married dear John, and that she hoped to be forgiven, and that she had slept at dear Mrs. Grimwade's as Mrs. Grimwade would testify, and that Mrs. Grimwade had lent her a silver bouquet-holder which Mrs. Grimwade had herself used at her own wedding – "the old bitch," said Uncle Montague. Anne hoped her dear Father would also forgive her dear John, and would receive them soon, and she remained his devoted daughter Anne Edgeworth.

When Uncle Montague had cursed as much as possible and had spilt his coffee which flew up and hit him as he banged the breakfast table, he went to his lawyer's where he revoked his allowance to his daughter and also changed his will; then he drove to the Works to roar at his brother Joseph. Joseph Edgeworth was not there, so Uncle Montague had himself driven to Elder House, where he found Father, Mother, and Topaz still in consternation. Topaz fled. Father had rallied, as he foresaw the coming of Uncle Montague with his rage upon him, and Father, a strong man of peace, had prepared himself for storm. Uncle Montague could not frighten the Stepmother, who drew herself up to the last proud and portly inch and at once took the part of Giovanni and of Anne, who thereafter became known in the family as Annie-John, or, sometimes, John's Annie.

Although Father and Mother were quite properly annoyed at the action of the preposterous young fellow John, they knew what circumstances had brought about this forbidden marriage. It had already been mooted, and John's parents and Anne's father had at once forbidden a marriage between the cousins. Having forbidden this marriage, these Olympians, accustomed to obedience, had dismissed so trivial a matter from their minds. Father did not propose to support John, and Uncle Montague had other plans for his daughter who was a bit of an heiress. Not only was Uncle Montague a wealthy and violent man, who blew where he listed, but he was a widower whose wife had gone to her peace, having made her own plans for her daughter's future beforehand. This rich and gentle woman, before she died, made her will, and left to her infant daughter Anne a pretty fortune, to be hers at the age of twenty-one. And here was Anne, a week after her twenty-first birthday, proceeding to London, and marrying her handsome and penniless young cousin, bringing with her a dowry which would support them both, very nicely indeed. True, John was a young man of integrity and he loved his cousin very much, but he was wise, and he and his bride chose this course which, although shocking even to themselves, was easier than facing the gales of family wrath wherein their little ship might founder.

Topaz, after much exclaiming and running about and relating the romantic news and writing on her own account an affectionate and welcoming letter to the culprits, was stricken with doubt. She withdrew to her bedroom to think, as the house seemed to be full of gasping exclaiming relatives.

Mr. Sandbach. John had been inconsiderate. Mr. Sandbach was entertaining the Baroness Burdett-Coutts at dinner on the following evening. Of course John and Topaz Edgeworth were both invited; and now John had gone off to London and got married without a word! Would Mr. Sandbach want her to come without John? Each evening with William Sandbach now filled her with misery, yet was her dearest joy. She would not relinquish this joy and this misery. She would not submit the problem to her Stepmother, who with dignity and spacious consideration was now deciding upon Stands to the taken in the future with John, with Anne, with Montague, with Mrs. Grimwade, with the daughters and sons, with the servants, with the aunts and uncles, with the cousins and with many other people. On the next evening Topaz, to the Stepmother's great surprise, ordered the brougham on her own account, put on her favourite green plaid taffeta with the many ruchings, and drove to Mr. Sandbach's house to dinner. During this very short journey she told herself again that the news of John's marriage must have spread quickly, that Mr. Sandbach would be prepared for John's absence and for her presence, since she had sent him no message. With a little apprehension she left the carriage, and rang the bell at Mr. Sandbach's well-known door, alone.

"Are you all right, Miss Topaz?" called Downs from the box. A maid took her mantle, and Topaz advanced smiling but uncertain into the drawing-room filled with talking people who immediately fell silent, and as immediately resumed talking with greater zest than ever.

"Yes, they do know. They are talking about John," she thought quickly and did not know how to proceed. But her host came up at once.

"Ah, Miss Topaz!" he said smiling (how often "Ah, Miss Topaz!"), "we were waiting for you impatiently! What is this we hear about your dashing young brother? But first let me take you to Baroness Burdett-Coutts, and then you must tell us . . ." and Topaz felt at home, and everyone turned their laughing friendly faces towards her.

There was in the mind of Topaz as she laughed and chattered and expatiated more and more lavishly an uneasy feeling of imminence. Imminence of what? Of something which would happen. Of a sign. This feeling grew throughout dinner-time, and afterwards became almost unbearable to her. "Yes, this evening will bring me a sign at last," she thought. Without looking, she watched William Sandbach. She saw – without seeming too much to observe – his every movement. She was not aware, then, that she, Topaz, was also observed. She, never self-conscious, did not feel that other guests watched with interest the possible crisis of a little play – a play of which they had grown, perhaps, after so long a time, rather tired. She saw Mr. Sandbach, with a gesture to the guest of honour, take her towards his little conservatory and his famous begonias. Then the Baroness led; he followed, impeccable, the host. *What happiness it might be, what unbelievable happiness!* Topaz renewed her animation and talked to Edmund Bond about the new Academy pictures which she intended to see when she visited Mrs. Grimwade in London – the same Mrs. Grimwade who so naughtily had contrived to help John. Edmund teased her.

"A very dangerous house to visit, Topaz, for your family," laughed little Edmund Bond, "you had better beware . . ."

"They are magnificent," said the Baroness, near at hand. "What richness of colour! So perfectly fringed! Have you seen them?"

"Would *you* like to see my begonias, Miss Topaz? They are at their best. May I take you?"

I must not show how I care. I must smile. No one shall see. And with her hasty eager tread which not even Mrs. Porter had been able to tame to the desired grace, Topaz stepped forward and laid her hand on Mr. Sandbach's sleeve. *Oh, I cannot come here again unless I come to stay!*

They went into the gloom, or it seemed at first to Topaz that it was gloom, of the little conservatory where light from the drawing-room showed the pink, the rose, the crimson, the white, the primrose of the great begonias. William stopped. Topaz stood facing him and fidgeted nervously with the ruching of her basque. They did not look at the begonias. It was evident that Mr. Sandbach had something to say. He looked down at her with the kind look that was to her so personal and tender. ("Oh, look at Holy Willie!")

"I hope, Miss Topaz," he said seriously, "that this sudden marriage of John's has not caused your parents real concern. I think, if I may say so, that it is a good marriage for John. His wife is a most estimable young lady and will, I feel, be a steadying and sensible influence on our young friend, on whom, so far, responsibility has sat lightly. You do not mind my saying this? I wished you to know how fully I sympathize with your parents – and yet I understand, believe me, and congratulate John heartily." He paused. Something in Topaz's uplifted face smote him, and caused him to be uncomfortable, and sorry, and ruthless.

"Oh," she thought, "he only wants to speak about John. It is only of John he is thinking, not of me."

"Thank you," she said at last. "I will tell John. Yes, I will tell him."

"Thank you . . . and I will write to him," said William. "And now . . . but Miss Topaz," he turned to her again and she stood and watched the shadows on his face, "I trust that when John and his wife return, and dine with me, as I hope they will often do, you will not neglect us altogether? Such a charming and lively young lady as you . . . we should miss you . . . I hope that . . ." He cursed himself. *How cold and clumsy I am! What am I saying? Yet I cannot speak otherwise. What am I trying to tell her?*

THE INNOCENT TRAVELLER

"Oh, he is too courteous, too cold!" thought Topaz despairingly. "He does not care whether I stay or whether I go. He doesn't care whether I live or die. This is plain to me now. This has been waiting for me. I need not deceive myself and put myself in this ridiculous position any longer. This is the sign. This is what was waiting for me." And she knew beyond any doubt that William Sandbach did not love her – not if she dined there for years and years and years would he ever love her. Her nervous fingers still played with the silk ruching and the frill of her bodice. She was glad that in the half-light he could not see her face clearly. She said with a pitiful dignity, with a little toss and agitation of her head, and with an unsure laugh, "I wanted to have this opportunity of telling you, Mr. Sandbach, that my Mother persuaded me to come tonight for fear lest I should disarrange your party, and that in future John's wife will, of course, accompany him – an extra woman does so much complicate your numbers. You see? You see? I understand these things," said poor Topaz. "This has been a very delightful evening," and the tears were near her eyes, "but I must keep my promise to my Mother, and go back to her, early. The event has been very trying for her. You understand? You will excuse me, I am sure. I will go, before Mrs. Beardmore begins to sing." She turned towards the door and stepped forwards with her swaying hasty tread.

I cannot stay and finish this evening. How best can I leave this place. I must go home. I must go home. There is no other sign. I know that I shall never come here again, for I cannot bear it any more. And she moved busily across the room towards the guest of honour. The faces of her friends were no longer the faces of friends. They were only talking, grimacing people. She had to be alone.

"Baroness," she said smiling, with death in her heart, "this has been charming, so charming! But my Mother is tired tonight, and I promised her that after I had filled my place at the table I would go home. You will forgive me if I leave before you? Goodbye. Goodbye . . . and Mrs. Beardmore, I am so sorry I shall not hear you sing!" *Is everything said? Can I escape without betraying myself?* And Topaz nodded and smiled and nodded, and made her exit, pale and smiling.

When Austin opened the door of Elder House, Topaz passed her headlong without word or sign. She hurried up the stairs, her long green skirt with its ruched frills trailing behind her. Half-way up the stairs she turned. "You need not come, Austin," she said in a choking voice, and proceeded hastily to her room. "I shall undress myself."

"Eh, what *has* happened to Miss Topaz! Not even going near the Master and Mistress, not to tell them about the party!" Austin said, and stood looking up the stairs. "It's all over then. . . . Nothing else could ever make her look like that. . . ." And, still looking up, she heard Topaz's door shut. And the silence.

In the great four-poster with its ocean of feather bed, Father and Mother lay comfortable in its billows and waited for their daughter to come in as usual, full of talk. They heard her at the front door, so early. The Stepmother raised herself slowly in the bed and lighted a candle. Topaz would come in and sit down and talk, and a candle would do. Some light shone in through the open door from the landing. But Topaz did not come. They heard her rapid tread. They heard the rustle of her silk. They heard her pass their door. They heard her own door close. Louder than words could tell, they heard that something was wrong.

"Why hasn't the girl come in to see us? I want to settle," said Father at last. "Is something the matter? Hadn't you better go?"

"Nay, Joseph, not yet," said Mother, and lay down again.

Inside Topaz's room the lamp was lighted. Topaz stood in the middle of the floor. So the impossible and outrageous had happened to her, Topaz Edgeworth. She had spent seven years of her life in the preoccupation of love, and there was no return but this emptiness. The placid bearded figure passed and repassed smiling before her eyes and she whispered "I hate him."

"Go, Jane, do," urged Father in the feather bed. The mountainous woman got up slowly, and silently and slowly passed through the door. She stood, holding her breath, outside Topaz's room. There was no sound. What was the girl doing in there. (She was still standing there, rigid, her hands clenched at her sides.) The Stepmother raised her hand to knock, and held it raised. She heard in a cold strong voice unknown before to her the fearful words "*Curse him!* I call Heaven to witness that I curse William Sandbach!"

Fear and compassion smote the Stepmother standing there. "Oh," she thought, "is that our Topaz? Our poor Topaz? I cannot help her now. I will let her be. She wouldn't want me to know." And she turned and went back to her bedroom.

She closed the door. She blew out the candle and mounted heavily into the bed and pulled on the covers and lay there looking into the dark.

"Well, Mother?" asked Father beside her.

"Oh, Joseph," said the big kind woman, "she cursed him!"

"Cursed who?"

"Cursed William Sandbach."

"Cursed William Sandbach? Our Topaz cursed William Sandbach?" Father repeated in amazement, while William Sandbach flitted past him and past again, the suitably bearded William in a frock-coat, William in a Prince Albert and striped trousers, William Sandbach, M.P., Holy Willie.

"What will you do, Jane?" he asked at last in dismay.

"I don't know," said Mother miserably.

There was a long heavy silence in the feather bed.

"Take the girl to Bloxum tomorrow and buy her a good mantle," suggested Father at a loss.

"A mantle! Oh, Joseph, sometimes you're very stupid," and Mother began to cry.

Joseph lay aghast. His enormous wife had never wept before. He reached out his hand and patted her great arm.

"Come, come, Mother. There then . . ." he said helplessly.

RECURRING PLEASURES

Of all the inventions human or divine which have been bestowed upon civilized peoples the one most taken for granted, yet the one most practical, is the division of Eternity – or is it of Time – into seven days of the week. Uncivilized persons, one supposes, do not feel the lack of this arbitrary division. The passage of Time is marked for them by such signs as the seasons if any, by day and night if any, by the lunar and solar changes at all events, and by the occurrence and duration of other physical phenomena such as hunger and gestation. These changes are enough; and to some indolent civilized people that is a very enviable kind of existence which they would willingly exchange for their own. For our existence which we call civilized becomes increasingly complex; so that 3 p.m. next Wednesday week has an entity and form and prognosis before ever it arrives; and instead of living in polar time and space like free Eskimos, we make prisoners of ourselves by appointments which we arrange for ourselves for 10 a.m. on Tuesday week and 5 p.m. on Thursday fortnight, and the first two weeks in July, and thus, between us, we murder our peace. The only thing in our changing world that we can now regard as being safe and sure is that next Monday will certainly be Monday, next Tuesday will be Tuesday and nothing else, and that Saturday afternoon will always be Saturday afternoon; and for this much stability we should be thankful.

Topaz was what might be called a civilized although not a conventional being. She was not indolent but she was idle. She seemed very busy, and for the most part she was busy in useless matters and recurring pleasures, so that if the book of her life had been shut up bang at an early age, history would have gone on much the same.

Between the time of her slow but complete and lively recovery from her one-sided love affair with William Sandbach and the time of her going to live in Canada as she ultimately did, there was a long stretch of years which had every right to be unbearably dull. Instead of being unbearably dull, these years were educative, amusing, and profitable, and this is a tribute to people who like Topaz are not particularly useful but are unquenchably gay.

While it is true that each year was very much like the last and the next and therefore the years slipped away uncounted and unmarked except by births, marriages, and deaths from old age, for no one was ever ill, the set and recurring pleasures of these years kept memory and anticipation alive.

During the winter months Topaz, since the age of seventeen, had met with other pleasant and knowledgeable people of the Pottery Towns at what were called the Book Meetings. Evening lectures were held at the grimy Bloxum Institute; but the evening journey was long for the family broughams, and so, among the Edgeworths and their friends, the Book Meetings were born. These continued for years to be among her recurring pleasures. I was never at a Book Meeting, because I was not alive and had not then been thought of, but I have heard so much about them that I am there with Topaz. There we sat, rising to greet with delight the Arkwrights, the Huntbachs, the Stocker girls, the Stalker boys, old Mr. Saddleback, the Greens, all the large Edgeworth family, and visitors. People came in their carriages, unless they lived very near at hand. The Book Meetings were held only once a month, because much real work had to be done beforehand. The standard of discussion of books, or of the performance of music, was good. Lecturers did not in those days rush about the country by plane and train and lecture at great pains and expense for half an hour after lunch to the time-driven citizens about Poland, Canadian Art, the University as I See It, and Political Changes in Our Time; nevertheless we are fortunate that they do this for us now, as thus we know more about more subjects, although less about less. The Book Meeting members did this for themselves, and they did it very well; so well that such early temporary members as young Mr. Kipling (later to be the surprised father of a poet), and the other lively and amusing in-laws of young Mr. Edward Burne-Jones were noticed to be bright, but not unusually bright nor potentially famous.

Topaz had a sweet singing voice, only moderately pleasing, because it was not so much like a singing voice as like a flute's note, or the notes of a thrush. She shone in the duet, because her voice was true; and she had absorbed on her way so much musical knowledge that she was able to harmonize nice airs which occurred to her or to other people, and to set them to music and to play the music too, while she warbled a flute-like true soprano and her younger sister Hannah (or after Hannah died Miss Arkwright or Mrs. Tennant) took a melodious contralto.

There was, of course, the busy and spreading family, political, and Chapel life which went on continuously, and which composed the background of the Book Meetings of the winter months, of Topaz's annual visits to old Mrs. Grimwade in London, of a short visit annually to the seaside which was held in only moderate esteem, and of an occasional journey to the continent of Europe. This sufficed for Topaz since she was congenitally lacking in any private or inner life and did not seem to miss or need it.

Father – who on account of James and Annie Hastings' growing young family was now established as Grandfather Edgeworth and was slipping almost unaware into being Great-Grandfather Edgeworth – had an esteem for Exhibitions. This dated from a visit to the Exhibition held in the new Crystal Palace in 1851. Father was a progressive manufacturer and had sent some teapots – brown teapots – to the section of the Exhibition devoted to china and pottery. His children's future as travellers on the continent of Europe was sealed at the moment when Father, standing aside with his two young sons, beheld the small Queen of England, escorted by her tall consort and the immensely popular Duke of Wellington and an entourage of ladies and gentlemen, advance to the stand on which were Father's teapots. Queen Victoria picked up each teapot and handled it. She almost caressed its rotundity as she discussed its merits with Prince Albert and the Duke who presumably were interested in brown teapots; she laid it down; and then amidst the hush of her subjects, she passed on. Father's business received a notable stimulus from this experience. The French next had an exhibition in Paris which they perversely insisted on calling an Exposition. Thither went Father and his sons. Next thing, Father was exhibiting in Amsterdam and in Rome; and next thing he had an agency in Naples.

As time went on and Father's sons grew up, it was obvious that John was the one for European travel, and so it was John who with a weak chest spent a year in Naples and developed a culture of Europe which blended very nicely with the natural charm which he possessed, which was English. It was John who was sent hither and yon to exhibit and report on each new Exposition and to develop business connections on the Continent. As a business man John was only fair; but since he spoke foreign languages easily and his manners were good, he made a worthy representative of his father, who was very able and much more useful at home. An odd but lucky thing was that Father could trust John completely and had no reason to feel uneasy about the debasing of the handsome young man's morals in the notoriously easygoing continent. John was a mirror of convention as he knew it; moral lapses were almost as serious to him as were lapses of good manners; so Father had no worries about John.

In the late summer of the year 1889, Topaz was in London. One day towards the end of her customary stay with Mrs. Grimwade, her brother John called and was admitted.

"Oh, here you are, John!" exclaimed Topaz, entering the drawing-room with a rush and finding her good-looking brother there. "What brings you to London?" and her brother told her.

Father had directed John to go to Naples to visit the factory's agent there, and had suggested that John should take with him his sister Topaz, as, although she had been to Switzerland, to Holland, and to France, she had never yet been to Italy. John had agreed, adding, "And I think it would do Topaz good, sir. I have noticed that she is in danger of becoming provincial."

"Is she indeed?" said Father indifferently; "well, I hadn't

noticed it." And that was probable, because Father himself was incurably and proudly a provincial of the finest kind.

"But Annie! Annie-John!" cried the delighted Topaz, when she heard the news, speaking not of her eldest sister Annie Hastings, who was far too busy with her own family of nine children to think of going to Europe, but of John's own wife, Annie-John. "How is it, John, that you are taking me, and are not taking Annie-John?"

John looked down his nose which was well modelled. He said, speaking with some importance, "A reconciliation has taken place between Annie and her father" ("Oh!" breathed Topaz with two round eyes and a round mouth), "and it seemed timely, as he wished Annie to accompany him on a visit to the Lakes, that she should go with him. I do not, however, feel that Uncle Montague" (his terrifying and reluctant father-in-law) "is yet completely resigned to me as Annie's husband, so I am taking this opportunity to go to the continent on business."

It would be a dull dog indeed who could call a life dull in which there suddenly occurred an unexpected visit to the Continent. Topaz, full of joy and anticipation, set out with brother John.

She exclaimed all the way across the Channel and in the train which puffed across the fair land of France, until they reached Paris. She exclaimed all day every day in Paris, and often John had to restrain and correct her. He became increasingly aware that ordinary convention which he so sincerely worshipped had no meaning for his sister. This placed John in many uncomfortable situations in which he felt that he was conspicuous not as the lordly and distinguished Englishman which he liked to be, but as the brother of an irreverent and carefree youthfully middle-aged sister from the Midlands; and before he arrived in Italy he often wished that he had left her at home to deteriorate.

The brother and sister began the ascent of the new and amazing Eiffel Tower. How delightful! What a wind! The skirts of Topaz whirled around her head obscuring her view, but she did not mind. John did. "We will descend, Topaz!" he said, tapping his cane sternly on the hand-rail.

"No, no, John!"

"Yes, yes!"

"No, no!"

"Yes, yes! This is no place for an Englishwoman of modesty with all these Frenchmen about. Descend! Descend!" he cried. With Topaz expostulating and backing down all the way, skirts whirling, they descended. Frenchmen watched with pleasure. This kind of thing happened continually.

John became more pallidly handsome and anxious as he escorted his sister about the continent of Europe. Topaz rejoiced too openly, she had no reticence; she did not seem to know the right people from the wrong people; she made friends with the wrong people without patronizing them suitably; she was openly entertained by the frank private habits of the wrong people. "Thank God," thought John, "that my sister is not physically attractive to men, or my position would be worse still; she is disgracefully natural." And Topaz thought – when she thought about it at all – "Really, how easily shocked John is! He does look silly with that martyred expression on! Oh dear, dear, John, I've put on odd boots, I do declare!"

And then, when they had reached Lyons, and John had decided that his sister was not physically attractive and that her particular kind of artlessness did not arouse the baser passions of men – especially of Frenchmen – he had a nasty jar, and resumed his anxious watchdoggery. Their plan in each new hotel in each new town was that John's room should adjoin the room of Topaz – an arrangement well suited to a brother chaperoning his unmarried sister through Europe. But in the thrifty little hotel found by John in Lyons there were no such rooms available. John could sleep just above Topaz, but not beside her. "Oh, I will, John. No, I won't, John. You see, Madame has given me a key! Yes indeed. If anything happens in the night, I shall stand on my bed at once and pound with my umbrella!" promised Topaz hopefully, and she slept soundly each night with her umbrella beside her in the bed, in case ("*Such* a comfort!"). But one day John, descending, paused aghast at the head of the narrow flight of stairs. There, outside his sister's half-open bedroom door, stood a man in earnest low conversation with the attentive Topaz. Out flew the Frenchman's hands, persuasive, this way, that way, flic-flac; out rushed the words; he paused for a moment and laid a hand upon Topaz's arm. Topaz dusted him off. She did not attempt to go away, but listened and interrupted with her usual eager vivacity. As John gathered himself together and bounded down the stairs like an avenging mountain goat he heard his sister say, "Mais, Monsieur, attendez un moment! Non, non, nous ne sommes pas froides, nous Anglaises! Pas du tout! Au contraire, je vous assure que . . ."

"An assignation!" roared John.

"Oh, is that you, John?" said Topaz, turning to her brother. "This gentleman no, I never saw him before . . . oh, where can he have gone? . . . tells me he finds the English cold, and I was only trying to reassure him that so far from that being the case we . . ." John stood silent, furious.

Then, "Into your room at once!" he hissed between neat teeth.

"Well I never, what a fuss to be sure! He was a very inter-esting young man . . . parted his beard in the middle in flour-ishes . . . east and west . . . like this . . ." twiddling her fingers each side of her face, "very peculiar!"

"And did he accost you?" asked John severely.

"Accost? Oh yes indeed he *did* accost! Never had such an accosting in my life! On the stairs! But I wouldn't have let him in, whatever he did, I do assure you, John, oh dear me, no!" said Topaz, delighted to be accosted, yet armed with all her gay purity.

"But you must have encouraged him!"

"*Me!* Encourage him! I did no such thing! I only greeted him politely as we met!"

"*Greeted* him . . . ! It's evident you don't know Frenchmen, Topaz!"

"Well, John," said Topaz shrewdly, "you don't give me much of a chance, do you?" which was true.

At dinner-times, John marked his sister as she drank the pleasant and sometimes unpleasant wines of France and Italy. He would lay his hand upon her glass.

"One glass is enough for you, Topaz; you are sufficiently intoxicated by nature without drinking wine."

"*Me!* Intoxicated by nature!" But so she was, like many another much more famous lady.

It was when Topaz lay flat on her back on the floor of the empty Sistine Chapel, better to observe the wonderful ceiling, in an attitude that John's idol, Ruskin, would have compre-hended, that John nearly started back home in a fury. Topaz had to do a little cajoling, at which she was not very good, to restrain him; she had to point out, for example, that Michael Angelo himself had had to take up unorthodox attitudes and had thereby actually developed a goitre while painting the great frescoes, until at last John spoke to her again and there was peace between them.

In the end they both went home as culprits. John had been unable to resist the opportunity of an audience with the Pope.

"Get Signora Castellani to give you a bit of black lace for your head, Topaz, and we will join the throng." And they did.

The pilgrims flocked in thousands. Every mind, every heart was high uplifted. The great spiritual and temporal power of the Church of Rome seized the imagination of these two intelligent English provincials, and in excitement and fervour they moved with the great throng. Gone were the scruples of John. Topaz had none. ("It is of course true, Topaz, that people died that England might become a Protestant country, and let us not forget that; and you know perfectly well also that our great-grandfather was made a class-leader by John Wesley. It is true, too, that Father and Mother will not be pleased. But in view of the opportunity to join in the service of this great historic church I prefer to become a casuist, and I shall not conceal it from my parents." "Oh do, John. Oh don't, John. Oh do, John!" cried Topaz, ready for everything. That is actually the way that John and Topaz talked to each other.)

It was fine to see John standing proud and erect in the presence of his parents when the travellers returned to England. Father did not seem to mind very much about the audience with the Pope, but the Stepmother was displeased. So Father spoke.

"And did you – bow the knee to the Pope of Rome, John?"

"I did, sir. To a great Prince of an historic Church." The green eyes of Topaz glanced quickly from parents to son.

"And did you commit yourself with any . . . remarks . . . or ritual during the ceremony?" asked the Stepmother, portentous with her girth and her black satin and her pug nose.

"I instructed my sister to repeat *sotto voce* the Apostles' Creed, and I did so myself," said John nobly.

The Stepmother raised her chin and looked down her proud pug nose across at her husband. She deferred, as always, to her mild lord. She trumpeted melodiously (as she so often did), "Then Lay your Commands upon them, Joseph!"

But Father laid no Commands upon them. He only said, "Let them be, Mother. I hope when I die that I shall have friends in the many mansions and they won't all think like me. Let them be."

All the journeys of Topaz, whether great or small, were packed with adventure and reminiscence. The world blossomed daily into incident; and so the years passed too quickly. Then suddenly, in all her opinion, rotundity, dignity, and integrity, the Stepmother died.

NUTS AND FIGS

Until the death of the Stepmother, the private life of Topaz, if life must be compared to a journey, had been like travelling on a canal. Topaz had never said to herself, "My private life is like a canal" ("A canal indeed! Whatever are they talking about!"), but nevertheless when for purposes of recollection or recapitulation she regarded her past and passing life, it was as a canal that she saw it. This canal had been soundly constructed by her progenitors, and was well administered by those now in charge. The banks of this smooth canal were pleasant, and presented much variety to her, not in scenery, but in people who were seen in passing – to whom Topaz eagerly spoke, nodded, or waved when possible, whatever their station or occupation – and objects, which she pointed out with many lively comments. Except for a period when she passed through a long and dark tunnel, when, distraught, she did not know where to turn (but the way led straight on regardless of her despair), her journey was comfortable and well-conditioned. Sometimes Topaz alighted and made an agreeable excursion. She went with Father to the Lake District ("Ah, Keswick, Keswick! Poor dear Ruskin!"), and she and Mother went to Manchester when Mother was very old (". . . and we took her to the Art Gallery, Austin and I, in the bath-chair, she would go! And Ellen Terry running like a girl from room to room, and coming in and meeting Mother again on purpose, and studying her, and laughing and saying, 'Oh, look, isn't she *perfect!*' And Austin *was* cross at anyone for laughing about Mother, Ellen Terry or no. Because Mother looked just as important as Queen Victoria in the bath-chair, you know, and far better dressed, and, of course, she had a pug nose, but Mother never noticed . . ." – just the same blessed obliviousness that preserved Topaz for a century). And a journey to France (". . . and we climbed the Eiffel Tower, and *such* a wind, oh, *such* a wind! And my skirts blowing above my head – such skirts! And John said, 'Topaz, turn and descend this instant! This is no place for a young Englishwoman with all these Frenchmen about! "). And a journey to Italy (". . . the ceiling of the Sistine Chapel! Wonderful! And there was hardly anyone there, so I lay down flat on my back to see better. And John hissed, 'Topaz, get up at once, I disown you completely!' and he walked away. Oh, John *was* annoyed! I thought he'd never get over it, but he did, he did . . ."). And a visit to Dartmoor (". . . and away went horse and trap down the hill, and over it spilled and when I came to, the horse and I were lying in each other's arms. Oh, Father *was* surprised!"). And a visit to Switzerland (". . . ah . . . Lucerne . . . beautiful . . . and the Prisoner of Chillon, Byron, you know, and *such* good cheese!"). And the annual visit to Old Mrs. Grimwade in London (". . . a very miserly woman indeed, but kind; but I took good care to have a tin of biscuits with me, *I* can tell you, and I always saw the Academy, and I saw Gladstone!").

After these journeys by the way, the leisurely travel down the canal was resumed once more under the general direction of the Stepmother, until Nature perversely had caused the Stepmother to die, and Topaz was left in a position for which, to tell the truth, she was not by experience prepared.

Topaz did not know that it was not an evil thing that her Stepmother should die in the ripeness of her age, for she loved her. What talk, now, of giving us twenty-five more years of life! Who would wish to live, Methuselah among a multitude of Methuselahs? Let us find another star. For unless aged persons have the very wisdom of God, if their authority has been exerted unquestioned upon adult younger persons, they may at last die, and leave those younger persons too old to have any youth, too young to have any age. And so it almost was with Topaz. It was perhaps as well, then, for her that her Stepmother at last left Topaz, still in her light-hearted minority at forty-five.

For the strange thing was that Topaz had never bought an essential thing for herself in her life. Ends of lace she had bought ("so pretty!"), and pictures of scenes which she had visited and enjoyed. She acquired boxes, and fans, and other pictures, too, when painted by cousins or friends, or by some artist whose nephew she had met at Torquay. She bought books, good and bad, although she preferred good ones. She bought china and glass, and sometimes extra chairs and tables. She bought "goodies." She bought, not from discrimination, but by reason of association, or, best of all, because she liked the looks of something.

But her mantles and dresses had been selected and paid for by the Stepmother, who was guided in choice not by beauty, nor by taste (of which she had none), nor by fashion (to which she was indifferent), but by "handsomeness," and by generosity, and by the time of day. Wool or alpaca for the morning; cloth (braided or bebuttoned) for the afternoon;

silk, satin or velvet lavishly trimmed for the evening. Without regard for the face or figure of Topaz, but with the agreement of Topaz, the Stepmother bought The Best. Food, also, had appeared upon the table as by the Stepmother's well-ordered magic, but Topaz knew little of the mechanics of ordering, marketing, selecting, planning, cooking, or serving. She saw food upon the table, she ate it, she loved it, she praised it, she digested it. Such things as railway tickets were obtained by brothers, or by such practical young women as Rachel, Annie's second daughter, or Elise, George's only girl, an effulgent beauty who feared neither man nor devil and captivated both – the only dazzling beauty in the family. Topaz had already become Aunt Topaz, and was now on her way to being Great-Aunt Topaz, without noticing it at all.

After the bewilderment of Mother's death Topaz cared for Father will all the love and inefficiency of which she was capable. The results were excellent. Austin became the house-keeper, and took over where Mother had left off, and Topaz became her Father's loving, constant, and talkative companion. Father was now a very old man. Now that Annie's eldest daughter Laura had given birth in South Africa to a child, he was always Great-Grandfather Edgeworth. Annie had in her turn become a Grandmother.

Great-Grandfather Edgeworth sat in the garden in the sunshine. A white handkerchief covered his face. Puff in, puff out, puff in, puff out. The white handkerchief, neatly secured under his round black skull-cap, rose and fell with the blasts from his wide ingenuous nostrils. Behind the concealing and expressionless handkerchief was the noble face of the sleeping old man. Happy, happy old man. He sat there, sleeping in security in the sunshine. His world was a good world. His

Queen was a good Queen. His country was a good country. His business was good. His health was good. His family was a good family and God was good. All this goodness flowed together in this strong and gentle old man. He had served his community well. He had never turned aside from recognized Duty. He had known consolable grief and inevitable worry, but not much grief and not much worry, and no doubts. None. God? God, invisible but real, was obscured from him only by the lofty and so often clouded English skies, but with spiritual eyes Great-Grandfather Edgeworth beheld his Maker. He even knew just what God looked like. He, like and yet how unlike Blake, beheld the Ancient of Days, bearded with majesty. How surprised Great-Grandfather Edgeworth would be if Death, the incalculable stranger, disclosed a different Being. Though God was ageless, God was old. For in the world in which lived Great-Grandfather Edgeworth and his daughter Topaz and his friends and his neighbours, wisdom was synonymous with bearded age, and the opinions of a beardless man were not worth attention, any more than the vague sweet songs of birds or the lashing of the wind in the trees. Great-Grandfather Edgeworth and his neighbours, practical bearded men though they were, lived deeply the life of the spirit. But they did not wander in uncharted spiritual ways. The great John Wesley remained their guide. He led them past the wayward phenomena of birds, winds, and stars, the calamitous inequalities of life, and the strange plaguings of beauty, to hard facts and spiritual certainties. Great-Grandfather Edgeworth was a kind and just employer, but he accepted without question what he saw, and he saw a world become at last static. His imagination, which flew beyond the bright blue sky to the invisible, did not pierce the squalor of the Poor so near at hand in the grim town. The Poor took their familiar deplorable place in squalor, and it would have seemed a novel and disturbing idea to Great-Grandfather Edgeworth that the Poor should reasonably aspire to eat well, drink well, live well, and die well. Not wrong, of course, but chimerical. Each age, like our own, has its large blind spots. The social conscience was stirring but not awake. Great-Grandfather Edgeworth was a product of the ages which preceded the young Victoria. Here he was, sleeping in the garden, ninety years old, an upright old man in a world which he really thought was upright.

Austin the old housemaid crept out to see if the master was asleep. The handkerchief puffed out and in rather uncertainly. The master stirred. He was waking. Where was he? Oh, in the garden. After lunch. *Such* a good lunch. But where was Topaz? Topaz! Topaz! Where are you? Oh yes. Topaz was coming home this afternoon from her visit in London to Mrs. Grimwade, bringing with her Mrs. Grimwade and bringing little old Miss Raphael too. Each year Topaz still spent a fortnight in London with Mrs. Grimwade. This austere and miserly lady did not offer to provide entertainment for the young girl of forty-eight, but at least Topaz could leave the narrow house in Lambeth and with her friend Tottie Hay visit the Academy, chatter in Piccadilly, whisper in St. Paul's, and return to the wiry grey curls of Mrs. Grimwade and the soft white curls of her little sister Miss Raphael and vivaciously recount and re-recount her day.

Great-Grandfather Edgeworth missed Topaz. She was his loving daughter and his comfort. A man needs comfort when he is ninety. She talked continuously. If no human ears were within range, she talked to animals or to birds. "Whee-whoo, whee-whoo," she called to the birds. "There, you see, it answered me, whee-whoo, whee-whoo!" She disliked silence. Silence existed only to be broken. If nothing new presented itself to be said, she said what she had been saying all over again. To Great-Grandfather Edgeworth Topaz's talking was an accompaniment of life like his skull-cap. He did not often notice it, but he was used to it, and he missed it when it was not there. He liked Topaz near him, or some woman. Austin the housemaid had been very good, very good. When one became old, women were really better to have near one than men. More comfortable. Men had been part of his responsible daily life, of course. But now women for comfort. Women in the house. A woman in the bedroom, and within the bond prescribed, a woman in the bed, as was natural. His mind turned slowly back to his first wife. He thought without surprise but with tenderness of Mary's death at the age of forty-two at the birth of their tenth child. He felt tenderness for Mary, and for himself, left with so many babes, immense pity. How lost he had been. But soft hands had been held out to help, and soft voices had said to the handsome man, "Oh, *poor* Mr. Edgeworth!" Not "Poor Mrs. Edgeworth!" but "*Poor* Mr. Edgeworth!" And he had turned to his stately Jane, and Jane had helped him, and he had become again strong, no longer poor Mr. Edgeworth with all those children. And now, after a lifetime together, Jane too had died and left him, an aged and lovable patri-arch, to the care of the young Topaz. And the young Topaz whose bonnets and mantles had been bought by Jane, and whose chest had been rubbed by Jane, was at the age of forty-eight the astonished and inexperienced young mistress of this orderly household which still ran on the momentum generated by Jane. But now Jane the autocrat was only a silent name in the cemetery. And on the upper half of the stone was the word Mary. Poor Mr. Edgeworth.

Great-Grandfather Edgeworth tugged the handkerchief from his skull-cap and rang the bell on a little table beside him. Obscurely the phantom thought passed, Topaz really needs a mother. She has been used all her life to a mother. She is very inexperienced. And it would be nice, very nice. "Eh," he sighed puffingly, "it would be nice to have a woman near me." This he said disregarding the proximity of Topaz and the constant nearness of Austin, Cook, and Betsy. A household of women, but lacking its head. "Aus*tin*, Aus*tin!*" he called with rising voice. "Oh, here you are. Scratch me back." Beside the bell on the little table lay a long slim ebony rod, and at the end of the rod was a small carved ivory hand, a little concave hand with fingers bent scratchingly inwards. This was The Backscratcher. Confiding as a child, Great-Grandfather Edgeworth leaned forwards and Austin loosened the back of his collar with her fingers. She slid the backscratcher down Great-Grandfather's back and drew it up and down discriminatingly. Austin was a good back-scratcher, she was. She knew just where. Scratch here, scratch there. Great-Grandfather Edgeworth shut his eyes in bliss and drew his breath inwards through his excellent old teeth. "Oh, nuts and figs," he murmured. And then "Nuts and figs, nuts and figs." "*There* then," said Austin. Great-Grandfather Edgeworth sighed comfortably. "Is Miss Topaz come yet?" he asked. "In about half an hour now, sir," said Austin. "Well, then, I'll go in. Help me up," said Great-Grandfather Edgeworth. "Eh, I'm stiff."

The evening was cold. Great-Grandfather and Mrs. Grimwade sat by the fire while Topaz helped little Miss Raphael to bed. As Topaz's rôle was that of young daughter, so little Miss Raphael's role was that of young sister. She was younger sister to the formidable Mrs. Grimwade who now sat

erect by the fire, her feet on a hassock, her black silk skirt lifted
a little, disclosing a phalanx of petticoats above her slippers.
Mrs. Grimwade always raised her skirt as she sat by the fire,
which at home was always a very small fire, believing that heat
was bad for silk. So severe were Mrs. Grimwade's cerements of
black, and so forbidding and lined and yellow was her face,
that the grey and wiry ringlets that hung down each side of
her face seemed to mock the aged features they adorned. They
bristled and mocked. Mrs. Grimwade was an exceptionally
ugly old lady, but to Great-Grandfather Edgeworth sitting
opposite her in the firelight she was neither ugly nor forbidding. She was just his old friend Maria Grimwade come to pay
him a visit. She was Jane's old friend, and the annual protec-
tress of his giddy Topaz. The same firelight that deepened Mrs.
Grimwade's wrinkles and could not soften her features, illu-
mined the majesty and repose of Great-Grandfather's handsome old face. The two old people spoke little. The fire, the
comfort, and the companionship were enough. At last Great-
Grandfather said, "I've been thinking, Maria. I've been thinking, Topaz needs a mother."

Mrs. Grimwade turned sharply and her ringlets swung.

"A mother? Don't be silly, Joseph. The girl's nearly fifty.
She doesn't need a mother, she needs a husband. If she needs a
mother at her age, she'll still be needing one when she's ninety!"

"Well, perhaps she will, Maria," agreed Great-Grandfather equably.

Silence while the coals glowed and shifted.

"I've been thinking, too, Maria," said the old man simply,
pursuing his thoughts, "I miss Jane. I miss Jane very much.
Topaz is a good girl, but it's not the same thing. Someone me
own age. There's nothing much left now, Maria, but to talk of
old times and just to sit together like you and I are sitting now.

You have Sarah and I have Topaz, but – well, I do miss Jane. I suppose you wouldn't marry me, would you, Maria? Just marry me and stay on. There'd be you and me, and Topaz and Sarah." (They could chatter together, the two girls, thought Great-Grandfather Edgeworth.) "There's plenty of room."

Never before had the imperturbable Mrs. Grimwade received such a shock, certainly not when Ebenezer Grimwade proposed to her, not when her brougham turned over at the foot of the hill, nor when her cook fell all the way down the stairs and broke her neck. But her lined yellow face showed no surprise. She gave Great-Grandfather Edgeworth a quick look. He gazed peacefully at the fire; his comfortable thoughts, the pleasant glow, the comfy chair, his good dinner, his old friend, all blended very well indeed.

"Joseph," said the old woman with sound sense, "you don't really mean this. You think you do because you see me sitting here and I'm your old friend. But you don't realize that you're over ninety and I'm eighty-seven and we'd be the laughing-stock of our families or at least upset them very much. You've got Topaz to look after you, and I've got Sarah to look after and we do very well as we are, you here and me in London, just the way we are. No, I won't marry you, Joseph." Through her clear mind passed quickly her gratification that Joseph Edgeworth, the man she had always admired above all men, should, even almost in his dotage, wish to marry her. There passed also the thought of her Will so carefully made, leaving her fortune in Consols to the Missions and leaving small bequests to the young Raphael nephews and their wives. What complications would ensue! There passed the thought of the genial comfort of this house, butter with bacon and no remarks passed, fires in your bedroom, little luxuries that her niggardly management could not endure, and so she spoke again emphatically, "No, Joseph, nonsense, Jane wouldn't like it, and it would never do. Put it out of your head."

"What did you say?" enquired Great-Grandfather Edgeworth, who had been nodding to the warmth of the fire. "Oh yes, yes. You really think it wouldn't do? Well, perhaps you're right, my dear, you always were a sensible woman. But it would have been very nice and comfortable." "*That* it wouldn't," thought Mrs. Grimwade.

The coals glowed and Great-Grandfather's eyelids began to close on the soft light. The two sat again in silence looking at the fire until Great-Grandfather slept in his chair. Mrs. Grimwade's tight mouth moved in speculation, her lips invisible. She almost smiled as her thoughts turned over and over and settled themselves down again. To think of it. She, Maria Grimwade, the third Mrs. Joseph Edgeworth. What a to-do there'd be! Nay, she'd keep it to herself. But what a triumph! Upstairs, Topaz and little Miss Raphael still chattered and laughed as Miss Raphael went to bed.

When on a bright late summer morning Mrs. Grimwade and Topaz went for a drive in the brougham, little old Miss Raphael and Great-Grandfather Edgeworth stood in the garden sunshine well muffled up.

"Shall we take a turn down the path, Miss Sarah?" suggested Great-Grandfather.

"Oh, that would be very nice, Mr. Joseph," said Miss Raphael. So Great-Grandfather, leaning on his stick, and the fragile little old Miss Raphael took a turn down the path. They walked slowly to the end of the path without speaking, little Miss Raphael's white silky curls bobbing as she walked. Then they walked back. Miss Raphael, who knew that gentlemen like to be entertained, searched her mind for something to say.

Her old friend seemed content not to be entertained, but Miss Raphael had been brought up in the ladies-must-talk school, so she began in her gentle way. She admired the petunias, she admired the roses, and she greatly admired Great-Grandfather Edgeworth's gold-headed cane and "Oh, what a pretty butterfly!" "She is a dear little creature," thought the old man, but he was feeling rather tottery. "Let us sit down, my dear," he said, and reaching the two garden seats they carefully sat down. Miss Raphael sat opposite Great-Grandfather Edgeworth, and as he looked at her it seemed that for the first time he saw how gentle was her look, and how pretty were the white curls that framed her sweet old face. "Sarah, me dear," he said, "how is it you never married?" Little Miss Raphael was not used to direct questions like this, especially from gentlemen. No one had ever before asked her why she had not married. What could she say? She could not tell the truth, that no one had ever asked her in marriage. "Oh, Mr. Joseph," she fluttered. "I've been so much with Maria, and I have never seen many gentlemen, and, as a matter of fact, Mr. Joseph, I'm very shy with gentlemen." And indeed she was, even with old Mr. Edgeworth whom she enshrined as the perfect man. An idea floated again to the surface of Great-Grandfather Edgeworth's mind. His rebuff from Maria Grimwade, which was no rebuff at all but the friendly statement of an old friend, had gone from his memory. He looked kindly at Miss Raphael. A glow of discovery warmed him. Here in Sarah Raphael was a sweet companion, really the suitable companion for his closing days. He saw no difficulties in the way and came straight to the point.

"Every woman should marry, my dear, especially a pretty woman like yourself. You are much too charming, my dear Miss Sarah, to continue in single blessedness."

Miss Raphael nearly suffocated. Never before had a

gentleman, sitting alone with her, said such exquisite and provocative things to her. And this from the perfect Mr. Edgeworth! She was fascinated but frightened. But Great-Grandfather continued.

"You see how alone I am, Sarah. My dear Jane has left me and I am a lonely old man –"

"Oh, Mr. Joseph, *surrounded* by Loved Ones!" murmured Miss Raphael.

"What is a daughter, what can children ever be, compared to a wife?" Great-Grandfather Edgeworth's face glowed as he looked upon the waste of sweet womanhood before him. "You should marry, Sarah," he said. "You should marry. Why not stay here and marry me and let us be old together? There's nothing much left now, Miss Sarah, me dear, for old people, except to sit together as we are sitting now, and talk over old times. To be companions, that's it, companions."

"But Maria . . ." said Miss Raphael faintly.

"Maria can look after herself very well," said Great-Grandfather Edgeworth. "Maria's a strong sensible woman."

"But Topaz . . ." faltered Miss Raphael.

"Topaz is a good girl, a very good girl, but it's time she got married herself." He had forgotten that Topaz needed a mother. "And Topaz is fond of you. Many's the time she's said to me . . ." and, using up far too much energy, he continued warmly his address to Miss Raphael.

While Great-Grandfather Edgeworth continued his speech to Miss Raphael, light steps came up the gravel walk. Into the garden came and out of the garden went a radiant young creature dressed in faded blue cotton. Pretty Milly, the dressmaker's daughter, brought Miss Topaz's jacket in a parcel to the side door. Milly's feet lightly crushed the gravel and she walked quickly to the door and away again out of the garden.

She wore no hat and her fair hair shone in the sunshine. Because the sun shone and she was young, and because she was happy and beautiful, sparkling smiles came to Milly's lovely face. And as she walked away from the house she looked carelessly at the two old people wrapped up and sitting in the sun, and to Milly they were hardly people. "Look at them two old mummies lapped oop like tha'. Eh, I'd as lief be dead as look like tha'." Her gay glance only touched them as she sped down the path, and as lightly out of the garden she went, shining.

But the two old people had not discovered that they were mummies. Great-Grandfather Edgeworth's long speech, which rather tired him, gave Miss Raphael a little time in which to collect herself. The moment of her life had arrived, and she must meet it suitably. Phrases heard, read, echoed in her head. She adored Mr. Edgeworth. Whether she loved him or not she did not know. Only one thing she knew, she could not marry, and only one thought confronted her – how to make a suitable refusal. This was unexampled. She was unprepared and alarmed. Absurd, at seventy-nine, still to feel inadequate. She wished Maria could do this for her but she had to do it for herself.

Great-Grandfather Edgeworth ceased speaking. He had said what he wanted to say, and to tell the truth he did not much mind what Miss Raphael decided, but he would abide by her decision and he was feeling a bit hungry.

Miss Raphael began, "Oh, dear Mr. Joseph, I cannot tell you how grateful, how honoured – I hardly know what to say – by you of all men. I cannot truly say, Mr. Joseph, that I do not requite your passion – that is, your feeling so kindly expressed – but I'm sure I should never enjoy being married to any gentleman, even – if I may say so – to you, dear Mr. Edgeworth, whom of all men I – well, Maria has always felt that I was too young for marriage and I think perhaps I am."

(Mr. Edgeworth received this statement without surprise from the aged maiden.) "I hope you won't think, dear Mr. Joseph, that I – oh, I beg of you, *do* understand that I appreciate – that I am fully aware of the honour you have done me – but I think that under the circumstances I would rather not – that is, I must regretfully beg to decline . . ."

She trembled. Her curls danced and trembled.

"All right, all right, me dear," said Great-Grandfather, who had made his little effort and was content, "there's no need to get excited; either you do or you don't, you know. Well, well, there's the brougham and I'm ready for me lunch *I* am."

But Miss Raphael put her hands to her breast. Her heart fluttered so.

The visit of the two sisters came to an end early as little Miss Raphael was not well, and Maria determined to get her home and into her own bed. The two ladies sat opposite each other in the train to London and had the carriage to themselves. Mrs. Grimwade's moment of human weakness came upon her. She became feminine and confiding. She could not resist telling her secret to her little sister now that they were safely alone together. She tasted her enjoyment. "*Won't* Sarah be surprised!" thought Mrs. Grimwade agreeably as she prepared to tell her tale.

"I do not usually discuss such matters with you, Sarah," she announced in her severe manner as though proposals were a daily occurrence to her, "and I trust you to regard with secrecy what I am about to tell you."

"Yes, Maria," promised Sarah, her soft look fixed on Maria's wrinkled yellow face.

"As things have turned out, we are travelling back to Lambeth together, but this might not have been the case."

"Oh?"

"I came to a very important decision last week, partly on your account, and partly for other reasons."

"Yes, Maria?"

"It may surprise you to learn that Mr. Joseph Edgeworth asked my hand in marriage but I declined."

Sarah's world spun round her. "Asked your hand in marriage, Maria?" she faltered.

"Yes, Sarah."

"Asked your hand in marriage?"

"That's what I said," snapped Maria.

"Are you sure it was *your* hand that Mr. Joseph asked in marriage, Maria?" timidly.

"Don't be ridiculous, Sarah. Why shouldn't he ask my hand in marriage? Don't act like a simpleton." Maria was annoyed. Sarah's surprise had the wrong sound.

"You're quite sure you didn't misunderstand Mr. Joseph?" persisted Sarah.

"Do I ever make mistakes?" said Maria quite furious.

"No, Maria," said Sarah simply. Poor Maria, so she had thought Mr. Joseph was asking for *her* hand, while, of course, it was her young sister's hand that he had demanded in marriage! Sarah had just been about to take her sister into her confidence, but now she could not disillusion her. Maria seemed so complacent about it. Poor Maria. And besides, weak as Sarah felt, she was unequal to facing Maria's anger on discovery of her mistake. Some other time perhaps, when she felt stronger. Not now. What could she say?

"Well, that was very kind of Mr. Joseph," she said at last placidly.

Maria looked sharply at her. What was wrong with Sarah? Where was the amazement, the admiration, the envy?

Maria was displeased. She looked out of the window. Sarah looked out of the window too.

"May I ask, Maria, just when this occurred?" asked Sarah, turning again.

"I am not prepared to discuss the matter further," said Maria huffily.

"Very well, Maria," and they finished the journey in silence.

Sarah was very tired when they reached the narrow house in Lambeth. "I feel poorly, Maria," she said. Into bed she went, and the next day Maria looked at her little sister and saw that she was ill.

On the day that Sarah died, Maria stood beside the bed. "Sit down, please, Maria," said Sarah weakly. Mrs. Grimwade sat down.

Sarah waited for a moment, collecting her little strength that was slipping from her. Then she spoke.

"Maria," she said clearly and sweetly, "I think that you should know that you are in error. It was not you, my dear sister, whom Mr. Joseph Edgeworth desired to marry. Your mistake was natural, that when he mentioned marriage you thought he referred to yourself. But dear Maria, it was I who had the great, great happiness of being desired in marriage by Mr. Joseph. I declined in spite of his protests, partly on account . . ." and she died.

"Well!!!" said Mrs. Grimwade. But it was too late. She could not put Sarah in her place. Lost satisfaction. Lost joy. Sarah was gently, irrevocably removed. Oh my little sister Sarah, what have you unaided done? You have died.

THE MAJORITY

When father died, Topaz attained her undesired majority and independence at the age of fifty. But she was only a girl grown old, however much strangers might take her for a woman. Life with her father had promised to be permanent, but the promise was broken. When Topaz, drying her reddened eyes, looked about her and found that decisions had now to be made by herself, and that people regarded her as an adult who should herself define her next move, she felt her weakness. Her spirit sought Father and the Stepmother in vain. They were not there any more. She no longer sat in their shadow.

John's Annie said to John in a melancholic voice, "Jee, dear" (Jee for Giovanni), "of course I should be *delighted* for Topaz to come and live with us."

John's distinguished face became clouded, and he said in an extremely religious tone, "That is very good of you, Annie, most kind indeed. I appreciate it. There is nothing I should like better than to give a home to my sister. But the fact is that she talks too much. I cannot *endure* to be out-talked at my own table."

John's Annie's face cleared. "Then she must come and stay with us for six months."

"Yes, or for one month at least," said John. "I will speak to George about Topaz." If John needed to atone for his natural reluctance to be out-talked at his own table, he atoned a hundredfold. He became for thirty years Topaz's faithful and valued correspondent while six thousand miles divided them. His letters were her tie with all that she had known and loved before. ("Look!" triumphantly waving an envelope, "another letter from John! Now, let me see!") For thirty years he gave her deep satisfaction and lasting pleasure, and thirty years is a long time.

And George said to his handsome wife Eleanor, "Hrrumph. What about Topaz coming to live with us? Uh? Mm? What?"

And Eleanor said, "Nothing would please me more than to have Topaz here. But I believe that Mrs. Williamson in the village has some very nice rooms that would suit Topaz well, and wishes to let. She could have her own furniture there, and Mrs. Williamson could Do for her. She would be near us all, and much more independent. I can think of nothing nicer."

George's worried look brightened and he said, "Hrrumph. Splendid! I will speak to John about it. Hum!"

But Annie, the eldest sister, came back post-haste from Llandudno, where in her new sad widowhood she had gone with her daughter Rachel, and came straight to Elder House. She entered the house in the dignity of her sorrow and of her black mantle and widow's weeds. "Where is Miss Topaz?" she enquired, and went swiftly to find her, calling "Topaz, where are you?" Annie tossed her black veil back over her little bonnet, and with all love and goodness in her face she looked at her grief-stricken sister. She ran up to her, and reached up – Annie was smaller than Topaz – and put her arms around her, saying in her gentle voice of comfort, "My dear sister. My dear dear sister. You will come to me, won't you? I need you."

And some months later a letter came from Blakey in Australia. It was not very well written and not very well spelled, but it shouted a welcome. "You must come and live with us, Topaz," it shouted. "We will get you a horse. How you and John and the rest of you can live in England when you could come to Australia I can't conceive. The children all want to see their English aunty and Maudie sends her love." Topaz looked sideways at this invitation (a horse?), but its kindness warmed her now established heart.

Rachel helped her to close up Elder House (a factory stands there now). And Annie said, "If we decide to go and join Frank and Stephen and Andrew in Vancouver – we can try it for a year – you will come with Rachel and me, won't you, Topaz? Now that the three boys here are settled, I feel I should go – for a while."

"Where thou goest, Annie . . ." said Topaz, with a tremulous laugh, and Rachel set about moving three women, instead of two, on the long journey.

Into her majority and for ever, Topaz took her three loyalties. Not religion, although she had an indigenous faith in God, for Topaz might well have been (and perhaps she had been) a heavy-footed Bacchante, a milder Maenad with satin white skin, dancing heavily and happily, excited before the flickering shrine, carefree among the olive trees, calling to the other boys and girls; not patriotism, although she loved her country; not love for a man – William Sandbach had become only a still interesting object seen from afar. But the Royal Family moved through her life with banners streaming. Mr. Gladstone stood for ever four-square in his integrity ("Yes, I shook his hand, I heard his wonderful voice – like an organ it was . . .") and through his spell she adhered in a wishy-washy way to the Liberal Party. And now her loyalty to her father lived as a loving memory – or perhaps it expanded, to include the person of her little eldest sister.

It was soon plain, however, that Topaz's majority was virtual, not real. Rachel slid by nature and unaware into the Stepmother's place. "Shall I take Mother's good black with me, Rachel, in case? And shall I take the little Portland Vase that Mr. Wedgwood gave Father? And, oh, shall I take John Lockwood Kipling's pen-and-ink sketch that he gave me?" The niece was fifteen years younger than the aunt, but Rachel was a woman grown, and older than Topaz in wisdom, and now took upon herself another care.

THE JOURNEY

When Miss Topaz Edgeworth, and her eldest sister Annie who was now several times the Grandmother, and the Grandmother's unmarried daughter Rachel left their homes in England, they embarked at Liverpool and crossed the Atlantic Ocean to a new home prepared for them in Canada. It was courageous of three women whose years added up to over one hundred and fifty, because, although they were going to make this new home with the Grandmother's welcoming sons in British Columbia, they were leaving behind them all the familiar safe things that had for so long composed their lives.

The Grandmother left behind her the happiness of familiar loves, dear places, and ordered days. She left bereavements, her great and only sorrows. But wherever she might go, in all circumstances and places, the Grandmother was at home, because she carried heaven in her heart and in her face.

Her daughter Rachel left nothing behind her, not even an unhappy love affair. Marriage? Not Rachel. Rachel, laughing and smug, used to say:

"Whene'er I take my walks abroad,
How many babes I see!
When I get home I thank the Lord
They don't belong to me."

And she meant it. She turned rejoicing towards Canada.

Rachel's Aunt Topaz left behind her much joy and most of the sorrow she would ever know. She left there the mordant years of unfulfilled love. They were finished. It was done. It was almost as if it had never been. And now she turned readily to the West and faced a fresh free life which she was eager to enjoy.

Aunt Topaz now looked forward with rising infectious spirits to every minute on this precious ship. She at once enjoyed talking to the exciting people who walked up and down and round and round the deck on the first day out, wearing important hats. It was exciting and unexpected also on the second day to meet a completely different lot of people walking about, facing the breeze in completely different hats. Some of these hats were humbler, some were more rakish, and their wearers were not identifiable. It was exciting on the third and subsequent days to totter in perfect health around the reeling windy deck, and stumble, laughing and apologizing, against passengers who with bowed heads charged into you, or against the protruding deck-chairs of passengers with only one eye partly open. Aunt Topaz got to know a great many people in this way and also at meals. Life extended immeasurably and intoxicatingly.

News about passengers was disclosed from hour to hour. It was said that there was an actor on board. His name was Mr. Otis Skinner. The fame of Mr. Otis Skinner sped round and round the ship. People tried to identify him. There was also a Lord. People tried to get into conversation with single men, so as to discover if they were the Lord. The determined Lord was never found throughout the voyage, and was probably one of two indistinguishable morose men who read books all day long. There was an English Admiral and an American Lecturer. They were soon discovered. Besides all these famous individuals, there were enough pleasant people to keep Aunt Topaz going for the rest of her life. Aunt Topaz spoke to everyone who could possibly be spoken to. She would hurry back with face alight to Sister Annie who was well tucked up on the breezy deck. "Annie! Just imagine! There's a Mr. and Mrs. Palfrey from St. Louis on board who know the Davises in Torquay!" How wonderful! The little Grandmother seldom spoke first to people, but people often spoke to her, and then she responded cordially.

One day the Grandmother leaned upon the rail of the ship with some other passengers and looked out to sea. Someone had seen a whale. She longed to see a whale. The passengers lingered at the side of the ship hoping that this phenomenon would graciously appear again. And oh, look, there was a ship against the horizon! Yes, look, a ship! The black veil of the Grandmother's widow's bonnet whipped about her in the wind.

"Would you please be so good as to tell me," she enquired of her next-door neighbour with circumlocution, "if that is what is generally known as 'the bulge'?"

The person at the Grandmother's right hand said disagreeably, "If what is what is generally known as the bulge?"

"That," said the Grandmother pointing with a small gloved hand at some dirty water that issued from the ship's side.

"What?" asked the disagreeable man.

"That dirty-looking water," explained the Grandmother.

"I don't know what in the world you're talking about," said the disagreeable passenger shortly and moved away.

The Grandmother was stricken. No one had ever been rude to her before. Really, for about fifty years, no one had ever been rude. She had seen and heard other people being rude to other people and she had deplored this. She had trained a large family in the practice of politeness. No wonder she looked stricken. She had seldom felt so exposed.

Her strickenness was written all over her. A passenger on her left hand (oh, such a nice man) had seen and heard all this, and said with a smile, "You are quite right, Madam. That, I believe, is the bulge, very frequently called the bilge. In fact it's nearly always called the bilge in seafaring language, but how could you be expected to know that!" The kind man smiled down at her with all the protection of a son. Grannie looked up prettily at him. "How kind of you! I was afraid perhaps I'd said something very stupid. But still I don't think I deserved to be spoken to like that, do you? I don't think anyone ever spoke to me quite like that before!"

The kind passenger with the nice voice told her soothingly No, that it was quite inexcusable. He took the affronted one by the arm, led her to her deck-chair, tucked her rug around her, said "Comfortable?" just like a nice son, and left her. "What a charming man!" thought the restored Grandmother, "I believe he's an American. How truly kind! What a delightful nation indeed!" The whole American nation had tucked her up.

On Saturday night the word went round that Mr. Otis Skinner was going to read the Lesson at the Church Service on Sunday morning. A great many people who had intended to stay in bed or out on deck joined the congregation shamelessly and sat there in solemn rows. Grannie sat there too, but, of course, she would have gone to Church whoever had read the Lesson. It grieved her that so many people seemed anxious to hear the Lesson only if it were read by Mr. Otis Skinner. And an actor! She did not feel sure about the rightness of this. When the time came for the reading of the Lesson, there was the kind passenger who had tucked up the Grandmother on the day before. So this was Mr. Otis Skinner! There he stood, grave of face, what a surprise. Otis Skinner then read the Sermon on the Mount. "Blessed are the pure in heart," he read gravely and the people listened. The Grandmother listened, luminous. People forgot the reader in the noble Word so nobly read. The Grandmother went quietly to her cabin after the service, spiritually refreshed but a little shaken too. A crack had appeared in one of her tiny strong bastions. Some stones had fallen out and a fresh air was blowing in. Through the aperture Grannie saw a disturbing view that she had not seen before. Her so-sure condemnation of the Stage was now not so sure.

Unknown to himself Mr. Otis Skinner forever shed a radiance on the Stage which to Grannie had hitherto been dark, and on the whole American nation which to Grannie had hitherto been unknown. Years afterwards she would say, "Yes, indeed. Americans are most charming. The very first American I ever met (not counting that very disagreeable person, of course) was an actor, Mr. Otis Skinner. So kind and, one felt, so good." This encounter with the Stage had a far-reaching determining effect. Ten years later, long after a young granddaughter Rose had joined this family in Vancouver, "some Shakespeare plays" came to the new Opera House. Polite and fashionable Vancouver attended, flattering William Shakespeare by evening dress or at least by a "fascinator" over the head, and even by a sprinkling of tiaras and pearl dog-collars (we have grown plainer since then). Of course, Rose wanted to go to a play. In spite of the hallowing influence of William Shakespeare, her Grandmother was mistrustful lest Rose, a girl so young, might through these delights "learn to get a taste for the theatre." Grannie, Great-Aunt Topaz, and Aunt Rachel debated, while the eager yet despairing girl prayed to each of them in turn. The die was really cast by the memories of Mr. Otis Skinner, "so kind, and, one felt, so truly good." Rose went to the Opera House and saw the play. She saw, too, the legendary beauty of Mrs. MacJames of the Klondike, sitting in her box, gleaming with white shoulders and diamonds, brilliant against the black coats and white shirt-fronts ranged behind her; sitting there dazzling and still, with her beauty shining across the sibilant Opera House; sitting there, accustomed to homage and to her own loveliness. Rose at once got a taste for theatre and the deceits of beauty. And all this miracle was being prepared unaware for the yet almost non-existent Rose by Mr. Otis Skinner, reading the Lesson on board ship to the Grandmother, to Topaz, to Rachel, and to all the other passengers.

On the last day of open ocean the seeming and delusive eternity of the voyage vanished. "Tomorrow we enter the St. Lawrence River!" Friendships suddenly ceased to have validity, or developed with ardour; flirtations became cool or poignant. Even the Grandmother, who lived neither in the present nor the past nor the future, not in Time at all but in a constant moment of Eternity, felt the approaching change. Her sister Topaz, taking down addresses, promising visits, recklessly giving invitations, running round to people's cabins, lending books, returning scarves, impeding stewards, collecting autographs at parties, hardly had time to regret the end of the journey across the famous Atlantic Ocean, in the anticipation of something imminent, new, and rare.

That night the sky was lit from zenith to horizon by Northern Lights. Rachel and Topaz, niece and aunt, leaning at the ship's rail, saw a long and wavering luminous plume of pale-golden colour ascend in the north. The light fanned out and raced to the midmost topmost sky where a black whorl took shape and poured forth a cataract of glowing green. Successive cataracts of light issued from the whorl and became banners which flapped in silence across half the sky made vaster by the antics of the unexplained and ungovernable heavens. From the left of the spreading whorl, which changed shape and character as the onlookers gazed upon it, came a glow of dull crimson. The crimson ran rapidly down to meet the black ocean, changing and doubling and spreading as it ran. The colossal performance of the Northern Lights was exaggerated up up up, on and on, down down and across; and beyond and behind the zenith it encroached upon the southern sky. For time immeasurable and lost the heavens continued to ripple and wave with light, sometimes ghastly, always incomparable, filling the diminutive travellers beside the ship's railing with unprecedented awe.

"Can we hear them?" marvelled Rachel to herself. "I can't believe that they don't crackle and bang, but with the noise of the waves . . ."

"A portent!" trumpeted Topaz happily. Rachel moved away. She wanted to contemplate the Northern Lights in silence, and to prolong this memorable moment of curious time alone.

Aunt Topaz looked round. Rachel had gone.

"A portent!" she said happily to an old man beside her. "We are coming to Canada for the first time, you know," she informed this listener, "and I certainly regard this as most favourable, an indication, I would say, that my sister and my niece and I have made the right decision in coming. A welcome indeed! Yes, I would call it a portent."

"A what?" asked the muffled-up old man.

"A portent, an omen," explained Aunty, waving her arm at the phenomenal heavens. "What the Greeks would regard as a sign. The Greeks watched the heavens very closely, you know, the stars and the planets, you know, and the flights of birds, geese for example – oh, very sensible – and I'm sure such a spectacle as this" – she again waved her arm at the resplendent and changing sky – "would have impressed them very deeply. I'm very fond of the Greeks myself. In fact I've read the Odyssey and the Iliad more than once, not in the original, you understand," she continued truthfully, developing a favourite theme to the muffled-up old man and the Northern Lights.

"I knoo a Greek," said the old man simply, willing to oblige. "He lived just a little ways down from our place when we was on the prairie and he kept a fish shop. Yes *sir*, he sure had good fish, that fellow. But he had a very bad nose and it got worse and they couldn't operate. It got to look like one of them lobsters. I sure felt sorry for that man."

As that was not the kind of Greek that Topaz had in mind she returned to the contemplation of the sky whose light now began to show a lessening and tremulous vitality, yet withal a threat or a promise. "I can do this again any minute that I want to. I can do more than this. I am independent of you, uncontrolled by you, indifferent to you, and you know nothing at all about Me. Behold!" said the mighty heavens rolling up like a scroll. The Grandmother went to bed, feeling with awe and rapture that she had had a foretaste of Heaven and Hell out of her own port-hole, which perhaps she had.

In the fresh morning the ship followed her course smoothly up the river, looking large in relation to the sometimes near banks as she had appeared small upon the wide ocean. On the banks of the St. Lawrence River were green trees, red trees, yellow trees, blazing signs of autumn. Everybody, homecoming Canadians and newcomers alike, exclaimed at the gorgeousness of hardwood maples set against the sombre utility of dark fir trees, and at the white villages which had grouped themselves cosily around the spires of churches. The river was immense, a prince among rivers. When at last the ship moving with stately slowness approached the city of Quebec, Mr. Otis Skinner stretched out his hand. "See!" he said, pointing, "over there are the Heights of Abraham." In Aunt Topaz, as in Mr. Otis Skinner, the spirit of History began to swell.

Mr. Otis Skinner spoke again. His voice was lower, and he spoke as it were unaware, to his own breast. "*There*," he said, "Wolfe fell." And he added, still more low, "And Montcalm." There was a moment of silence. Everybody looked respectfully and with deep interest at the steep Heights of Abraham.

The spirit of History swelled in the bosom of the well-informed Topaz, rose into her throat and nearly suffocated her. She gobbled a little and cried, "See, Rachel, see! The Heights of Abraham! That is where Wolfe fell!"

"Well, well, well," said a fat man, "so *that's* where Wolfe fell! Well, I don't blame him! I don't mind saying I'd a fallen there myself!" And he looked round laughing, courting applause, his shoulders shaking as he laughed.

Aunt Topaz glared at him, astonished. The hound! The base fellow! To jest at death and history! Her eyes flashed a dangerous green; she opened her mouth wide and held it open as Rachel turned quickly and with a bright anxious look stilled her. Then she remembered to close her mouth, and swallowed back some of the most enjoyable things she would ever have said in her whole life.

The ship resumed her lordly passage up the stream, and at Montreal, among the bedlam of landing and leave-taking, travelling companion cast off travelling companion and the unity of the ship was gone. The last friend waved and was gone. Gone. Oriented to his home or journey, each traveller moved away. Here the three ladies, a little experienced in European travel but novices in the New World, were met by a friend of the Grandmother's sons in Vancouver. Away went Rachel with this helpful Mr. Jackson and returned, saying, "Well, Mother, the Boys were able to get a drawing-room for us on the train."

"Did you say 'a drawing-room,' love?" enquired the Grandmother with surprise.

"Yes, Mother, a drawing-room."

"I wonder why the Boys got a drawing-room?" queried the Grandmother. "A bedroom would be quite enough. I think it would be more convenient and more generally useful. We could, I think, dispense with a drawing-room."

"I think a drawing-room *is* a bedroom, Mother," explained Rachel.

"Then why is it called a drawing-room, I wonder! Indeed," continued her mother, "I would really have preferred a bath-room. On so long a journey I feel sure I shall often feel the need of a bathroom, dear, but I suppose the Boys know best."

"But I understand the drawing-room *is* a bathroom, Annie," said Topaz pounding up hastily from the book-stall, magazines under her arm. "I have had *such* an interesting time! The man at the book-stall speaks French! Imagine! I said to him, 'Parlez-vous français alors?' and he said, 'Mais naturelle-ment, Madame!' What could be more delightful?"

"Then," said her Sister Annie, with her luminous and guileless smile, "if the drawing-room is not a drawing-room, but is a bedroom and a bathroom, I foresee a good deal of con-fusion. We shall have to try and learn new ways, dear, and I for one am quite ready." And she walked away, and stood, a small cone-shaped figure in black, alone and minute in the now empty centre of the big station. With her gentle enquir-ing gaze she looked around her at the new scene which was indisputably Canada, where a drawing-room was not a drawing-room, but a bathroom and a bedroom. She would accept it.

As the Grandmother walked, her long black circular skirt, topped by her black mantle, concealed the fact that she had feet. Since her steps were small and level, it appeared that the Grandmother moved smoothly upon wheels like a toy mouse. Her foot-work, unlike that of her sister Topaz, was impercep-tible. She returned, composed, to her family and Mr. Jackson who now escorted them along the platform to the train.

"Ah! Negroes!" exclaimed Aunt Topaz with delight, has-tening ahead. "How do you do! How do you do! I'm sure I'm very glad to see you! Have you a wife, yes? And family? This is a charming surprise!"

"Yassum," said the porter, presenting to Aunt Topaz his unusually wide swelling nostrils and a preposterously fine set of dazzling white teeth. Aunty gazed at them, admiring. "Splendid!" she said. "Magnificent! Much better than ours! What do you use? I understand that in Africa they use a stick! It is very efficacious! Or is it diet?"

"Oh, Anty, get on, *do*!" begged Rachel. Aunty clambered up and they made their way to the drawing-room. "Well, this *is* nice, I do declare!" said Aunt Topaz, looking around her. Assisted by Mr. Jackson and the exciting porter ("I *do* hope he's a Christian!" thought the Grandmother), surrounded and almost eclipsed by hand-baggage and Aunty's extra parcels, they settled, crying and exclaiming, like shore birds, and said goodbye to Mr. Jackson. "All Aboard!" cried someone. ("Listen to that! 'All Aboard!'" said Aunty.) The train creaked, groaned, shuddered, and started on its long journey West.

When the three women got onto the train in Montreal station, their visible baggage filled seats, racks, and floor, but was as nothing compared to the baggage not immediately visible which they brought with them. The Grandmother took onto the train her powerful spiritual awareness and lasting gentle domination, and her other-worldliness. Her daughter Rachel took all her anxieties, her fierce sense of duty, her integrity, and a great deal of practical irritable commonsense which, although hampered as yet by inexperience, could readily be applied in nearly all circumstances which affected those who were in her charge at any place or time. Of herself, Rachel never had time to think, and so in her the habit of anxious responsibility to which she was disposed had taken root and was to grow. It became as a beech tree, and, under its fine shade, unessential flowers of ease and frivolity were apt not to flourish, and luxury could not grow where the beech leaves fell.

Topaz got on the train with practically nothing at all. She travelled light. A native toughness enabled her to carry her few strong loyalties without inconvenience to herself, but for the rest, the joy of living was daily renewed in her and was seldom checked by things, people, or events. This joy, which was concerned only with the veriest surface of material and psychic being, allowed her to amuse herself like those "water-gliders" which we see in summer running about on the top of pleasant weed-fringed pools. Unencumbered by boots or boats they run, seldom wetting their feet and, one supposes, unaware of the dreadful deeps below them, in which other beings more heavily weighted are plunged, and swim or sink, caught in the mud or entangled by the debris of circumstance and human relations; and sometimes these heavier beings encounter acute sorrow or acute joy or dull despair of which the water-gliders know nothing. Two or three times in her hundred years Aunty's foot slipped below the surface of her pool, but only for a moment – albeit a long moment – and then she got caught in entangling sorrow and this caused her personal suffering. She at once, on recovery, resumed her running to and fro, and, quite unaware of the realities of the lives of the people whom she met day by day, she went eagerly laughing on. So, equipped as lightly as a water-glider of considerable education, she got on the train.

(It was about half a century later that a great-grandson of the Grandmother's, walking home beside the Rideau Canal in Ottawa, stopped to light a cigarette and looked over the railing at the rather still water of the canal. There came a small invisible wind which ran rapidly along the surface of the water and made its presence known by the sudden pretty dimpling and wrinkling of the stream, and by the deflection of some dry leaves whose time had come to fall. The leaves were carried by the small vagrant wind down the slow-moving canal and sailed for a while until the sluggish current bore them to a cluster of waste twigs and lately fallen leaves at the canal's edge, and no one noticed them any more after that. The wind passed, and the water was again still, and the disturbance was forgotten.

"My Great-Grandmother," thought the great-grandson for some reason or other, looking idly at the water, "needs no memorial. There are forty of us – why, there must be over fifty of us now! – Canadians, up and down the country, who have issued from her or from her issue, and for better or worse we are her memorial. And my Great-Aunt Rachel, whom I just remember, needs no memorial either, because there are still people who knew her and honoured her quite a lot, and anyway, a person like my Great-Aunt Rachel has her own memorial. But Great-Great-Aunt Topaz, who outlived these two, and outlived all her generation, and many of the next generation, and some of the next generation, and who defied these generations in her later days – don't I remember her! – she has gone; there is no mark of her that I know, no more than the dimpling of the water caused by the wind a few minutes ago. She is only a line on granite, 'Sister of the Above.' Yet she lived a hundred years, and is not long dead. Already she is seldom mentioned, and when we meet together as we sometimes do, all so busy, all so occupied, perhaps no one remembers, until afterwards, to mention her name. And the little ones will not even know her name. It is really a shame," thought the great-grandson idly, "that one can live a hundred years with gusto, and be happy, and agitate the stream, and pass at once out of memory. So she has no memorial. . . . I'd better hurry or I'll be late. . . ." The breeze blew and rippled the waters of the canal here and there, and the great-grandson set off briskly and thought of nothing in particular after that until the house was reached. . . . It is pleasant walking home beside the Rideau Canal in Ottawa in the fall, to a good meal and an amusing family and a warm house, especially when there is a nip in the air.)

The forests bordered the railway tracks and ran away up the hills. The forests were more brilliant in colour than any that the travellers had ever imagined. Sunlight was reflected from the gold and flame of each leaf of each tree. The forests seemed to blaze with harmless fire. The travellers' vision was intent on the rose, flame, and yellow that shot towards them, passed them, and fell behind them, remaining stationary and identifiable only on the distant hills they could not see and did not know that away towards the north (and southwards too) beyond and beyond the northern horizon there was a still world of red, rose, and yellow trees, and they did not think that in a few weeks these forest branches would be thin and bare. And because Time was bounded by yesterday, today, and tomorrow as the train slid and rocked along paralleling Time, they could not know that, decades later, a young grandson of the Grandmother's (not yet imagined, not yet born) would be a bush pilot and would fly in a slow, rather rackety plane above such forests. He would fly above the brilliant woods of the Maritime Provinces, and of Quebec, and of Ontario, and would see below him a flaming earth of boundless maple trees, coloured the tender warm rose and fabulous crimson of a carpet of Ispahan; and he would see small and great rivers shining like steel, widely curving through the bright trees; and he would look down on lonely lakes, great and small, shining like mercury, lying as mirrors to the clouds and the blue sky, and reflecting the rose and flame of the maple woods. The grandson would see all this in a newly discovered dimension as old as Time; yet it would be the same brilliance which they now saw with amazement, and which had transformed autumnal Canadian forests for centuries unknown.

"Oh, look!" and "Oh, look!" they said, as tree after tree flashed shining past in perfection of colour and beauty and was for ever lost. The Grandmother began to tire, and so she took out from her bag her book, Ranke's *History of the Popes*. She fell to reading, reading and looking, reading and looking, until she slept, and the book slid from her sleeping hands and fell upon the floor, and she slept for a long time.

The train jerked, pulled, slowed down, and stopped with a jolt that wakened her, and she found that Topaz had left the drawing-room, and that she and Rachel sat opposite to each other and that Rachel was still looking out of the window. Rain fell fast now and it fell in a straight, vertical curtain that muted the scene which they now looked upon and which they saw as through a fine steel curtain.

The scene upon which the mother and daughter looked had great beauty. They did not recognize it as great beauty because they had always acquiesced in what they saw, not distinguishing beauty unless it presented itself in familiar, obvious, and inescapable form; but there was something strange and old and new in this scene which pleased them. Their coach had come to a standstill opposite a small square field of green which was bounded on its three remaining sides by a shabby once-painted white wooden fence. Beyond the far side of the square, opposite to them – behind the far fence, that is – was a large white wooden church. The church had a belfry and, on the top of the spire, a cross. In spite of the rain and the greyness of the atmosphere they saw plainly, in the belfry, a large bell and a wheel, outlined against the heavy sky. At right and left of the square field, and at right angles to the church, and also behind the fence which enclosed the field, two rows of tall wooden houses faced each other across the intervening grassy space. These houses were painted. One was green, the next was a chartreuse colour, the next was yellow, the next was white, one was blue, and the roofs were red. Never before had Rachel and her mother seen wooden houses painted in random colours. The brightness of the colours was drenched a little and silenced by the driving vertical rain. The green square field across which the coloured houses looked upon each other was a graveyard, and, very strangely, all the tombstones and all the obelisks were of red granite, and all appeared to be new. The red granite shone wetly and the green grass gleamed and satisfied the eye and the scene was complete in its colour and its vertical and horizontal beauty of proportion. Down fell the rain.

"It looks," said Rachel, "as if everyone had died together and everyone had died rich."

"I think it looks very pretty, and very peaceful," said her mother, whose heart warmed to this place which she understood. "Do you think that the people in these houses are rich or poor, love? I cannot quite make out."

"I don't know. Somehow I think they all speak French though."

"French . . . ? Oh . . . ? We must get a history at once." The train jerked, groaned, and started, and the unity of the small and homely scene was left behind where it remains to this day in its simplicity.

"That place was Saint Something," said Rachel.

"What a many saints they do have, to be sure!" exclaimed her mother.

"I think most people in these parts are probably Roman Catholics."

"Roman Catholics . . . ! I see . . ." said the Grandmother. She pondered this for a while and then said within her heart, "There are many ways to God. We shall all meet there."

Suddenly the door of the drawing-room was flung open and Topaz burst in.

"So there you are, Annie!" she said (as though the Grandmother was likely to be anywhere else). "What *do* you suppose! Oh, I've had *such* an interesting conversation! I have been sitting in the gentlemen's smoking-room . . ."

"Topaz!" said her sister, and into the eyes of Sister Annie and of Rachel came a rare angry obsidian look.

"Yes," continued Topaz heedless and unwarned, "it has a curtain, you know, and as I passed I heard – oh, only by chance! – one of the gentlemen mention the Palmer House! So, of course, I put my head inside and said, 'What a coincidence! My brother-in-law stayed at the Palmer House when he came to America!' (because James did, you know), and before you could say Jack Robinson I was sitting there, and we had *such* a nice talk!"

"Topaz," said her little elder sister sternly, "I forbid you, do you hear, I *forbid* you ever to do such a thing again! That my sister would invade the privacy of the gentlemen's smoking-room – not that I like their smoking," said Sister Annie sitting erect and almost vibrating, "but it is their prerogative! You never did such a thing in your life before and pray do not begin now. You are altogether too free!" Topaz had never heard her mild Sister Annie sound so cross.

"Well, what a fuss, I do declare!" said Topaz swaying in the doorway of the swaying coach. "This is a free country, isn't it? We've come to a free country, haven't we? I didn't say I was smoking, did I? Really, Annie, and you too, Rachel – it's no good looking at me like that – now that you've come to Canada, you know, you'll have to be less conventional, you know. You're both very conventional, I don't mind telling you. The gentlemen were very nice indeed and I think they were pleased to see me."

"Not they! Anty," said Rachel, "you don't know anything about men at all! Even if they seemed nice, that was just politeness, and *next* time . . ."

"Topaz," said Sister Annie, "you are right. This is a free country. And gentlemen are free to gather together, if they wish to, without intrusion by you or anyone else. Let this be the last occasion. I do beg of you . . ."

"Well," said Topaz, hurdling her rebukes, "I learned a great deal, I can tell you, more than *you* did, sitting here reading Ranke's *History of the Popes*! They say we shall come in a few days to a part of the country called the Rolling Prairie, all humps and hollows, and Mr. Tomack told me it's caused by thousands and millions of bison, or buffaloes he called them, rolling over and over and causing these humps and hollows – some years ago, of course. We shall not see them actually doing it at the moment, I'm afraid."

"Why ever did they do that?" asked Sister Annie, curious, and forgetting that she was annoyed.

"Come in, Anty, *do,* and sit down for goodness sake," said Rachel. "It must have been fleas, of course, and anyway I don't believe it." The vision of millions of large brown woolly animals rolling over and over seemed improbable. Aunty began to argue.

The train ran on and the countryside ran to meet them and was left behind. The comfortable farms and broad meadows of Ontario which now they saw, pleased the Grand-mother. She understood them and the human toil and planning and thrift which had given them their prosperous dignity. They had a look of home. Here were elms. Here were sheep and cattle. Here was lazy smoke rising from chimneys of white farms. The sheep grazed in an international manner. They did not seem to know or care that they were Canadian sheep and should perhaps behave differently in a characteristic way, like the bison. They might indeed have been sheep of Staffordshire. Neither were the cows different from English beasts in their behaviour, the dear familiar cows. And the horses gossiped silently together as they did in the fields of England, communing secretly head to head through the soft intimate skin of their noses as the train fled past them. "I am rather old," thought the Grandmother, looking at the swiftly passing familiar animals, "to be able to assimilate great change." And the train ran on and on. And the day grew dark. And the windows became black. And they prepared with pleasure for the great adventure called Sleeping on the Train.

The couch of the drawing-room was piled with hand-baggage, of which they had far too much. Rachel and her mother lay in the lower berth, and Aunt Topaz climbed up above with agility and delight, and from the top bunk leaned over in her white calico nightdress, declaiming, "Romeo, Romeo, wherefore art thou Romeo?" and they were all merry. Rachel slept fitfully. She awoke each time the train stopped, and lay looking into the dark until it started again, jolting. How sad and how lonely the train sounded in the night. "O-o-o-oh," it cried on its way in the dark. "Oh oh o-o-oh," mourned the train. Aunty slept and woke lightly too, and climbed up and down at intervals. She enjoyed it.

"What *are* you doing, Anty?" whispered Rachel testily. "That's three times you've been up and down now!"

"Well, I need a goody," said Aunty. "Mr. Tomack gave me some goodies, only he called them candies. Have a goody." And she thrust a rustling paper bag at Rachel, sucking noisily.

"And I *do* wish, Anty, you'd stop flicking your light off and on all night."

"Well, keep your eyes shut then," said Aunty, who was accustomed to the miracle of gas-light but had never had such a nice little electric light to play with before. "Have another goody. This is all very cosy." And she clambered gustily up again.

If Rachel had kept a diary (but she never could, not being that kind of person, except "May 3rd, Mending shoes

2/6. Stamps 6d."), she should have noted down that something very important happened to her the next morning, and
it was simply this. The obligation of disposing of unnecessary
possessions in England, of equipping her mother, her aunt,
and herself with adequate and quite superfluous wardrobes of
a thrifty nature (six pairs of long woollen combies apiece
because they were going to Canada; three flannel petticoats
apiece for the same reason; a new umbrella In Case, the
number one umbrella, and the number two umbrella In Case,
and so forth), of making all decisions, of taking nearly all the
responsibility for nearly all the details of travel for her co-operative parent and her unpredictable aunt on board ship, the
embarkation onto the train – all this had knit Rachel's brows
and tensed her spirit. But when she awoke after the first night
on the train, dressed, looked out of the window, and saw that
they were indeed still speeding westwards (this time through
a world entirely different, through millions upon millions of
sombre and indistinguishable jackpines), the worry and fret
dropped away from her, and she felt a new lightness of heart
and a release. She loved even the jack pines which in their rank
dark millions are hard to love.

"Anty," she said, turning and smiling at Aunt Topaz who
was head downwards uttering muffled cries, trying to get her
address-book out of a suitcase which was under the seat, and
whose bottom was therefore her only visible part, "I'm so glad
I came to this country I can't tell you! Why didn't we come
before? It's my kind of country and I never want to go back
home again. There's something . . ." Rachel wanted the simple word "free," although no word could express her all-pervading release of spirit – ". . . well, I feel Canadian, just as if
I'd been born here. I don't care if we stop – here – now – or
if we go on, as long as I can live here all my life." And it was

true. Although Rachel would always be prone to anxiety, she had for ever, now, a fundamental peace – because she was where she liked to be. She was in essence as much a Canadian as those who had trodden Canada's wooded shores two hundred years before, or their descendants. The whole thing was an accident of time. "I wish I'd come two generations ago."

Aunty scrambled to her feet, scarlet and puffing. "I can't find it," she said, "and how could you come here two generations ago, what a ridiculous thing to say! I can't find it." But instead of helping, admonishing, and rebuking her, Rachel sat smiling at the jackpines which rushed past and vanished in myriads.

"Poufff!" said Aunty, blowing out her cheeks, and pulling the address-book and a great many other things out of the third lowest of a pile of heavy leather cases. "Here it is. McLeod. Winnie-Peg. Perhaps she has a telephone, they all seem to. A very lady-like woman. What a name! Winnie-Peg!"

"You'd better be careful what you say about names in a new country, Anty," laughed Rachel, "or they'll say 'What about Amen Corner and Petticoat Lane and . . . Cirencester? . . .'"

"And Much Dewchurch!" said her mother.

"And Little Gidding and Sixpenny Handley, to be sure," said Aunty. "And, oh, did I tell you what that Mr. Mawdsley from Newfoundland told me on the boat? In Newfoundland there's Bare Need, and Seldom-Come-By, and Heart's Ease, and Heart's Delight, and Heart's Content!"

They smiled at each other and at the lovely names. The train rocked on through the serried jackpines and they were all in good humour.

"Heart's Content, Heart's Content," murmured the Grandmother with her shining look. "But, oh, what a many trees! I didn't know there were so many trees! What do the people do with them all? But there are not many people!"

And far to the north, and to the south too, unnumbered, uncountable, stood the crowded jackpines, and among them lay dark, unreachable, anonymous lakes of blank water. And soon all this country and north to Hudson's Bay and beyond would be sealed with iron cold, and with silence broken only by the ultimate shot-like crack of frozen wood or water. And the train ran on and on, and the jackpines showed no sign that they would ever come to an end.

Next day the jackpines had come to an end as though they had never been. During the night as the train had hurried along, mourning as it went, the character of the country had changed, and they awoke to find flat distance – space, space, space. "Why, this must be the prairie!" they exclaimed to each other.

Sometimes they stopped at groups of dwellings so small that they did not conform to the words town or village or hamlet, and so short was the wait at the little station that the porter had continually to prevent Aunt Topaz from getting off the train to "walk upon the prairie," and getting left there. Some of the small wooden houses, which had two eyes, a nose, and a mouth, held a malevolent expression. Some leered out of their windows at the train as it ran past. Some with false pride had false fronts, which concealed and then drew attention to the absence of a second storey. "Well, it may be all very nice, but I'm sure I wouldn't like to live here," said Topaz.

"I would," said Rachel, "I'd love it. Look at all that space! Not *here*, I mean," as the train left behind a melancholy grouping of dolls' houses, "but on a farm – over there," and she pointed to the horizon. "I should like to live on a farm." And she saw herself living on a lonely prairie farm with everything dependent upon her and her industry, and upon her

companions and their industry. She would live on this hypothetical farm with a hypothetical brother, not with a husband
or a lover. To Rachel all men were indeed brothers, not husbands or lovers. So she saw herself on the farm with her little
house and her chickens and her turkeys and a well in the yard
and a hypothetical someone, and around her – space.

"Whatever are those? Bones?" said Aunty peering at
white piles of bleached something which rushed past them.
"Bones I do declare! Well! They must be bison bones!" And,
of course, they were.

The train slowed down and stopped. "Regina!" called the
porter. "Twenty minutes to Regina!" and they all got out
except the Grandmother.

"I didn't quite hear. May I ask you the name of this
place?" Aunty asked politely of a tall sombre young man who
felt uneasy with elderly women.

The young man looked at her distastefully. "Formerly
Pile of Bones, now Regina. I much prefer Pile of Bones," he
said, turning and striding to the other end of the platform.

"Whatever *is* he talking about?" Aunty asked her new
friend Mrs. Knox.

"He said it used to be called Pile of Bones and now the
name is changed to Regina. When the Indians made pemmi-
can out of buffalo meat they left great piles of bones, and that's
how it got its name. I rather like the old name, but some
people didn't, and the Governor-General's wife, Princess
Louise I think, suggested Regina," Mrs. Knox told her.

"Oh, Regina – Regeena – the Romans, very remarkable,
I'm sure," said Aunty vaguely, deferring to royalty. But as they
looked abroad on the bare prairie and over the little groups of
small angular buildings, she could see nothing to confirm the
queerly Latin name in this so very new prairie town. But then

Aunty could not look forward and see a vigorous city of brick and stone and wood, of industries, of grain elevators, and a seat of government, with a man-made lake, and hand-planted parks, and a thriving centre of a far-flung community of prosperous wheat farmers. She could not see the courage and vision that absurdly dared to call this place Regina. She could see only the bare sun-drenched prairie, waiting for the wheat and for people.

"Nevertheless I cannot understand," she said to an elderly man, who stood near, "how it is, with all this open space, that the inhabitants of the Old World, crowded as they are, do not flock to this new country, with space and to spare," forgetting as she spoke that only family and circumstances had wrenched her from the cosy crowding of the Old World which she loved so well.

"Jever tend stock 'n keep the fires goin' 'n melt the ice for watter with the thermometer forty below?" asked the elderly man, whose face was tanned and wrinkled and a little sad.

"Well, no, but . . ." began Aunty.

"Jever spend the winter on a prurrie farm, outer sight of any human bean?" continued the man.

"No, but . . ."

"Well, I spent twenny-five of them. There's women can't stand it. Asylums full of farmers' wives can't stand it. Drives 'em crazy. The prurrie don't always look like this," said the elderly man pointing with his open hand to the far-flung sunny land. He turned and moved away.

"Oh, now, Miss Edgeworth," said Mrs. Knox to the horrified Topaz, "that's not what you'd call really true. Some people can't stand it. There were times I found it pretty bad myself. Tom and I had nearly twenty years of it, but I stood it all right – it was hard work and it *was* lonely, and now we're older Tom and I don't feel equal to it so we moved down to the Coast. But what he said would make you think what isn't just right . . . oh, here he comes."

The elderly man walked towards them, stopped, and said, "My wife died in an institution near a year ago," and moved on.

"There . . . you see . . . oh, the poor man, that's why he said what he did," said Mrs. Knox. And she and Topaz walked down the platform together, Topaz rearranging her feelings. "Oh, Indians!" she exclaimed suddenly.

On the grass, wrapped in blankets, with a plait of hair over each shoulder, squatted two Indians. Aunty hastened up, and stopped as one would at a stone wall. The stolid faces of the two Indians showed no knowledge that she or any other human being was in the world. How did one address Indians? "Parlez-vous français?" "How do you do?" all the customary forms of greeting seemed useless. The two Indians defeated Aunty. "Well!" she said.

"Come on, Anty, *do*," urged Rachel. "Don't keep looking at those Indians. They won't like it. They've got a right to sit there, they were here first."

"Rachel, *did* you hear what that poor man said?"

"Yes, and still I'd like to live on the prairie. It's the most exciting thing I've ever seen in my life."

"*All aboard . . . !*" came the cry, and they turned and ran like chickens.

All day the illimitable prairie spread before them and slipped behind them. Far to the north (and to the south) the prairie spread, defeating imagination, like eternity. They did not know that further north still were great irregular lakes, and rivers, and a great river flowing to the Arctic Ocean, where only a few of the hardiest white men had been. They could not tell, speeding comfortably across the yellow stubble of the prairie, that winter would come and seal, and petrify, and drive away birds, and exact a difficult life and death from fur-bearing animals and their hunters, and maintain in rigidity and without mercy a whole empire in the north. They did not think of these things. "From what I gather, I don't *think* Vancouver will look like this, do you, love?" asked the Grandmother uncertainly. And the train ran on.

At night Rachel was wakeful. She could not see, but she imagined the dark endless prairie lying about them as they ran. "O-o-oh," mourned the train sadly, "oh oh o-o-oh." "Why does the engine blow on the open prairie?" wondered Rachel. "I suppose it's level crossings." "*Oh*," moaned the train, pushing on.

And the next day they still ran along the prairie, but now the land broke into rolling country ("This *must* be the Rolling Prairie!"), and the world became lightly wooded again. Then, beyond increasingly high hills they looked westwards and saw, coldly blue and white against the sky, a tumult of mountains.

In the gullies of the little hills through which they now passed there were aspens and birches whose leaves the early frost had turned from green to gold. The birches with their white maidenly stems and honey-yellow leaves shone against the dark conifers. Far to the north of them, but still east of the Rockies, east of Jasper House, the Athabasca River flowed widely through a land that was all gold. Golden golden golden shone the birch trees in the sunshine in that northern land from north to south, from east to west, spiked here and there by dark conifers. Few travellers along the brave steel way had ever heard of this golden world. But here, as the train hurried towards the mountains, Rachel looked up at the railway cutting and saw, for one moment, poised alone against the blue sky, a single slender white-stemmed aspen tree whose golden leaves trembled and shone and sang in the sunshine. It was there. It was gone. It was hers.

Quickly the mountains were upon them. Each of the travellers had been to Switzerland and the word "Alps" sprang from mouth to mouth, but soon they ceased to speak of the Alps. "This ain't all of it, no, ma'am," said the coloured porter huskily. "It goes 'way 'way up north and down south. This ain't only a little patch of it."

The great peaks advanced upon them and they were as nothing amongst the confusion and welter of the mountains. The train began to pant and toil. What wild extravagance of nature was this. Mist came down, or was it rain or snow, and sometimes blotted the great indifferent torrent-spilling mountains from their sight. "I think, love, that they are rather too big! I could appreciate the mountains better if we had come upon them before we'd seen all the other bignesses. I think," laughing a little, "that my appetite for big things is gone," said the Grandmother.

The mountains ranged themselves on either side of the railway track, peak after peak. The Grandmother looked up murmuring vaguely, "The mountains skip like rams." She would have regarded this statement as hyperbole if the Bible had not said it first. But that is exactly what the mountains did. Silently, silently, they moved one behind the other with surprising speed considering their age and size. They changed their positions as the pushing train sped curving along their bases; so that first one mountain, then another, moved silently, in order, one behind another. The mountains only remained static when the train stood still; but when the train raced along their bases the mountains skipped like rams. "The Lord doeth wonderful things," marvelled the Grandmother gazing up at the moving peaks as they rearranged themselves against the sky, and then gave place to still more mountains which behaved in the same way. This occurred for a whole day, for these were the Rocky and Cascade Mountains. They did not see the gorges of the Thompson River (for night had fallen) nor Hell's Gate.

Morning came in the widening Fraser Valley. The train was running for home now, and the long journey was nearly done. It ran along the shores of Burrard Inlet. As the travellers approached Vancouver they hardly saw the swelling line of the mountains across the Inlet, nor the first waters of the Pacific Ocean, nor the masted schooners and brigs which stood off from Hastings Mill, nor the sea-gulls wheeling and wheeling above the salt water – they sat there ready with their gloves on and their handbags on their knees and their minds forerunning them.

At last the train slowed up and clanked into a modest railway platform. The three women searched the faces and forms of the little crowd.

"Oh, Rachel, I see the Boys!" cried the Grandmother, tremulous. "I see the Boys! I see Andrew!"

"Well, I do declare!" said Aunt Topaz, quite beside herself.

Rachel wrote to her cousin Elise, ". . . it is so lovely, Elise, that I feel I've wasted my life in not living here before. Housekeeping with a Chinaman in the kitchen is odd but I'll soon get used to it. People are so kind. I was rather amused at the church social when a Canadian lady admired my pound cake and said I was so capable you'd never think I was English! It was supposed to be a compliment, I think! Wasn't it funny? Perhaps we're all funny like that because I found myself saying to a Mrs. Barrett the other day that you'd never know she was a Canadian, and I don't believe she was pleased. And Mother couldn't understand it when the bank manager's wife said flatteringly that you'd never think we were Methodists, and then again I heard Aunt Topaz say you'd never dream that Mrs. Shafto was a Roman Catholic! All these preconceived ideas! There seems to be more mixing-up of people here than in Ware, and I like it. And it's so beautiful, you *should* see Stanley Park! . . ."

Aunt Topaz wrote to her friend Miss Peacock – or was it to her other friend Miss Pocock? – ". . . and we have a Chinese cook called Yow with a queue with green silk plaited in to make it longer wound round his head in the house and let down and caught up somehow under his right arm when he walks in the street with Chinese slippers turned up a bit in front and a very good black silk coat and trousers indeed quite expensive with a high neckband. He wears a hat. I can't understand a word he says but he seems very good I'm sure. Our house is called The Hawthorns and we have the only hawthorn trees in Vancouver each side of the door. Fancy that! You will hardly believe it but Stephen drove us carriage and all into a hollow tree where we sat in the carriage and had our pictures taken. I will send you one. Such a size! Oh my dear Lily, you *should* see Stanley Park. . . ."

And the Grandmother wrote to her son George, ". . . we are thankful indeed for Journeying Mercies. I shall never get quite used to being away from you all, love, and the children, and from all the dear associations of England and of home. . . . But this place is beautiful beyond description. The boys have been so thoughtful and we have a deal to be thankful for. The nice house that the boys got for us all is close to the chapel, or church as it is called here. . . . I can, from my bedroom window, see the mountains! The trees here are remarkable. You should see Stanley Park. . . ."

Topaz had at last reached open country. British Columbia stretched before her, exciting her with its mountains, its forests, the Pacific Ocean, the new little frontier town, and all the new people. Here was no time limit, no fortnight's holiday. Here she had come to live; and, drawing long breaths of the opulent air, she began to run about, and dance for joy, exclaiming, all through the open country.

OPEN COUNTRY

I f you arrive in Vancouver on a fine day and go up into a high place, to Little Mountain perhaps or even to the top of some high office building, you will come under the immediate spell of the mountains to the north of you, and of dark coniferous forests. You will see high headlands sloping westwards into the Pacific Ocean, and islands beyond. And then you will turn again and look across the blue inlet at the mountains which in their turn look down upon the grace and strength of the Lions' Gate Bridge, upon the powerful flow of the Narrows, upon English Bay, upon the harbour, and upon the large city of Vancouver.

When Topaz came to Vancouver there were no high places built for people to climb into. Modest one- or two-storeyed buildings rose, to everyone's admiration, where the nobler forest had lately been. The forest still was, and winding trails through the woods ended at small hidden shacks, almost within the town itself. Vancouver was only a little town, but prophetically it called itself a city. It was soon to bear the marks of the Klondike Rush. It was the "end of steel," the beginning of the Pacific, and people thought that possibly the place had a future. Who could tell. There was more sail than steam coming into the harbour, but the elegant *Empresses* with their shapely bows came and vanished again into the dim Orient, and the *Islander* crossed the Gulf to Vancouver Island. In the days of tents and shacks by the water edge, and of Gassy Jack Deighton's saloon, the settlement had been called Gastown. Then with a rush of self-consciousness it became Granville. And then came the perfect inevitable name of meaning and destiny – Vancouver. Broad wooden sidewalks bordered the few main streets, but in front of the houses there were just three-plank-wide wooden sidewalks. If you were a little boy or girl you counted your steps to a plank as you walked. You said, "Step across a crack, Break your mother's back," and then you avoided or stepped on the cracks, according to your disposition.

Down came the forests. Chop. Chop. Chop. The blessed forests came down. The men of the chain-gang were driven up in a waggon and with lumbering movements cleared away the fallen trees while their guard stood near, and interested passers-by watched them and speculated on their past and their future. The forests vanished, and up went the city.

Aunt Topaz's nephew Stephen soon began to build a large house halfway between the town and English Bay. This was very pioneering of him, as there was yet no streetcar near there. He built a stable also, and had a fine hitching-post for his horse, and a mounting-block which remains there to this day for children going home from school to play upon. Blackberries rampaged over the adjoining land which itself adjoined the forest. The West End was wooded. Shaughnessy Heights was virgin forest without a name. Stephen's house was painted red. It was with a doll's-house kind of pleasure that Topaz, fresh from bricky England, saw painters painting little wooden houses red, white, green, and even yellow among the standing cedars, fir trees, and maples. The houses all had wooden trimmings and verandahs, and on the verandah steps when day was done the families came out and sat and talked and counted the box pleats on the backs of fashionable girls' skirts as they went by; and visitors came and sat and talked, and idly watched the people too, and watched the mountains grow dark, and the stars come out above the mountains. And then they all went in and made a cup of cocoa. It was very pleasant and there seemed to be no trouble anywhere upon the face of the earth, that you could discern.

Topaz and her sister and her niece all thought that Vancouver was a beautiful name. It was not long before the contours of the mountains became part of their lives. There was the Sleeping Beauty, lying nobly to the sky. There were the Lions rising sculptured, remote, indifferent. Smoke of fires trailed delicately through the trees. Along the topmost generous curve of the westward hills, pine trees cut sharply against the coloured evening skies, and there were always the sounds of the sirens of ships and the cries of the sea-gulls – sounds of ocean.

This, at last, then, was the Canadian city which they came to know. Topaz had hardly observed the towns and cities of Canada, for each one, as is the custom of cities, had presented only its sprawling and unpleasing posterior to the railway travellers, and its face and person could not be seen by them. Now, in Vancouver, whose face and person they soon came to know so well, they also knew for the first time the growth of a young frontier town into a real city.

"Listen, Annie!" cried Topaz, ten years later, "we have a slogan!"

"What is a slogan, Topaz?" asked Sister Annie, looking up from her fine white cotton knitting.

"A slogan is a war-cry for wild Highland clans (or is it Irishmen?), I believe," answered Topaz, perusing the newspaper in a mutter "m-m-m-m-m," as was her custom, "and someone has just discovered the word."

"But we are not Irishmen," said Sister Annie truthfully, "and I am sure we need no war-cry."

"Yes, ah, yes. Here it is," said Topaz, loudly folding and unfolding the paper. "Listen to this:

'In nineteen-ten,
Vancouver then
Will have one hundred thousand men.
Move her! Move her!
Who? – Vancouver.'

There then, fancy that, one hundred thousand men! I wonder if that includes women and children! *There's* a slogan for you, Annie!"

Sister Annie shook her head. "No, Topaz. I like it very well the way it is. I don't want a slogan." And indeed when the Grandmother arrived in Vancouver, and for some years afterwards, it was a very comfortable little place to live in. But no one could stop the changes that came, not even if they had used a slogan to keep people away.

Very soon Aunt Topaz made a great many friends in the little church which was so conveniently near, and her genius for acquaintanceship and activity sparkled and flew about. Societies disclosed themselves, asking to be joined. She joined the Ladies' Aid, the Women's Auxiliary, and the Women's Council, and as time went on, the Y.W.C.A., the Victorian Order of Nurses, and the Anti-Tuberculosis Society and the Ladies' Minerva Club, which had a distinguished book-plate for its small library, but in spite of that could not survive. She went to the Public Library every other day and carried home books. And read late into the night, and before the Public Library became the Carnegie Library she had read every book in it except two on engineering and one on jurisprudence. She had conveyed the entire Library bit by bit, home and back again in a string bag, bursting into the house, loud with exhaustion. She took sketching lessons, and china-painting lessons (bunches of lilac and other suitable flowers, with gilt trimmings, upon cups and saucers), and joined, tentatively, a glee club.

It was not long before Aunt Topaz and Rachel bought bicycles. Rachel bought a light slim bicycle, red, of Canadian manufacture, easy to ride; and on this bicycle she did her errands, riding about the wooden sidewalks among the pedestrians of Vancouver when she had time to do so, saluting with politeness and a smile other cyclists whom she met riding on the wooden sidewalks too; and, for pleasure, she and her various new friends sometimes pedalled in twos and threes around Stanley Park. Their skirts were a little inclined – despite protective inventions – to fly up in front. Their men friends made up for this by wearing natty cycling costumes, trim and manly about the leg. Aunt Topaz bought a noble English bicycle. It was magnificent and too heavy, as if built for Boadicea. It was proud, sexless in spite of its shape, intractable, and would throw you as soon as look at you. It had a large lamp with heavy bevelled glass sides, which was not necessary as Topaz never took the bicycle out at night. It had a bell like a sweet clarion which she delighted to ring; and that was almost all the good she ever got out of it. She became devoted to her bicycle but it never returned her love. It threw her nearly every time she tried to get on it. As she never succeeded in staying comfortably on, even in the most wobbling fashion, she took to leading her bicycle about because it seemed a pity to waste it. It spent more and more time sulking in a dust-sheet. Fifteen years later, when the bicycle appeared rarely, it had acquired under the dust-sheet, over which the years slid by, the look of a grande dame of an early mechanical era, and it attracted attention and comment, which always pleased her.

Aunt Topaz soon became an ardent shopper but was so employed by Rachel only when absolutely necessary, as Aunty was not economical and was usually late in returning home. Together with the other shopping ladies she would go to Cordova Street, meeting and greeting, and arriving at last at Mr. Fader's fish shop.

"Oh, Mr. Fader, how do you do! What a beautiful salmon! It reminds me exactly of a Scottish salmon I once met in, or I should say on, the Tay. . . ." This Scottish salmon was to Aunty the criterion of all fish, and it did not occur to her, as it does to ordinary people, that one fish wears much the same expression as another. The similarity of her salmon to other salmon always surprised her.

Life was further enlivened by the discovery of the Hudson's Bay Lunch Room. There had been no lunch room in Ware, only the Leopard pub, to which Aunty could not or did not go, though she would have loved it and would have met her match there. To the Hudson's Bay Lunch Room she repaired eagerly, any morning that she had nothing better to do, sometimes accompanied by her bicycle, sometimes alone; and she ate elevenses, a kind of superfluous mid-morning snack, in the cosy publicity of the Lunch Room. She made many friends of many kinds there and would return and tell Sister Annie and Rachel all about them.

"Rachel, I met *such* an interesting American woman! I

said to her, 'I see you are an American, you cut up your meat and then lay your knife down and eat it with your fork.' She *was* surprised. "

"Well, I should think she was very much annoyed with you! That is no business of yours, you know, Anty, going round telling people about their knives and forks."

"Oh, she was intensely interested, and told me all about her sister. I joined her and I asked her to come to Annie's next At Home day. I said, 'My sister Mrs. Hastings would be delighted to see you. She is At Home on the first and third Tuesdays, and she is very fond of Americans.'"

"*Anty!*" Rachel would exclaim, helpless and aggravated.

For by this time the Grandmother and her family were established with At Home days, like all the other people who knew what was what. Aunty derived a great deal of pleasure from dressing herself with unusual care (she was indifferent about clothes, yet "dressy"), and paying and returning calls, but most of all she loved the first and third Tuesdays. There was a fearful pleasure in considering whether no one would call, and they would have to sit alone with the best tea-things all afternoon, or whether the room would be proudly overflowing. It was found best to have something or some-body in the kitty, and most ladies took the precaution of asking a trusted friend or two to come in as a nucleus and to save face if necessary on their At Home days. True, Aunty loved what was beginning to be called Society, but she found people who were not designated as In Society equally delightful.

One day, when about five years had passed, Rachel and Topaz looked up to see the Grandmother walk into the sitting-room with tears running down her face. She held a letter in her hand.

"Mother, what is it?" asked Rachel.

"Robert has died," said her mother speaking through tears. Her face was convulsed with grief.

"Rose must come to us at once," said Rachel decisively.

"Robert *dead*!" exclaimed Topaz in distress.

Here was a young death, not one of those old deaths with which Topaz was now familiar. When the tall dark handsome Robert had walked straight into the family affections and had married Laura, who was the Grandmother's eldest daughter and a second mother to all the Grandmother's sons, he had become one of the family. It had been forgiven him for his charm and sincerity that he had taken Laura to a benighted Africa where in her second childbirth she had died. And now Robert, who had returned to England with his baby daughter Rose, had died, too, and the small eight-year-old Rose was left alone. Wholehearted plans were at once made by the family of six adult people to bring the child to Canada, and Rose, after spending some months with compassionate relatives in England, arrived, a small surprised child, dressed in black. "Take off that black," said the uncles, "and let the child wear colours!"

"We can't waste her *best* black," said Rachel, "but she shall have colours for every day." And now Rachel added to her duties the great care of a child.

It was about the time that Rose arrived in Vancouver that Aunt Topaz, in whom the success of belonging to so many societies had mounted to the head, ran herself into trouble. Since it was obvious that she was a great deal better educated – in her own peculiar way – than most women, and since she had great affability and was particularly get-on-able-with, and since she had unlimited leisure, executive committees in several societies decided separately but simultaneously that

Miss Topaz Edgeworth must not be wasted out of office. Aunty therefore accepted, with almost delirious enthusiasm, nominations to office in three or four societies at the same time. The experience was novel and exhilarating, until she gradually became entangled in the horrible web of the responsibility which goes with office. Then began the period of the Great Moan. As decisions had to be made, succinct letters had to be written, reports had to be made out and read, and exact information ascertained, Aunty's pleasant life dimmed and became uniquely horrible. A blackness crept upon the bright and lighted chamber of her mind. She awoke in the morning, and while her nephews were still in the house, she moaned softly. The Hudson's Bay Lunch Room saw her no longer, and the bicycle stayed in the shed and its bright bell remained unrung. Aunty went to her bedroom after lunch, closed the door, lay upon her bed, and then went to work moaning in good earnest. She moaned and moaned and moaned whenever her nephews were out of the house, and the sound of her moaning was heard everywhere by all except the Grandmother, who was becoming very deaf.

One day Rachel found Rose standing outside Aunt Topaz's closed bedroom door, listening to the uninhibited bellowing that went on inside.

"Aunty Rachel, why does Aunt Topaz moo?" asked the child.

"Aunt Topaz isn't moo-ing, Rose," said Rachel genially, "she is moaning because she is the head of a committee to select the new carpets for the new church." And Rachel went about her work. She found Aunty's low spirits rather a relief. It seemed to equate things somewhat. To Rachel, always reserved, always controlled, except for surface irritation, Aunty's indifference to her listeners was funny and very astonishing.

Rose, entranced, remained listening. Words were mingled with the moans.

"Oh. Oh. Oh," roared Aunty like a suffering bull. "Those carpets. Oh. Oh. Oh." And she buried her face in the pillow and continued to roar, which gave her moans a fog-horn note.

Rose did not analyse her feelings about her Great-Aunt's moaning, but nevertheless her feelings were mixed. She was a child who was already schooled to change. She had discovered that grown-up people were not all the same. In Father there had been all that was more gay than grave, more kind than severe, and in him a dearness and a oneness that was simply "Father." She could say her silliest word to him and it was not too silly. But since the world which was Father had gone, she had lived in a world of many different grown-up people who all regarded her with the compassionate kindness and love which they felt for Laura and Robert's little girl and which an orphaned child inspires. But she had already begun to lose the habit of blurting everything out, and had begun to consider. And as she stood outside Aunt Topaz's door with her hands behind her back and her head rather on one side, she considered.

"O-o-o-oh," moaned Aunty.

"Imagine a grown-up making a noise like that," considered Rose. "I don't think it hurts her. I think she likes it. I don't feel sorry like if it was a cat. I couldn't bear it if it was a cat. Aunt Rachel wouldn't do that, nor Grannie, nor Uncle Frank, nor Uncle Stephen, nor Uncle Andrew, and Father never would and they wouldn't let me if I wanted to." At that moment Aunt Topaz, moving as usual with precipitation, blew her nose loudly, let out one more moan, got up, and burst out of her room to go to the bathroom and Rose only just had time to skip.

As soon as the church carpets were bought, and each Annual Meeting came round in turn, Aunty resigned from her offices. She took her delightful unresponsible place again as an ordinary member of society and societies, and resumed running about the open country in a way which she now more than ever appreciated. The Hudson's Bay Lunch Room welcomed her again, and the superb and indifferent bicycle was wheeled abroad. Rarely, in the years that followed, did she allow herself to become entangled in responsibility.

One only office she cherished. During the visit of the Duke and Duchess of York to Vancouver, Aunty had assisted in the pleasant task of presenting the Duchess with a Book of Views. She had talked as volubly to the Duchess as her allotted space of time would allow, and had recalled to the Royal memory the name of her friend Miss Peacock (or was it Miss Pocock?) who helped the Duchess in her own private charities. And so it was that Aunty was asked to establish a branch of a Needlework Guild in Vancouver with Royal encouragement. It was, to begin with, a one-woman affair, and Aunty joyously collected knitted garments from her knitting acquaintances, and forwarded them to the Duchess. And as years went on, Aunty was joyously sending knitted garments to the Queen of England, for which she received charming and grateful letters through the Queen's Lady-in-Waiting. Aunty gave these letters with all speed to the newspapers, and then rejoiced to read in the news:

Miss T. E. P. Edgeworth of Vancouver has received the following letter from the Lady-in-Waiting to Her Majesty the Queen:

Buckingham Palace

Dear Miss Edgeworth,
The Queen commands me to thank you for . . .

And friends and strangers would accost Aunty and say, "Oh, Miss Edgeworth, I see you've had another letter from the Queen!" and Aunty would be gratified.

And friends and strangers would accost Aunt Rachel and say, "Oh, Miss Hastings, I see that your Aunt has had another letter from the Queen!"

And Rachel would go home and say crossly, "Anty, I do wish you'd stop putting the Queen's letters in the paper. They are really personal letters, and I don't think the Queen would like it at all. It's very self-important of you."

And Aunty would retort, "Everyone but you likes to see them! The trouble with you is, you have no loyalty! No loyalty whatever!" "Me! 'No *loyalty*!'" Rachel would splutter, and an argument would begin.

And late, very late in Aunty's life, when Rachel and Annie were dead and gone, and Aunty was more alive than ever, and had entered into her apotheosis, she was commanded to go to see the Queen. And the Queen, dressed in blue, with glorious sapphires, received her kindly in Buckingham Palace, and Aunty lived happy ever after. She could not have dreamed that her future might hold such bliss.

"I HAVE A FATHER IN THE PROMISED LAND"

Yes, love, I understand," said the Grandmother at the head of the table, soothing one of her sons who made strong objections to going to the revival meeting, "indeed I do understand that you prefer another way of worshipping God. But since Mr. Pratt is our new minister and he has called his congregation together for this service, it ill behooves us to stay away. Nay, and if the Lord should speak to us and bless us, we shall be well repaid. Come, let us all go." Grandmother spoke in her little careful ornate way that was her natural form of expression, and looked with such sweet sincerity upon her household, that, of course, they all went to the revival meeting, willy-nilly.

They walked into the pew, pushing a little, but decorously. There were the Grandmother, the Great-Aunt Topaz, Aunt Rachel, Uncle Frank, Uncle Stephen, and Uncle Andrew. There was also the lovely Miranda, fiancée to Uncle Frank. There was Rose, aged eight, small, curly-haired, still wearing the good black in which she had been warmly and suitably dressed following her adored father's death the year before. They all sat down, then they dropped upon their knees. The uncles remained there for a brief and manly instant. The Grandmother became charged with emotion immediately on closing her eyes. The Aunts communed silently and respectfully for a moment, and Rose stayed down as long as they. On rising they settled themselves on the long pew which curved at the side of the church. The lovely Miranda, knowing herself the object of interest to her young friends as she sat among her dignified relatives-to-be, gazed pleasantly round, acknowledging charmingly and almost imperceptibly the bright glances that shot to her across the church. Radiant she sat there among her dignified relatives-to-be. The Grandmother gazed at nothing, rapt and suffused by her own inner vision, unaware of the congregation. Rose looked this way and that with youthful interest. She noted the bonneted old ladies as they stole to their pews, their plain and bearded husbands, the pretty Miss Moores, the fathers, the mothers, the families that streamed in. Most of them dropped to their knees. Fleetingly she wondered what they all really did there. But some, oh horrors, sat smack down and looked round frankly and with interest upon their neighbours. No stained glass shed its warm and romantic radiance upon the congregation. The amenities of coloured windows, pulpits, surplices and the like were not there. No, they were suspect a little of the delightful worldliness of the Church of England.

A door opened. On to the platform, garnished with chairs and a reading-desk, strode the Pastor. When this man of God was sent from Ontario to minister to the West, doubtless the Fathers in Israel shaded their eyes and gazed towards Vancouver. They looked west across the Great Lakes. They looked across the prairies, all wheat, cattle, cowboys, and Indians. They looked again across the foothills, the forests, the Rocky Mountains, the mining camps, the saloons, the gambling hells, to the wild shores of the Pacific Ocean where a young and turbulent city was growing. They looked towards the Klondike Rush. They looked, and then they said to each other, "Let us send the Rev. Elmer Pratt, he's just the man for the West." So now here was the Rev. Elmer Pratt, full of zeal, swarthy, black-visaged, and violent of feature. Beneath his black hair shone his bright black eyes. Beneath his bright black eyes jutted his large nose. Beneath his large nose sprang and flourished his magnificent black moustaches. Beneath his vigorous chin rose up his high and stiff white collar, with a splendid white four-in-hand tie. The face, coarse and vigorous, was perpetually at war with the sanctity of the starched white collar and tie beneath. He used strange words. Rose, accustomed to the suave tones of her native England, was constantly amazed at the flat and grating voice of the Rev. Elmer Pratt. Whereas the ministers of the Gospel to whom she had listened Sunday by Sunday since infancy spoke gently of the love of God, the Rev. Elmer Pratt thundered about brothels. She supposed that brothels were places where broth was made and decided that the broth must be very bad or the Rev. Elmer Pratt would not be so angry. He also spoke frequently about "foaming out your shame upon your city streets" (see Hosea), in a way that made her feel personally responsible, and she could only conclude that he had reference to the nasty habit of spitting that she had noticed and disliked among men in the streets of this little western town. There seemed to be no other explanation. Many strange things were uttered by the Rev. Elmer Pratt, and little of it did Rose understand. But once his sermons of wrath and denunciation were over, he became a human and kindly being.

This evening as he mounted the platform he was almost in tender vein. He prayed long and enjoyably. Chiefly he desired

God's blessing upon the week of revival services on which the congregation was entering. Much stress was laid upon the Last Chance. For example, it might be that Tuesday night next had been selected for some dear brother (or sister) to be saved, and if they stayed away on Tuesday night the chance might pass by for ever. This became very important. Rose had never before been to a revival service, in fact there had been some discussion at home as to whether she was too young to come. But, the Grandmother having been saved at the age of five, here she was.

By the time they were again vertical in their seats, the church was filled with a lively emotion. The congregation rose and sang, their thoughts uplifted, "There is a fountain filled with Blood," a terrifying hymn to Rose, because she had seen fountains. Then they sat down, their gaze upon Mr. Pratt. Even the lovely Miranda, her thoughts forcibly removed from her trousseau, gazed upon Mr. Pratt. He became as one a little transfigured by darkness. His grating and powerful voice was subdued, vibrant, and touching. His black glances played over the congregation, loving them, frightening them, yearning over them. He held up to them their lives of sin and shame. He showed them the dreadful, the almost inescapable doom. Strident his voice rose to the horrors of the hereafter. Softened and vibrating with tenderness he described to them as if he had been there the Kingdom of the Blessed where they fain would be. Did they not, urged the Rev. Elmer Pratt, as a strong inducement, wish to see their Dear Ones who were undoubtedly waiting for them in the Heavenly Home? "Is there no one waiting for you?" thrilled Mr. Pratt. "My brothers, my sisters, have you no one waiting in Heaven for you? Come now," said he encouragingly, "who has a Father in the Promised Land? Who has a dear dear Father waiting in the Promised Land? Come now, stand! Stand up now, any person who has a dear dear Father waiting in the Promised Land; do not be afraid; stand up, ah, bless you, my brother; bless you, my sister!" Thus exhorted people began to stand up, one here, one there, looking downwards. Rose's heart was ready to burst. Her Father, her dear dear Father, whom she loved better than anyone on earth, Father with the dear voice and the kind laughing eyes, was waiting, waiting. She slipped to the floor and stood up. "Bless you, my child," said the Rev. Elmer Pratt kindly.

Rose burst into tears.

"Let us sing," said the Rev. Elmer Pratt, "let us sing together." And he sang in his grating voice:

"I have a Father in the Promised Land,
I have a Father in the Promised Land,
My Father calls me, I must go
To meet him in the Promised Land."

"Come now," said Mr. Pratt, "all those standing, sing – 'I have . . .'" and everybody sang.

Rose sang sobbingly, sniffingly, to the mute distress of Great-Aunt Topaz, Aunt Rachel, Uncle Frank, Uncle Stephen, Uncle Andrew, and the lovely Miranda. The Grandmother, touched and pleased, wept gently beside her.

The song finished. Relieved, the bereaved ones sat down. Rose wiped her eyes.

"Now then," said the Rev. Elmer Pratt, rubbing his hands in a pleased way, "who has a Mother, a dear dear Mother, waiting for them, waiting to welcome? Stand up, those who have a dear Mother in the Promised Land."

This startled Rose. She had thought the affair was over, and had settled down comfortably in the pew to her grief. But

others, the more knowing among the congregation, had sus-
pected this. Sadly Rose stood up again. Her mother had died
when she was eighteen months old, at the birth of a little son.
In fact, as far as Rose was concerned, she had never had a
mother and felt no grief at her loss. However, there she stood,
still weeping for her father. One by one the people stood.
More handkerchiefs came out. The Rev. Elmer Pratt with innocent ghoulish pleasure welcomed and encouraged them as
they stood. "Bless you, my brother; bless you, my sister. Bless
you, bless you, my child." Thus blessed, they stood, looking
downwards. "Let us sing," said Mr. Pratt, "let us sing, my dear
folks, those who have lost a Mother.

> "I have a Mother in the Promised Land,
> I have a Mother in the Promised Land,
> My Mother calls me, I must go
> To meet her in the Promised Land."

They sang. "Sit down, sit down," said the Rev. Elmer
Pratt. The bereaved ones sat. Well, that was over.

"Has anyone," said the Rev. Elmer Pratt enquiringly,
"lost a dear brother?" Now this came as a surprise to everybody, and hastily the congregation tried to remember if they
had lost a brother. A bit of mental fumbling here. Rose recol-
lected that Father had once told her that her baby brother,
christened Edward, had died when he was three days old, and
lay buried beside her mother in South Africa. Once only her
father had spoken of his grief. "Did I ever see little Edward,
Father?" she had asked. "No, dear," had said her father. And
now, here was little Edward! Did she have to stand up for
Edward? He must have been so very small, hardly worth
standing for. Time was pressing. Poor little Edward, no one

to stand up for him! But, strictly speaking, would little Edward be able to welcome her in the Promised Land, being so very small? This was puzzling, but there was no time for advice. Little Edward won. Rose stood up again. The family looked up in surprise. They had forgotten about little Edward. "Sing, friends," commended the Rev. Elmer Pratt, sing together,

"I have a Brother in the Promised Land,
I have a Brother in the Promised Land,
My Brother calls me, I must go
To meet him in the Promised Land."

They sang. The tune, now familiar, rang out cheerfully. The bereaved ones sang sturdily and without sobs. Apparently, inured as they now were to loss, they could more easily support the presence of a brother in the Promised Land.

"Sit down, folks," said Mr. Pratt with real satisfaction. They sat down. "Well," thought Rose, "I'm down now safely, for I never had a sister." But poor Miranda! Her turn was coming. Rose looked along the pew at the lovely Miranda. Miranda was turning her engagement ring this way and that. She tilted her charming head with its pretty pointed chin. She looked at her ring. Rubies and diamonds, rubies and diamonds. Look up, look up, Miranda, it's your turn next! Miranda looked at the ring and smiled sweetly, dreamily. Only yesterday, as Rose had sat admiring her while she brushed her beautiful hair, they had talked about Miranda's family. "And was that all of you, Aunt Miranda?" Rose had said. "Yes, dear," said the lovely Miranda, her mouth full of hairpins, "except a tiny tiny baby sister, but she died, stillborn," murmured the truthful young Miranda through the hairpins. Rose had enquired further, "Did you say 'stillborn'? What does 'stillborn' mean?" Miranda had not answered. Her mouth was full of hairpins. All this Rose now remembered. She looked along the pew. The tiny tiny sister, stillborn, how sweet! She yearned over Miranda, so soon to be haled to her feet by the inexorable Pratt. Even now he was speaking tenderly, tenderly. "Any person here lost a sister?" he said, "a dear dear sister, stand, stand up!" Heavily, without alacrity, people stood. Rose looked at Miranda. Miranda looked fondly upon her ring. Rubies and diamonds, rubies and diamonds. Oh, the little stillborn sister – forgotten – Miranda, how could you? You couldn't have heard Mr. Pratt! But indeed now the people were singing glibly, pleasantly,

> "I have a Sister in the Promised Land,
> I have a Sister in the Promised Land,
> My Sister calls me, I must go
> To meet her in the Promised Land."

Rose looked along the pew. Her whole mind besought Miranda. The little stillborn sister! But the lovely Miranda tilted her charming head with the pretty pointed chin the other way and gazed upon her ring.

Rubies and diamonds, rubies and diamonds.

After the service was over they all walked home.

Aunt Topaz, standing in front of her mirror and drawing the hatpins out of her boat-shaped hat, was frozen in her attitude by a thought. It had not occurred to her during the revival meeting that perhaps she, Topaz Edgeworth, was also a bona fide orphan, and should have done something about Mr. Pratt's appeal.

"I do declare!" she exclaimed aloud. "Father's in the Promised Land, and so's Mother and Mother Jane, and so's Mary and Joe and what a many uncles and aunts – they've been there for years, some of them – and I never thought to stand up! *Wouldn't* Father be annoyed, oh dear! Well, what a bobbing up and down that would have been, to be sure!" She laughed merrily, but she felt that she had missed an opportunity.

DOWN AT ENGLISH BAY

Once upon a time there was a negro who lived in Vancouver and his name was Joe Fortes. He lived in a small house by the beach at English Bay and there is now a little bronze plaque to his honour and memory near-by, and he taught hundreds of little boys and girls how to swim. First of all he taught them for the love of it and after that he was paid a small salary by the City Council or the Parks Board, but he taught for love just the same. And so it is that now there are Judges, and Aldermen, and Cabinet Ministers, and lawyers, and doctors, and magnates, and ordinary business men, and grand-mothers, and prostitutes, and burglars, and Sunday School superintendents, and dry-cleaners, and so on whom Joe Fortes taught to swim, and they will be the first to admit it. And Joe Fortes saved several people from drowning; some of them were worth saving and some were not worth saving in the slightest – take the man who was hanged in Kingston jail; but Joe Fortes could not be expected to know this, so he saved everyone regardless. He was greatly beloved and he was respected.

Joe Fortes was always surrounded by little boys and girls in queer bathing suits in the summer-time. The little boys' bathing suits had arms and legs not to speak of bodies and almost skirts on them; and the little girls were covered from neck to calf in blue serge or alpaca with white braid – rows of it – round the sailor collar and the full skirt, and a good pair of black wool stockings. This all helped to weigh them down when they tried to learn to swim, and to drown the little girls, in particular, when possible.

Joe had a nice round brown face and a beautiful brown body and arms and legs as he waded majestically in the waves of English Bay amongst all the little white lawyers and doctors and trained nurses and seamstresses who jumped up and down and splashed round him. "Joe," they called, and "Look at me, Joe! Is this the way?" and they splashed and swallowed and Joe supported them under their chins and by their behinds and said in his rich slow fruity voice, "Kick out, naow! Thassaway. Kick right out!" And sometimes he supported them, swimming like frogs, to the raft, and when they had clambered onto the raft they were afraid to jump off and Joe Fortes became impatient and terrible and said in a very large voice, "Jump now! I'll catch you! You jump off of that raff or I'll leave you here all night!" And that was how they learned to swim.

Rose was one of the children who learned to swim with Joe Fortes, and she was one of the cowardly ones who shivered on the raft while Joe roared, "You jump off of that raff this minute, or I'll leave you there all night!" So she jumped because the prospect was so terrible and so real, and how threatening the wet sea by night, and who knows what creatures will come to this dark raft alone. So she jumped.

Aunt Rachel did not let Rose go swimming in her good blue serge bathing costume with white braid and black wool stockings unless some grown-up was there. Aunts and guardians feel much more responsible for children than parents do, and so they are over-anxious and they age faster. Aunt Topaz was not very much good as a guardian because she did not bathe, could not swim, was irresponsible, and usually met friends on the beach with whom she entered into conversation and then forgot about Rose.

One day, however, Rose persuaded her Aunt Rachel to let her go to the beach with Aunt Topaz who was quite ready for an outing, and in any case wanted to take her bicycle for a walk. So Rose and her Great-Aunt started off down Barclay Street in very good spirits on a sunny July afternoon. Tra-la-la, how happy they were! They talked separately and together. Aunt Topaz wheeled her bicycle, which gave her a very sporting appearance, and she wore her hat which looked like a row-boat. She carried some biscuits in the string bag which was attached to the shining handle-bars of her noble English bicycle. Rose carried a huge parcel in a towel and swung it by a strap. She further complicated her walk by taking her hoop and stick. So Great-Aunt and Great-Niece proceeded down Barclay Street towards English Bay, Rose bowling her hoop whenever she felt like it.

When they arrived at English Bay Rose rushed into the bath-house with five cents, and Aunt Topaz got into conversation with a young man called Eustace Flowerdew, with whose mother she was acquainted. Eustace Flowerdew wore a stiff straw hat attached to him somewhere by a black cord, so that if in his progress along the sands the hat should blow off, it would still remain attached to the person of Eustace. He wore pince-nez which made him look very refined. His collar was so high and stiff that it hurt him, and his tie was a chaste and severe four-in-hand. He collected tie-pins which were called stick-pins. Today he wore a stick-pin with the head of a horse.

"Oh, good afternoon, Eustace," said Aunt Topaz, "how nice you do look to be sure. How is your mother what a nice horse!"

After taking off his hat and putting it on again, Eustace hitched up each of his trouser legs and sat down beside Aunt Topaz, and looked over the top of his collar. In so doing he jiggled the bicycle which was unusually heavy and was inexpertly propped against the log on which he and Aunt Topaz were sitting. The bicycle intentionally fell on them both and knocked them down. This bicycle was very ill-tempered and ingenious, and was given to doing this kind of thing when possible on purpose. Aunt Topaz lay prone, and Eustace Flowerdew crawled out and lifted the bicycle off her and led it away to a tree where it could not touch them any more. Aunt Topaz exclaimed a great deal, got up, dusted the sand off herself, and Rose was as forgotten as though she had never existed.

"What are you doing on the beach at this time of the afternoon, Eustace?" asked Aunt Topaz.

Eustace did not want to tell Aunt Topaz the truth, which was that he hoped to meet a girl called Mary Evans in whom he had become interested, so he told her a lie.

"I have come here to forget, Miss Edgeworth," he said, looking at the ocean over his collar.

"And what do you want to forget? . . . Oh, I suppose I shouldn't ask you if you want to forget it! How very interesting!"

The young man took his hat off and passed his hand over his forehead wearily. "He is good-looking, but he looks rather silly," thought Topaz.

"The fact is that I am writing a play," he said at last.

Topaz was frightfully excited. She had never before sat on a log with someone who was writing a play. Memories of

Sir Henry Irving, Ellen Terry and the Lyceum Theatre in general romped through her mind and she did not know where to begin. She bubbled a little but the young man did not seem to hear. He was still looking out to sea. How beautiful it was, beyond the cries and splashings of children who crowded round Joe Fortes. There is a serenity and a symmetry about English Bay. It is framed by two harmonious landfalls. Out stretches Point Grey sloping to the south-west. Undulations of mountain, mainland, and island come to a poetic termination on the north-west. Straight ahead to the westward sparkles the ocean as far as the dim white peaks of Vancouver Island. Sea-gulls flash and fly and cry in the wide summer air. Sitters on the beach regarded this beauty idly.

"What are you calling your play, Eustace?" asked Aunty when she had recovered.

"*Break, Break, Break,*" said the young man. "Who is this uncommonly plain little girl standing in front of us? How very wet she is!"

"That?" said Aunt Topaz, suddenly seeing Rose. "Oh, there you are. How do you do, Rose? That is my great-niece. Yes, she is plain, isn't she? When wet. When dry she looks better, because her hair curls. Now run away and enjoy yourself and make sure you don't drown. Well what is it?"

"May I get a biscuit?" asked Rose, who had come up full of rapture and talk now quenched.

"Yes, yes. Get a biscuit but be careful of the bicycle. It's against the tree."

Rose looked hatingly at Eustace Flowerdew and went over to the bicycle, dripping as she went. No sooner did she touch the heavy bicycle than it rushed violently away from her down the beach and hurled itself into the sand where it lay with its pedals quivering. Rose looked, but the two had not seen this. So she went and pulled up the bicycle and led it over to the tree again. She propped it up against the tree as best she could, dusted some of the sand off the biscuits, ate them grit and all, and ran off again to the heavenly waves and children surrounding Joe Fortes.

"What does your mother say about your writing a play? I should think she would feel very nervous. Are you introducing the sex element at all . . . illicit love, so to speak . . . or are you, if I may say so, keeping it thoroughly wholesome?" asked Topaz.

"My dear Miss Edgeworth," answered the young man pityingly, "I trust that you do not still regard Art as being in any way connected with morality!" He saw in the distance a figure that looked like Mary Evans, and his muscles were already flexing to rise. A shadow fell across Aunty and Eustace.

"Well, I do declare!" exclaimed Aunty joyously. "If this isn't Mrs. Hamilton Coffin! Mrs. Coffin, let me present to you a rising young . . ." but the rising young playwright was no longer there. He was striding away down the beach.

"Do sit down, Mrs. Coffin!" said Topaz. "This *is* nice! How very athletic you do look!" She was filled with admiration. Mrs. Coffin was tall and the black serge bathing suit which she wore did not become her. On this fine summer day Mrs. Coffin, warmly dressed for swimming, displayed no part of her body except her face and ears and her arms as far up as her elbows. "How delightful!" exclaimed Topaz sincerely.

"I have lately, Miss Edgeworth," said Mrs. Coffin, who was a serious woman, "come under the influence of Ralston's Health Foods, and so has my husband. We are making a careful study of physical health and exercise and right thinking. We eat Ralston's Health Foods and a new food called Grape Nuts" ("'Grape Nuts!' that sounds delicious!" said

Topaz) "twice a day. Already complexion is brighter, our whole mental attitude is improved, and I *may* say," she lowered her voice, "that faulty elimination is corrected."

"Faulty elimination! Well, well! Fancy that!" echoed Aunt Topaz, and wondered "What on earth is she talking about?"

"I have also made an appointment with Mr. Fortes for a swimming lesson and I hope very soon to have mastered the art. This is my third lesson."

"Never too old to learn! Never too old to learn!" said Topaz merrily but without tact. She had no intention of taking swimming lessons herself. "I will come down to the water's edge and cheer you on." "I wonder if it's her costume or her name that makes me think of the tomb," she thought cheerfully.

Mrs. Coffin and Aunt Topaz went down to the water's edge. Joe Fortes disentangled himself from the swimming, bobbing, prancing, screaming children, and came out of the ocean to speak to Mrs. Coffin. He looked very fine, beautiful brown seal that he was, with the clear sparkling water streaming off him.

Mrs. Coffin advanced into the sea, and unhesitatingly dipped herself. "How brave! How brave! Bravo!" cried Topaz form the brink, clapping. Joe Fortes discussed the motions of swimming with Mrs. Coffin, doing *so* with his arms, and then *so* with his big legs like flexible pillars, and Mrs. Coffin took the first position. Joe Fortes respectfully supported her chin with the tips of his strong brown fingers. He dexterously and modestly raised her rear, and held it raised by a bit of bathing suit. "How politely he does it!" thought Topaz, admiring Joe Fortes and Mrs. Coffin as they proceeded up and down the ocean. When Mrs. Coffin had proceeded up and down supported and exhorted by Joe Fortes for twenty minutes or so, with Topaz addressing them from the brink, she tried swimming alone. She went under several times dragged down by her bathing suit but emerged full of hope. She dressed, and came and sat with Aunt Topaz.

"I understand, Miss Edgeworth," said Mrs. Coffin, "that you are the President of the Minerva Club!"

"I! President! Oh dear no!" said Topaz laughing merrily. "Never again will I be President of anything as long as I live! I was for a year President of our Ladies' Aid, and the worry nearly killed me! I'd as soon be hanged as be President of anything – much sooner, I assure you! No, Mrs. Coffin, I am the Secretary of the Minerva Club – Honorary you understand – and Mrs. Aked, the President, promises that I can toss it up! toss it up! at any moment that I wish!"

Mrs. Coffin seemed to be about to say something further when a miserable-looking object appeared in front of them. It was Rose, blue and dripping.

"J-J-oe F-F-Fortes s-s-says that I'm b-b-b-blue and I must g-g-go home," stuttered Rose shivering. "I d-d-d-don't want to. D-D-Do I have to?"

"Oh dear me, what a sight!" said Aunt Topaz who had forgotten Rose again. "Certainly, certainly! Rush into your clothes and we'll walk home briskly and have some tea! What a delightful afternoon!"

On the way home the two pushed their impedimenta. Rose took the superfluous hoop, and Aunt Topaz wheeled her bicycle. The bicycle kicked her with its large protruding pedals as often as possible, and became entangled in her long skirt from time to time, so she often had to stop. When she was disentangled they went on. The bicycle bided its time, and then it kicked her again. Their minds were full of their own affairs, of which they talked regardless.

"A very silly young man, I'm afraid, but he may grow out of it. It is possible, however, that he has talent. . . ."

"I swam six strokes alone. I swam six strokes alone . . ."

"I'm sure Mrs. Hamilton Coffin deserves a great deal of credit at her age. . . ."

"Joe Fortes says that if I can just master the . . ."

"But what she meant by 'faulty elimination' I cannot imagine. It may have something to do with the Mosaic Law. . . ."

"Joe Fortes can swim across English Bay easy-weasy. A big boy said that Joe Fortes could swim across the English Channel easy-weasy . . ."

"I do wish you'd stop saying 'easy-weasy' . . . oh . . ." The bicycle, behaving coarsely, swerved, turned, and tried to run Aunt Topaz down.

"And Geraldine has been swimming longer than me and she can't swim as good as me. . . ."

"As well as I. 'Grape Nuts' sound delicious! A combination of grapes and nuts no doubt. . . ."

This kind of conversation went on all the way home, and after they reached home too, until Rose went to bed. It was plain to Rachel and her mother that Aunty and Rose had enjoyed going down to English Bay, and Rachel was greatly relieved that Rose had not been drowned.

On the next afternoon Aunt Topaz prepared to go to the meeting of the Minerva Club. She dressed very prettily, and wore a feather boa. Her success in dress was a matter of luck rather than taste, but today she looked uncommonly well. "How nice you look, Anty!" said Rachel admiringly. Aunty was very happy. She pranced up Barclay Street, carrying her Minutes of the previous meeting – which were brief – in her hand.

There were nine ladies gathered at Mrs. Aked's house for

the meeting of the Minerva Club. Tap, tap went Mrs. Aked on a little table. "We will now call the meeting to order, and our Honorary Secretary will read the Minutes of the previous meeting – Miss Edgeworth."

Everybody admired the experience and aplomb of Mrs. Aked.

Topaz arose and smiled at the ladies. Nine of them. When it came to reading aloud, even Minutes, she enjoyed herself thoroughly. But if she had to utter a single impromptu word in public, on her feet, she suffered more than tongue could tell. Therefore she was careful never to place herself in a position where she might have to make a speech. Considering that she had spent her whole life in speaking, this was strange. But human beings are very strange, and there you are.

Topaz reported, smiling over her Minutes, that at the previous meeting the Minerva Club had listened to a paper on Robert Browning and that selections from that great man's less obscure poems had been read aloud. It had been decided that today's meeting should include a brief comprehensive paper on "Poets of the Elizabethan Era" by Mrs. Howard Henchcliffe who certainly had her work cut out, and that selections from the verses of Elizabethan poets would be read by Mrs. Isaacs, Mrs. Simpson, and – modestly – Miss Edgeworth. Then Aunt Topaz sat down. How she enjoyed this!

"Any business, ladies?" enquired Mrs. Aked. "Ah, yes, one vacancy in the Club. The name of Mrs. Hamilton Coffin is up for election. Any discussion before we vote Mrs. Hamilton Coffin into the Club? I think not."

But a rather pudding-faced lady raised a tentative hand. She cleared her throat. "Pardon *me*," she said. "I hope we are all friends here, and that discussion may be without prejudice?"

Mrs. Aked nodded, and the ladies murmured and rustled and adjusted their boas.

"Before voting on the name of Mrs. Hamilton Coffin," said the pudding-faced lady, "may I remind ladies present that the reputation of our members has always been beyond reproach?"

"I'm sure Mrs. Hamilton Coffin . . ." began a small lady with sparkling eyes, in outraged tones. "Whatever can this be?" wondered Topaz.

The pudding-faced lady again held up her hand.

"Pardon *me*," she said, "I have nothing at all to say against the personal reputation of Mrs. Hamilton Coffin. But *do* the Ladies of the Minerva Club know that Mrs. Hamilton Coffin has been seen more than once in a public place, bathing in the arms of a black man?"

A rustle of indignation ran through the room, whether at the pudding-faced lady or at Mrs. Hamilton Coffin it was impossible to say.

Suddenly in that inward part of her that Topaz had not known to exist, arose a fury. She who did not know of the existence of private life because she had no private life of her own, she who feared so greatly to speak in public, she who was never roused to anger, rose to her feet, trembling and angry. She was angry for Joe Fortes; and for Mrs. Hamilton Coffin; and for herself, a spectator on that innocent blue day. She was aware of something evil and stupid in the room.

"Ladies," she said, shaking, "I shall now count ten because I think I shall then be better able to say what I want to say and because I am very frightened. Excuse me just a minute." And Topaz was silent, and they could see her counting ten. All the ladies waited; emotions were held in check. Then the plain and interesting face of Topaz lighted with its usual friendly smile.

"Ladies," she said, "I was present yesterday when that admirable woman Mrs. Hamilton Coffin had her swimming lesson from our respected fellow-citizen Joe Fortes. I know that the lady who has just spoken," and Aunty smiled winningly upon the pudding-faced lady, "will be quite properly relieved to hear that so far from swimming in the arms of Mr. Fortes, which any of us who were drowning would be grateful to do, Mrs. Hamilton Coffin was swimming in his finger-tips. I feel that we should be honoured to have as a fellow-member so active, progressive, and irreproachable a lady as Mrs. Hamilton Coffin. I therefore beg to propose the name of Mrs. Hamilton Coffin as the tenth member of the Minerva Club." And she sat down scarlet-cheeked, shaking violently.

"Hear-hear, hear-hear," said all the ladies – including the pudding-faced lady – with one accord and very loud, clapping. "Order, order," cried the President, enjoying herself immensely. "I hereby declare Mrs. Hamilton Coffin a member of the Minerva Club, and I instruct our Honorary Secretary to write a letter of invitation. I will now call upon Miss Topaz Edgeworth to read the introductory selection from one of the poets of the Elizabethan Era."

The ladies slipped back their boas and emitted releasing breaths of warm air (the room had become close), adjusted their positions, and adopted postures suitable to those about to listen to the poets.

Aunt Topaz stood and read. This was her great day. How beautifully she read! Her chattering tones were modulated and musical. The training of the classical Mrs. Porter had made Aunty a reader in the classical style. She was correct, deliberate, flowing, unemotional, natural. She was very happy, reading aloud slowly to the Minerva Club. She read clearly –

"Even such is Time, that takes in trust
Our youth, our joys, our all we have,
And pays us but with earth and dust;
Who, in the dark and silent grave,
When we have wandered all our ways,
Shuts up the story of our days.
But from this earth, this grave, this dust,
My God shall raise me up, I trust."

Everybody clapped.

Aunty went home disturbed and happy; and that evening she told her sister and Rachel about the meeting, and her indignation rose and fell and was satisfied. She told it several times.

The Grandmother said, "I am glad you spoke as you did, my dear sister. You were right."

Rachel put down her work. She thought, "How often I am angry with Aunty! How often I scold her! She *is* aggravating, but just see this!" Rachel looked across at Aunt Topaz with eyes at once sombre and bright that were Rachel's only beauty. "Yes, Anty," she said, "that's true. I have never heard you say an unkind thing about anyone. I have never heard you cast an aspersion on anyone. I really believe that you are one of the few people who think no evil."

Aunty *was* amazed! Rachel, who seldom praised, had praised her. She – Topaz – who was never humble and embarrassed became humble and embarrassed. What could she say. "I think," she said, "that I will go to bed. I will take the newspaper." And she stumbled upstairs in her hasty way.

Above, in her bedroom, they heard her singing in that funny little flute voice of hers.

CHRISTMAS EVE

When Frank and Stephen were married and living in their own homes near by with their wives ("Yes, charming charming girls, Canadians, born in this country!" which seemed to establish the whole family as finally and indisputably Canadian), the Grandmother, Topaz, Rachel, Andrew, and Rose moved to a smaller and peculiar house. Andrew was now the man of the house; but as he went before long to live in Montreal where he established connections for the firm, Rachel herself became and remained the man of the house. At the time of his marriage, Andrew returned again to Vancouver, and the family branched out again. Thereafter it continued to branch, and the history of families like the Hastings family is to some extent the history of the city of Vancouver, but it will not be written for a long time.

The house in which the Grandmother now lived had a bastard architectural excrescence at its corner which resembled both a Norman turret and a pepper-pot but was neither. Houses with assertive pepper-pots may still be seen in the older sections of Canadian cities, and date from aspirations held in the eighteen-nineties. Although from the outside the pepper-pot was a nasty bit of work, from the inside it provided many windows and much light, and a pleasant more than semicircular window-seat in the Grandmother's bedroom. This window-seat was the perfect place for a household of women to gather in, and read their letters to each other, drink tea, sew, mend, and turn sheets sides-to-middles. And below the Grandmother's bedroom was a similar curve and a similar window, which changed an uninteresting small square drawing-room to a room of considerable charm, in which, on the first and third Tuesdays, the Grandmother's At Home days were prinked out.

This was now a household of women in which the usual filaments of pull and push, understanding and failing to understand, love and forbearance grew, and grew stronger than hawsers, binding the four together and pushing them apart. But their faces often turned outwards too, and the ties which bound them to their old home held steady. The Grandmother wrote industriously in her delicate hand to her sons in England – Lancelot, Samuel, and George – and to their wives, and their children, and to Rose's paternal relatives to whom she felt responsibility. Rose's letter-writing was negligible. Topaz wrote furiously and continuously. She and her surviving correspondents were the kind who upon receipt of a letter sit down in short order and write a voluminous answer, and thus drive dilatory correspondents mad. They belonged to the dwindling generation of letter-writers. So in the curved upper window of the pepper-pot, Aunty triumphantly read aloud letters from Mme Roux in Grenoble, old Signora Castellani in Rome, Mr. Heaton (a widower) in Ware, Miss Pocock, and also Miss Peacock, the never-yet-seen but ageing and indistinguishable twins Tilly-and-Sassy in India (the babies of Mary), Brother Blakey in Australia, Brothers George and John in England and their wives, and several assorted ladies throughout Canada.

When Brother John and Topaz had both lived in Ware, John had tried to sneap Topaz whenever he thought it good for her, which was often. But now that six thousand miles separated them, John's letters flew with a lover's frequency, and Aunty in the pepper-pot happily read to the others of John's encounters with Members of the House of Commons and the House of Lords, with the Lord-Lieutenant of the County, and other Great Ones, his roarings against the present policy of the Government, pious memories of Mr. Gladstone, news of his cold and of his wife's cold, and of their visitors of whom they had a great many.

Rachel disliked writing letters and so she wrote none. At Christmas-time, duty made her send a few non-committal cards. In any case she was far too busy.

Those were days of agreeable simplicity in Vancouver. Since then we have learned to wrap our Christmas parcels in coloured and decorated papers, have tied them with prodigal tinsels, have adorned them with stickers, stars, and bells, and have outwitted ourselves in the enfolding of lingerie, decanters, and face powders. But we remember a time when we wore not lingerie but underclothes, when reputable noses went bare, when we offered not decanters but bedroom slippers, as again we do. Then people wrapped their parcels neatly in brown paper, and tied them with good string.

Rose returned home with a rush, after delivering most of the tidy and identifiable parcels at the homes of Uncle Frank and Uncle Stephen. At each house there was a baby or two, and at each house there were gay greetings and rushings about and the delicious mounting excitement of Christmas Eve. But the treat of the day lay ahead. Every Christmas Eve Aunt

Rachel and Rose had their own special and peculiar celebration. After the hall and downstairs rooms had been decorated with greenery, and the last carefully observed preparations for the large family Christmas Day gathering had been made; after the Grandmother had been escorted to her rest, behind drawn window blinds; after the Grandmother had been awakened and helped to dress for the evening; after the completion of a multitude of details of which Rachel alone knew the meaning and necessity, she – Rachel – was ready.

Evening had come, and with it a light pretty snowfall. When Rachel stepped out into the dark exciting air with Rose, and closed the house door, she shut the door on a small, warm, and well-conducted world which she had created and which she maintained. Grannie, the admired and titular head of the house, was now really the child of her daughter Rachel. It was Rachel who, with a selfless filial piety, and sometimes with sharp admonishings, was still her mother's proud servant. It was Rachel who was the only subduer of the effervescent Aunt Topaz. It was Rachel who had cared for her younger unmarried brother Andrew. It was Rachel who looked after her orphaned niece Rose, and made her hair shine, and disciplined her, and loved her. It was Rachel who controlled the wily and violent Chinese cook, Yow. And it was Rachel who was regarded by the family as the responsible person in her wonted place. And for what reward did Rachel spend her days? For no reward other than the fulfilment of her own fierce integrity and sense of order, and the confidence and placid affection of her family.

Rachel and the young Rose walked arm in arm down the snowy sidewalk, and waited at the street corner for the tram. They would have walked to town, but that their planned and joyous occupation when they reached town was to be the peculiar one of twice walking slowly the length of Hastings Street, from Granville Street to below Cambie Street and back. Rachel was already tired, and so they took the tram.

When they jumped off the tram at the corner of Granville and Hastings Streets, and began walking, there was the stirring feeling of something shared and gay in the air. Snow sparkled on the roofs of the small shops. The streets and the shops were bright, and the people walking slowly on Hastings Street in twos and threes with no regard for right or left, laughed, talked, and gave themselves up to the pleasure of Christmas Eve in a random strolling fashion. On this respectable street there was no noisy behaviour and no drunkenness. Families and friends walked happily, just as Rachel and Rose also walked. It is true that on near-by Cordova Street, when Rose accompanied her aunt on Saturday morning shoppings, she sometimes saw glorious ladies dressed in fashionable black, who sauntered, often in pairs. These ladies were beautiful. They did not shop. They sauntered lazily with a swaying of opulent hips and bosom, looking softly yet alertly from lustrous eyes set in masks of rose and white. "Aunt Rachel, Aunt Rachel, *look* at those pretty ladies, who are they, just look!" Rose had sometimes whispered. But Aunt Rachel did not look. She behaved as if she were blind and deaf. It appeared that she did not know the pretty ladies at all. The town was small, and Aunt Rachel knew everybody, at least by sight, so this struck Rose as queer. But tonight, on Christmas Eve, these ladies were not to be seen. Only the families strolled and talked and laughed and gazed at the shops along Hastings Street. Well, that is all that Rachel and Rose did too. And then they got on the tram and went home again. Even the tram was full of Christmas.

Aunt Topaz was impatient for them. She had just helped

the Grandmother to bed, and was in the kitchen munching. "Well, who did you see?" she enquired eagerly.

"Anty, what *are* you eating?" asked Rachel as she set about making some cocoa for them all.

"Oh, just a bitta cheese and some mustard pickle," said Aunty airily.

"It's a marvel to me that you don't have nightmares," said Rachel, measuring the cocoa.

"Well, I don't have nightmares, and that's a fact," said Aunty. "A little gas sometimes perhaps, but no nightmares," laughing and patting her diaphragm elegantly with her spread fingers and continuing to eat pickles and cheese. Aunty had the gift of belching delicately, when and where and as often as she chose. She enjoyed this. It amused her. Rachel was not amused when Aunty belched, because the example was bad for Rose, who thought it funny.

Over and through the small things of home flowed the excitement that was Christmas Eve. In a gust of secrecy and love Rose kissed her aunts good-night. She took Grannie her cocoa, and sat carefully on the edge of Grannie's feather bed. As she talked to the Grandmother, Christmas hung and glittered in the air, just as if the slow walk along Hastings Street had been a festival, just as if the parcels lay wrapped in silver. Tomorrow is Christmas Christmas Christmas! She went to bed.

When Rachel came upstairs, long after the lively Aunt Topaz had proceeded with ejaculations up the stairs to her room, the Grandmother called sleepily, "Is that you, Rachel? Tuck me feet up, love," and Rachel reached in her capable and accustomed hands under the bedclothes and wrapped a shawl around the Matriarch's tiny feet. "Now go to bed, love, do." "Good-night, Mother."

Rachel lay tiredly awake for a time, and then turned her face into the pillow and slept. She was the daughter, the maiden. Never having known the lights and music of marriage, never having known the joy and care of being a mother, she was yet the wife and mother of her household. She was to this home as the good bread upon the table, as the steadfast light upon the stair.

FAMILY PRAYER

One day Rachel walked up to her mother who was sitting in the pepper-pot window of her bedroom mending some lace, and said in a tone of grave announcement, "Yow is going to China."

Her mother looked up dismayed and said, "Yow going to *China*? Why?"

"Because," Rachel said, "he is going to have a baby. In three months."

"But, my dear Rachel, that is impossible. Yow cannot possibly . . ."

"I know, I know," said Rachel irritably because she had just had a scene with Yow. "Just the same he is going to China for the purpose of having a baby. He will live with his wife for three months, and at the end of that time he assures me that he – or I suppose she – will . . . will . . ."

"Of course. I understand," said her mother who did not think it was nice of Yow to have discussed with her daughter the probabilities and mechanics of his having a baby. "But if Yow has a baby, I think we should invite him to bring it here, and then it would be a little Christian."

"What's this, what's this?" exclaimed Aunt Topaz coming hastily into the bedroom. "Yow having a baby! Well, what next! What a surprise, to be sure!"

"Hush," said Rachel, "here's Rose coming!" But Rose was already there, and the sealed faces of her three elders added another mystery to her expanding but muddled mind.

Down in the kitchen Yow and a thin Chinese friend sat on two chairs opposite each other at the kitchen table and kept up a rapid Chinese conversation in the Cantonese dialect. The door opened with a rush and Topaz bounced in.

"Well, Yow, what's this I hear! How do you do, how do you do!" to the second Chinaman who showed that he knew how to behave in a white house by standing up and taking off his round hat. He was neatly dressed but much smaller and thinner than Yow. His queue was not bound around his head for working purposes as Yow's was, but hung down in a neat plait which was augmented and lengthened by a twist of green cotton, so as to reach up and be hooked invisibly under his right arm. Yow did not stand up, because he enjoyed being ill-mannered.

"And is this a friend of yours, Yow?" enquired Aunt Topaz gracefully.

"No. He not my friend. He my kah-san," said Yow rather sullenly.

"But how can he be your cousin and not be your friend? I should think . . . at least in *our* family, cousins are closer even than friends!" This was true.

Yow proceeded to be rude. "Canadian people no savee nothing. China people more different. Last February China New Year my family have large party seven hundred people. All my kah-san. All my generation. You no care. You not ask all your famuly. I not hear you go telephone seven hundred people, all your generation. You not know all your generation. You not care. I care. I know all my generation. I all same Queen Victoria."

For a moment Aunt Topaz could not answer, because she was trying to discover any likeness between Yow and Queen Victoria.

"Queen Victoria he know he generation eight hundred year," continued Yow, while the other Chinaman remained impassive, standing. "Queen Victoria generation King in England eight hundred year. My generation King in China eight hundred year." "I think he means 'relations,' not 'generations,'" explained Rose who had joined her Great-Aunt in the kitchen doorway.

An idea had blossomed in the mind of Topaz. She forgot all about her intended enquiries about Yow's absence, his baby, and his successor, and turned. She hastily climbed the stairs and entered the room with the pepper-pot, taking a good deal of breeze in with her.

"Yow says he is like Queen Victoria," she announced.

"Now *that* is *quite* impossible," said the Grandmother, smiling at all these careless statements flying about. Rachel stopped her dusting, and listened.

"No. It is credible,"' said Aunt Topaz. "And he has given me a very good idea, with which I hope, Rachel, that you will agree and co-operate." Rachel looked at her Aunt, but was already set to disagree with any idea born under these auspices.

"He says," continued Aunty, "that his ancestors were kings in China at the same time that Queen Victoria's ancestors were kings in England. He seems to set a great deal of store by family, and I'm sure I for one don't blame him. He says that last Chinese New Year his family – or clan, I suppose – anyway all his cousins had a party of seven hundred people in Chinatown. He seems to think very badly of us because we don't do the same kind of thing."

"Well, he can think badly of us for all I care. I'm not going to ask seven hundred people to this house in order to keep Yow's good opinion, I'm sure," said Rachel, "and I'm telling you now."

"Wait, wait," implored Aunty. "Can't you wait! In this new country it is very important that we should not lose track of family history. Tradition tends to die." Rachel went on dusting.

"My suggestion is this. I have reason to believe that my ancestors came over with William the Conqueror" ("What about mine, then, I'm your niece," said Rachel.) "and I'm sure, Annie, that the same must be true of the Hastings family. It stands to reason! Look at the name! I shall write to *The Times*. I shall ask all those who can trace their descent from the Norman Knights who came over with William the Conqueror" ("How can they tell? They might have been kitchen boys," said Rachel.) "to have a meeting. We could call it a rally. We could meet on the beach at Hastings, or in Normandy, or even here! I shall certainly write to *The Times*!"

"And I shall certainly leave home if you do!" said Rachel vehemently. Her dark eyes flashed. This was too much in one morning.

"I think I'd wait a little, love," said the Grandmother gently. "Why not try to substantiate your own claim first? That would be very interesting, I'm sure. You could write to the Staffordshire Archives and you might get some splendid information about the family."

"Yes, and she might get some information she wouldn't like," said Rachel, shutting a drawer with a bang.

While this conversation continued upstairs in the room with the pepper-pot, the Chinese conversation went on in the kitchen. Yow was smoking a very stinking small cigar. He only did this to show off, as he was not supposed to smoke in the kitchen. Translated into simple pidgin, the Chinese conversation went something like this.

"All right. I give you this job for three month. You give me ten procent wages," said Yow.

The small thin Chinaman, whose name was Fooey, blinked his mild eyes behind his steel-rimmed spectacles.

"I give you five procent."

"You give me ten procent."

"Lady Fowkes down by Stanley Parks like me go cook for her. She give me forty-five dollars a month. No procent."

"You lie. I know Lady Fowkes. I know her cook. He heap smart. Lady Fowkes pay fifty-five dollars a month. Six children. Three housemaid nurse. Three breakfast. Three lunch. Afternoon tea with sandwich and hot biscuit and small cake. Three dinner. You no can do. You very small. You very thin. You not strong. You all time cough. I think pretty soon you die."

Fooey sat respectful and silent. All this was true.

"You come here," said Yow wheedling a little. "This very easy job. Not much cooking. Bossee lady" (this was Rachel) "heap stingy. All the time milk pudding. Very easy. Dinner very oily" (early). "Dinner Lady Fowkes half-past seven. All time wash dish Lady Fowkes' house."

"What time dinner here?" asked Fooey.

"They say dinner half-past six. I say dinner six. I make dinner six. They no like. I no care. You get out oily. Every night I go Chinatown play fan-tan. Sunday I go two o'clock go Lung Duck play fan-tan all day all night."

"Lung Duck tell my kah-san you lose plenty money."

"He lie. Sometime I lose twenty-five cent. Sometime I win one two dollar. He crazy."

Fooey thought for a minute. "All right," he said, "I take this job three month while you go China get baby."

"Ten procent?"

"Ten procent."

Something else occurred to Yow.

"Listen," he said, "you care for old Mrs. Hastings. She good. She all same God. You care for her like she your sister." Yow was too proud to say that he loved the Grandmother. Just the same he loved her beyond anyone; far more than he loved his wife or his mother. "Two times every day you go Famuly Prayer."

"I not know what you call Famuly Prayer," objected Fooey.

"Old Mrs. Hastings heap like talk to Jesus Christ," said Yow, only Yow said "Jee Kly." "After breakfast she talkem Jee Kly. After dinner she likee talk Jee Kly."

"Why she all the time talk Jee Kly? What she say?" asked Fooey.

"I not know what she say," said Yow crossly, putting out his stinking cigar. "I no care. You no ask. After breakfast she tell you come. You come."

"What I do?" enquired Fooey.

"You look see. Very easy. After dinner you go Famuly Prayer too."

"How long time Famuly Prayer?" asked Fooey dubiously.

"Maybe five minute. Maybe seven minute. Not long."

"All right. I go Famuly Prayer,'" said Fooey. He slipped fifty cents to Yow for letting him have the job, and the bargain was sealed. Yow was well pleased. Fooey was not strong and could not aspire to a difficult or expert job, and he was so poor a cook that Rachel would not want to keep him when Yow returned. Everything, then, was right; Yow would go to China for three months and do his best to have a baby, and would return to Mrs. Hastings to this comfortable billet which was only a side-line to his game of fan-tan.

The family had now descended to the sitting-room. Yow went in, followed by the mild thin Fooey, hat in hand. Yow led Fooey up to the Grandmother.

"Missee Hasting. This Fooey. He my kah-san. He very good cook. He likee work for you. I tell him be good boy. I show him everything. He care for you. He likee Famuly Prayer. He not usem much cream. He heap stinge."

Thus introduced and qualified, Fooey bowed, and the Grandmother looked up at him confidingly, sensitively, kindly, and he knew and trusted her.

"I hope you will be happy here, Fooey," she said. "Yow is *so* good, *so* kind." (The Grandmother really believed this, and perhaps he was.) "We shall miss him very much, but I know you will look after us."

Fooey was very much surprised to learn that anyone thought that Yow was good and kind; but as the two races had always to understand or believe in each other across a great area of fog-like confusion and misconception, he was prepared to try to believe anything at all.

"Well, he looks very thin, I'm sure," said Aunt Topaz.

"He welly strong. He more strong than me," said Yow and swaggered out of the room with Fooey following submissively.

Only a day or two after Yow left, the imitative Fooey was performing all Yow's duties in such a way that hardly any change could be observed in the conduct of the house. This was what Rachel, who was conservative, desired; and this was what Yow, who was conservatism itself, would have desired too. There was the added advantage to Yow that although the atmosphere of the house in general was more peaceful, Fooey's cooking was tasteless, and his cough was incessant; otherwise Rachel would have preferred to keep Fooey.

Time passed peacefully enough, with friends and family coming and going, and the At Home day on the first and third Tuesdays; but always there is something ahead, isn't there. And now the family looked forward to the visit to Vancouver of the eminent Dr. Carboy.

Dr. Carboy was the President of the Methodist Conference, and he came from Toronto. Both these attributes elevated him in the estimation of the Grandmother, and her estimation of him spread downwards through the family, until at last Dr. Carboy's psychic presence preceded him and hovered all over the house. His name was constantly on the tongue of Aunt Topaz. Dr. Carboy was asked to dinner. Dr. Carboy, by letter, accepted. He accepted gladly, because of the goodness and fame of the Grandmother, who was indeed a Mother in Israel, and because the Grandmother had given a home to a young nephew of his during the previous winter and Dr. Carboy was grateful.

"I shall be very glad indeed to accept your gracious hospitality, dear Mrs. Hastings," wrote Dr. Carboy. "Dr. Fensom, the Executive Secretary, thanks you for your inclusion of him in your kind invitation to dinner, but will, on that occasion, visit his mother-in-law, who is very aged and resides in Vancouver. He deeply regrets . . ."

"Well, well. 'Gracious hospitality!' Very nice, I'm sure," said Aunt Topaz, and proceeded to talk of Dr. Carboy every day until her niece Rachel nearly went out of her mind.

The Grandmother's hospitality forever outran her means. Her table – simple enough to excite the scorn of Yow – was always ready to receive the guest without a real home; and in this small seaport town, where transient travellers came and went, many visitors having a tenuous connection with the Grandmother's long life in England were made welcome. And on Sunday afternoons came the Boys and their own young families. Poor Fooey! Yow could manage all this small hospitality with ease and disdain; but poor coughing Fooey could hardly keep up, and so it was that Rachel and her mother decided that Dr. Carboy should come alone, and there should be no dinner-party. Just Dr. Carboy.

How nice Dr. Carboy was! A small pleasant stubby old man who made you feel at home at once. They had been warned that Dr. Carboy, coming from Toronto which had a peculiar and unfair fame, might show a little cultural and spiritual "side." But no, there was none.

As long as the volatile Topaz would permit it, the Grandmother and Dr. Carboy talked the same spiritual language, though in a different dialect. The Grandmother's was the dialect of the soul; the minister's was the dialect of the executive officer of the Church, dry and succinct; but they comprehended one another, and would have communed long together if Topaz had not been on hand to show Dr. Carboy her photograph album, where relatives appeared serious or with dehydrated smiles, and her birthday-book, which by this time was of unusual interest because it contained the autographs of several suicides.

During dinner the supersensitive Rachel was aware, and so was the young Rose, that, although Aunt Topaz was very amusing, and kept Dr. Carboy in a dry crackle of laughter, she overstepped a good deal. But they could do nothing about it. And so, when the time came for Family Prayer, Rachel welcomed the imposed silence.

The Grandmother, so small that her granddaughter had begun to overtop her, moved with her accustomed gentle stateliness to her accustomed place. Dr. Carboy was ushered to the large easy-chair on which Great-Aunt Topaz usually knelt at prayer-time. ("*Why* do you have to be different, Anty?" Rachel used to say. "*Why* do you have to kneel on an easy-chair when everybody else kneels on the floor?" "I have a perfect right to kneel upon a chair. Do you suppose that your posture is the only one acceptable to the Lord? Mohammedans put their heads on the floor and Quakers stand up, and if the Lord doesn't mind, why should you? Anyway, it's because of mice." "*Mice!!* What a . . ." "Now, now, love. What does it matter where Aunty kneels, as long as she prays from a full heart?") So tonight Topaz was dislodged from her big chair and had to sit and kneel like other people.

What is it, Oh God of Love and Battles, that you have given to the saints of the earth and that you have withheld from the earth-bound of the earth? Dr. Carboy read from the Word. The Grandmother leaned forward. Her soft eyes were upon him. She listened with her ears and with her soft eyes and with her luminous countenance and with the other-worldliness and selflessness and consecration that made her a saint, as if she had never heard the familiar holy words before. Her earth-bound granddaughter Rose, who was young but alert, would have been quick to detect the least scent of hypocrisy or of self-awareness in her Grandmother. There was none. Rose marvelled. She could not enter, but she marvelled. (She thought, "It must be a gift like music. It must be a special gift of religion that other people haven't got. Aunt Rachel has it a lot, but not like Grannie. Aunt Topaz hasn't got it at all. And I? No, I haven't got it.") When Dr. Carboy ceased reading and closed the Book, they all got up, turned round, knelt down, folded their hands, closed their eyes, and Dr. Carboy began to pray.

"We thank Thee, oh Lord," he prayed. "We thank Thee for . . ." and Dr. Carboy thanked the Lord for twenty-five different things. He then prayed for Country, King, Church, Heathen, Family – both the Grandmother's and his own – using a perfected formula for each petition.

("It's very hard for him," thought Rose as she knelt, watching him with bright eyes, "to find anything fresh to say, isn't it. But he seems to mean it. I wonder how they made the pattern in the back of this little cane chair." She poked. "The cane goes in here and out here and the other piece goes out there and in here. I like this little chair. I wonder if it's ebony. No, there's some paint off here. Do they paint ebony? Gild the lily and refine the what. Oh, look at Dr. Carboy's beard going up and down. He's praying for *us* now. I must pay attention." And she shut her eyes very tight.)

("Oh God," prayed Rachel, "enable me to keep my temper with Anty. Enable me to bring Rose up properly, and give me a gift of true goodness and make me worthy. That joint was far too big. We'll have it cold tomorrow, and Italian Delight – or Cecil – on Friday if it keeps this weather. If Yow had only been here we could have had Frank and Miranda and the Johnsons and little Percy Beardmore in to eat it up. I think Fooey has consumption. If he has, what had I better do? What am I thinking of? Oh, my God, I am no better than a heathen with wandering thoughts." And she pressed her hands over her eyes and listened to Dr. Carboy. Italian Delight – made with minced ends of meat, and tomatoes, and the macaroni that was supposed to delight Italians, and a baked meatloaf with the surprising name of Cecil, were the final states of any joint entering the Hastings home. Rachel often had to banish the cares of housekeeping from her prayers. It was one of her "besetting sins"; so – "Save me," she prayed, "from my besetting sins.")

("Carboy, Carboy," thought Topaz. "I forgot to ask him if he could be any relative of that old Mr. Carboy that Father did business with. He used to wear a square hat. A most unusual name. Irish?" She looked at Dr. Carboy. "He doesn't look Irish. No brogue. I would call that an Ontario accent myself, but it's all the same in the sight – or sound I should say – of God, no doubt. It's very difficult, I must say, to keep one's mind intent during a long prayer. I feel quite sure that God – who made us and not we ourselves when all's said and done – will quite understand. Ah, the *Rubaiyat*! Beautiful and so true!

'Oh Thou who didst with pitfall and with gin
　　Beset the path I was to wander in,
　　Thou wouldst not with whatever is it
Enmesh me and impute my Fall to Sin.'

I quite agree. Oh, look, grapes! I didn't see that fine bunch of grapes! Rachel must have hidden it. I *would* like a grape!")

("Our Dear Heavenly Father," breathed the Grandmother, "Thou hearest this good man Thy servant. Pour down Thy Blessing upon Thy children gathered here and upon all Thy poor children gathered everywhere. Give us all a sense of the close reality of Thy Presence. Draw us near to Thee. Purify us. Yes, indeed we thank Thee, dear Father, in the Name of Thy Beloved Son." And the Grandmother listened to the prayer of Dr. Carboy, and her communion spread like a natural radiance straight to God, either in that room or wherever He might be. Posture of body did not change her heart. When she stood up or walked she was as close to God as when she sat or kneeled or lay down.)

The Chinaman Fooey knelt with his head bowed, eyes squeezed tight shut, and his thin hands knitted together, thinking in Chinese of God knows what.

When Dr. Carboy's voice fell, and ceased, all those kneeling except Fooey collected themselves and joined reverently in the sublime words of the Lord's Prayer. A short pause, and they rose. Fooey departed. Rose took away the Bible. Dr. Carboy stood still. He seemed to be thinking. The Grandmother, still looking through a mist, sat down.

"Ah! A grape!" exclaimed Topaz, darting. She went through the half-closed sliding doors into the dining-room, and returned with the best Spode comport laden with green and purple grapes, peaches, and pears. Rachel looked desperately at her – this fruit was destined for later in the evening – and then she fetched plates and fruit-knives and forks.

"Let me show you how to eat a grape, Dr. Carboy," said Topaz merrily. "You impale it – so! – on the fork. You lift the skin a little, and – you see – off it comes! Then you cut the grape in half – out pop the seeds! – and you eat it. Delicious! Delicious!"

"Thank you, Miss Edgeworth," said Dr. Carboy in his deliberate dry and rather grating voice, "I can handle this prahposition myself." And he swallowed down the grapes one at a time, stems, skins, seeds and all. Rose laughed so hard that she had to be sent out of the room.

About a month later Yow returned and said he had had a good time.

"And what about the baby?" enquired Great-Aunt Topaz with gay interest.

Yow shot her a dark look and went into the kitchen and made banging noises. Rachel began to talk. "Anty, you are outrageous!" she said.

Every few weeks whenever the thought happened to enter her mind, Aunty nevertheless enquired of Yow if there was any word of the approaching baby. After some months Yow announced that his wife had given birth to twin boys. Topaz congratulated him warmly and gave him two dollars each to send to the babies. Rachel and Rose, however, believed that Yow had made it up. There did not seem to be the right ring about his announcement. They felt quite sorry for him, because he had done the best he could.

The family settled down into its place once more. They settled down to one At Home day a month instead of two. They were busy people now. Yow jockeyed them into early dinner again, but always came in to Family Prayer. Family Prayer continued as a loving reality to the Grandmother, and as a "very good thing" and an accustomed order to Topaz and Rachel. Rose was inclined to dodge Family Prayer. She did not care for it, except for her Grandmother's sake, and yet in after life she affectionately treasured the memory and the sincerity of the communion. It all seemed to centre in and radiate from her Grandmother.

THE INNUMERABLE LAUGHTER

W hat a lovely morning! Oh, look, there's a bird!"
said Aunt Topaz as she hastened down the steps
from the verandah of the small summer cabin
which her nephews had caused to be built upon the high rocky
shores of Benbow Island. "And the sea, oh, look!" she said to
no one in particular, for there was no one there. "'The many-
twinkling smile of ocean!' 'The innumerable laughter of the
sea!' Just like the Greeks I do declare! I wouldn't be at all surprised! Who would think that this is the Pacific Ocean! Much
the same rocky . . . What is that? Voices? Voices? Who *can* it
be?" and she quickened her steps towards the rock which over-
looked the lonely bay.

Aunt Topaz, hurrying forwards, reached the rock and
looked down. "Well!" she said.

On the smooth expanse of the little bay below her
floated two small yachts, and in the bay, swimming about
with lusty and happy shouts, were several young men with
nothing on.

"Well I never!" exclaimed Aunt Topaz, bending down
so as to see better. "Nothing on! Very pleasant, I'm sure! Oh,

can that be Mr. Morland? Good-morning, Mr. Morland, goodmorning! And *can* that be that nice young man in the Bank? I do believe it is!" said Aunty, delighted to recognize two young men of her acquaintance so far from home, even though they had nothing on.

At the sight of Aunty who smiled and called and waved the handkerchief which she had rummaged from the front of her blouse, Mr. Morland and the nice young man in the Bank uttered warning cries. All the swimmers immediately turned face downwards and swam about, vainly trying to escape from the orbit of Aunty's vision. Aunty now saw nothing but posteriors swimming vainly away.

"Oh," said Aunty, vexed, "if only they'd turn right side up, I'd be able to see if it really *is* Mr. Morland! I *must* tell Rachel!"

Aunt Topaz, who was a great imparter of news, turned and went back at top speed to the cottage, where she saw her niece Rachel standing in the doorway.

"Rachel, Rachel, what *do* you suppose," she cried, "there are nine young men swimming about the bay with nothing on, and I do believe that one is Andrew's friend Mr. Morland, and I *do* believe that one of them is that nice young man in the Bank! If they would only turn right side up I might be able to see! I called and called but they did not reply!"

"What does it matter if it *is* Mr. Morland?" said Rachel wrathfully. "A great pity if young men can't have a bit of a swim without people staring at them. I sometimes think, Anty, that you have no modesty."

"*Me!* No modesty!" exclaimed Aunty with indignation. "Well, really! Here I am clothed from head to foot, and they haven't got a stitch on! Who's immodest, I'd like to know! Oh, Annie, so *there* you are! What do you think, there are nine . . ."

Just as the Grandmother appeared at the door, Yow, dom-ineering as usual, came round the corner with a large break-fast tray.

"I puttem breakfast verandah. Plenty sun," he announced, without asking them whether they wanted to have breakfast on the verandah or not.

"Ah, bacon, bacon! How nice!" said Aunty. "Delicious! Annie, did you know that there are nine young men . . . Oh dear me, there's a serpent!"

"Why, there's a snake!" said Rachel, looking over the verandah railing at a snake which lay curled on the warm grass.

"A serpent?" said the Grandmother in surprise.

The garter snake slid, coiled, stopped. It slid, coiled, stopped, and slid shining away through the grasses.

"Well!" said the ladies, who had seldom seen snakes before, except in a zoo.

"Can it be poisonous?" asked Rachel.

"Is it venomous, do you think?" asked the Grandmother. They all left their bacon and peered over the verandah railing after the vanished snake.

"Mr. Oxted says that snakes in this part of the world are never poisonous," said Aunt Topaz. "Mr. Oxted has lived in British Columbia for years and years and years. Mr. Oxted says that Mrs. Oxted . . ."

"*Anty*," said Rachel in extreme exasperation, "if I hear you mention Mr. Oxted once more . . . if I hear you quote Mr. Oxted once more . . . I've heard nothing but Mr. Oxted ever since we started coming up here, for two whole months. You'd think that no one but Mr. Oxted had ever gone camping before!"

"Mr. Oxted is a very nice man and a very *fine* man," said Aunt Topaz. And then she proceeded to give a good example of the way she could shift an argument to suit herself. Since no one could prove whether the snake was poisonous except by being bitten by it, and being sent down as a corpse to Vancouver, Aunty adroitly shifted her stand.

"His wife is a very handsome woman, and she sings in St. Andrew's choir. A fine contralto. Some people say that St. Andrew's choir is the best choir in Vancouver."

This was not kind of Aunty. Rachel had been for five years a faithful choir member and a leading soprano in Wesley Church. But Aunty achieved her end, which was to irritate Rachel just a little. Rachel had rebuked her in the matter of the young men, and Aunty was still mildly annoyed. She succeeded in irritating Rachel.

"How can you say such a thing!" cried Rachel. "Everyone who is anyone and knows anything about music knows quite well that Wesley Church choir is the leading choir in Vancouver, and if St. Andrew's . . ."

The Grandmother held up her hand. "Let us have no rivalry," she said gently. "Although we do not belong to the Presbyterian Church, there is no doubt but that, in their own way, the Presbyterians praise God with equal . . ."

"Oh, do look at Yow!" exclaimed Aunt Topaz.

Yow stood nonchalantly in the doorway. He looked at the ladies with his peculiar facial cynicism. This was not difficult, as his right eyelid drooped by nature with a sinister effect, and gave to his face a cynical and even diabolical appearance without any effort on Yow's part. Between his fingers he held the tail of a snake. The snake, hanging head downwards, looked uncomfortable, and squirmed in an angular and unnatural manner, quite unlike its usual fluid performance.

"I catchem snake. I puttem stew," said Yow, looking with

indifference upon the breakfast party. Cries arose, but Yow did not stay to listen. He departed, taking the snake with him.

"I do believe he will!" they breathed one to another.

It was the habit in this family of three ladies that even the slightest move on anyone's part should be prefaced by a brief and candid explanation. If Rachel should at any time arise, and go out of the room without some such announcement as "I am going to get my sewing cotton," the Grandmother and Aunt Topaz would say mutually in amazement, "Where *can* Rachel have gone?" as if she might have gone to China or to Peru or to bed.

Aunt Topaz therefore did not surprise anyone when she said, "I have a call," and got up and walked in her hasty pounding fashion in the direction of the rear of the cottage.

She returned by way of the lean-to kitchen where Yow was making loud noises in the dish-pan.

"Yow," said Aunt Topaz, "you wouldn't *really* put that serpent into the stew, would you?"

"Sure," said Yow rudely, and went into the house.

As Aunty returned dismayed to the verandah, Rachel arose and said, "I am going to get some more hot water." She then repaired to the lean-to kitchen. Yow looked at her malevolently.

"Yow," said Rachel, using her mixture of pidgin-English which she admired but could not achieve, and the King's own English, "I absolutely forbiddem you puttem snake in stew. If you puttem snake in stew, I shall tell Mr. Andrew when he comes next Saturday. If you puttem snake in stew, Mr. Andrew will be extremely angry."

"I no care," said Yow, and went on being noisy.

When Rachel got back to the breakfast table, the Grandmother stood up in all her small dignity and said, "I am going to speak to Yow about that serpent," and sailed like a little black schooner into the house.

"Yow," she said, lifting her limpid brown gaze to the Chinaman, "*please* don't put that little serpent into the stew! I shall not relish my stew at all if you do. Please, Yow!"

Yow looked upon his darling. "I no puttem snake stew, Missy Hasting," he said. "You no likee, I no puttem. I makem little fun. I foolem. They heap clazy. They no savvy nothing. I no puttem stew."

"Oh, I do thank you, Yow," said the Grandmother gratefully. She returned, saying to her sister and daughter, "Yow declares that he does not intend to put the serpent into the stew. He says . . ." but her sister and her daughter did not hear her.

"I have every intention of doing so!" declared Aunt Topaz. "Mr. Oxted says that Mrs. Oxted says that she finds it most beneficial. She says that he says, I mean he says that she says . . ."

"Oh, for goodness *sake*, Anty!" said Rachel.

"What can this be?" asked the Grandmother, diverted from the serpent.

"I am going to sleep on this verandah tonight," said Aunt Topaz. "It will be most delightful. Mrs. Oxted sleeps on their summer cottage verandah all summer. She sleeps like a top. I shall sleep like a top too. I shall sleep on this little couch. It will be quite comfortable and it will be very invigorating."

"Yes, and you will be going around with one of your sniffly colds for the rest of the summer. *I* know," said Rachel, "and breakfasts in bed and the wash full of those pocket-handkerchiefs of yours."

"Now, love," said the Grandmother mildly, "let Aunty do what she likes. Let her try it for one night. I'm sure if I were young I should enjoy it."

"Young!" said Rachel, and she looked at the shining spacious sea, and the sky, and at the fringe of the dark bright forest. *If I had been here when I was young. If I had come here before I was an elderly woman looking after two older women, and my brother; and my sister's child . . . all this beauty. If I had married Tom Shaw, or Mr. Calverley when he asked me, I might have been a married woman and important like my sisters-in-law . . . but I could never have married Tom Shaw or anyone else. Only this life that I lead is tolerable to me. I could not endure to be other than I am. Oh, what a beautiful beautiful morning!*

There was within Rachel a virgin well into which beauty silently seeped. She could receive the beauty of the morning without speaking. She did not have to transmute this beauty into conversation. So, now, she did not need to say to her mother, "Look, the smooth bark of the arbutus tree is like copper in the sunshine, isn't it? See how the draped branches of the cedars wave seriously! Listen to 'the innumerable laughter of the sea!'" But she turned to her mother, content, and then cried in her anxious way, "Mother, what *are* you doing! Come, Anty, let us move Mother's chair out of the sun!"

When the evening came, Aunty's plans for the night caused so much confusion that no one could sit upon the verandah couch without being asked, several times, to get up. Even the mild Grandmother felt that the experiment demanded too much fuss.

"I shall take my walking-stick," declared Aunty, pounding in and out with her busy tread.

"Whatever for?" asked Rachel.

"Well, I might want to walk down the steps in the night. And I shall take my umbrella and my parasol that belonged to Elijah's wife."

"Both of them, love?" asked the Grandmother.

"Yes, both of them. In Case. Because it might rain in on me, or in the morning the sun might prevent me sleeping. And, you see, I shall take a glass of milk."

"That will attract slugs," said Rachel.

The slugs of Benbow Island are large and gross. They appear to be inert, but are really very mobile; they cover long distances at night and may be found in the morning glued to the edges of containers of food. They are very intelligent, although they do not look it.

"Slugs! Oh. Then I shall take some biscuits and a little bit of chocolate instead," Aunty announced.

Rachel did not say "That will attract mice," although she felt that it should be said.

"I shall take my quilt and Grandfather's shawl," continued Aunty, plumping up her pillow. "And I shall take a hat."

"A hat! Whatever for?" enquired Rachel.

"Because I should like to have my hat with me. In Case. I might wish to sit up during the night, and then it would be nice to have my hat on," said Aunt Topaz.

"Anything else?" asked Rachel.

Night drew on, and the coal-oil lamp was lighted. Yow, the protector, had gone to bed in his outside room. Night finally declared itself, dark and moonless. The lamp shone reflected in the jet-black windows. This was the time when the three women felt within themselves a turning towards sleep. The Grandmother was settled by Rachel; Rachel settled herself; and Aunt Topaz at last closed the door on the warm small room, instinct with habitation, and went out into the uncharted dark. She was excited.

After some stumbling, and some rearrangement on the floor of her equipment, she turned back her neatly made bed, got in, and pulled the bedclothes up to her chin. She looked up into the dark. "This is most delightful," she announced to herself.

She lay for some time looking into the darkness which did not become less opaque. Objects did not emerge from this darkness. Sometimes she turned and regarded a patch of starred sky which the slope of the verandah roof disclosed. All was very still, except for the small continuous sound of ocean upon the rocks. There had been a wind earlier in the day. The wind had died, but a slight wash of the salt sea remained, and with the wash against the shore only a small continuing sound, which grew more faint. The usual commotion and breeze caused by Aunt Topaz in the business of living had ceased abruptly with getting into bed and pulling up the bedclothes. She would have liked to cough, for something to do, but the austere solitude of the night forbade her. Her own stillness and the dark cosmic and planetary silence outside the cabin really disturbed and deprived Aunty a good deal, but she determined to enjoy herself.

"This is indeed *most* delightful," she thought again, but she was restive, feeling a need of someone to express herself to. There was no one. Even the young men in the bay had long since sailed away. She lay awake. She was not afraid, but, with her genius for communication, she felt deeply the need of a listener, to whom she could explain how delightful everything all was. This became more needful as she continued to lie awake. But there were no human ears at hand to oblige her; so she conversed with herself, within, or fell silent, pinioned in the bedclothes.

There are on Benbow Island many deer of small and medium size. These beautiful bucks and does – with their elegant heads, their poetic and nonsensical eyes, their delicate feet and their fine russet or beige rumps – together with their pretty dappled children inhabit the forest where they stray safely, because there are no predatory beasts indigenous to Benbow Island. The only predatory beast is man, occasional man, and the deer are reasonably safe from man except for a few months in the year. Knowing and suspecting man, the deer stray in the forest in the day-time, but when night comes they emerge from the woods, and enjoy cropping tender shoots in the grass that often surrounds the small houses where men seem to keep themselves at night; and, if possible, the deer enter men's enclosed vegetable gardens and eat up their green peas, and sometimes get shot out of season for doing this.

Around Aunt Topaz's nephews' cottage which was in solitude, there were no green peas, but there was some good lush grass. The deer knew this, and because they were as conversant with the dark as with the day, they came out by night one by one, to the number of three or four, and cropped this good grass undisturbed, but Aunt Topaz did not know this. She soon heard an alien sound.

For there were now, near her, sounds as of small footsteps, a little movement, a little rustling. Aunty raised herself cautiously on her elbow and peered. She could see nothing, nothing. These small sounds came from in front of the cottage, and from either end of the verandah. They were closing in. Crop, crop, crop. Rustle, chump, and a nipping of grasses. "Dear me," thought Aunty, "it sounds like a very little cow! But there are no cows. Or a sheep! Certainly it sounds like a grass-eating animal. Could it be a deer? Or an elk? Or a moose? Or *could* it be a bison? Is it dangerous if surprised? However, since it seems to be a vegetarian it is unlikely to attack me." She began, nevertheless, to feel nervous. The sounds ceased. They began again. Aunty strained her eyes this way and that into the unrevealing night.

In the woods, so near the cottage, owls began to cry. Hoo-oo-oo, came the sweet quavering cry. Hoo-oo-oo, came the answer out of the forest. "Owls," thought Aunt Topaz, "I do believe! I hope indeed that they will not think of pecking out my eyes! . . . And if owls, then mice, and what else – rats, perhaps, and weasels. This is, when all is said and done, a very wild country, and only newly inhabited. Truly the New World. Oh, there's the owl again!" She began to wish that she had never met Mr. Oxted, and as the unexplained, unexplainable rustlings continued near the verandah, she wanted to gather up her bedclothes and go in from the unknown and elemental to the comfortable familiarity of the cabin. She was wide awake, and her usually impercipient senses were alert. But she was too proud to get up and go inside.

A great shooting star tore red across the patch of silent sky and went out. Aunty felt elated, and then subdued. "And to think that Rachel is sleeping, and Annie too!" she reflected, bitterly.

"If I thought about Father, perhaps I could go to sleep," she decided, and reverted easily to her life's habit of youngest daughter. She saw at once his noble bearded head. "What a fine beard! You never see a beard like that now. How queer those nine young men would have looked today swimming about with beards on! Very odd. Very much in the way. There must be some reason for it, I suppose." She now indulged her favourite habit of enumeration. "Let me see, beards, beginning with Father. And then Uncle Montague. And Uncle Edward. And Sam Rathbone – all long and well-combed except Uncle Edward's, a very unpleasant beard. And *not* Matthew Arnold – side-whiskers when we knew him, very peculiar. And all my brothers, little pointed ones – the decline of the beard, I suppose. Mrs. Porter's husband hadn't got a beard, but then he was a very unprincipled man. And, oh, William Sandbach – the most *beautiful* beard!" She tried to evoke tenderness at the thought of Mr. Sandbach and his beard, his benign, deceiving, heartless, hypocritical beard. But no, her love for him was long dead. She who had wept so much could not now evoke even a spurious sigh. "How could he have made me so unhappy?" she asked herself with surprise. A dreadful cry grated and rent the night. Aunt Topaz stiffened and her eyes started. She did not know that a blue heron was protesting as it awoke, and was now beating its great wings slowly against the adjacent air. She had never heard of a blue heron. The harsh and frightful cry was repeated near at hand. "That is not human!" thought Aunty trembling, and, of course, it was not. What Aunty meant was that it was hellish, which it was. All her bearded company had flitted, like the lot of silly shadows that they were. They had never been. The only reality was the dark and preposterous night. "If I turn over," thought Topaz unhappily, seeking refuge in a phrase, "I shall sleep like a top."

The owls had ceased their whistling, the deer had moved slowly on, and with the passing of time even the slight sound of the sea against the rocks was stilled. Aunt Topaz turned over, and it was when she began to pull the flannelette sheet about her ears that she heard the voice.

A voice? Voices? Sweet, high, clear, and very faint. A dropping cadence of semitones. A foreign tongue? A sound never heard before, followed by a light sigh, a groan. Aunty listened with her whole being. Again the sweet, descending, unmeaning cry, followed by a sigh, a groan. It came from the shore. No, it came from the ravine. No, it was nearer than that. It was farther away. In the dark was no proportion, no guide. Whence did it come? From the ravine? Again! Is it a voice, is it a cry, or is it music? Is it a flute? Yes, it is a flute. "Oh, my God!" thought Aunty, and cowered in the dark, remembering.

(Yes, said Mrs. Porter when she had finished reading to her young pupils sitting safely about her beside the fire, now, girls, you understand where the word Panic comes from. The Greeks, you see, believed that whoever should hear the fluting of the pagan god Pan was in danger of a revelation which would turn him mad, and whoever should see Pan – who was not even a human type of god, if I may say so, but resembled also a goat – might die from the experience. How much more fortunate are we than the Greeks – we who have the benefits of the Christian religion, that we do not suffer from these and other unsatisfactory superstitions!

But, Mrs. Porter, asked Eliza Pinder and Topaz Edgeworth, both speaking together, and only half convinced, wasn't there really a god Pan in those days? The Greeks were quite sure of it!

No, certainly not, replied Mrs. Porter turning her fine eyes upon them, except . . . well . . . it may be possible . . . that before they had the benefit of the Christian religion, when their world of rocks and trees was so new . . . and in its natural state who can say . . . no, we cannot say . . . why, even Homer . . . Benbow Island is as new as Greece ever was, and newer, newer, much newer.) Again the descending notes of the flute, and a groan, dropping into the night.

Inside the white satin body of Topaz – satin white until the day of her death – there opened a dark unknown flower of fear. Slowly it opened, and through the orifice of this flower fear poured into the darkness. Her whole body dissolved listening into fear which flowed into the terrible enclosing night. She, all alone, became only a frightened part of the listening elements.

The high sweet sound continued again into a groan. She could not tell whether the fluting came now at regular intervals. It came. It came. It was light but clear, and stronger than the silence into which it fell. "Oh God Our Help. Oh God Our Help," said a residuum of Topaz blindly. She could not remember anything more to say. But the sweet sound came again, undefeated and unperturbed by the Holy Name. *Then I must go or I am lost this is Panic I have heard it now at any moment I shall see him close in the darkness I shall feel his breath!* And she sprang up, not knowing what she did, and seized soft quilt and Grandfather's shawl, and stumbling, trailing, upsetting, she found the door. She wrenched the door open and rushed in. She shut the door and locked it. How dark was the room!

"What on earth *are* you doing?" said Rachel crossly from the bedroom.

Topaz stood against the wall, breathing heavily, her quilt fallen about her. Directly she stood within this frail unlit shelter of walls, doors, windows, and humanity, even before she heard the comfortable crossness of Rachel's voice, Pan, so very near at hand, became impotent and withdrew into his own place. Her living family and all her bearded memories rushed about her in confusion.

Rachel lit a candle and, blinking from sleep, saw Topaz standing there, white and staring. "Were you frightened, Anty? What frightened you?" she asked curiously.

"I have a cold, I think," said Topaz, chattering. "I think I have a chill. "She laboured across the floor dragging her quilt and cast herself upon her naked and deserted bed. She pulled the quilt over her.

Rachel got up and stood with the candle in her hand. "Would you like a bit of a rub?" she asked.

"Yes," said Topaz, with her eyes closed, and still shivering, "I would like a bit of a rub." She longed to feel the hard comfort of Rachel's capable hand upon her.

"What is it, love?" murmured the Grandmother, stirring distantly in sleep.

"Nothing, Mother, turn over, turn over."

Rachel bent down and rubbed and rubbed. She wondered amazedly "She isn't talking! She isn't saying a word! Why is she so quiet?" Her knowing capable hands swept up and down the flaccid white back and shoulders of her lively, voluble, silent aunt. Aunt Topaz felt their solace, mournfully.

"There then," said Rachel, and stood up. She looked down on Topaz who still lay without speaking. "She looks as though she were suffering," she thought.

"Anty," Rachel said at last, "why did you lock the door?"

But Topaz did not answer.

The wind having so long dropped, the ocean became at last still, and there was no movement at all in the waters of the bay. Long before dawn broke and there came the sounds of birds and of day, the faint regular musical rub of the boom log against the little wharf, wood against wood, wood against wood with the slow sway of the water, ceased its clear petulant cry, its chime, its rhythmical sighing.

RATHER CLOSE IN THE SITTING-ROOM

They always had dinner earlier than they wanted to because Yow, whose domination had increased over all these years, wished to get out. When he got out he walked with his swaggering gait straight to Vancouver Chinatown and shed his cloak of West End respectability. He belonged to a very fast set. He became deeply and darkly a Chinese gambler. This occurred every night of the week, but his nicest and most gambling day was Sunday when he got out very early. Yow looked like a dangerous criminal, and later in life he had, unfortunately, to go to prison. No one knew what his early life had been. He was in some ways a very bad and unscrupulous man, but during the day-time he guarded the interests of his blameless household of ladies in a bullying and efficient way. Such is the power of goodness, that Yow (who was quite the wickedest person that the Grandmother had ever seen, only she did not know this) revered the Grandmother deeply. Each morning and evening this scoundrel continued to "come in" to Family Prayer, and as the little Grandmother knelt and raised her earnest and tremulous petitions to the Lord, he also knelt without either compulsion or contempt.

When they all arose from their knees, Yow swaggered out of the room in a more bullying manner than usual, probably in order to re-establish himself in his own esteem, and also in order to reimpose himself on his ladies.

Between Aunt Rachel, since she was the housekeeper, and Yow, there was for ever war. Sometimes one of them lost ground, sometimes the other. When Yow lost in the great kindling dispute (he liked to cut it too long for the grates), Aunt Rachel lost in the thick-toast-for-afternoon-tea battle. Each was daily comforted by some small victory. When Aunt Rachel showed her superiority by ordering fifteen cents' worth of soup-meat from the butcher instead of the twenty-five cents' worth demanded by Yow, then it was music in her ears to hear the defeated Yow muttering as he went about his work, "Stinge, stinge, stinge, no can make good soup fifteen cents soup meat, all a time velly stingy." When she heard this, she affected not to hear, but she enjoyed it as Yow's admission of defeat. And Yow, when he succeeded in announcing dinner at six, at twenty minutes to six, at twenty-five minutes to six, at half-past five instead of at half-past six, regarded Aunt Rachel's annoyance and bafflement with sneering satisfaction.

Between Yow and Great-Aunt Topaz nothing existed. She was the freelance of the family. She gave no orders, and received none, and although she set forth daily on her own immaterial and engrossing affairs, often leading with her the obstinate bicycle, she returned more or less in time for meals. She talked continuously when the presence of any other person, Christian or heathen, made this profitable. And in the solitude of her bedroom, for lack of any immediate listener, she talked to herself. During Aunty's flings at public office, when she used to retire to her room and bolt the door and moan there, Yow would stand and listen and then confide to

Rose, "He clazy," and depart swaggering to the kitchen. Yow regarded her incuriously when she addressed him, answered her briefly, and was often heard to say as he departed, "He clazy." But Great-Aunt Topaz never heard him say this, as, of course, she was still talking. Neither did the Grandmother hear him, as a great deal of her time was spent in listening deafly, charmingly, and attentively to her sister. Aunt Rachel and Rose, who were not deaf, charming, or attentive, felt as time went on that Yow should not be allowed to say this, even in the hall, and that something should be done about it. But, on the other hand, they each felt that they were getting a bit of their own back, as Great-Aunt Topaz's rather continuous monologue used to drive them silly, but unlike Yow they were unable to say "He" (or she) "clazy," and get up and go into the kitchen and make unnecessary and deafening noises there. A little thing like this shows plainly the disadvantages of a good upbringing. Or put it another way – what is civilization?

Between Rose, now nearly grown up and a very innocent young lady who had only lately begun to pry into life, and Yow, there was a kind of camaraderie. They sometimes disliked each other, but they were united by a common tug against Aunt Rachel who was a little prone to command. That, however, was her rôle. Yow was fairly polite to Rose, except when she was ironing. It was understood that Rose should iron her own silk blouses. When Rose prepared to iron her blouses, she clamped the handle on each iron in turn, as the irons lay heating on the top of the kitchen stove. She raised each iron in turn to her cheek to test the heat, but she could not tell. So she spat on the iron, a delicate spit, sizzle, sizzle, that told her exactly how hot the iron was. This always enraged Yow. He would not allow Rose to spit upon his irons. When Rose spat upon his irons Yow roared, "No Spitty Iron!"

in such a menacing way that Rose was quite frightened. She used to try guile. She would go through the form of putting the irons to her cheek, while Yow watched her closely, and then, apparently making her selection, she would go into the little laundry with the chosen iron. There she would cautiously spit upon it to see if it were really right. A very little spit indeed, sizzle, sizzle. But Yow never trusted her. Like a cat he would follow her into the laundry, just in time to catch her spitting. Then he would roar with ferocity, "No Spitty My Iron!" and the simple girl was caught again. Sometimes Rose would brazen it out. She simply could not iron her blouses if the irons were not just right. Defiantly she would spit upon the iron. But Yow had two dreadful punishments for her. One was that he would pull his loose eyelids away from his eyes, above and below, exposing large unpleasant red areas. Then he would roll his bloodshot eyes in all directions apparently independent of each other. As in any case he was violent of face, this was formidable, but somehow Rose could not help gazing upon him. She had to look. Yow did another thing. With a quick flick of his fingers he turned both eyelids inside out, and advanced into the little laundry with what looked like two great gobs of raw meat hanging where his eyes should be. The effect of this as he advanced upon Rose so terrified her that she always cried submission at once, and untruthfully promised never to spit upon the irons again. Sometimes in consequence she scorched her silk blouses past repair, but Yow did not mind. He just unflicked his eyelids and returned to his business. This was queer of Yow, because it is well known that his compatriots in the laundry business are not so finicky.

This, then, was the tyrant who induced the four ladies to sit down unwillingly to dinner at five-thirty instead of at half-past six, and to whom the game was this night conceded. Yow was thus ensured a good long evening with his fellow-rowdies, but for Rose this particular evening was unendurably lengthened thereby. From this early meal both Aunt Rachel and Rose therefore got up in middling humour. Their ill-humour had been increased by the garrulous Great-Aunt, who, finding little response from her niece and great-niece, had been driven to repeat some of her observations an irrelevant number of times. This mood did not always prevail at the table. There were times when the irrepressible Great-Aunt was very funny; when, indeed, they were all funny together, wittier and wittier. Then they laughed and laughed until the tears ran down their faces, and until the little Grandmother, who mistrusted too much laughter, looked around with some concern and said kindly, "There, there, that will do. We have laughed," and they stopped being so divinely silly.

But on this evening Rose got up from Family Prayer in the sitting-room after dinner in a haughty and irritable frame of mind. She was aware that the veil of her irritability hung between herself and her Maker, but she clung to her veil and wrapped it round her in defence against her Grandmother's piety, the Great-Aunt's impervious loquacity, and the domination of Aunt Rachel. As Rose put away her Grandmother's Bible she looked enviously at the retreating Yow. He was on his way to a gambling hell. He was lucky. Tomorrow he would approach her, black with temper and lack of sleep, and would borrow twenty-five cents from her. Lucky unlucky gambler Yow. What, oh, what should she do? She wandered over to the piano. "Oh, for goodness' sake," exclaimed Aunt Rachel, "let us have a little peace! What with Anty talking, talking all dinner-time, I want to read my book in peace." The Great-Aunt was offended. She became superior.

"It is well known," she said, "that the difference between civilized and uncivilized man is that civilized man converses with his meals, and uncivilized man eats his in silence. Except, I suppose, for grunting. I at least prefer intelligent conversation."

"To sit and listen to you telling us about Miss Jackson's brother's bedroom slippers several times isn't conversation," said Aunt Rachel. "I like to eat my meals in peace, they digest better. And, anyway, that's not conversation, that's monologue."

"Well, if you can't take your part in an intelligent conversation, I can't do anything for you," said Aunty, still nettled. "Where's the newspaper? Nobody speak a word, if you please." Decidedly everyone was in a bad humour.

"Rachel doesn't mean it, Topaz," said the peace-making Grandmother ("I do," said Aunt Rachel.), "but perhaps it would be nice to have a little quiet." ("'Quiet'! Heavens above!" murmured Rose, dramatizing.) "Rose, love, what is that book you have, is it a novel?"

"Yes, Grannie," said Rose. "It is a novel."

"What is it called?" asked Grannie.

"*Poppy*, darling," said Rose.

"Is it a good book, dear?"

"Well, it's all about Africa, you know, darling," said Rose. And so it was. Dark, sensual, amorous Africa, night on the veldt, Poppy in Africa, plagued by dangerous Love.

"That's nice, dear," said Grannie, thinking, Rose knew, of missionaries. "Where are me reading glasses, and where's the Missionary Magazine? *Now* we're all settled. Poke the fire, love."

"Well, well, *well*," exclaimed Great-Aunt Topaz in agitation, "the Duke of York!" They all looked up.

"Well what?" asked Aunt Rachel. "Oh, a cold," said Aunty indifferently, rattling the newspaper. She was sucking a plum stone.

"I *do* wish, Anty," said Aunt Rachel desperately, "that you'd put that plum stone out!"

"I'll do no such thing," said Aunty, "a plum stone gets sweeter and sweeter and – dear me! 'Arm broken in three places!'"

Everyone tried to fix their looks downwards. Grannie went on reading a report from the Congo with living interest. Aunt Rachel turned a page of *Adam Bede*, and Rose read to herself, "I am not beautiful," said Poppy, "but I have good bones." "Good bones. Have I got good bones?" thought Rose. She looked at her wrists, and saw that she had not got good bones.

"Well!" said Aunt Topaz. She sucked loudly, and they could hardly hear her words on account of the plum stone. "Did you see this?" The newspaper always excited her dreadfully. "This must be *our* Mrs. Bromley! It says –" They all looked up: Mrs. Bromley was one of their more exciting friends. "Oh no," said Aunt Topaz, "it can't be our Mrs. Bromley because this one lives in Kansas and it says 'a widow aged 64.'" Aunt Rachel glared at Aunty, but Aunty did not see. She was engrossed in the newspaper. She sucked and rattled her plum stone.

"Eh," said Grannie wistfully, "if some of you would take a little more interest in these articles from Dr. Mawdsley. They're good, so good – I can't think why you –"

"Her own mother!" exclaimed Aunty with indignation. "Listen to this!"

She rustled the paper furiously, folding it this way and that.

"Is it in Kansas, Aunty?" said Rose in a tired way, "because if it's in Kansas –"

"Yes, listen," said Aunty, "it says 'Adeline Leavenworth, formerly of Liverpool, but now residing in New York, when asked whether –'"

"Oh, Anty, *will* you be quiet, we've all read the paper!" said Aunt Rachel.

"A pretty funny way you read the paper," said Aunty looking at Aunt Rachel. "None of these things that are so interesting have you read a word of, it seems to me. You must read the paper very badly, it seems to me. You miss a great deal."

"Well, I miss what I want to miss and I read what I want to read," said Aunt Rachel.

"I miss nothing," said Aunty loftily. "I read everything. You never know what . . . Well!!"

For a few minutes there was silence broken only by the plum stone. Everyone read.

"Here's a letter," said Aunty, "a very good letter 'From One Who Knew Gladstone.' I wonder *who* that could be! I'm sure I could write about Gladstone. I shook hands with him when he came to Ware. Father was on the Committee. He –"

"I think I'll go to bed," said Rose getting up with "Poppy" who was being rather sensual in Africa. Rose could not concentrate. She went over to her Grandmother, stooped and kissed her.

Grannie looked up from her reading. "Going, dear? So early? Not tired, are you?" "Not exactly," said Rose. She turned to her Aunt Rachel.

"Would it be all right if I went to stay with Marcella Martin over Easter?"

"Oh . . . Easter . . ." said Aunt Rachel slowly. "I hoped you and I might go away for the week-end together. Perhaps to Chilliwack."

Rose was silent. "Well . . ." she said. She wanted to stay with Marcella.

"When you say 'week-end,'" said Grannie gently, "it grieves me a little to think that we can speak of the Lord's Day as being the week-*end*. It is the *beginning* of the week, the beginning of a new week of endeavour and of service to our Loving Heavenly Father."

"Well, Mother, the week-beginning then," said Aunt Rachel, still looking up at Rose. Her eyes were bright and a little anxious.

"This week-end habit," said Aunty coming out from behind the newspaper, "is pernicious. It's growing. Everyone says it's growing. What my father would have said! A fortnight, I always had. A fortnight once a year with Mrs. Grimwade to go to the Academy, and then a week sometimes . . . Why, off to Bermuda!"

"Who?" asked Aunt Rachel, diverted for the moment. But Aunty had moved on. "Who? Who what?" she said, "oh . . . Bermuda! Some people from Nanaimo, I believe. Walker it said."

"Anty, you are aggravating!" said Aunt Rachel passionately, but Aunty did not hear her.

"M-m-m-m-m-m," she read secretly, "well I never! Well I *never*. Oh, nothing, nothing." And she sucked her plum stone. She would take it to bed with her.

Rose went slowly upstairs with "Poppy" to Africa. She didn't want to hurt Aunt Rachel but she did want to spend the week-end with the laughing and popular Marcella.

"Did you see *this*?" said Aunty violently. "Well, of all the outrageous statements! A man in Australia . . ." and she went on reading to herself.

"Is there something wrong with Rose?" asked Grannie.

"She seems to want a change," said Rachel. "But she gets plenty of change, I'm sure, more than ever I used to get. Last Sunday Stephen and Margaret and the children came to tea and next Sunday Frank and Miranda and their children are coming to tea. And she was out with Marcella Martin on Tuesday. And last week young Mr. Anthony called."

"*I* think she's in love with him," said Aunty, looking up from her paper and sucking hard.

"She *says*," said Rachel, "that she can't bear the sight of him. She *says* she hopes he never comes to the house again, and she *says* that if he does, *she's* going to bed."

"Well, I'm sure, I tried to make it a pleasant evening, I'm sure," said Aunty. "Rose sat as mum as a mouse, and I had to talk to him all evening. He stayed and stayed. I found him a very intelligent young man though. I asked him all about his aunt at Dunstable. I know Dunstable well. Father and I were there in '84. There are some very fine gardens in Dunstable. I'm sure we were all very polite. Why, even Annie waited up to see him. What more could Rose want?"

"She says he wants to take her for a drive," said Rachel.

"A *drive*!" said the startled Grannie. "Do you mean a drive alone with a horse?" Rachel nodded.

"I call such an idea ridiculous, and very *common*," said Aunty, suddenly censorious for the fun of the thing. She resumed sucking operations and furled and unfurled her paper at arm's length. "Well, what does this say? Ostrich feathers! The Duke of Sutherland! Laughing gas! Ah, here we are. But I do call that very ridiculous."

"I don't want Rose to begin that kind of thing," said Grannie. "I hope that young man is not going to be troublesome. Oh dear, I do find it a responsibility, Rachel. . . . Well, shall we have a little game of dominoes? That would have been nicer for Rose. We are too quiet, I think sometimes, for young people . . . Three's not so good quite, but would you mind having a little game, Topaz, and Rachel?"

"Dominoes? Dominoes?" said Aunty folding the paper

noisily. "Good, a little game before we go to bed. But what's this?" with rising excitement. "It says Puccini's new opera, oh no, that's in London! Well, where are the dominoes?"

And as they rattled the dominoes Rachel thought, "I believe she doesn't want to go with me. Oh no, no, it can't be that. She's all the youth I have. I've always done everything for her. She couldn't not want to go with me! How thankless, how selfish they can be!"

"*There* then," said the Grandmother, "now, who has double six?"

"I have," said Aunty with a flourish.

Upstairs Rose read, "The stars glowed like lamps in the scented African night. Poppy could almost hear . . ." Without taking her eyes off the romantic page Rose reached vaguely for another sweet. The hasty trampling steps of Aunt Topaz were heard upon the stairs. Quickly the damsel turned out the light.

SATURDAY MORNING

Nothing exciting ever happened on Saturday afternoon, nor, come to that, on Saturday evening. Nevertheless there was a delicious air of preparation about Saturday morning. They walked quickly along the narrow dark passage that led to the bathroom (there was a lot of traffic to and from the bathroom on Saturday morning, and some impatience and knocking . . . "Anty, are you taking all the hot water?"), and as they met each other going and returning they enquired, "What are you going to do this morning?" and the news was relayed.

Grannie, having finished her breakfast, sat up in bed reading her devotional books. She looked up at her daughter Rachel. Grannie was such a pretty old lady. Later, when she got up, she wore a morning-cap of white net in Mary Stuart design. It had no streamers. From tea-time on she wore a white net cap of similar design that had two long white net streamers. But for morning wear in bed she had white lace over her head. For sleeping, she put on a tiny frilled white spotted muslin nightcap that tied under her chin. Never had she been seen bareheaded. As she sat up in her bed she wore shawls. One shawl in summer, mounting to four or even five in winter. Her Bible, her Prayer Book, her Hymn Book, a little pile of devotional books and some small religious magazines lay beside her. All these books looked alike to her granddaughter Rose. They were just "Grannie's books." But to the Grandmother they were strikingly and thrillingly various. She read these manuals to a soft cooing accompaniment of praise and sorrow. "Oh Lord." "How great indeed is Thy Mercy to us, Oh Lord." "Oh, indeed we *do*, Lord." Her soft brown eyes were dewed with tears. Her spiritual life was all-pervading. Communion with God, a great and infinitely loving Father, was the great fact of Grannie's life. Morning and evening, indeed throughout her conscious life, Grannie communed.

From this gently solemn occupation she looked up at her daughter Rachel, and wiped her misty eyes. "And what are you going to do, dear?" she asked.

"I am going to make a Milk Jelly," said Aunt Rachel rather importantly. She did well to sound important. Around this simple delicacy had grown up a legend. Rachel's Milk Jelly could have been made by anybody else, certainly by the capable Yow, who could make anything, but it was only made by Rachel. If the visiting minister came to dinner on Sunday, a Milk Jelly was considered suitable. Or perhaps on Saturday evening some young friend of Rose's might (on invitation) come to dinner, or some of the family. Then the Milk Jelly was felt to be just the thing. Grannie's sons and their exhilarating wives and children were the delight of this family. Their visits brought infinite pleasure and variety to this sedate household of three ageing ladies and one young girl.

This is the way that Aunt Rachel's Milk Jelly was made:

1 oz. gelatine (nearly)

½ lb. white sugar

1 breakfast cup of milk

2 lemons

2 eggs

Put the gelatine into a breakfast cup of hot water until dissolved. Add the beaten eggs and the juice and the grated rind of the lemons to the sugar. Stir all together, adding the milk last. Pour into a mould and set.

It will be seen that the Milk Jelly was not a complicated dessert. The theory that Yow could not make it was untenable. In its scrupulous simplicity it typified this innocent household. It was fresh, clean, sweet, tart, economical, clear and sparkly in places, in other places opaque, of a pale-primrose distinction, and the recipe was English. Also it had been poured into a mould and had set. Also it was controlled by Aunt Rachel.

"Oh, *here* you are, Annie. Did you now that Rachel is going to make a Milk Jelly?" enquired the lively Topaz, bouncing into the Grandmother's bedroom after a hasty pounding progress along the passage. "Oh, *there* you are, Rachel! Who is coming?"

"Well," said Rachel, "it's just In Case. And what are *you* going to do this morning, Anty?"

Aunt Topaz went to the window. "It's such a lovely day, I think I shall go for a ride," she said. "Oh, look, there's a bird! Whee-whoo! Whee-whoo! There, he answered me. Such a pretty bird! And there's Mrs. Andrews, I *do* declare! She's got a string bag! She must be going to the town! I think I shall go to the town! Yes, I shall ride to the town!"

"*Do* be careful, Topaz," begged Grannie. Only last week a young man pedalling merrily down the Long Hill in Stanley

Park had lost control of his machine and with pedals whizzing madly had pitched over at the bottom of the hill and had broken both his legs. But Grannie need not have cautioned Aunt Topaz. It was unlikely that she would break a leg, as it was rarely now that she tried to mount her bicycle. She usually led it all the way to town and pushed it all the way back again. Before being taken for a walk, Aunty's good English bicycle, whose organs were laced into a kind of flat corset, and whose beautiful lamp shone, was dusted off with care. Aunty led it through the garden gate. She then gave one or two abortive hops as of one about to mount a bicycle. This was done for the benefit of anyone who might be looking out of windows. Then as if dismissing for the moment the idea of mounting, she set off, wheeling her bicycle. Thus, throughout her ride, Aunty presented to the passer-by the appearance of a lady who, owing to the heat of the day perhaps, is for the moment wheeling her bicycle which she may at any instant decide to remount. Aunty rather enjoyed "going for a ride." Many opportunities occurred to stop and chat with friends, and it would have been a great pity always to leave such a good bicycle at home. Aunt Rachel and Rose had been inclined to tease Aunty about taking her bicycle for an airing, but they realized that they would spoil things for her, so they had stopped long ago.

A door was heard to slam. There were young steps coming down the hall and Rose came quickly into the bedroom. She looked young and fresh and eager as she joined her elders. "Oh, hello, Aunt Rachel, I thought you were in the kitchen. Yow told me you were going to make a Milk Jelly. Who's coming?"

"Well, it's just In Case," said Aunt Rachel.

"Come here, love," said Grannie. She reached up to smooth Rose's billowing fair pompadour from her brow. Rose and her young friends were rather stylish and wore their hair in an extravagant fashion with a swoop up and a dip down over the brow. The brow was mostly concealed, as though it were an immodest thing, a sort of second bosom.

"Couldn't you take your hair straight back from your face, dearie? I should like it so much better."

"Oh, Grannie, it would look perfectly *awful.*"

"I wish, love, that you would try not to use those slang words. 'Perfectly awful!' I know it is fashionable, but it is not pretty nor suitable," said Grannie gently. "I even heard Mrs. Bromley say the other day that she felt 'awfully well.' How could one feel awful and well at the same time?"

"*Awfully well* indeed," said Great-Aunt Topaz, "what a contradiction! But there is no need to copy Mrs. Bromley. She even shakes hands high up – like this" (and Aunty minced about the room in a burlesque of the fashionable Mrs. Bromley shaking hands), "in a most affected way. How d'you do! How d'you do!" mimicked Aunt Topaz holding up her right hand in an affected manner. "But what are *you* going to do this morning, Rose?"

Rose was readjusting her prized pompadour at Grannie's mirror and laughing at Aunty's performance. "Marcella Martin is calling for me and we are going to town."

"To the *town,* dear?" asked Grannie, "what takes you to the *town*?"

"Marcella is going to buy a new hat, and she asked me to help her." Rose tried to make this pleasant expedition sound virtuous, but the fact was that she and the beautiful Marcella were young and vain, and the nicest thing that they could possibly think of on this fine morning was to tie on their new blue veils over their fresh unpowdered complexions and their tilted sailor hats and go to town and try on something dashing.

"Poor Marcella has, of course, no mother and no aunts to help her to choose her hats, so I'm glad you are able to help her, dear." Rose knew that this speech meant "No going off with Marcella to choose *your* hats. That is Aunt Rachel's prerogative."

The door-bell rang. It was the ravishing and elegant young Marcella. Rose patted her pompadour and the front of her blouse, settled her waistline, smoothed down her hips, kissed her Grandmother, and flew for her hat, veil, and gloves. Aunty watched from the window.

"Well, they look very nice to be sure, those two tall girls, but a little inclined to attract attention. They should know by this time that no lady puts her gloves on in the street. I don't know that I quite like them walking about the town together like that, I *must* say, do you, Rachel? It may perhaps be all right in Vancouver, but in Ware I know it would never do. However. Well, I must be off," she said busily, the gay idler.

Before Aunty led her bicycle down the path and out onto the sidewalk, she tested the sweet-voiced bell which she so enjoyed ringing, and attached the little string bag to the handle-bars. It was convenient for carrying things home. You never knew what Aunt Topaz would find to buy. All sorts of things took her eye. "Anty, what *have* you bought now!" the thrifty Rachel would exclaim. And Aunty would protest.

As Great-Aunt Topaz wheeled her good bicycle up Barclay Street this bright June morning, two little boys across the road were trying out their new words. "Skidoo," they said to each other, "skidoo skidoo, twenny-three for you, twenny-three for you, skidoo skidoo skidoo." They liked saying it. The words wafted after Aunty as she pushed her bicycle up the street. "Skidoo for you, skidoo, skidoo," and fainter and fainter, "twenny-three skidoo."

Aunty smiled. "What funny little boys! Why, there's Miss Butterworth ahead, I do declare! I believe I can catch her if I try. What a *beautiful* morning!"

THE VOICE

Suddenly Rose surprised her grandmother and aunts by growing up and getting married. No sooner had they begun to recover from their surprise than the German armies marched unwarranted into Belgium. This event made apparent the continuous fusing of Time and Place and Effect everywhere, and people (startled and rallying from shock) in all places found that their lives were not their own and were no longer assured, because the Germans (who had not consulted them) had decided to march into Belgium. Rose's husband left, and went overseas. She, in common with other innocent dwellers on the Pacific coast and elsewhere, had long since relegated war to the old pages of history. And here was war, violent and not to be denied, taking away her husband and jouncing her out of her delightful new existence, back into the too cosy seclusion of the house with the pepper-pot, hurt and anxious. Life in the pepper-pot house thereupon seemed to close down again and settle into its old simple yet involved forms. "Something," thought Rose, "is unreal about this . . . I have had nightmares. . . ."

From August the fourth, nineteen hundred and fourteen,

until November nineteen hundred and eighteen, were days of severe trial and sorrow. Each evening – in that war – the newspapers published a casualty list of the last recorded day, in round numbers. The lists would read thus – killed 385, wounded 979, missing 211.

Rachel and Rose, who had too much imagination, read daily with unwilling eyes these dreadful lists, and felt in their bodies the loss and anguish of wives and parents. Aunt Topaz, who had almost no imagination at all, read the lists also, and to her the numbers were not people but numbers. She was not susceptible to the depression which afflicted Rachel and Rose as they unwillingly read these numbers which to them were people, and she often chided them.

"Dear me, we'll never win this war if people give way to their feelings like that! Take the long view, like me! These lists will only serve to stiffen the determination of our men!" And, noisily folding and unfolding the newspaper, "Well, what's this? 'Lady Haig visits hospital for Canadian soldiers.' Good. Good." Rachel and Rose looked at her and thought her incomprehensible. It is true that if Aunty had been allowed to march into battle with "our men" she would have marched joyously. But she could not do that. So she knitted linear miles of scarves, bought raffle tickets lavishly, and won two raffles; when she did that, you would have thought that "our men" had carried two major victories. Aunty did what she could, and as she often remarked, there is no virtue in feeling low.

One morning late on in the war Rachel went to her mother's bedside to awaken her, and her mother did not answer.

When it was made clear to them that the Grandmother would continue to lie there, unknowing, unseeing, unspeaking, for an indefinite time, Rachel and Rose divided the care of her between them. Aunt Rachel slept in the Grandmother's room and cared for her during the night. Rose did the active nursing during the day. There were times in the afternoons when both Rachel and Rose were away, and then, provided that everything had been done for her sister, Aunt Topaz took her books and her knitting and sat beside the bed. Now, when young men were lying on beds of pain, the once-beautiful Grandmother, with her long and good life behind her, lay without suffering, with eyes closed, unspeaking, cared for by the loving devotion of three women. Rose's tenderness overflowed to her Grandmother, yet she saw with envy the young men and a few young women going away to where the war was, and her mind was continually divided.

One afternoon Rose sat beside her Grandmother's bed knitting and not knitting, wondering when the war would be over, wondering about her own engrossing problems, wondering if Aunty would come in time to let her go and play tennis, wondering where her Grandmother really was, wondering if there would be another mail today. The vagrant, unsatisfactory, familiar wonderings came and went. She was bored. She got up abruptly and went and looked out of the window of the pepper-pot.

"It's not fair," she thought rebelliously. (Rose often seemed to think "it's not fair.") "It's not fair. Look at this war. Going on and on and on. And us separated. And me *doing* nothing. It's been nearly four years now." (Four years seemed to be all her life, then.) "Every day people getting killed and crippled. Every day people made miserable. When's it going to stop? When are they coming home? Look at Grannie. She's no more than a bit of broken china in that bed. She's never done one unkind thing in her life or said one unkind word" ("Not like me!" she thought with a gust of shame), "and she gave

209

Aunt Topaz a home at once when she needed one and look at Aunt Topaz! Oh, she *can* be aggravating! And she gave me a home when I needed one and all the love there is, and she'd give anyone a home. And she's never bought one extra thing for herself, she gives every bit away." ("The tithe belongs to the Lord, love," Grannie had said simply. "We don't begin to give until we have given our tithe and until we do without things.") "And she hasn't any spiritual pride like she might have. She's not a bit a prig. She's just like crystal. She's got the gift of religion like Paderewski has music. I haven't got it but I can see it. And look at her!" (The girl turned again and looked at the small figure in the bed.) "Where is she? Where is she now, this minute? It's not fair. I wish the war would stop. I *do* wish . . . If Aunty doesn't come I won't get any tennis. Oh, blast." And she knelt on the window-seat of the pepper-pot and drummed on the window-ledge. She was furiously bored. Life was a mystery; so was death. She wished Aunty would come. She wanted to play tennis.

The door opened and Aunt Topaz tiptoed noisily in. "Oh, so *there* you are, Rose!" she said. "Am I late? Is everything all right? Did you feed her? I've got my books. You can go, you know."

"All right, Aunty," said Rose, gathering up her knitting. She bent over her grandmother, lifted the little mask-like head, softened the pillow, and set the inanimate head with its closed eyes gently on the pillow again. "She's all right. I gave her her milk, and Aunt Rachel or I will be back. But do keep the fire in, won't you." So often, now, Rose, the young one, felt immeasurably older than Topaz, the old one.

Rose left, and Aunty took her place beside the bed with her pile of books. She chose a book and began to read. Sometimes she looked at her sister. The Grandmother lay unmoving, as always now. Aunty went on reading until the light faded; but like an owl, if an owl could read, Aunty could read in the dusk. She did not put on the light. She read on and on.

She laid down the volume of Frazer's *Golden Bough* and took up her book of Sherlock Holmes stories. "Let me see, now," she thought, flicking the pages, "*The Speckled Band.* Yes, *The Speckled Band.*" And she continued to read.

A young voice in the room called urgently, "*Rachel!*"

Topaz slowly lowered her book and looked over the top of it through the dusk at her sister. The room was still except for a dropping of ashes in the grate. The Grandmother lay as ever, eyes closed, unmoving. Her face, which was not any more the serene face of sister Annie, had gradually become a shadowed anonymous mask of extreme age and approaching death – infinitely tragic in its mystery and anonymity. Over the top of the book Topaz gazed upon the ivory shadowed mask of her dear sister.

The Grandmother's lips moved, and the voice, which was clear and young, said urgently, "*Rachel! I want you.*" The eyes remained closed. It was very strange.

"Oh, dear," said Aunty within herself, "whatever shall I do? Annie wants Rachel! If I try to tell her that Rachel isn't here and that she's coming I shall muddle things and spoil it . . . she might never speak again. . . . But *is* it Annie speaking? Oh dear, why isn't Rachel here! Whatever shall I do?"

The mysterious voice called again, "*Rachel!*"

Topaz made her decision.

"Yes . . . yes . . . Mother . . ." she faltered.

"*Did you marry him, Rachel?*" asked the voice.

"No . . . Mother . . ." said Topaz leaning forwards, her hands flat out on her open book.

"*Then are you happy?*" asked the voice.

"Yes . . . Mother . . . I am very *very* happy . . ." said Topaz, breaking into a sob. "Oh," she thought, "what is it? Oh, Annie."

"*I am very thankful, love. God bless you always, Rachel,*" said the clear mysterious voice, and ceased.

The book slid to the floor. Topaz fell on her knees beside the bed. "Annie," she said. Then "Annie, Annie!" she cried in distress. "Annie, speak to me too! It's me! It's Topaz! It's your little sister!" Aunty put her hands almost roughly on the little form and, "Annie," she cried, "won't you *please* speak to me too? Just one word to me! I'm Topaz, Topaz, calling you! Oh, Annie! I'm Topaz, the youngest one!"

"How many hours," the thought flooded through her, "Annie and I have sat and talked together, and now can't I have just one word? This is our last chance," she thought desperately.

But whatever had come had also gone away again, and the Grandmother made no sign. It was as though she had never spoken.

Topaz stood up and looked wildly round the darkened room. "What shall I say to Rachel when she comes?" Shock had given way to compassion. Pity for Rachel crowded out pity for herself and for her dear sister lying so still. Rachel was good; she was constant and devoted, and after all these years of service she had not received her mother's message and her blessing. This pity for Rachel, which was in itself an unfamiliar emotion to Topaz, wiped out her natural curiosity and quickened an unusual sensibility in her, disclosing to her a sure knowledge that something in human relations of which she was unaware, or which she was incapable of feeling, existed between Rachel and her mother. Aunty knew blindly that she had stumbled into some private ground that belonged to the reserved Rachel, and with this sensibility that was rare in her she felt that she must not disclose the whole of the strange scene, or Rachel would feel her life (which was all that she had) invaded and deprived by Aunty.

She sat down. She rehearsed herself. I shall say, "Your mother called your name, Rachel, and then she said, 'God bless you always.' . . . She called your name, and then she said, 'God bless you always.'"

Aunty did not see that the fire had gone out. She had been close to a mystery, and her mind was confused. She wiped her face with her handkerchief, pulled her skirt over her knees and tried to compose herself.

Before long the bedroom door opened and Rachel came in briskly. "What are you in the dark for? Oh, Anty, you've let the fire go out! Is everything all right?" and she turned on the light and went over to the fireplace.

Aunty sat blinking. She said rather stupidly, "Rachel, your mother spoke."

Rachel stood still. "Spoke?" she said, "Mother spoke? You're imagining, Anty!"

"Your mother spoke . . . loudly," said Aunty, nodding her head, hardly believing her own words.

"What did she say?" asked Rachel.

Aunty said her part. "She called *you*. She said your name twice and called you 'love,' and then she said, 'God bless you, Rachel, always.'" Then Aunty said with a rush, "I was so surprised, I couldn't . . . but she didn't say any more after that. I *asked* her and *asked* her!" She gazed up at Rachel.

Rachel looked down for a minute at the little ivory and shadowed face which lay upon the pillow, and which was her mother who was so saintly, and was her care and so dear to her, and was soon going to leave. Then she turned and went out of the room, and down the passage, and into the little room that used to be Andrew's bedroom before he was married. She looked through the dark window at nothing but darkness, and her heart felt hot and sad and proud within her. "Oh," she thought, "It's me she asked for . . . after all these years it was me she wanted. . . ." She stood there a long time and then she went back and made up the fire.

It was weeks later that the Grandmother died. The mysterious voice was not heard again.

Rose knew that this death was not really sad, although it made everyone of the family sad because they had all always loved the Grandmother ever since they could remember, and she was their mother. She knew that the right time had come; but she and Topaz and Rachel were very unreasonably sorrowful.

With the death of the Grandmother, the house with the pepper-pot tower was "broken up." Rose and her husband, now returned from the war, went to live in a house on the hill opposite a green open park. Rachel and Topaz after much discussion left on a visit to England, which cheered and excited Topaz very much. Yow became cook to a newly married couple and stole all the bride's trousseau bit by bit to give to a white lady-friend of his. He would never never have done anything like this if he had still been with the Grandmother. Yow had to go to prison in spite of everything and the white ladyfriend formed other connections.

APOTHEOSIS

During the year after the Grandmother died, when Rachel and Topaz went to England, certain events induced a sort of catharsis in Rachel, and her small complaints and impatiences were shed away. Rachel became very gentle but Aunty did not notice this. New relations had gradually established themselves between aunt and niece, and Aunty became the leader and decider, although of course it was always upon Rachel that the brunt of arrangements fell.

The following year Rachel and Topaz left England and travelled to Italy. They went with Elise, still the unrivalled beauty of the family among young or old, and now a widow, living sometimes in Florence. Aunt Topaz often took much pleasure in recalling that forty years ago she (as chaperon) and Rachel, and the haughty beautiful young Elise had gone to Paris with Elise's father, Aunt Topaz's brother George. Topaz and the two young girls had stuffed their bustles (which were not Frenchily large enough for Paris) with newspapers, and had crackled wherever they went, until some young Frenchmen had poked them in the bustle, and Elise had flashed round and enchanted the young Frenchmen with her

fury and it was worse than ever (but wherever Elise went there
was this kind of trouble), and they had had to go back to the
hotel with bits of newspaper sticking out of their behinds, and
take it all out. What adventures for three young women from
Ware in the eighteen-seventies!

This time it was Elise, still, at her age, in brilliant scornful beauty, who led, followed by Rachel (her occupation gone)
and by the hastily pounding Aunt Topaz whose gait had
become more vigorous in motion than ever. There were many
tilts and flashes between Aunty and Elise, but there was much
laughter too, as Elise had by nature and experience a disturbing sense of humour. They all laughed a good deal but, afterwards, Aunty forgot the laughing, and remembered the
picture galleries, and the encounters with people, in the trains,
and in the pension dining-rooms, and on excursions. They
went as far as Rome.

It was about two months after their return to England
that the dreadful event – too tragical to contemplate –
occurred which took the life of Rachel with great suffering,
and spared Aunt Topaz. The impossible had happened. Rachel
had left her and was dead.

Aunty lay in her last phoenix fire of sorrow. She did not
know that it was a phoenix fire which consumed her, and that,
in her own remarkable way, she would arise from this fire and
become more resilient, more strong, impervious to grief and
even to love, and that now, at the age of seventy-five, she was
entering into her own little apotheosis, and nothing mortal, not
even death itself, would be able to move her or hurt her any
more. And so it was that one day, as she uttered her constant
and touching cry, "However can I live without her? Oh, if only
Rachel were here to scold me! Why wasn't I taken too? I wish I
was dead. Oh, Rachel, Rachel, I am a poor old woman and I

shouldn't be here," she suddenly thought with surprise, "That isn't true! I'm only pretending now! I am not a poor old woman at all! I'm not afraid of anything!" It was as when, after a dire illness which might have reduced her to the lowest in human weakness and dependence, and which might have continued through weeks of disheartening and uncertain convalescence, a day had come in spring and she had looked at the poignant world of buds and birds and sky (which appeared somehow different) and felt, with life in her body and in her face, "I am better! Oh, I am well again!" So it was with Great-Aunt Topaz after her weeks in the valley of the shadow of Rachel's sudden and violent death. She looked around her with interest, and was immune for evermore from chance and mischance. And it was at this moment that a large square envelope arrived, with a crown on the back of it, and Aunty was commanded to go to Buckingham Palace to see the Queen. Topaz instinctively turned at once to Rachel, but Rachel was not there.

Uncle John hurried up to London. Here he was, a Justice of the Peace, and County Councillor, a sitter on Boards of Directors, an industrious and valuable public servant, dropping at once his multiple activities and coming to the help of his inexperienced sister Topaz in London. "I will manage the whole affair. I shall take charge." Aunty moved from the nursing home where she had been taken after Rachel's death, to a repulsively respectable hotel in Bloomsbury which you would really think that Uncle John owned, by the way he treated it. You could use the old-fashioned phrase "he patronized that hotel," because Uncle John patronized the hotel and everyone in it, and began by patronizing Aunt Topaz. He found that although he had patronized her, off and on, for seventy-five years, Aunty was no longer patronizable, and this disconcerted him.

Uncle John at the age of seventy-eight was still a handsome man whose trouble was that he had always looked like an earl, much more like an earl than earls do, and was thus usually taken for one when in places frequented by earls, and that he had been called Giovanni ever since he was twenty. He had a habit of fluttering his eyelids, which looked sublime and put one a little in one's place. At concerts, before taking his seat, he would stand and turn round (sometimes in an opera cape) and, gazing about him with pure delight and looking very distinguished, would, across invisible nobodies, discover a friend and would exclaim, "Ah, do I see my dear old friend Forsyth?" These attributes caused affectionate admiration, pleasure, and amusement among acquaintances, and among coarse people something like fury. He had an undeniably kind heart as many in need could testify, and he came up to London well equipped in every possible way to help his poor sister – who had recently suffered so frightful a bereavement and had, herself, barely escaped the grave – through the overwhelming emergency of going to Buckingham Palace.

After four or five days of coping with Aunty, Uncle felt that something had become unmanageable; but his mind was not supple enough to understand that his sister could no longer be coped with, and so he went on trying.

"I will order a good carriage, Topaz," said Uncle John, "and *I* will take you to Buckingham Palace myself. It would not be suitable for you to go without an escort, and I had better go in with you to see the Queen. I could tell you what to do." Aunty opened her mouth and shut it again. She had no intention of giving John the glory. Uncle John knew the idiosyncrasies of a man's wardrobe and was always well dressed and well groomed, but he did not know about the details of women's dress and prayed that Topaz would look "right" for this grand occasion, for she often looked "wrong."

On the great morning, Aunt Topaz emerged jangling from her bedroom, looking right and also looking wrong. Rachel would have curbed her here and there, especially in the matter of necklaces and bracelets to which Aunty was addicted. However, Aunty looked nice in her own particular unfashionable yet individual way, and she was very happy indeed. She stopped each chambermaid whom she met, and announced (because she couldn't help it and because such an announcement was bound to give them pleasure), "And where do you suppose I am going? You'd never guess! I'm going to Buckingham Palace! There! I knew you'd be surprised!" And the chambermaids regarded this happy old lady prancing along the hall with a warming of heart or with disbelief.

"Ah, John, so *there* you are!" exclaimed Aunty, radiant, "what a beautiful carriage! Oh dear, I haven't got me other little bag with me other hanky! Well, this will do! How do you do, how do you do," to the doorman, "where d'you suppose I'm going? I'm going to Buckingham Palace!" And to the cabby, "Ah, what a beautiful day! I'm sure it isn't every day you drive someone to Buckingham Palace, is it!" And bent down and laboured happily into the cab.

All this effervescence disturbed and annoyed Uncle John; in fact the past few days had made him very nervous, as Aunty had caused him, in his passion for correct behaviour, to suffer. He recalled their Italian journey together. Association with Topaz would be a trial, he felt, in public, to any man of position. No longer could he thunder, "Topaz, be silent! May I not be permitted to speak at my own table?" for several tries of this sort of thing had been easily squashed by his sister.

"I do wish, Topaz," he said in a pained way as he settled himself beside her on the carriage seat, putting his stick between his knees and leaning upon it in an elegant manner, "that you would try to control yourself, and – er, *conform* a little. You really sound very Colonial sometimes."

Aunty flew to battle. Her words leapt like little jangling jaguars onto Brother John.

"'Colonial!'" she said sarcastically, "'Colonial!' You do indeed make me laugh, John. You're too conventional to breathe. 'Colonial!' You don't know what the word means! You say the word as if it were something to be ashamed of! Well, it isn't. I'm Colonial and I'm proud of it."

"I only –" began Uncle John.

"Yes you did," continued Aunt Topaz. "You have no sense of history, that's what's the matter with *you*! When colonists left Greece and colonized every corner of the Mediterranean" (Aunty flung out her arms and batted Uncle John on the pince-nez with a bag flying from her wrist) "you don't suppose those colonists were ashamed of the word 'colonial'? No, indeed, it was their pride . . ."

"I only –" said Uncle John.

"And," Aunty went on, giving her necklaces a toss (the carriage rolled pleasantly along) "those who left this country as colonists, and established colonies in the New World have a deal more to be proud of than you who stayed at home and were comfortable . . . a deal too comfortable, I don't mind telling you! It's a word that anyone should cherish and be proud of if they've any sense of history at all, whether they stayed here in comfort or are descendants of those colonists who so nobly landed on those rugged shores." Aunty blew a gust of breath. She had become an orator. She trumpeted at her brother who sat with immaculately gloved hands on the silver head of his walking-stick, his handsome face with its pince-nez and its Van Dyck beard looking straight ahead like that of a well-bred martyr. "If they haven't any sense of history," Topaz continued, "I'm sorry for them and I'm sorry for *you*, but I can't do anything about it." You would have thought that Aunty had hewn down the forest and raised the home and killed the wolves and planted the garden herself.

"My dear Topaz . . ." said Uncle John in a tone of defence, "I only –"

"That will do, John," said Aunty grandly and kindly. After all, who was going to Buckingham Palace, she or John? "Well, look at all the people, I do declare. *Wouldn't* they all be surprised if they knew that we were going to Buckingham Palace!" Aunty had indeed won, because they were back exactly where they had started the argument, and not a word from Brother John.

When the tiff had subsided, Great-Uncle John and Great-Aunt Topaz, seeming to any observer to be an old gentleman and an old lady (although, of course, they were actually only little John Edgeworth and his sister Topaz, grown old), rolled along in the nice carriage, looking out at the London crowds and buildings, all familiar to John but always fresh to Topaz. Topaz rolled along in the heaven of happiness reserved for one specially commanded to Buckingham Palace, but Uncle John was only in the second-class heaven reserved for the relations.

"It must have been very funny," laughed Aunt Topaz to Miranda when she was back in Vancouver a few months later. "I didn't notice it at the time because I was very excited – oh yes, very excited indeed – but when John said to the nice young man in a lordly way, '*I* will escort my sister to see Her

Majesty!' I don't remember what happened but the nice young man was very polite and the next thing I knew John was left sitting in a beautiful room, waiting, you know, and I was walking with the nice young man along wide corridors with fine carpets on, oh very fine carpets, and large paintings on the walls. John *was* sneaped, I can tell you," said Aunty retrospectively and very much pleased. "John had always been so important and a J.P. and a County Councillor and exactly like a lord to look at, and *he* had to wait! And me, *I*, his little sister that many's the time he'd sneaped, walking with this handsome young man all along those corridors – we *did* have a nice talk – and going to see the Queen."

Aunty stopped for a moment and savoured her memories. Miranda looked at Aunty whom she had known so long – although she was only a niece-in-law – and pictured, smiling to herself, the figure of Aunty pounding busily down the palace halls, all her necklaces dancing, the pearls, the amethysts, the jet, and perhaps the amber underneath for luck, and catching up with and passing and falling behind the escorting young man, telling him meanwhile about herself, about Vancouver, and that she remembered seeing the great exhibition of Winterhalters in 1873 – " . . . that *is* a Winterhalter, I think!" as she pointed here and there at a Royal portrait with her best walking-stick.

"And when we got to the door of the large drawing-room – oh, tremendous – me knees trembled and I thought they wouldn't support me, and there was the Queen standing, oh such a long way off it seemed to me, all in blue and she had on those blue stones – sapphires they were" (Aunty had telescopic vision) "she looked *beautiful* and I thought, oh dear me, how shall I ever get there, and I went forward, and would you believe it, the Queen came forward to meet me! And she took my hand and led me to a chair and sat down in front of me and said (and I thought to meself, this is *The Queen* speaking to me, Queen of Great Britain and Ireland and of the Dominions Overseas), yes, she said, 'Now, Miss Edgeworth, we have just half an hour and then the American Ambassador is coming. Tell me all about Vancouver. I remember how beautiful it was. I suppose the city has grown out of recognition.' And she put me at me ease and I told her all about you, Miranda, ("Oh my goodness!" thought Miranda) "and about Rose, and Rose marrying Charles, and Charles coming back from the war, and about the Boys and all about the children, and about everybody, and Annie and Rachel, of course. Oh, Her Majesty *was* interested!"

"I'm sure she was!" said Miranda politely.

"And then," said Aunty, "it seemed like two minutes and I had a deal more to say" (now that Topaz was old, she used old colloquialisms and Staffordshireisms, "jannock" she would say for "kind and pleasant"), "and Her Majesty was very jannock with me, and then she told me that the half-hour was gone and she must receive the Ambassador, and she got up and, of course, I got to me feet too, and I suddenly remembered again where I was at the end of that long room, and how would I get to that door, backing all the way as John had told me, and I would bump into the furniture and me knees turned to water and I thought oh dear. But the Queen didn't let me do it. She walked all the way down the room with me to the door and made it oh so easy and then she stopped and picked up this photograph – she'd written her name on it – and said, 'I should like you to have this, Miss Edgeworth,' – and here it is! Look!" said Aunty in effulgence of pride.

Miranda took up the picture of the Queen, who stood superbly dressed for an occasion of State, wearing a small diamond crown, and jewels, and orders. Her eyes looked steadily out of the photograph, the eyes of a woman who could bear pomps, and cares, and dignities, and the anxieties of a wife and of a mother; and could be an example to her people; and could keep her own counsel; and could summon to her an old woman who, six thousand miles away, had served, a little, the Queen's poor people of London, over a long period of years; and she could crown this old lady's life, and walk with her to a door, and send her away with undying happiness. This was the photograph of Queen Mary that Miranda now held in her hand and looked at, thinking of these things.

"And John," laughed Aunty, "poor John! I think he enjoyed himself after he got over feeling sneaped. When we drove away in the carriage – because we kept the carriage waiting, John said spare no expense – and after I had told him all about the interview as we were driving back to the hotel, John said, 'I will admit to you, Topaz, that I felt a certain pang of envy. But that is gone, and I can assure you of my deep satisfaction for you.' John was really very good," Aunty said kindly, "I can see him now," and she sat back and closed her eyes in a lofty manner and regarded inwardly that memorable day.

Now, for the first time in her life, Aunty had her own home. She reigned for the first time alone, and in her own apartment. And yet not alone, for there was a constant struggle for mastery with her companion Mme Brizard. Life was always exciting. Aunty enjoyed her duels with Mme Brizard, because she always felt that she (Aunty) won, and because she was fond of Mme Brizard as a worthy friend and adversary, and because Mme Brizard was related to a Cabinet Minister.

Mme Brizard she would introduce thus. "This is Mme Brizard . . . my Companion . . . ma dame de compagnie," airily, "English. Of very good family. Well connected.

Sometimes speaks French." And Aunty would flip an explanatory hand as if Mme Brizard were a waxwork, and then would hiss whisperingly in parenthesis, "Her husband was French, you see, poor man!" Why Aunty was sorry for M. Brizard was because he was dead, not because he was French. She had a high opinion of the French, and felt that the inclusion of even an imitation Frenchwoman in her household conferred on her – Topaz – a good deal of chic. "Mme Brizard is the sister-in-law of a Cabinet Minister," Aunty (vague as to whose Cabinet) continues ineffably, "and comes from West Africa."

"Argentine, Argentine, Miss Edgeworth," protests Mme Brizard.

"Very well then, the Argentine, if you insist," says Aunty in a fatigued manner, closing her eyes, and putting Mme Brizard almost in the wrong. This she could do quite unfairly whenever she chose, simply by closing her eyes, although she had noisier methods. Mme Brizard seemed to admire Aunty's adroitness, as one would say "Ts – ts! Well, well! Behold!" In fact, each admired the other – a sound basis. . . . Mme Brizard, alternating between exasperation and devotion, managed Aunty very well.

Topaz spoke often of Rachel. Then, as time went on – you know how it is – her memory reverted and reverted until she spoke very seldom of Rachel, and more of the friends of the moment or of the friends of her youth.

AUNTY SPENDS THE DAY

Great-Aunt Topaz now ruled from her eyrie in the tall apartment house over her whole world, which was small; yet she did not know that it was small, for it extended as far as her interested vision could reach. She not only ruled her own world, but she took it, and tossed it off like a drink, and it intoxicated her, and, renewed daily, it intoxicated her again. Around and beyond her spun the barren and often silly 'twenties. She knew little enough about them; but that she could amble with the times was evident as, laughing, she passed cigarettes to her younger great-nieces Carlotta, Helen, Peggy, Isabel, and Anne. Ten years before, she would as soon have passed them strychnine. She ran about her world in her relatives' cars or in taxis. The proud and obstinate bicycle had long since been sold at a loss after many years of monastic retirement in a shed, and Aunty's age and unsure bounce prohibited the use of street-cars. Each week rose to two peaks of happy personal excitement (what more can one wish for at eighty? At eighty-five? At ninety?) – her Sunday visit to one of her nephews and their spreading families, and the regular Friday afternoon visit to Rose. This Friday visit, originally scheduled for early afternoon, soon began at mid-morning. Mme Brizard, fighting a losing battle and urged on by Aunty since daybreak ("Now then, this is the day I go to Mrs. Forrest's, you know!"), compromised on ten-thirty, and so did Rose. All the preparations, dispute, and commotion involved, added the pinch of conflict required by Aunty to season her day and make it perfect. She arrived alone each Friday morning in the captious good humour of a ruffled and recent victor.

Rose hears her Great-Aunt mounting the front steps and runs to receive her multiple burden. Great-Aunt Topaz, small, resolute and aged, thunders up the steps on large and important feet. This grand and ancient woman carries a parasol ("it belonged to Elijah's wife"), a walking-stick, a large chintz bag, a small leather bag, and a tiny black silk bag. She carries a muff of grey fur. Protruding from the largest bag, which contains books, papers, shawls, slippers, and sweets, is a garden hat trimmed with a mauve ostrich feather. In Case. She talks as she pounds resolutely up the steps. A taxi-man dodges anxiously behind her with a rug and an umbrella.

Rose begins, "Oh, Aunty, I'm so sorry, I didn't hear the taxi . . ." but Aunt Topaz is speaking and does not listen. She seldom listens. She enjoys speaking. She enters the front door. She fills the house. She casts everything down.

"Well," says Aunt Topaz in a powerful and carrying voice, "so here we are. Friday again. I've had some very interesting letters this week . . . catch . . ." (the letters fall like snow) "a very good letter from Tilly-and-Sassy, and one from Miss Peacock and one from Miss Pocock, and one from Elise who seems to be very much annoyed, and, oh, such a good one from Sam Skadding, very fond of me is Sam Skadding. He's an orphan, you know, he's had that school in Surrey for over forty years."

"He can't be a very young orphan," suggests Rose, helping Aunty off with her coat and hat.

"Young? Of course he's young. He's my second cousin. He can't be more than fifty . . . sixty . . . well, seventy years old." At what age does one cease to be an orphan? wonders Rose, who, although an orphan at the age of eight, hasn't felt like one for years and years. This orphan is also a widower, it appears, and has a long life-history. So have all his relations. Up wag the dogs. "Oh, doggie, *there* you are! Come and be scratched. You see, they like to be scratched. What? Lunch? Out of the way, doggie, out of the way. I want to wash me hands."

The bathroom door closes on Aunt Topaz. Peace descends upon the house. Then the door opens. Aunt Topaz comes out. She rubs her hands vigorously, refreshed. Bracelets jangle. Necklaces of jet become entangled in necklaces of gold, of amber, of pearls. She wears five necklaces. She is small, she is shrinking in size, but she fills the house from the front door to the back.

"There then," continues Aunt Topaz, "give me me stick. Well," sinking heavily into a dining-room chair and dropping some bags, "it's nice to be here again, I'm sure. You haven't told me what you've been doing since last Friday. Oh, been in bed with a cold. You should be like me. I'm never ill. Well, I think I had a headache once, but I'm not sure, and here I am over eighty and I can read and sew without glasses! Oh, what's this? Soup! Mushroom soup! Good! Good!" says Aunt Topaz, stirring her soup with relish. "Do you know Bishop Empey? A fine old man Bishop Empey. My age. Walks with a stick. Well, he came to see me yesterday, and he came in and said, 'Ah, Miss Edgeworth!' and I held out me hand and Bishop Empey took it and he shut his eyes and raised his other hand and began giving me a sort of introduction to God, and he went on praying over me hand . . . you know the sort of thing . . . and I looked at Mme Brizard and I began to laugh, and I covered me face with me other hand," and Great-Aunt Topaz spreads her gemmed and crooked fingers over her face and looks wickedly through her fingers, gulping with laughter (she has not tasted her soup yet) "and the good man thought I was weeping and he went on praying all the more. And I wrenched me hand free and I *ran* along the hall," picture to yourself Aunt Topaz's frail but heavy flight, "and rushed into me bedroom and flung meself upon me bed and laughed into me pillow. And when I'd got over it and wiped me eyes I went back. And Bishop Empey thought I'd been overcome with emotion and weeping in me bedroom. Oh, he *was* pleased!" She stirs her soup. "What do you say? Cold? I like it cold. How you *do* gobble your food, to be sure! No wonder you're not strong. What do you say?" stirring harder than ever, "I can't hear what you say. I never could endure to sit silent at a meal. It's uncivilized to sit mum as a mouse. Don't hurry me. I can't bear to be hurried at me meals."

Rose continues to sit with a hostess expression above her long-emptied soup-plate while Aunty continues to pour out the racier news of the week. Then, piteously, "I can't eat all this soup. I'll just have a bitta cheese. Oh, but oysters! . . . good! . . . Did you know that oysters are an aphrodisiac? Oh yes, indeed. It's well known. What big oysters! Charles Dickens said he'd as soon eat a baby as one of these large oysters!" She prods her oysters.

Aunty talks of Charles Dickens and the joy of reading the instalments of his stories as they came out in *Household Words* and *All the Year Round*. She continues prodding her oysters. They are perforated, but not eaten. Information about

Dickens and his family. Information about Thackeray and his family. Trollope . . . "*Please*, Aunty . . . !" implores Rose. "*Do* eat your lunch!"

"These oysters are too big," Aunt Topaz says plaintively. "Rhubarb? Well, eat your rhubarb then. It's good for the blood, doctors say. No, my blood's all right. Whatever does Anna want now? To clear away? Well, then, clear away, Anna! Oh, a cup of tea. Yes, I'd rather have it in the drawing-room. I'll take me cheese with me." Commotion of removal. Aunty. Stick. Bags. Cheese. Tea. Aunty continues in the drawing-room.

"A fire! That's nice. Well, and what have you been doing with yourself? I haven't heard a word of what you've been doing. You must have been doing *something*. You should be more lively, Rose, more interested in everything. Look at me! Always interested, never dull! Not a word have you said all lunch-time –"

"But, Aunty –" breaks in Rose.

"Don't argue," kindly, "it doesn't suit you to argue. The fact is you smoke too much. Look at you now, lolling in an armchair half naked and smoking a cigar! What your Grandmother would have said!"

This time Rose really exerts herself (and the shade of her Great-Uncle John thunders within her, "Let me speak! Be silent, Topaz! May I not be permitted to express myself in my own house?") "*This*," she says coldly, "is a tennis dress, as worn by everyone who plays tennis, and I warn you I'm going next door to play tennis in a few minutes. And this isn't a cigar, it's a cigarette. You know that very well, you're just being naughty. I am *not* half naked and I am *not* smoking a cigar!"

Wasted, wasted, for Aunty is not listening; she has moved on. "You remember your uncle's old friend Mr. Pontifex with a moustache? I saw him last week at Miranda's.

Has a tear duct. Oh, a very handsome man! And he said, 'Is it true that you are still Miss Edgeworth?' Oh, very gallant. He thought I had married, of course. So I told him I was indeed Miss Edgeworth, but I was never very still! How Miranda laughed! You should take more notice, Rose. You're inclined to sit mum as a mouse." Aunty is fond of Rose in a way; but this great-niece whom she has known through childhood has, she feels, defied her and nature by growing up and becoming a married woman and running a house, and this irks Aunty just a little. Rose suggests a nap, a little sleep for Aunty, as she, Rose, is going to play tennis for one hour by the clock.

"Do I want a sleep after me lunch? No, I don't want a sleep. And who have you asked for tea?" Autocratically. "Who? Gray? Gray? What Gray? I don't know any Gray. Oh, GRAHAM. Yes, and a very pretty woman, but her husband is that young man who presumed to speak in that way of Gladstone in this house. I curbed me temper, I curbed me temper, but I told him a few things and I could have said a many more. Oh, several coming in to tea! Good! I brought me birthday-book In Case. It's almost full now. Many's the great name I've got in me birthday-book. There's Lord and Lady Aberdeen and Gladstone himself and Rudyard Kipling and his father and mother, and the Archbishop of Canterbury, and Sir Garnet Wolseley, and Several Suicides. Oh, I must have at least six suicides now," says Aunty, very proud. "There was that poor young man who . . . what? Well, go, then, go! Charm, charm! Sparkle, sparkle! Scintillate, scintillate! I shall play Beethoven." And she does, resoundingly.

It is half-past nine. The master of the house sits reading by the fire. Dinner is just over, a protracted affair, but shorter than lunch owing to ruthlessness on the part of Rose. Aunty has enjoyed her audience and her dinner. The afternoon tea-party has been discussed in all its implications. Some criticism has been spoken and some praise. Old tales have been retold. Always with Aunty one thing leads to another and everything is new under the sun.

And now this pleasant dinner is over and the master of the house sits reading by the fire. Aunty admires him, the man, the nephew-by-marriage, the surprising husband of the great-niece to whom she has so long been accustomed. "How you came to get such a good husband *I* can't imagine!" He treats Aunty with the right blend of indulgence and authority. He admires her, and she becomes more and more entertaining. She becomes intoxicated with her success and with her own wit and funniness. He teases her. He gives her all his flattering attention, and then he suddenly withdraws into his own mind and into his own books as if she did not exist. What a phenomenon! He sits there reading and note-taking, and she does not exist! She is in the room, racy, amusing, important, but she does not even fret the outside edge of his consciousness! This phenomenon, so unusual in Aunty's experience, does not annoy her. It pleases her; she admires it. Rose has for some reason gone quiet. She is knitting. She is inattentive. Aunty, a reader with taste and discrimination, makes choice from the shelves of books to take home with her. Gibbon, Rabelais. A gap here. A gap there. Book leans upon book. The books will return littered with Aunty's marginal notes ("Yes, I, too, remember that magnificent scene, because Father and I were there in 1874. We . . .")

Elusive, unheard, some significant moment of Time has just struck. She will go home.

Tossing herself into a chair, with books slipping to the floor from her tiny lap, Aunty leans back with the fatigued air of one who is being detained against her will. She closes her eyes, but she continues speaking with gusto, a recapitulation. "Well, a very pleasant day, I'm sure, though I must say that once I got into a fine bad temper with your wife, Charles! But I enjoyed it, I enjoyed it. I *think*," with eyes closed and with the infinitely grand air that she can summon, "I think those young people were all very much interested in all I had to tell them at tea-time, very nice people. But," a little aggrieved, "it's time you took me home, you know. I'm not young, you know. I can't stay up talking till all hours the way you do, you know. Where are me things?" And Aunty, ancient, important, a delight and disturbance to her family, still talking, goes home.

The day is over. The earth turns, and seven times turning brings Friday again. The weeks hasten by. Where are the weeks? They are lost in the years. Aunty's long life inscribes no sweeping curves upon the moving curtain of Time. She inscribes no significant design. Just small bright dots of colour, sparkling dots of life.

GUSTO

Aunty and Mme Brizard continue to live together in the tall apartment house overlooking the mountains. Great-Aunt Topaz looks frail but she has bursts of unsurpassed energy. Her visits to the family are intermittent now but still she dearly loves a party.

A niece has come to see her. Aunty is sitting up in bed vigorous, vibrating, still talking. She has talked for ninety years. She is no longer John's youngest sister ("*Silence*, Topaz! Let me speak. May I not speak in my own house?") She is the Great-Aunt. She is the Great-Great-Aunt. She is important. She sits up in bed mourning for her King. She wears a black lace cap, crooked; she wears a mauve dressing-jacket and a black woollen shawl; she wears jet bracelets and necklaces and a mourning ring of hair. Mourning mitigates her grief. She enjoys her mourning. She sees herself, pathetic, superb, ancient, historic, suitably mourning for her King. "I am mourning, you see!" she says with dignified satisfaction. She is brilliant and autocratic and her family is important too because it is her Family and has its place in her life like Monday, Tuesday, Wednesday. She is no longer just the beloved Mrs. Hastings' unmarried sister or Rachel's aunt. She is listened to and admired. "Oh, Miss Edgeworth, how wonderful you are!" She knew Rudyard Kipling and his parents (whom she introduced to each other at a "Book-Picnic" at Rudyard Lake). She nearly knew all the Pre-Raphaelite Brotherhood. She still remembers the death of the Duke of Wellington. ("Pull down the blinds, Topaz, the great Duke is dead.") As she talks she moves her head bowingly and with vigour. She gesticulates with her little hands, the fingers spread, crooked with age, loaded with rings. She has become very small. She closes her eyes as she talks, which conveys a vast importance. She does not flutter her eyelids like Uncle John. She closes them with an air. She can, and does, say what she will. Life is a party and she is at the party. She is the guest of honour. She is sitting up in bed surrounded by books, newspapers, woolwork, apples, and letters. She is recounting an episode to the visiting niece.

"Yes, wasn't it exciting, Georgia? But life *is* very exciting. I'm really in a vortex," says this small being who now spends four-fifths of her life against her pillows. "Something happening all the time . . . look. I found these two old letters today, one from Miss Peacock and one from Miss Pocock."

"What a coincidence!" murmurs the visiting niece.

"Not a coincidence at all. What's coincidence about it?"

"Well, I mean the similarity of the names – Peacock and Pocock," explains the niece.

"They're not similar at all, Miss Peacock was Miss Peacock and Miss Pocock was Miss Pocock. They're not in the least alike," says Aunty, who is not sensitive to the queer tricks played by sound, and does not know that to her nephews and nieces who never saw Miss Peacock or Miss Pocock, Miss Peacock is usually Miss Pocock, and Miss Pocock is Miss Peacock. "Yes . . . Mme Brizard? What is it . . . what is it? She wants something.

Whatever does she want? To dinner? Mrs. Forrest? When? When? Tonight? Oh, good, good, I'll wear me black lace. Or shall I wear me crimson velvet? Because, you see, with the crimson velvet I can wear me garnets and – Mme Brizard, Mme Brizard, get out me crimson velvet, I want to have a look at it. And get out me old purple. I can mourn in that very nicely. I want to have a look at that too. Out to dinner and ME ninety-three. You know Mr. Jordan? Well, he's an old rip, that's what he is." "Old rip" is a new word for Aunty, but she likes it. "I was getting into me taxi yesterday with Mme Brizard and he came up. We were going for a little drive in Stanley Park. Have you been in the Park lately? Oh, beautiful, beautiful. Such vistas. The flowers are beautiful and *such* a lot of people. And Mr. Jordan came up and swept off his hat and was full of admiration at me going for a drive and not looking me age. And I said, 'Well, I'm over ninety.' And," says Aunty, flinging her arms wide in mocking imitation of the admiring Mr. Jordan and tossing her head with scorn, "he professed to *swoon* with surprise, he professed to *swoon,* the old rip. Did I tell you that I'm going to have me miniature painted? Oh yes. Well, I am. Why don't you have *your* miniature painted? What? Too expensive! Nonsense, that's just an excuse. Nose? What's wrong with your nose? Too big for a miniature you say? Of course it's not too big. Why, does it feel too big *on*? Oh, here's me crimson dress. And bring out the purple!"

It is seven o'clock. Rose and Aunty's friend Miss English sit talking in the drawing-room. Sounds are heard of Aunty approaching. Commotion. Talking. The front door bursts open. Aunty enters, supported by the overladen Mme Brizard.

"Well, here we are," announces Aunty agreeably. "Oh, so *there* you are, Miss English, in that nice dress too. It *is* a nice dress. Well, Rose, have I seen that before? What a many dresses you do have to be sure. I *told* you," addressing Mme Brizard vehemently, "I *told* you I should have put on me black lace. Well, where's Charles? Late? He often seems to be late! What? Gone to Victoria? I made sure Charles would be here. Whatever did you want to ask us for when Charles isn't here? Well, then, who *is* coming? What men, I mean? WHAT, NO MEN? I thought we were going to have a right good time!"

Aunty is escorted to the bedroom still talking. She is not pleased. Mme Brizard will take off her things. Sounds of argument are heard from the bedroom.

Aunty hastens back into the drawing-room leaning on her stick. Mme Brizard follows her. Aunty is not handsome but she looks very interesting in her purple velvet, her black lace cap, and a great sparkle of jewelry. Her jewelry makes more noise than most jewelry. She is still speaking. She has not ceased speaking.

"Mme Brizard calls this a party. Well, I don't. Very nice, I'm sure," says this ancient and privileged woman, "but not a party. Oh, so here's Anna with something. How are you, Anna? Oh, what a pretty tray! Well, Anna, what's this you've got?"

"Cocktails, Miss Edgeworth," murmurs Anna politely.

"Cocktails indeed!" says Aunty. She looks superbly around the man-less room. She looks lightly upon the three laughing ladies. "Cocktails indeed. *I'd* call them hen-tails. Here, give me one."

THE 'THIRTIES

T opaz has for the last time left Vancouver for her summer holiday, but, of course, she does not know this. We do not know these things. Henceforward she will stay at home.

"Yes, indeed. Victoria is very nice. I always like a cathedral city. But altogether too much bridge. Bridge at that little hotel all day long. No intelligent conversation." Rose pictures the bridge players massed for defence, formed four-square against the prowling Topaz who seethes with conversation. "And tea at the Empress! You know that fine hotel? A very fine foyer; it is called a Rotunda, oh very long, and at each end a portrait, one of the King and one of the Queen. . . ." Rose has heard the story from a friend at the hotel. . . .

Aunt Topaz, weary of waiting for her tea, looks with sparkling green eyes around the rotunda. American visitors sit on chairs and loll back on chesterfields. So do Canadian visitors. No doubt they are all divided into the two classes of persons who sit in hotel lobbies – those unutterably bored persons who detest sitting in hotel lobbies but for some reason have to, and those who enjoy it. The rotunda is quiet, except for a slight busyness of waiters arranging with their peculiar deft swish and grace the afternoon-tea tables. The visitors follow the movement of the waiters with glazed eyes. Aunty does not look glazed; she is spoiling for commotion. She spies the portrait of the King. She spies the portrait of the Queen. Before Mme Brizard can put out a detaining hand, Aunty is in the middle of the floor, and with her nimble yet pounding gait is hastening down the long expanse between the visitors sitting on chairs, toward the King, all her necklaces dancing. By the time she reaches the portrait of the King, every eye has become unglazed and has turned on Aunty, who drops a deep curtsy to the portrait, wobbling a little, and says for the benefit of those near at hand, "I bow to my King!" Then she turns, and pounds happily down the long distance of the rotunda, dodging and being dodged by waiters. The hotel visitors have come alive, and watch her heavy dancing progress with interest. Will she do it again? Aunty reaches the portrait of the Queen. Again she curtsies, saying in a semi-religious way for the benefit of those near at hand, "I bow to my Queen!" Having stirred up a bit of excitement and brought some action into the rotunda, she returns delighted to the suffused Mme Brizard, who, although the relative of a Cabinet Minister, dares not risk scolding her in public, for Aunty could give back handsomely.

"There, that woke them up a bit," says the aged Topaz, laughing and pleased. "Where's me tea? . . ." Aunty feels sublime for days afterwards and does not very much mind that Mme Brizard refuses to take her to the Empress Hotel again for tea.

That is one of the last sallies of Topaz, whose world now contracts to her apartment and to her pouring flood of memories. Vague news of an outside world comes in. She reads the newspaper, exclaiming. What is this of young men who ride up and down the country on freight cars; who live in jungles; who have no work, no money, no food; who cannot hope to have a wife, nor a home, nor a family; to whom all legitimate ambitions are closed? ("There should be someone like Gladstone!") The young men ride from east to west and west to east on the freight cars, and drop off at cities and walk to people's doors and ask for work or food. Where do they spend the night? They are baffled. They have no past and they certainly have no present, and cannot see a future; neither can the housewives who say regretfully, "I have no work for you, but would you like some lunch?" Yes, the young men would like some lunch, but a lunch does not last long, and they would rather have a job. There are no jobs.

A rehearsal is being arranged in Europe. There will be something to do in Europe and Asia and Africa and on some of the oceans and rivers and in the sky. It appears that things are being planned. The patterns on the curtain of Time are confused, but we are aware of something alarming which is about to begin.

THE BURIED LIFE

Rose entered Aunty's bedroom with a guilty feeling. Too long had passed since she had visited Aunt Topaz; but Aunty never showed resentment at this, however much she might, a few minutes later, provoke and enjoy a good tiff with you. She looked up from her book, and her face lighted with the particularly well-mannered winning look which always accompanied her greetings, which were never dull. Aunty was becoming rather attached to Rose, whom she had regarded until lately as still a person of fourteen who had accidentally been married and had no real status. She had suddenly begun to regard Rose as an adult and a genuine married person, indeed as a contemporary, but above all as a surviving symbol of Annie and Rachel. "What a many years of memory we share!" And it was true.

"So *there* you are!" she exclaimed joyously. "You're just in time to hear something. Listen to this! It's poetry. You like poetry, you know," as if this were Rose's odd peculiarity. And she read aloud from the book which she held in her left hand. She read in a very special voice:

"The unplumb'd, salt, estranging sea."

And again, more slowly:

"The unplumb'd, salt, estranging sea."

"Mrs. Porter used to say," said Aunty, "that there was everything that anyone could think, know, or say about the sea in that line. And many's the time I've shaken the hand that wrote that line! He used to come to our house to dinner whenever he came to Ware, and very good he was to me once when he came to dinner. Matthew Arnold, you know. Nobody reads Matthew Arnold now, do they, but they should, they should. Listen to this," and she riffled the pages over until she came to her place. She raised her crooked little gemmed hand (something like a gemmed claw) and, the little crooked hand held up, said, "Listen! Mark this!" and Rose listened.

"How well Aunty reads poetry!" she thought. "With all her love of rattle and bang you'd think she would trumpet it, or read with windy eloquence. But her voice is slow and musical when she reads, and her tone is level and plain. She lets the words and phrases speak for themselves. This must be the training of the classical Mrs. Porter of whom I have heard; eighty years ago and more."

Aunty read, and her hand with its glittering rings remained upraised:

"Only – but this is rare –
When a beloved hand is laid in ours,
When, jaded with the rush and glare
Of the interminable hours,
Our eyes can in another's eyes read clear,

When our world-deafen'd ear
Is by the tones of a loved voice caress'd –
A bolt is shot back somewhere in our breast,
And a lost pulse of feeling stirs again . . ."

She raised her voice and dulcetly she read on:

"The eye sinks inward, and the heart lies plain,
And what we mean, we say, and what we would,
    we know.
A man becomes aware of his life's flow,
And hears its winding murmur; and he sees
The meadows where it glides, the sun, the breeze . . .
. . . And then he thinks he knows
The hills where his life rose,
And the sea where it goes."

There was quiet in the room, and then Aunty descended briskly from poetry. "That's from 'The Buried Life.' Read it. Read it. It's very good, a good man Matthew Arnold. My life rose in Staffordshire and I suppose it's going out into the Pacific Ocean. Well, well! But as for a Buried Life," said Aunty pertly, "I suppose some people have them. Couldn't say, I'm sure. I never did, myself, only for a time I suppose when I loved Unrequited for seven years. It isn't everyone who can love for seven years . . . Unrequited," said Aunty complacently. "Could you do that?"

"No," said Rose honestly, "I don't believe I could."

"There, you see," said Aunty scornfully, "you and your happy marriages! Any simpleton can do that. But to love Unrequited," she continued with satisfaction, "your generation hasn't got the guts to do it. Not a one of you could do it! Have I told you about it before? . . . Oh, I have." (Rose knew the story well.) "Well, here's tea! Good, good! You pour it out. And get down that picture of William Sandbach. That's him. Hasn't he got a handsome nose?"

"I'm always inclined to suspect a handsome nose," said her great-niece.

"What a ridiculous remark! Suspect a nose indeed! He was a widower, the handsomest man in Parliament they used to say. They lost their only son and then she went a little queer before she died. I'm not surprised, I'm sure.

"He gave me that picture. In Court dress with a white ostrich feather along his hat. Oh, I *was* proud when he gave me that picture. No, another lump, I like it sweet. Why don't you take sugar in your tea? You'd be fatter. You'd be a deal better-looking if you were fatter. Well, whenever distinguished people came to the Potteries, Mr. Sandbach gave a dinner-party. And he always asked John and me until John married Annie-John. John and I used to drive there in the brougham and we always Dressed. No one Dressed in Ware except at Mr. Sandbach's dinner-parties. Oh, I met Gladstone there (I worshipped Gladstone) and the Prince and Princess Colonna and Burne-Jones and Sir Garnet Wolseley and Baroness Burdett-Coutts and all the Foreigners. I could always talk, you see, English and French, oh yes. I could always talk and so could John, and so we were always asked. I never could bear to sit mum as a mouse. Very dull I call it. Just like Charles Lamb said, 'A party in a parlour, all silent and all damned!'"

"Wasn't it Wordsworth or wasn't it . . ." interrupted Rose.

"Don't argue so much," said Aunty. "You argue. Very unattractive in a woman, arguing, anyone will tell you. But I'd as lief go to bed as sit mum as a mouse. That young woman here last week. Not a word did she-say. I talked to her all afternoon and not a word did she utter."

"Well, Aunty . . ." began Rose, defending.

"A bit more cake. . . . No, that one. And the result was that people said, 'You'll see, William Sandbach will marry Topaz Edgeworth!' Oh, it became very painful to me, very painful." Rose knew what was coming next. If she had not known, it would have shocked her, coming as a disclosure, a secret. But Aunty was enjoying herself. "Oh yes, I fell in love. How I suffered! Driving down with John to dinner and driving home again. My greatest joy and misery too. I loved him for seven years of my life, and it was wasted, wasted. I'm proud of it now, not everybody could do it! But then I said to myself, 'No, it's over,' and it *was* over. And I well remember, in me bedroom I raised me fist to heaven and I CURSED HIM!"

If ever a face flashed, Aunty's face flashes now. If ever a crooked jewelled hand was raised and shaken to heaven, it is hers. She lives through the distant dreadful moment again. Her face is contorted in pleasurable rage. Rose, curled up in the armchair, watches. She has seen this before. She has heard it before. "Wherein is it," she wonders, "that our generation is different? I'd feel a fool, shaking my fist to heaven. Aunty doesn't feel a fool and, moreover, she doesn't look it. She's enjoying herself. Don't we feel as deeply? Yes, we do. But we're different."

"How strange!" thought Rose, looking at Topaz. She marvelled again at the unquenched vitality of the small ancient being who was her Great-Aunt. This vitality had been preserved and untroubled by Aunty's lack of awareness of the human relations which compose the complicated fabric of living. The limitless treasure and absorbing motions of a con- tinuous hidden life had neither enriched nor depleted her. Rose began to admire the candour of Aunt Topaz, who now had passed the zenith of her wrath.

"But," said Aunty, "I'll never forget, when I came back to England in nineteen-twenty, I was driving up Port Hill in John's brougham and I saw William Sandbach walking up alone, and ill he looked, and very very old. And I bade the coachman stop the horse, and I leaned out of the brougham and said, 'Mr. Sandbach, may I offer you a lift home?' And he came up to the brougham and he took off his hat. We looked at each other. It was a strange moment," said Aunty gently, "very strange. And he got in. And as we talked I thought, 'How could I curse him? How could I be so wicked, and how could he make me suffer so?' It was all washed away except that I had cursed him. I regretted it bitterly, bitterly, when I saw him old and ill. We drove him home and I never saw him again, and I could not read his thoughts."

Aunty sat quiet for a moment, but not for long. "Well, and how's Charles? . . . Oh, here's someone. Who is it? Who? Visitors? Oh, good. I like visitors. Now . . . do I know . . . ? Oh!" with delight. "Oh-h-h," in a downward ripple of pure joy. "It's Frank, I do declare! *And* Stephen! Well, I do declare!" And with her winning greeting face she offered a fresh welcome.

SEA-GULLS IN THE CITY

There came a day when those who strained their eyes and looked forwards could see the forms of designs blocked out upon the future. These designs took shape and meaning with the present and with the past. Men did not need to be prophets to discern these patterns. Bombs would explode, men would drown, cities would burn, peoples would flee, dissension and faith would prevail, the pattern of suffering was clear. The future ceased to be a peaceful obscurity blocked by a concrete tomorrow which could be reached out to and almost touched as the planet revolved. The future (which was really one with the present and the past) became shockingly discernible. And beyond visibility it was to a point implicit and to be believed. As the planet revolved making day and night against the patterned curtain of Time, men painted daily in violent colours of noise and flame and with an infinite unexpected detail of private living the terrible designs upon the curtain. With the revolving of the planet the painted many-dimensioned curtain slipped slowly by and joined the past while men busied themselves painfully about the present and the future. Or it seemed that as the curtain on which men were painting, with extreme difficulty, slipped backwards, men proceeded forwards against the curtain at a snail's pace into a future already in being. The voice speaking from the field of battle had always, in the nature of things, been prepared to speak. The battle had always been, and was completed before it had begun. The mother sat with the bit of paper not an hour old, and her heart which failed within her told her, "I have always known this, it has always been; when he was so high, this was approved in Time and I sat here with this paper."

While these events were disclosed in the world of Time, there was a timeless and impersonal world to which men turned and in which they found momentary refreshment. The permanence of the fleeting and prodigal joy of this timeless world was without responsibility or question. The unearthly light of morning on the flank of the hill departs and is eternal and no one can prevail against it. The permanence of the impermanent frail flower is for ever. So is the sunshine on clover and the humming bees. The teasing whisper of the little wave on the shingle turns and always creeps in again. The beauty of structure of a tree or of a mountain changes but will never change. In these satisfying things men refreshed themselves painfully yet with delight.

Aunt Topaz had always been too much occupied with living to notice the existence and relation of these two worlds of man. The nature of her world did not change, although it had become constricted, which made it more closely packed with interest. Hence she was never lonely nor anxious. She is cared for diligently. She is visited by the family, but rarely visits the family now. Each night she unfurls the newspaper and rattles it this way and that, and reads, exclaiming to Mme Brizard, the very bad news and all the advertisements with equal attention. She is busy with these things, and seldom turns to observe the dreadful sights which appear upon the great painted moving curtain of Time. Nor does she passionately require the comfort of the sunset or the bird on the wing. She waits for the newspaper with all the beautiful advertisements. "Is it come?"

In the green park opposite the house on the hill where Rose lives there are trees where small birds build and fly and sing. In the late afternoon the ascending songs of evening spiral into the still air. There is a good large space of green there. Legally, it is owned by the city. But actually it is possessed by the people who live around the park, by children who fly kites there, by dogs, and by sea-gulls who have no regard for anybody else. Let us turn and look at these white birds who take no heed of the war.

The sea-gulls walk proudly in this park. They stand still. Then with the air of one taking up the collection they walk away majestically. They then turn and walk back again. The rain pours down and the sea-gulls stand and walk in the rain with indifference. The people who live around the park look through their rainy windows at the sodden park and at the sea-gulls standing there looking fatter than usual, like white sheep on the grass. The people like the sea-gulls to be there. They think it gives the tame and planted park a look of wildness and what-will-happen-next. These sea-gulls fly in from the Pacific Ocean. The people who live around the park always debate when they see the sea-gulls like sheep grazing there. They say, "There must be a dreadful storm at sea or the sea-gulls would not be here." But they can never prove it, because there is not a dreadful storm every time the sea-gulls come. There is some secret reason why they come to the city parks, and indeed further inland, in varying weather. They are not always seeking for food in the grass and furrows.

Sometimes they come in fine breezy weather. Then woe to the sea-gulls, because Rose's two dogs, Johnny and Tuppence, will drive them about the park and give them no peace. Johnny and Tuppence are two wire-haired terriers, but when they see the sea-gulls in the park they become, not two dogs, but a gang, a pack, an army of avenging dogs. They tear from end to end of the little park, driving away the sea-gulls. The sea-gulls wheel about and settle again idly, flapping and folding their great wings. The defeated dogs bear down upon them again, but the sea-gulls elude the dogs and fly away, settling down again, flapping and folding their great wings. This drives the dogs mad. They cannot endure to see the sea-gulls standing and walking in their park. But the big white birds do not seem to notice the frenzied dogs. Simply they rise and fly and settle again.

On a very wet day, however, Johnny and Tuppence, who love comfort, lie in two compact and similar curves in front of the fire, and the gulls walk in dignity unmolested. Rose looks out of the window. "If I were not a person," she thinks, looking through the streaming window-pane at the devilishly indifferent gulls walking in the rain, "I should like to be a dog in a nice family, or else I should like to be a sea-gull." A dog looks at his own people and his heart is full of love for them. The good smell of his own people fills him with content and often with rapture, and by his soft brown gaze, by his leaping, by his vibrating tail, he tells his love to his dear people. The big white sea-gull has no heart of love. He is beautiful, strong, calculating, and rapacious. He does not love his own kind or humankind. He barely tolerates them. This carnal and lawless bird is slave to nothing but his own insatiable appetite. But just the same, there is something about a sea-gull.

Vancouver runs down to the sea. This way it runs down to the salt inlet. That way it runs down to the salt creek. East to west it runs to the Pacific Ocean. The hungry arrogant sea-gulls possess the water-front. Ships come into the harbour from up the coast, from down the coast, from across the gulf, and again from the Orient, too, they come. The arrogant greedy birds escort the ships to harbour, screaming and wheeling about the stern. Sometimes the sea-gulls fly over the city streets, and their mewing cries disturb the busy or abstracted minds of townspeople going about their business. Something shakes for an instant the calm of a man crossing the street when he hears the cry of a gull above the traffic, something that is not a sound but a disturbing, forgotten, unnamed desire, a memory. Java, Dubrovnik, the Hebrides. What is it?

Rose walks down Granville Street, and the gulls, so scornful of the traffic, swoop between the walls of grey buildings. Their cries sound high above the traffic in the sunlight, like the call of the muezzin in the minaret at the end of the crowded Galata Bridge. Someone, not everyone, hears the voice above the crowd. Rose is going to buy the new hat. She sees the wheeling birds in the sunshine. Then her thoughts fly away as the gulls swoop and cry over the city streets. Land's End, the gusty Channel, the sun on the striped awnings at Ostend. The cry of the wheeling gulls in the city streets.

The gulls know on which side their bread is buttered. For all that they are lawless birds of the sea and shore, they frequent the domestic windows of high buildings, hoping that people will put food out on the window-ledges, and sometimes people do.

Great-Aunt Topaz still lives with Mme Brizard at the top of the seven-storey apartment house, and from her bedroom window she can look out across the salt water of the Inlet to the enchanting mountains north of Vancouver. She has nearly forgotten the mountains (which so enchanted her half a century ago). One does, except when visitors come. "Yes, haven't I a marvellous view!" Then she sees them again. In winter they are white almost to their base, and very glorious against the clear sky. In summer they hold hardly any snow. They lie vaporous, low, unreal, almost dissolving in the warm coloured air. In wet weather no one can see them. No, the mountains are not there. But the sea-gulls come. They fly and turn and fly again past and past the high windows. Great-Aunt Topaz watches for them. She does not like eating crusts, and so she pokes her crusts out onto the window-ledge beside her bed. Down swoop the gulls. Two of them sit on her window-ledge, bowing and flapping and balancing. They look very cruel. They would eat up the little Great-Aunt if she were smaller and inanimate. Aunty laughs with delight and talks to them through the window. She pokes out more and more bread and cake, and the gulls gobble and balance and look at her with their predatory stare.

"Oh, Miss Edgeworth,"says Mme Brizard coming in for the tray, "every bit gone! You *have* done well." "Yes, haven't I?" says Aunt Topaz, and the gulls fly past the window and back again.

One gull, however, really settles on the window-ledge. He bows and bows, and presses himself against the pane, staring at the Great-Aunt in his avaricious way. He is not interested that she talks and laughs to him. He is completely interested in food. There is no more food. At last the sea-gull accepts and despises this fact, so he flies away. He looks grey from beneath, but the breaking sunlight from above outlines his strong wings in bright transient silver. He has a fine life, but he is too earnest.

Vancouver people going home from work in the late afternoon who chance to look upwards, see the sea-gulls flying out to sea singly, and in twos, threes, and companies, through the changing skies of evening. On come the gulls, flying steadily westwards and seawards to the places where they will spend the night. If you scatter your pieces now, the gulls will not turn, descend, alight, and devour. Food does not tempt them as they proceed together on their appointed flight. Only a wind disturbs them, and when a west wind blows furiously in from the sea on a bright evening, the sea-gulls, caught in its power, fly high, and higher, wheel, negotiate, gather and disperse. There is an exultation communicated to the evening watcher who lifts his eyes to the mysterious sight.

In the evening while the sea-gulls fly westwards with lazy purposeful flight, and great and terrible events are massed by Time and Plan upon the slow-moving curtain, Aunt Topaz gathers the rattling newspaper together and with her embroidery scissors cuts out a picture of the King and Queen, an account of a wedding, and an advertisement for garlic pearls because they sound so odd. She may send for these pearls some day. She puts the newspaper cuttings into a large overfull box with a red plush cover on which some sea-shells still remain. She is very old. She will soon be a hundred.

UNLIKE THE SAINTLY ELIJAH

The fourth day of intense heat came. "Oh, this heat," thought Rose, pushing back her hair. "And I have to meet the train and bring John and Annabel up to the house, and settle them in, and go to the meeting, and take Annabel to the luncheon, and go to the wedding, and here's Mme Brizard away and Aunty's Miss Cox in a state and I must find someone to take her place this afternoon. I'll ring up that Miss Umplethwaite who used to look after old Mrs. Dickenson. Umplethwaite, Umplethwaite. Here it is."

Rose telephoned.

"Oh, Miss Umplethwaite, is that Miss Eleanor Umplethwaite? Oh, Miss Umplethwaite, it's Mrs. Forrest. Do you remember I asked you if you would be able to help with my Great-Aunt Miss Edgeworth some day? Yes, I know, you looked after old Mrs. Dickenson, yes, they told me. Yes, delightful, oh, so nice. Well, so is Miss Edgeworth. Perfectly charming, yes, indeed. Well, we're rather in a fix, her companion Mme Brizard is away on her holidays, and we have little Miss Cox with her, and Miss Cox's sister has just broken her arm and Miss Cox feels she has to go out there but she'll be back this evening, and I'm going to a wedding, I really have to, and so has Mrs. Hastings, in fact we've no one to go in and sit with Miss Edgeworth. Oh no, no trouble. Just to sit with her and get some tea, and be there. Oh no, she's up and dressed today, I really wouldn't ask you if – Yes, it is, isn't it? Really dreadful. Cold I *can* stand, but this heat! No. Really exhausting. I quite agree. *How* kind! You'll find the apartment very cool and pleasant. I envy you I'm sure. I say I quite envy you! Yes, as soon as you can, and I'll drop in later if possible, and, anyway, Miss Cox will be back before six. Oh, thank you, that *is* nice, Miss Umplethwaite, I'm so relieved you can't imagine."

And then she telephoned again.

"Hello, hello. Oh, Miss Cox, it's all right, I've got Miss Umplethwaite, no – Umplethwaite, and she'll be there about two. Yes, I told her. Oh, very nice; she used to be with old Mrs. Dickenson. I told her only tea to get, and just *be* there, and, of course, it's so nice and cool in the flat. I told her Miss Edgeworth would be no trouble. Yes, isn't it hot! Oh, I'm sure you do, oh, really, your poor sister! It *is* too bad . . . above the elbow! . . . such a simple thing too, anyone might . . . yes, I quite understand . . . Yes, you must be . . . terribly . . . in this heat – yes, indeed. It is, isn't it, most exhausting, you could fry an egg on the pavement. I said you could fry – oh, nothing."

"Well," said Aunt Topaz to the agitated Miss Cox, "what's all this fuss about an elbow? Whose elbow? Well, run along, run along. Hot? It's not hot. Very pleasant I call it in this flat with all the windows open. Who? Never heard such a name. Never heard such a name in my life. Umplethwaite? I don't need any Miss Umple to look after me. There's the bell. I suppose it's that young woman with the peculiar name. Oh, how do you do?" with the utmost winningness to the polite Miss Umplethwaite.

Miss Cox and Miss Umplethwaite exchange instructions, lamentations about the heat, and hasty farewells and promises. And as fast as Miss Cox puts on her hat and reaches for her hand-bag Miss Umplethwaite takes off her hat, lays down her hand-bag, and sits down opposite Great-Aunt Topaz ingratiatingly but very much fatigued by her haste and obligingness on this sultry day. Miss Cox departs with lightning speed to her sister.

"Well," says Aunt Topaz, "have I ever seen you before? That's a nice brooch you have on, to be sure, a very nice brooch. Hair in it. I have one with hair in it too. You see! And pearls. This hair belonged to old Mrs. Grimwade; very stingy she was but very kind to me. I have a ring too. Hair in it. What a many things they did put hair in, I do declare. I have some embroidery done with hair. Very sentimental I call it and far from hygienic. Now, let me see, what did you say your name is, Umple-something? Oh, yes, Yorkshire. A very fine county Yorkshire. Oh, the Minster, glorious, glorious" (signs of emotion and desiring to speak on the part of Miss Umplethwaite but she does not succeed), "many's the time I've stayed in York before we came to Canada. My Great-Uncle George Mallet married the daughter of a Canon of York – Canon Tillyard. No!!!" By this time Aunty and Miss Umplethwaite are dewy with the happiness of shared memories of loved places and name. On they go. Suddenly Miss Umplethwaite remembers her duties.

"Wouldn't you like a cup of tea, Miss Edgeworth?" she asks pleasantly.

Great-Aunt Topaz stops short and looks at her. She has thought of something.

"No, I wouldn't like a cup of tea," she says, "but I *would* like a nice bit of ice-cream. Get me me hat and me stick, and me little bag with me purse in, and we'll just walk to the drug-store and sit down and have a nice ice-cream; you can help me, you know."

Now this is very wily of Great-Aunt Topaz, because although it is only one long block it is really much too far for her to walk to the drug-store, and she knows it, especially on this hot day. But Mme Brizard is away, Miss Cox is away, Miranda and Rose, those two lynx-eyed ones, are not here, and innocent Miss Umplethwaite is at Aunty's mercy.

Miss Umplethwaite is dismayed. This is the first time she's been cool to-day. "Oh, Miss Edgeworth!" she exclaims, "you've no idea how hot it is outside! It's so lovely and cool in here. The sidewalk's like a stove, and the sun beating down. It's like an oven! It's most unusual. Exhausting. Everyone complaining. Indeed my sister's husband forbade her absolutely to go out in this heat." Miss Umplethwaite delicately mops her brow and upper lip on which the perspiration starts. She invokes the superior sex.

"If I had a husband and he forbade me to do anything," says Aunty, "I should – well, let me see – I should kick him. I *need* a bit of ice-cream," piteously, "many's the time . . . ," and she pounds busily to her bedroom. She reappears with her hat on, with her stick, two hand-bags, and a pair of white cotton gloves. She will go to the ice-cream. It shall not come to her. The already defeated Miss Umplethwaite is still anxious not to go out into the heat; she is anxious not to betray Mrs. Forrest's trust in her; and she really is afraid that Great-Aunt Topaz or she (Miss Umplethwaite) may have a stroke in the street. The heat is intense. She will say the dread word, stroke.

"Aren't you afraid, Miss Edgeworth, that the heat might be too much for you, that you might be overcome by the heat? And um . . . ?"

"What do you mean?" says Aunty, who uses plain English. "Do you mean shall I have a stroke? No, I shan't have a stroke. Not one in my family ever had a stroke. It runs in some families. Not in mine. Come along, come along now," rather testily. She is afraid of the return of the preventing Miss Cox.

Leaning heavily upon Miss Umplethwaite, who perspires freely though unwillingly, Aunty pounds in her own peculiar way down the street. She leans thus heavily upon her companion because she uses her stick chiefly for pointing, either at merchandise in the shop-windows, or at people and other objects. She is a menace. People wince as she points. People walk languidly along the hot street; dogs pant in the shade, rise, lie down and pant again. The pavement feels like a stove-top. The heat beats upwards. Aunty indulges a life-long passion of hers.

"Oh," she says, "there's Mrs. Tibbett, I do declare! How do you do, how do you do, there, you see, she's smiling at me. Oh, it's not Mrs. Tibbett. Well, well, it is pleasant out, to be sure. People complaining about a little sun. Oh, there's Mr. Clark, the Rev. Mr. Clark, he comes to see me, how do you do? Oh, it isn't Mr. Clark, he hasn't got his collar on, a very nice man though, I'm sure. Well, *can* that be Mrs. Hogg? Strawberries," she says, pointing dangerously at a shop-window with her stick. "We'll get some strawberries on the way back; I always have a little pepper on me strawberries. And a pineapple! What a treat! Well, I do declare, isn't that old Mrs. Meredith?" And so, smiling, bowing, rejoicing, Aunty goes to the drug-store with the exhausted Miss Umplethwaite.

Their progress back is slower. Miss Umplethwaite, refreshed with ice-cream, turns gratefully homewards. On Aunty the heat and the exercise and all the excitement have begun to tell. Walking becomes difficult. She leans more heavily on her companion.

"You walk very fast," says Aunty who had gaily trampled down to the drug-store almost dragging Miss Umplethwaite with her. "You'll have to go a deal slower. I'm not so young as you, you know. I can't go tearing along the way you do, you know. I'm feeling tired. I don't feel well." Aunty is still expert in accusation.

"Oh, Miss Edgeworth," Miss Umplethwaite says anxiously, "I told you you shouldn't have come, I said –"

"Don't begin saying 'I told you so,'" says Aunty with asperity. "I can't bear being rushed along in the heat. You're rushing me. Me legs don't seem to be functioning. There's something wrong with me legs."

"Oh, Miss Edgeworth," says the alarmed companion (the very first time out!), "lean on me, I'll help you along. I'll put my arm round you!" And so they walk, sweltering, each clutching the other.

"It's paralysis," says Aunty, irritated. "Never before in my family. I can't make it out. I can't feel me legs. I can't use them. OH! Elijah Jones was paralysed, he was a very saintly man was Elijah, handsome too; there were three Elijah Joneses in wheel-chairs, two of them with water on the knee and one paralysed, in three generations. That's why they stopped using the name Elijah in the Jones family. Oh, this is terrible. I can't even use me feet! Miss Umple, Miss Umple! I'm going to fall!"

Miss Umplethwaite is distracted. She seizes Aunt Topaz more firmly. She glances down. Wreathed around Aunty's feet are her good white calico drawers. Descending, they had impeded her. Descended, they wrap her feet around. She is helpless to move.

"Lift up a foot, Miss Edgeworth, lift up a foot," implores Miss Umplethwaite, hotter than ever. Passers-by rouse from their lethargy and take interest. People turn and smile kindly enough.

"I can't lift a foot. I'm paralyzed! I've had a stroke, I do declare!" says Aunty, shocked.

"Oh yes, you can, Miss Edgeworth. Try. Try. It's only your . . . ," murmurs Miss Umplethwaite, wrestling. She bends down and lifts up one of Aunt Topaz's strangely large and heavy feet, and wriggles the garment off; she lifts up the other foot, and wriggles the other part of the garment off; she whips the calico drawers up into a bundle, tucks them under her arm, and faces the world with a flush.

Great-Aunt Topaz is amazed. "Eh, it's me knickers!" she says astonished. She kicks out with one leg, kicks out with the other, and finds them free and active. Distress fades to surprise, to pleasure on her face. She steps out nimbly. She is pleased.

"This is a deal more comfortable," she says. "Well, what people wear all these clothes for, *I* can't think, this weather. This *is* comfortable, I'm sure. No, I won't put them on again. Well, what are you waiting for? I made sure it couldn't be a stroke. Something told me. Well, here we are. Oh, *there* you are, Rose!"

Aunt Topaz prances into the elevator, and up they go to the flat. She laughs merrily, and proceeds with heavy hasty tread to her apartment. Rose and Miss Umplethwaite are nearly fainting, Rose with the heat and Miss Umplethwaite with the heat and Aunty's knickers. Aunty is not fainting. "You see," she says, plucking the bundle from under Miss Umplethwaite's arm, "you see," holding up the calico drawers and flourishing them, "these are me knickers! The button came off, and down they came! And I thought, Rose, I was getting paralysis, just like poor Elijah Jones, a very saintly man and *such* a long beard, and his father and his great-uncle Elijah with water on the knee all in a bath-chair. Miss Umple, Miss

Umple, will you get us some tea? And Miss Umple, take these away. I don't want them. A very nice young woman that. Has a brooch with hair in it. Well, that *was* a Do!" She laughs with delight, and, as she talks, Rose is aware that not the least of Aunty's triumph is that she is still one up on the saintly Elijah.

Miss Umplethwaite brings in some tea. She is silent and a little offended. Rose is sure that Miss Umplethwaite feels that she has been deceived, and that she will not come again.

Because Great-Aunt Topaz is a hundred years old and is still little Topaz Edgeworth with a strong infusion of *grande dame*, she is invincible. Small and great lapses from convention do not dismay her. Why should they? They entertain her. She is impatient of illness but not at all dismayed by death, which now can almost be heard approaching, it is so near. She has had a pleasant afternoon. Her enjoyment fills the room and dispels the chagrin of Miss Umplethwaite. "Miss Umple," Topaz says with good humour, "pull up your chair and have a cup. Well, that *was* a bit of a Do, to be sure!"

Miss Umplethwaite begins to smile again and to regard the whole thing as simply a bit of a Do.

A HUNDRED YEARS GONE, AND
THE 'FORTIES AGAIN

Chopin's Raindrop Prelude beats heavily through the room. Those are not drops of rain; they are drops of lead. Down go the keys, "RUM-ti-too (tum tum tum tum tum). . . ." A deputy in a white apron rushes in, protesting. Aunty is sitting on the piano-stool, playing vigorously. She has nipped out of bed in her cotton nighty and is playing the Raindrop Prelude. Both feet are firmly down on the pedals of the small piano. The window is open. No, go away; she will not stop playing and put her arms in her dressing-gown; no, she will not go back to bed, and she will not catch cold; go away. This bit of conflict satisfies her. Soon she is glad to be helped back to bed, a little tired, after all.

Now her world is bounded by one room. Where are the mountains which one sees from her windows? They do not exist in her world; there is no rain driving against the window-panes; there are no neon lights reflected on Granville Street, looking so pretty in the rain at night; there are no sea-gulls; there are no armies and no torpedoed ships. There is only her room and a friend ("Who is it?") coming in at the door, to be greeted with tremulous delight. Come to think of it, she has enjoyed about nine thousand consecutive days of her apotheosis beside the Pacific Ocean. She has been healthy and amused for ninety hundred days. Is she not lucky?

Her world continues to shrink. It is a bed; it is a cup of milk; it is a voice which she essays to greet with customary friendliness. Her memories have flowed away. Wherever can they be? Only habit remains.

Her world has closed down to a point; it is a point of departure. She is restless and ill at ease.

In the middle of the last century, when Topaz was a young girl, at the seasons of the great bird migrations, large areas of the Argentinean plains, "the green floor of the world," were covered by birds as by a carpet, and, when the birds took wing, the sky was invisible. As the time for departure drew near, the vast myriads of birds became nervous and restless to the point of anguish. This spirit of unrest "was marked in the most volatile species, the swiftest of wing and the wildest." One of the greatest of all field naturalists formed the theory that the birds of these migrations – leaving their habitat at a season when food was ample and the climate salubrious, leaving as it were against their will – were drawn in migration by a sense of polarity, that is, by the strong influence of the magnetic poles exerted upon their species at certain times. The birds are uncertain, restless; they are forced to go. One last bird remains alone, restless, nervous, undecided, wishing to go, awaiting something. After pitiful agitation the bird at last rises and follows the flight with confidence. There are certain things about which one can only form a theory.

If there is a sense of polarity which exerts an influence on the winged creatures of the pathless and unpreventing air, it seems reasonable that a polarity should exist, different in kind, to which the unknowing human spirit, through its own atmosphere more tenuous than air itself, responds.

Topaz is dying, there is no doubt of that. She – gay, volatile, one hundred years old, the last of her generation, long delayed – is uneasy. She is very restless. She shows no fear and yet she seems to be in some kind of anguish. Plainly she is awaiting something, an affirmation or release. What is that she is saying? She wants to go, she says. She is being prevented. The poor volatile bird.

"Let me go immediately . . . immediately . . ." she murmurs in her imperious way. "A hundred years . . . I shall be late . . . me, the youngest." Then the small face lightens. "Quick, get me some fresh lace for me head, someone! I'm going to die, I do declare!" Evidently she is pleased and confident. What an adventure, to be sure!

Away she went. Now she is a memory, a gossamer.

After the summing up, after the questions and answers ("O Death, where is thy sting?"), after the fusion of the large family standing together, life again became diffused and urgent; the scene which had bound them together ceased and the family dispersed. Something remained and something was ended.

"Do you want a lift?" asked Ruth. "The men are mostly going back to their offices, and Don's taking Ellen and Aunt Miranda, and Helen's looking after the boys, and Uncle Stephen is taking the others. I'm going up Granville Street." So Georgia and Rose got in and Ruth drove away in her little car. She drove for blocks and they were all three silent. Then they passed a little boy who blew a tin trumpet.

"Did I hear that Allan wants to learn the clarinet?" asked Georgia, suddenly amused.

"Yes," laughed Ruth, "won't it be awful!"

"I don't see why, if you can bear it at first. . . . Oh dear, I never never *never* shall forget the flowers all going to the wrong place. . . ."

". . . Wasn't it terrible? And we could do nothing at all. There it was . . . I shall never forget . . . the poor little thing . . . I still can't see how it happened . . . and Aunty of all people . . ."

"Yes, *wasn't* it terrible? I felt *awful,* you could feel *everybody* feeling awful all round you," said Ruth driving neatly through the traffic. Her thoughts ran forward to the children and their supper. Should she stop and get ice-cream because they had not wanted to stay at Miss Gam's? Rose and Georgia sat pensive but not sad, thinking backwards. . . . They were away from the shops now and up Granville Street hill.

"Shall I drop you at the corner or will you come on with me? I have to pick up the children. . . . I can stick them in the back. . . . I didn't like to take them to the funeral. . . ."

They drove along under the trees in the late sunshine. The sunshine was reflected from the leaves of the trees whose branches would soon be grown to touch across the road. First Georgia got out; then Rose. The sea-gulls were flying westwards in their ordained evening flight, in twos, threes, and companies, high overhead on account of the wind; but neither Rose nor Georgia noticed, because of the funeral, and because they were each preoccupied. The customary westward flight of the sea-gulls over the sea, through the evening sky, was, however, as always, a curious and ravishing sight.

(The Bell rings out; the pulse thereof is changed; the tolling was a faint and intermitting pulse, upon one side; this stronger, and argues more and better life. His soule is gone out. . . . His soule is gone; whither? Who saw it come in, or who saw it goe out? No

body; yet every body is sure, he had one, and hath none. . . . This soule, this Bell tells me, is gone out; Whither? Who shall tell mee that? . . . mine owne Charity; I aske that; and that tels me, He is gone to everlasting rest, and joy and glory.

. . . We are . . . transported, our dust blowne away with pro-phane dust, with every wind.

(FROM THE EIGHTEENTH DEVOTION OF JOHN DONNE)

AFTERWORD

Twenty-three years after the publication of *The Innocent Traveller*, in a characteristically modest letter to John Gray, her publisher, Ethel Wilson wrote: "it is well written, I like it . . . I value it. . . ."

How different from her doubts in November of 1944 when she first submitted the manuscript to the Macmillan Company:

> Dear Sir – I shall venture to send you a few stories, three of which appeared in the New Statesman and Nation, the fourth in the Canadian Forum, the others not at all . . . I send these, not with expectations of acceptance, but with plain humility, as I am not sure whether they are good, a little good, or no good, or whether they would interest a public at all.

Two days later, even less secure, she wrote again:

> Dear Sir – I sent you lately a bundle of short stories which had suddenly begun to burn a hole in my pocket.

I think I told you of my own uncertainty as to whether they are at all good.

Distance has, I think, lent a proper perspective, and also the enormous events which agitate the country now. And my stories have dwindled into their proper size – the matter is so trifling, old fashioned, and of personal interest only, perhaps. One can hardly blame a public that requires "social awareness" in its reading, or something truly funny and entertaining –

So this leads me to say that when you send me these little pieces – *collect* – I will welcome them into obscurity again.

Of such confidence and misgivings are good writers made! And Ethel Wilson was a very good writer indeed – a quirky and sophisticated writer with an individual style, tilting and elliptical. Witty as well as funny. Unique. But as yet unproven.

"If you cannot make something out of that Topaz saga you're not the writer we think you are," read the note accompanying the returned stories. It was not an outright rejection, but for Wilson it might as well have been. "When you definitely refused Topaz for the good reason of being short stories," she wrote in reply, "and I definitely knew that I can't and won't change her form, I sent them to . . . Simon and Schuster." And so began the discussions with Macmillan which were to continue over the succeeding five years.

In today's literary climate, it is difficult to understand why Macmillan took so long to decide to publish. One feels anyone with half an eye would have jumped at such a book. And it is clear from the correspondence that Macmillan *had* half an eye. The trouble lay with the other eye and a half, which could see a book as a book only if it was a novel. Linked stories, however consecutive, would not do. This attitude was not peculiar to Macmillan. In Canada few collections of stories, other than anthologies, had appeared before the sixties.

Then in 1946 Wilson wrote *Hetty Dorval*. Unarguably a novel, it was published by Macmillan in 1947. Two years later, her first-born, *The Innocent Traveller*, appeared. Wilson was sixty-two years old.

The Innocent Traveller is both family chronicle and fiction. "The persons and incidents are true," Wilson said of it in 1957, "or, when I made some up (as I did), they are so truly characteristic of certain persons that they approximate to truth." And she was right. Her characters *are* true – fictionally true. Flesh and blood.

"One day I will write down my stories," she is reported to have said to a friend, "but not until Granny, Aunt Eliza and Aunty Belle are dead." The last of them, Aunt Eliza, died in 1943, aged one hundred. Wilson must have meant "publish," not "write," for it is evident from her papers that she had been writing and revising *The Innocent Traveller* (originally called *Topaz*) for nineteen years. During that time its title was changed and changed again, as was the order of its chapters. What remained unchanged was Eliza herself, the book's central character, and energy. "I called her Topaz," Wilson wrote. "There had to be a 'z' in her name, for she had sudden small dazzles and sparkles, and . . . she was like a semi-precious stone . . ."

Let us have a look at Topaz in the book's opening paragraph as she first appears and makes her presence felt:

Far away at the end of the table sat Father, the kind, handsome and provident man. At this end sat Mother,

her crinoline spread abroad. On Mother's right was Mr.
Matthew Amold. On each side of the table the warned
children ate their food gravely, all except Topaz on
Mother's left. Topaz, who could not be squelched, was
perched there on the top of two cushions, as innocent as
a poached egg. Mother sat gracious, fatigued, heavy
behind the majestic crinoline with the last and fatal child.

Already we are caught in the spell of the prose, in the pull of
the plot. Who cares if this is fiction or memoir, short stories
or novel? A world has been created in six sentences. A
Victorian world. *Pater familias*, kind, handsome, provident,
friend of Mr. Matthew Arnold. Mother about to die. (What a
great deal is suggested about men and women of the period.
Husbands and wives!) And the warned children – were they
indeed not warned in Victorian England, children who should
be seen and not heard – gravely eating their food. All, that is,
except Topaz, impervious then, impervious always, to the limitations and conventions of her narrow world.

In real life, whatever that is, Topaz would drive one to
distraction. She is talkative, trivial, tiresome – overwhelmingly
unaware of the feelings of those around her. She is one of those
unmarried women who stay "girls" all their lives, who are good
sports, game for anything. Chattering and merry. Infuriating.
At the same time she is unexpectedly flexible, unwaveringly
kind, and, due to an almost total lack of imagination, endlessly surprised by life. She moves uncomplainingly through a
hundred years of rapidly accelerating change, from Victorian
England to post-Second-World-War Canada, only once
raging at her fate.

"I am afraid that if I depart from the life of Topaz as it
was," Wilson wrote to her publisher, "and begin to make a

story, either rather violent or rather psychological out of it, I have to introduce someone who *does* something to Topaz, or to whom Topaz *does* something. But the point about her, I find, is that having no touch with reality below the top layer, she does nothing to anyone! She is incapable of it." She is, indeed, the innocent traveller of the well-chosen title.

With such material to work with, why is Topaz so memorable, so endlessly fascinating, so – lovable? The answer must lie in the fact that Wilson's inscribing eye – her incising, incisive eye – is sufficiently infused with a loving spirit that we catch her love. Literate Ethel Wilson, master of implication, mistress of delicate balances, is incapable of a boring thought. She carries us lightly, as though bearing no weight at all, through a myriad of interweaving mini-stories, deftly skirting the real pain, burning us only a little, but burning us just the same. Letting us touch the flame so we know how it feels. But not dwelling on it anymore than does Topaz herself.

"The drop of water, the bird, the water-glider, the dancer, the wind on the canal, and Topaz, are all different and all the same," she says in the "Author's Note." And as this sharp and gentle book unfolds, she shows us their dance – back and forth in time, back and forth again – weaving an intricate fabric into which, while the spell is upon us, we are woven too. We become part of that Victorian community of women – of widows and unmarried aunts; part of that ordered, harmonious world: upper middle-class, reading Greek, travelling abroad, knowing our place. *Knowing our place.* Yet the detached and thoroughly modern mind of the author writes, at the same time, a wry, invisible gloss.

So Topaz, then, is wonderfully drawn, as are the splendid others. And that includes the author herself who appears first, as a disembodied "I" – surprisingly – before she is born. Later, as the orphaned, third-person Rose, she adds a younger voice to the Grandmother's house, even though she is usually off in her bedroom, hidden or half hidden (but observing, observing), while Topaz stamps about centrestage congenitally insensitive to everything – well, almost everything – around her.

But what of the book itself, what of its shape? For it *has* a shape, this collection of stories (or is it a novel, after all?). So delighted are we by its style, by its characters who have become our friends, that we have altogether forgotten shape. We have been carried along – like Topaz herself – absorbed, unthinking, until towards the end, the book gathers itself together, and we see by its circularity and lift that it is, in fact, a spiral. Echoes of its beginning sound once more, altered as echoes have to be. Topaz speaks poetry again not, as in chapter 1, *to* Mr. Matthew Arnold but *by* Mr. Matthew Arnold. And as the first poem might anticipate Topaz's single life, so the second anticipates her death:

> A man becomes aware of his life's flow,
> And hears its winding murmur; and he sees
> The meadows where it glides, the sun, the breeze . . .
> . . . And then he thinks he knows,
> The hills where his life rose,
> And the sea where it goes.

Three short chapters from the end when, as through a scrim, we glimpse the brutalities of war, Wilson suddenly confronts us with what previously she has repeatedly hinted at – the enigmatic nature of time – and which we now see as the theme of the book. "The future," she tells us, "[is] really one with the present and the past."

And as we confront "a timeless and impersonal world"

and are asked to consider "the permanence of the impermanent frail flower," the retreat and return of the little wave on
the shingle, we watch the gulls, which have unexpectedly invaded the book, circle and rise and fly off to sea. And we
know that it will not be long before Topaz, "poor volatile
bird," will follow.

BY ETHEL WILSON